Global Fintech Institute - World Scientific Series on Fintech

Print ISSN: 2737-5897
Online ISSN: 2737-5900

Series Editors: David LEE Kuo Chuen *(Global Fintech Institute, Singapore & Singapore University of Social Sciences, Singapore)*
Joseph LIM *(Singapore University of Social Sciences, Singapore)*
PHOON Kok Fai *(Singapore University of Social Sciences, Singapore)*
WANG Yu *(Singapore University of Social Sciences, Singapore)*

In the digital era, emerging technologies such as artificial intelligence, big data, and blockchain have revolutionized people's daily lives and brought many opportunities and challenges to industries. With the increasing demand for talents in the fintech realm, this book series serves as a good guide for practitioners who are seeking to understand the basics of fintech and the applications of different technologies. This book series starts with fundamental knowledge in finance, technology, quantitative methods, and financial innovation to lay the foundation for the fundamentals of fintech, and understanding the trending issues related to fintech such as regulation, applications, and global trends. It is a good starting point to the fintech literature and is especially useful for people who aspire to become fintech professionals.

Published:

/ol. 2 *Finance for Fintech Professionals*
edited by David LEE Kuo Chuen, Joseph LIM, PHOON Kok Fai and WANG Yu

l *Foundations for Fintech*
edited by David LEE Kuo Chuen, Joseph LIM, PHOON Kok Fai and WANG Yu

ing:

Finance Professionals
avid Lee Kuo Chuen (Global Fintech Institute, Singapore & Singapore iversity of Social Sciences, Singapore), Joseph Lim, Phoon Kok Fai and ng Yu (Singapore University of Social Sciences, Singapore)

d Trends in Fintech I: Governance, AI, and Blockchain Design Thinking
Lee Kuo Chuen (Global Fintech Institute, Singapore & Singapore ity of Social Sciences, Singapore), Joseph Lim, Phoon Kok Fai and ı (Singapore University of Social Sciences, Singapore)

is series can also be found at https://www.worldscientific.com/series/gfiwssf

(Continued at end of book)

Finance for Fintech Professionals

Global Fintech Institute - World Scientific Series on Fintech 2

Finance for Fintech Professionals

Editors

David LEE Kuo Chuen

Global Fintech Institute, Singapore

Singapore University of Social Sciences, Singapore

Joseph LIM

Singapore University of Social Sciences, Singapore

PHOON Kok Fai

Singapore University of Social Sciences, Singapore

WANG Yu

Singapore University of Social Sciences, Singapore

Global Fintech Institute   CFtP   World Scientific

Published by

World Scientific Publishing Co. Pte. Ltd.
5 Toh Tuck Link, Singapore 596224
USA office: 27 Warren Street, Suite 401-402, Hackensack, NJ 07601
UK office: 57 Shelton Street, Covent Garden, London WC2H 9HE

and

Global Fintech Institute Ltd.
80 Robinson Road, #08-01, Singapore 068898

Library of Congress Cataloging-in-Publication Data
Names: Lee, David (David Kuo Chuen), editor. | Lim, Joseph, editor. |
Phoon, Kok Fai, editor. | Wang, Yu, editor.
Title: Finance for fintech professionals / editors, David Lee Kuo Chuen (Global Fintech Institute, Singapore, Singapore University of Social Sciences, Singapore), Joseph Lim (Singapore University of Social Sciences, Singapore), Phoon Kok Fai (Singapore University of Social Sciences, Singapore), Wang Yu (Singapore University of Social Sciences, Singapore).
Description: Singapore ; Hackensack, NJ : World Scientific, [2022] | Series: Global Fintech Institute - World Scientific series on fintech, 2737-5897 ; vol. 2 | Includes bibliographical references.
Identifiers: LCCN 2021041939 | ISBN 9789811241048 (hardcover) | ISBN 9789811241857 (paperback) | ISBN 9789811241055 (ebook) | ISBN 9789811241062 (ebook other)
Subjects: LCSH: Finance. | Finance--Problems, exercises, etc. | Finance--Technological innovations. | Financial engineering.
Classification: LCC HG173 .F4878 2022 | DDC 332--dc23
LC record available at https://lccn.loc.gov/2021041939

British Library Cataloguing-in-Publication Data
A catalogue record for this book is available from the British Library.

For any available supplementary material, please visit
https://www.worldscientific.com/worldscibooks/10.1142/12389#t=suppl

Desk Editors: Balasubramanian Shanmugam/Yulin Jiang

Typeset by Stallion Press
Email: enquiries@stallionpress.com

Preface

The Finance for Fintech Professionals Volume provides a significant underpinning to the CFtP qualification. While the topics are familiar to professionals who are traditionally trained in Finance, these topics continue to be relevant as one needs to appreciate the financial problems that technology is being developed to solve. Without an evident appreciation of finance concepts and practice, any professional will have difficulties solving such issues the traditional way, let alone incorporating recent technological breakthroughs. In this Finance for Fintech Professionals Volume, we have systematically written up the basic concepts and knowledge required in Finance for a Fintech professional. We must remind ourselves that while Finance has a long tradition, new problems and applications in the financial sector continue to develop at a swift pace.

This Finance volume comprises four sections, with Section 1 being Economics. In this part, we cover Microeconomics, Macroeconomics, and Macro-Finance. The Volume starts with a coverage of economics, which is crucial for understanding Finance and selected Fintech areas, including Cryptocurrency and Fintech Strategy. Coverage includes game theory, central banking, and financial institution risk management. The next section focuses on understanding how business information is created, organized, and used in financial analysis. This part is titled Financial Statement Analysis that focuses on understanding the income statement, balance sheet, and statement of cash flow. We also discuss the use of these statements in equity and credit analysis. The third section is on the financial management of businesses and discusses key corporate decisions and the concepts behind how such decisions are made. The coverage includes critical concepts like the time value of money and risk. The last section is on Investment Management. This section comprises four parts. The first three parts contain the introduction and valuation of the equity and fixed income asset classes and derivatives fundamentals. The remaining parts include portfolio analysis, investing in alternative assets, like hedge funds, private equity, and real estate; and lastly on the portfolio management process includes short discussions on current asset allocation methods.

This book is a companion volume to the book titled *Fintech for Finance Professionals* that covers the fundamental concepts in Fintech. Together, these two books form the foundation for a good understanding of Finance and Fintech applications which will be covered in subsequent volumes.

About the Editors

Professor David LEE Kuo Chuen is a professor at the Singapore University of Social Sciences and Adjunct Professor at the National University of Singapore. He is also the founder of BlockAsset Ventures, the Chairman of Global Fintech Institute, Vice President of the Economic Society of Singapore, Co-founder of Blockchain Association of Singapore, and Council Member of British Blockchain Association. He has 20 years of experience as a CEO and an independent director of listed and tech companies and is a consultant and advisor to international organizations on food supply chain, blockchain, fintech, and digital currency.

Associate Professor Joseph LIM is with the Singapore University of Social Sciences where he teaches finance. He has also taught at the National University of Singapore and the Singapore Management University. Joseph obtained his MBA from Columbia University and PhD from New York University. In between his stints in academia, he worked in various advisory positions in the areas of private equity and valuation. Joseph, who is a CFA charter holder, has served in various committees at the CFA Institute and as President of CFA Singapore. In addition, he was on the board and committees of various investment industry associations. In the non-profit sector, he was on the board of a pension fund and several endowment funds. He is a coauthor of several popular college finance textbooks.

Associate Professor Kok Fai PHOON teaches finance at the School of Business, Singapore University of Social Sciences (SUSS). He received his PhD in finance from Northwestern University, MSc in Industrial Engineering from the National University of Singapore, and BASc in Mechanical Engineering (Honours) from the University of British Columbia. His research interests focus on the use of technology in portfolio management, wealth management, and risk and complexity of financial products. In addition to his current position at SUSS, Kok Fai has taught at other universities in Singapore and at Monash University in Australia. He has worked at Yamaichi Merchant Bank, at GIC Pte Ltd, and as Executive Director at Ferrell Asset Management, a Singapore hedge fund. He has published in academic journals including the *Review of Quantitative Finance and Accounting* and the *Pacific Basin Finance Journal* as well as practice journals like the *Financial Analyst Journal*, the *Journal of Wealth Management*, and the *Journal of Alternative Investments*.

Ms Yu WANG (Cheryl) is a fintech research fellow at the Singapore University of Social Sciences FinTech and Blockchain Group. Her main research interests are fintech, machine learning, and asset pricing. Prior to SUSS, she worked at the National University of Singapore, Business School as a research associate on corporate governance and sustainability. She graduated with an MSc in Applied Economies from Nanyang Technological University and BSc in Financial Engineering from Huazhong University of Sciences of Technologies. She has multiple journal papers, including an empirical study on sustainability reporting and firm value published on an SSCI journal, *Sustainability*, and one investigating cryptocurrency as a new alternative investment published on *Journal of Alternative Investments* that has been cited for over 200 times and recommended by *CFA Institute Journal Review*. She also serves as referee for various journals such as *Singapore Economic Review*, *Quarterly Review of Economics and Finance*, and *Journal of Alternative Investments*.

Contents

Section 1: Economics

Part A: Microeconomics

Chapter 1

Demand and Supply Analysis

1.1 Introducing the Market

1.1.1 *Defining a Market*

A market consists of buyers and sellers cognisant of each other, agreeing to a price to exchange goods and services.

Learning Objectives

- Recognize the characteristics of a market.

Main Takeaways

Main Points

- Markets help match buyers and sellers.
- There are many markets, including the market for finished goods and services, the factor markets, and capital markets.

Main Terms

- **Price:** Payment or compensation given by one party in exchange for goods or services.
- **Intermediate goods:** Goods to produce final goods.

In an economy, a market enables players to bid and offer and transact after agreeing on a price. In other words, a market is a virtual or physical place that helps match buyers and sellers. Many markets exist.

We characterize each market by what is exchanged, who can participate, how transactions are processed, and the regulations.

The markets comprise markets for factors of production (factor markets) and markets for services and finished goods (goods markets or product markets). For example, energy and human resources are production factors, while automobiles, wine, and clothing are finished goods sold to consumers. In general, firms are buyers in factor markets and sellers in product markets. Samsung produces LED panels used in the manufacture of televisions. LED panels are intermediate goods used to make televisions that are the final goods sold to consumers.

1.2 Demand

1.2.1 *Demand Curve*

We define a product's demand curve as the quantity that consumers of the product want to buy at each possible price, holding all else the same. At a given price, the quantity demanded is a good or service that a consumer is willing or able to purchase.

Learning Objectives

- Understand the demand curve and the Law of Demand.
- Differentiate between a shift in the demand curve with movement along the demand curve.
- Construct and understand the demand curves.

Main Takeaways

Main Points

- An economic agent's price-to-quantity relation or demand schedule can be represented graphically as a "demand curve."
- Underlying the demand curve are the economic agents' preferences, substitution potential, and income, as well as other characteristics that impact their ability to assess their willingness to pay for goods and services.
- Aggregate demand is the total quantity of a good or service demanded at a specific price over a group of economic agents.
- A movement along the demand curve results from a price change.
- A shift in the demand curve can arise from a non-price variable change.

- An outward shift in demand will occur for a normal good if income increases. For an inferior good, the demand curve will shift inward as a consumer will only purchase the good after not being able to afford a preferred good.

Main Terms

- **Demand curve:** A graphical representation of the price to quantity choice of an economic agent for a specific good or service.
- **Marginal benefit:** The benefit that each buyer gains from each additional unit of a good or service in the goods and services market or that each business gains from each additional unit of input in the factor market.
- **A normal good:** Price remaining constant, demand for a normal good increases when income increases and falls when income decreases.
- **An inferior good:** Demand for an inferior good decrease when consumer income rises.

1.2.2 *Individual Demand*

How will a price reduction in mobile phone prices affect sales? To find out, we need to know how the price reduction will affect individual buyers' purchases. We would like to see how an individual's purchases are related to the item's price. The individual demand curve displayed on a graph shows the buyer's quantity at each possible price point.

In most cases, economic agents will likely decrease consumption as the price of a good increase. The demand curve in these cases shows a negative price to quantity relationship. Graphically, the demand curve typically slopes downward from left to right. Abnormal goods like certain luxury goods exhibit an upward sloping demand.

1.2.3 *Demand and Other Factors*

The demand schedule is defined as the amount of good, *X*, that a buyer is willing and able to purchase over a range of prices. We define the demand schedule, assuming that the income levels, price of substitute goods, and price of complementary goods are held constant.

The demand curve depicts the demand schedule graphically. The downward-sloping demand curve is sometimes referred to as "the law of demand." It merely means that as the price of a good decreases, consumers will buy more of that good.

1.2.4 *Market or Aggregate Demand*

If an individual agent's demand curve is combined with other economic agents, we will obtain a market or aggregate demand curve. The quantity demanded per individual can be summed for a specific price, giving the total demand. If we continue aggregating the amount at different price points, we obtain an aggregate demand curve. In this manner, the economy's demand curve is constructed from every individual consumer's demand curve.

The market demand curve is a graph that shows the quantity that all buyers will purchase at different prices. We expect the market demand curve's properties to be similar to those of the individual demand curve. Since each buyer's marginal benefit diminishes with the quantity consumed, the market demand curve will be downward sloping. The equivalent is that the market as a whole will buy a larger quantity at a lower price.

1.2.5 *Business Demand for Input (Factor Market)*

A business produces items for sale to consumers or intermediate goods to other businesses. In return, the business earns revenue from such sales. The company can have a larger output and raise revenue by increasing inputs. Thus, the business' marginal benefit from the input is the increase in revenue from an additional input unit.

We can construct the demand curve for an input using its marginal benefit. This demand curve shows how the business will purchase for a range of input prices. A business should buy up to the "optimal" quantity when its marginal benefit equals the (input or factor) price.

If the business buys one more unit than the optimal amount, the additional unit provides a smaller increase in revenue, diminishing marginal benefit. On the other hand, if the input price is lower, the business will acquire a larger quantity. Thus, the demand curve for input is downward sloping.

1.2.6 *What Changes Business Demand?*

A change in the input price results in a movement along the demand curve. On the other hand, reasons for shifting the entire demand curve include factors like prices of complements and substitutes in the business's production. Compared with consumer demand, business demand does not depend on income but rather on the output of the item being produced. The larger the output, the more the business will increase its demand for inputs and vice versa.

We examine the demand for trucks in the transportation business. Since delivery trunks and truck drivers are complements, an increase in drivers' wages will reduce demand for trucks. So, if drivers' wages increase, we will observe a downward shift in trucks' demand curve in a goods delivery business.

1.2.7 *Changes in Demand and Shifts in the Demand Curve*

We can define demand as the relationship between an economic agent's willingness to purchase a good or service quantity at a given price. The demand curve is a graphical representation of such a relationship at a given point in time-based on preferences, income, and other prevailing factors.

We can also depict supply curves that show the price to quantity relationship of producers graphically. In combination, the demand and supply curves represent the goods and services market. We define market equilibrium as the price to quantity when demand equals supply. Graphically, this is the point where the demand and supply curves intersect.

Graphically, a point (P_0, Q_0) can change to another (P_1, Q_1) due to a movement along a single demand curve or a shift of the entire demand curve.

If the price of a good increase, holding other variables like the price of a substitute unchanged, then the quantity of that good is expected to decline. All else being unchanged, we will see a movement along the unchanged demand curve to the increased price point and reduced quantity (see Figure 1.1). This movement describes a consumer who is less willing or able to purchase a quantity of goods due to its price increase resulting in demand for a lower quantity.

If non-price underlying factors like income, preferences, and price of substitutes and complements affect consumer demand changes, shifts in the demand curve, for example, from D_0 to D_1, occur (see Figure 1.2). If an individual just received a pay increase, we can expect an outward shift in demand (to the right). This shift describes when the good or service assessed is a normal good, which is a desirable good, positively correlated with income. However, if we have an inferior good, that one, where the good is only acceptable to a consumer who cannot afford a more desirable

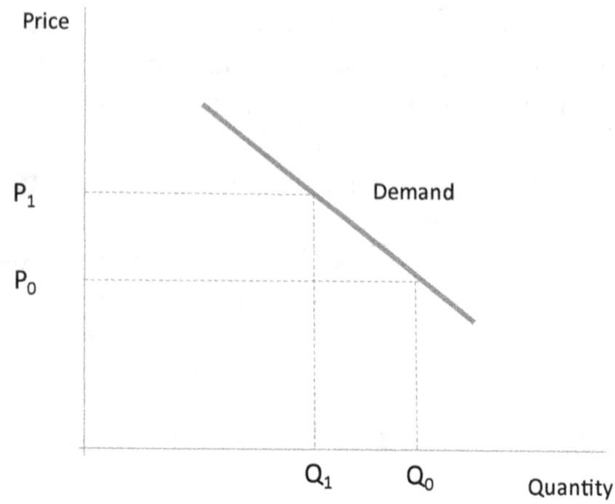

Figure 1.1: Movement along the demand curve.

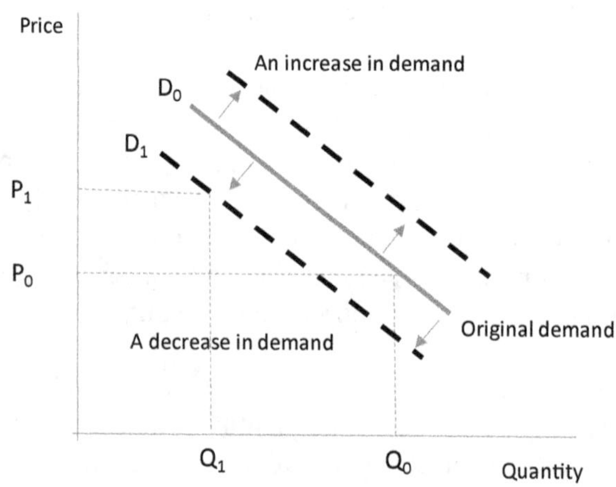

Figure 1.2: Shifts in the demand curve.

one (i.e., constrained by income), then an increase in income could result in an inward shift of demand (to the left).

1.3 Supply

1.3.1 *Supply Curve*

We now turn to discuss supply. Like demand, supply is a behavioral relationship that looks at suppliers' ability and willingness to offer quantities of a good or service at different sale price points. The supply curve represents the price to quantity relationship that is upward sloping.

Learning Objectives

- Explain the supply curve and the law of supply.
- Construct and understand the supply curves.

Main Takeaways

Main Points

- Quantity supplied increases as product price increases.
- With higher prices, producers increase production resulting in higher revenues and profits.

Main Terms

- **Supply curve:** The supply curve is upward sloping due to the potential increase in profitability with a price increase.
- **Surplus:** This is used in the context of either producer or consumer surplus. In producer surplus, the difference between the market price of a good and the lowest price that a producer will accept. In consumer surplus, they are willing to pay versus what they have to pay.
- **Shortage:** This involves a lack or deficiency.
- **Equilibrium:** A system's condition is in balance and does not change unless due to external influence changes.
- **The law of supply:** All else be held the same; a price increase will increase the quantity supplied.

Graphically, the supply curve of a product depicts the quantity of goods that sellers want to sell at each possible price, all else that affects supply remains unchanged. Figure 1.3 shows the supply curve of a product, for example, chocolate cake. The law of supply states that the supply curve is upward sloping.

1.3.2 *Movement along the Supply Curve and Shift in the Supply Curve*

Similar to our previous discussion on demand curves, a price increase, all else being unchanged, will result in a demand curve movement. Figure 1.4 illustrates an increase in the quantity supplied from Q_0 to Q_1 in response to an increase in price from P_0 to P_1.

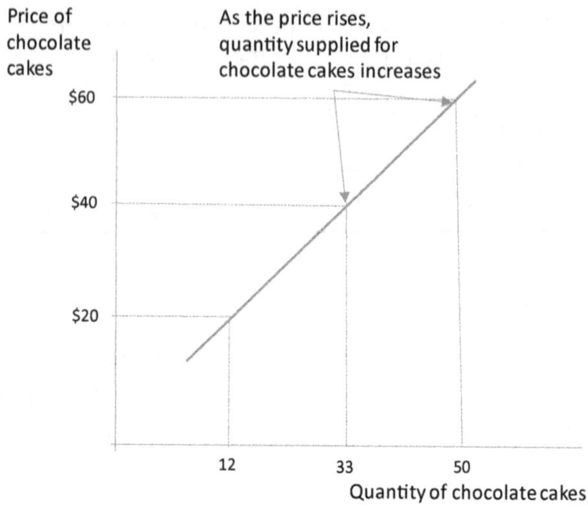

Figure 1.3: A supply curve for chocolate cakes.

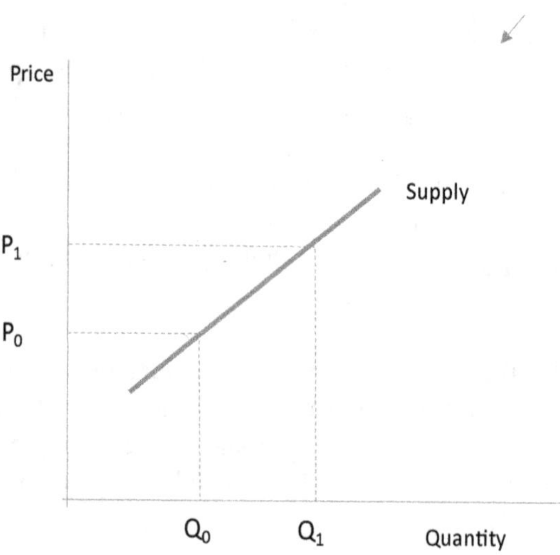

Figure 1.4: Movement along the supply curve.

Figure 1.5 shows both the increase in supply resulting from a decrease in input price. It also offers a reduction in supply, resulting from an increase in the input price. The supply curve decline from the original supply curve S_0 to the new supply curve S_1.

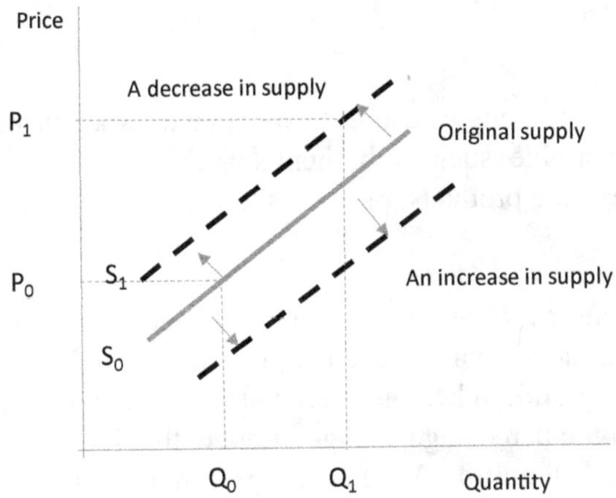

Figure 1.5: Shifts in the supply curve.

References/Further Readings

Mankiw, N.G. (2020). *Principles of Economics*, 9th edn., Cengage Learning, Chap 4, pp. 60–85.

Png, I. (2016). *Managerial Economics*, 5th edn., Routledge, pp. 21–42 and pp. 44–65.

1.4 Elasticities

1.4.1 *Introduction*

In this section, we discuss the concept of elasticity. Elasticity describes how demand and supply respond to price and other economic variables. The economic variables include income and prices of substitute and complementary goods.

Learning Objectives

- Understand the elasticity of demand and the determinants of it.
- Construct and understand the graphs of price elasticity and calculate the price elasticity from a demand and supply curve.
- Explain the concept of cross-price elasticity of demand.

Main Takeaways

Main Points

- The demand elasticity measures how demand responds to changes in an economic variable, such as the item's price, the prices of complementary or substitute products, or buyers' income.

Main Terms

- **Elastic demand:** When the percentage change in quantity demanded is greater than the percentage change in price, that is $\varepsilon_x > 1$.
- **Inelastic demand:** When the percentage change in quantity demanded is less than the percentage change in price, that is $\varepsilon_x < 1$.
- **Unit-elastic demand:** When the percentage change in quantity demanded is equal to the percentage change in price, that is $\varepsilon_x = 1$.

1.4.2 *Elasticity of Demand*

The demand elasticity measures how the demand responds to the change in an underlying variable, including the price of the item, the prices of complements or substitutes, and the buyers' income. We can define an elasticity to correspond to each economic variable or factor affecting demand.

1.4.3 *Own-Price Elasticity*

The own-price elasticity of demand measures how the quantity of that item demanded responds to changes in the item's price. With the own-price elasticity, a seller can estimate the impact of an increase or reduction on buyers' expenditure and revenue. Formally, the price elasticity of demand is

$$\varepsilon_x = \frac{\text{Percentage change in quantity demanded for good } x}{\text{Percentage change in price of good } x}$$

Example:
If the price of a tub of ice cream falls by 5% and the quantity demanded rises by 2%, then the price elasticity of demand for ice cream has a value of –0.4. Note that since the demand curve for a normal good like

ice cream is downward sloping, its own-price elasticity of demand will always be negative (or zero). We usually ignore the negative sign and focus on the absolute value of demand's price elasticity.

The following defines the terms elastic, inelastic, and unit-elastic demands:

- **Elastic demand:** When the percentage change in quantity demanded is greater than the percentage change in price, that is $\varepsilon_x > 1$.
- **Inelastic demand:** When the percentage change in quantity demanded is less than the percentage change in price, that is $\varepsilon_x < 1$.
- **Unit-elastic demand:** When the percentage change in quantity demanded is equal to the percentage change in price, that is $\varepsilon_x = 1$.

1.4.4 *What Determines the Price Elasticity of Demand?*

The following variables impact how the change in quantity demand respond to a change in price, that is, the price elasticity of demand:

1. **Substitutes:** With more close substitutes, the greater the price elasticity of demand as consumers can replace with a comparable, less expensive alternative.
2. **Time:** Demand becomes more elastic with time.
3. **Discretionary versus necessities:** The price elasticity for a good that is discretionary is more elastic than the price elasticity for a necessity.
4. **Big-ticket items versus small ticket items:** The larger the share of the good or service comprises the consumer's budget, the more elastic the demand for that good or service.

1.4.5 *Graphical Interpretation of Price Elasticity*

If the price change is small, we calculate the price elasticity of demand by dividing the percentage by which quantity demanded changes by the corresponding percentage by which price changes. The formula for the price elasticity of demand is as follows:

$$\varepsilon_x = \frac{\Delta Q_x / Q_x}{\Delta P_x / P_x}$$

This formula is interpreted graphically in Figure 1.6.

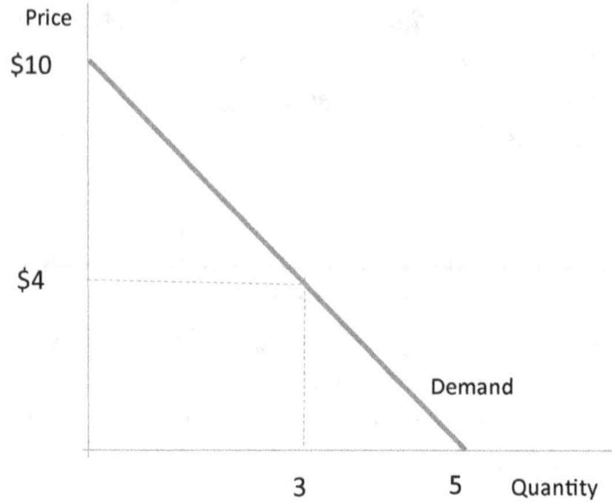

Figure 1.6: Price elasticity of demand calculation (point A is coordinate (3,4)).

The slope $\frac{\Delta P_x}{\Delta Q_x}$ of this demand curve is 10/5 = 2. So, $-\frac{\Delta Q_x}{\Delta P_x}$ of demand for x is 1/2. The ratio of P/Q at point A is 4/3. Using the formula, the price elasticity formula for point A is $(4/3) \times (1/2) = 2/3$. This result's interpretation is that a 3% price reduction will lead to a 2% increase in quantity demanded at the current price of $4.

In a linear demand, curve demand can be elastic, unit elastic, and inelastic at different points. Specifically, demand is elastic on the top half, unit elastic at the midpoint, and inelastic on the bottom half, as shown in Figure 1.7.

We now look at two special cases: (1) a horizontal demand curve is perfectly elastic, and the price elasticity is infinite at every point, and (2) a vertical demand curve is perfectly inelastic at every point, and the price elasticity is zero. Figure 1.8 shows the perfectly elastic and perfectly inelastic demand curves.

1.4.6 *Income Elasticity of Demand*

The income elasticity of demand for good measures how the quantity demanded responds to income changes. We calculate the income elasticity of demand as the percentage change in quantity demanded divided by the percentage change in income as follows:

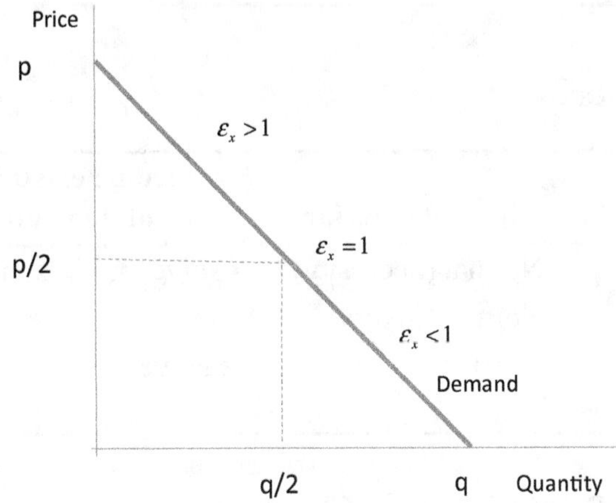

Figure 1.7: Price elasticity of demand along the demand curve.

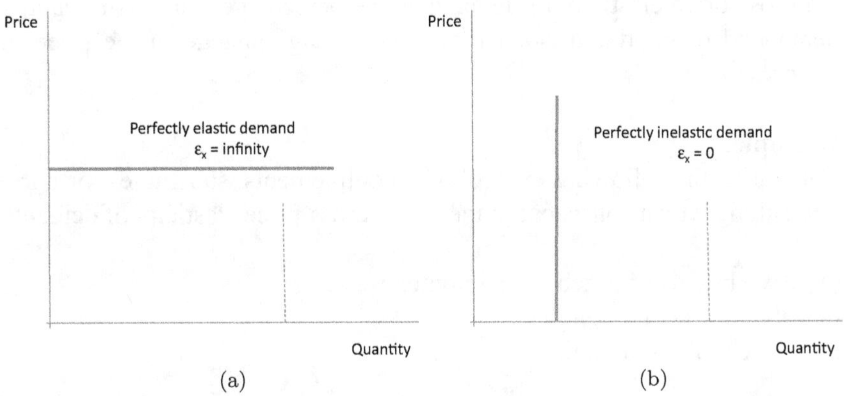

Figure 1.8: (a) Perfectly elastic and (b) perfectly inelastic demand curves.

$$\varepsilon_m = \frac{\text{Percentage change in quantity demanded for good } x}{\text{Percentage change in income}}$$

Example:

Categorize the following goods as normal and inferior along with a consistent range for its elasticity of demand:

(1) Eggs;
(2) Truffle;
(3) Canned meat.

Good	Normal/Inferior	Income elasticity of demand
Eggs	Normal (necessity)	Positive, but less than 1
Truffle	Normal (luxury)	Positive and greater than 1
Canned meat	Inferior	Negative

1.4.7 *Cross-Price Elasticity of Demand*

The cross-price elasticity of demand for good measures how the quantity demanded responds to changes in its related goods' prices. We calculate the cross-price elasticity of demand as the percentage change in quantity demanded of good x divided by the percentage change in the price of good y.

Example:
Categorize the following examples as complements, substitutes, or unrelated along with a consistent range for its cross-price elasticity of demand:

(1) Two brands of notebook computers;
(2) Notebooks and dongles;
(3) Notebooks and vanilla ice cream.

Example	Complements/ Substitutes/ Unrelated	Cross price elasticity of demand
Two brands of notebook computers	Substitutes	Positive
Notebooks and dongles	Complements	Negative
Notebooks and vanilla ice cream	Unrelated	Zero

1.4.8 *Price Elasticity of Supply*

Price elasticity of supply measures how the quantity supplied responds to a change in price. We calculate the price elasticity of supply as the percentage change in the quantity supplied of a good divided by the percentage change in the good's price as follows:

$$\varepsilon_x^s = \frac{\text{Percentage change in quantity supplied for good } x}{\text{Percentage change in price of good } x}$$

The formula for price elasticity of supply is the same as the corresponding expression for price elasticity of demand. The main difference for supply is that elasticity is positive due to the upward-sloping supply curve.

1.4.9 *What Determines the Price Elasticity of Supply?*

The following variables impact how the change in quantity supplied respond to a change in price, that is, the price elasticity of supply:

1. **Skill and flexibility of workforce:** Production that requires a highly skilled workforce is likely to be more inelastic in terms of its supply. For example, flying an airplane requires highly skilled and experienced pilots means that the resumption of air travel is likely to be constrained by the ability to requalify pilots to fly.
2. **Production capacity:** Supply is more elastic with excess capacity that can be brought online quickly. Spare capacity is why some expect the V shape recovery after the pandemic, with a quick increase in production, despite minimal price increases.
3. **Time to adjust:** Producers may require a significant lead time to switch from one activity to another, especially when there is a steep learning curve in the new activity. The substantial lead time is likely to be exacerbated if the new activity requires setting up a new plant and equipment.

References/Further Readings

Mankiw, N.G. (2020). *Principles of Economics*, 9th edn., Cengage Learning, Chap 5, pp. 86–108.

Png, I. (2016). *Managerial Economics*, 5th edn., Routledge, pp. 43–65.

1.5 Sample Questions

Question 1

Examine the four graphs below. Choose the graph representing the market of crops affected by a cyclone hitting Australia's northern states?

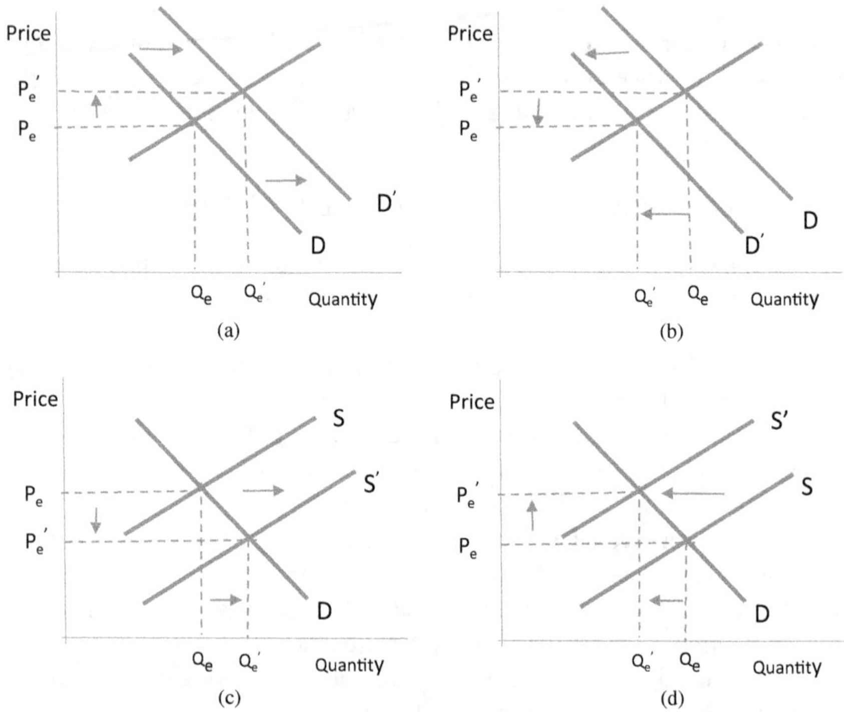

(a) Chart A
(b) Chart C
(c) Chart D

Question 2

Tables made from teak wood in Indonesia are considered normal goods. An initiative to stop half of all logging operations in Brazil saw tropical hardwood prices, including teak wood, increasing. There are more buyers for teak tables. Also, the price of wood saws has increased. What would happen to the equilibrium price and quantity in the teak tables market?

(a) Price will fall, and the effect on quantity is ambiguous.
(b) Price will rise, and the effect on quantity is ambiguous.
(c) Quantity will fall, and the effect on price is ambiguous.

Question 3

New cars are normal goods. What will happen to new cars' equilibrium price if gasoline prices rise, the price of steel falls, public transportation becomes cheaper and more comfortable, auto-workers accept lower wages, and automobile insurance becomes more expensive?

(a) Price will rise
(b) Price will fall
(c) Price will stay the same

Question 4

The percentage change in quantity demanded divided by the percentage change in price is known as the

(a) Price elasticity of demand
(b) Income elasticity of demand
(c) Cross-price elasticity of demand

Question 5

If the price of 1kg of durian increases by 20%, resulting in a decrease in quantity demanded by 10%, the price elasticity of demand for durians is

(a) 0.5
(b) 1.0
(c) 2.0

Question 6

Consumer staples like rice have _________ price elasticity of demand than consumer durables like a high-end television.

(a) higher
(b) lower
(c) unitary

Solutions

Question 1

Solution: Option **c** is correct.

The demand is not affected by the cyclone. The supply shifts to the left because of the damage caused by the cyclone.

Question 2

Solution: Option **b** is correct.

When the price of tropical hardwood tables rises, the demand for teak tables will shift to the right since they are substitutes. When the teak wood price rises, the supply for teak tables will shift to the left. With more buyers, the demand will shift to the right. When the price of wood saws increases, the supply will shift to the left. Therefore, the demand curve shifts to the right, and the supply curve shift to the left. The price will rise while the effect on quantity is ambiguous.

Question 3

Solution: Option **b** is correct.

If gasoline prices rise, new cars' demand will shift to the left. If the price of steel falls, new cars' supply will shift to the right. If public transportation becomes cheaper and more comfortable, new cars' demand will shift to the left. If autoworkers accept lower wages, new cars' supply will shift to the right. If automobile insurance becomes more expensive, new cars' demand will shift to the left. Therefore, the demand curve shifts further to the left, and the supply shifts to the right. Supply and demand Intersect at a lower equilibrium, prices will fall.

Question 4

Solution: Option **a** is correct.

The price elasticity demand for a good is calculated as the quantity demanded of that good divided by its price changes. Income elasticity measures responsiveness to income, and cross-price elasticity measures responsiveness to price changes to a related good.

Question 5

Solution: Option **a** is correct.

The price elasticity demand for durian is calculated by dividing the percentage change in the durian quantity demanded by the percentage change in durian price. 10%/20% = 0.5.

Question 6

Solution: Option **b** is correct.

The price elasticity demand for a good is calculated by dividing the percentage change in the quantity demanded of the good by the percentage change in the good price. When the price changes, consumer staples' quantity is smaller than consumer durables.

Chapter 2

Firm Decision-Making

2.1 Production, Revenue, Costs, and Profits of the Firm

2.1.1 *Production Function*

The production function is the relation between the maximum quantity of output obtained from a given amount of inputs.

Learning Objectives

- Define the production function.

Main Takeaways

Main Points

- Graphically, the production function is the boundary or frontier representing the maximum output that a feasible combination of inputs can produce.
- A production function relates the output of goods to the input factors of production.
- The production function provides valuable information on production conditions, such as increasing or decreasing returns to scale and the marginal products of labor and capital.

Main Terms

- **Marginal cost:** Increase in total cost from one more production unit.
- **Production function:** Relates the number of inputs used to make a good and the quantity of output of that good.
- **Output:** The quantity produced, created, or completed.

In economics, a production function is a relationship between the number of inputs, e.g., workers, and the quantity of output, e.g., refrigerators. The production function is a mathematical relation between the maximum amount of output obtained from a given number of inputs, generally capital and labor. Graphically, the production function is the boundary or frontier representing the maximum output that a feasible combination of inputs can produce.

Firms use the production function to determine: (1) quantity of output to produce given the product price, and (2) the optimal combination of inputs for production, given the input prices.

The traditional view of the production process is that it is subject to diminishing returns to scale. Firms typically find that their marginal costs increase at high production levels. Diminishing returns to scale arise because of increasing the number of inputs; for example, capital creates a less-than-proportional increase in output quantity. The implication of diminishing returns to scale is that supply cannot expand without limits without the need to increase output prices.

2.1.2 *Revenue*

Revenue is the "income" generated by normal business operations. It is the top line from which costs are subtracted to obtain net income in the income or profit and loss financial statement.

Learning Objectives

- Calculate, interpret, and compare total, average, and marginal revenue.

Main Takeaways

Main Points

- For a firm operating in a perfectly competitive market, all units are sold at the same price regardless of quantity, AR = MR = price.

- Firms that do not operate under perfect competition must decide the price to charge for their products. To sell a greater quantity, price-searcher firms must decrease the price.

Main Terms

- **Total revenue (TR):** the amount a firm receives for the sale of its output. In the case where a firm charges a single price (P), TR is calculated as price (P) multiplied by the quantity (Q) sold or TR = P x Q.
- **Average revenue (AR):** is equal to TR divided by the quantity sold, or AR = TR/Q.
- **Marginal revenue (MR):** It is the change in TR from an additional unit sold.

For a firm operating in a perfectly competitive market, all homogeneous product units are sold at the same price regardless of quantity. Figure 2.1 illustrates that in a perfectly competitive market, the firm's AR and MR are both equal to the market price, or AR = MR = price.

In a perfectly competitive market, all firms charge the same price of that homogeneous product to all buyers. With a downward-sloping market demand curve, to sell one more unit in the market requires that the price of all units sold must be decreased. With the assumption of a single price, AR and price must be equal.

Firms that do not operate under perfect competition must decide the price to charge for their products. These firms face downward-sloping

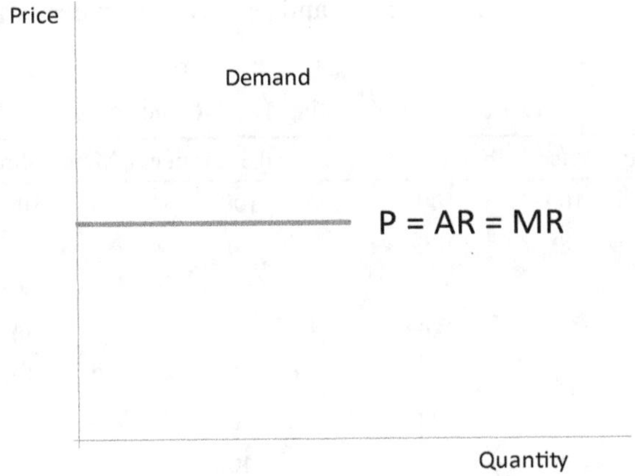

Figure 2.1: Average and marginal revenue under perfect competition.

demand curves and are called “price searchers”. To sell a greater quantity, price-searcher firms must decrease the price.

Under imperfect competition, AR and MR will decline as the quantity sold increases. If the firms charge the same price, selling one more unit requires that all units’ prices be reduced. So, MR < P for quantities more than 1. Also, AR is not equal to MR for any quantities greater than one. The decrease in MR (or the rate of change in TR) is more than the decrease in price or AR. TR is maximized when MR equals zero (Table 2.1).

Example: TR, AR, and MR (Imperfect competition)
The demand schedule for firm X is provided below:

Quantity	1	2	3	4	5	6	7	8
Price	100	90	80	70	60	50	40	30

Calculate the TR, AR, and MR for the different number of units in the demand schedule and draw the AR and MR curves for units 1 to 8.

Solution:
Figure 2.2 illustrates the marginal and AR for a firm facing the downward sloping demand shown in the table. Note that AR is equal to a firm’s price that charges a single price to all customers.

2.1.3 *Costs*

Cost is the monetary value of goods and services producers and consumers purchase.

Table 2.1: Calculating TR, AR, and MR.

Quantity	Price	Total revenue	Average revenue	Marginal revenue
1	100	100	100	100
2	90	180	90	80
3	80	240	80	60
4	70	280	70	40
5	60	300	60	20
6	50	300	50	0
7	40	280	40	–20
8	30	240	30	–40

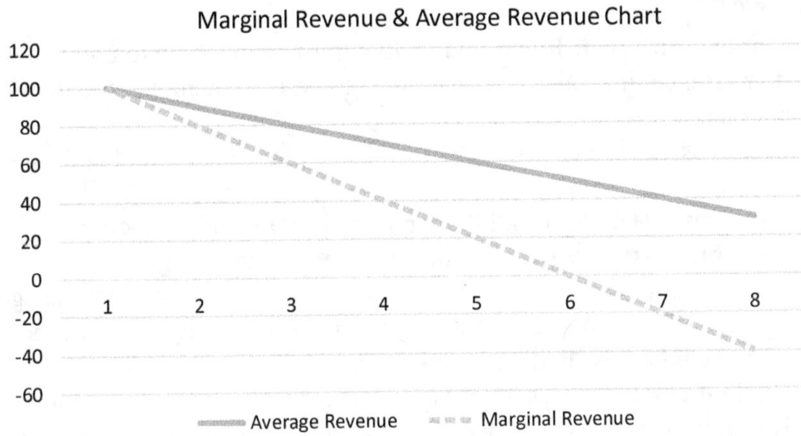

Figure 2.2: Marginal revenue and average revenue for a firm facing downward sloping demand.

Learning Objectives

- Calculate, interpret, and compare total, average, and marginal cost.

Main Takeaways

Main Points

- An item's opportunity cost is what you give up to get that item. The opportunity cost of an activity is the value of the next-best alternative that must be forgone to undertake that activity.
- Sunk cost to a firm is a cost that the firm has already committed and cannot be recovered. Because nothing can be done about sunk costs, firms should ignore them when making business decisions.
- The firm's total product shows how the output varies with the number of workers employed. The average product is the total product divided by the number of workers employed. The marginal product is the change in total product from one additional unit of a worker.
- The firm's production function is the relationship between the firm's inputs and the maximum output. The production function is short-run if the period is too short to vary at least one of the inputs.
- To accountants, profit is defined as the difference between the revenue it takes in a year and its explicit costs for that year. Profit is defined as the difference between the firm's TR and its explicit costs and implicit costs.

Main Terms

- **Opportunity cost:** It is whatever that must be given up to obtain some item. Hence, it is based on scarcity, a trade-off, giving up one item for another.
- **Sunk cost:** It is a cost that the firm has already committed and cannot be recovered.
- **Total cost:** The cost of all the inputs a firm uses in production.
- **Variable cost:** It is a cost that changes as output changes.
- **Fixed cost:** It is a cost that remains constant even as output quantity changes.
- **Economic cost:** It is a cost defined as the opportunity cost of production, including explicit and implicit costs.
- **Explicit cost:** It is a cost defined as actual cash payments for inputs.
- **Implicit cost:** It is an opportunity cost, defined as the cost of non-purchased inputs
- **Accounting profit:** The TR less explicit costs.
- **Economic profit:** The TR less explicit costs and implicit costs.
- **Economies of scale:** When long-run average cost (LRAC) declines with a firm's operation's size (scale).
- **Economies of scope:** Similar to economies of scale, but the total cost is reduced in joint production.

(a) Opportunity Cost

An item's opportunity cost is what you give up to get that item. The opportunity cost of an activity is the value of the next-best alternative that must be forgone to undertake that activity. The opportunity cost principle is based on scarcity, hence, a trade-off, giving up one item or activity for another.

Decision-makers should take into account the opportunity cost of each possible action. The concept of opportunity cost applies to both an individual's daily decisions and a firm's. There is always a trade-off because resources are scarce and can be utilized differently.

In discussing the firm's cost, we use the term "economic cost," which is defined as the opportunity cost of production, including explicit and implicit costs.

A firm's explicit cost is defined as its actual cash payments for inputs.

Example: Explicit and implicit cost

Restaurant X spends a total of S$25,000 per month on wages, raw material, and space plus equipment rental. The S$25,000 is its explicit cost.

This explicit cost is an opportunity cost because the $25,000 spent cannot be used for something else.

The firm's implicit cost is also an opportunity cost. It can be defined as the cost of non-purchased inputs such as the restauranteur's time or money.

Now, let us examine more closely the implicit cost. Assume that the restauranteur's next best alternative is to work as a top restaurant manager that pays a monthly salary of S$12,000 per month. Hence, the opportunity cost of his time is S$12,000. The restauranteur had used his savings that were earning interest of $10,000 per month to start restaurant X. The opportunity cost of using the savings is the interest it could have earned. Hence, the implicit cost for restaurant X is $12,000 + $10,000 = $22,000. The economic cost in this example is S$25,000 + S$12,000 + S$10,000 = S$47,000 per month.

(b) Sunk Cost

It is essential to note the difference between opportunity cost and sunk cost. Sunk cost to a firm is a cost that the firm has already committed and cannot be recovered. Because nothing can be done about sunk costs, firms should ignore them when making business decisions.

Example of sunk cost

Farmer Salleh considers the planting of his land. Due to the low expected prices, he decides not to plant this season. The land cost is one of Salleh's fixed costs, and if he leaves the land plant fallow (unplanted) this season, he cannot recover this cost. In deciding to plant or not plant this season, his land's cost is a sunk cost. It is so because, in the short run, there is nothing that Salleh can do about this cost, and the cost does not impact his decision to plant or not to plant. We note that the land cost is not a sunk cost if Salleh decides whether to stop farming altogether.

(c) Short Run and Long Run

A firm's technology is how inputs are converted into outputs of goods and services. Positive technological change results in a firm producing more output from any given combination of inputs. Simple examples include faster or more reliable machinery, better workflows, and information dashboards for decision-making.

On the other hand, technological change for a firm can be negative, such as less-skilled workers and cumbersome rules and bureaucracy.

For many firms, the division of total costs between fixed and variable costs depends on the time horizon. So, we describe the short run to mean a period in which one or more of the firm's factors of production is fixed and cannot be varied.

For example, over a few months, a carmaker cannot adjust its manufacturing plants' number or size. The only way to produce more cars is to hire more workers in the plants it already has. The cost of the plants is fixed in the short run. On the other hand, over several years, the carmaker can expand its existing plants, build new plants, or close inefficient ones. In the long run, the cost of its manufacturing plants is variable.

(d) Short-Run Production and Diminishing Returns

The production process is subject to diminishing returns in the short run. To illustrate this, let us look at a cloth mask maker. For simplicity, let us assume that the raw materials are scrap from apparel makers and available free of charge. The cost incurred is the workers' wages and the lease payments on a cloth mask-making machine. Table 2.2 shows the firm's short-run production function using only one cloth mask-making machine; specifically, how total product, average product, and marginal product vary with the number of workers.

The firm's total product is the firm's output, while the average product is the total product per worker and the marginal product is the change in total product from one additional worker. We observe that marginal product increases when we add a worker. The increase in the marginal product is sometimes explained by the workers being able to specialize, leading to productivity increases. In this example, we observe diminishing returns

Table 2.2: Total product, average product, and marginal product of firm.

Workers	Total product	Average product	Marginal product
0	0	0	
1	10	10	10
2	30	15	20
3	57	19	27
4	72	18	15
5	80	16	8

when adding the fourth worker. In the short run, the process uses only one cloth mask-making machine, resulting in output increasing at a decreasing rate when we increase the number of workers.

(e) Fixed Cost and Variable Cost

We first begin by defining the following:

1. Total cost is the cost of all the inputs a firm uses in production.
2. Variable cost is the cost that changes as output changes.
3. Fixed cost is the cost that remains constant even as output quantity changes.

Next, the following cost variables are defined.

The firm's average cost (AC) equals the total cost divided by the quantity of output produced.

Average fixed cost (AFC) equals TFC divided by total output, q.

Average variable cost (AVC) equals TVC divided by total output, q.

Marginal cost (MC) is the change in total cost (ΔTC) from producing one more unit of output (Δq) and expressed as follows:

$$\text{Marginal cost (MC)} = \frac{\Delta \text{TC}}{\Delta q} = \frac{\Delta \text{TFC}}{\Delta q} + \frac{\Delta \text{TVC}}{\Delta q} = 0 + \frac{\Delta \text{TVC}}{\Delta q}$$

We will look at the following example to gain insights into the above cost definitions and their relationship. For a better insight into the relationships between these production costs, it is helpful to consider a firm confronting how much to produce without affecting the output price with this decision. The firm in question is the small cloth mask-making company. Table 2.3 shows how the firm's production costs vary with its mask production.

We have also calculated the AFC, AVC, and AC of the firm and summarise the results in Table 2.4.

Figure 2.3 shows that:

1. MC intersects AC when AC is minimum.
2. When MC < AC, AC is decreasing.
3. When MC > AC, AC is increasing.
4. Observations (1) to (3) holds for MC and AVC (replacing AC).

Table 2.3: Fixed cost, variable cost, and total cost.

Masks per day ('000)	Fixed cost (S$'000/day)	Variable cost (S$'000/day)	Total cost (S$'000/day)	Marginal cost (S$/mask)
0	40.0	0	40	
80	40	12	52	0.15
200	40	24	64	0.1
260	40	36	76	0.2
300	40	48	88	0.3
330	40	60	100	0.4
350	40	72	112	0.6

Table 2.4: Average fixed cost, average variable cost, and average cost and marginal cost.

Masks per day ('000)	Average fixed cost (S$/masks)	Average variable cost (S$/mask)	Average cost (S$/mask)	Marginal cost (S$/mask)
0		0	0	
80	0.50	0.15	0.65	0.15
200	0.20	0.12	0.32	0.10
260	0.15	0.14	0.29	0.20
300	0.13	0.16	0.29	0.30
330	0.12	0.18	0.30	0.40
350	0.11	0.21	0.32	0.60

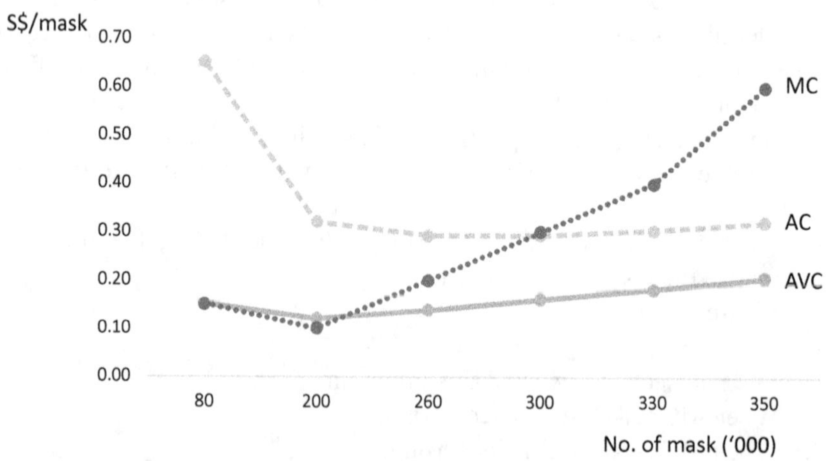

Figure 2.3: Graph of AVC, AC, and MC.

(f) Accounting Profit versus Economic Profit

In Economics and Finance, we traditionally state that the firm's goal is to maximize its profit. We also notice that there are several ways to define profits. One may use the term profit to mean accounting profit or economic profit. Economists understand profit differently from accountants. Accountants define profit as the difference between the revenue over time and its explicit costs for that same time frame.

Explicit costs are the actual payments a firm makes to its factors of production and other suppliers. Accounting profit is defined as

$$\text{Accounting profit} = \text{Total revenue} - \text{Explicit costs}$$

Economists, on the other hand, define profit differently. Economic profit is the difference between the firm's TR and explicit and implicit costs, such as the opportunity costs of the firm's owners' resources. Economic profit is thus defined as

$$\text{Economic profit} = \text{Total revenue} - \text{Explicit costs} - \text{Implicit costs}$$

Figure 2.4 is a chart to show the difference between accounting profit and economic profit. Of the TR in panel (a), it can comprise accounting profit and explicit cost panel (b) or comprise economic profit plus the explicit cost and implicit cost as shown in panel (c).

Example:

A firm had $4 million in total annual revenue in 2019. It paid $3 million for raw materials, wages, and rent during the same period. This firm's

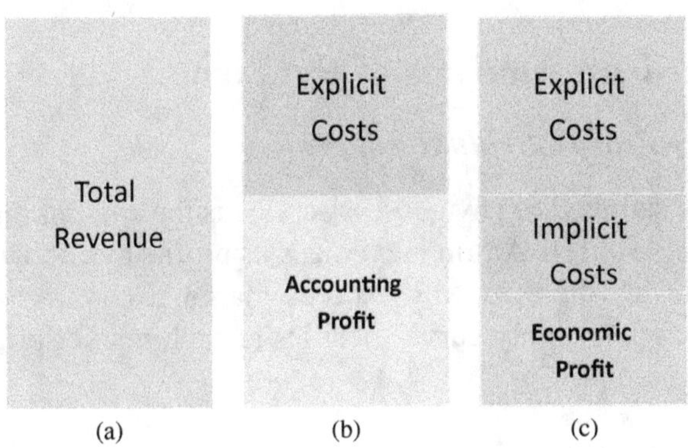

Figure 2.4: The difference between accounting profit and economic profit.

owner has supplied machines and other equipment with a total resale value of $10 million. What are the firm's accounting and economic profits for 2019?

Solution:
The firm's accounting profit is the difference between TR and total explicit costs. Therefore, the firm's accounting profit is $1 million, i.e., $4 million minus $3 million.

The calculation of economic profit requires more information. To calculate the firm's economic profit, we must first calculate the opportunity cost of the owner-supplied machines and other equipment with an estimated resale value of $10 million. If the machine and other equipment were sold, the owner could put the proceeds in a savings account, earning 3% per annum. In this case, the opportunity cost is $0.3 million. If we assume that there are no other implicit costs, the firm's economic profit is $0.7 million, i.e., $4 million minus $3 million minus $0.3 million.

We note that the economic profit calculated is less than the accounting profit by exactly the firm's implicit costs of $0.3 million. This difference between the accounting profit and the economic profit is also known as the normal profit. It is just the opportunity cost of the resources that can include time and funds supplied to a business by its owner.

References/Further Readings

Gregory Mankiw, N. (2020). *Principles of Economics*, 9th edn. Cengage Learning, pp. 242–258.

2.2 Short-Run Analysis of the Firm

2.2.1 *Short-Run Individual Supply*

The quantity supplied of any good or service is the amount that sellers are willing and able to sell. A firm maximizes its profits by choosing to supply the output level where its MR exceeds marginal cost. As such, in the short-run, a firm's supply curve specifies at each market price its profit-maximizing output.

Learning Objectives
- Understand the concept of profit-maximizing output.

Main Takeaways

Main Points

- A perfectly competitive firm's profit-maximizing output is when the price is equal to marginal cost. If the firm is producing above/less than the profit-maximizing output, the firm should reduce/increase output to that level.
- When deciding whether a business should continue operating, a firm compares the profits from two alternatives: (1) from continuing production and (2) shutting down.
- Critical decisions made by firms like (1) whether to continue operation and (2) how much to produce involves considerations of both revenue and costs.

Example: Profit maximization

We consider a perfectly competitive firm where the profit maximization output is obtained when the price is equal to marginal cost or P = MC. The firm should increase output to the profit-maximizing level. Let us see if this is the case for a firm with increasing marginal cost (diminishing return) and unable to influence the price, as shown in Figure 2.5. The profit-maximizing output for the price of $25 is 270 units. Should the firm produce this output?

Suppose the firm sells only 200 units for $25.
If the firm expands by one unit, revenue will increase by $25.
The cost to produce that one unit will increase the cost by $16.

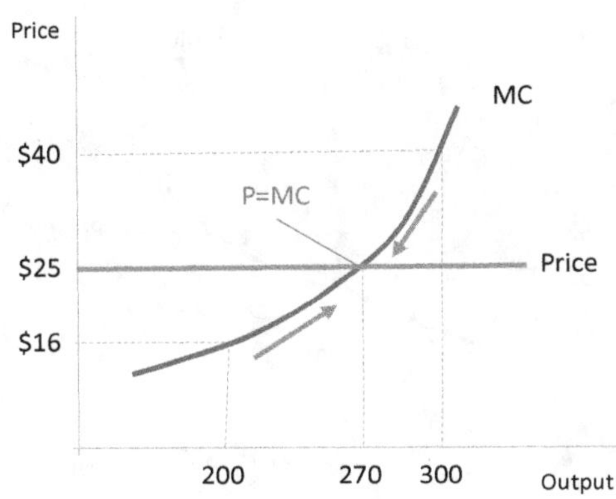

Figure 2.5: Profit maximizing output, P = MC.

In this case, producing one more unit will increase profit by \$25 – \$16 = \$9.

Using the same argument, we can show that for any quantity with P > MC, the firm can increase profit by expanding production.

Now suppose the firm produces and sells 300 units for \$25 instead. We see that the marginal cost is S\$40 per unit. So, each additional unit contributes –\$15 to profits. We can show by the same argument that the firm can increase profit by reducing production as long as P < MC. It follows that the firm maximizes profit and produces 270 units when the market price is \$25.

Example: Calculation of firm profit

We can demonstrate graphically in Figure 2.6 the firm's profit computation. We are using the numbers from the previous example and the AC curve (as shown). If the price is \$25 per unit, profit is the difference between price (P) and AC multiplied by the number of units sold (*q*). For the example, P = \$25 and AC = \$20, profit per unit is (P – AC) = \$5 and total profit is \$5 × 270 units = \$1,350 represent by the shaded rectangle in Figure 2.6.

(a) The Firm's Short-Run Shutdown Condition

We have so far been analyzing the question of how much a competitive firm will produce. In some circumstances, however, the firm will decide to shut down and not produce anything at all.

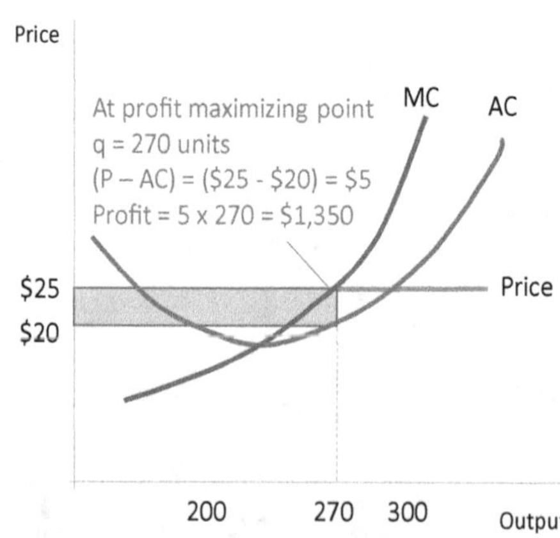

Figure 2.6: Example of profit maximization.

Example:

Consider the same farmer Salleh again. The example discusses the short-run decision to plant or not to plant for the season.

Suppose the farmer decides to plant and yet suffers a loss. (There is no issue if he plants and makes a profit). The loss from planting is as follows:

$$\text{Loss (Continue planting)} = \text{TFC} + \text{TVC} - \text{TR}$$

where TR is the total revenue,TFC is the total fixed cost (farm equipment, but not land that is a sunk cost), and TVC is the total variable cost (fertilizers and wages for harvesting).

If the seller decides not to plant for the coming season, Salleh has no revenue but does not incur any TVC. The farmer continues to pay in some form for farm equipment. Therefore, the loss associated with not planting is

$$\text{Loss (Not planting)} = \text{TFC}$$

The farmer should plant if the loss from not planting is at least as low as the loss from planting, i.e.,

$$\text{Loss (Continue planting)} \leq \text{Loss (Not planting)}$$

Meaning that

$$\text{TFC} + \text{TVC} - \text{TR} \leq \text{TFC}$$

which can be simplified to

$$\text{TR} \geq \text{TVC}$$

Since TR = P × Q and TVC = AVC × Q, we can reduce the condition to P ≥ AVC.

Therefore, the profit-maximizing rule, together with this shut-down rule, implies that the firm's short-run supply curve is simply the portion of MC that lies above AVC (see Figure 2.3). We will discuss profit maximization under perfect competition, monopolistic, and oligopolistic markets in Chapters 3 and 4.

2.3 Long-Run Analysis of the Firm

2.3.1 *Overview*

For many firms, the division of total costs between fixed and variable costs depends on the time horizon. In this section, we look at the long run where a single firm can achieve facilities of different sizes. A single firm's long-run cost curves show the relationship between production cost and different size facilities. As for the time horizon, the long run is defined such that a firm is perfectly flexible in its choice of all inputs, including manufacturing plants or staff of much greater capabilities.

Learning Objectives

- Analyze long-run cost curves.
- Distinguish between LRAC and long-run marginal cost.
- Understand the economies of scale and economies of scope.

Main Takeaways

Main Points

- Because many decisions are fixed in the short-run but variable in the long run, a firm's long-run cost curve differs from its short-run cost curve.
- The shape of the LRAC curve conveys important information about a firm's production processes. So, if the slope of a firm's LRAC curve is negatively sloped, it is experiencing economies of scale.
- The Economy of scope gives a cost advantage to firms that produce a complementary range of products that leverage their core competencies.
- In the long run, firms should continue operating if it makes an economic or normal profit.

(a) Long-Run Average Cost versus Long-Run Marginal Cost

Because many decisions are fixed in the short run but variable, a firm's long-run cost curve differs from its short-run curve in the long run. For example, in the long run, a firm is entirely flexible in choosing its manufacturing plants' size and number.

In the discussion on long-run cost, we define the following:

- LRTC is the total cost of production in the long run when a firm is perfectly flexible in its choice of all inputs.

Table 2.5: LR limited's long-run projections.

Output	Labour	Labour cost (S$/day)	Capital cost (S$/day)	Long-run total cost (S$/day)	Long-run average cost (S$/day)
5	3	150	100	250	50
10	4	200	100	300	30
15	6	300	200	500	33
20	8	400	200	600	30
25	10	500	300	800	32
30	12	600	300	900	30

- The LRAC is the LRTC divided by production units.
- LRMC is the cost increase due to increasing production by one unit.

Example:
Firm LR Limited has forecast that it can produce a different quantity of output using different equipment and workers. The projections for different quantities of the output of 5, 10, 15, 20, 25, and 30 units per day are shown in Table 2.5.

Given the project labor, labor, and capital cost required, LRTC and LRAC are calculated for the different output levels. Plot the LRAC curve and explain its shape.

Solution:
The plot of LRAC against output is shown in Figure 2.7. The benefits of labor specialization explain the resulting plot. The LRAC declines with increases in output at a certain point, ten units of output in this example. Beyond that point, the firm continues to benefit from specialization by replicating its operations. LRAC remains unchanged with increasing output beyond that particular point.

Long-run marginal cost (LRMC) is the cost increase due to increasing production by one unit.

Unlike the short run, the firm is entirely flexible in choosing its inputs in the long run. In particular, LRMC is the additional cost that results in a firm increase in operation scale by adding more workers to a given factor and building a larger factory or new factories.

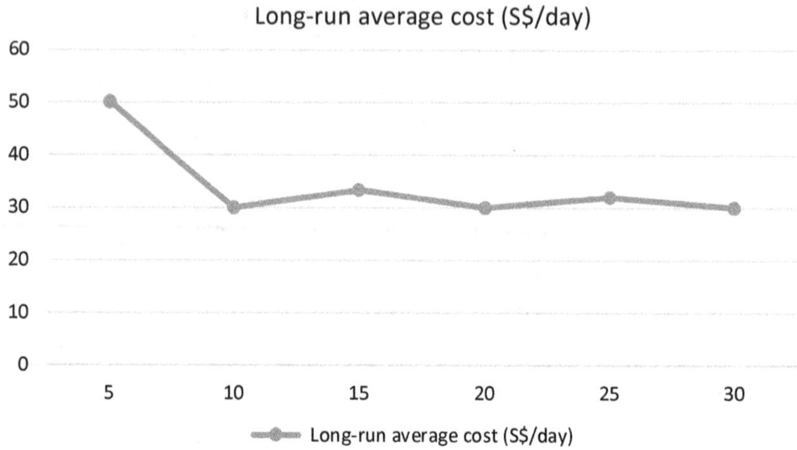

Figure 2.7: Long run average cost curve.

(b) Economies of Scale

The shape of the LRAC curve conveys important information about a firm's production processes. It also tells us how costs vary with a firm's operation scale. So, if the slope of a firm's LRAC curve is negatively sloped, it is experiencing economies of scale. If the LRAC rises as output increases, there are diseconomies of scale. When the LRAC does not vary with the output level, there are constant returns to scale.

With the diminishing return, one helpful information in analyzing the extent of economies of scale of a firm is the "minimum efficient scale," or the level of output at which the LRAC curve becomes flat or horizontal. That is the level of output at which economies of scale are exhausted.

What might cause economies or diseconomies of scale? Economies of scale often arise because higher production levels allow specialization among workers, allowing them to be better at specific tasks. However, diseconomies can occur because of coordination problems in large organizations. Further, the increasing output can stretch management teams resulting in them being ineffective at keeping costs down.

For most firms, the LRAC is U-shaped. At low production levels, increasing production allows for their workforce specialization, while coordination problems are not severe. In contrast, at high production levels, benefits of specialization have already been harnessed, while coordination issues have become more severe.

(c) Economies of Scope

Economies of scope are conceptually similar to economies of scale and help firms manage their costs. Economies of scope focus on the total cost of producing a variety of complementary goods. In other words, the economy of scope gives a cost advantage to firms that produce a complementary range of products that leverage their core competencies.

Economies of scope occur when there are cost savings from products in the production process. One example in banking is a common information production cost component to lending and underwriting securities. Combining the functions will result in economies of scope. For financial institutions, information about borrowers and know-how (like analytics) can develop products or variants without additional costs.

(d) Long-Run Break-Even Condition

Similar to firms' critical decisions in the short run, firms also make long-run decisions to (1) continue to operate and (2) the quantity to produce. The key difference is that all production factors are variable in the long run, whereas one or more may be fixed in the short run.

In the long run, a seller should continue in operation if he is making at least zero economic profit (sometimes called normal profit), offsetting the owners' implicit or opportunity cost. The profit of the firm is given by

$$\pi = \mathrm{TR} - \mathrm{TC}$$

Then, the firm continues to operate if

$$\mathrm{TR} - \mathrm{TC} \geq 0$$

Rearranging gives:

$$\mathrm{TR} \geq \mathrm{TC}$$

Since $\mathrm{TR} = \mathrm{P} \times \mathrm{Q}$ and $\mathrm{TC} = \mathrm{AC} \times \mathrm{Q}$, we rewrite the condition as $\mathrm{P} \geq \mathrm{AC}$.

Hence based on profit-maximization and the need to break even in the long run, a firm's long-run supply curve is simply the portion of MC, that lies above the AC curve.

References/Further Readings

Gregory Mankiw, N. (2020). *Principles of Economics*, 9th edn. Cengage Learning, pp. 263–275.

2.4 Blockchain and Firm Decision-Making

Given the advantageous features of blockchain technology, we expect to increase applications in processes facilitating firm decision-making.

Learning Objectives

- Understand the role that blockchain can play in firm decision-making.

Main Takeaways

Main Points

- Blockchain technology can revolutionize organization design and allow organizations to create value better.

Main Terms

- **Blockchain:** It is a system of recording information that makes it difficult or impossible to change, hack or cheat the system. It is essentially a ledger of duplicated transactions and distributed throughout its computer system.
- **DAO:** Decentralized Autonomous Organizations. Created by developers to automate decisions and facilitate transactions.
- **Internet of Things:** Interconnection via the internet of computing devices embedded in everyday devices enables them to send and receive data.

Blockchain technology archives and permanently manage data that can't be tampered with or changed. It engages in "smart contracts" and consensus mechanisms that oversee the process of automation, development, evaluation, and execution of the decisions. Blockchain technology can revolutionize organization design with its decentralized and distributed characteristics. An example is in the making or buys decisions that firms make. The decision is now to make, buy, or network.

Companies that apply Blockchain are progressively unifying with a distributed network organization, as part of the Internet of Value'. When companies commence using smart contracts deployed on a blockchain, they proceed towards becoming a DAO where actors of all classes self-organize to create value. Governance, either implemented within a code or ensured through its acceptable practices, is crucial because of the irrevocable code deployed and the data stored in the blockchain. Moreover, DAOs must ensure they adhere to regulatory requirements, which may or may not be contradictory.

Overall, economics allows for exploring how blockchain technology can shape competition and innovation in digital platforms. Blockchain offers immense possibilities for organizations to create value, develop different products and services, automate strategic decision-making and lessen intermediaries, resulting in new organization concepts. However, considerably more research is needed to overcome the governance and technological challenges.

References/Further Readings

Catalini, C. & Gans, J. S. (2016). Some Simple Economics of the Blockchain [Ebook]. NBER Working Paper Series. Retrieved from https://www.nber.org/system/files/working_papers/w22952/w22952.pdf.

Potts, J., Berg, C., & Davidson, S. (2019). Blockchain Technology as Economic Infrastructure: Revisiting the Electronic Markets Hypothesis. Retrieved from https://www.frontiersin.org/articles/10.3389/fbloc.2019.00022/full.

van Rijmenam, M. (2019). A Distributed Future: Where Blockchain Technology Meets Organisation Design and Decision-Making. Retrieved from https://medium.com/swlh/a-distributed-future-where-blockchain-technology-meets-organisation-design-and-decision-making-ce7430e1a196.

2.5 Sample Questions

Question 1

Aggregating the production possibilities frontiers of firms that produce the same product shows:

(a) How the products should be allocated to consumers.
(b) How the products should be produced in the future.
(c) How many products can be achieved using different available inputs.

Question 2

Assume Firm X's explicit costs are $10,000/month. The firm's owner could earn $1,000 in his next best alternative job. Firm revenue is $12,000/month. What is Firm X's accounting profit?

(a) 1000
(b) 2000
(c) 11000

Question 3
Which of the following situations best describes the concept of opportunity cost?

(a) Taking advantage of investing opportunities involves cost.
(b) The firm is planning to shut down because it expects to earn negative economic profits.
(c) The firm expects costs to reduce due to many technological opportunities.

Question 4
Daniel was a supermarket manager, where he earned $4,000 per month. If he started a food delivery business, he would earn $7,000 in revenue. Daniel owns a mid-size truck that he uses to commute to work; the truck can be sold for $10,000. Daniel will probably put the proceeds in a savings account, earning 3% per annum if it were sold. His expected expenses to run the business is $1000 per month to cover fuel and other costs.

Daniel's total economic profits per month are ________.

(a) $1,700
(b) $2,000
(c) $6,000

Question 5
Economies of scale exist when:

(a) Market size is important.
(b) Short-term input prices are expected to decline.
(c) Average costs fall as output increases.

Question 6
A firm operating in a perfectly competitive market expects that its AR will exceed its AVC but not its average total cost. What should the firm do?

(a) Shut down immediately.
(b) Shut down in a short period.
(c) Shut down in the long run if the situation is not expected to change.

Solutions

Question 1

Solution: Option **c** is correct.

The production possibilities frontier is a graph that shows the various combinations of output that can be produced given available factors of production and technology.

Question 2

Solution: Option **b** is correct. Accounting profit is the difference between TR and explicit costs.

Question 3

Solution: Option **b** is correct. Economic profit is net of implicit costs, including opportunity cost to the business owners.

Question 4

Solution: Option **a** is correct. Total economic profit = \$7,000 − \$1000 − \$300 − \$4,000 = \$1,700.

Question 5

Solution: Option **c** is correct.

A firm is experiencing economies of scale when its LRAC curve is negatively sloped.

Question 6

Solution: Option **c** is correct.

If the firm is generating enough to cover its variable cost and part of its fixed cost, it should continue to operate in the short run. If this situation is expected to persist long term, the firm should shut down.

Chapter 3
Market Structure

3.1 Analysis of Market Structures

The firm's decision-makers are presented with a different set of choices depending on the type of market structure their firm is operating in. Important decisions such as the pricing of the firm's product and determining strategies to increase profits depend on the firm's market structure. Since choices for a competitive market differ from, let's say, a monopoly, we are required to have a clear understanding of market structure to help guide decisions facing firms.

Learning Objectives

- Describe the characteristics of perfect competition, monopolistic competition, oligopoly, and pure monopoly.
- Understand the factors that determine the market structure.

Main Takeaways

Main Points

- In the long run, a firm's profitability will be determined by the forces associated with the market structure within which it operates.
- In a highly competitive market, long-run profits will be driven down by competition forces. In less competitive markets, large profits are possible even in the long run; while in the short run, any outcome is possible.
- Market structure can be divided into four distinct categories: perfect competition, monopolistic competition, oligopoly, and monopoly.

Main Terms

- **Price takers:** Parties that must accept whatever the price the market dictates.

3.1.1 *The Types of Market Structure*

Economists define a market as a group of buyers and sellers who know each other and exchange goods or services with each other upon an agreed price. Some markets are highly concentrated, with most total sales coming from a small number of firms. For example, in the market for internet search, three firms control 98.9% of the US market (Google 63.5%, Microsoft 24%, and Oath (formerly Yahoo) 11.4%) as of January 2018. Other markets are very fragmented, such as automobile repairs, where small independent shops often dominate, and large chains may or may not exist.

Market structure can be categorized into four distinct categories: perfect competition, monopolistic competition, oligopoly, and monopoly.

The most competitive environment is perfect competition. Perfect competition is demonstrated in actual markets and is seen in several commodities markets, where sellers and buyers trade a homogeneous product. None of the producers are large enough to influence market prices. Under perfect competition, profits above required returns to the entrepreneur or investor are challenging to attain as they compete away. However, on average, firms in competitive markets are expected to be fairly compensated and survive, if not thrive, in a challenging competitive environment.

While highly competitive, monopolistic competition is a case of imperfect competition. This market structure comprises a mix of competition with elements of monopoly-like conditions. This market structure consists of many firms in which products are differentiated. As a result, some degree of pricing power can be attained for products that consumers perceive are distinctly different from other "similar" ones. One example is the soft drink, with brand loyalty enjoyed by Coca-Cola.

The oligopoly market structure is characterized as one that is populated by a relatively small number of firms. The small number of firms supplying the market requires that each's strategic decisions are made with the other firms' strategies and actions in mind. Consider the pricing behavior of supermarkets, especially for perishables. Pricing strategies and the products on promotion are based on the expected reaction of the other supermarkets nearby. Suppose one of the competitors has a promotion on a seasonal item. In that case, a supermarket may consider retaliating with a similar promotion, or have a promotion on a close substitute or do nothing.

Finally, the monopoly market structure is the least competitive. There are no other suitable substitutes for the given product or service in a pure monopoly. A single seller, if unconstrained, can exercise considerable power over pricing and output. As such, pure monopolies in market-based economies are usually regulated by the government. An example of a regulated monopoly would be the train system in major cities. Operators of the trains are allowed to earn a normal return on their investment, and fares are set by the regulatory authority (like the Land Transport Authority in Singapore) to enable that return. Also, other operating incentives are set up to ensure service quality.

3.1.2 *Aspects that Determine Market Structure*

The main aspects that determine the market structure are as follows:

1. The number and relative size of firms supplying the product.
2. The degree of differentiation and uniqueness of products.
3. The power of the seller over pricing decisions.
4. The ease or not of entering and exiting the market.

The number and relative size of firms in a market influence market structure. Suppose there are many firms, the degree of competition increases. With fewer firms supplying a good or service, consumers are limited in their market choices. One extreme case is the monopoly market structure, with only one firm supplying a unique good or service. Another extreme is perfect competition, with many firms providing a similar product.

Many firms provide products to the market in monopolistic competition, as with perfect competition. However, one firm's product is differentiated in some way that makes it appear better than similar products from other firms. If a firm successfully differentiates its product, the differentiation will provide pricing leverage. The more dissimilar the product appears, the more the market will resemble the monopoly market structure. A firm can differentiate its product through aggressive advertising campaigns, frequent styling changes, linking its product with other complementary products, or a host of different methods.

With production differentiation, we are likely to see non-price competition. An example of non-price competition is product differentiation through marketing. In other circumstances, non-price competition may

Table 3.1: Characteristics of market structure.

Market structure	Number of sellers	Degree of product differentiation	Barriers to entry	Pricing power of firm	Non-price competition
Perfect competition	Many	Homogeneous/Standardized	Very Low	None	None
Monopolistic competition	Many	Differentiated	Low	Some	Advertising and Product Differentiation
Oligopoly	Few	Homogeneous/Standardized	High	Some or Considerable	Advertising and Product Differentiation
Monopoly	One	Unique Product	Very High	Considerable	Advertising

occur because the few firms in the market feel dependent on each other. Each firm fears retaliatory price changes that would reduce total revenue for all market firms. Because oligopoly industries have so few firms, each firm feels dependent on the others' pricing strategies. Therefore, non-price competition becomes a dominant strategy.

In a market where aggregate supply and demand dictate prices, the individual firm has no control over pricing — they are price takers. That is, they must accept whatever price the market dictates. Price taking is the case under the market structure of perfect competition. In the case of monopolistic competition, product differentiation's success determines the degree to which the firm can influence the price. There are so few firms in the market that price control becomes possible in an oligopoly. However, the small number of firms in an oligopoly market invites complex pricing strategies. Collusion, price leadership by dominant firms, and other pricing strategies can result.

Table 3.1 shows the characteristics of the market structure.

From the firm's owners' perspective, the most desirable market structure is with the most control over price because this control can lead to significant profits. Monopoly and oligopoly markets offer the greatest potential control over price. The monopolistic competition offers less control. Firms operating under perfectly competitive market conditions have no control over price. On the other hand, consumers desire markets with the highest degree of competition and lower prices. Consumers generally prefer that most goods and services are offered in competitive markets. In the subsequent sections, we will focus on Perfect Competition and Monopoly. Oligopolies will be discussed in Section 4.6 of Chapter 4.

3.2 Competition

3.2.1 *Perfect Competition*

Perfect competition is usually viewed as a benchmark against which other market structures are compared.

Learning Objectives

- Understand the demand analysis and supply analysis under perfect competition.
- Learn to calculate the optimal output and price.

Main Takeaways

Main Points

- Five conditions characterize perfect competition.
- Compare with other market structures, the quantity sold is highest in perfect competition, and the price is usually the lowest. Having the lowest price among the types of market structures depends on the demand elasticity and increasing returns to scale, reducing the producer's marginal cost.

Main Terms

- **Opportunity cost:** Measured by determining the resource's next best opportunity.
- **Economic profit:** The difference between the total revenue (TR) and total cost (TC). economic profit differs from accounting profit because accounting profit does not include opportunity cost.
- **Law of diminishing returns:** Each additional unit of input produces a progressively smaller increase in output.

We characterize perfect competition using the five conditions presented:

1. The number of potential buyers and sellers is large.
2. The products are more or less identical.
3. Sellers can easily enter or exit the market.
4. Sellers cannot set prices.
5. There is no non-price competition.

Perfect competition is usually viewed as a benchmark against which other market structures are compared. The most typical example of perfect competition is found in certain aspects of the agriculture industry, such as many farmers growing corn for animal feed. Corn is a primary food source for pork, beef, and poultry production. Farmer Brown's bushel is virtually identical to a bushel of corn from Farmer Lopez. If a hog farmer needs corn to feed his hogs, it does not matter whether it comes from Farmer Brown or Farmer Lopez.

Furthermore, in a well-functioning aggregate corn market, with active futures and spot markets, price and quantity information is easily accessible and inexpensive to acquire. The corn product is not easily differentiated. While agribusiness is capital intensive, the abundance of arable land and water availability makes it relatively easy for new players to enter the corn production market.

(a) Demand Analysis

Demand and supply in that market. Economists usually represent demand and supply in a market through demand and supply curves in a two-axis plane. Quantity and price are shown on the *x*-axis and *y*-axis, respectively. Economists believe that demand functions have negative slopes, as shown in Figure 3.1. At high prices, less is demanded.

As the price declines for normal goods and services, the quantity demanded increases. This concept is based on two effects: the income effect and the substitution effect. The income effect results from the increased purchasing power the consumer has when prices fall. With lower prices, the consumer can afford to purchase more of the product. The substitution effect comes from the increasing attractiveness of the lower-priced product. If soybean prices are unchanged and corn prices decrease, hog farmers will substitute corn for soybeans feed for their animals.

Assume the demand for this product can be specified as $Q_D = 50 - 2P$, where Q_D is the quantity of demand, and P is its price.

We rearrange the demand function in terms of price:

$$P = 25 - 0.5Q_D$$

In this form, total revenue (TR) is equal to price times quantity, or $P \times Q_D$. Thus,

$$\text{TR} = PQD = 25\ Q_D - 0.5Q^2{}_D$$

Average revenue (AR) can be found by dividing TR by QD. Therefore,

$$\text{AR} = \text{TR}\ QD = (25\ Q_D - 0.5\ Q^2{}_D\ )\ QD = 25 - 0.5\ Q_D$$

Marginal revenue (MR) is the total revenue change per extra increment sold when the quantity sold changes by a small increment, ΔQ_D.

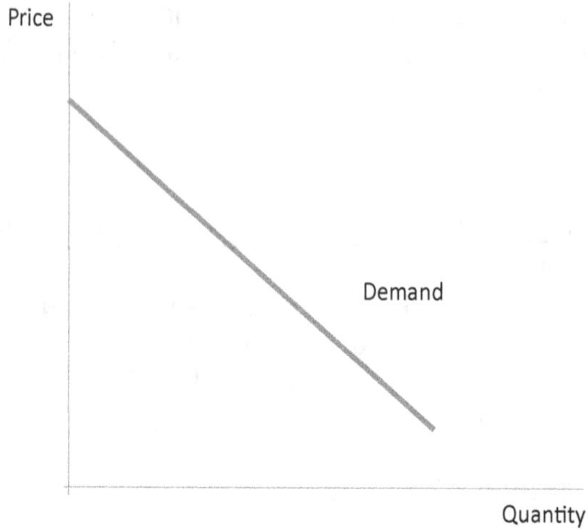

Figure 3.1: Market demand in perfect competition.

Substituting $(Q_D + \Delta Q_D)$ into the TR equation, marginal revenue can be expressed as

$$\text{MR} = \frac{\Delta \text{TR}}{\Delta Q_D}$$

$$= \frac{[25(Q_D + \Delta Q_D) - 0.5(Q_D^2 + 2Q_D \Delta Q_D + \Delta Q_D^2)] - [25Q_D - 0.5Q_D^2]}{\Delta Q_D}$$

$$= \frac{[25\Delta Q_D - Q_D \Delta Q_D - 0.5\Delta Q_D^2)]}{\Delta Q_D} = 25 - Q_D - 0.5\Delta Q_D$$

(b) Supply Analysis

Consider two palm oil farmers, Mr. Ahmad and Mr. Salleh. They both have land available to grow palm oil and sell at one price, say three currency units per kilogram. They will try to produce as much oil palm as is profitable at that price. If the price is driven up to 5 currency units per kilogram by new consumers entering the market — say, fuel producers — Mr. Ahmad and Mr. Salleh will try to produce more corn. To increase output levels, they may use less productive land, increase irrigation, use more fertilizer, or all options. So, production costs are likely to increase.

They will both still try to produce as much corn as possible to profit at the new, higher price of 5 currency units per kilogram. Figure 3.2 illustrates this example. Note that the supply functions for the individual firms have positive slopes. Thus, as prices increase, the firms supply greater product quantities.

Notice that the market supply curve is the sum of the individual firms' supply curves — Ahman, Salleh, and others — that make up the market. Assume that the supply function for the market can be expressed as a lincar rclationship, as follows:

$$Q_S = 10 + 5P, \text{ or } P = 2 + 0.2Q_S$$

where Q_S is the quantity supplied and P is the product's price.

Optimal Price and Output: Carrying forward our examples from the discussion on (a) demand analysis, and (b) supply analysis, we can now combine the market supply and demand functions to solve for the equilibrium price and quantity, where Q^* represents the equilibrium level of both supply and demand.

$$\begin{aligned} P = 25 - 0.5Q_D &= -2 + 0.2Q_S = P \\ 25 - 0.5Q_D &= -2 + 0.2Q_S \\ 27 &= 0.7Q^* \\ Q^* &= 38.57 \end{aligned}$$

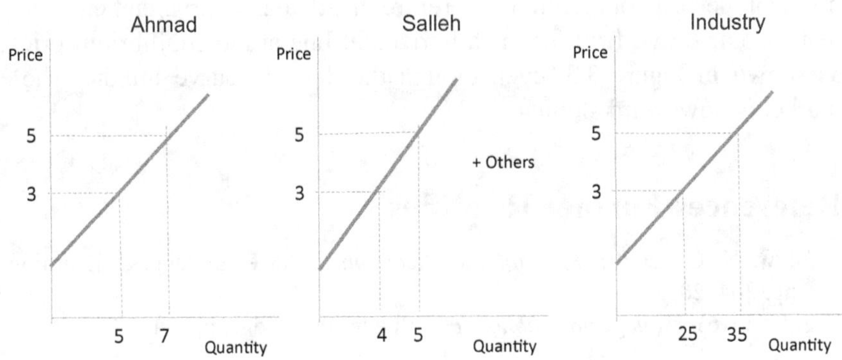

Figure 3.2: Firm and market supply in perfect competition.

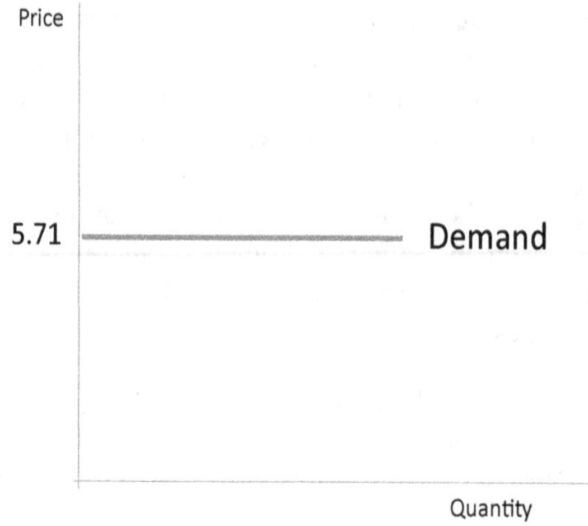

Figure 3.3: Individual firm's demand in perfect competition.

According to the market demand curve, the equilibrium price is:

$$P = 25 - 0.5Q^* = 25 - 0.5(38.57) = 25 - 19.29 = 5.71$$

With many firms in the market and total output in almost 39 units of the product, the effective market price would be 5.71. P = 5.71 is then the demand curve for each perfectly competitive firm. If a few producers expand production, it will have no impact on the market equilibrium price. If anyone could change the equilibrium market price, the market would not be in perfect competition. Therefore, the demand curve that each perfectly competitive firm face is a horizontal line at the equilibrium price, as shown in Figure 3.3, even though the demand curve for the whole market is downward sloping.

References/Further Readings

Mankiw, N. G. (2020). *Principles of Economics*, 9th edn. Cengage Learning, pp. 264–285.

Png, I. (2016). *Managerial Economics*, 5th edn. Routledge, pp. 21–42.

3.2.2 *Monopoly*

A monopolistic market structure has a single firm and substantial barriers against firms trying to enter the market.

Learning Objectives
- Understand the demand analysis and supply analysis under monopoly.
- Learn to calculate the optimal output and price.
- Note the differences between monopoly and monopolistic competition.

Main Takeaways

Main Points
- There are five characteristics of monopoly markets.
- Compared with other market structures, monopolists sell a smaller quantity at a higher price. Unless constrained, monopolies demonstrate large profit margins and strong positive cash flows that benefit shareholders.
- To charge higher prices, monopolists, oligopolists, and producers in monopolistic competition try to differentiate their products.
- Price discrimination has many practical applications when the seller has pricing power.

Main Terms
- **First-degree price discrimination:** Charging the highest price that the customer is willing to bear.
- **Second-degree price discrimination:** Inducing customers to reveal how highly they value a product via a menu of quantity-based pricing options.
- **Third-degree price discrimination:** Segregating customers by demographic or other traits.

Monopolies are on the opposite end of the spectrum to perfectly competitive firms. Due to significant barriers to enter the market, a single firm produces a specialized, unique product or service and faces no competitive threats. With no substitutes for its unique product or service, its demand curve is the same as the market demand curve, in contrast with a firm in a perfectly competitive market. The distinguishing characteristics of a monopoly are that a single firm represents the market, and significant entry barriers exist. The features of monopoly markets are as follows:

1. There is a single seller with a unique, highly differentiated product.
2. There is no close substitute for the product offered for sale.
3. Difficult to enter the market due to high costs and other significant barriers.
4. A single firm has strong pricing power.
5. Product differentiation being reinforced by non-price means.

(a) Demand Analysis

The monopolist's demand schedule is the aggregate demand for the product in the relevant market and is downward sloping. The general form of the demand relationship is

$$Q_D = a - bP \qquad \text{or, rewritten,} \qquad P = a/b - (1/b)Q_D$$

$$\text{Therefore, total revenue} = \text{TR} = P \times Q = (a/b)Q_D - (1/b)Q_D^2$$

Marginal revenue is defined as the change in revenue given a change in the quantity demanded. Intuitively, since the price has to be lower to induce an increase in quantity, the marginal revenue schedule is steeper than the demand schedule. As shown in Figure 3.4, the marginal revenue curve is twice as steep as the demand schedule for a linear demand schedule.

$$\text{MR} = \Delta\text{TR}/\Delta Q = (a/b) - (2/b)Q_D$$

Suppose a company operating on a remote island is a single natural gas seller. Demand for its product can be expressed as

$$Q_D = 400 - 0.5P, \text{ which is rearranged as}$$

$$P = 800 - 2Q_D$$

Total revenue is $P \times Q = \text{TR} = 800Q_D - 2Q^2_D$, and marginal revenue is $\text{MR} = 800 - 4Q_D$.

Also shown in Figure 3.4, the demand curve's intercept is 800, and the slope is –2. The marginal revenue curve has an intercept of 800 and a slope of –4.

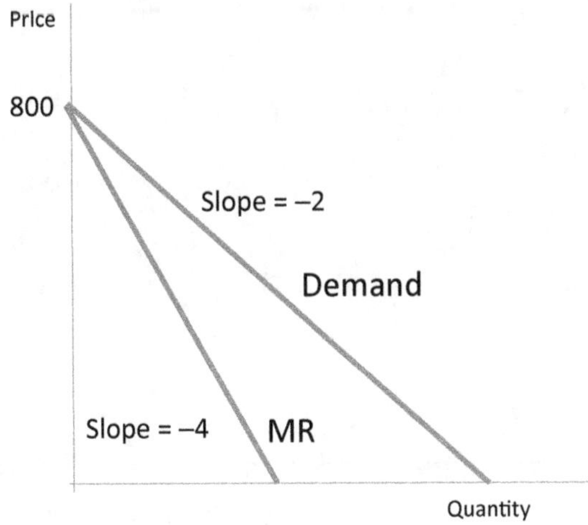

Figure 3.4: Monopolist's demand and marginal revenue.

The average revenue is TR/Q_D; therefore, AR = 800 – $2Q_D$, which is the same as the demand function. In the monopoly market model, the average revenue is the same as the market demand schedule.

(b) Supply Analysis

A monopolist's supply analysis looks at the firm's cost structure. A well-defined supply function to determine optimal output level and the price to charge is not available for the monopoly (as well as monopolistic competition and oligopoly).

However, to compute the optimal output, we recall that the optimal output is the profit-maximizing output level. The profit-maximizing output level occurs where marginal revenue equals marginal cost, MR = MC.

Example:

Assume the Natural Gas Company has determined that its total cost can be expressed as

$$\text{TC} = 20{,}000 + 50Q + 3Q^2$$

Marginal cost is $\Delta\text{TC}/\Delta Q = \text{MC} = 50 + 6Q$.

Supply and demand can be combined to determine the profit-maximizing level of output. Figure 3.5 combines the monopolist's demand and cost functions.

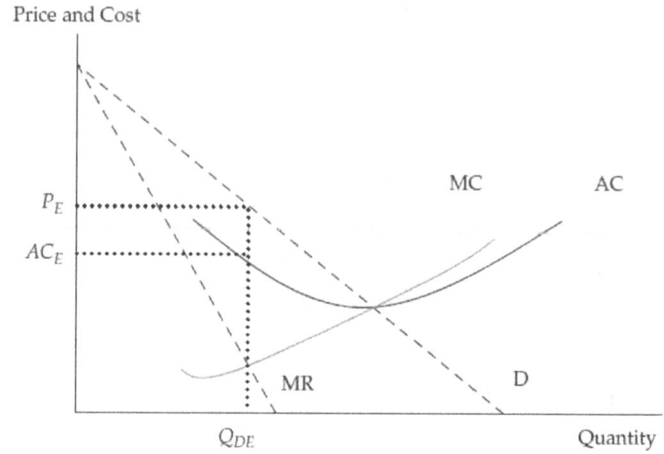

Figure 3.5: Monopolist's demand, marginal revenue, and cost structures.

In Figure 3.5, the aggregate market demand and marginal revenue functions are clearly defined. However, the monopolist does not have a supply curve. The quantity that maximizes profit is determined by MC and MR's intersection, Q_{DE}. The price consumers are willing to pay for this output level is PE, as determined by the demand curve, P_E.

The profit-maximizing level of output is MR = MC: $800 - 4Q_D = 50 + 6Q_D$; therefore, $Q_D = 75$ when profit is maximized.

Total profit equals total revenue minus total cost:

$$\pi = 800Q - 2Q_D^2 - (20{,}000 + 50Q_D + 3Q_D^2) = -20{,}000 + 750Q_D - 5Q_D^2$$

Profit is represented by the difference between the rectangle $Q_{DE} \times P_E$ area, representing total revenue, and the rectangle QDE × ACE area, representing total cost.

(c) Optimal Price and Output

We continue with the natural gas example from above. The total profit function can be solved using the quadratic formula. Another method to solve the profit function is to evaluate $\Delta\pi/\Delta Q_D$ and set it equal to zero. The method identifies the point at which profit is unaffected by output changes. Of course, this will give the same result as we found by equating marginal revenue with marginal cost. The monopoly will maximize profits when $Q^* = 75$ units of output and the price is set from the demand curve at 650.

$$P^* = 800 - 2(75) = 650 \text{ per unit}$$

To find total maximum profits, substitute these values into the profit function above:

$$\pi = -20{,}000 + 750Q_D - 5Q^2_D = -20{,}000 + 750(75) - 5(752) = 8{,}125$$

Note that the price and output combination that maximizes profit occurs in the demand curve's elastic portion. The result must be so because marginal revenue and marginal cost will always intersect where marginal revenue is positive. This fact implies that quantity demanded to respond more than proportionately to price changes, i.e., demand is elastic, at the point at which MC = MR. The relationship between marginal revenue and price elasticity, E_P, is[1]:

$$\text{MR} = P[1 - 1/E_P]$$

In a monopoly, MR = MC; therefore,

$$P[1 - 1/E_P] = \text{MC}$$

The firm can use this relationship to determine the profit-maximizing price if it knows its cost structure and the price elasticity of demand, E_P. For example, assume the firm knows that its marginal cost is constant at 75, and recent market analysis indicates that price elasticity is estimated to be 1.5.

We solve for the optimal price as

$$P[1 - 1/1.5] = 75 \quad \text{and} \quad P = 225$$

Figure 3.5 indicated that the monopolist wants to produce at Q_E and charge the price of P_E. Suppose this is a natural monopoly operating as a government franchise under regulation. Natural monopolies are usually found where production is based on significant economies of scale and

[1]Retrieved from https://socialsci.libretexts.org/Bookshelves/Economics/Book%3A_The_Economics_of_Food_and_Agricultural_Markets_(Barkley)/03%3A_Monopoly_and_Market_Power/3.03%3A_Marginal_Revenue_and_the_Elasticity_of_Demand.

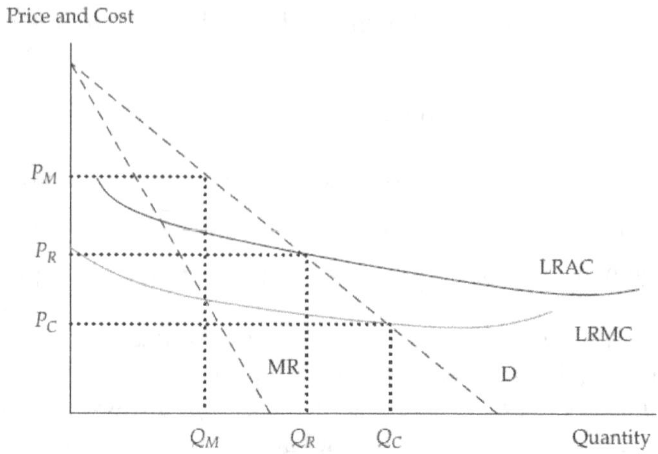

Figure 3.6: Natural monopoly in a regulated pricing environment.

declining cost structure. Examples include electric power generation, natural gas distribution, and the water and sewer industries (the public utilities). Figure 3.6 illustrates such a market in long-run equilibrium.

Monopolists can either be more or less effective in taking advantage of their market structure. At one extreme, we have a monopolist that charges prices and supplies quantities that are the same as they would be in perfect competition. This scenario may result from regulation or threat of entry (if the monopolist charged more, another company could come in and price the former monopolist out of the market). At the opposite extreme, hated by all consumers and economists, the monopolist extracts the entire consumer surplus. This scenario is called first-degree price discrimination, where a monopolist can charge the highest price that the customer is willing to bear.

In second-degree price discrimination, the monopolist induces customers to reveal how highly they value a product via a menu of quantity-based pricing options. Examples include volume discounts, volume surcharges, coupon discounts, product bundling, and access or use restrictions.

Lastly, third-degree price discrimination segregates customers by demographics or other traits. An example is when different software versions are sold to students, households, small offices, and enterprises. Each version of the software has varied functionality and is sold at various price points for a user license.

References/Further Readings

Mankiw, N. G. (2020). *Principles of Economics*, 9th edn. Cengage Learning, pp. 286–307.
Png, I. (2016). *Managerial Economics*, 5th edn. Routledge, pp. 167–192.

(d) Monopolistic Competition

Monopoly is to be distinguished from monopolistic competition. The monopolistic competition market structure has characteristics of both a monopoly and a perfectly competitive market. It differs from perfect competition in those products sold are differentiated.

Characteristics of Monopolistic Competition include:

1. A large number of potential buyers and sellers.
2. Products with close substitutes that are differentiated to some extent.
3. A reasonably low-cost entry and exit from the market.
4. Some degree of pricing power.
5. Products being differentiated with the use of advertising and other non-price strategies.

While the market comprises many firms that sell substitutable products, each producer tries to differentiate its product to some extent. Success in doing so contributes to the producer's pricing power in the market. If the differentiation effort is successful, like creating a recognizable brand name, a market structure resembles the single-seller market (monopoly) attains. In the long run, because of the relatively low entry and exit costs, the competition will drive prices and revenues down, akin to perfect competition. Thus, this market displays characteristics found in both perfectly competitive and monopoly markets.

References/Further Readings

Mankiw, N. G. (2020). *Principles of Economics*, 9th edn. Cengage Learning, pp. 318–325.
Fritz, R. & Gambera, M. (n.d.). *The Firm and Market Structures. In CFA Level 1 2020*. John Wiley & Sons, Incorporated.

3.3 Identifying Market Structure

Different market structures can have different degrees of efficiency in that less of a good may be produced and consumed along with higher selling prices. A Monopoly and situations in which firms gain significant pricing power can be inefficient because increasing prices constrain the output. As a result, many countries have introduced competition laws to regulate competition in many industries.

Learning Objectives

- Understand the measures to calculate market power.

Main Takeaways

Main Points

- Regression analysis and cross-sectional regression analysis can be used to calculate market power. However, these approaches have limitations.
- Simpler measures such as the concentration ratio are used as it is easier to calculate, although it may have some drawbacks.

Main Terms

- **Market power**: A firm's ability to raise and maintain prices relative to a situation when the market is competitive.

3.3.1 *Econometric and Simpler Approaches*

The theoretical answer to identify the market structure is to estimate demand and supply elasticity in a market. In the case of a market very close to perfect competition, demand will be estimated to be very elastic. If companies have significant market power, demand is likely to be estimated to be inelastic.

One empirical approach uses regression analysis with a large data sample to estimate elasticity using a historical time series or cross-sectional data. Using time-series data, we may use 20 years of quarterly sales data for a market. However, twenty years is a long time, and the market may change over this time frame, and the estimated elasticity may not represent that of the current situation. Further, if there are significant consolidations in a market, the supply curve's elasticity may have changed drastically. An example is the US airline market over the last twenty years.

The alternative uses regression analysis to look at data of a cross-section of different companies in the same year. This approach requires more granular data like sales data from other companies during the same year. One can also use more granular data like transaction data from many companies and individual buyers. Data collection of such granularity is time-consuming and prone to inaccuracies.

Trying to avoid the above drawbacks, analysts often use more uncomplicated measures to estimate elasticity. The most straightforward measure is the concentration ratio, defined as the largest N firms' total market shares. The concentration ratio is obtained by summing the largest of the ten largest firms' sales and divide by total market sales. The result will be between zero and one hundred, from pure competition to monopoly. The result does not directly quantify market power. Another index to measure market concentration is the Herfindahl Hirshman Index (HHI).

References/Further Readings

CFI (n.d.). Herfindahl Hirshman Index (HHI): How to Access the Degree of Market Concentration in An Industry. Retrieved from https://corporatefinanceinstitute.com/resources/knowledge/finance/herfindahl-hirschman-index-hhi/.

3.4 Fintech and Market Structure

Given the advantageous features of blockchain technology, we expect to increase applications in processes facilitating firm decision-making.

Learning Objectives

- Understand the debate of the impact of Fintech on market structure.

Main Takeaways

Main Points

- The debate on the invasion of Fintech companies into the banking market is ongoing, and an important question is if the market structure of banking will be changed. This question's answer has a crucial longer-term impact and signals current participants to prepare for such changes.

Main Terms

- **Digitalization:** It is a system of recording information that makes it difficult or impossible to change, hack or cheat the system. It is essentially a ledger of duplicated transactions and distributed throughout its computer system.
- **Blockchain:** It is a system of recording information that makes it difficult or impossible to change, hack or cheat the system. It is essentially a ledger of duplicated transactions and distributed throughout its computer system.

FinTech has started to revolutionize how traditional financial services providers work and interact with their customers. It is changing the dominant paradigms with which traditional financial services are provided, resulting in a fundamental disruption in applicable business models, blurring the boundaries established in the traditional financial sector.

Digitalization or the Fintech companies' invasion into the banking market is ongoing. It is essential to assess whether the banking sector's market structure (from a microeconomic point of view) will be changed during the Fintech market encounter. If yes, what type of market structure will be established. A change in the structure may mean significant long-term effects and shall signal present participants to prepare in advance.

According to Catalini (2017), Fintech companies' solutions differ significantly from the traditional banking solutions, introducing new methods, cost-saving possibilities, and much higher customer satisfaction. Incorporating blockchain technology may lower the cost of verification, ensuring markets are more secure and efficient and expand the types of transactions users are willing to engage in.

As a result of network effects and economies of scale, the digital platforms that shape our lives today have accumulated a high degree of market power. They often act as the default "shared infrastructure" within their industry.

Still, the actual effect on the market remains an unresolved question. The goal is to reveal, with Digitalization and Blockchain, what type of market structure will be established and how Blockchain or Digitalization creates a more competitive market.

References/Further Readings

Catalini, C. (2017). Why Blockchain Can Be Good for Competition. Retrieved from https://www.forbes.com/sites/christiancatalini/2017/10/30/why-blockchain-can-be-good-for-competition/?sh=76e89b14768e.

Mate, N., Laszlo, C., & Sandor, G. (2019). Fintech Companies and Banks — Encounter of Two Different Market Structures in Hungary — Economics & Working Capital. Retrieved from http://eworkcapital.com/fintech-companies-and-banks-encounter-of-two-different-market-structures-in-hungary/.

3.5 Fintech and Competition

FinTech has revolutionized how traditional financial services providers work and interact with their customers. It is changing the dominant paradigms with which traditional financial services are provided, resulting in a real disruption in applicable business models, blurring the boundaries established in the traditional financial sector.

Learning Objectives

- Understand the impact of Fintech on the ability to analyze and assess anticompetitive behavior within the financial services market.

Main Takeaways

Main Points

- Difficulties in analyzing potential anti-competitive behaviors are due to traditional instruments' inappropriateness.
- Adding to difficulties in assessing anticompetitive behavior includes the diversity of competitors and relatively new users.

Main Terms

- **Anticompetitive behavior:** business practices in which a firm or group of firms may restrict competition amongst firms to improve market position and profits while not providing goods at a lower cost or higher quality.

With the disruption of traditional markets, competition instruments' application to analyze potential anticompetitive behaviors faces several challenges. The most relevant challenge is applying traditional competition law instruments to assess competition issues to this relatively new and innovative market segment. The difficulties include (1) describing the relevant market, (2) defining the market power for a type of service, and (3) analyzing anticompetitive behaviors and their root causes. Moreover, market power assessment cannot solely rely on traditional indicators such as market share, prices, or profit margins. These indicators fail to explain the economic relationships between supply and demand in the provision of FinTech services, given that some of these services are offered at zero price or are provided through multi-sided platforms with several stakeholders intertwined (see Carmona *et al.*, 2018).

Adding to the challenges is the FinTech services' market's current state. Unlike other fields, where markets are well-established and the relevant players and their features are well-known, FinTech services are characterized by the confluence of start-ups, large financial institutions, and large tech companies as relevant competitors. The diversity of origins and potential sources of competitive advantages means that the different markets' state is in flux. This diversity means that firms may swiftly change their services portfolio depending on the activities they consider similar and susceptible to synergies. Simultaneously, users are relatively new and slowly getting used to the different offers for these services. Users being new means that their perception of which offers are comparable and which services are substitutes is continuously changing. It is challenging to identify advantages and sources of market power durable throughout time or even to talk about incumbents in this context. In the case of strategies being in constant change and market power being contestable and contested, the default option should be cautious.

References/Further Readings

Carmona, A. F. *et al.* (2018). *Competition Issues in the Area of Financial Technology* (*Fintech*). Policy Department for Economic, Scientific and Quality of Life Policies, pp. 48–80. Retrieved from https://www.europarl.europa.eu/RegData/etudes/STUD/2018/619027/IPOL_STU(2018)619027_EN.pdf.

Other Readings

Cao, L. (2020). *AI in Fintech: A Research Agenda.* [ebook] University of Technology Sydney, Australia. Retrieved from https://arxiv.org/pdf/2007.12681.pdf.

3.6 Sample Questions

Question 1

If you have a few sellers of little differentiated products, you have a market structure that is best described as

(a) oligopoly
(b) monopoly
(c) perfect competition

Question 2

A market where firms have little incentive to use advertising as a tool of differentiation will have a structure identified as

(a) monopoly
(b) perfect competition
(c) monopolistic competition

Question 3

Neptune Energy, Inc. enjoys very high entry barriers in its national market. Its marginal cost is \$40, and its average cost is \$70. The price elasticity of demand is estimated at 1.5. The company will most likely set its price at

(a) \$40
(b) \$70
(c) \$120

Question 4

The demand schedule in a perfectly competitive market is given by $P = 93 - 1.5Q$ (for $Q \leq 62$), and the long-run cost structure of each company is

Total cost: $256 + 2Q + 4Q^2$
Average cost: $256/Q + 2 + 4Q$
Marginal cost: $2 + 8Q$

New companies will enter the market at any price greater than:

(a) 8
(b) 66
(c) 81

Question 5
If companies can earn economic profits in a perfectly competitive market, over the long run, the supply curve will most likely:

(a) shift to the left
(b) shift to the right
(c) remain unchanged

Solutions

Question 1

Solution: Option **a** is correct.

Few sellers of a little differentiated product characterize an oligopoly.

Question 2

Solution: Option **b** is correct.

The product sold in a perfectly competitive market is unlikely differentiated by advertising.

Question 3

Solution: Option **c** is correct

Profits are maximized when MR = MC. For a monopoly, MR = $P[1 - 1/E_p]$. Setting this equal to MC and solving for P:

$$\$40 = P[1 - (1/1.5)] = P \times 0.333$$
$$P = \$120$$

Question 4

Solution: Option **b** is correct.

The long-run competitive equilibrium occurs where MC = AC = P for each company. Equating MC and AC implies $2 + 8Q = 256/Q + 2 + 4Q$. Solving for Q gives $Q = 8$. Equating MC with price gives $P = 2 + 8Q = 66$. Any price above 66 yields an economic profit because P = MC > AC, so new companies will enter the market.

Question 5

Solution: Option **b** is correct.

The economic profit will attract new entrants to the market and encourage existing companies to expand capacity.

Chapter 4

Game Theory (Strategic Games and Oligopoly Models)

4.1 Introduction to Game Theory and Oligopoly

4.1.1 *Introduction*

> *If you know the enemy and know yourself, you need not fear the result of a hundred battles. If you know yourself but not the enemy, for every victory gained, you will also suffer a defeat. If you know neither the enemy nor yourself, you will succumb in every battle.*
>
> —*Sunzi: The Art of War*

Learning Objectives

- Learn the basics components of game theory and oligopoly.

Main Takeaways

Main Terms

- **Oligopoly:** A market environment with a small number of competing firms is called an oligopoly.

Game theory is the formal analysis used to predict outcomes for a group of decision-making agents, allowing for strategic interactions. In such a situation, a single agent directly affects other participating agents' payoffs (profits). In other words, an essential feature of this situation is that each agent's payoff depends on all the other agents' actions, rather than being solely determined by his action. To comprehensively describe what a strategic game is, we need first to specify:

1. **Players:** Who the decision-makers are;
2. **Strategies:** What actions each decision-maker can do;
3. **Payoffs:** Each decision-makers possible payoffs resulting from the players' actions.

Game theory is especially useful when the number of interacting agents is small. For this reason, game theory is constructive in analyzing an oligopolistic market consisting of a few competing firms. Specific to the study of oligopolies, we denote the component of a strategic game as

1. **Players:** The set of firms;
2. **Strategies:** The set of outputs, or the set of prices;
3. **Payoffs:** The firms' profits.

Many product and service markets neither consist of many suppliers with no market power (perfect competition) nor are entirely controlled by a single supplier (monopoly). Instead, a few competitors have all or most of the market share in an industry. For example, there are only a few brands of personal computers (Apple, Dell, HP, and Lenovo), soft drinks (Coca-Cola, Pepsi), TV sets (LG, Samsung, Sharp, Sony), and even electric toothbrushes (Oral-B, Philips), to name a few.

Large firms have seized a significant share of the respective markets they are operating in. They cannot be described as price takers or pure price-makers since they cannot ignore their competitors' behavior. Such a market environment with a small number of competing firms is called an ***oligopoly***.

Usually, in most markets, a few suppliers will compete for many potential buyers. Besides large firms, even small firms are often part of oligopolistic market structures and can play a role in influencing the actions of other players. Many markets are geographically local. Local banks, supermarkets, and restaurants in isolated market areas (such as a small community, university campuses) are good examples. Hence, firms operating in an oligopoly are the most common occurrence.

4.2 Prisoners' Dilemma

4.2.1 *Prisoners' Dilemma*

The prisoner's dilemma is a paradox in decision analysis in which two individuals acting in their self-interests do not produce the optimal outcome.

Learning Objectives
- Understand the prisoner's dilemma and the example provided.

Main Takeaways

Main Points
- In normal form games, all players choose all their actions simultaneously.
- The typical prisoner's dilemma is set up so that both parties choose to protect themselves at the other participant's expense.

Main Terms
- **Game theory:** It is a theoretical framework for conceiving social situations among competing players. In some respects, game theory is the science of strategy, or at least the optimal decision-making of independent and competing actors in a strategic setting.
- **Normal form games:** It is a description of a game. Unlike an extensive form, normal form representations are not graphical but represent the game by way of a matrix.
- **Prisoner's dilemma:** It is a paradox in which two individuals acting in their self-interests do not produce the optimal outcome.
- **Best response:** In game theory, the best response is the strategy (or strategies) that produces the most favorable outcome for a player, taking other players' strategies as given.

A game can be represented in its *normal* form. Simplistically, in normal form games, all players choose all their actions simultaneously. We start with the classic example of a strategic game in the normal form called the prisoners' dilemma problem. This example shows how the key elements are modeled in a game. A game with two players is displayed in Table 4.1.

Table 4.1: Prisoners' dilemma game.

		Suspect B	
		Silent	Confess
Suspect A	Silent	–1, –1	–3, **0**
	Confess	**0**, –3	**–2, –2**

This table describes a strategic game in which two prisoners, A and B, are suspected of committing a crime. However, the police lack sufficient evidence to convict either suspect. The prosecutors offer each suspect a bargain. The offer is:

- If A and B both remain silent, both of them will serve only one year in prison, i.e., the payoff is –1;
- If A and B both confess, both of them will serve two years in prison, i.e., the payoff is –2;
- If A remains silent but B confesses, A will serve three years in prison while B will be set free, i.e., the payoff of A is –3, but the payoff of B is 0; vice versa.

We argue that Table 4.1 contains all the data needed to display all of the information in a condensed format, which will be used extensively in this chapter's remaining context. First, we have two players, called suspect A and B. Second, suspect A's strategies are Silent and Confess, and suspect B's strategies are Silent and Confess as well.

There are exactly four outcomes for this game: {Silent, Silent}, {Silent, Confess}, {Confess, Silent}, {Confess, Confess}. Third, the table cells contain the payoffs to suspect A (the first number in each cell) and to suspect B (the second number in each cell), corresponding to the associated strategy profile. For example, if suspects A and B both confess, we would be in the bottom-right cell (–2, –2).

4.3 Nash Equilibrium Concept

4.3.1 *Nash Equilibrium*

Nash equilibrium is a concept within game theory where the game's optimal outcome is no incentive to change its initial strategy.

Learning Objectives

- Understand the essential components of the Nash equilibrium concept.
- Apply the best response functions to find Nash equilibria.

Main Takeaways

Main Points

- A Nash equilibrium is a strategy profile (list of strategies, one for each player). With the property, no player can obtain a higher payoff by changing to a different strategy, given the other players' strategies.
- In other words, a Nash equilibrium is a situation in which neither player has an incentive to change their strategy based on the other players' strategies holding consistent beliefs about the decision of other players.

Main Terms

- **Nash equilibrium:** It is a strategy profile (list of strategies, one for each player) with the property that no player can obtain a higher payoff by changing to a different strategy, given the other players' strategies.

Once the game is appropriately defined, we ask the following:

- What actions will be chosen by the players in this game? And
- How is the game ended?

Informally, suppose that suspect A asks himself: "Knowing the strategies of suspect B, and treating his strategies as set in stone, what is the best strategy that I should choose?"

Ideally, we would like to find a method that would select desirable and reasonable outcomes of a strategic game for players such that:

1. each player chooses the strategy that is best for him, given his beliefs about the other players' strategies;
2. each player's belief about the other players' strategies is correct.

(a) Finding Nash Equilibria: Best Response Functions

The "best response" functions facilitate the finding of Nash equilibria.

Firstly, we formulate the notion of a Nash equilibrium for a two-player game and call the best response function (or reaction function) of player 1 as $R_1(s_2)$, that for every given strategy s_2 of player 2 determines player 1's strategy $s_1 = R_1(s_2)$ maximizes player 1's payoff $\pi_1(s_1 = R_1(s_2), s_2)$. Similarly, we define $R_2(s_1)$ as player 2's best response function to every player 1's strategy, s_1.

Given this definition of best responses, a strategy profile $\{s_1, s_2\}$ is a Nash equilibrium if and only if:

1. Player 1's strategy s_1 is the best response to player 2's strategy s_2;
2. Player 2's strategy s_2 is the best response to player 1's strategy s_1 in turn.

Thus, the procedure for finding a Nash equilibrium is now straightforward: First, we calculate the best response function of each player. Second, we check which strategy profiles lie on all players' best response functions. For the two-play game, we now have the strategy profile $\{s_1, s_2\}$ is a Nash equilibrium if and only if:

$$s_1 = R_1\,(s_2) \quad \text{and} \quad s_2 = R_2\,(s_1)$$

We now turn to the Prisoners' Dilemma game to search for the Nash equilibrium outcome. Suspect A's best response to suspect B's strategy {silent} is {confess} because of 0>–1, and A's best response to B's {confess} is also {confess} because of –2>–3. Similarly, suspect B's best response to A's {silent} is {confess} because of 0>–1, and his best response to A's {confess} is also {confess} because of –2>–3. Thus, we have:

$$R_1(s_2) = \begin{cases} \text{confess}, & \text{if } s_2 = \text{silent} \\ \text{confess}, & \text{if } s_2 = \text{confess} \end{cases}$$

and

$$R_2(s_1) = \begin{cases} \text{confess}, & \text{if } s_1 = \text{silent} \\ \text{confess}, & \text{if } s_1 = \text{confess} \end{cases}$$

Therefore, we see that only the strategy profile {confess, confess} satisfy the property that $s_1 = R_1(s_2)$ and $s_2 = R_2(s_1)$, which is the desired result according to the principles set out. It is worth noting that in this

Nash equilibrium {confess, confess}, both suspects are worse off than they are in the strategy profile {silent, silent}. Therefore, the game is given its name, ***Prisoners' dilemma***.

4.4 Oligopolistic Output Competition: Cournot Model

4.4.1 *Cournot Model*

The oligopoly theory originated from French mathematician Augustin Cournot (1801–1877). The reviewer was another French mathematician, Joseph Bertrand (1822–1900). He was quite critical of Cournot's achievements, especially the market game's hypothetical rules.

The main point of debate was the pricing mechanism. Cournot supposed that each firm decides how much to produce, which means that oligopolists set output as strategies. However, Bertrand argued that letting oligopolists themselves set their products' prices to maximize profits seems more reasonable. He raised this issue and suggested that his proposed modifications would lead to very different conclusions. The real-world examples of Cournot oligopoly are the OPEC countries in which those countries decide how much oil they will produce because the amount of oil produced affects the price of oil in the market.

Learning Objectives

- Discuss the strategic behaviors of firms in an oligopoly market.
- Describe the Cournot oligopoly model assuming homogeneous and differentiated products.

Main Takeaways

Main Points

- Cournot began by assuming that firms produce a single homogeneous good and simultaneously choose production. Each firm decides how much to produce by assuming that its rivals will not alter their production level in response.
- In the Cournot model, firms' profits increase when they become more differentiated.

Main Terms

- **Strategic behavior:** Usually refers to decision-making that considers other economic agents' actions and reactions. Its essential feature is recognizing the direct interdependence between one's behavior and others.
- **Cournot model:** An economic model in which competing firms choose a quantity to produce independently and simultaneously, assuming rivals will not alter their production level in response.
- **Homogeneous product:** Cannot be distinguished from competing products from different suppliers.
- **Differentiated products:** These are products (and services) that are distinguishable from others, with differences in appearance, quality, and even location.
- **Oligopoly:** It is a market structure with a small number of firms, none of which can keep the others from having significant influence.
- **Duopoly:** It is a type of oligopoly where two firms have dominant or exclusive control over a market.

(a) Cournot with Homogeneous Product

Cournot began by assuming that firms produce a single homogeneous good, and they simultaneously choose the production quantity (i.e., the output level is the strategic variable). Each firm decides how much to produce by assuming that its rivals will not alter their production level in response. To simplify matters, we focus on the Cournot competition with two firms (duopoly), and it can be easily extended to $N \geq 2$ firms. For a more generalized analysis, the reader can refer to Kreps (1994) *A Course in Microeconomic Theory* and Varian (1992) *Microeconomic Analysis*.

We assume that the market inverse demand function is linear and is given by

$$P = 100 - (Q_1 + Q_2)$$

and that both firms' marginal cost is 10 with no fixed cost of production, i.e., the firm's cost functions are

$$TC_1 = 10Q_1$$
$$TC_2 = 10Q_2$$

where the variables of choice Q_1 and Q_2 represent the output levels chose by firms 1 and 2, respectively.

(b) Representation of the Game in Normal Form

There are two players, firm 1 and firm 2; any non-negative amount of output Q_i would serve as a strategy for firm $i = 1, 2$. The payoff obtained by each firm at the combination of strategies (Q_1, Q_2) is

$$\begin{cases} \pi_1(Q_1, Q_2) = PQ_1 - TC_1 = (90 - Q_1 - Q_2)Q_1 \\ \pi_2(Q_1, Q_2) = PQ_2 - TC_2 = (90 - Q_1 - Q_2)Q_2 \end{cases} \quad \square$$

Previously, the procedure that we follow to obtain the Nash equilibrium is used in the Prisoners' Dilemma game. Applying that concept, we derive the best response function (also known as reaction function) of each firm to its rival's possible strategies and then look for combinations of strategies that are mutually best responses to each other.

Given a strategy of firm 2's output level Q_2, we look for the strategy that yields the most profit for firm 1; that is, firm 1's best response is to choose a strategy Q_1 to maximize its profit

$$\pi_1(Q_1, Q_2) = (90 - Q_1 - Q_2)Q_1$$

taking the first partial derivative with respect to Q_1 and holding Q_2 as constant, set equal to zero, we have firm 1's reaction function $R_1(Q_2)$ as a function of Q_2

$$Q_1 = R_1(Q_2) = 45 - \frac{Q_2}{2}$$

In the same way, applying similar reasoning to firm 2, we have its reaction function $R_2(Q_1)$

$$Q_2 = R_2(Q_1) = 45 - \frac{Q_1}{2}$$

The Cournot–Nash equilibrium is a strategy profile of both firms' output level (Q_1^C, Q_2^C) (here, the superscript C represents Cournot competition) such that the strategy of each firm is its best response to the rival's plan. That is,

$$\begin{cases} Q_1^C = R_1(Q_2^C) = 45 - \frac{Q_2^C}{2} \\ Q_2^C = R_2(Q_1^C) = 45 - \frac{Q_1^C}{2} \end{cases} \quad \square$$

which yields $(Q_1^C, Q_2^C) = (30, 30)$ at equilibrium.

We then have, at equilibrium, the market output level is equal to:

$$Q^C = Q_1^c + Q_2^c = 60$$

which implies that the equilibrium price level is

$$P^C = 100 - Q^C = 40$$

Substituting these outcomes into the profit functions yields

$$\pi_1^C = \pi_2^C = 900$$

The Cournot–Nash equilibrium requires that the strategy profile lies on both firms' reaction curves. Only one point that is shown in Figure 4.1 is the intersection of the two reaction curves.

(c) Cournot with Differentiated Products

Most industries produce similar but not wholly identical products; consumers can also distinguish among different producers of similar goods and treat the products as close substitutes. Also, most industries producing

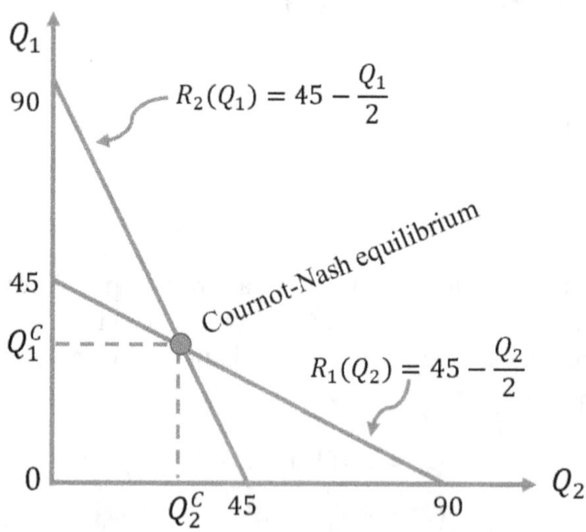

Figure 4.1: Cournot–Nash equilibrium.

differentiated products are concentrated. For example, think of Adidas and Nike, AMD and Intel, Boeing and Airbus, Coke and Pepsi, etc. These products are not identical, but they do compete with each other.

In the following discussion, we allow for differentiated products made by firms 1 and 2. We assume the following linear inverse demand functions for products from each of the two firms:

$$P_1 = 100 - Q_1 - \frac{Q_2}{2}$$

and

$$P_2 = 100 - Q_2 - \frac{Q_1}{2}$$

These demand functions are realistic, assuming that a product's price is more sensitive to a change in its quantity than a change in its competing product. For instance, both Adidas and Nike decided to produce fewer sneakers by similar amounts, increasing sneakers' price. However, we expect the price increase of Adidas sneakers resulted more from its reduced quantity.

Assuming again these two firms have no fixed costs, and their marginal costs are equal to 10

$$TC_1 = 10Q_1$$
$$TC_2 = 10Q_2$$

We now use the same approach as before, starting with firm 1's best response to firm 2's strategy by choosing a strategy Q_1 to maximize its profit

$$\pi_1(Q_1,Q_2) = P_1Q_1 - 10Q_1 = (90 - Q_1 - Q_2/2)Q_1$$

Taking the first-order condition (taking the derivative of π_1 with respect to Q_1 and equating to zero) yields the reaction function for firm 1

$$Q_1 = R_1(Q_2) = 45 - \frac{Q_2}{4}$$

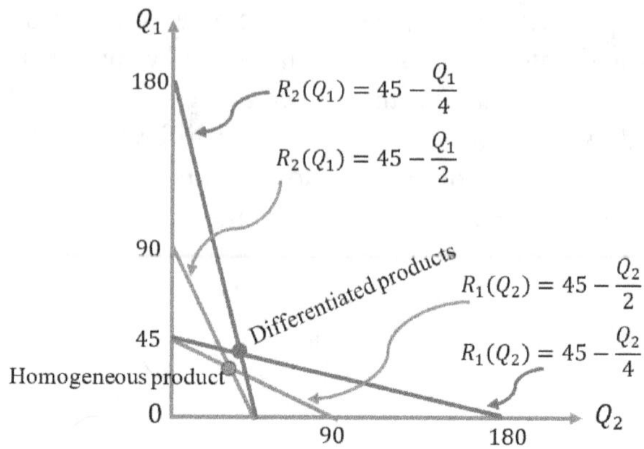

Figure 4.2: The Cournot model with differentiated products.

Using the same argument, the reaction function for firm 2 is now

$$Q_2 = R_2(Q_1) = 45 - \frac{Q_1}{4}$$

As you can see from Figure 4.2, these reaction functions are similar to those obtained for the Cournot competition with homogeneous products in Figure 4.1, except that these curves are steeper.

Solving the reaction functions, using symmetry, we have that

$$Q_1^{CD} = Q_2^{CD} = 36, \;\; P_1^{CD} = P_2^{CD} = 46, \;\; \pi_1^{CD} = \pi_2^{CD} = 1296$$

where superscript *CD* denotes the Cournot equilibrium with differentiated products.

As the products become more differentiated (for example, for firm 1, its demand function change from $P_1 = 100 - Q_1 - Q_2$ producing an identical product to $P_1 = 100 - Q_1 - Q_2/2$ producing differentiated products), the individual and aggregate quantity produced, and the profits all rise. Although the preceding analysis is a numerical example, this property extends to the use of the following inverse demand functions:

$$P_1 = a - bQ_1 - cQ_2$$
$$P_2 = a - cQ_1 - bQ_2$$

whereas c converges to b, we say the product is less differentiated.

The intuition for this result is straightforward. As the products become more differentiated, the competition between firms becomes less intense. This reduced competition explains why firms in many markets spend considerable amounts on building their brands, believing that branding lead to product differentiation, alleviates competitive pressure, and increase profits.

4.5 Oligopolistic Price Competition: Bertrand Model

4.5.1 *Bertrand Model*

Unlike the Cournot model, consumers here would favor their preferred products at the lowest price. A firm in these market's price choices affects not only its profits but its opponents' profits as well. This circumstance is known as the Bertrand model that postulates that oligopolists simultaneously choose their unit price to maximize profits. Hence, this is interpreted as a game where prices are the strategic variables.

Learning Objectives

- Describe the Bertrand oligopoly model assuming homogeneous and differentiated products.

Main Takeaways

Main Points

- In the Bertrand model with a homogenous product and identical marginal costs, firms charge prices equal to marginal cost. Thus, competing on prices is sufficient for the competitive outcome, called the Bertrand paradox.
- In the Bertrand model with differentiated products, firms enjoy more market power, and firms' profits increase when products become more differentiated.

Main Terms

- **Bertrand model:** Postulates that oligopolists simultaneously choose their unit price to maximize profits, and hence, is interpreted as a game where prices are the strategic variables.
- **Homogeneous product:** Cannot be distinguished from competing **products** from different suppliers.

- **Differentiated products:** These are products (and services) that are distinguishable from others, with differences in appearance, quality, and even location.

(a) Bertrand Model with a Homogeneous Product

We will assume that two firms have the same constant marginal cost for simplicity.

$$MC_1 = MC_2 = 10$$

and the market demand function is given by

$$P = 100 - Q$$

From the consumers' perspective, the relationship between these two firms' prices is determined as the products are identical. Buyers will patronize only the firm offering the lower price. If a tie occurs, market demand is shared evenly by all firms. Therefore, depending on the prices P_1 and P_2 offered by firms 1 and 2, firm 1's demand function $Q_1(P_1, P_2)$ is given by

$$Q_1(P_1, P_2) = \begin{cases} 100 - P_1 & \text{if } P_1 < P_2 \\ (100 - P_1)/2 & \text{if } P_1 = P_2 \\ 0 & \text{if } P_1 > P_2 \end{cases}$$

which is illustrated in Figure 4.3.

By similar reasoning, we can derive firm 2's demand function.

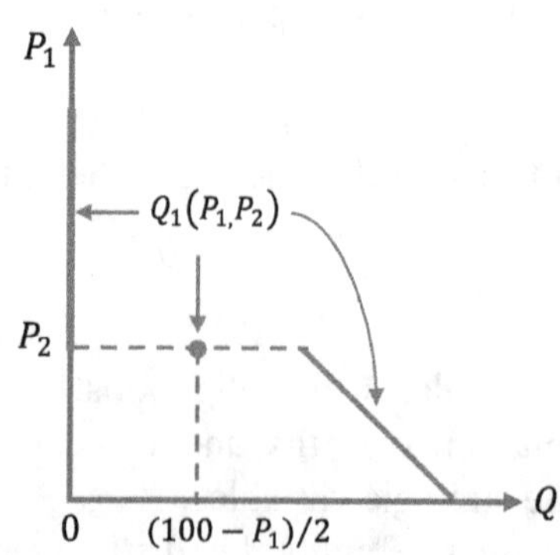

Figure 4.3: Firm 1's demand function.

(b) Representation of the Game in Normal Form
There are two players, firms 1 and 2, and any non-negative price serves as a strategy for firm $i = 1,2$. The firms' payoffs corresponding to the strategy profile (P_1, P_2) are:

$$\pi_1(P_1,P_2) = (P_1 - MC_1) * Q_1(P_1,P_2) = \begin{cases} (100 - P_1)(P_1 - 10) & \text{if } P_1 < P_2 \\ (100 - P_1)(P_1 - 10)/2 & \text{if } P_1 = P_2 \\ 0 & \text{if } P_1 > P_2 \end{cases}$$

and

$$\pi_2(P_1,P_2) = (P_2 - MC_2) * Q_2(P_1,P_2) = \begin{cases} (100 - P_2)(P_2 - 10) & \text{if } P_2 < P_1 \\ (100 - P_2)(P_2 - 10)/2 & \text{if } P_2 = P_1 \\ 0 & \text{if } P_2 > P_1 \end{cases}$$

Using a similar procedure to solve the Cournot case, we derive the firms' reaction functions. For firm 1, its best response is to charge a price P_1 just below the price P_2 of firm 2 to attract all consumers and maximize its profits. Notice that if $P_2 = 10$, then firm 1 will set $P_1 = 10$ as undercutting firm 2 indeed attracts all consumer but would yield negative profits as illustrated by its profit function and that if P_2 is less than 10, then firm 1 will set $P_1 = 10$; otherwise, it would entail losses again. Thus, firm 1's reaction function is given by

$$R_1(P_2) = \begin{cases} 10 & \text{if } P_2 < 10 \\ 10 & \text{if } P_2 = 10 \\ P_2 - \varepsilon & \text{if } P_2 > 10 \end{cases}$$

where ε represents a minimal value.

By similar reasoning, we can derive firm 2's reaction function. These two reaction functions are superimposed in Figure 4.4, which demonstrates that the Bertrand-Nash equilibrium is

$$P_1^B = P_2^B = 10$$

where the superscript B denotes the Bertrand competition equilibrium.

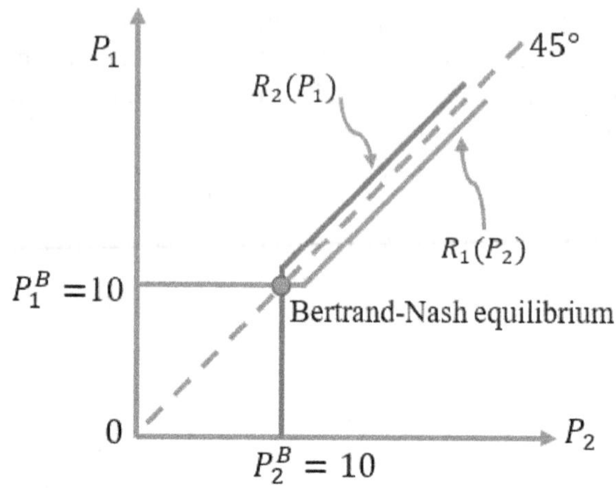

Figure 4.4: Bertrand–Nash equilibrium with homogeneous product.

We then have the following equilibrium outcomes characterized by

$$Q_1^B = Q_2^B = Q^B/2 = (100-10)/2 = 45$$
$$\pi_1^B = \pi_2^B = 45*(10-10)/2 = 0$$

From the result, we can see that the above Bertrand-Nash equilibrium is that where competition between the two firms end in complete dissipation of profits (i.e., $\pi_1^B = \pi_2^B = 0$ and hence the industry profit is zero). The market power of oligopolists (i.e., $P_1^B = P_2^B = MC = 10$) is eliminated. These two results are the foundation of the "Bertrand paradox." The intuition behind this result is clear. Competing firms cannot charge a price higher than marginal cost 10 because they can obtain higher profits by slightly undercutting its price.

(c) Bertrand Model with Differentiated Products

In many markets, products that compete with each other are not identical. For example, think of the market for midsize family cars, for example, Toyota's Camry and Honda's Accord. These products are not identical, but they do compete with each other. Some families will prefer Accord over Camry even if Accord's price is higher than Camry's. However, we would expect that such demand for Accord will fall as Honda raises Accord's price and will eventually buy Camry. The next question is the implication of product differentiation in Bertrand competition?

We leave unchanged the rest of the assumptions of the Bertrand model (two firms, simultaneous choice, constant and identical marginal cost = 10, price competition), but now we consider that firm 1 and 2 faces the following inverse demand functions as in the Cournot model with differentiated products, respectively

$$P_1 = 100 - Q_1 - \frac{Q_2}{2}$$

$$P_2 = 100 - Q_2 - \frac{Q_1}{2}$$

To find quantity demanded as functions of products' prices, we reformulate the above two inverse demand functions to direct demand functions

$$Q_1(P_1, P_2) = \frac{200}{3} - \frac{4}{3}P_1 + \frac{2}{3}P_2$$
$$Q_2(P_1, P_2) = \frac{200}{3} - \frac{4}{3}P_2 + \frac{2}{3}P_1$$

For firm 1, its demand function depends on its price and its rival's price level. Also, when firm 1 raises its price, this increase in P_1 will lead to a decrease in the demand for its product Q_1; while when firm 2 charges a higher price, this increase in P_2 will lead to an increase in the demand for firm 1's product Q_1. For firm 2, we have similar results. Notice that we assume that products are substitutes throughout this chapter.

(d) Representation of the Game in Normal Form

There are two players, firm 1 and firm 2; any non-negative price level P_i would serve as a strategy for firm i = 1,2. The payoff obtained by each firm at the combination of strategies (P_1, P_2) is

$$\begin{cases} \pi_1(P_1,P_2) = (P_1 - 10) * Q_1(P_1,P_2) = (P_1 - 10)\left(\frac{200}{3} - \frac{4}{3}P_1 + \frac{2}{3}P_2\right) \\ \pi_2(P_1,P_2) = (P_2 - 10) * Q_2(P_1,P_2) = (P_2 - 10)\left(\frac{200}{3} - \frac{4}{3}P_2 + \frac{2}{3}P_1\right) \end{cases} \quad \square$$

Following the same procedure to obtain the Nash equilibrium in Cournot competition, we first derive each firm's reaction function to its rival's possible strategies. Then we look for combinations of strategies that are mutually best responses to each other.

Given a strategy of firm 2's price level P_2, we look for the strategy that yields the most profit for firm 1; that is, firm 1's best response is to choose a strategy P_1 to maximize its profit

$$\pi_1(P_1,P_2) = (P_1 - 10)\left(\frac{200}{3} - \frac{4}{3}P_1 + \frac{2}{3}P_2\right)$$

Taking the first partial derivative with respect to P_1 and holding P_2 as constant, set equal to zero, we have firm 1's reaction function $R_1(P_2)$ as a function of P_2

$$P_1 = R_1(P_2) = 30 + \frac{P_2}{4}$$

In the same way, applying similar reasoning to firm 2, we have its reaction function $R_2\ (P_1)$

$$P_2 = R_2(P_1) = 30 + \frac{P_1}{4}.$$

The Bertrand-Nash equilibrium of product differentiation is a strategy profile of both firms' output level (P_1^{BD}, P_2^{BD}) (here, the superscript BD represents Bertrand model with differentiated products) such that the strategy of each firm is its best response to the rival's strategy.

That is,

$$\begin{cases} P_1^{BD} = R_1(P_2^{BD}) = 30 + \frac{P_2^{BD}}{4} \\ P_2^{BD} = R_2(P_1^{BD}) = 30 + \frac{P_1^{BD}}{4} \end{cases} \square$$

which yields $(P_1^{BD}, P_2^{BD}) = (40, 40)$ at equilibrium.

Diagrammatically, the Bertrand–Nash equilibrium of product differentiation for this duopoly game can be represented by the intersection of these two reaction curves in Figure 4.5.

We then have, at equilibrium, both firms' products are:

$$Q_1^{BD} = Q_1^{BD} = 40$$

substituting these outcomes into the profit functions yields

$$\pi_1^{BD} = \pi_2^{BD} = 1200 > 0$$

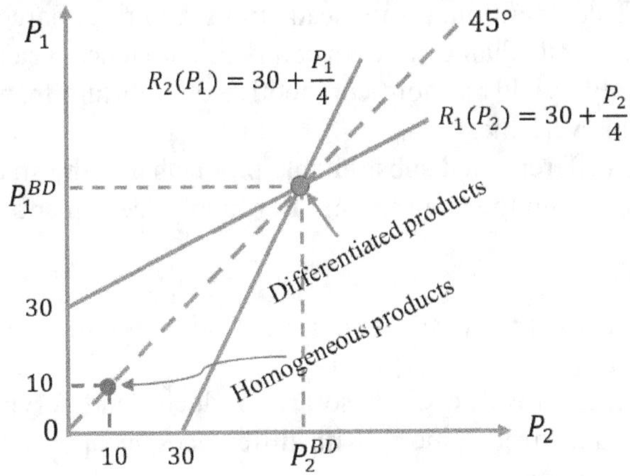

Figure 4.5: Bertrand–Nash equilibrium of product differentiation.

Notice that the price level is now higher than marginal cost, and firms become more profitable than that in the Bertrand equilibrium with the homogeneous product. This result demonstrates that product differentiation increases price-competing firms' market power by loosening up price competition.

4.6 Comparisons within Oligopoly and among Monopoly, Oligopoly and Perfect Competition

In the above two classic oligopoly models, we first observe that the results are different from monopolies or perfect competition due to market power. We also observed marked differences between Cournot (quantity) and Bertrand (price) competition inhomogeneous and differentiated products. In the rest of this section, we will refine these observations analytically and graphically.

Learning Objectives

- Compare oligopolies, monopoly, and perfect competition.

Main Takeaways

Main Points

- With a homogeneous product, price is higher, quantity is lower, and profits are higher under Cournot competition than under Bertrand competition.

- Bertrand's competition always leads to lower prices, larger quantities, and lower profits than Cournot's competition. Hence, price as the strategic variable yields a more competitive equilibrium than quantity as the strategic variable.
- The more differentiated substitutable products are, the smaller the differences between the Cournot and Bertrand prices, quantities, profits.

Main Terms

- **Homogeneous product:** Cannot be distinguished from competing **products** from different suppliers.
- **Differentiated products:** These are products (and services) that are distinguishable from others, with differences in appearance, quality, and even location.
- **Cartel:** It is a group of independent market participants who collude with each other to improve their profits and dominate the market.

4.6.1 *Homogeneous Product*

As we have shown in the homogenous product market with demand function:

$$P = 100 - Q$$

A firms' costs function with no fixed costs and constant marginal costs 10. The above two competing oligopoly models demonstrated different equilibrium outcomes regarding the firm's profits, consumer surplus, and total surplus. Total surplus is the sum of a firm's profits and the consumer surplus of the firm's customers. Consumer surplus is defined as the difference between the value that a consumer places on the units purchased and the amount of money required to pay for them. It is a measure of the buyer's value from the transaction. With a downward sloping demand curve, the consumer surplus is the shaded area in Figure 4.6.

Note that after some algebra, we have consumer surplus is equal to

$$S = \frac{1}{2} * (100 - P_E) * Q_E = \frac{1}{2} * (100 - (100 - Q_E)) * Q_E = \frac{1}{2} Q_E^2$$

where subscript E represents the associated price and quantity level at equilibrium.

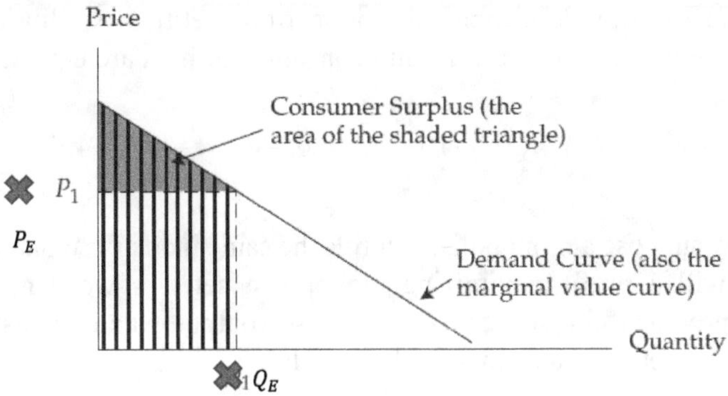

Figure 4.6: Consumer surplus on the demand curve.

Note: Consumer surplus is the area beneath the demand curve and above the price paid.

This formula is straightforward to calculate the consumer surplus under Cournot and Bertrand competitions with the homogeneous product. Thus, we have:

$$S^C = \frac{1}{2}(30+30)^2 = 1800$$

and

$$S^B = \frac{1}{2}(45+45)^2 = 4050$$

The results under the Cournot and Bertrand oligopoly models (for homogeneous products) are summarized. Those values are given in Table 4.2 and depicted in Figure 4.6. Next, we turn to the perfect competition market and calculate the corresponding values of market price, market output, firms' profits, consumers' surplus, and total surplus at equilibrium. Recall that firms in a perfectly competitive market maximize their profits by producing an output such that their marginal cost equals the market price. That is, we have

$$P^{PC} = 10$$

which yields the market output:

$$Q^{PC} = 100 - P^{PC} = 90$$

where superscript *PC* denotes the perfect competition equilibrium. It is easy to show that firms' profits and consumer surplus are equal to:

$$\pi^{PC} = P^{PC} * Q^{PC} - 10 * Q^{PC} = 0, \ \ S^{PC} = \frac{1}{2}90^2 = 4050$$

Now suppose a monopolist controls the same industry. What price and output will a profit-maximizing monopolist set? As we demonstrated in the previous chapter, the firm will set output where industry-wide marginal revenue equals marginal cost. That is,

$$\mathrm{MR}^M = \frac{d\mathrm{TR}^M}{dQ} = \frac{d}{dQ}(P * Q) = \frac{d}{dQ}((100 - Q)Q) = 100 - 2Q = \mathrm{MC}^M = 10$$

where *TR* and superscript *M* denote total revenue and monopoly equilibrium, respectively. Thus, we have the market output level,

$$Q^M = 45$$

which implies that the price level in the monopolistic market is

$$P^M = 100 - 45 = 55$$

Substituting these above two values into the firm's profit and consumer surplus functions, we have

$$\pi^M = (P^M - 10) * Q^M = 2025, \ \ S^M = \frac{1}{2}45^2 = 1012.5$$

From Table 4.2 and Figure 4.7, we can see that being a monopolist will rake in the most significant profits, while the lowest profits accrue to those a Bertrand competition or perfect competition. Consequently, we have:

$$\pi^M > \pi^C > \pi^B = \pi^{PC}$$

Ranking by consumer surplus, Bertrand competition, and perfect competition is highest. The monopolist has the power to charge the highest price and produce the lowest level of output among all these market structures. Therefore, the monopoly market results in the lowest consumer

Table 4.2: Equilibrium outcomes inhomogeneous product market.

	Cournot	Bertrand	Monopoly	Perfect competition
Price	40	10	55	10
Output	60	90	45	90
Profits π	1800	0	2025	0
Consumer surplus S	1800	4050	1012.5	4050
Total surplus $TS = \pi + S$	3600	4050	3037.5	4050

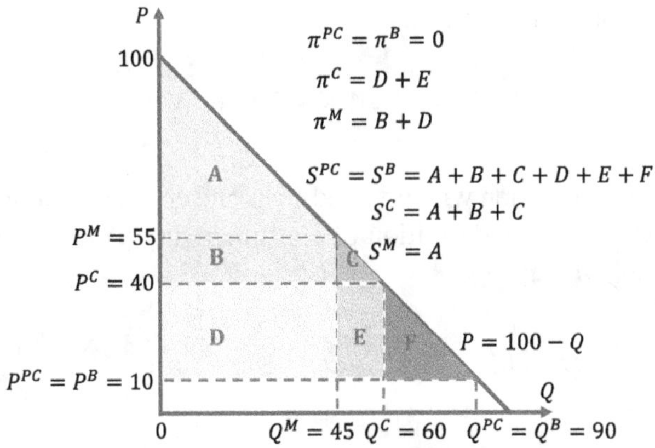

Figure 4.7: Equilibrium outcomes inhomogeneous product market.

surplus. Cournot competition results in less consumer plus than Bertrand competition. In short, we have

$$S^{PC} = S^B > S^C > S^M$$

Finally, ranking by total surplus, we can get the same ranking as the one sorted by consumer surplus

$$TS^{PC} = TS^B > TS^C > TS^M$$

Moreover, one finds that firms operating in the Cournot market produce less, charge higher prices, and obtain higher profits than those competing in the Bertrand market. The intuition behind this result is given in Vives (1985): Under the Cournot market structure, each firm would maintain a low output since it knows that quantity expansion would result in a price drop and lowers profits. However, each competitor in the Bertrand market knows that quantity expansion would not result in a price drop since its opponents hold price constant. Hence, the Cournot competitors produce less than the Bertrand competitors and thus charge higher prices and obtain larger profits.

4.6.2 *Differentiated Products*

It is natural to ask if the foregoing result still holds when we allow product differentiation. The accumulative market demand of differentiated products market can be rewritten as

$$P = 100 - \frac{3}{4}Q$$

Firms' costs function with no fixed costs and constant marginal costs 10.

We first follow the definition of consumer surplus again to obtain the corresponding value:

$$S^D = \frac{1}{2}Q_E * (100 - P_E) = \frac{1}{2}Q_E * \left(100 - 100 + \frac{3}{4}Q_E\right) = \frac{3}{8}Q_E^2$$

where superscript *D* represents the market with differentiated products.

Substituting associated output levels of Cournot and Bertrand competitions at equilibrium, we have

$$S^{CD} = \frac{3}{8}(36 + 36)^2 = 1944,\ S^{BD} = \frac{3}{8}(40 + 40)^2 = 2400$$

which are summarized in Table 4.3 combined with other equilibrium outcomes.

As we did in the previous subsection, a few computation lines give us the corresponding monopoly and perfect competition results, respectively. Those values are shown in Table 4.3 and depicted in Figure 4.8.

From Table 4.3, we once again see that the monopolist will rake in the most significant profits. However, Bertrand's competition with differentiated products yields positive profits. Consequently, we have

$$\pi^{MD} > \pi^{CD} > \pi^{BD} > \pi^{PCD}$$

where superscript MD denotes monopoly equilibrium, and PCD denotes perfect competition equilibrium in the market with differentiated products.

Table 4.3: Equilibrium outcomes in differentiated products market.

	Cournot	Bertrand	Monopoly	Perfect competition
Price	46	40	55	10
Output	72	80	60	120
Profits π	2592	2400	2700	0
Consumer surplus S	1944	2400	1350	5400
Total surplus $TS = \pi + S$	4536	4800	4050	5400

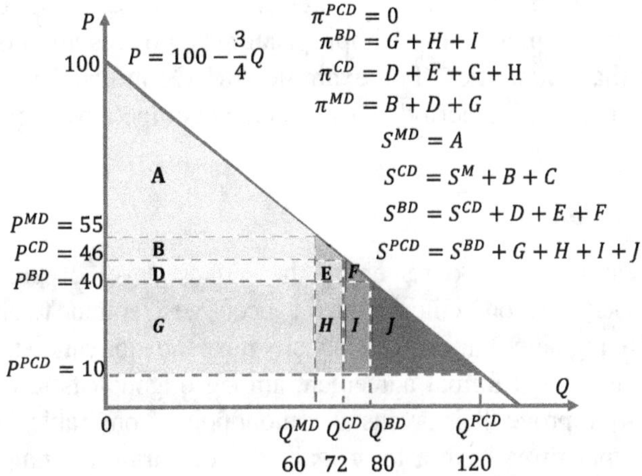

Figure 4.8: Equilibrium outcomes in differentiated products market.

Ranking by consumer surplus, perfect competition is highest, while monopolies provide the lowest consumer surplus. Also, Cournot competition again results in a lower consumer surplus than Bertrand competition. In short, we have

$$S^{PCD} > S^{BD} > S^{CD} > S^{MD}$$

Finally, ranking by total surplus, we can get the same ranking as those ranked by consumer surplus

$$TS^{PCD} > TS^{BD} > TS^{CD} > TS^{MD}$$

As you may expect, in the differentiated product markets, the above results establish that firms quote lower prices, produce more products, and obtain higher profits under Bertrand competition than under Cournot competition.

How would changing the degree of product differentiation affect the differences between the two oligopolistic competitions in terms of price, output, and profits? The answer to this question is straightforward. Comparing Tables 4.2, 4.3 and Figures 4.7 and 4.8, we observe that the more differentiated the substitution products, the smaller the difference between the two market structures.

The appropriate modeling choice depends on the case. The quantity competition appears to be the more appropriate choice when quantities are more challenging to change than prices, for example, travel ticket price competition during China's Spring Festival holidays. On the other hand, price competition may be more appropriate when prices are more difficult to change than quantities. For example, IMAX movies' price remains fixed over an extended period. Most cinemas compete over quantity.

4.6.3 *Collusion*

As noted earlier, monopolists enjoy the highest level of profits. Would Cournot or Bertrand competitors have the incentive to collude to obtain higher profits? (If unregulated) firms in an industry have the motivation to coordinate to form a cartel — a formal agreement among oligopolists to collude with each other to improve their profits as a monopoly. From Tables 4.2 and 4.3, we can see that firms have a lot to gain by conspiring to attain monopoly profits rather than competing under an oligopolistic market structure.

The most well-known example of a cartel is the Organization of Petroleum Exporting Countries (OPEC). It began restricting the quantity of oil extracted since the mid-1970s, which has led to a dramatic rise in oil prices and OPEC members' revenue and wealth.

References/Further Readings

Mankiw, N. G. (2020). *Principles of Economics*, 9th edn. Cengage Learning, pp. 335–356.

Png, I. (2016). *Managerial Economics*, 5th edn. Routledge, pp. 249–276.

Belleflamme, P. & Peitz, M. (2015). *Industrial Organization: Markets and Strategies*, 2nd edn. Cambridge University Press.

Church, J. R. & Ware, R. (2000). *Industrial Organization: A Strategic Approach*. McGraw-Hill.

Pepall, L., Richards, D., & Norman, G. (2014). *Industrial Organization: Contemporary Theory and Empirical Applications*, 5th edn. Wiley.

4.7 Application of Game Theory in Fintech

Game theory is widely applied in recent developments of Fintech in terms of the business model and the fundamental technologies. Game-theoretic concepts and methods underpin solutions that provide an incentive(s) for participants to behave well in Fintech-related activities and interactions.

Learning Objectives

- Understand the application of game theory in Fintech.

Main Takeaways

Main Points

- Game theory can improve newly developed financial models that incorporate Fintech.
- Game theory provides fundamental incentive design thinking in Fintech.

Main Terms

- **Mechanism design:** Refers to the design of mechanisms or incentives for desired outcomes, given that all the players are rational.
- **Reverse game theory:** Game theory in reverse where it starts at the end of the game and works backward.

Financial technology (Fintech) is related to innovative technology applied to change traditional financial services. Game-theoretic concepts and methods can help establish mathematical mechanisms to achieve optimal strategies and designs in Fintech.

For innovated business models, game theory can develop reliable mechanisms and improve the overall designs. Peer-to-Peer (P2P) network lending, a new Internet finance model, is one typical example. The P2P network facilitates collecting small amounts of idle funds and matches businesses with capital needs to establish a loan relationship among multiple online parties. However, risks such as breach of contract and fraudulent operation of P2P lending in actual financial activities would be of great concern (Martina and Miroslav, 2016). To reduce misconduct, game theory can be introduced, supported by insurance and regulation to improve the business model (Zhong, 2018).

While Blockchain technology can improve existing financial networks, game theory provides the blockchain design's incentive mechanism. In the traditional finance sector, trust can be a missing component among financial players and a lack of transparency in financial transactions. The traditional model can be inefficient and incur costs due to regular audits. The use of blockchain technology will integrate trust with traditional banking functions. As a result, audits are unnecessary, with all records made immutable, securely stored, and traceable.

To better appreciate how game theory appends Blockchain technology, we start by describing the context with a Blockchain as a distributed public data recording ledger and maintained by using a P2P network to achieve consensus among multiple nodes. Specifically, the data is recorded in a chain of blocks, and the new blocks with updated data would be appended to the miners' main chain. However, malicious nodes might still launch attacks and damage the decentralized blockchain system. Game theory can be applied to analyze the consensus and interactions among the nodes, thus providing prediction on mining behavior, allowing for the optimal reaction using equilibrium analysis (Liu, 2019). More importantly, game theory can help develop incentive mechanisms to discourage misconduct from malicious nodes utilizing the idea of mechanism design (also called a reverse game theory). Overall, game theory helps improve blockchain in its fundamental structure, workflow, and compatible incentive design.

References/Further Readings

Liu, Z. *et al.* (2019). A Survey on Applications of Game Theory in Blockchain. Retrieved from https://arxiv.org/pdf/1902.10865.pdf.

Martina, P. & Miroslav, S. (2016). Social Lending and its risks. Procedia-Social and Behavioral Sciences. Retrieved from https://www.sciencedirect.com/science/article/pii/S1877042816306073.

Zhong, L. (2018). The Game Strategy of Sustainable Development of P2P Internet Loan. *International Journal of Engineering and Applied Sciences.* Retrieved from https://www.ijeas.org/download_data/IJEAS0504010.pdf.

4.8 Sample Questions

Question 1

Consider the following game with a normal form representation in the table below. The first row is the situation that firm 1 sets a high price, and the second row is the situation that firm 1 sets a low price; the first column is the situation that firm 2 sets a high price, and the second column is the situation that firm 2 sets a low price. The cells provide the payoffs under each situation. The first number in a cell is firm 1's payoff, and the second one is firm 2's payoff. In this game, if both firms set high prices, each earns 36, while if both set low prices, each earns only 32. But if one's price is high while the other one's price is low, then the firm with the higher price earns 30, while the other earns 40.

		Firm 2	
		High price	Low price
Firm 1	High price	36, 36	30, 40
	Low price	40, 30	32, 32

What is the Nash equilibrium for this game?

(a) {High price, High price}
(b) {High price, Low price}
(c) {Low price, Low price}

Question 2
You are a manager of one of two identical mask-producing firms. Each firm produces the same good and faces the same production costs described by the following cost function: Total Cost = $4Q$, where Q is the output of an individual firm. The market demand for masks can be characterized as $P = 130 - 2Q$, where $Q = Q_1 + Q_2$, where Q_1 is your output and Q_2 is your rival's output. If competition is Cournot, what output level will you choose to maximize your profit?

(a) 15.75
(b) 21
(c) 31.5

Question 3
Return to Question 2, what is the consumer surplus at equilibrium?

(a) 441
(b) 1764
(c) 3969

Question 4

Consider that a university community has two milk tea stores owned by Alice and Bob. Market demand is described by the inverse demand function $P = 50 - 0.1Q$. Each store has a constant unit cost of production equal to 2. If competition is Cournot, what is Bob's price at the Cournot–Nash equilibrium?

(a) 18
(b) 22
(c) 26

Question 5

Return to Question 4, what is the total surplus at equilibrium?

(a) 10240
(b) 11520
(c) 15360

Question 6

Assume that two ballpoint pen suppliers, 1 and 2, sell differentiated models and face the following demand curves:

$$Q_1 = 24 - 5P_1 + 2P_2 \quad \text{and} \quad Q_2 = 24 - 5P_2 + 2P_1.$$

Suppliers have equal and constant marginal cost $c = 0$ and compete over prices once. What is the equilibrium set of prices in this ballpoint pen market?

(a) 0
(b) 3
(c) 4

Question 7

Return to Question 6, what is the output level of ballpoint pen supplier 2?

(a) 12
(b) 15
(c) 24

Question 8

Suppose that two firms compete on quantities (Cournot) in a market in which demand is described by $P = 260 - 2Q$ and that each firm has a constant marginal cost of 20. What profit does each firm earn if they conspire to produce the monopoly output and evenly share the market demand?

(a) 3600
(b) 4200
(c) 5400

Question 9

Singtel, Mobile One, and Starhub are the only three companies in Singapore today that provide mobile services. Singtel is a dominant player with more than 80% market share. Singtel also provides packaged services that include mobile, WiFi services, and movie packages that translate to mobile contracts enjoying a 10% discount compared with stand-alone contracts. The *best* characterization of the Singapore telecommunications industry is

(a) oligopoly
(b) perfect competition
(c) monopoly

Solutions

Question 1

Solution: Option **c** is correct

If firm 2 chooses {high price} then firm 1's best response is to choose {low price} due to 40 > 36; while if firm 2 chooses {low price} then firm 1's best response is to choose {low price} due to 32 > 30. Similarly, if firm 1 chooses {high price} then firm 2's best response is to choose {low price} due to 40 > 36; while if firm 1 chooses {low price} then firm 1's best response is to choose {low price} due to 32 > 30. Therefore, the strategy profile {low price, low price} is the Nash equilibrium.

Question 2

Solution: Option **b** is correct

First, write down firm 1's profit-maximizing problem as

$$\pi_1\,(Q_1, Q_2) = (130 - 2(Q_1 + Q_2) - 4)\,Q_1$$

Then taking the first derivative with respect to Q_1, which yields firm 1's reaction function

$$R_1(Q_2) = \frac{1}{2}(63 - Q_2)$$

Similarly, firm 2's reaction function is given by

$$R_2(Q_1) = \frac{1}{2}(63 - Q_1)$$

Therefore, your output level that maximizes profits is equal to

$$Q_1 = \frac{1}{2}(63 - Q_1), \text{ i.e., } Q_1 = 21$$

Question 3

Solution: Option **b** is correct

Based on Question 2, we know that the industry-wide output level is equal to 42. Then using the consumer surplus formula $S = \frac{1}{2}Q*(130-(130-2Q)) = = Q^2$ we have $S = 42^2 = 1764$.

Question 4

Solution: Option **a** is correct

First, write down Alice's profit-maximizing problem as:

$$\pi_A(Q_A, Q_A) = (50 - 0.1(Q_A + Q_B) - 2)Q_A$$

Then taking the first derivative with respect to Q_A, which yields Alice's reaction function

$$R_A(Q_B) = 240 - \frac{1}{2}Q_B$$

Similarly, Bob's reaction function is given by

$$R_B(Q_A) = 240 - \frac{1}{2}Q_A$$

Therefore, both Alice and Bob maximize their profits by producing

$$Q_A = Q_B = 160$$

which implies Alice and Bob charge the same price for milk tea at

$$P_A = P_B = 18$$

Question 5

Solution: Option: **c** is correct

Recall that the total surplus is the sum of consumer surplus and industry profit, where the consumer surplus is equal to

$$S = \frac{1}{2}Q(50-(50-0.1Q)) = 0.05Q^2 = 0.05 * 320^2 = 5120$$

and the industry profit is equal to

$$\pi = 2 * (P - MC) * Q = 2 * (18 - 2) * 320 = 10240$$

Thus, the total surplus is equal to 15360.

Question 6

Solution: Option **b** is correct.

First, write down supplier 1's profit-maximizing problem as

$$\pi_1 (P_1, P_2) = (P_1 - 0) * (24 - 5P_1 + 2P_2)$$

Then taking the first derivative with respect to P_1, which yields supplier 1's reaction function

$$R_1 (P_2) = 2.4 + 0.2P_2$$

Similarly, supplier 2's reaction function is given by

$$R_2 (P_1) = 24 + 0.2P_1$$

Therefore, both suppliers maximize their profits by charging

$$P_1 = P_2 = 3$$

Question 7

Solution: Option **b** is correct.

Based on the price level at equilibrium, we have:

$$Q_2 = 24 - 5 * 3 + 2 * 3 = 15$$

Question 8

Solution: Option **a** is correct.

If firms agree to the cartel arrangement, they will play as a monopoly and share evenly the monopolistic profits, which is given by

$$\pi^M = (P^M - MC) * Q^M = (240 - 2Q^M) * Q^M$$

where $Q^M = 60$ maximizes the monopoly's profits.
Thus, each firm's profit is equal to

$$\pi = \frac{1}{2}\pi^M = \frac{1}{2}(240 - 2 * 60) * 60 = 3600.$$

Question 9

Solution: Option **a** is correct.

Singtel operates as an oligopoly. The number of contract customers will be affected by its two competitors' strategy. The packaged deal is an attempt to product differentiation and compete on price.

Part B: Macroeconomics

This section introduces macroeconomics and the various aggregate economic output measures, including real and nominal GDP, national income, personal income, and personal disposable income. Essential concepts covered include aggregate demand (AD) and short-run and long-run aggregate supply. We also discuss the causes of a shift in AD and aggregate supply and long-run economic growth sources.

Chapter 5

Aggregate Output, Prices, and Economic Growth

5.1 Measures of Output

5.1.1 *Gross Domestic Product*

Gross domestic product (GDP) is the market value of all final goods and services produced within a country within a given period. We also use GDP as a comparison tool.

Learning Objectives

- Differentiate the income and expenditure approaches to assessing GDP and explain how we calculate GDP.

Main Takeaways

Main Points

- GDP is measured using the expenditure approach as: $Y = C + I + G + (X - M)$.
- The income approach measures GDP by summing up national income and adjusting for depreciation, taxes, and subsidies.
- For an economy as a whole, income must equal expenditure.

Main Terms

- **Equilibrium:** A situation in which the marketplace has reached the level of which quantity supplied equals quantity demanded.

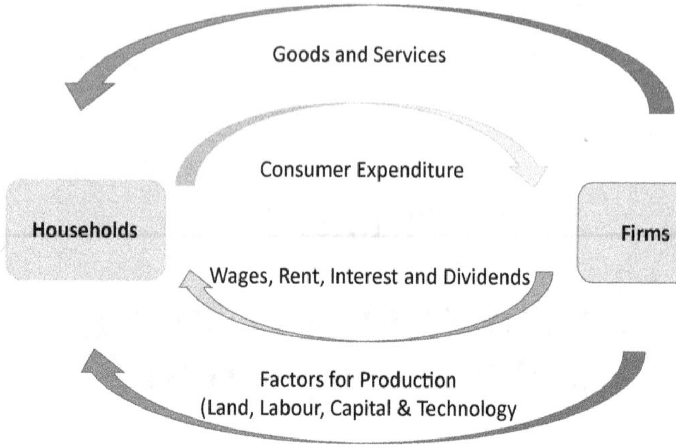

Figure 5.1: Schematic of flows in a closed economy.

GDP is the market value of all final goods and services produced within a country within a given period. GDP measures two things at once: the total income of everyone in the economy and the total expenditure on the economy's output of goods and services. For an economy as a whole, income must equal expenditure as a buyer spends and a seller paid in any transaction. Figure 5.1 shows a schematic of the flows of goods and services, factors of production, consumer expenditure and wages, rents, and dividends.

(a) Looking at Expenditure

In a simple economy, the main economic agents are households and firms. We assume that households buy all goods and services from the firms for simplicity. When households purchase goods and services from firms, these expenditures flow through the markets for goods and services. Firms receive money from the sale of goods and services to pay workers' wages, landowners' rent, and owners' profits. This income flows through the markets for factors of production. GDP thus measures this flow of money.

The expenditure approach attempts to calculate GDP by evaluating the sum of all final goods and services purchased in an economy. The GDP denoted as "Y" is divided into four components: consumption (C), investment (I), government purchases (G), and net exports (X – M):

$$Y = C + I + G + (X - M)$$

- "C" (consumption) is spending by households on goods and services. Goods include durables, such as cars, and non-durables, such as food and clothing. Services include medical care and education. Consumption is usually the most significant GDP component in the economy.
- "I" (investment) is the purchase of goods (called capital goods) that will be used to produce more goods and services. Investment is the sum of business capital purchases (such as factory and office buildings and equipment), residential capital (housing for rent and own stay), and inventories. "Investment" in GDP does not mean the purchases of financial products. Buying financial products is classified as 'saving' instead of an investment.
- "G" (government purchases) is spending by the government on final goods and services. It includes salaries of government workers, the purchase of weapons for the military, and government investment expenditure. Transfer payments like social security, unemployment benefits are not counted as government purchases; since GDP is intended to measure income or expenditure from the production of goods and services. Since transfer payments do alter income, they are captured in "C" when the payments are spent.
- "(X – M)" (net exports) represents exports minus imports. It means the foreign purchases of domestically produced goods minus the domestic purchase of foreign goods. We subtract M because other components, "G," "I," or "C," include import of goods and services and so the deduction to avoid counting foreign supply as domestic.

Sum-of-Value-Added and Value-of-Final-Output: In the expenditure approach, we calculate GDP by summing the values of all final goods and services produced. We can also calculate GDP by summing up the value created at each production and distribution stage. The second approach is called the "sum-of-value-added." We present an example of the calculation for a product like a wooden coffee table below:

Stage of production	Sales value ($)	Value added ($)
Raw materials (processed wood)	$200	$200
Manufacturing (cutting, sanding, assembly, painting, packing)	$450	$250
Retail (distribution, display and delivery)	$600	$150
Sum of value-added		$600

The example shows that the final wooden table's price is equal to the value-added at each stage of production (harvesting and processing raw wood, manufacturing the table, and distributing the table to the consumer).

(b) Nominal and Real GDP and the GDP Deflator

GDP measures the total spending on goods and services in all markets in the economy. If total expenditure rises from one year to the next, at least one of two things must have happened: (1) the economy produces more output, or (2) goods and services sold at higher prices. When we study the economy, we would like to know the quantity of goods and services produced by the economy, independent of price changes. Under the expenditure approach, nominal GDP is the total value of all goods and services produced by an economy, valued at current market prices. For an economy with *N* different goods and services, we can express nominal GDP as

$$\text{Nominal GDP}_t = \sum_{i=1}^{N} (\text{Price of good } i \text{ in year } t) \times (\text{Quantity of good } i \text{ in year } t)$$

Based on the current prices, inflation will increase nominal GDP even if the physical output of goods and services remains constant from one year to the next. Using prices from a base year, real GDP measures the economy's output at constant prices, and inflation is not counted as economic growth.

Assuming the base year prices are those for *x* years ago, we calculate real GDP as:

$$\text{Real GDP}_t = \sum_{i=1}^{N} P_{i,t-x} Q_{i,t}$$

The GDP deflator measures the current prices relative to prices in the base year. We calculate The GDP as

$$\text{GDP deflator for year } t = \frac{\sum_{i=1}^{N} \text{P}_{i.t} Q_{i,t}}{\sum_{i=1}^{\text{N}} \text{P}_{i.t\text{-}x} Q_{i,t}} = \frac{\text{Nominal GDP in year } t}{\text{Value of year t output at year } t\text{-}x \text{ prices}} \times 100$$

Example: Nominal and real GDP, GDP deflator

Consider a simple two goods market as follows:

Prices and Quantity

Year	Price of pizza	Quantity of pizza	Price of drone	Quantity of drone
2018	$4	100	$8	50
2019	$5	150	$9	100
2020	$6	200	$10	150

The nominal GDP is as follows:

Year	GDP in year t = $(\text{Price} \times \text{Quantity})_{\text{pizza}} + (\text{Price} \times \text{Quantity})_{\text{drone}}$
2018	$4 × 100 + $8 × 50 = $800
2019	$5 × 150 + $9 × 100 = $1650
2020	$6 × 200 + $10 × 150 = $$2700

The GDP in 2018 prices is as follows:

Year	GDP in year t = $(\text{Price}_{2018} \times \text{Quantity})_{\text{pizza}} + (\text{Price}_{2018} \times \text{Quantity})_{\text{drone}}$
2018	$4 × 100 + $8 × 50 = $800
2019	$4 × 150 + $8 × 100 = $1400
2020	$4 × 200 + $8 × 150 = $2000

The GDP deflator is as follows:

Year	$\frac{\text{Nominal GDP in year } t}{\text{Value of year } t \text{ output at year } t\text{-}x \text{ prices}} \times 100$
2018	100
2019	(1650/1400) × 100 = 117.9
2020	(2700/2000) × 100 = 135.0

(c) Income Approach

The income approach estimates GDP as the sum of incomes receivable by each institutional sector from the domestic production of goods and services. In Singapore, the income approach's estimated GDP and its main components include compensation of workers and gross surplus from financial and non-financial corporations, unincorporated enterprises (including imputed rental of owner-occupied dwellings, non-profit institutions. Also included are taxes on the production like workers' levy, import and excise taxes, business registration fees, stamp duties, and property taxes paid by businesses and households to the government.[1]

Other Measures of Income: Other measures to get a better picture of what goes on in the economy include national income, personal income, and disposable personal income.

- **National income** is the total income earned by a nation's residents in the production of goods and services:
- **Personal income** is the income that households and non-corporate businesses receive. Personal income differs from national income in that retained earnings in corporations, indirect business taxes, corporate income tax, and contributions for social insurance are excluded. On the other hand, interest income for households holding government debt and income that households receive from government transfers are included.
- **Personal disposable income (PDI)** is the income that households and non-corporate businesses have left after satisfying all their government obligations. It equals personal income minus personal taxes and certain nontax payments (like traffic fines). PDI measures the amount that households have available to save or spend on goods and services and is an important economic indicator of consumers' ability to spend and save.

(d) The Relationship between Savings, Investment, Fiscal Balance, and the Trade Balance

Private savings are related to investment, government, and foreign trade. This relationship combines the income and expenditure approaches to measuring GDP.

Based on total expenditure, GDP equals C + I + G + (X – M). Based on total income, GDP (income) ultimately comes back to households who use it for consumption, savings, and government taxes. Hence, GDP equals C + S + T, where C is consumption, S is household and business savings, and T is net taxes, i.e., taxes minus transfer payments received.

Because total income equals total expenditures, we can write:

$$C + I + G + (X - M) = C + S + T$$

[1]Retrieved from https://www.singstat.gov.sg/-/media/files/publications/economy/gdi.pdf (accessed September 20, 2020).

Solving for S (household and business savings), we get:

$$S = I + (G - T) + (X - M)$$

Solving for the fiscal balance, (G – T), we get:

$$(G - T) = (S - I) - (X - M)$$

From this equation, we can see that a government deficit (G – T > 0) must be financed by some combination of a trade deficit (X – M < 0) or an excess of private saving over private investment (S – I) >0.

References/Further Readings

Mankiw, N.G. (2020). *Principles of Economics*, 9th ed., Cengage Learning, pp. 467–486, 530–549.

5.2 Introducing Aggregate Demand and Aggregate Supply

Economies in the longer-term experience increase in the production of goods and services because of increases in the labor force, capital, and technology advances. In some years, however, economies contract, firms suffer losses and may even go out of business, and more, workers become unemployed.

A key question in economics is "what causes these short-run fluctuations?" The critical variables to analyze this question include GDP, unemployment, interest rates, and the price level. While a great deal of debate surrounds this question, the primary tool used to analyze output fluctuations in the short run is the model of aggregate demand (AD) and aggregate supply. We start the section by defining aggregate supply and AD and describing the aggregate supply curve and AD curve.

Learning Objectives

- Define aggregate supply and AD.
- Discuss economic fluctuations.

Main Takeaways

Main Points

- Aggregate supply is the total amount of goods and services that firms are willing to sell at a given price in an economy. The AD is the total amounts of goods and services purchased at all possible price levels.
- A standard aggregate supply–aggregate demand (AS-AD) model focuses on the behavior of two variables, the economy's output of goods and services (Y) and the average level of prices (P).
- David Hume, a classical economist, observed that when the money supply expanded after gold discoveries, it took some time for prices to rise. In the meantime, the economy enjoyed higher employment and production.

Main Terms

- **Nominal:** Without adjustment to remove the effects of inflation (in contrast to real).
- **Unemployment rate:** The percentage of the labor force that is unemployed.
- **Price level:** Average price of all goods and services produced in an economy.
- **Interest rates:** The nominal interest rate is the monetary return to savings and investment and the financial cost of borrowing; the real interest rate is the nominal rate adjusted for inflation.

5.2.1 *Aggregate Supply and Aggregate Demand*

The aggregate supply is the total amount of goods and services that firms are willing to sell at a given price in an economy. The AD is the total amount of goods and services purchased at different price levels in an economy.

A standard AS-AD model focuses on the behavior of two variables, the economy's output of goods and services (Y) and the average level of prices (P). We can then analyze fluctuations in the economy using aggregate supply and AD, illustrated in Figure 5.2, with Y on the x-axis and P on the y-axis. The AD curve shows the quantity of goods and services that households firms, the government, and customers abroad want to buy at each level. The aggregate supply shows the quantity of goods and services that firms produce and sell at each price level. The equilibrium output and equilibrium price level is the point where aggregate supply

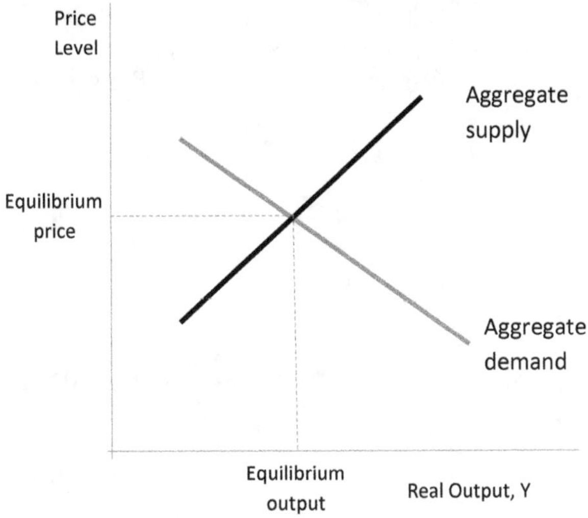

Figure 5.2: AS–AD model.

equals AD. According to the AS–AD model, the price level and quantity of output adjust to bring aggregate supply and AD into balance.

The AS–AD model is different from the market demand model and market supply introduced in microeconomics. In the market model, agents' behavior depends on resources' ability to move from one market to another. For example, when the price of pizza increases, the quantity demanded falls as buyers move to other products like frozen yogurt. The substitution is not possible for the economy as a whole. The AS–AD model's quantity of concern is the total quantity of goods and services produced by all firms in an economy.

5.2.2 *Economic Fluctuations*

Short-run fluctuations in economic output have occurred throughout history. Long-run economic activity changes are only affected by labor, capital, and technology differences. Otherwise, in the long run, economies are assumed to be optimal. The aggregate supply curve is vertical, so fluctuations in AD impact only the long run's price level.

Over the short run, economic fluctuations are irregular and unpredictable. Secondly, most macroeconomic quantities fluctuate together, and lastly, as output fall, unemployment rises. These are the stylized facts surrounding economic fluctuations.

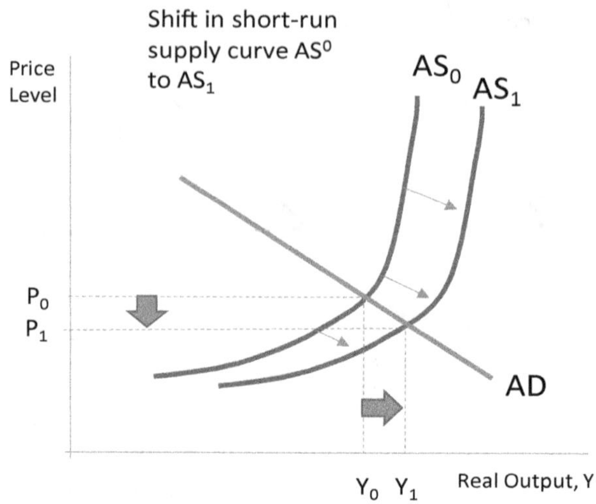

Figure 5.3: AS-AD model with a shift in short-run aggregate supply (SRAS).

Most importantly, economists have realized that to explain economic fluctuations in the short run. The analysis must include the price level and real output. David Hume, a classical economist, observed that when the money supply expanded after gold discoveries, it took some time for prices to rise. In the meantime, the economy enjoyed higher employment and production.

Figure 5.3 illustrates Hume's observation. In the short run, an increase in money will increase production due to a shift in the aggregate supply (from AS_0 to AS_1). The output has increased (from Y_0 to Y_1) and increased purchases because of the lower prices (from P_0 to P_1).

5.3 Aggregate Demand Curve: IS and LM Curves

5.3.1 *The Aggregate Demand Curve*

The AD curve tells us the quantity of all goods and services demanded in the economy at any given price at a specific time. The AD curve slopes downwards. All else unchanged, an increase in the price level results in reduced demand for goods and services. Conversely, a decrease in the price level will increase demand.

Learning Objectives

- Explain the downward-sloping AD curve.
- Understand the I-S and LM models.

Main Takeaways

Main Points

- AD can be represented as: AD = C + I + G + (X – M).
- To explain the downward sloping demand curve requires us to look at how each component of AD changes with the price level.
- The IS and LM models essentially show why the AD curve shifts.

Main Terms

- **Aggregate demand:** The total demand for final goods and services in the economy at a given time and price level.
- **Asset markets:** The entire set of markets in which people buy and sell real and financial assets.
- **IS curve:** Depicts the set of all levels of interest rates and output (GDP) at which total investment (I) equals total saving (S); in other words, when the market for goods and services is in equilibrium.
- **LM curve:** Shows the combinations of income and the real interest rate for which demand for money (or desired liquidity) equals money supply. Hence, the domestic economy is in asset (or stock) equilibrium.

(a) Demand Sources

It is useful to recall that an economy's GDP (which we denote as Y) is the sum of its consumption (C), investment (I), government purchases (G), and net exports (X – M). Each of these components contributes to the AD. AD can be represented as: AD = C + I + G + (X – M). The AD curve is normally depicted on a price-output diagram, as shown in Figure 5.4.

As the components contribute to the AD for goods and services, and each of them depends on the price level, to explain the downward sloping demand curve requires us to look at how each component of AD changes with the price level.

An increase in the price level reduces the real value of money and makes consumers poorer, reduces consumer spending, and demands the quantity of goods and services. On the other hand, a decrease in the price level increases the real value of money, increases consumer spending, and demands the quantity of goods and services.

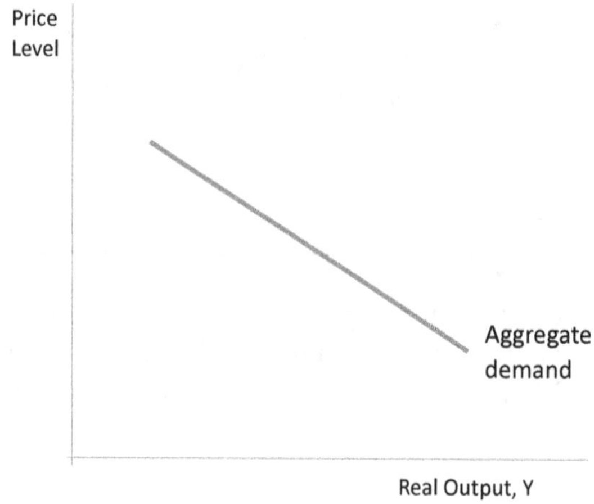

Figure 5.4: Aggregate demand (downward sloping demand curve: the AD curve is derived via consumption, investment, government spending, and net export).

The price level affects the quantity of money demanded. With lower price levels, households need to hold less money to buy goods and services. So, households hold less money and lend or save more. Financial institutions have more funds to lend out. As households convert to more interest-bearing assets, interest rates will be driven down, resulting in greater spending on goods and services by lowering borrowing costs. Firms will also borrow more to invest in plants and equipment; households will borrow more to purchase a dwelling, and big-ticket items, like automobiles and white goods. Hence a lower interest rate increases the amount of goods and services demanded.

Domestic price level decline causes domestic interest rates to fall. Fund flow to seek better returns in foreign asset markets, resulting in depreciation of the domestic currency. The depreciation then alters the real exchange return, with each domestic currency buying less foreign goods while the foreign currency buys more domestic goods. With foreign goods more expensive, consumers will buy less, while foreigners will buy more domestic goods. The depreciating domestic currency results in exports minus imports increasing.

For the three components, as price level declines, C + I + (X – M) increases, and as price level increases, C + I + (X – M) declines. It is not clear how price level impacts government purchases, usually government policy decisions. We should note that the three key components are magnitudes larger than government spending. For the reasons above, as price level increases, AD declines, and as price level decreases, AD increases, i.e., the AD curve is downward sloping.

(b) The IS–LM Model

The following discussion will be on the **IS–LM model** or **Hicks–Hansen model** that shows why an AD curve can shift, i.e., to analyze economic fluctuations. The model formally demonstrates the link between AD with the market for goods and services and the asset markets. IS stands for "investment" and "saving", and the IS curve represents what is going on in the market for goods and services. LM stands for "liquidity" and "money", and the LM curve represents what is happening to the supply and demand for money. Because the interest rate influences both investment and money demand, it is the variable that links the IS and LM curves.

(c) The IS Curve

The **IS curve** depicts the set of all levels of interest rates and output (GDP) at which total investment (I) equals total saving (S); in other words, when the market for goods and services is in equilibrium.

When total expenditure equals total income, the relation between saving, investment, the fiscal balance, and the trade balance is S = I + (G – T) + (X – M) as shown in Section 5.1. Rearranging by subtracting I from both sides of the relation, we get:

$$(S - I) = (G - T) + (X - M)$$

Each of the variables in this equation is a function of economic output/aggregate income. All else being equal, higher aggregate income causes the fiscal deficit (G – T) to decrease, or a fiscal surplus, to increase because taxes increases with income. (X – M) decrease, or a trade deficit to increase because imports increase with income. Thus, we represent the sum (G – T) + (X – M) as a *decreasing* aggregate income function. The plots of (S – I), (G – T) + (X – M) against aggregate income as shown in Figure 5.5.

At any given real interest rate, the excess of private savings over private investment (S–I) is represented as an *increasing* function of aggregate income, assuming that an increase in income will increase household

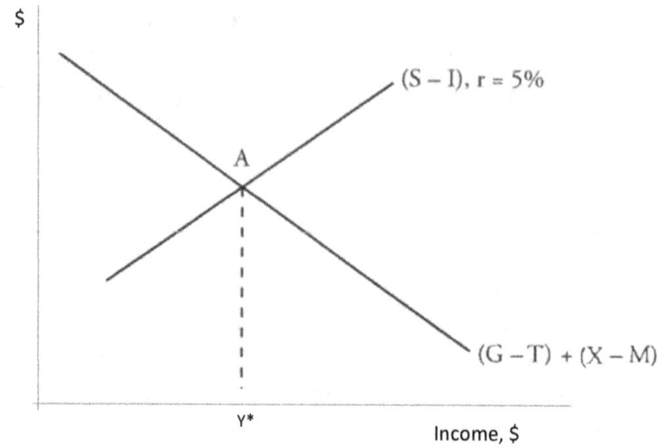

Figure 5.5: (S–I), (G–T) + (X–M) against aggregate income (the essential relationship between excess private saving over private income and fiscal deficit and trade balance against aggregate income for a fixed level of the real interest rate).

and business savings more than it increases investment. Figure 5.5 also shows the (S–I) plot.

What happens if we change the real interest rate? Other things equal, a decrease in the real interest rate will decrease financing costs and increase businesses' investment. Because we are holding the fiscal and trade balances unchanged, the excess of savings over investment (S–I) is also unchanged. An equal increase in savings accompanies an increase in investment. Holding the marginal propensity to save unchanged, the increase in savings can only result from an increase in income.

As shown in Figure 5.6, a decrease in the real interest rate from r_A to r_C results in point C as the new combination of real interest rates and real aggregate income that balances the equation. Real aggregate income increases from Y_A to Y_C.

An increase in the real rate has the opposite effect. Higher rates will decrease the real aggregate income.

If income and expenditure remain in equilibrium, there must be an inverse relationship between the real interest rate and income. This relationship is called the I–S curve (as shown in Figure 5.7) because investment (I) and savings (S) are the primary variables that adjust to maintain the balance between expenditure and income. The I–S curve plots the combinations of income and real interest rates for which total income equals total expenditure.

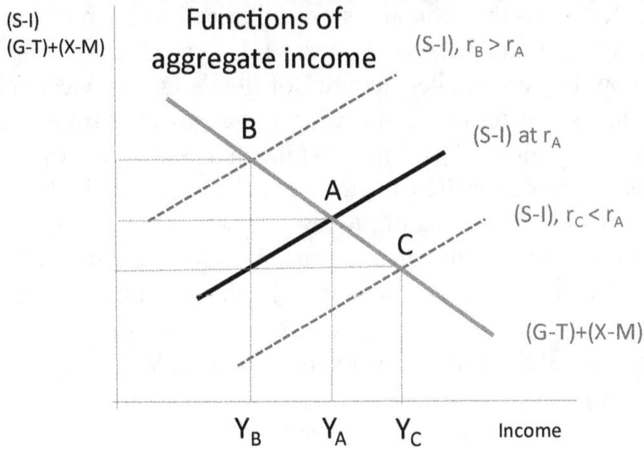

Figure 5.6: (S–I), (G–T) + (X–M) against aggregate income (changing real interest rate) (the relationship between excess of private saving over private income and government and trade balance against aggregate income changing real interest rate (e.g., with $r_B > r_A > r_C$)).

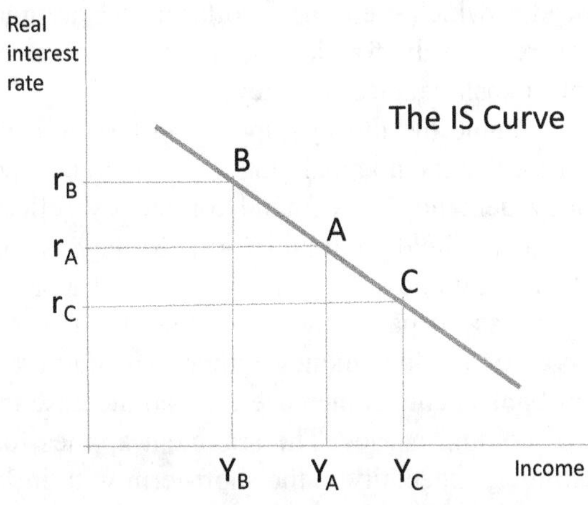

Figure 5.7: The I–S curve (aggregate income against real interest rate) (if income and expenditure are to remain in equilibrium, there must be an inverse relationship between income and interest rates).

(d) The LM Curve

The LM curve shows the combinations of income and the real interest rate for which demand for money (or desired liquidity) equals money supply. Hence, the domestic economy is in asset (or stock) equilibrium.

We will discuss the economy's overall price level as a monetary value measure. A rise in the price level means a lower value of money because a dollar now buys a smaller quantity of goods and services. Now, how the price level is determined and why it changes over time is called the "quantity theory money." It states that the quantity of money available in an economy determines the value of money, and growth in the quantity of money determines the value of money.

One perspective of the quantity theory is to calculate the velocity of money. To do so, we divide the nominal value of output (nominal GDP) by the quantity of money, M. If P is the price level and Y is the quantity of output (real GDP), then the velocity of money, V is

$$V = (P \times Y)/M$$

and

$$1/V = (M/P)/Y$$

V is the speed at which the typical dollar travels around in the economy. 1/V is interpreted as the fraction of real income that people desire to hold in the form of cash balances (money).

Let us now examine the money supply and money demand. In most analyses, we assume that the nominal money supply to be a policy variable.

As for money demand, the demand for money reflects how much wealth people want to hold in liquid form. Money is the medium of exchange and the most liquid asset available. There is a preference to hold money even if other assets pay a higher interest rate. However, if interest rates rise, the cost of holding money rather than putting it in interest-bearing bonds or bank accounts increases. So, an increase in interest rates raises the cost of holding money. The argument applies for both real or nominal interest rates, especially in the short-term with inflation stable.

Demand for money decreases when real interest rates increase, and demand for money increases when real income rises. We hold the real money supply (M/P) constant. If real income increases, the real interest rate must adjust upwards for the money supply and money demand to be in balance.

Concerning the quantity theory, holding money supply (M/P) constant, increase in real income, Y is offset by a decrease in 1/V, due to an increase in real interest rates. Figure 5.8 shows this relationship. Holding (M/P) constant, the relationship between real income and real interest rate

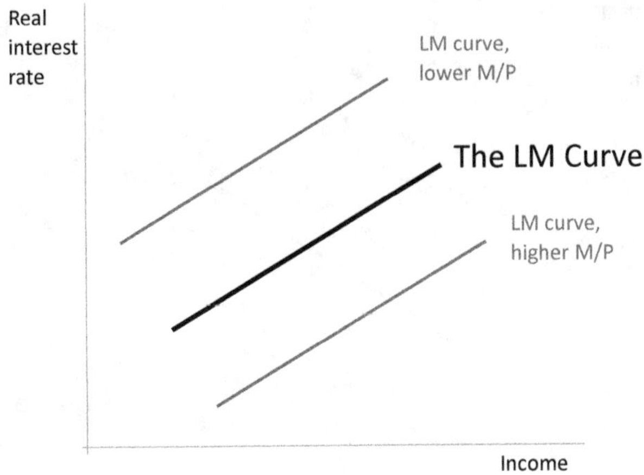

Figure 5.8: The LM curve (real interest rate against real income) shows a positive relationship between income and real interest rate for a given level of M/P.

is upward sloping. The curve is called the LM curve, where the asset market is in equilibrium.

(e) IS–LM Model and the Aggregate Demand Curve

Recall that the **AD curve** represents the total quantity of all goods (and services) demanded by the economy at different price levels.

Figure 5.9 shows the combined IS and LM curves. The point at which they intersect represents the real interest rate and income levels consistent with an equilibrium between income and expenditure (the IS curve) and equilibrium between the real money supply and the real interest rate (the LM curve). The intersection between the IS and LM curves determines the equilibrium levels of prices and real income (real GDP) for a given level of the real money supply.

The AD curve shows the relationship between the quantity of real output demanded (which equals real income) and the price level.

Example: Holding nominal money supply, M constant

The real money supply (M/P) is constant along the LM curve. If the nominal money supply (M) is held constant, the real money supply can change due to changes in the price level (P). An increase in the price level will decrease the real money supply (M/P), and a decrease in the price level will increase the real money supply (M/P).

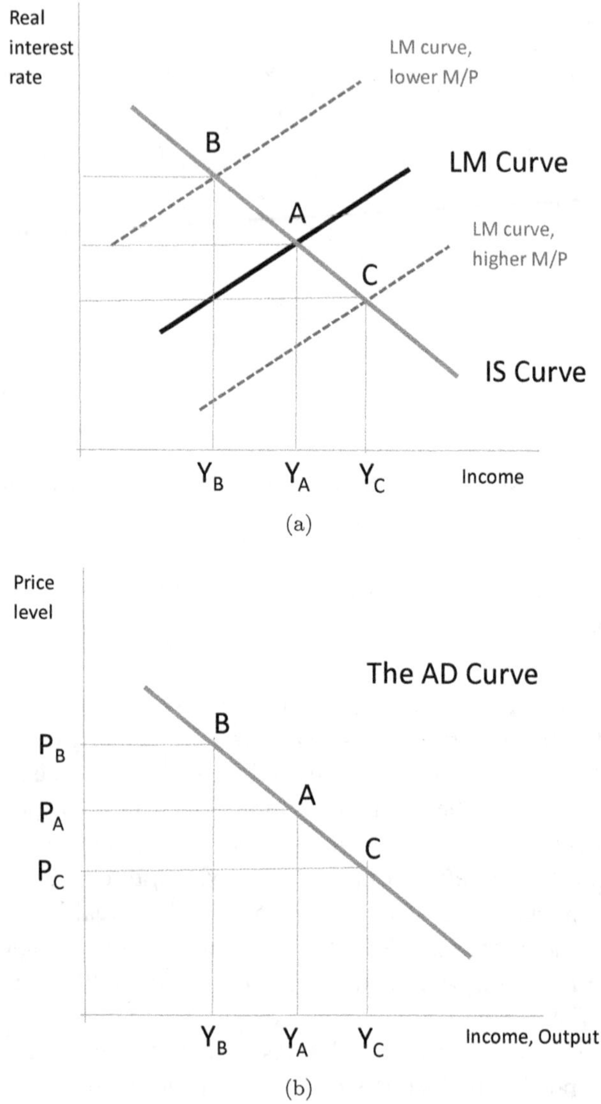

Figure 5.9: Combining the IS–LM curves and implications for price level and income. (a) The IS–LM model takes investments and savings and compares liquidity and the overall money supply. (b) The AD curve.

In Figure 5.9(a), Point B is on an LM curve for a lower real money supply (and therefore a higher price level) than Point A. Point C is on an LM curve for a higher real money supply (and thus a lower price level) than Point A. We assume that the IS curve is unchanged. With income equal to expenditure (the IS curve) and money demand equal money supply (the LM curve), even if nominal supply M remaining unchanged, the relationship between the price level and real income is downward sloping. The resultant AD curve in Figure 5.9(b).

References/Further Readings

Mankiw, N..G. (2020). *Principles of Economics*, 9th edn., Cengage Learning, pp. 683–694, 720–736.

5.4 Aggregate Supply Curve in the Short and Long Run

5.4.1 *Aggregate Supply Curve*

The aggregate supply curve tells us the total quantity of goods and services firms produce at any given price level.

Learning Objectives

- Describe the aggregate supply in different time frames.
- Describe the relationship between the price level and the quantity of real GDP supplied.

Main Takeaways

Main Points

- Aggregate supply is the relationship between the price level and the economy's production.
- The aggregate supply is graphed vertically on the supply curve in the long-run.
- The equation used to determine the long-run aggregate supply (LRAS) is $Y = Y^*$. In the equation, Y is the economy's production, and Y^* is the natural level of output of the economy.
- The aggregate supply is graphed as an upward sloping curve in the short-run.

Main Terms

- **A factor of production:** A resource employed to produce goods and services, such as labor, land, and capital.
- **Output:** Production; quantity produced, created, or completed.

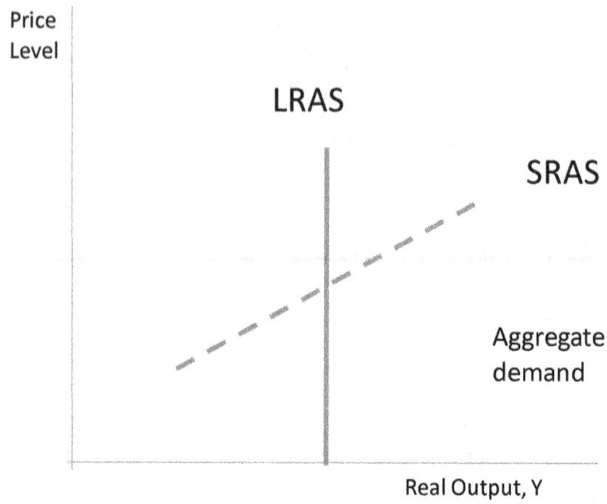

Figure 5.10: The aggregate supply curves (the LRAS curve is inelastic, while the SRAS curve is upward sloping).

(a) Aggregate Supply Curves over Different Time Frames

We will focus on the SRAS curve and the LRAS curve, as shown in Figure 5.10.

In the long run, we have already mentioned that an economy's production of goods and services depends on its supply of labor, capital, natural resources, and available technology. All prices can vary in the long run, and the LRAS curve is perfectly inelastic. In the long run, the amount of money supply that determines the price level does not affect technology nor the inputs mentioned above. As such, the price level has no long-run effect on aggregate supply. We refer to this level of output as potential GDP or full-employment GDP.

In the short run, the price level affects the output. Market imperfections can cause the short-run supply curve to behave differently from the long-run curve. Examples of market imperfections are sticky wages (where nominal wages adjust slowly), sticky prices (where prices of some products are slow to change), and misperception (where the overall price level is not reflective of the individual firms' market that they serve). When the price level rises above the price level that economic agents expect to prevail, output increases above the "natural" level. If the price level falls, the output will decline below that "natural" level. The result is an upward-sloping SRAS curve.

5.5 Shifts in Aggregate Demand and Supply Curves

5.5.1 *Reasons for Shifts in the Aggregate Demand Curve*

An increase in any of the four inputs into AD (consumption, investment, government spending, and net exports) will result in higher real output or increased prices.

Learning Objectives

- Describe exogenous events that can shift the AD curve.

Main Takeaways

Main Points

- There are four essential inputs to consider in calculating AD: consumption (C), investment (I), government spending (G), and net exports (NX, which is exports (X) – imports (I)).
- There are a variety of direct and indirect consequences in AD shifts. For this discussion, it is most important to keep in mind the changes in output and price.
- As the system moves closer to the highest potential output (optimal utilization of resources, or Y*), scarcity will naturally cause prices to increase more than the system's overall output.
- As the system moves closer to the highest potential output (or optimal utilization of resources, or Y*), scarcity will naturally see the prices increase more than the system's overall output.

Main Terms

- **Exogenous:** received from outside a group.

Recall that the AD curve reflects the total expenditures in an economy by consumers, businesses, governments, and foreigners. This section aims to discuss the factors that cause the AD curve to shift. Of course, a change in the price level is represented as a movement along the AD curve.

Graphically, an increase in AD is represented by a shift to the right, as shown in Figure 5.11. In the diagram, the new AD curves show that the quantity of goods and services demanded has increased for any given price level.

Recall that, from the expenditure point of view, GDP = C + I + G + (X – M). Many factors can affect the quantity of goods and services demanded at a given price. These factors can be categorized according

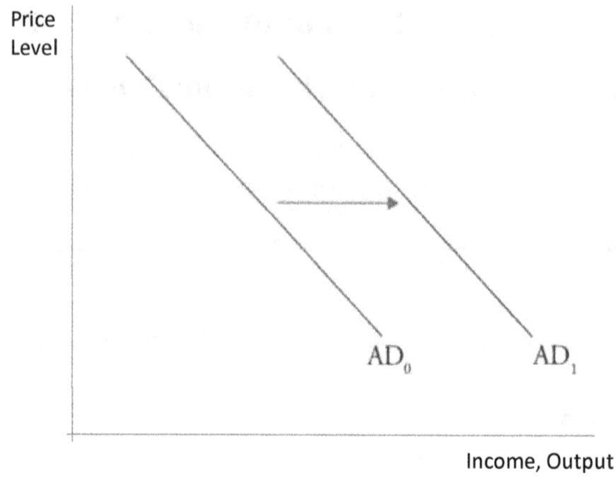

Figure 5.11: Increase in aggregate demand. The relationship between price and output within a given economic system. Changes in factors resulted in a shift in AD.

to the most directly affected expenditure factor. Below are some of the exogenous driving forces that will shift AD to the right:

Shift arising from:

(a) Changes in Consumption (C)

- **Increase in consumers' wealth:** Events like a stock market boom or continuous increase in house prices make people feel wealthier and less concerned about saving, which can result in increased spending, and rising AD.
- **Consumer expectations of future income:** When consumers expect higher future incomes due to a belief in greater job stability, expectations of rising wage income, or even a tax cut, they save less for the future and increase spending now, increasing AD.

(b) Changes in Investment (I)

- **Business expectations:** When businesses are more optimistic about future sales, they tend to increase their investment in plant, equipment, and inventory, which increases AD (I increases).
- **High-capacity utilization:** When companies produce at a high percentage of their capacity, they tend to invest in more plants and equipment, increasing AD (I increases).
- **Business tax credits:** Investment tax credit (tax rebate tied to investment spending by businesses) increases the demand for business goods.

(c) Changes in Both Consumption and Investment

- **Expansionary monetary policy:** When the rate of growth of the money supply is increased, banks have more funds to lend, which puts downward pressure on interest rates. Lower interest rates increase investment in plants and equipment because the cost of financing these investments declines. Lower interest rates and greater credit availability will also increase consumers' spending on consumer durables (e.g., automobiles, large appliances) that are typically purchased on credit. Thus, expansionary monetary policy's effect increases AD (C and I increase).

(d) Changes in Both Consumption and Government Purchases

- **Expansionary fiscal policy:** Expansionary fiscal policy (a decreasing government budget surplus or an increasing budget deficit) from decreasing taxes, increasing government expenditures, or both. A decrease in taxes increases disposable income and consumption, while an increase in government spending increases AD directly (C increases for a tax cut, G increases for spending increase).

(e) Changes in Net Exports

- **Exchange rates:** A decrease in the relative value of a country's currency will increase exports and decrease imports. These effects tend to increase domestic AD (net X increases). Also, speculators cause movement in the exchange rate, for example, during the Asian Financial Crisis.
- **Global economic growth:** GDP growth in foreign economies tends to increase the quantity of imports (domestic exports) foreigners demand. Domestic export demand will increase AD (net X increases). For example, continued US recovery since 2008 lifted the net exports of many exporting countries.

5.5.2 *Reasons for Shifts in the Long-Run Aggregate Supply Curve*

The LRAS curve is vertical (perfectly inelastic) at the potential (full-employment) level of real GDP. Changes in factors that affect the real output that an economy can produce at full employment will shift the LRAS curve. The potential (full-employment) level of output is called the natural output level.

Learning Objectives

- Identify common reasons for shifts in the LRAS curve.

Main Takeaways

Main Points

- In the long run, the aggregate supply is affected only by capital, labor, and technology.

Main Terms

- **Long-run:** Fixed at the full-employment level of GDP.

Any change to the economy that alters the potential output shifts the LRAS curve. Since output depends on labor, capital, natural resources, and technological knowledge, we can categorize shifts in the LRAS as arising from these four sources:

(a) Changes in Labour (L)

- **Increase in labor supply:** Suppose the economy experiences an increase in immigration and an increase in the number of workers. Because LRAS reflects output at full employment, an increase in the labor force will increase the full-employment output and the LRAS.
- **Increase in human capital (or skill of the workforce):** Suppose that through training and education, skills and hence productivity increases. The output is the productivity of the economy multiplied by the workforce. An increase in productivity results in increasing potential real output and increasing LRAS.

(b) Changes in Capital (K)

- **Increase in the stock of physical capital:** An increase in the economy's capital stock increases productivity. For a given size labor force, an increase in an economy's productivity will increase potential output and LRAS.

(c) Changes in Natural Resources (N)

- **Increase in the supply of natural resources:** An economy's production depends on the availability of natural resources like its land;

minerals, and weather. The Discovery of a mineral deposit will shift LRAS to the right, while weather change damaging its arable land will move LRAS to the left.

(d) Changes in Technological Knowledge (A)

- **Technology:** Improvements in technology, such as technology upgrades and digital transformations, increase labor productivity (output per unit of labor), and thereby increase the real output that can be produced from a given amount of productive inputs, increasing LRAS. While not technology, many developments deliver a similar impact on productivity, including countries specializing in their comparative advantage. On the other hand, restrictive government regulation (sometimes for the overall good, like those due to safety and environmental concerns) can reduce LRAS.

Examples: Various shifts in aggregate supply

John Donovan is a portfolio manager for a global mutual fund. Currently, his fund has 10% of its assets invested in Chinese equities. He is considering increasing the fund's allocation to the Chinese equity market. His decision will be based on an analysis of the following economic developments and their impact on the Chinese economy and equity market. What is the effect on SRAS and LRAS from the following factors?

1. Global oil prices, currently near their longer-run trend at $75 a barrel, have increased from $35 a barrel over the last three years because of strong demand from emerging markets.
2. The number of students studying engineering has dramatically increased at Chinese universities over the last decade.
3. Wages for China's workers are rising, leading some multinational companies to consider shifting their investments to Vietnam or Cambodia.
4. Recent data show that business investment as a share of GDP is over 40% in China.
5. The People's Bank of China is likely to permit the yuan to appreciate by 10% over the next year.

Solutions:

Solution to 1: Higher energy prices cause a decrease in short-run AS and shifts the SRAS curve to the left. Because oil prices are back to their longer-run trend, the leftward shift in SRAS essentially reverses a previous change that occurred when oil prices fell to $35, and there will likely be no impact on the LRAS curve. Lower output and profit are likely to hurt Chinese equity prices.

Solution to 2: More students studying engineering indicate improved labor force quality (an increase in human capital). As a result, AS increases, and the AS curve shifts to the right. Both short-run and long-run curves are affected. Higher output and profits may be expected to affect Chinese equity prices positively.

Solution to 3: The increase in wages increases labor costs for businesses, causes SRAS to decline, and shifts the SRAS curve to the left. Lower output and profit should harm Chinese equity prices.

Solution to 4: The high level of business investment indicates that China's capital stock is growing rapidly. This fast-growing capital stock means that workers have more capital to use, which increases their productivity. Thus, AS increases, and the AS curve shifts to the right. Both short-run AS and long-run AS are affected. The higher output should have a positive effect on Chinese equity prices.

5.5.3 *Reasons for Shifts in the Short-Run Aggregate Supply Curve*

The SRAS tells us the quantity of goods and services supplied in the short run for any given price level. This curve is similar to the LRAS curve, but it is upward sloping rather than vertical. Shifts are related to changes in price level and production.

Learning Objectives

- Identify common reasons for shifts in the SRAS curve.
- Explain the consequences of shifts in the SRAS curve.

Main Takeaways

Main Points

- The short-run supply curve is similar to the LRAS curve. Still, it is upward sloping rather than vertical because of sticky prices, sticky wages like contractual wage rates, and misperceptions that may not fully adjust to the economy's state, as discussed previously.

- Factors that shift LRAS and SRAS to the right include decreased wages, an increase in physical stock, or technology advancement.
- An increase in the expected price level results in a reduction in the output of goods and services. This change also shifts the SRAS to the left.

Main Terms

- **Short-run:** When one or more factors are fixed.

The short-run supply curve is similar to the LRAS curve. Still, it is upward sloping rather than vertical because of sticky prices, sticky wages like contractual wage rates, and misperceptions that may not fully adjust to the economy's state, as discussed previously. While considering what shifts the SRAS curve, we should consider those same factors that move the LRAS plus other factors. Figure 5.12 shows an increase in aggregate supply by shifting to the right as the quantity supplied at each price level increases.

Factors that shift LRAS and SRAS to the right include decreased wages, an increase in physical stock, or technology advancement. When SRAS moves right, output increases, and price level declines. On the

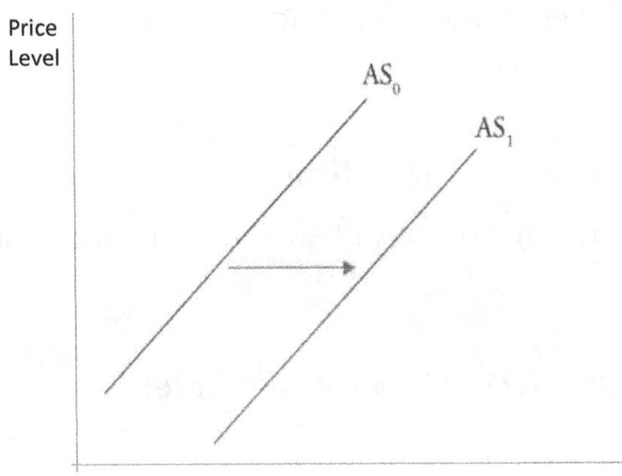

Figure 5.12: Shift in SRAS. The relationship between price and output within a given economic system where factors resulted in a shift in SRAS.

other hand, an increase in minimum wages will result in a shift left with the opposite impact on output and price levels.

In addition to changes in potential GDP (shifts in LRAS), several factors can cause the SRAS curve to shift to the right.

In the short-run, examples of events that shift the aggregate supply curve to the right include a decrease in wages (increase in wages bring in more workers), increased physical capital stock, or technology advancement. The short-run curve shifts to the right, the price level decreases, and the GDP increases. When the curve shifts to the left, the price level increases, and the GDP decreases.

Factors that affect the production cost of an economy can shift the SRAS. These factors include taxes and subsidies, the price of raw materials, and even changes in the mix of capital and labor. Appreciation of a country's currency will decrease the cost of imports. If the input to production is imported, the resulting decrease in production costs will increase output, shifting the SRAS curve. Of course, a change in natural resource availability, like extreme weather conditions, will also move the SRAS curve.

Lastly, a variable that affects the SRAS curve's position is the price level that economic agents expect to prevail. We note that wages, price, and perceptions are based on the expected price level. As an example, consider sticky wages. When the price level is expected to be high, workers are likely to bargain for higher nominal wages resulting in higher firm costs, reducing the output of goods and services. As a result, the SRAS curve shifts, and in this case, to the left. Conversely, an expected decrease in the price level will result in a shift in the SRAS to the right.

References/Further Readings

Mankiw, N. G. (2020). *Principles of Economics*, 9th edn., Cengage Learning, pp. 695–717.

5.6 Using the AD–AS Supply Model

5.6.1 *Macroeconomic Equilibrium*

In economics, the macroeconomic equilibrium is when aggregate supply equals AD.

Learning Objectives

- Understand the implications of AD and aggregate supply equilibrium.
- Describe how fluctuations in AD and supply cause short-run changes in the economy and the business cycle.

Main Takeaways

Main Points

- Equilibrium is the price-quantity pair where the quantity demanded is equal to the quantity supplied.
- Phases of the business cycle are shown as deviations of short-run equilibrium real GDP below full-employment GDP (recession) and above full-employment GDP (expansion leading to inflationary pressure).
- The AD and aggregate supply model explains the Phillips curve's outcomes.

Main Terms

- **Disequilibrium** is when internal and external forces prevent market equilibrium from being reached or cause the market to fall out of balance.
- **Adjustment:** The process by which prices and quantity supplied and demanded are reduced or increased.

In economics, equilibrium is when the market price has reached the level in which quantity supplied equals quantity demanded. Without external influences, price and quantity will remain at the equilibrium value. Figure 5.13 demonstrates that macroeconomic equilibrium is when aggregate supply equals AD.

(a) Equilibrium in Aggregate Supply–Aggregate Demand Model

Let us examine macroeconomic equilibrium in the short run and the long run.

In Figure 5.14, the long-run equilibrium is at the intersection of the LRAS curve and the AD curve. Changes in the price level of final goods and services can move the economy to a long-run macroeconomic equilibrium.

To see this, if we are at a short-run disequilibrium with the price level, say P_H, there is excess supply, sometimes termed a "recessionary gap",

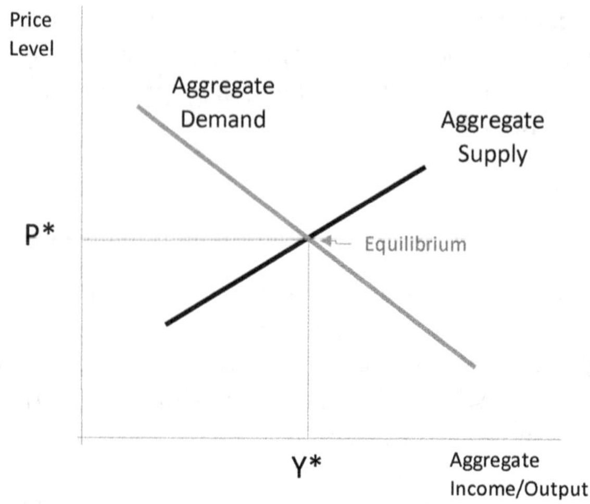

Figure 5.13: Equilibrium. The macroeconomic equilibrium is similar to microeconomic equilibrium when the aggregate supply intersects the AD.

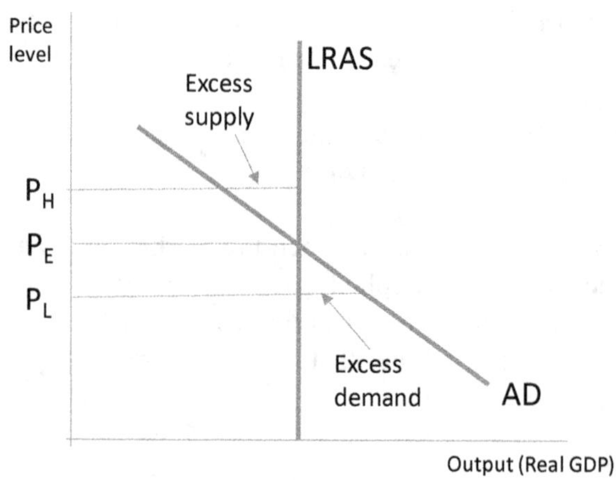

Figure 5.14: Long-run equilibrium real output. The relationship between price and output within a given economic system in the context of LRAS.

and there will be downward pressure on prices. This excess supply decrease the price level toward the long-run equilibrium price level, P_E. If the price level were P_L, there would be excess demand for goods and services, sometimes referred to as an "inflationary gap". Businesses experiencing decreases in inventories respond by increasing output and prices.

As the price level increases, the economy moves along the AD curve toward long-run equilibrium.

We next examine the situation when the economy is in short-run equilibrium. Still, at a level of output above or below the long-run equilibrium output, i.e., the economy is in long-run disequilibrium. These two situations are illustrated in Figure 5.15.

In Figure 5.15(a) the short-run equilibrium GDP_R is less than the full employment GDP_E on the LRAS. Figure 5.15 illustrates two situations where the economy is in short-run equilibrium but not in long-run equilibrium. In Figure 5.15(a), short-run equilibrium real GDP, GDP_R, is less than full-employment GDP_E (along the LRAS curve). The economy is said to be in recession or below full-employment equilibrium. (GDP_E – GDP_R) is called a recessionary gap or output gap. Being below full employment puts downward pressure on money wages and resource prices, decreasing the equilibrium price level from P_R to P_E.

Figure 5.15(b) shows a situation where short-run equilibrium GDP_B is greater than full employment GDP_E. This situation shows the case of an expansion that overshot the LRAS. This situation puts upward pressure on prices resulting in inflation increases the price level from P_B to P_E.

The adjustments are shown in Figure 5.15 describe short-term economic fluctuations, sometimes called the business cycle. The recessionary phase of the business cycle is shown as a deviation of short-run real GDP below the full employment level. The business cycle's late expansionary

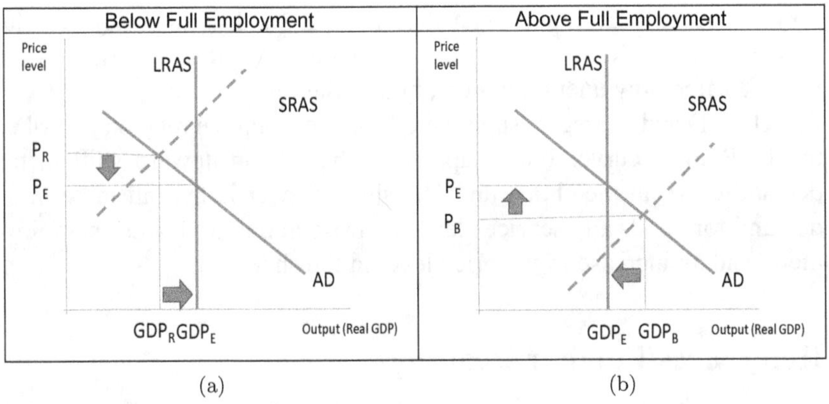

Figure 5.15: Long-run disequilibrium. The relationship between price and output within a given economic system in the context of SRAS.

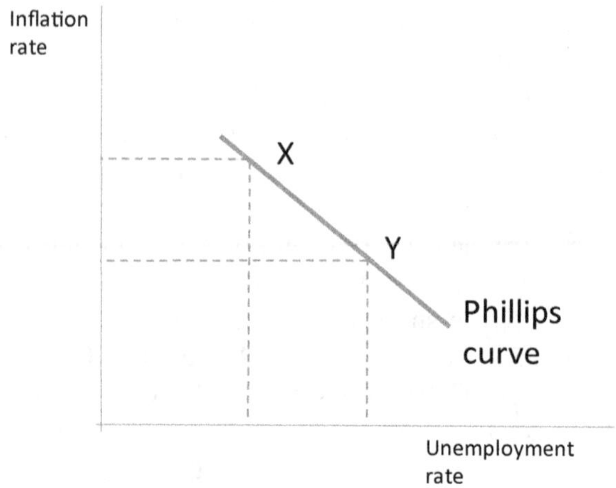

Figure 5.16: The Phillips curve. The Phillips curve shows a negative relation between the inflation rate and the unemployment rate.

phase is shown as a deviation of short-run real GDP above the full employment level. The departure above full employment led to inflationary pressure.

Example:
Let us examine the Phillips curve that shows the short-run relation between inflation and unemployment. Figure 5.16 shows an example of a Phillips curve. Policymakers can alter monetary and fiscal policy to influence AD. Point X offers high unemployment and low inflation, while Point Y offers low unemployment, high inflation.

The AD and aggregate supply model can explain the relation described by the Phillips curve. What happens if there is an upward shift in the demand curve in the short run? The short answer is that an increase in demand for goods and services leads to a rise in output, lower unemployment, and an increase in the price level in the short run.

References/Further Readings

Mankiw, N. G. (2020). *Principles of Economics*, 9th edn., Cengage Learning, pp. 745–758.

5.7 Economic Growth

Economic growth is an increase in the production of economic goods and services. Three main factors that affect economic growth are increases in labor inputs, capital stock accumulation, and technology advancement.

Learning Objectives

- Understand the drivers of economic growth.

Main Takeaways

Main Point

- Aggregate supply will change because of changes in labor supply, human capital, physical capital stock, technology, and natural resources; these factors are also important sources of economic growth.

Main Terms

- **Production function:** Relates production output to inputs (or factors of production) to a production process.

This section examines the discussion on LRAS in more detail. In an earlier section, we mentioned that the LRAS curve is vertical and does not change with the price level. Aggregate supply will change because of changes in the following factors that are also important sources of economic growth:

1. **Labour supply:** The labor force is the number of people over the age of 16 who are either working or available for work but currently unemployed. The labor force's growth (via population growth, net immigration, and increase in participation rate) is a crucial economic growth source.
2. **Human capital:** Workers who are skilled and well educated (possess more human capital) are more productive and better able to adapt to technological advances. Investment in human capital leads to more significant economic growth.
3. **Physical capital stock:** A high investment rate increases a country's supply of physical capital, allowing for increased labor productivity and higher potential GDP. An increased rate of investment in physical capital can boost economic growth.

4. **Technology:** Improvements in technology increase productivity and potential GDP. More rapid progress in technology leads to greater rates of economic growth.
5. **Natural resources:** Raw material inputs, such as energy and land, are necessary to produce economic output. Countries with large amounts of productive natural resources can achieve greater economic growth rates.

5.7.1 *Economic Growth around the World*

The living standard measured by real GDP per capita varies widely from country to country. In some cases, the disparity is extreme where Pakistan has the same GDP per capita in 2017 as the UK in 1870.[2] Further, we also note that while developing countries do rise over time, the rich countries do decline and are not guaranteed to remain prosperous in the long run.

The critical reason living standards vary across the world is "productivity". The GDP of an economy measures the total income earned and the total expenditure on the economy's output of goods and services. Since an economy's income is its output, a nation can only enjoy a high living standard if it produces many goods and services.

5.7.2 *Sustainability of Economic Growth*

We first define the term potential GDP as the highest output an economy can sustain over some time. Technically, the OECD defines it as the output level an economy can produce at a constant inflation rate. In contrast, other economists have described it as what an economy can make if operating at its natural unemployment rate. For ease of discussion, we will state potential GDP as:

$$\text{Potential GDP} = \text{Aggregate hours worked} \times \text{Labor productivity}$$

and in terms of growth:

$$\begin{aligned}\text{Growth in potential GDP} = {} & \text{Growth in labor force} \\ & + \text{growth in labor productivity}\end{aligned}$$

[2] *Source*: Barro and Sala-I-Martin (1995). *Economic Growth*. McGraw-Hill; World Bank Online Data and Mankiw (2021). *Principles of Economics*, 9th edn. Cengage Learning.

Example:
Japan has been experiencing low actual growth over the last several decades. Most attribute this to an aging population. Its potential economic growth rate is obtained by estimating labor productivity and labor force growth separately. These separate studies project Japan's labor force to shrink by 1% and its labor productivity to grow by 2%.

Hence, the estimated growth in potential GDP is $-1\% + 2\% = 1\%$.

From the study, Japan's slow potential GDP growth is due to negative labor force change, which is likely attributed to numbers leaving the labor force exceeding new entrants.

5.7.3 *Production Function and Economic Growth*

We can use a production function to describe the relationship between the quantity of inputs used in production and the output quantity.

The quantity of output can be thought of as a function of labor, physical capital, human capital, and available natural resources and their productivity, which depends on the available technology. That is

$$Y = A \times F(L, K, H, N)$$

where F is the function that shows how factors are combined to produce output, Y is the quantity of output, L is the labour, K is the physical capital, H is the human capital, N is the natural resources, and A is the available production technology.

As technology improves, A rises, and the economy's output improves from a given combination of inputs, L, K, H, and N.

The production function can be stated on a per-worker basis by dividing by L:

$$Y/L = A \times F(1, K/L, H/L, N/L)$$

where Y/L is the output per worker (labor productivity), K/L is the physical capital per worker, H/L is the human capital per worker, and N/L is the natural resources per worker.

The relation demonstrates that whether we have an individual, a simple or complex economy, labor productivity, or only "productivity", is increased by four key factors: improving technology, increasing physical capital per worker, increasing human capital per worker, and increasing natural resources per worker.

With physical capital, we mean that workers can be more productive if they have tools to work with. Equipment and structures to produce goods and services are called physical capital. Human capital is the knowledge and skill that workers acquire through training and experience. Lastly, natural resources are provided by nature, namely land, water, minerals, renewable, and non-renewable.

Technological knowledge is an essential determinant of productivity as well. It is an important determinant and takes on many forms: shared experience, proprietary knowledge, open-source, patented, etc.

The production function is assumed to exhibit diminishing marginal productivity for each input. Holding other inputs constant, the amount of additional output produced by each additional unit of input declines. Based on this assumption, sustainable long-term growth may not be achieved simply by increasing physical capital per worker overtime.

References/Further Readings

Mankiw, N. G. (2020). *Principles of Economics*, 9th edn., Cengage Learning, pp. 504–512.

5.8 Sample Questions

Question 1

An investor expecting a decrease in AD that will result in a recessionary gap should:

(a) Increase investment in cyclical companies
(b) Increase investment in investment-grade fixed-income securities
(c) Both (a) and (b)

Question 2

Equality between aggregate expenditure and aggregate output implies that the government's fiscal deficit must equal:

(a) Private saving – Investment – Net exports.
(b) Private saving – Investment + Net exports.
(c) Investment – Private saving + Net exports.

Question 3
Which of the following is most likely to cause the LRAS curve to shift to the left?

(a) Higher nominal wages.
(b) A decline in productivity.
(c) An increase in corporate taxes.

Question 4
The component least likely to be included in the measurement of gross domestic product (GDP) is:

(a) the value of owner-occupied rent.
(b) The annual salary of a local police officer.
(c) environmental damage caused by the production.

The following information applies to Questions 5 and 6

An economic forecasting firm has estimated the following equation from historical data based on the neoclassical growth model:

Potential output growth = 1.5 + 0.72 × Growth of labor + 0.28 × Growth of capital

Question 5
The intercept (1.5) in this equation is best interpreted as:

(a) the long-run sustainable growth rate.
(b) the growth rate of total factor productivity.
(c) above-trend historical growth that is unlikely to be sustained.

Question 6
The coefficient on the growth rate of labor (0.72) in this equation is best interpreted as:

(a) the labor force participation rate.
(b) the marginal productivity of labor.
(c) the share of income earned by labor.

Question 7
An increase in the price level would shift the:

(a) IS curve.
(b) LM curve.
(c) aggregate demand curve.

Question 8
As the price level declines along the AD curve, the interest rate is most likely to:

(a) decline.
(b) increase.
(c) remain unchanged.

Question 9
Which of the following would be included in the Malaysian GDP for a given year? The market value of:

(a) durians grown in Malaysia by Singapore citizens.
(b) electronics made in Japan and sold in Malaysia.
(c) movies animation produced outside Malaysia by a Malaysian artist.

Question 10
Suppose a painting is produced and sold in 2018 for $5,000. The expenses involved in producing the painting amounted to $2,000. According to the sum-of-value- added method of calculating GDP, the value added by the final step of creating the painting was:

(a) $2,000.
(b) $3,000.
(c) $5,000.

Solutions

Question 1

Solution: Option **b** is correct.

From the choices given, investment-grade fixed-income securities are less likely to default. On the other hand, cyclical companies are likely to experience a greater decline in earnings and more affected than defensive and investment-grade bonds. Since b is a clear choice, we need not consider choice c.

Question 2

Solution: Option a correct.

The fundamental relationship between saving, investment, the fiscal balance, and the trade balance is S = I + (G – T) + (X – M). This relationship shows that private saving must fund investment expenditures, the government fiscal balance, and net exports (= net capital outflows).

Rearranging gives G – T = (S – I) – (X – M). The government's fiscal deficit (G – T) must be equal to the private sector's saving/investment balance (S – I) minus net exports.

Question 3

Solution: Option **b** is correct.

Productivity measures labor efficiency and is the amount of output produced by workers in a given period. A decline in productivity implies decreased efficiency, increased labor costs, reduced profitability, and lower output at each output price level, causing a leftward shift in both the SRAS and LRAS curves.

Question 4

Solution: Option **c** is correct.

By-products of production processes with no explicit market value are not included in GDP.

Question 5

Solution: Option **b** is correct.

The estimated equation is the standard growth accounting equation developed by Solow. The intercept is the growth rate of total factor productivity.

Question 6

Solution: Option **c** is correct.

In the standard Solow growth accounting equation, each factor's growth rate's coefficient is its share of income.

Question 7

Solution: Option **b** is correct.

The LM curve represents combinations of income and the interest rate at which the demand for real money balances equals the supply. For a given nominal money supply, an increase in the price level implies a decrease in the real money supply.

To decrease the demand for real money balances, either the interest must increase or fall. Therefore, at each level of the interest rate, income

(= expenditure) must decrease—a leftward shift of the LM curve.

Question 8

Solution: Option **a** is correct.

A decrease in the price level increases the real money supply and shifts the LM curve to the right. Since the IS curve is downward sloping, the IS and LM curves will intersect at a higher income level and a lower interest rate.

Question 9

Solution: Option **a** is correct.

Malaysia's GDP is the total market value of all final goods and services produced in a given period within Malaysia. The durians were grown in Malaysia and counts towards the Malaysian GDP.

Question 10

Solution: Option **b** is correct.

This is the value added by the artist: $5,000 – $2,000 = $3,000.

Part C: Macro-Finance

Chapter 6

Financial Development and Financial Markets

6.1 Financial Development

6.1.1 *Banks and Financial Institutions*

Banks, insurance companies, fund management companies, stockbrokers, and many other financial institutions (FIs) are operating in the financial sector.

Learning Objectives

- Understand the need for financial markets (FMs) and FIs (or intermediaries) and their services.

Main Takeaways

Main Points

- FMs and intermediaries exist because they help us to address market imperfections, namely imperfect information, limited enforcement, and transaction costs when we conduct financial transactions. They help to reduce friction and provide convenience in our financial lives.
- These market imperfections inhibit the flow of society's savings to those with the best ideas and projects, thus curtailing economic development.
- The existence of these market imperfections and costs creates incentives for the emergence of financial contracts, markets, and intermediaries.

Main Terms

- **Imperfect information:** Acquiring and processing sufficient information about potential investments is difficult and costly.
- **Limited enforcement:** Costs and uncertainties associated with writing, interpreting, and enforcing contracts.
- **Transaction costs:** Costs associated with transacting goods, services, and financial instruments.

Banks and other financial intermediaries provide the following financial services (not exhaustive list):

(a) savings and investment schemes;
(b) payment and remittance services;
(c) loans and advances (maturity transformation and volume transformation);
(d) documentary credit and trade finance services;
(e) risk management services (risk transformation);
(f) corporate finance and advisory services.

6.1.2 *Financial Development*

Financial development occurs when financial instruments, markets, institutions, and intermediaries mitigate the effects of imperfect information, limited enforcement, and transaction costs.

Learning Objectives

- Understand what financial development means.
- Provide examples of financial development.
- Understand the traditional and growing alternative view of the relationship between the financial sector and economic growth.
- Learn what does financial development involves and how to measure it.

Main Takeaways

Main Points

- Financial development can be defined as an improvement in specific FMs' functions.
- There are a traditional view and a growing alternative view of the relationship between financial and economic growth.

- Financial development is challenging to measure as it is a vast concept, but proxy variables measure four financial system characteristics: depth, access, efficiency, and stability.

Main Terms

- **Financial intermediation:** The process performed by banks or other financial intermediaries of taking in funds from a saver and then lending them out to a borrower.
- **Financial markets:** Encompass foreign exchange, financial derivatives, equity and bond markets
- **Financial access:** The ability of individuals or enterprises to obtain financial services, including credit, deposit, payment, insurance, risk management, and others.

At the economic level, financial development can be defined as improvements in the quality of five key functions of the financial system:

(a) mobilizing and pooling savings;
(b) producing and processing information about possible investments and allocating capital based on these assessments;
(c) monitoring performance of firms and exerting corporate governance after allocating capital;
(d) facilitating the trading, diversification, and management of risks;
(e) easing the exchange of goods and services.

Financial development involves developing infrastructure, policies, and institutions that lead to effective financial intermediation, with FMs providing broad access to capital and financial services.

For example, credit bureaus or registries tend to improve the acquisition and dissemination of information about potential borrowers and improve financial resource allocation with positive economic development effects.

Countries like the US and UK with effective institutions such as legal and regulatory systems and enforcement machinery have instilled investors' confidence and facilitated the development of equity and bond markets that help the economy grow and investors to hold more diversified portfolios.

The traditional view is that the financial sector is a by-product of broader economic development, leading to a reactive financial sector policymaking approach.

However, there is a growing alternative view that a robust financial sector can stimulate broader economic growth or that a well-functioning financial system plays an independent role in promoting long-run economic growth. Countries with better-developed financial systems tend to grow the economy faster over a long period. A well-functioning financial system eases the external financing constraints that impede firm and industrial expansion.

The IMF commented in a publication entitled "Finance & Development" in September 2011 that "more varied and more accessible financial services permit larger pools of savings to be channeled with increasing efficiency toward various productive investments that result in stronger economic growth."

For example, Grameen Bank (also known as "Bank for the Poor"), established in 1976 by Muhammad Yunus in Bangladesh, grants poor people small loans on easy terms known as microcredit. Such microcredit reduces the widespread rural poverty and creates economic and social development in Bangladesh. In 2006, Muhammad Yunus was awarded the Nobel Peace Prize.

Financial development is a vast concept and has several dimensions. Empirical work done so far is usually based on standard quantitative indicators available for a long-time series in most countries, e.g., the ratio of private sector credit granted by FIs to GDP, ratio of FIs' assets to GDP, or ratio of total financial assets (stocks, bonds, and loans) to GDP, etc.

An example of studies with such standard quantitative indicators is provided here. Countries with higher private credit levels (the value of credits by financial intermediaries to the private sector divided by GDP) tend to enjoy faster growth rates over the 1960–1995 period than countries with lower financial intermediary development levels. Regression results also indicate an economically large impact of financial development on growth (see Figures 6.1 and 6.2).

The World Bank launched a more comprehensive online database on financial systems — the Global Financial Development Database focusing on proxy variables that measure the four financial system characteristics: Depth, Access, Efficiency, and Stability for FIs and FMs. See Table 6.1.

To overcome the shortcomings of proxy variables as single indicators, the IMF developed a new comprehensive Financial Development Index, capturing all four proxy variables for FIs and FMs (see Figure 6.3).

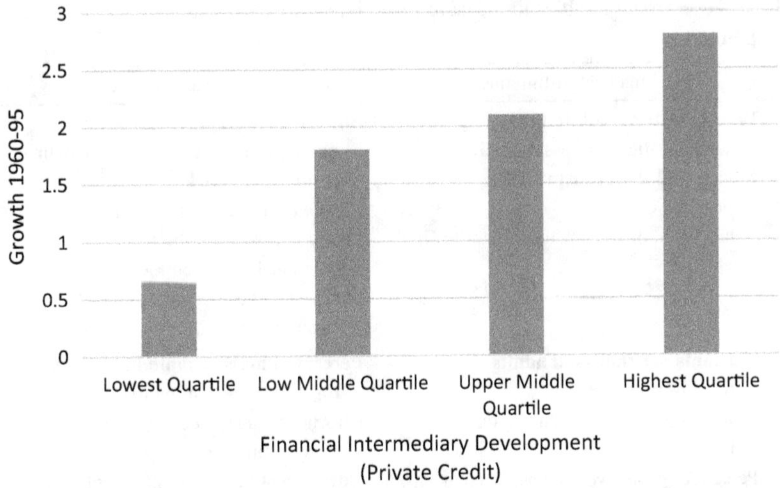

Figure 6.1: Relationship between financial intermediary development (proxied by the level of private credit) and growth.

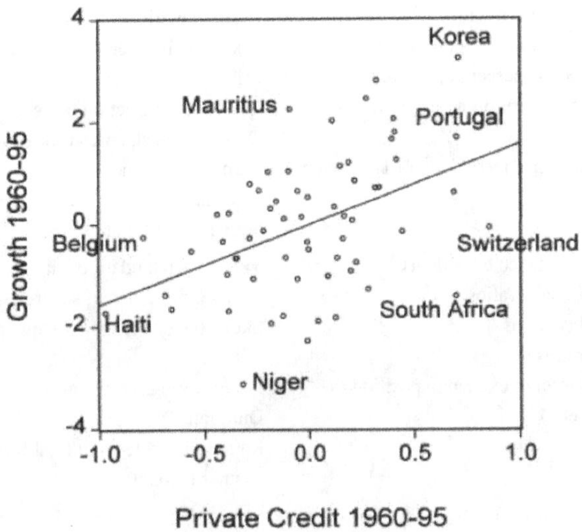

Figure 6.2: Regression results of the impact of financial development on growth.

Source: Beck, T., Loayza, N. V., & Ross, E. L. (2000). Financial Intermediation and Growth: Causality and Causes. *Journal of Monetary Economics*, 46(1), 31–77.

Table 6.1: Proxy variables to measure financial development (depth, access, efficiency, and stability).

	Financial institutions	Financial markets
DEPTH	**Private sector credit to GDP** Financial institutions' assets to GDP Money IM2 aggregate to GDP Deposits to GDP Value-added of the financial sector to GDP	**Stock market capitalization plus outstanding domestic private debt securities to GDP** Private debt securities to GDP Public debt securities to GDP International debt securities to GDP Stock market capitalization to GDP Stocks traded to GDP
ACCESS	**Accounts per thousand adults** (commercial banks) Branches per 100,000 adults (commercial banks) Percent of people with a bank account (from user survey) Percent of firms with line of credits (all firms) Percent of firms with line of credits (small firms)	**Percent of market capitalization outside of top 10 largest companies** Percent of value traded outside of top 10 trade companies Government bond yields (3 month and 10 year) Ratio of domestic to total debit securities Ratio of private to total debit securities (domestic) Ratio of new corporate bond issues to GDP
EFFICIENCY	**Net interest margin** Lending deposits spread Noninterest income to total income Overhead costs (percent of total assets) Profitability (return on assets, return on equity) Boone indicator (Herfindahl, or H-statistics)	**Turnover ratio** (turnover/capitalization) for stock market Price synchronicity (co-movement) Price impact Liquidity/transaction costs Quoted bid-ask spread for government bonds Turnover or bonds (private, public) on securities exchange Settlement efficiency
STABILITY	**z-score** (or distance to default) Capital adequacy ratios Asset quality ratios Liquidity ratios Other (net foreign exchange position to capital, etc.)	**Volatility** (standard deviation/average) of stock price index, sovereign bond index Skewness of the index (stock price sovereign bond) Price/earnings (P/E) ratio Duration Ratio of short term to total bonds (domestic, international) Correlation with major bond returns (German, United States)

Source: Global Financial Development Report 2013 (5 September 2012), Rethinking the Role of the State in Finance, World Bank.

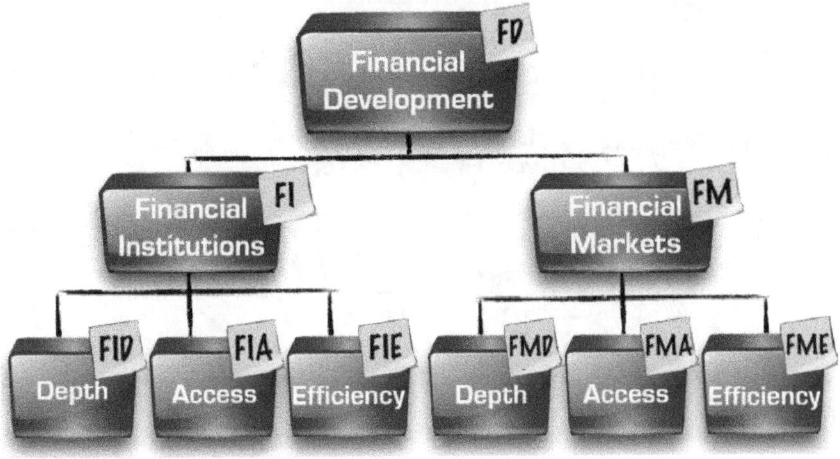

Figure 6.3: Financial Development Index capturing all four proxy variables (depth, access, efficiency, and stability) for both the FIs and FMs.

6.2 Functions of Financial System

6.2.1 *Financial System*

The financial system is a system that enables the gathering, distribution, and trading of funds, financial assets, and other financial instruments.

Learning Objectives

- Understand the financial system and its essential functions.

Main Takeaways

Main Points

- A financial system enables the gathering, distributing, and trading of financial instruments in both direct and indirect FMs.
- In Asia, banks generally dominate the financial sector as they develop first.

A financial system is where the FIs, as agents or intermediaries, operating in the FMs, using various delivery channels, delivering multiple financial products and services. Recipients of products and services are the market participants such as individuals, households, business enterprises, governments, and other organizations who need to conduct

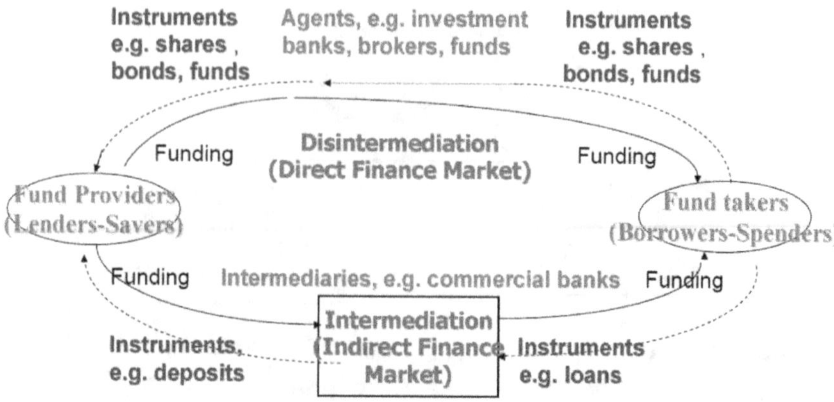

Figure 6.4: Intermediation and disintermediation of FMs.

financial transactions. More established financial systems have ultimately achieved efficient gathering, distribution, and trading of funds, financial assets, and instruments to better the economy.

The FMs can broadly be divided into direct and indirect finance markets. The indirect finance market is where the borrowers borrow funds from savers through a financial intermediary such as banks (this process is also known as financial intermediation). The direct finance market is where the borrowers issue securities such as bonds or shares directly to the savers acting as investors. For example, in an initial public offering (IPO) where the security is sold to the public for a set initial price (this process is also known as financial disintermediation). See Figure 6.4.

Key functions of the financial system are:

(a) mobilizing and pooling savings;
(b) producing and processing information about possible investments and allocating capital based on these assessments;
(c) monitoring investments and exerting corporate governance after providing finance;
(d) facilitating the trading, diversification, and management of risks;
(e) easing the exchange of goods and services.

In general, banks dominate the financial sector in the most developed and emerging Asian markets, as they do in Europe. Unlike in the United States, equity and bond markets have a larger role.

Using total financial assets (including the amount of bank credit, bonds, and stocks) as a percentage of GDP as a yardstick, in Asia, the highly financially developed (over 300%) countries include Hong Kong, Korea, Japan, Singapore. Countries with an intermediate level of financial development (100%–300%) include China, India, Indonesia, Malaysia, Philippines, Thailand, Viet Nam, and the rest are countries with low financial development (>100%). See Table 6.2.

The bank dominance in Asian FMs comes at the cost of under-developed equity and bond markets in many countries. Short-term

Table 6.2: Total financial assets as a percentage of GDP in Asia, 2015.

Economy	Bank credit	Bonds	Stocks	Total
Bangladesh	41.0	N/A	24.9	65.9
Brunei Darussalam	40.1	N/A	0.0	40.1
Cambodia	56.5	N/A	N/A	56.5
People's Republic of China	140.4	62.6	64.1	267.2
Hong Kong, China	212.2	N/A	1029.1	1241.3
India	50.2	32.4	71.5	124.7
Indonesia	31.5	24.6	71.5	127.6
Japan	102.5	208.1	85.9	396.6
Republic of Korea	136.6	146.3	99.8	376.7
Lao PDR	18.9	N/A	N/A	18.9
Malaysia	119.6	108.7	26.3	254.6
Mongolia	55.2	N/A	24.9	80.0
Myanmar	16.0	N/A	4.0	20.0
Nepal	56.7	N/A	26.5	83.1
Pakistan	14.9	35.8	27.1	77.8
Philippines	39.5	50.5	25.2	115.2
Singapore	127.9	97.5	88.4	313.9
Sri Lanka	27.5	11.5	29.3	68.3
Thailand	114.6	77.7	97.7	290.1
Vietnam	102.8	24.2	53.6	180.5

Notes: Bank credit calculated from bank deposit to GDP and bank credit to bank deposit ratio. Lao PDR data for 2010, GDP = Gross domestic product, Lao PDR = Lao People's Democratic Republic, N/A = Not available.

Source: World Bank Financial Development Index Database.

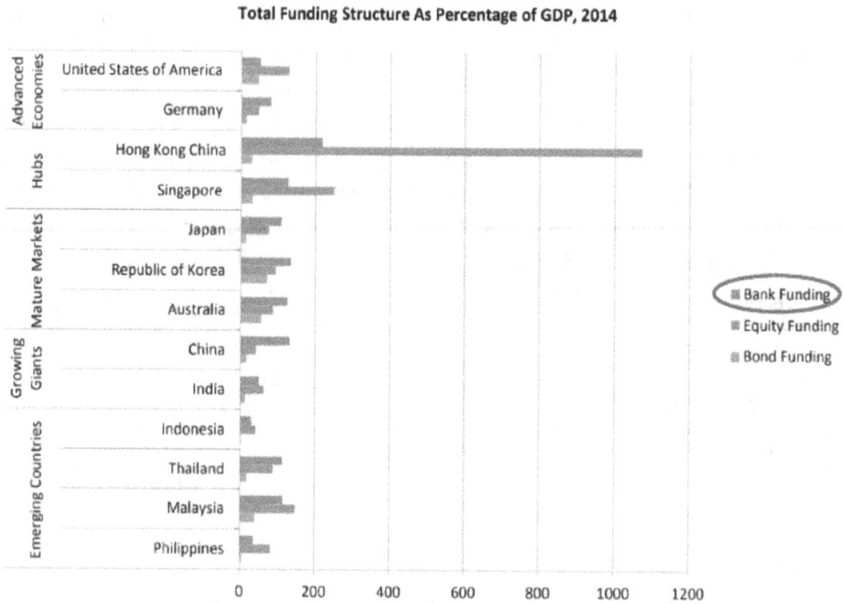

Figure 6.5: Total funding structure as a percentage of GDP in Asia, 2014.

Source: UN Economic and Social Commission for Asia and the Pacific (April 2017), The State of Finance in Asia and the Pacific, background document for the fourth High-Level Dialogue on Financing for Development in Asia and the Pacific.

liabilities limit the banks' capacity to finance long-term investments. As one of the fast-growing regions, Asian FMs should be developed further to provide adequate, stable funding for long-term investment and risk capital for innovation and entrepreneurship. See Figure 6.5.

6.3 Financial Liberalization and Deepening

6.3.1 *Financial Repression*

Financial repression retarded many less developed countries during the 1960–1970s.

Learning Objectives

- Learn about financial repression, how it is manifested, and its symptoms.

Main Takeaways

Main Points

- Financial repression includes directed lending to the government, interest rate caps, regulation of capital movement between countries, and a tighter association between government and banks.
- Today, the government's actions to intervene in monetary and interest rate policies or restrict financial services are considered financial repression acts.

Ronald McKinnon and Edward Shaw were the first to explain the notion of financial repression in a seminal study entitled "Money and Capital in Economic Development", published in 1973. McKinnon and Shaw argue that historically, many countries, including developed ones but especially developing ones, have restricted competition in the financial sector with government interventions and regulations. According to their argument, a repressed financial sector discourages saving and investment because the return rates are lower than what could be obtained in a competitive market. In such a system, financial intermediaries do not function at their full capacity and fail to channel savings into investments efficiently, thereby impeding the overall economic system's development.

Financial repression refers to the notion that a set of government regulations, laws, and other non-market restrictions prevent an economy's financial intermediaries from functioning at their full capacity. Financial repression acts include interest rate ceilings, liquidity ratio requirements, high bank reserve requirements, capital controls, restrictions on market entry into the financial sector, credit ceilings or restrictions on credit allocation directions, and government ownership domination of banks.

Some of the symptoms manifested in the FM as a result of financial repression include:

(a) the over-sized and dominating state-owned banking sector;
(b) non-bank sector, i.e., undeveloped or underdeveloped direct finance market;
(c) businesses rely mainly on self-funding or loans from state-owned banks (if they can get loans at all);
(d) besides bank deposits, generally, there is a lack of public investment products;

(e) inefficient and poor service standard of banks due to lack of competition;
(f) the emergence of a vibrant shadow banking which is unregulated or even illegal fund gathering and financing activities;
(g) market forces do not determine prices of financial variables such as the interest rate and exchange rate. As a result, dual pricing is not uncommon, i.e., official rate and unofficial or black-market rate.

6.3.2 *Financial Liberalization and Deepening*

Financial liberalization leads to financial deepening and financial innovation, two essential financial development elements.

Learning Objectives

- State some standard measures for financial deepening.
- Understand that financial deepening may not always be good for the economy.

Main Takeaways

Main Points

- Financial depth in most emerging market economies remains low, though it has been growing.
- Key findings of an IMF study showed the "too much finance" effect where it showed a marginally decreasing relationship between financial development and growth. The study noted greater risk-taking could happen if financial development is too fast and a premium on developing useful institutional and regulatory frameworks.
- Another study by the Mckinsey Global Institute attributed the Global Financial Crisis in 2008 to the equity market bubbles and unsustainable increases in debt and leverage by FIs, which inflated financial depth with non-productive financial transactions.

Main Terms

- **Financial liberalization:** It is defined as removing government intervention and restrictions on FMs and institutions to permit financial deepening and innovation to promote economic growth.
- **Financial deepening:** It refers to the increased provision of financial services with a broader choice of services geared to all social levels.

The degree of financial deepening is known as "Financial Depth", which by some measures captures the financial sector's size relative to the economy.

Financial liberalization is defined as removing government intervention and restrictions from FMs and institutions, such as bank interest rate ceilings, compulsory and high reserve requirements, barriers to entry, particularly by foreign financial intermediaries, and credit allocation decisions, etc. Financial liberalization can lead to the privatizing of state-owned banks, introducing the convertibility of the currency on the capital account (i.e., capital account liberalization), improving prudential regulation, and promoting stock and bond markets.

Common measures of "Financial Depth" for FIs include:

(a) Private Sector Credit to GDP, which refers to domestic private credit to the real sector by banks as a percentage of local currency GDP. It excludes credit issued to governments, government agencies, and public enterprises and credit issued by central banks.
(b) Total Banking Assets to GDP, a more comprehensive measure of size, because itincludes credit to the private sector, credit to the government, and bank assetsother than credit.

Key findings of an IMF study revealed the "too much finance" effect.

(a) Financial development increases growth, but the effects weaken at higher levels of financial development and eventually become negative. This observation can be attributed to financial deepening, i.e., excessive finance, rather than to higher financial access or greater financial efficiency:
    i. too much finance increases the frequency of booms and busts and leaves countries ultimately worse off and with lower real GDP growth;
    ii. too much finance diverts talent and human capital away from productive sectors and toward the financial sector;
    iii. a substantial financial sector may be particularly susceptible to moral hazard or rent extraction, which lead to a misallocation of resources.
(b) If the pace of financial development is too fast, it may encourage greater risk-taking and higher leverage, which is poorly regulated and supervised, may lead to economic and financial instability.

(c) There is, therefore, a premium on developing good institutional and regulatory frameworks as financial development proceeds.

Key findings of a McKinsey Global Institute report showed that an increase in financial depth could also be due to bubbles in asset prices or unsustainable increases in debt and leverage. Using equity and debt as a percentage of GDP to measure financial depth, the increase in financial depth between 1995 and 2007, the period before the Global Financial Crisis in 2008, was mainly attributed to:

(a) Financial Sector accounted for 37%, mainly bonds and other debt securities issued by FIs to fund their lending and purchase of financial assets. Hence leverage of these institutions increased.
(b) Rising equity market valuations accounted for 25%, due mainly to inflated investors' expectations and low-interest rates.
(c) Financing for households and non-financial corporations accounted for 28%, mainly due to increases in mortgage lending during the housing bubble period in several large countries like the US, UK, Spain, etc.

The above shows that standard quantitative measures of financial depth may not be perfect as the quality of the financial depth, such as the ability of the financial system to allocate financial resources to the most productive uses in the economy, are not considered.

References/Further Readings

IMF Staff Discussion Note (May 2015). Rethinking Financial Deepening: Stability and Growth in Emerging Markets.

McKinsey Global Institute (March 2013). Financial Globalization: Retreat or Reset?

6.4 Financial Innovation

Financial Innovation involves creating and popularizing new financial instruments, technologies, institutions, markets, processes, and business models, thus promoting and benefiting financial development.

Learning Objectives

- Understand the motivations for financial innovation and what financial innovation includes.
- Appreciate that there are different perspectives on whether financial innovation is good.

Main Takeaways

Main Points

- The motivations for financial innovation are globalization and capital mobility, financial regulations and taxes, risk management, and technological advances.
- Financial innovation includes institutional innovation, product (or technique) innovation, and process innovation.
- Successful innovation in financial services can improve capital productivity with beneficial effects that permeate through the wider economy, while unsuccessful and excessive innovation may disrupt financial services and harm the economy.
- The self-governance mechanism of financial firms and the regulation and supervision by the financial regulator are important to ensure the positive result of financial innovation.

Main Terms

- **Financial Innovation:** The act of creating and then popularizing new financial instruments, technologies, institutions, markets, processes, and business models.

The motivations for financial innovation include:

(a) **Globalization and capital mobility:** This increases competition among financial firms to meet the higher expectation from customers who demand more efficient services, as they face new risks arising from globalization and capital, are more mobile looking for higher return globally.

(b) **Financial regulations and taxes:** This motivates financial firms to innovate to circumvent regulations to lower compliance costs or to avoid taxes for a higher return.

(c) **Risk management:** Volatility in FMs due to financial liberalization or changing economic conditions give impetus to the innovation of risk management products and the techniques that transfer or share risks.

(d) **Technology advances:** Advances in emerging technologies such as cloud computing, big data, distributed ledgers, and artificial intelligence, etc. change or revolutionize how financial firms conduct their business.

Financial Innovation includes:

(a) Institutional innovation relates to the creation of new types of financial firms or structures, e.g., internet banks, Alibaba's Ant Financial Services Group.
(b) Product (or technique) innovation relates to the creation of new products such as Yu'E Bao by Ant Financial, credit default swap, carbon trading, longevity swap, catastrophic and weather derivative, Islamic bonds (Sukuk), CDO, and various payment products like Google Wallet, Alipay, etc., or financing technique innovation like securitization.
(c) Process innovation relates to new ways of conducting financial business, including biometric facial or voice recognition, mobile banking applications, dark pools, high frequency, and algorithmic trading.

Successful innovation in financial services can improve capital productivity with beneficial effects permeating the broader economy.

Unsuccessful and excessive innovation can have the opposite effect. An example of excessive innovation was the complex synthetic securities known as CDO^2 and CDO^3 related to poorly underwritten mortgages which partly caused the 2008 Global Financial Crisis. The crisis was also aggravated by the high interconnectedness between financial services and firms and the rest of the economy.

Corporate governance mechanisms such as new product approval, the risk management process, and remuneration policy, etc., of financial firms, along with regulation and supervision by financial regulators, play essential roles in channeling innovation efforts properly so that the economy and society as a whole can enjoy the benefits of innovation. At the same time, exposure to the negative outcome is kept to the minimum.

6.5 Trends in Financial Markets

6.5.1 *Global Financial Markets*

The rise of financial technologies (Fintech) and greater awareness of sustainable development goals advocated by the Department of Economic and Social Affairs, United Nations (https://sdgs.un.org/#goal_section) are driving changes in FMs, boosting competition and innovation, especially after the Global Financial Crisis.

Learning Objectives

- Understand the transformation driven by Fintech and the emerging new forms of financing and investments such as "inclusive finance", "socially responsible investment", and "impact investing", etc. driven by greater awareness of sustainable development goals.

Main Takeaways

Main Points

- Technologies transform financial services, making them more efficient, low-cost, and convenient for consumers. Fintech has lowered the entry barrier into the financial sector for new entrants.
- Due to the lessons of senior executives' greed learned from the Global Financial Crisis, people are more aware of and demand more social responsibility by banks. The timely arrival of digital and mobile technologies and Fintech" have given the impetus to push for "inclusive finance" and a "shared economy", benefiting a wider group of population.
- Inclusive finance focuses on expanding services to the poor, the vulnerable, and the "underserved" populations.
- Due to greater awareness of sustainable development goals, there is an emerging movement to promote sustainable finance, which includes "socially responsible investment", "impact investing", and "green finance", etc. Such financial investments integrate environmental, social, and governance (ESG) criteria into financial services to bring about sustainable development outcomes, including mitigating and adapting to the adverse effects of climate change, for the lasting benefit of the society at large.

The rise of digital technologies and Fintech is putting pressure on traditional FIs to increase competition and compress margins. Banks are the most disrupted by Fintech as telcos and tech firms have rushed into banking.

Examples include internet-only banks in China such as WeBank by Tencent Holdings and MyBank by Ant Financial. Amazon Bank in the US could also emerge soon.

In wealth management, "Robo-advisors" like Wealthfront, Betterment, and Nutmeg have automated a full suite of wealth management services, including asset allocation, investment advice, and even complicated tax minimization strategies, all offered to customers via an online portal at much lower fees than the traditional wealth management firms.

Increasingly, more and more countries in the world are warm to the idea of having non-banking entities provide financial services. Telcos are seen as one non-banking sector that could benefit from the liberalization of the financial services sector because telcos are seen as older trusted brands, and telcos can mine their subscriber base to layer on payments and credit services. The recent COVID-19 pandemic has been the biggest driver of digital banking.

Regulators are gradually opening up to the idea of non-banks such as telcos and tech companies positioned between the banks and the customers, capturing the aspect of the customer relationship. Hong Kong and Singapore are issuing virtual bank licenses to non-bank players such as telcos and tech companies.

Banks themselves are embracing and capturing the value of digital technology to compete with the new players:

(a) increase connectivity with clients, from online interactivity and payment solutions to mobile functionality and opportunities to boost bank brands in social media;
(b) draw on big data, advanced analytics, and artificial intelligence to sales, product design, and pricing, etc. to deliver amazing customer experiences and drive revenue growth;
(c) create value by enabling straight-through processing — that is, automating and digitizing many repetitive, low-value, and low-risk processes, e.g., process apps boost productivity and facilitate regulatory compliance, while imaging and straight-through processing lead to paperless, more efficient work-flows;
(d) foster innovation across products and business models, e.g., social marketing and crowdsourced support, as well as digitally-centered business models.

Inclusive finance focuses on expanding services to the poor, vulnerable, and "underserved" populations. Mobile technology and Fintech present opportunities in deposit collection, money transfer, and microfinance.

Examples include:

- M-PESA, a mobile phone-based money transfer, financing, and micro-financing service in Kenya,
- Aadhar (digital identity in India),
- Unified Payment Interface (direct money transfer between banks in India), and
- India Stack stores personal data, facilitates KYC and allows digital signing of documents.

Socially responsible and sustainable investment is closely associated with "green" or ethical investment strategies. It takes on a passive and indirect approach to doing good. For example, "Equator Principles" is a financial industry benchmark for determining, assessing, and managing environmental and social risk in project financing to support responsible risk-taking. Another industry benchmark is for the wealth management industry — UN Principles for Responsible Investment — which promotes the incorporation of environmental, social, and corporate governance factors (ESG) into investment decision-making. In Singapore, the Association of Banks in Singapore (ABS) also issued responsible financing guidelines in 2015 to raise the bar for sustainable finance.

Impact financing involves investments made to generate quantifiable social and environmental benefits while delivering financial returns, e.g., clean energy investing, microfinance, etc. It takes on a more active approach to doing good and has a clear measurement matrix. For example, in the Impact Investment Exchange (IIX), Singapore provides social enterprises in Asia with access to capital to expand their impact.

6.5.2 *Asian Financial Markets*

Due to the above trends in the global FMs and the changing economic strategies and demographics in Asian countries, new opportunities are emerging in Asian FMs.

Learning Objectives

- Understand the opportunities emerging in Asian FMs.

Main Takeaways

Main Points

- Many Asian countries need to transit from an export-based economy reliant on global growth to economic growth fostered by domestic consumption and investment spending.
- Infrastructure and retirement financing needs to increase to cope with urbanization and the aging population.
- Sustainable investment in Asia ex-Japan accounted for only 0.8% of total global AUM. However, active engagement is underway, such as government pension funds and sovereign wealth funds, which offer a big boost for ESG investing across Asia.
- The rise of a wealthy middle class in Asia opens up financial services opportunities in consumer finance and wealth management.
- In Family Offices, there is a growing interest from PB clients in investments with social impact. Impact investing is also happening in PE and VC firms for various reasons, including investors' pressure and reputation.

Many Asian countries need to transit from an export-based economy reliant on global growth to economic growth fostered by domestic consumption and investment spending especially given recent anti-globalization sentiment in the US and European countries, the US–China trade conflict, and most recently COVID-19.

Underdeveloped infrastructure in many Asian countries necessitates significant investment to match the pace of urbanization and the need for the aging population to support internal growth.

According to an estimate by ADB, in 2009, the infrastructure deficit across the Asia Pacific economies was a substantial US$8 trillion, which required spending between 2010 and 2020. Little was done between 2010 and 2013 apart from China's infrastructure program. To sustain current growth levels, PWC estimated in 2014 that a sum between US$800 billion and US$1.3 trillion annually would have to be injected into infrastructure projects right up to 2020. The breakdown is shown in Table 6.3.

Table 6.3: Breakdown of sectors of infrastructure projects.

Sector	US$ trillion
Telecommunications	1.1
Transporation — Roads	2.3
Transporation — Rail	0.05
Transporation — Other	0.1
Power	4.1
Water and Sanitation	0.4
Total	**8.05**

Source: PWC (2014), Developing Infrastructure in Asia-Pacific: Outlook, Challenges, and Solutions.

In another estimate, ADB predicted Asia would need US$1.7 trillion in infrastructure investment annually up to 2030 to maintain growth.

Expanding domestic demand is a primary policy goal for Asian governments. Many Asian countries need to transition from export-based economy to economic growth fostered by domestic consumption and investment spending.

The rise of Asian consumers could turn out to be the next megatrend in the global economy and is likely to create an expanding consumption — a new engine of growth.

By 2030, 2/3 of the global middle class will be residents of the Asia-Pacific region (see Table 6.4), while Europe's share of this population will have dropped by 14%. The emergence of a wealthy middle class will open up financial services opportunities — consumer finance and wealth management.

Sustainable investment in Asia ex-Japan accounted for only 0.8% of total global AUM. However, active engagement is underway, such as government pension funds and sovereign wealth funds, which offer a big boost for ESG investing across Asia. Stock exchanges in Singapore, Hong Kong, Malaysia, and Thailand have mandated sustainability reporting from their listed companies. Banks increasingly include ESG risks as part of the assessment in financing proposals. Also, governments grant financial incentives for green and sustainable bonds and other financing schemes.

Table 6.4: Size of the middle class by regions.

(Millions of people and global share)						
	2009		2020		2030	
North America	338	18%	333	10%	322	7%
Europe	664	36%	703	22%	680	14%
Central and South America	181	10%	251	8%	313	6%
Asia Pacific	525	28%	1.740	54%	33,228	66%
Sub-Saharan Africa	32	2%	57	2%	107	2%
Middle East and North Africa	105	6%	165	5%	234	5%
World	1,845	100%	3,249	100%	4,884	100%

Source: Kharas, H. & Wolfensohn, G. G. (2010). *The New Global Middle Class: A Cross-Over from West to East.* Center for Development at Brookings.

Singapore case studies on ESG lending:

(a) **Case 1:** In March 2018, Olam, a company majority-owned by Temasek Holdings, took Asia's first sustainability-linked club loan, a revolving US$500 million credit facility. DBS Bank is one of the lenders.
(b) **Case 2:** In June 2018, OCBC Bank and Wilmar International inked a deal that pegged the interest rate of the agribusiness giant's US$200 million revolving credit facility to its sustainability performance.

Both Olam and Wilmar are committed to achieving pre-set targets for a wide range of environmental, social, and governance (ESG) metrics. If achieved, the loan interest will be reduced. An independent party, Sustainalytics, will conduct the assessment.

In Family Offices, there is a growing interest from private banking clients in investments with social impact. As reported in Bain and Company's report, investors' discomfort has morphed into genuine alarm among fund customers and investors. An investment survey by Shroeders of 25,000 investors in 2019 found that more than 60% of investors under the age of 71 believe that all investment funds must consider sustainability factors when making investments.

References/Further Readings

Bain and Company (2020). Global Private Equity Report 2020 Section 2.2. Retrieved from https://www.bain.com/insights/esg-investing-global-private-equity-report-2020/.

Olam Press Release (26 March 2018). Olam International secure Asia's first sustainability-linked club loan facility of US$500 million. Retrieved from https://www.olamgroup.com/news/all-news/press-release/asias-first-sustainability-linked-club-loan-facility-us500million.html.

OCBC and Wilmar Media Release (8 June 2018). OCBC Bank Partners Wilmar on Largest Sustainability-Link Bilateral Loan by a Singapore Bank. Retrieved from https://www.wilmar-international.com/docs/default-source/default-document-library/sustainability/resource/WIL_News_Release_dd8June2018_OCBC_Sustainability-Linked_Bilateral_Loan.

6.6 Sample Questions

Question 1

Commercial banks intermediate your financial transactions. Which of the following are considered financial intermediation?

1. Taking deposits from you to meet your savings' need.
2. Collecting sales proceeds for your export on your behalf and provide export-related.
3. Financing to you via documentary trade credit.
4. Underwriting and sale of your company's IPO shares.
5. Making loans to you to meet your financing needs.
   (a) (1) and (4) are correct.
   (b) (1), (2) and (4) are correct.
   (c) All of the statements are correct.

Question 2

Which of the following is (are) not the signs and symptoms of financial repression?

1. State-owned banks dominated the nation's FMs.
2. Underground money lending activities are rampant.
3. Several banks from private sectors are serving the needs of SMEs well.
4. Besides bank deposit and investment schemes, a variety of investment products are available from the direct finance market for investors.
   (a) Statements (1) and (2).
   (b) Statements (3) and (4).
   (c) All of the statements are correct.

Question 3

Which of the following statements is correct?

(a) Intermediaries like commercial banks usually have a much larger balance sheet because of their function of taking deposits and making loans. Agents like investment bankers typically have a smaller balance sheet because they provide mainly corporate finance advisory services and help corporate clients in the listing and trading of securities.

(b) Interest income is usually the largest income item for Agents in the direct finance market, and fee income is usually the largest income item for Intermediaries in the indirect finance market.

(c) Intermediaries in the indirect finance market provide mainly financial advisory services such as company valuation in merger and acquisition activities. Agents in the direct finance market mainly take deposits and make loans to their customers.

Solutions

Question 1

Solution: Option **b** is correct.

(Underwriting and sale of your company's IPO shares are made by an investment banker or stockbroker in the direct finance market)

Question 2

Solution: Option **b** is correct

(3 and 4 are usually the signs of a vibrant direct finance market, reflecting financial liberalization rather than financial repression)

Question 3

Solution: Option **a** is correct.

(Activities such as corporate finance advisory services and helping corporate clients in listing and trading of securities do not require funds to flow investment banker's balance sheet)

Chapter 7

Central Bank and Monetary Policy

7.1 Functions of Money

According to Wikipedia, Money is any item or verifiable record that is generally accepted as payment for goods and services and repayment of debts in a particular country.

Learning Objectives
- Understand the functions of money.

Main Takeaways

Main Points
- Money can be anything that serves as a unit of account, medium of exchange, and store of value.
- Money had evolved from ancient agricultural commodities such as gold, silver, and other metals, to paper money, plastic cards, electronic cash, and now cryptocurrencies.

Main Terms
- **Unit of account:** Provide a common base for prices.
- **The medium of exchange:** It is something that people can use to buy and sell goods or services.
- **Store of value:** People can save it and use it later — smoothing their purchases over time and anywhere.
- **Fiat currency:** The currency that government regulation or law has declared legal tender is not backed by a physical commodity or any

other assets. The term derives from the Latin word — fiat, used in an order or decree.

- **Legal tender:** It is a medium of payment recognized by a legal system to be valid for meeting a financial obligation. Paper currency and coins are common forms of legal tender in many countries.
- **Cryptocurrency:** It is a digital or virtual currency secured by cryptography that makes it nearly impossible to counterfeit or double-spend. Many cryptocurrencies are decentralized networks based on blockchain technology — a distributed ledger enforced by a disparate network of computers.

7.2 Monetary Systems

7.2.1 *Definition of a Monetary System*

A monetary system is defined as a set of policies, frameworks, and institutions by which a central bank provides money and controls the exchange of money in a country's economy.

Learning Objectives

- Understand international currency and the necessary conditions to be satisfied as an international currency.
- Understand monetary systems — Bretton Woods system and Jamaica Accord, and why they are created.

Main Takeaways

(a) International Currency

Main Points

- International currency is a currency used between countries for cross-border trade and investment.
- There are mainly four conditions to be satisfied as an international currency: convertible and widely circulated, a sizable economy with close links with the global economy, strong and stable value, and well-developed financial markets.

International currency is a currency used between countries for cross-border trade and investment. For example, when China (RMB is its currency) buys oil from Saudi Arabia (Riyal is its currency), China does not pay in RMB or Riyal but instead pays USD to Saudi Arabia. USD is said to be used as the payment currency for international trade.

Necessary conditions to be International Currency:

1. The currency is convertible and widely circulated in international markets.
2. Has a sizable economy that is closely linked with the global economy with significant trade and investment.
3. The currency is generally strong and stable to facilitate the transfer of purchasing power internationally and for investment purposes, e.g., backed by substantial reserves and strong institutions such as the rule of law, central bank's independence, good governance structure, etc.
4. Has sizable, deep, and well-developed financial markets that provide various investment avenues and good liquidity.

Mark Carney, former BOE Governor, urged that some form of global digital currency would be better than the USD, a national currency, as a global payment and reserve currency. His view is that the US accounts for only 10% of international trade and 15% of global GDP but half of world trade invoices and two-thirds of global securities issuance. Countries are forced to self-insure and hoard dollars to guard against potential capital flight, leading to excess savings and lower global growth. He felt that some form of global digital currency, similar to Facebook's proposed Libra, would be a better option than allowing the USD's reserve status to be replaced by another national currency such as China's renminbi.

(b) Bretton Woods Agreement

Main Points

- The Bretton Woods Agreement aimed to have exchange rate stability after World War II by setting up a system of rules, institutions, and procedures to regulate the international monetary system.

Main Terms

- **Gold standard:** It is a monetary system whereby a country's currency or paper money has a value directly linked to gold. With the gold standard, countries agree to convert paper money into a fixed amount of gold.

The Bretton Woods Agreement was signed in July 1944, setting up a system of rules, institutions, and procedures to regulate the international monetary system. It also established the International Monetary Fund (IMF) and the International Bank for Reconstruction and Development (IBRD), which today is part of the World Bank Group.

Exchange rate stability was the prime goal. All currencies were linked to the USD and maintained fixed exchange rates within the possible plus or minus 1% movement. In turn, the USD was linked to gold at one ounce of gold = US$35 ("Gold Standard"). At that time, the US controlled 75% of the world's gold stock.

In the 1960s, the US Government faced inflation due to excessive money printing to pay for massive spending on the Vietnam War and domestic social welfare. Other countries were worried about the US dollar devaluation and demanded to exchange USD for gold.

On 15 August 1971, due to the shrinking gold stock, the US unilaterally terminated convertibility of the USD to gold, which effectively brought the Bretton Woods system to an end and rendered USD a fiat currency ("Nixon shock"), putting an end to the monetary system based on Gold standard.

(c) Jamaica Accord

Main Points

- The "Jamaica Accord" legitimized floating exchange rates.

Main Terms

- **USD standard:** After the fall of the Gold Standard, the US Dollar is considered a benchmark currency and is the most-used currency in transactions across the world. Outside the US, many countries use the USD as the official currency. Others use it alongside their own as an unofficial currency.

The "Jamaica Accord" was reached in January 1976, legitimizing floating exchange rates. A member country is free to choose its exchange rate system, either freely floating, managed float, or pegged to a currency or a group of currencies but not to gold.

Due to its economic and military powers, the US Dollar is still held as an international reserve currency after World War II. Hence, the "USD Standard" is in practice. For instance, about 64% of all known central bank foreign exchange reserves are in USD, 85% of forex trading involves the USD (BIS Triennial Survey, 2016), and 52% of international trade is settled in USD (Swift, 2014)

7.3 Functions of Central Bank

A central bank, reserve bank, or monetary authority is an institution that manages the currency, money supply, and interest rates of a state or formal monetary union and oversees its commercial banking system.

Learning Objectives
- Understand the main functions of central banks.

Main Takeaways
There are six main functions of central banks:
- Issuing currency notes
- Acting as banker to commercial banks
  - Imposes and manages the deposit reserve requirement
  - Acts as "lender of last resort" to banks, usually against high-quality collaterals
  - Manages the clearing system for local currency payments
- Acting as banker to the Government
  - The Government keeps cash balances in the current account with the central bank, and the central bank accepts receipts and makes payments on behalf of the government
  - Acts as agent for the issuance of government or treasury bills and bonds
- Formulating and implementing monetary policy
- Holding and managing official foreign exchange reserves
- Supervising financial sector
  - Responsible for macro-prudential supervision concerned with overall financial stability
  - Responsible for micro-prudential supervision concerned with the safety and soundness of individual financial firms

  (*Note*: This will vary by country and not be part of a central bank's responsibilities, e.g., China Banking and Insurance Regulatory Commission (CBIRC) and China Securities Regulatory Commission (CSRC) in China, Financial Services Agency (FSA) in Japan, and

Financial Services Authority (OJK) in Indonesia are responsible for micro-prudential supervision and not their central banks).

7.4 Money Supply and Money Creation

7.4.1 *Money Supply*

The money supply is the entire stock of currency and other liquid instruments in a country's economy at a particular time.

Learning Objectives

- Understand the concept of money supply and the money supply's standard measures.

Main Takeaways

Main Points

- The money supply includes cash, coins, balances held in checking, the term (fixed), and savings accounts.
- There are several standard measures of the money supply, namely M_0, M_1, M_2 and M_3.
- Central banks analyze the economic conditions and money supply situation and formulate and execute monetary policy, expansionary or contractionary, to ensure the economy's price stability and healthy growth.

Main Terms

- **Money supply:** The entire stock of currency and other liquid instruments in a country's economy at a particular time.

The US Federal Reserve's definition of the money supply is "commonly defined to be a group of safe assets that households and businesses can use to make payments or to hold as short-term investments." For example, US currency and balances held in checking accounts and savings accounts are included in many money supply measures.

Because of the money supply's impact on the price level, inflation, and the business cycle, central banks analyze the money supply and formulate monetary policy, expansionary or contractionary. Central banks influence the amount of money flowing in the economy and market interest rates to ensure that the money supply and interest rates are appropriate in maintaining price stability and economic growth.

Different countries may differ slightly in the measures and classifications of money due to their financial landscape and development stage in financial markets. However, the various types of money in the money supply are generally classified as follows:

M_0 = Monetary Base (aka high-powered money or 'narrowest measurement of money')

(defined as the amount of currency notes and coins in circulation and reserve cash balances, i.e., deposits held by banks and other depository institutions in their accounts at the central bank and banks' and depository institutions' vault cash in hand).

$M_1 = M_0$ + Demand deposits (Checking account)

(narrower definition of money, emphasizing medium of exchange function of money).

$M_2 = M_1$ + Fixed deposits + Saving deposits

(broader definition of money that includes the money's function as a store of value, apart from being a medium of exchange).

$M_3 = M_2$ + Other short-term liquid assets

(also known as the "broadest measure of money," e.g., transferable certificates of deposits, money market funds, commercial bills, etc.).

Most central banks today monitor $\mathbf{M_2}$ as an important guide in formulating monetary policy.

7.4.2 *Money Creation*

Money creation is the process by which banks increase the money supply of a country or an economic or monetary region.

Learning Objectives

- Understand the process of money creation and the factors affecting the money multiplier.

Main Takeaways

Main Points

- Money supply = Monetary Base × Money Multiplier
- Depending on the demand for loans, central banks use various monetary policy tools to adjust the overall money supply.

Main Terms

- **Statutory deposit reserve ratio:** It is a central bank regulation that sets the minimum amount of reserves held by a commercial bank in its account at the central bank. The central bank generally determines the minimum reserve requirement to be no less than a specified percentage of the amount of deposit liabilities the commercial bank owes to its customers.
- **Money multiplier:** Aactual observed quantity of money supply usually M2 (broad money) Over M0 (base money or monetary base).

Four factors affect the Money Multiplier:

1. Deposit reserve ratio (both statutory and volunteer)
2. "Leakage" from the banking system by way of cash withdrawals
3. Loan demand
4. Banks' willingness to lend

Suppose the loan demand by businesses and households is strong, and banks are short of funds. In that case, the central bank can increase its monetary base via various monetary policy tools to increase the overall money supply.

Example:
Say we start with an original deposit of a $1,000 cheque and assume a statutory deposit reserve ratio of 10% (see Figure 7.1).

7.5 Monetary Policy

7.5.1 *Objectives of Monetary Policy*

Monetary policy is the demand side of economic policy, which refers to the actions undertaken by a nation's central bank to control the money

Money Creation

(Assuming statutory deposit reserve ratio of 10%)

Bank	Increase in Demand Deposit*	Increase in deposit reserve	Increase in Loans**
A	1,000	100	900
B	900	90	810
C	810	81	729
D	729	72.9	656.1
...		...	...
Total	10,000	1,000	9,000

Money Multiplier = 1/r = 10 times

$\Delta D = 1/r \times \Delta R = 10{,}000$

ΔD : Total increase in demand deposits ($10,000)

ΔR : Change in initial deposit ($1,000)

r : Statutory deposit reserve ratio (10%)

Derivative deposit = $9,000, created by the banks' credit expansion

* Assuming not cash is withdrawn and recipients deposit all monies back into demand deposit accounts.

** To have maximum money multiplier, there must be loan demand in economy and banks are willing to lend.

Figure 7.1: Example of money creation.

supply to achieve macroeconomic goals that promote sustainable economic growth (*Source*: Investopedia).

For example, the objectives as mandated by Congress in the Federal Reserve Act in the US promotes (1) maximum employment, which means all Americans that want to work are gainfully employed, and (2) stable prices for the goods and services Americans purchase. (*Source*: Federal Reserve website)

Learning Objectives

- Explain the objectives of monetary policy.
- Learn some examples of monetary policies used in practice and what objectives they seek to achieve.

Main Takeaways

Main Points

- The monetary policy objectives include ultimate objectives, intermediate objectives, and operating targets.
- In practice, monetary policy can have a single target of inflation-targeting, dual targets, or multiple targets.

Main Terms

- **Price stability:** According to Alan Greenspan, former Chairman of the US Federal Reserve, "For all practical purposes, price stability means that expected changes in the average price level are small enough and gradual enough that they do not materially influence the economic decisions of businesses and households."
- **Inflation targeting:** A central bank estimates and makes public a projected or "target" inflation rate and then attempts to steer actual inflation toward that target, using such tools as interest rate changes.

The ultimate objectives are the final goals but not operation targets, including:

- Price stability (refers to medium-term price stability, i.e., low and stable inflation)
- Full employment
- Economic growth
- Balance of international payments
- Others

Intermediate objectives are closely related to final goals, usually monitoring targets. They include:

1. Money supply
2. Interest rate
3. Exchange rate
4. Others, such as China, use "Total Social Financing Amount" in addition to the money supply.

Operating targets are directly responsive to and can be varied by monetary policy

1. Monetary base
2. Policy (interest) rate
3. The spot price of the currency (or a basket of currencies)
4. The statutory deposit reserve ratio
5. Others

"*Inflation is always and everywhere a monetary phenomenon*" is the famous quote by Nobel Prize-winning monetary economist Milton Friedman, who held that excessive money creation spawns inflation. Empirical studies show that inflation usually accelerates when money supply growth exceeds the economy's growth rate for an extended time.

7.5.2 *Monetary Policy Objectives in Practice*

Refer to Table 7.1 for some examples of monetary policy objectives in practice.

Inflation targeting is when a central bank estimates and makes public a projected or "target" inflation rate and then attempts to steer actual inflation toward that target, using such tools as interest rate changes. Most developed economies target CPI change of 2% or thereabout as a proxy for price stability.

For example, the Reserve Bank of New Zealand (1989) uses monetary policy as defined in its Policy Targets Agreement (PTA). The current PTA requires Banks to keep inflation between 1% and 3% on average over the medium term.

Some examples of dual-target monetary policy include the Bank of England's monetary policy objective to deliver low inflation and, subject

Table 7.1: Monetary policy objectives in practice.

Objective(s)	Operating target	Example
Inflation targeting: Certain rate of change in CPI (price stability)	Interest rate (Policy rate)	New Zealand
Dual targets: Certain rate of change in CPI (price stability) and economic growth/employment	Interest rate (Policy rate)	USA, UK
"... sustained non-inflationary economic growth ..." (no explicit target on CPI)	Certain range of exchange rate against a basket of currencies	Singapore
Multiple targets: price stability, employment, economic growth and balance of payment	Money supply	China

to that, support the government's economic goals, including those for growth and employment. Price stability is defined by the government's inflation target of 2%. In the US, the monetary policy goals are to ensure price stability and maximum sustainable employment, known collectively as the "dual mandate".

For multiple-target monetary policy, such as in China, the country aims to target price stability, employment, GDP growth, and payment balance. However, in practice, likely, the People's Bank of China, the central bank of China, has to prioritize the multiple targets according to the needs of its economy at a particular time.

Maintaining price stability remains the main official objective for most central banks in Asia.

References/Further Readings

Jahan, S. (28 March 2012). *Inflation Targeting: Holding the Line*. IMF.

7.6 Monetary Policy Tools

7.6.1 *Conventional Tools*

Conventional monetary policy tools include general and targeted tools.

Learning Objectives

- Understand the three main conventional monetary policy tools, the effect they seek to achieve, and the pros and cons of each tool.
- Learn the monetary transmission mechanism.
- Appreciate communication as a policy tool.

Main Takeaways

Main Points

- General conventional tools tend to have an overall effect on the financial markets. There are three such tools: the Statutory Deposit Reserve Requirement, Rediscount Window, and Open Market Operations.
- Targeted conventional tools use a more targeted and selective approach by controlling or expanding the amount of credit available

or applying a "preferential lending rate" targeted at particular industries or groups.
- Communication with the central bank's market about the likely future monetary policy course is known as "forward guidance".

(a) General Conventional Tools

The Statutory Deposit Reserve Requirement directly affects the amount of money banks hold and varies the monetary base.

The Rediscount Window refers to the central bank's financing facility. Commercial banks could discount commercial bills with the central bank or borrow short-term loans from the central bank against acceptable collateral such as treasury bonds and bills. From a policy perspective, the Rediscount Window's importance is through the changes made in the rates or terms of discounting or short-term loans. The central bank sends a signal to the market that it is now leaning towards an expansionary or contractionary monetary policy stance and thereby assert influence on the market interest rates.

The Open Market Operations (OMO) refers to the central bank (a) buying and selling outright, or (b) conducting repurchase agreements ("repos") or a reverse repo of government securities with commercial banks in the open market. It is the most important and commonly used conventional monetary policy tool. It affects the monetary base and interest rates, and usually, it is the primary source of fluctuation in the money supply. By varying the "policy rate," the central bank's rate to implement or signal its monetary policy stance will lead to changes in the market interest rates via OMO.

The monetary transmission mechanism is illustrated in Figure 7.2.

(b) Communication as a Policy Tool — "Forward Guidance"

Communication as a policy tool has seen a clear trend since the 1990s in central banking, aimed towards greater transparency, and driven by:

(a) A growing recognition that monetary policy is essentially about managing expectations.
(b) Increasing adoption of inflation targeting also spurs advances on the transparency front to anchor longer-term inflation expectation, which in turn increases the effective scope of monetary policy to stabilize output and employment in the short run.

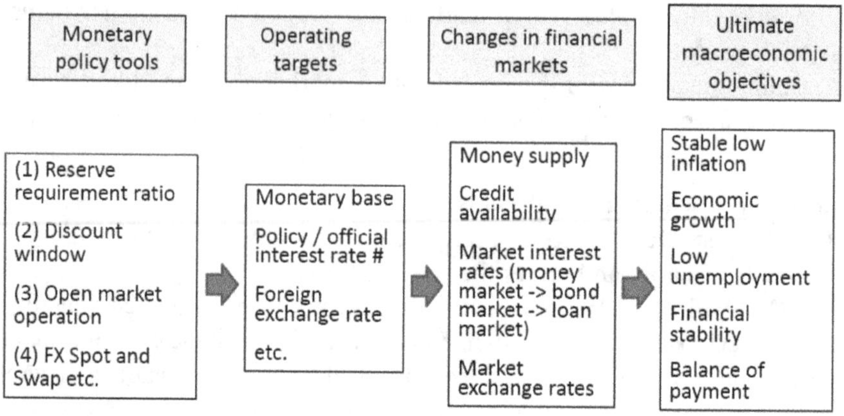

Figure 7.2: Monetary transmission mechanism.

Notes: US: Federal Funds Rate — the interest rate at which depository institutions (banks and credit unions) lend reserve balances (held at the Federal Reserve to maintain reserve requirements) to other depository institutions overnight, on an uncollateralized basis.
UK: Official Interest Rate (a.k.a as Bank Rate) at which the Bank of England (BoE) pays on reserve balances held by commercial banks and building societies. The BoE can influence a range of other borrowing and lending rates set by commercial banks and building societies, hence spending in the economy.

Many central banks communicate regularly and frequently with the public about the economy, the economic outlook, and the likely future monetary policy course. Communication about the possible monetary policy course is known as "Forward Guidance".

When central banks provide forward guidance about the future monetary policy course, individuals and businesses will use this information in making decisions about spending and investments. Thus, forward guidance about future policy can influence financial and economic conditions today. Also, forward guidance provides clarity and transparency of the central bank's monetary policy, help reduce uncertainty and market volatility, and in turn, is promote market confidence and financial stability.

7.6.2 *Unconventional Tools*

Quantitative easing (QE) is an unconventional monetary policy tool and mainly targets the monetary base. It is used when conventional monetary policy tools lose effectiveness.

Learning Objectives

- Understand that quantitative easing is an unconventional tool in monetary policy.
- Learn how quantitative easing works and how it differs from conventional monetary easing.
- Understand the possible challenges or unintended consequences arising from quantitative easing.

Main Takeaways

Main Points

- Quantitative easing (QE) is an unconventional tool in monetary policy.
- QE is used when conventional monetary policy tools lose effectiveness. It differs from traditional monetary easing in terms of scale, scope, counterparty, asset type, and the central bank's bond-purchase operation's maturity.
- QE's possible new challenges include fiscal dominance, quasi-fiscal policy, the buyer of the last resort, and moral hazard.

Main Terms

- **Helicopter money (drop):** This is an unconventional monetary policy tool to bring a flagging economy back on track. It involves the central bank printing large sums of money and distributing it directly to individuals, households, businesses, and other economic agents. American economist Milton Friedman coined this term. It denotes a helicopter dropping money from the sky. Friedman used the word to signify "unexpectedly dumping money onto a struggling economy to shock it out of a deep slump". It is a last resort type of monetary stimulus strategy to spur inflation and economic output.

QE is used when conventional monetary policy tools lose effectiveness. For example, the central bank conducts conventional OMO by buying government securities from banks, increasing banks' liquidity, and lowering policy rates or short-term interest rates to near-zero or zero. However, banks are risk-averse and could fall into a "liquidity trap and not lend," resulting in the risk of a severe deflation in the economy.

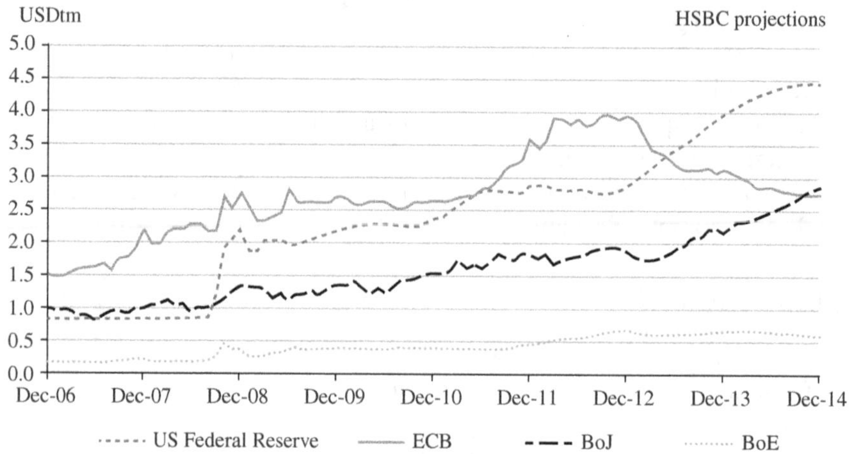

Figure 7.3: Aggressive monetary policy adopted by the G4 central banks since the 2008 Financial Crisis.

Source: HSBC Global Research (June 2014) Asia Central Banks Guide 2014.

QE differs from traditional credit easing in terms of scale, scope, counterparty, asset type, and maturity of the central bank's bond-purchase operation. Apart from buying government securities in the open market, the central bank might resort to "printing money" in large amounts. Such printing then buys up large quantities of other financial assets such as commercial loans, asset-backed securities, or even stocks from banks and private sector institutions to expand lending and investment. The central bank may also lower the longer-term interest rates or yields of those assets the central bank bought, e.g., US Fed bought mortgage-backed securities (MBS) to support the sagging mortgage market.

Figure 7.3 shows the unprecedented aggressive monetary easing program by G4 since the 2008 Global Financial Crisis (GFC) boosted their central banks' balance sheet by some US$6.5 trillion between the end of 2007 and 2014.

During the GFC, many countries such as the US, UK, Japan, and Europe all looked to the central banks to do the heavy lifting of the economy in the short term, becoming what Barry Eichengreen, a University of California professor, called the "policymakers of last resort". Some of the reasons contributing to this are:

- Unlike politicians, unelected central bankers can act quickly without parliamentary debate.
- Some economic ills have to be addressed by structural economic reforms, which require medium to long term effort and are sometimes hard or painful to implement.
- After the demise of the Gold Standard, central banks but not the governments could print new money in unprecedented amounts to stimulate the economy.

However, it is generally acknowledged that monetary easing alone is insufficient to address the economic ills and ensure long-term sustainable and healthy economic growth. Depending on the nature of economic ills, it requires appropriate monetary policy, fiscal policy, and economic structural reform policy to work in tandem to restructure and reinvigorate the economy.

Besides, there are also possible challenges or unintended consequences arising from implementing QE:

1. *Fiscal dominance*: The high level of government debt pushed up by QE could well constrain the central bank's ability to set the policy rate higher to control inflation. The lower interest rate helps lighten the cost of government debt. It also creates a moral hazard for governments to borrow more as QE artificially depresses borrowing costs.
2. *A quasi-fiscal policy with distributional effects*: QE pushed up the prices of financial assets such as bonds and equities and real assets such as properties. The distributional implication that the rich get richer and the poor such as low-skilled workers and those without assets, get poorer. Also, direct purchase of financial assets by the central bank from non-bank corporates, such as AIG, stockbrokers, Fannie Mae, Freddie Mae, etc. in the case of the US during GFC blurred the line between monetary policy and fiscal policy.
3. *"Buyer of last resort"*: During QE, central banks took more financial risks by buying up risky financial assets, deviating from its traditional role of "lender of last resort" to lend against quality collaterals such as government securities. The central banks' actions gave rise to a potential controversy where the central bank participates in a financial market that it supervises and manages.

7.7 Central Bank Independence

The central bank needs to maintain independence from the influence of the government. Empirical studies have shown that an operationally independent central bank is also a more effective central bank.

Learning Objectives

- Understand in democratic countries why the central bank's independence from government influence is essential, what kind of autonomy it should strive for, and how to remain independent.
- Consider central banks' accountability and what they should do to earn that independence.

Main Takeaways

Main Points

- Without independence, central banks could be pressured by politicians to implement a short-term expansionary monetary policy which may be at the expense of longer-term price stability, or politicians could abuse money-printing power to finance budget deficits. Central banks also need to maintain independence to allow for effective and swift undertakings of a "lender of last resort" operation to address a financial crisis.
- Central banks everywhere are struggling to stay above politics, as we see the politicians have been making comments threatening the central bank's independence.
- To remain independent, central banks need to ensure that they do not depend on governments for funding. It is also crucial for central banks to be transparent in their policy formulation. For its policy independence to be democratically legitimate, the central bank must be accountable to the public for its actions, so it is essential to explain the monetary policy.
- The monetary policy goals are usually established by the legislative, but the conduct (or operation) of monetary policy should be free from political control.

Independence from politicians or government is essential because:

- It insulates monetary policy from political interference and from electoral pressure to pursue short-term expansionary monetary policy and deliver short-term economic growth at the expense of longer-term price stability.

- Politicians may abuse the central bank's money-printing powers to help finance its budget deficit, resulting in the national debt's monetization.
- With objectives of price stability with maximum sustainable growth and employment, monetary policymakers must attempt to guide the economy over time toward a growth rate consistent with the expansion in its underlying productive capacity. As monetary policy works with time lags that can bc substantial, achieving these objectives require monetary policymakers to take a longer-term perspective when making their decisions. Anti-inflationary measures like hiking interest rates can be highly unpopular. Maintaining such unpopular commitments is difficult for politicians when the benefits only arise over a horizon longer than an electoral cycle.
- To allow a more rapid and effective response in a crisis, central banks' ability to independently undertake "lender of last resort "operation and undertake it swiftly is critical, e.g., it must delay disclosure about the recipients of its funds. Otherwise, banks worry about being seen as fragile will not borrow, perpetuating the financial system's liquidity shortfall and panic.

It is useful to distinguish two types of independence for central banks: goal independence and operational independence. If a central bank is free to set the final monetary policy objectives, it has goal independence. If a central bank is free to choose its instruments and decide how to implement monetary policy to pursue its ultimate objectives, it has operational independence.

Most central banks have specific legislative mandates and therefore do not have goal independence. However, in democratic countries, central banks should have operational independence. Operational independence refers to the central bank's ability to select and use monetary tools with the autonomy to pursue the objectives mandated by the legislature without seeking permission from the executive or the legislature. However, countries vary considerably in the specificity of the required goals and central banks' discretion in monetary policy.

Empirical studies support the views:

1. That more-independent central banks tend to deliver better inflation outcomes than less-independent central banks.

2. That insulating monetary policy from short-term political pressures helps foster desirable macroeconomic outcomes and financial stability.

Figure 7.4 shows consistently there is a negative relationship between inflation and independence across time and countries.

To remain independent from politicians or government:

1. There is a need to ensure the "purse strings" is not controlled by politicians. For example, the Federal Reserve in the US does not receive funding through the congressional budgetary process. The Fed's income comes primarily from the interest in government securities acquired through open market operations. After paying its expenses, the Federal Reserve turns the rest of its earnings over to the US Treasury.

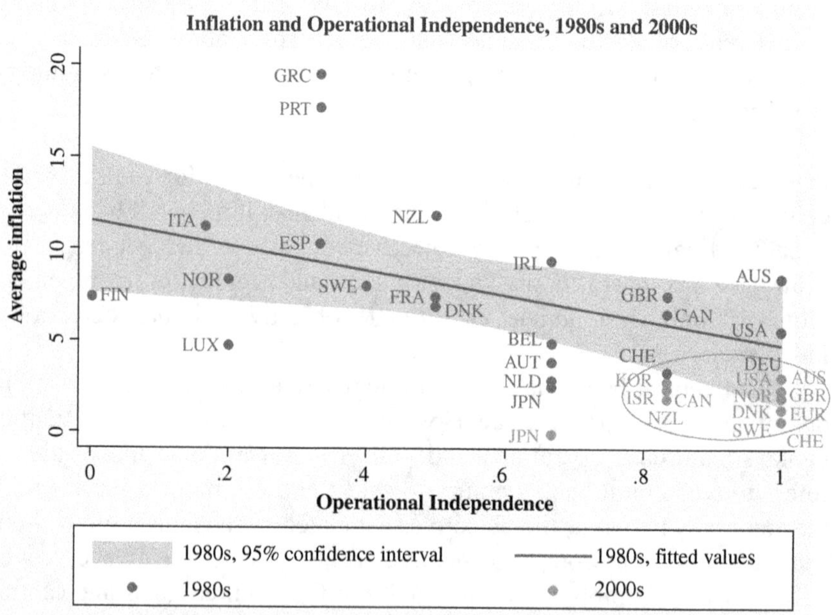

Figure 7.4: Inflation and operational independence in advanced economies, the 1980s, and 2000s.

Source: Balls, E., Howat J. and Stansbury, A. (Nov. 2016) Central Bank Independence Revisited, Harvard Kennedy School Mossavar-Rahmani Center for Business and Government.

From the Federal Reserve, What does it mean to be "independent within the government?" Retrieved from: https://www.federalreserve.gov/faqs/about_12799.htm\

2. For its policy independence to be democratically legitimate, the central bank must be accountable to the public for its actions, so it is crucial to "Taking Monetary Policy to the People," whereby monetary policies are explained to the public in the UK.

   "...Independence demands higher degrees of accountability and transparency, whereby policies are explained to the public. To its credit, the Bank of England has been showing the way forward with a series of open forums around the UK. Taking monetary policy to the people is time-consuming, but it is essential if the necessary political consensus to sustain independence is to be maintained...."

Central banks' independence needs to come with accountability and transparency. Central banks should seek to achieve goals such as:

1. The central bank must be accountable to the people via legislation, just like the government is accountable to the people for the economic well-being of the country, e.g., US Fed to issue monetary policy report to Congress and testimony by Fed Chairman before Congress.
2. Monetary policy must be coordinated with fiscal policy to present a cohesive program that promotes economic performance and stability.
3. Transparent about its economic outlook and policy strategy to demonstrate its fidelity to its mandated goals, this helps make central banks more accountable.

References/Further Readings

Bernanke, B. S. (25 May 2010) Central Bank Independence, Transparency and Accountability, The Federal Reserve. Retrieved from: https://www.federalreserve.gov/newsevents/speech/bernanke20100525a.htm.

Davies, H. (25 October 2016). *Taking Monetary Policy to the People*. Project Syndicate.

Mankiw, N. G. (2020). Principles of Economics, 9th edn. Cengage Learning, pp. 589–637.

7.8 Central Bank Digital Currency

The development of technologies has changed the commerce industry, the payment system, and money. The cashless society is trending. With the prevalence of digital currencies such as cryptocurrencies and stable coins, many are concerned that such an emerging form of money will challenge the sovereign currencies or fiat money. Under this circumstance, many central banks have started to work on digital currencies or central bank-issued digital currencies (CBDCs). This section will introduce this form of money.

Learning Objectives

- Understand the concept and design of central bank digital currency.
- Formulate the benefits and risks associated with central bank digital currency.

Main Takeaways

Main Points

- According to the distribution model, CBDC can be categorized as wholesale CBDC and retail CBDC.
- Based on the different trust components, there are three types of digital currencies: central bank-issued, the central bank authorized, and non-central bank.
- Issuing a CBDC has various benefits, but it does come with risks. Jurisdictions should carefully plan and design the model before the launch.

Main Terms

- **Central bank digital currency:** A form of a digital currency issued by the central banks and a digital form of legal tender. It can be CBI or CBA.
- **Central bank issued (CBI):** A form of a digital currency issued directly by the central bank, and the trust component is only the central bank. It is a legal tender and a direct liability of the central bank.
- **Central bank authorized (CBA):** It is authorized but not directly issued by the central banks. It is also a form of legal tender.

7.8.1 *Definition of CBDC*

As the name suggests, **central bank digital currency (CBDC)** is a form of digital currency that the central banks issue, and it is a digital form of legal tender. It does not have a physical state but is also supported by monetary reserves and a liability to the central banks like fiat money. The development of blockchain technology contributes to the global development of CBDC in governments around the world. Still, distributed ledger technology such as blockchain is not a must for a CBDC. It depends on the jurisdiction's objective and architecture design (although many CBDCs use blockchain technology).

Unlike most cryptocurrencies that use blockchain technology and are decentralized (without any authorized third parties), CBDC is centralized. It is governed by the central bank or centralized authority delegated by the government (such as commercial banks).

7.8.2 *Types of CBDC and Digital Currency*

Based on the issuance and distribution model's design, CBDCs have two categories: wholesale CBDC and retail CBDC. With **wholesale CBDC**, central banks do not directly interact with the public or issue the digital currency to the general public. For wholesale CBDCs, central banks delegate agents such as commercial banks or financial institutions so that individuals can gain access to the CBDC, similar to the current system. **Retail CBDC** refers to the type that central banks or monetary authorities directly issue to the public.

Based on the trust component, CBDCs can be issued or authorized by the central banks, with the trust lies in central banks. All other digital currencies can be viewed as "non-central banks". In summary, there are three types of digital currencies as follows:

1. **Central Bank Issued (CBI):** Legal tender and a direct liability of the central bank. The trust component is the central bank (only). CBDCs that fall in this category are wholesale CBDC.
2. **Central Bank Authorized (CBA):** Authorized but not directly issued by the central banks. It is also a form of legal tender. The trust lies in the central bank and the agencies it delegates and central banks in other jurisdictions if foreign currencies are involved.
3. **Non-Central Bank (NCB):** All other digital currencies that are not CBI and CBA. It is not legal tender and not a type of CBDC. The trust components include central banks (if fiat currency is involved), companies or entities, and algorithms or protocols (for a decentralized public network). Examples include platform tokens, stable coins, and cryptocurrencies on a public blockchain (decentralized).

7.8.3 *Pros and Cons of CBDCs*

There are various reasons why a country or jurisdiction should consider launching a CBDC. First of all, it provides a potential solution to the currency payment system's pain points, especially in fulfilling the need to go cashless. For example, allow offline transactions or transfer via eWallets like physical money but with greater convenience and lower cost. Also, transactions do not require contact, which is especially important in a pandemic like COVID-19. It creates more opportunities in payments and makes smart contracts and tokenization possible.

In terms of overall economic and social welfare, CBDCs contribute to financial inclusion as people in the rural areas or currently unbanked have a greater likelihood of benefitting from the digital economy. Also, with CBDCs, economic activities within a country or region will be more accurately reflected and tracked.

However, before a CBDC can be launched, the jurisdiction needs to plan carefully and select a model that fits its objective and resources. CBDCs are associated with certain risks and can bring many challenges to the financial system and economy, especially if poorly designed. First, the country or region needs to decide which type of CBDC to issue and what technologies should be in place. How to avoid technical or system failure to ensure data privacy and system security are vital questions to be answered and are of considerable challenge.

Despite security and privacy issues, we consider the identification problem to be manageable while allowing a certain anonymity level. On the other hand, illegal activities such as money laundering are more likely to happen with CBDC. The cost of counterfeit may be lower than using the physical notes. There remain broader issues like increased risks of bank runs and ineffective monetary policies with the introduction of CBDCs.

References/Further Readings

John, Kiff *et al.* (2020). A Survey of Research on Retail Central Bank Digital Currency. International Monetary Fund. IMF Working Papers. Retrieved from https://www.imf.org/en/Publications/WP/Issues/2020/06/26/A-Survey-of-Research-on-Retail-Central-Bank-Digital-Currency-49517.

David K. C. Lee, & Ernie G. S. Teo (2020). The New Money: The Utility of Cryptocurrencies and the Need for a New Monetary Policy. Working Paper. Retrieved from https://papers.ssrn.com/sol3/papers.cfm?abstract_id=3608752.

David K.C. Lee, Li Yan, & Yu Wang (2020). A Global Perspective on Central Bank Digital Currency. Working Paper.

Orla Ward & Sabrina Rochemont (2019). Understanding Central Bank Digital Currencies (CBDC). Institute and Faculty of Actuaries. Retrieved from https://www.actuaries.org.uk/system/files/field/document/Understanding%20CBDCs%20Final%20-%20disc.pdf.

7.9 Sample Questions

Question 1
Which of the following statements is correct?

1. Keeping more cash at home by households will not affect the money multiplier
2. Imposition of overall lending limit or quota on commercial banks by a central bank can affect the money multiplier
3. In conventional open market operations, central banks usually buy or sell corporate bonds to inject or withdraw liquidity in the banking system

(a) (1)
(b) (2)
(c) (3)

Question 2
Which of the following statements about quantitative easing (QE) is correct?

1. QE usually targets the money multiplier
2. QE is usually activated when the policy rate or short-term interest rate is at a very high level
3. QE involves the central bank buying up large quantities of risky financial assets from non-bank institutions
4. All of the above

(a) (3)
(b) (2) and (3)
(c) All of the above

Question 3

Why are central banks increasingly expected to become "superheroes" helping to lift the economy in a time of crisis?

1. Central banks can act quickly with their rescue package without the need to go through parliament or congress.
2. Central banks can carry out structural economic reforms with the electorate or relevant interest groups' support.
3. After the gold standard's demise, central banks (but not the governments) can print new money in unprecedented amounts to pump into the economy.

    (a) All of the above.
    (b) (1) and (2)
    (c) (1) and (3)

Solutions

Question 1

Solution: Option **b** is correct.

Households keeping cash at home is considered "leakage" from the banking system and hence less usable funds for banks, affecting the money multiplier. Imposing credit quota on banks will restrain banks' ability to extend loans and, therefore, the money multiplier. In OMO, banks usually buy and sell risk-free government securities as their primary purpose is to regulate the liquidity in the banking system.

Question 2

Solution: Option **a** is correct.

QE targets the monetary base and not the money multiplier and usually used when conventional monetary policy tools are no longer sufficient. For example, the policy rate has been lowered to near zero and still unable to stimulate the economy.

Question 3

Solution: Option **c** is correct.

Structural economic reform is the government's economic policy and none of the central bank's business.

Chapter 8

Financial Regulation and Supervision

8.1 Introduction

Financial institutions need to understand financial regulation and supervision. They need to appreciate what regulators expect of them to be better able to formulate and execute their business plans in a sound and safe manner, ensuring regulatory compliance while doing well for their business.

Main Terms

- **Regulation:** Refers to the establishment by regulating specific legally enforceable rules on financial institutions' behavior.
- **Supervision:** Means monitoring and assessment by the regulator of the risk profile, financial strength, governance, risk management and control procedures, regulatory compliance and business conduct of financial institutions, and if necessary, take legal and supervisory actions by the regulator against financial institutions to require them to rectify irregularities or weaknesses.

8.2 Virtuous Cycle between Financial and Economic Development

There is a need to actively develop, regulate and supervise the financial sector to achieve the virtuous cycling of funds between the financial markets and the real economy through savings by the population, investment channeled through the financial markets, and wealth produced by the economy.

Learning Objectives

- Understand the ideal outcome of virtuous cycling of funds.
- Understand what might derail the attainment of this virtuous cycling of funds.

Main Takeaways

Main Points

- The ideal outcome is that the financial markets can collect all the population's savings. The financial system's well-functioning distributes the financial resources optimally to the most productive and most profitable industries in the economy to produce maximum national economic output. With maximum economic output, more wealth is created in income, rent, profit, etc. Increased output increases the population's savings, and such savings can then be recycled into the real economy again. However, this ideal outcome is not automatic. It requires the financial markets to be carefully curated and cultivated and also regulated and supervised at the same time.

Note

Figure 8.1 shows the ideal outcome of the virtuous cycling of funds.

However, such cycling of funds may be derailed, preventing the ideal outcome's attainment. For example:

1. Lack of necessary infrastructure to encourage and collect savings, interest rates are controlled by the government due to financial repression, or investors would have no confidence investing in securities markets due to insider trading, price manipulation, lack of liquidity, etc.
2. Banks do not serve SMEs well and lack other means or channels such as private equity and venture capital firms, micro-finance firms, etc., to meet SMEs' financing needs.
3. Financial derivatives not well developed to help businesses to manage financial risks which affect their investment plans
4. Banks over-lend to some sectors, e.g., real estate in certain China cities, resulting in excess capacity, or banks don't lend to infrastructure

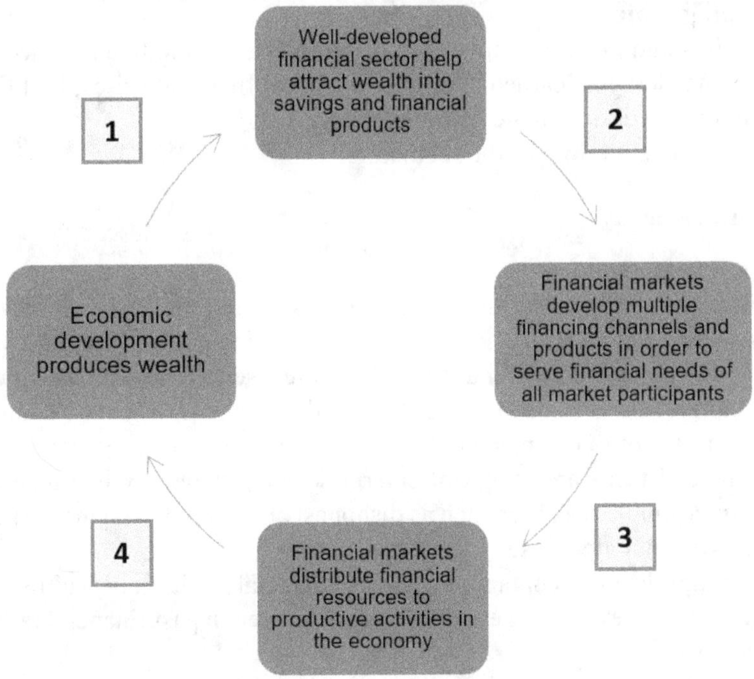

Figure 8.1: Virtuous cycling of funds between financial markets and the real economy.

projects, productive industries, or creative sectors. These borrowers lack acceptable collateral.

Therefore, there is a need to actively cultivate and develop and regulate and supervise the financial sector to help achieve the virtuous cycling of funds.

8.3 Why Supervise and Regulate Financial Markets

8.3.1 *The Need for Regulation*

Some potential issues and problems require regulatory intervention within the financial markets, such as information asymmetry, undesirable behavior of financial intermediaries, and concerns about financial markets' stability to ensure financial markets and financial intermediaries' well-functioning.

Learning Objectives

- Understand the importance and vulnerabilities of the financial sector.
- Discuss lessons learned from the historical financial crises, highlighting the need to regulate financial markets.
- Appreciate the role of the regulators.

Main Takeaways

Main Points

- Finance is the core of the modern economy, but the financial services industry is inherently unstable. Financial institutions' activities are closely connected and intertwined, giving rise to potentially high contagion levels. It is also vital for the regulator to ensure healthy competition to benefit customers and avoid concentration risk.
- Financial firms are for-profit enterprises, and they may be vulnerable to undesirable behavior such as dishonesty and greed. And the financial markets may not be self-correcting.
- The high level of contagion between financial institutions had resulted in vast and devastating economic costs, as seen in past financial failures and crises.
- The role of the financial regulator, through regulation and supervision, is to ensure smooth functioning of financial markets and to prevent and mitigate costs of financial crises.

Apart from information asymmetry and potential undesirable behavior of financial intermediaries, the following are some crucial reasons why financial services as an industry need to be closely regulated and supervised:

1. Finance is at the core of the modern economy. It provides "blood circulation" to ensure the productive industries' well-functioning. It has an impact on almost every part of the economy and society.
2. The financial services industry is inherently unstable because:
   (a) The nature of financial intermediaries such as banks, having substantial short-term liability in deposits, gives rise to high leverage and liquidity risk due to maturity mismatch in deposits and loans.
   (b) Financial intermediaries such as banks take on and house various financial risks from their customers, such as risk in interest rate, exchange rate, commodity prices, etc.

(c) The globalized trading environment and technological advances mean financial assets are being traded "round the clock," and their prices can be affected by developments globally, and hence more volatile than other investments.
(d) Financial firms bear the risk of each other because of inter-bank funding and trading activities, and as a result, the failure of one firm can affect the viability of other firms.
(e) Financial innovation such as risk transfer instruments and asset securitization techniques bring financial firms and financial sectors such as banking, insurance, and securities closer together. Being closer together amplifies the contagion risk, especially in a liberalized and open market environment.

The financial services industry is also prone to monopoly due to the high entry barrier, huge investment required, and the tendency for economies of scale, so there is a need to regulate the industry to ensure a level playing field for healthy competition. Healthy competition benefits customers and reduces concentration risk, which is good for financial stability.

(a) Financial Crisis

A financial crisis happens when financial markets face severe stress or collapse, resulting in malfunctioning critical functions. These functions include the settlement and payment system, resource allocation, and market pricing of financial products and services, which brings about a severe negative impact on the real economy.

Past financial crises have resulted in vast and devastating economic costs. Figure 8.2 shows the history of the financial crises, Figure 8.3 shows the costliest financial crises from 1970 to 2012, and Figure 8.4 shows the past unemployment cycles arising from banking crises.

The Global Financial Crisis in 2008 has given greater credence to the idea that active state involvement in the financial sector can help maintain economic stability, drive growth, and create jobs. Even the crisis subsides, the state has a vital role, especially in providing supervision, ensuring healthy competition, and strengthening financial infrastructure. One of the crisis lessons is the importance of robust, timely, and anticipatory supervisory action, complemented with market discipline and necessary to address distorted competition, improve the flow of information, and strengthen the contractual environment.

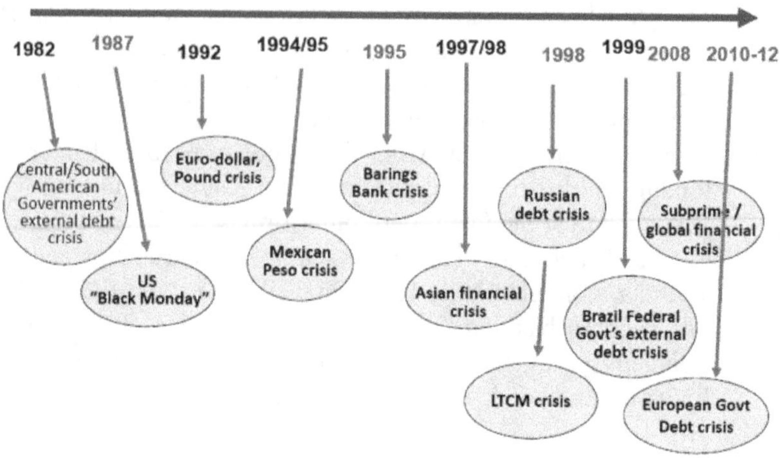

Figure 8.2: History of financial crises.

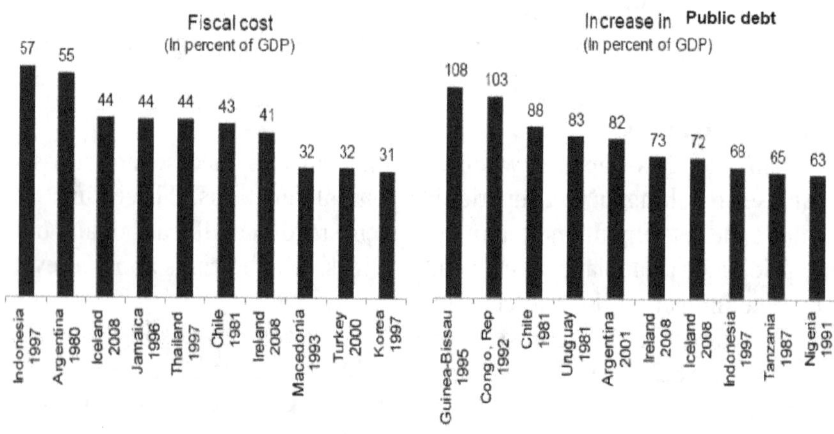

Figure 8.3: Costliest banking crises since 1970 (to 2012).

Source: Laeven, L. & Valencia, F. (June 2012). *Systemic Banking Crises Database: An Update*. IMF.

References/Further Readings

Global Financial Development Report 2013 (5 September 2012) Rethinking the Role of the State in Finance, World Bank Series. Retrieved from https://books.google.com.sg/books/about/Global_Financial_Development_Report_2013.html?id=zmTv7BofRbMC&printsec=frontcover&source=kp_read_button&redir_esc=y#v=onepage&q&f=false.

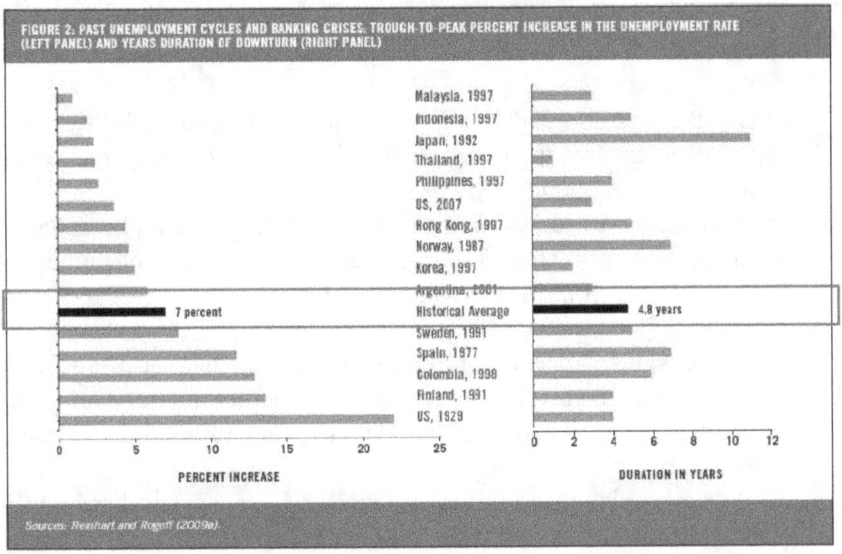

Figure 8.4: Past unemployment cycles and banking crises: Trough-to-peak percent increase in unemployment rate and duration.

Source: Reinhart, C.M. (December 2009). *The Economic and Fiscal Consequences of Financial Crises*. World Bank Institute, Development Outreach.

8.4 Objectives of Financial Supervision

Based on different objectives, there are broadly three types of financial supervision: macro-prudential, micro-prudential, and market conduct supervision.

Learning Objectives

- Understand the objectives of financial supervision and look at Singapore as an example.

Main Takeaways

Main Points

- There are three types of financial supervision: macro-prudential, micro-prudential, and market conduct supervision, which focuses on financial stability, high prudential standards of financial firms, and sound conduct-of-business financial markets and financial firms, respectively.
- In Singapore, these objectives are related to and reinforcing each other.

The three types of financial supervision with their respective objectives:

1. Macro-Prudential Supervision to achieve financial stability. Such supervision ensures the entire financial system's smooth functioning contributes to economic growth.
2. Micro-Prudential Supervision to achieve high prudential standards. Such supervision is to ensure the safety and soundness of individual financial firms to protect the interest of customers, e.g., depositors, policyholders, and investors.
3. Market Conduct Supervision to achieve sound conduct-of-business. Such supervision ensures market integrity, market intermediaries and companies' ethical conduct, fair dealing, and providing consumer protection.

   For example, ensuring that the market is transparent has an efficient price discovery, no price manipulation, and no front-running. Further supervision ensures that intermediaries conduct business professionally, disclose product information thoroughly, and "sell suitable products to suitable customers," etc.

In Singapore, the objectives of financial supervision are:

1. A stable financial system;
2. Safe and sound financial intermediaries;
3. Safe and efficient financial infrastructure;
4. Fair, efficient, and transparent organized markets;
5. Transparent and fair-dealing intermediaries and offerors;
6. Well-informed and empowered consumers.

Objectives 1 and 3 contribute mainly to financial stability. Objective 2 is a result of maintaining high prudential standards of financial firms. Objectives 4, 5, and 6 contribute to sound conduct-of-business by financial markets and market intermediaries. These objectives are related to and reinforce each other. Lastly, sound financial intermediaries help promote the ultimate goal of financial stability.

References/Further Readings

The Monetary Authority of Singapore (September 2015). *Objectives and Principles of Financial Sector Oversight in Singapore.*

8.5 Financial Supervision and Financial Development

Financial markets need to be supervised and regulated. Still, we need to maintain the right balance between self-discipline and self-regulating the markets and regulation and supervision by regulatory agencies.

Learning Objectives

- State the pros and cons of regulations.
- Learn from financial history balancing between financial development and financial supervision and regulation.

Main Takeaways

Main Points

- We learn earlier that financial markets need to be regulated and supervised. But, as with everything, regulation has pros and cons. It is therefore essential to balance financial regulation and development.
- The Basel Capital Accord II sets out the three pillars for sharing supervisory responsibility for banks, namely sound regulation, good corporate governance of banks, and appropriate market discipline.
- We learn from financial history that balancing between financial development and financial regulation and supervision is like a "Regulatory Pendulum"; it has been a continuous process in seeking a dynamic balance between the two.

Main pros and cons of regulations:

<u>Pros</u>

1. Help ensure a level-playing field to promote healthy competition.
2. Maintain minimum prudential standards.
3. Promote market orderliness.
4. Instill confidence in the market

<u>Cons</u>

1. Tend to stifle creativity and innovation.
2. Can become too much red tape which increases compliance cost.
3. Tend to be "one size fits all" which does not consider individual circumstances, hence less flexible.
4. Regulation creates moral hazard and rent-seeking.

Basel Capital Accord II advocates three pillars in sharing supervisory responsibility for banks. The need for sharing is because the regulator cannot and should not micro-manage the banks. Instead, they can leverage other stakeholders to achieve supervisory objectives. While sound regulation is essential, appropriate market discipline and incentive and good corporate governance (self-regulation) of banks, when used in combination with the right measure, can produce better outcomes than sole reliance on regulation alone.

Financial regulation has evolved over the years, from the time before the 1930s to the present.

Before the 1930s ("Free Banking"): Consistent with the then prevailing free economic system, financial markets were not supervised in most countries. Central banks focused mostly on managing the money supply.

1930–1970 ("Financial Repression"): The Great Depression with the stock market crash of 1929 and thousands of banks and market failures in the US allowed Keynes economics to become prevalent and form mainstream economic theory. With advocates of "Market Failure Theory," the state pushed for heavy control and interference over the financial markets. Banks were subject to prescriptive, one-size-fits-all rules, including interest rate controls in many countries, such as the 1933 Glass-Steagall Act in the US.

1970–1990 ("Financial Deregulation"): The previous era's financial repression led to inefficiency, sub-optimal capital allocation, and discouraged creativity by financial institutions because government interference stifled market innovation and development. During this period, there was more deregulation, and financial institutions were subject to fewer rules. For example, the Gramm-Leach-Bliley Act (Financial Services Modernization Act) in 1999 was passed to repeal the US's Glass-Steagall Act. The repeal allowed markets to innovate; hence financial derivatives flourished.

1990–2000 ("Financial Reform"): During the Savings and Loan Crisis, many banks failed in the US, and financial crises also happened in Nordic countries, Mexico, Brazil, and Asia, resulting from too much deregulation. Authorities saw the need to focus on systemic and contagion risks. Emphasis shifted to balancing the needs between safety/stability and efficiency, and macro-prudential surveillance was introduced in many countries.

2001–2009 ("Complacency and Hubris"): Improvements of the previous decade were thought to have contributed to benign conditions, resulting in complacency and hubris. Few, especially the Western economies, were prepared for the 2008 financial crisis.

2010–Current ("Financial Reform"): The 2008 financial crisis exposed the over-confidence of authorities on market discipline and the self-correcting financial markets' ability, resulting in unrestrained credit expansion and financial institutions' leverage. The "Volker Rule" effectively reinstated The Glass-Steagall Act's elements in the US. The "Volker Rule" prohibits commercial banks from proprietary trading and investing in hedge funds and private equity. It also enhanced prudential supervision for securities firms. Basel Capital Accord III was also introduced, which requires banks to have higher and better quality capital, higher liquidity, including for off-balance sheet exposures, and control of leverage. However, through Treasury Secretary Mnuchin, President Trump had reversed many reforms.

The above financial history demonstrates that it is not easy to balance financial regulation and development. It is more of a continuous process in seeking a dynamic balance between the two, like a "Regulatory Pendulum." The key is to calibrate policies carefully and get the right balance. Where possible, adjust policies in time, avoid drastic policy changes to maintain consistency in regulatory objectives and principles, and reduce "policy risk" to the industry.

8.6 Why Do Banks Hold Capital and Basel Accords

8.6.1 *Why Do Banks Hold Capital?*

Holding adequate capital is essential to banks for various reasons, including buffer for unexpected losses, protecting creditors and depositors, and disincentivizing excessive risk-taking by banks.

Learning Objectives

- Learn the reasons why banks hold capital.
- Understand the trade-off between holding high and low amounts of capital, i.e., balancing the needs for profitability and solvency.

Main Takeaways

Main Points

- Banks hold capital for various reasons, including buffer for unexpected losses, protecting creditors and depositors when unexpected losses occur, and disincentivizing excessive risk-taking by banks.
- A bank's capital base is the concern of all stakeholders, including bankers, shareholders, depositors, creditors, and regulators.
- Delicate capital management is essential because there is tension between holding less capital to show profitability and holding more capital for solvency or efficiency and safety.

Main Terms

- **Credit risk:** risk of loss arising from the failure of an obligor, e.g., borrower, the issuer, or trading counterparty, to perform according to the terms and conditions of his contract or agreement with the bank, as well as a loss in value of the institution's assets due to deterioration in the credit quality of the obligor.
- **Market risk:** the adverse effect on asset value due to adverse movements in the level and volatility of the market rates or prices, e.g., interest rates, exchange rates, equity prices, commodity prices, credit spreads, etc., of underlying assets.
- **Operational risk:** risk of loss arising from complex operations, inadequate internal controls, processes and information systems, organizational changes, fraud or human errors or negligence, or unforeseen catastrophes, including terrorist attacks and natural disasters. According to the Basel Committee on Banking Supervision (BCBS), it includes legal but excludes reputational, strategic, and business risks.

Banks hold capital for a variety of reasons:

- Acts as a buffer against "unexpected" losses.
- Protects creditors and depositors in the event a bank nonetheless fails.

- Creates a disincentive to excessive risk-taking by bank owners and managers as equity capital is an expensive source of capital.
- A well-capitalized bank can take advantage of growth opportunities such as supply credit to consumers and businesses and fund investment opportunities during an economic boom.

The BCBS approach assumes that reserves and provisions held on the bank's balance sheet should adequately cover and compensate for "expected" loss caused by normal operating conditions. Capital should primarily cover the "unexpected" portion of the loss distribution.

There is a need to recognize a divergence of views among various bank stakeholders, such as management, shareholders, regulators, depositors, and creditors, regarding the desired capital level. For example, if financial assets are impaired, the bank's capital (i.e., shareholders) takes the first hit, whereas creditors and depositors will be impacted after the bank's capital is exhausted. Hence, it is understandable that creditors and depositors would prefer the bank to have as much capital as possible.

The capital of banks, mainly in the form of common equity as required by Basel Accords, is more expensive than liabilities. When there is too much capital, banks face a higher cost of funds, affecting competitiveness, and bank management may find it challenging to produce good operating results. There is a greater risk of insolvency when there is too little capital, affecting public confidence in the bank's financial strength, hence threatening the bank's interest and depositors. The need for banks' financial stability is why regulators need to step in to prescribe a minimum level of capital for banks.

Therefore, capital management is vital as there is tension between profitability and solvency, or banks' efficiency and safety.

8.6.2 *Key Milestones of Basel Accords*

Basel Accords prescribe minimum regulatory capital requirement as global standards for banks to absorb potential unexpected losses so that banks can continue to operate as a going concern to contribute to the economy and the interest of depositors is protected.

Learning Objectives

- Understand the key development milestones of Basel Accords.

Main Takeaways

Main Points

- Basel I, Basel I Plus, and Basel II together prescribed minimum regulatory capital requirement for banks on their credit, market, and operational risks.
- The Global Financial Crisis exposed banks' significant weaknesses, and Basel III is meant to strengthen banks' capital and liquidity position further and limit the banks' leverage. There are also more stringent capital and other requirements on G-SIBs (Global Systemically Important Banks).
- Basel III also introduced the requirements of (a) Capital Conservation Buffer to ensure that banks have an additional layer of usable capital that can be drawn down when losses are incurred, and (b) Countercyclical Capital Buffer to address systemic risks.

Main Terms

- **Basel accords:** To date, there are a series of three global banking regulations (Basel I, II, and III) set by the BCBS. The committee provides recommendations on banking regulations, particularly on banks' regulatory capital requirements, to ensure banks have sufficient capital to absorb unexpected losses.

Figure 8.5 shows an overview of milestones of Basel Accords.

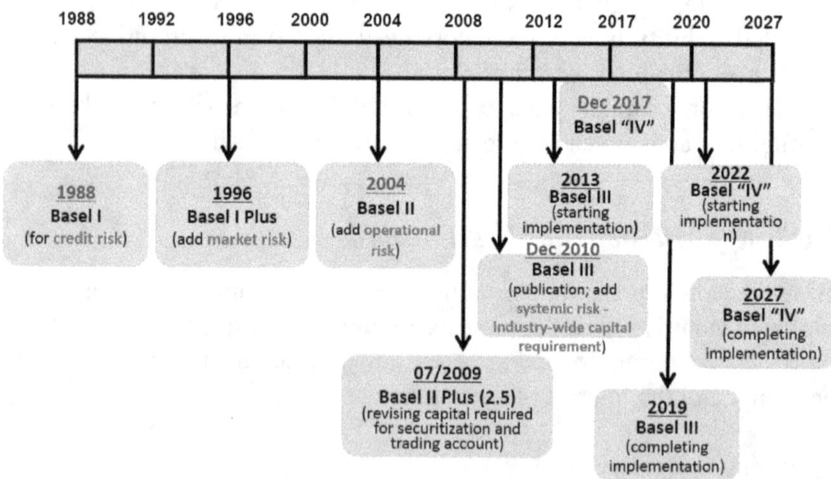

Figure 8.5: Overview of milestones of Basel Accords.

As explained earlier, regulators need to step in to prescribe a minimum capital level for banks and encourage banks to maintain an adequate capital level commensurate with the banks' risk profile and risk management capabilities. So, BCBS has to date published Basel Accord I, II, and III for this purpose. These are guidelines, but member countries are expected to implement them.

If a bank takes on more risks, the regulator must require the bank to hold more capital (hence known as regulatory capital) to absorb the potentially more unexpected losses. To date, Basel Accords has prescribed minimum regulatory capital requirements for banks on their credit, market, and operational risks in Basel Accord I & II. There is also a regulatory capital requirement on systemic risk in Basel Accord III.

(a) A Brief Overview of Basel I and Basel II

Basel I, published in 1988, sets minimum capital adequacy ratio (CAR) of capital to risk-weighted assets (not accounting assets), both on and off banks' balance sheets, of 8%, and it covers only credit risk

Basel I Plus, published in 1996, sets a capital requirement for market risks arising from banks' exposures to foreign exchange, traded debt securities, equities, commodities, and options.

Basel II, published in 2004, improves credit risk sensitivity, sets a capital requirement for operational risk, and introduces the concept of "three pillars" where it emphasizes banks' supervision as the shared responsibility of regulators, banks themselves, and market discipline.

(b) A Brief Overview of Basel III and "Basel IV"

The Global Financial Crisis exposed some significant weaknesses of banks. Briefly, banks (a) held too little capital of sufficient quality during economic downturns, (b) had excessive leverage, and (c) had insufficient liquidity buffers to withstand stress scenarios

Basel III, published in 2010, is meant to further strengthen banks' capital and liquidity and limit their leverage. There are also more stringent capital and other requirements on G-SIBs (Global Systemically Important Banks).

Key recommendations of Basel III:

1. **Capital conservation buffer:** An additional layer of 2.5% of common equity which provides a capital cushion that can be drawn down

during periods of stress without violating minimum CAR. If the buffer is breached, the bank will be restricted from paying out earnings to help it protect and rebuild the buffer.

2. **Countercyclical capital buffer:** The additional capital requirement of 0%–2.5% of common equity during periods of system-wide credit booms to rein in excessive credit expansion by banks to reduce losses in credit busts during an economic downturn.
3. **Leverage ratio:** A minimum amount of loss-absorbing capital of 3% relative to total bank's assets, including off-balance sheet exposures (should generally follow accounting measure) regardless of risk-weighting.
4. **Liquidity requirements:** A minimum liquidity ratio to provide enough cash to cover funding needs over 30 days of stress and a longer-term ratio to address maturity mismatches over the entire balance sheet.

Basel III and Financial Stability Board (FSB), an international body that monitors and makes recommendations about the global *financial* system. They also made the following recommendations on banks whose failure would threaten the entire global banking system, also known as Global Systemically Important Banks (G-SIBs).

1. Additional loss absorption capacity, ranging from 1% to 3.5% of risk-weighted assets (in addition to Basel III requirement) corresponding to their default's systemic impact, to be met with common equity.
2. More intensive and effective supervision of all G-SIBs, including more robust supervisory mandates, resources and powers, and higher supervisory expectations for risk management functions, data aggregation capabilities, risk governance, and internal controls.
3. Requirements for recovery and resolution planning for G-SIBs, and development of institution-specific cross-border cooperation agreements. Home and host authorities of G-SIBs are better prepared for dealing with crises and have clarity on how to cooperate in a situation.

In December 2017, BCBS announced revisions to the Basel III framework (or commonly dubbed by industry as "Basel IV"), intending to bring more consistency in using internal models among banks. We note that under Basel II, subject to regulator's approval, banks are allowed to use their internal models to calculate regulatory capital:

- To restore credibility in the calculation and reduce the variability of risk-weighted assets as observed in banks from different regions.
- To improve the comparability of banks' capital ratios by aligning and harmonizing the applications of approaches across regions and countries.

References/Further Readings

"Basel III: An International Regulatory Framework for Banks." Retrieved from https://www.bis.org/bcbs/basel3.htm#:~:text=Basel%20III%20is%20an%20internationally,and%20risk%20management%20of%20banks.

FSB (4 November 2011). Policy Measures to Address Systemically Important Financial Institutions.

BCBS (December 2017). High-Level Summary of Basel III Reforms.

8.7 Sample Questions

Question 1

Which party's interest will be the first to get affected when a bank's assets are impaired?

(a) Bank shareholders
(b) Bank creditors
(c) Bank depositors

Question 2

Which of the following statements is correct?

(a) A bank should have more and more capital
(b) Basel Accords set rules for the optimal level of capital for banks
(c) A bank's capital level should be commensurate with its risk profile and risk management capabilities.

Question 3
Which of the following statements is correct?

(a) The regulatory capital set by Basel Accords is meant to cover all losses of a bank.
(b) Basel Accords do not concern only with capital requirement.
(c) Basel I set minimum capital adequacy ratio (CAR) of capital to accounting assets, both on and off banks' balance sheets, of 8% for credit risk.

Solutions

Question 1

Solution: Option **a** is correct.

When a bank's assets are impaired, the bank shareholders who own the bank's equity capital take the first hit. The interest of the bank's creditors and depositors will be impacted only after the equity capital is exhausted.

Question 2

Solution: Option **c** is correct.

Banks, mainly in the form of common equity as required by Basel Capital Accords, are more expensive than liabilities.

There is a divergence of views among various bank stakeholders, such as management, shareholders, regulators, depositors, and creditors, regarding the desirable bank capital level. For example, when there is too much capital, banks face a higher cost of funds, affecting competitiveness, and bank management may find it challenging to produce good operating results. There is a greater risk of insolvency when there is too little capital, affecting public confidence in the bank's financial strength, hence threatening the bank's interest and depositors.

As a result, regulators set rules for the minimum (not optimal) level of capital for banks and expect the bank to ensure capital level should be commensurate with the bank's risk profile and risk management capabilities.

Question 3

Solution: Option **b** is correct.

The regulatory capital set by Basel Accords is meant to cover only unexpected losses of a bank. Basel III also concerns with the liquidity and leverage positions of banks. Basel I measures CAR based on risk-weighted assets and not accounting assets.

Section 2: Financial Statement Analysis

Part D: Financial Statement Analysis Foundations

Preliminaries

The objective of financial statement analysis is to understand the trend and relation between key financial statement variables. Specifically, financial statement analysis tools are used to assess a firm's financial health, risks, and prospects to help manage a firm and help potential investors make their investment decisions.

Before using the financial statements' data, one needs to understand how the financial statement is constructed. Part D of this module is devoted to the accounting process mechanics and critical accounting principles underlying financial statements. Part D aims to understand the three financial statements: the Income Statement, the Balance Sheet, and the Statement of Cash Flows.

This module's coverage continues with Part E that discusses financial analysis and evaluation. Part E covers three chapters that discuss financial analysis techniques, quality of financial reporting, and evaluation and applying financial statement analysis. This second part's essential purpose is to provide the professional with a clear understanding of how data is constructed and analyzed. Understanding the foundation for analyzing the data better can be developed and improve data communication between the data source and end-users to be more effective and efficient.

Chapter 9

Understanding Income Statements

9.1 Revenue Recognition

The first thing that a company typically reports in its Income Statement is its revenue. Decisions about measuring and reporting revenue are decisive factors for determining whether financial statements are an accurate representation of a company's financial health. Preparers of financial statements must be equipped with a comprehensive understanding of revenue reporting complexities — a.k.a revenue recognition. It is also essential for readers of the reports to assess if a company's revenue recognition approach delivers an accurate depiction of its cash flows and income.

9.1.1 *Decisions of Revenue Recognition*

Revenue recognition is an accounting principle that identifies the specific conditions in which revenue is recognized and determines how to account for it.

Learning Objectives
- Understand General Principles of Revenue Recognition.

Main Takeaways

Main Points
- The Income Statement reports the company's revenues and expenses, which equals net income (or net loss) for a period.

- The Income Statement provides details of a company's expenses, revenues, gains, and losses that occurred in an accounting period. The fundamental relationship can be expressed as Revenues − Expenses = Net Income.
- A vital accounting principle governing the measurement of elements in the income statement is the accrual basis of accounting.
- There are two fundamental concepts related to accrual accounting: revenue recognition and expense matching.
- Revenue is recognized in the income statement when (a) **Earned** (Earnings process substantially complete) **and** (b) either **Realized or Realizable** (Cash collection reasonably assured).

Main Terms

- **Accrual accounting:** Recognizes the impact of value-producing transactions in the period that they occur, which is not necessarily when the company receives or makes any payments.
- **Revenue:** The expected inflow or inflow of economic resources to a company from the implementation of production, the sale of goods, and services provision.

(a) Revenue Recognition

Typically, the first thing reported in an Income Statement is its revenue. Decisions about measuring and reporting revenue are decisive factors for determining whether financial statements are an accurate representation of a company's financial health. Preparers of financial statements must be equipped with a comprehensive understanding of revenue reporting complexities — a.k.a revenue recognition. It is also essential for readers of these statements to assess if the company's revenue approach delivers an accurate depiction of its cash flow and income.

(b) What is Revenue?

Revenue is the income that a business obtains from its daily business activities, usually from sales of products and services to customers and other profit-generating activities, like fees. Revenue is reported for accounting purposes when a company earns it. It is often used to show the business's revenue in its normal operations. Generally, revenue is not recorded until the income generation is almost complete and close to little uncertainty of collection of the payment due. Revenue is recognized when it is earned or when the work is fulfilled.

(c) Decisions for Revenue Recognition

One of the most critical aspects concerning revenue recognition would be that revenue recognition can happen independently of cash movements. Revenue is recognized in the Income Statement when it is (a) earned and (b) either realized or realizable. For the first condition, revenue is considered earned if the company has carried out its part through its delivery of goods or services. When the company has substantially accomplished what it must do to be entitled to the benefits, the revenue earning process is said to be complete, and thc firm has the right to receive the amount earned.

The second condition relates to the certainty of the amount receivable. Revenue is realized when cash is received. Revenue is realizable if the future economic benefits associated with the assets being created are reasonably certain to be realized, e.g., the future collection of cash from accounts receivable. Judgment is a crucial part of accrual accounting.

Note that there may be measurement errors in some rare cases when determining the amount to be taken up as revenue due to miscellaneous contingent liability that may appear with the revenue. An illustrative case of this is the existence of money-back guarantees or product guarantees where the amount of contingent liability is unable to be correctly approximated. A real-life example of this is installment sales, where the eventual receipt of cash is uncertain.

Similarly, it is also possible to collect cash in advance and later deliver the goods or services. In this scenario, the firm will record a liability for unearned revenue when the money is initially collected. Revenue would be recognized as being earned over time as products and services are delivered. Unearned revenue is recorded as a liability in the balance sheet.

(d) Methods of Revenue Recognition

Revenue is usually recognized at the point of sale or point of delivery, using the revenue recognition criteria given above. There are, however, some instances where revenue is recognized before or after the delivery of goods and services.

- **Sales basis:** Revenue is recognized at the moment of the sales action, either for cash or to creditworthy customers.

In some circumstances, revenue shall not be recognized at the time of sale if there is a substantial amount of uncertainty on the ability to receive the sales price or the remaining costs. In such a scenario, the Installment Method, which recognizes revenues and expenses in proportion to cash collections, or the Completed Contract Method, which recognizes profits only after recovering all costs through cash collections, can be used.

- **Percentage of completion method:** Realizes costs and revenues in proportion to and as work is completed. The approach's application includes long-term contracts, or when reliable estimates of production are completed, cost and revenues are made possible. The determination of progress is based on engineering approximates or the ratio of costs incurred to expected total costs.
- **The completed contract method:** Realizes revenues and expenses only after the contract and is used when terms necessary for applying the Percentage of Completion approach are not feasible.

9.2 Expense Recognition

A company's expenses reflect its cash outflows, the incurrence of liabilities, and depletions of assets generated from a business's activities. Subject to some specific requirements, expenses can be grouped and reported in several different formats.

9.2.1 *Decisions of Expense Recognition*

Expense recognition refers to converting an asset into an expense, usually done when the utility of an asset has been consumed.

Learning Objectives
- Understand the Matching principle of Expense Recognition.

Main Takeaways

Main Points
- Expenses are recognized when incurred and are matched with their corresponding revenues.
- Examples of expenses include product costs, which are naturally linked with revenues (e.g., cost of goods sold, sales commissions), period costs incurred over a specific period (e.g., wages, rent, utilities), etc.

- One of the general principles of expense recognition is the matching process. Expenses can be matched to either to revenue (such as cost of goods sold) or to the time the expenditure occurs (period costs) or to the time of the expected benefits of the expenditures (such as depreciation).

Main Terms

- **Expenses:** The amounts incurred by a firm to generate revenue.
- **The matching principle:** Refers to the accounting practice of recognizing expenses (used to generate revenue) in the same period.
- **Accrual basis accounting:** An accounting method in which income will not be recorded until received and expenses will not be recorded until incurred.

(a) What is an Expense?

Following the IASB Conceptual Framework, expenses are "decreased" in economic benefits during the accounting period in the form of outflows, depletions of assets, and incurrences of liabilities generated from the activities of a business. Technically, an expense refers to an event in which an asset is used up, or a liability is incurred. In terms of the accounting equation, expenses deduct the owners' equity. Subject to some specific requirements, expenses may be grouped and reported in several different interpretations.

(b) General Principals of Expense Recognition

A company recognizes expenses within the same period that it depletes the economic benefits joined with the expenditure or lost previously recognized economic benefits. The matching principle is one of the general principles of expense recognition. Strictly speaking, instead of naming it "matching principle", IFRS refers to it as a "matching concept" or a methodology of "matching of costs with revenues".

A business recognizes certain expenses (e.g., cost of goods sold) under the matching principle rule each time the associated revenues are recognized and after that matching the expenses and revenues. Matching requires an organization to recognize the cost of goods sold in the same period as the revenues from the goods' sale.

Period costs are outgoings that match revenue less straightforwardly. Period costs are also reflected in the period in which the business has the expenditure or an increment of a liability.

The matching principle means that operating performance can only be measured when the related revenues and expenses are accounted for in the same period ("let the expense follow the revenues"). Expenses are recognized when the work (service) or the product contributes to revenue instead of when wages are paid when the work is performed or when a product is produced. Therefore, expense recognition is correlated to revenue recognition.

When the revenues are recognized, expenses incurred to generate revenues need to be matched to those revenues.

If revenues are recognized in the present period, the joint expenses should be recognized in the same period and reported in the income statement.

If revenues are expected to be recognized in the future, the associated expenses are capitalized (reported in the present period's balance sheet as an asset). When the revenues are recognized in future periods, the asset will be converted to an expense.

For costs that are not directly linked to revenues, accountants must develop a "rational and systematic" allocation approach similar to the matching principle. However, when these costs may not have future benefits, matching allows some costs to be deferred and reported as assets on the balance sheet. This new principle authorizes the balance sheet to become a "dumping ground" for unmatched costs if abused.

(c) Financial Analysis Implications

In expense recognition, a company's reported income can be affected by choice of method (i.e., the depreciation method and the inventory method) as well as estimates (i.e., uncollectible accounts, warranty expenses, assets' useful life, and salvage value). An analyst should recognize the differences in companies' expense-recognition methods and adjust reported financial statements if possible to facilitate comparability. Suppose the available information does not permit adjustment. In that case, an analyst can characterize the policies and estimates as more or less conservative and, therefore, qualitatively assess how financial ratios and judgments about companies' performances can be affected by different policies.

9.3 Income Statement Elements

The income statement, or profit and loss statement (P&L), gives information about a company's revenue, expenses, and net income over a period.

Learning Objectives

- Describe the elements of the income statement.

Main Takeaways

Main Points

- Companies usually report net income at the bottom of the income statement.
- The businesses consolidate subsidiaries over which they have control. Each company presents additional items below net income: information about the proportion of the net income attributed to the company itself and the proportion attributable to non-controlling interests, also known as minority interests.
- Gains and losses, which are increases and decreases in economic benefit, are also included in net income. They may or may not emerge in the ordinary activities of a business.
- Apart from presenting net income, income statements also depict items, including subtotals, which are essential to users of financial statements. For example, the cost of goods sold, operating expenses (research and development, marketing and advertising, depreciation, other operating expenses), interest expenses, income taxes, etc.

Main Terms

- **Gains:** Inflows of assets that are not associated with the business's ordinary activities directly.
- **Losses:** Outflow of assets that are not associated with the business's ordinary activities directly.
- **Consolidation:** Means that all the subsidiaries' expenses and revenue are included, even if they own less than 100%.
- **Net income (loss) attributable to non-controlling interest:** Refers to the proportion of income attributable to the minority shareholders of the consolidated subsidiaries, as opposed to the parent company itself.

9.3.1 *Income Statement*

An enterprise's income statement is a financial statement used to analyze the historical financial performance, predict future performance, and assess its ability to generate future cash flows. The income statement is also known as the profit and loss statement (P&L), statement of operations, or statement of earnings.

Following both US GAAP and IFRS, the income statement can be presented as a separate statement followed with the statement of comprehensive income, which starts with profit or loss from the income statement, or otherwise as a segment of a single statement of comprehensive income.

9.3.2 *Elements of Income Statement*

IFRS requests for various items, such as revenue, finance costs, and tax expense, to be separately shown in the income statement. IFRS also requires that line items, headings, and subtotals pertinent to understanding a business's financial performance to be spelled out even if not specified.

However, there is flexibility for companies to present the income statement in different ways. Therefore, the reader of the statements must justify information on reporting matters such as the order of years, how the expense items are grouped and reported, and the meaning of parenthesized items presented in parenthesis.

As an illustration, Table 9.1 shows a consolidated income statement for company ABC.

Table 9.1: Company ABC consolidated income statement (Reported in millions of SGD).

	Year ended 31 December	
	2019	2018
Net revenue	12,345	9,629
Cost of goods sold	(7,345)	(5,729)
Gross profit	5,000	3,900
Selling, general and administrative expenses	(1,345)	(1,049)
Other revenue (expense)	2,100	1,638
Operating profit	5,755	4,489
Interest revenue	1,178	919
Interest expense	(1,056)	(824)
Earnings before tax	5,877	4,584
Income tax	(1,918)	(1,496)
Income from fully consolidated companies	3,959	3,088
Share of profits from associated companies	1,200	936
Net income	5,159	4,024
Attributable to the group	3,869	3,018
Attributable to minority interests	1,290	1,006

Table 9.1, one can observe that there are multiple components to be found in an income statement. Which include:

- **Revenue:** Refers to the company's sales or turnover commonly presented on the first line of any income statement. The terminology' net revenue' is typically used after revenue is reported for any adjustments on cash or volume discounts.
- **Expenses:** Refers to the outflows, depletion of assets, and incurrences of liabilities generated from normal activities. Subject to different requirements, expenses can be sorted by their function or nature and presented in various formats. For instance, some companies may want to show a specific expense as a separate line item, when others may sum that same expense with other costs and present the total in a single line item. Businesses can also adopt either one way to show an amount on the income statement, such as how an expense is reflected as a decrease in net income. Companies can also choose to present expenses, such as the cost of goods sold or selling expenses, in parenthesis, which helps indicate that these are subtracted from revenue and will decrease net income explicitly. In contrast, other companies may not use parenthesis but assume that the reader understands that the item is an expense that will ultimately have to be subtracted before tabulating net income.

The amount of revenue available after deducting the costs of delivering goods or services is called the gross profit. Instead of a single-step format, an income statement that shows a gross profit subtotal uses a multi-step format. One will deduct other expenses associated with a firm's operation after gross profit.

Operating profit is often introduced to as the Earnings Before Interest and Taxes (EBIT), derived by gross profit less operating expenses such as selling, general, and administrative expenses. The EBIT reflects a business's earnings from its normal business activities before making deductions for taxes or interest expense (in the case of non-financial companies). One exception will be financial companies, which include interest expense in their operating expenses and, therefore, deducted before deriving operating profit.

Net income is commonly referred to as "net earnings" or "profit or loss." It is presented at the lower section of the income statement and can also be cited as the "bottom line" for the same reason. Usually, net income is the most critical number in the income statement as it provides a picture of a business's performance over a period.

Information on the proportion of net income attributable to a company or minority interests or non-controlling interests is typically reported below net income.

When a firm presents the income statement in a consolidated format, the information on all subsidiaries over which it has control over will be consolidated. The consolidated form means that its subsidiaries' revenues and expenses will all be included even when the company owns less than 100%.

Net income can also include "gains" and "losses", which refer to the increases and decreases in economic benefits, respectively.

Effectively, net income is derived by (i) revenue less expenses in the normal activities of a business, summed with (ii) other income less other expenses, and (iii) gains less any losses.

References/Further Readings

Robinson, T., Henry, E., Pirie, W., Broihahn, M., & Cope, A. (2015). *International Financial Statement Analysis*, 3rd edn. Wiley, Chap. 4.

Subramanyam, K. R. (2014). *Financial Statement Analysis*, 11th edn. McGraw Hill, Chap. 1 and 2.

9.4 Earnings Per Share Computations

9.4.1 *Basic and Diluted Earnings Per Share*

Earnings per share (EPS) and diluted EPS are profitability measures used in the fundamental analysis of companies.

Learning Objectives

- Describe how EPS are calculated.
- Calculate and interpret a company's EPS (both basic and diluted EPS).

Main Takeaways

Main Points

- Basic EPS is the amount of income available to common shareholders (i.e., net income minus preferred dividends) divided by the weighted average number of common shares outstanding over a period.

- The difference between complex and simple capital structure is relevant to deriving EPS since financial securities that are potentially convertible into common stock can potentially dilute (i.e., decrease) EPS due to conversion or exercise.

Main Terms

- **Complex capital structure:** A firm is said to own a complex capital structure when it issues any financial instruments that are potentially convertible into common stock. Some financial instruments that are potentially convertible into common stock include convertible bonds, convertible preferred stock, employee stock options, and warrants.
- **Simple capital structure:** A company is said to have a simple capital structure if its capital structure does not comprise potentially convertible financial instruments.
- **Basic EPS:** refers to the net earnings available to common shareholders (i.e., net income minus preferred dividends) divided by the weighted average number of common shares outstanding.
- **Diluted EPS:** Refers to the EPS when all dilutive securities are converted into common shares.
- **Diluted shares:** The number of outstanding shares when all potentially dilutive claims on common shares (e.g., convertible debt, convertible preferred stock, and employee stock options) have been exercised.
- **If-converted method:** An accounting method to determine the effect of convertible securities on EPS *if* the convertible securities had been converted at the beginning of the period, taking into account the impact of the conversion on net income and the weighted average number of shares outstanding.
- **Treasury stock method:** An accounting method to determine the effect of options (and warrants) on EPS that specifies what EPS would have been *if* the options and warrants had been exercised and the company had used the proceeds to repurchase common stock.

(a) EPS and Capital Structure

Presenting a firm's EPS on the income statement for net profit or loss (net income) and profit or loss (income) from continuing operations is a requirement from both the IFRS and US GAAP. However, the calculation of EPS depends on the company's capital structure.

An analyst should distinguish between a simple and a complex capital structure. A simple capital structure has only common stock, non-convertible debt, and non-convertible preferred stock. It does not have any potentially dilutive securities. A complex capital structure contains potentially dilutive securities such as options, warrants, or convertible securities. These are known as "dilutive" securities because they will potentially decrease EPS when they are exercised or converted to common stock.

Firms with simple capital structures report the basic EPS solely. All firms with complex capital structures must report both basic and diluted EPS. The expressions are as follows:

$$\text{Basic EPS} = \frac{\text{Net income} - \text{Preferred dividends}}{\text{Weighted average number of shares outstanding}}$$

$$\text{Diluted EPS} = \frac{\text{Net income} + \text{After tax interest on convertible debt} - \text{Preferred dividends}}{(\text{Weighted average number of shares outstanding} + \text{Additional common shares that would have been issued at conversion})}$$

The basic EPS is derived by using reported earnings available to the parent company's common shareholders divided by the weighted average number of outstanding shares. The amount of earnings made available to common shareholders is equal to net income minus off preferred dividends (if any) that have been paid. The weighted average number of shares outstanding is a time weighting of outstanding common shares.

On the other hand, a diluted EPS refers to the EPS derived if all dilutive securities are converted. If a business owns a simple capital structure (one that does not hold any potentially dilutive financial securities), its diluted EPS is equivalent to its basic EPS. Conversely, if a business has potentially dilutive financial securities, its diluted EPS may vary from its basic EPS. Diluted EPS, by definition, is always less than or equal to the basic EPS.

Below lists three common types of potentially dilutive financial securities that determine a diluted EPS:

1. Suppose a company has convertible preferred outstanding stock (if-converted method). In that case, the method determines the convertible preferred shares' effect if converted at the start of the period.

Diluted EPS is defined as net income minus preferred dividends divided by the sum of the weighted average number of shares outstanding from the basic EPS calculation and the additional shares of common stock that would be issued at the conversion of the preferred stock.

$$\text{Diluted EPS} = \frac{\text{Net income} - \text{Preferred dividends}}{\begin{array}{c}(\text{Weighted average number of shares outstanding} + \\ \text{New common shares that would have} \\ \text{been issued at conversion})\end{array}}$$

2. When a company has convertible debt outstanding (if-converted approach), diluted EPS is derived, assuming that convertible debt had been converted at the beginning of the period. The debt securities would no longer be outstanding if the convertible debt had been converted; otherwise, additional shares of common stock would be outstanding.

$$\text{Diluted EPS} = \frac{\begin{array}{c}\text{Net income} + \text{After tax interest on convertible} \\ \text{debt} - \text{Preferred dividends}\end{array}}{\begin{array}{c}(\text{Weighted average number of shares outstanding} + \\ \text{Additional common shares that would have} \\ \text{been issued at conversion})\end{array}}$$

3. When a company has stock options, warrants, or any other equivalents (treasury stock approach), the assumed exercise of these financial securities would have the following results for the computation of diluted EPS using this approach:
   - The business is assumed to receive cash upon exercise and issue shares in exchange.
   - The weighted average market price during the period, the business is assumed to utilize the cash proceeds to repurchase shares.

$$\text{Diluted EPS} = \frac{\text{Net income} - \text{Preferred dividends}}{\begin{array}{c}[\text{Weighted average number of shares outstanding} + \\ (\text{New shares that would have been issued at option} \\ \text{exercise} - \text{shares that could have been purchases} \\ \text{with cash received upon exercise}) * (\text{Proportion of year} \\ \text{during which the financial instruments were outstanding})]\end{array}}$$

Specific potentially convertible securities can be anti-dilutive (i.e., their inclusion in the calculation would conclude in an EPS higher than the firm's basic EPS). Due to IFRS and US GAAP regulations, anti-dilutive securities are not included in calculating diluted EPS. The diluted EPS should reflect the maximum potential dilution from conversion or exercise of potentially dilutive financial securities. Also, diluted EPS is always less than or equal to basic EPS.

Changes in the numerator and denominator illustrate the differences in EPS arithmetically. Understanding the business drivers of those changes requires further research. The next section presents analytical tools that an analyst can use to highlight additional examination areas.

References/Further Readings

Subramanyam, K. R. (2014). *Financial Statement Analysis*, 11th edn. McGraw Hill, Chap. 6, pp. 385–389.

9.5 Common Size Statements and Financial Ratios Based on Income Statements

The profitability ratios and the common-size income statement present insights about changes in a firm's performance.

9.5.1 *Common-Size Analysis of the Income Statement*

A common-size income statement refers to an income statement in which each line item of the statement is expressed as a percentage of revenue or sales.

Learning Objectives

- Convert income statements to common-size income statements.

Main Takeaways

Main Points

- The profitability ratios and the common-size income statement present insights about changes in a firm's performance.

- The income statement's common-size analysis can be presented by expressing each line item on the income statement as a percentage of revenue.
- Common-size statements provide a comparison across periods (time series analysis) and between companies (cross-sectional study) since the standardization of each line item offsets the size effect.

Main Terms

- **Common-size analysis:** The restatement of financial statement items using a common denominator or reference item enables one to identify trends and significant differences. One case; will be an income statement in which all items are stated as a percentage of the revenue.

A common-size analysis of the income statement is presented by stating each line item in the income statement as a percentage of revenue. Common-size statements allow the analyst to compare across different periods (time series analysis) and various companies (cross-sectional study) since the standardization of each line item disables the effect of size.

In a common-size statement, all items in the financial statement are displayed as percentages of a common base amount. Regarding an Income Statement, it is typical to select total sales as the common base because sales impact almost all expense categories. Whereas with the Balance Sheet, it is usual to choose total assets as the common base.

Common-size financial statement analysis enables easy analysis across firms or between periods of a given firm. For example, by presenting all of the balance sheet statement amounts as a percentage of total assets for different financial years, an analyst can easily observe changes in accounts within groups of assets and liabilities over time. By recasting different companies' financial statements in the common-size format, an analyst can also compare different companies or compare a firm's common-size accounts with industry averages. An analyst can attribute individual performance items to aspects in the internal management or the operating environment associated with the industry-level analysis. Such analyses can be valuable input in a credit or equity analysis to devise strategies at the industry level.

Using common-size financial statements may help analysts spot trends that are not apparent from reading raw financial statements.

Therefore, analysts can reach some helpful conclusions about attributes of a firm's operating performance, for instance, profitability margins, expense ratios, or a firm's deployment of resources in current and non-current assets over prior reporting periods. Also, the common-size income statement highlights differences in organizations' strategies.

Note that common-size financial statement analysis also provides valuable input to more advanced financial analysis tools such as asset composition analysis and assessing a firm's capital structure's riskiness.

(a) Preparing Common-Size Statements

An example of converting a financial statement to a common-size format is presented below.

Example: Income statement for the year ended 31 December 20XX:

	Year ended 31 December	
	2019	2018
Revenue	560,000	400,000
Cost of goods sold	350,000	240,000
Gross profit	210,000	160,000
Selling, General and Administrative expenses	100,000	89,000
Depreciation expense	80,000	50,000
Other operating expense	6,000	4,500
Operating profit (EBIT)	24,000	16,500
Interest expense	2,000	1,500
Income before tax (EBT)	22,200	15,000
Provision for income tax	6,000	4,000
Income from continuing operations	16,000	11,000
Earnings from discontinued operations, net of tax	1,000	0
Net income	15,000	11,000

To convert this to a common-size format, we first have to determine what common base to use. Per convention, we select total sales as the common base for a common-size Income Statement. Dividing all the items by the top-line total sales revenue, we arrived at:

Example: Common-size Income statement for the year ended 31 December 20XX:

	Year ended 31 December	
	2019	2018
Revenue	100%	100%
Cost of goods sold	63%	60%
Gross profit	38%	40%
Selling, General and Administrative expenses	18%	22%
Depreciation expense	14%	13%
Other operating expense	1%	1%
Operating profit (EBIT)	4.3%	4.1%
Interest expense	0.4%	0.4%
Income before tax (EBT)	4%	4%
Provision for income tax	1%	1%
Income from continuing operations	3%	3%
Earnings from discontinued operations, net of tax	0.2%	0.0%
Net income	2.7%	2.8%

We see from the above example that the firm earned around 2.7 cents per dollar of sales in 2019 and 2.8 cents per dollar of sales in 2018. Note that these figures of 2.7% and 2.8% are, in fact, the net profit margins (i.e., net income/total sales) that are calculated as part of ratio analysis. Accordingly, the analyst can derive useful information on a firm's profitability from its common-size Income Statement.

9.5.2 *Financial Ratios Based on Income Statements*

Financial Ratios can be used to conduct quantitative analysis and assess a company's liquidity, leverage, growth, margins, profitability, rates of return, valuation, etc.

Learning Objectives

- Evaluate a company's financial performance with common-size income statements and financial ratios based on the income statement.

Main Takeaways

Main Points

- Two income-statement-based measures of profitability are gross profit margin and net profit margin.

- Net profit margin is otherwise called profit margin and return on sales. It calculates the amount of income a business can generate for each dollar of revenue.
- The gross profit margin calculates the gross profit that a business generates for each dollar of revenue.

Main Terms

- **Net income:** The difference between revenue and expenses; the amount of cash that remains after subtracting all expenses (including depreciation, interest, and taxes) from revenue.
- **Net profit margin:** Calculated as net income divided by revenue, which indicates a company's profitability. Net profit margin also shows how much of each dollar of revenue is left after all costs and expenses have been deducted, otherwise called profit margin or return on sales.
- **Gross profit:** Calculated as sales minus the cost of sales (i.e., the cost of goods sold for a manufacturing company).
- **Gross profit margin:** refers to the ratio of gross profit to revenue.

Profitability demonstrates a firm's financial performance. Financial ratios and common-size income statements are helpful in determining this profitability and at the same time provide some insights into changes in a business's financial performance.

Many financial ratios can contribute to measuring profitability. The gross profit margin and net profit margin are two examples. They can be found by common-sizing the income statement.

(a) Net Profit Margin

A business's return on sales or net profit margin calculates the amount of income that the business is capable of generating for each dollar of revenue in the form of an equation:

$$\text{Net profit margin} = \frac{\text{Net income}}{\text{Revenue}}$$

A higher net profit margin suggests a higher level of profitability.

(b) Gross Profit Margin

The gross profit margin is another measurement of profitability. It is determined in the following way:

$$\text{Gross profit margin} = \frac{\text{Gross profit}}{\text{Revenue}}$$

Gross profit equals revenue less the cost of goods sold.

As indicated in the equation, the gross profit margin scales a business's gross profit from each dollar of revenue. Likewise, with the net profit margin, a higher gross profit margin suggests a higher profitability level.

References/Further Readings

Robinson, T., Henry, E., Pirie, W., Broihahn, M., & Cope, A. (2015). *International Financial Statement Analysis*, 3rd edn. Wiley, Chap. 4.

Subramanyam, K. R. (2014). *Financial Statement Analysis*, 11th edn. McGraw Hill, Chaps. 1 and 2.

9.6 Sample Questions

Question 1 (Revenue Recognition)
In which of the following scenarios will revenue be recognized?

(a) Xiaomi receives an order from Best Denki for high-definition flat-screen televisions.
(b) Runner's World magazine ships out magazines that subscribers paid for in advance last quarter.
(c) Liverpool sells tickets and receives cash for a soccer game next month.

Question 2 (Revenue Recognition)
The following transactions occurred during July:

1) Received $900 cash for services provided to a customer during July.
2) Issued shares for $2,200 cash.
3) Received $750 from a customer in partial payment of his account receivable, which arose from sales in June.
4) Provided services to a customer on credit, $375.
5) Borrowed $6,000 from the bank by signing a promissory note.
6) Received $1,250 cash from a customer for services planned to be rendered next year.

What was the amount of revenue for July by following revenue recognition principles?

(a) $900.
(b) $1,275.
(c) $2,525.

Question 3 (Expense Recognition)
Select the expense scenario that should be recorded in this period by following the expense recognition principles.

(a) ZARA purchases T-shirts from a vendor with cash.
(b) A major movie production company gives the entire Star Wars cast cash advances for a future movie sequel.
(c) A new employee at Shaw theater has worked an entire month and has not been paid yet.

Question 4 (Income Statement Elements)
Given the ABC company's following information, compute net income including non-controlling interest and net income attributable to the ABC company.

Interest expense	3,000
Sales Revenue	100,000
Rent expense	2,800
Wages expense	80,000
Supplies expense	4,000
Interest income	7,100
Non-controlling interest	1,000

Which of the following is the correct answer?

(a) Net income, including the non-controlling interest, is 17,300 and net income attributable to the ABC company is 16,300.
(b) Net income, including the non-controlling interest, is 10,200 and net income attributable to the ABC company is 9,200.
(c) Net income, including the non-controlling interest, is 20,300 and net income attributable to the ABC company is 19,600.

Question 5 (Basic EPS Calculation)
For the year ended 31 December 2019, the ABC company had a net income of $38,000 thousand. The company declared and paid $2,000 thousands of dividends on preferred stock.

ABC company had 8,000 thousand shares of common stock outstanding on 1 January 2019 and 12,000 thousand shares of common stock outstanding on 31 December 2019. During the year, the company issued 2,000 thousand shares on 1 October 2019.

Which of the following is correct on the company's time-weighted average number of shares outstanding and basic EPS?

(a) The time-weighted average number of shares is 10,000 thousand shares, and basic EPS is $3.6.
(b) The time-weighted average number of shares is 9,000 thousand shares, and basic EPS is $4.
(c) The time-weighted average number of shares is 9,000 thousand shares, and basic EPS is $4.22.

Question 6 (EPS Calculation)
As of 29 November, it appears that Notel will report EPS of $1.15 for the quarter ended November 30. Which of the following events would cause this EPS measure to decrease, assuming the event occurs on the morning of November 30?

(a) The company pays a supplier for inventory bought on account.
(b) The company purchases ten ordinary shares of another company.
(c) The company reissues the treasury shares it holds.

Question 7 (Diluted EPS Calculation)
For the year ended 31 December 2019, the ABC company had a net income of $1,200,000. The company had an average of 500,000 common shares outstanding, 20,000 shares of convertible preferred, and no other potentially dilutive securities. Each share of preferred stock pays a preferred dividend of $2 per share and is convertible into two shares of the companies' common stock.

Which of the following about the company's basic EPS and dilutive EPS is correct?

(a) The Basic EPS is \$2.20, and the diluted EPS is \$2.22.
(b) The Basic EPS is \$2.4, and the diluted EPS is \$2.32.
(c) The Basic EPS is \$2.32, and the diluted EPS is \$ 2.22.

Question 8 (Basic Understanding EPS versus Diluted EPS)
Which of the following statements is not correct?

(a) If a business owns a simple capital structure (in other words, one that includes no potentially dilutive financial instruments), its basic EPS is equivalent to its diluted EPS.
(b) When a business has convertible debt outstanding, diluted EPS is computed as if the convertible debt had been converted at the beginning of the period. The debt securities would no longer be outstanding if the convertible debt had been converted; on the contrary, additional shares of common stock would be outstanding. If such a conversion had taken place, the company would not have paid interest on the convertible debt, so the net income available to common shareholders would increase by the after-tax amount of interest expense on the debt converted.
(c) Diluted EPS is less than basic EPS in all scenarios.

Question 9 (Common Size Income Statement)
Which statement on the common-size income statement is correct?

(a) Common-size statements facilitate comparison across companies (cross-sectional analysis) because each line item's standardization eliminates the sizing effect. Still, it cannot help compare the same company across periods (time series analysis).
(b) A common-size income statement restates each income statement line as a percentage of net income.
(c) An analyst can infer some information from common-size statements to identify its strategies.

Question 10 (Net Profit & Gross Profit)
The ABC company has the following income statement information:

Revenue	100,000
Cost of goods sold	30,000
Other operating expenses	28,000
Interest expense	2,100
Tax expense	1,000

What are the company's gross profit margin and net profit margin?

(a) The company's gross profit margin is 70%, and the net profit margin is 20%.
(b) The company's gross profit margin is 42%, and the net profit margin is 20%.
(c) The company's gross profit margin is 70%, and the net profit margin is 21%.

Solutions

Question 1

Solution: Option **b** is correct.

The two conditions to realize revenue are (1) earned and (2) realized or realizable. Both conditions need to be satisfied before revenue can be recognized. Revenue is recognized when the impact of value-producing transactions in the period occurs, which is not necessarily when the company receives or pays cash. Xiaomi and Liverpool have not performed their services, so the revenue has not been earned. Only Runner's World's revenue has both been earned and realized.

Question 2

Solution: Option **b** is correct.

Recall the conditions for revenue to be recognized, transaction (1) and (4) satisfies both requirements.

1) + Cash 900 + Revenue 900
2) + Cash 2200 + Share Capital 2200
3) + Cash 750 − Accounts Receivables 750
4) + Revenue 375 + Accounts Receivable 375
5) + Cash 6000 + Notes Payable 6000
6) + Cash 1250 + Unearned Revenue 1250

Total will be $900 + $375 = $1275

Question 3

Solution: Option **c** is correct.

The matching principle of expense recognition requires that resources consumed to earn revenues in an accounting period should be recorded in that period, regardless of the cash payment time. ZARA and the major movie production company- cannot realize the revenue yet (the revenue is either not earned or not realizable). Therefore the corresponding expenses can also not be recorded.

Question 4

Solution: Option **a** is correct.

Sales Revenue	100,000
Interest income	7,100
Expenses:	
• Rent expense	2,800
• Wages expense	80,000
• Supplies expense	4,000
• Interest expense	3,000
Net income, including non-controlling interest	**17,300**
Non-controlling interest	1,000
Net income attributable to the ABC company	**16,300**

Question 5

Solution: Option **b** is correct.

The time-weighted average number of shares outstanding is determined by the length of time each amount of shares was outstanding.

Weighted average number of shares outstanding:

8,000∗(9 months/12 months) + 12,000∗(3 months/12 months) = 9,000

Basic EPS = (Net income-Preferred dividends)/time weighted average number of shares = ($38,000 thousands − $2,000 thousands)/9,000 thousands shares = $4.

Question 6

Solution: Option **c** is correct.

Reissuing treasury shares will cause the average ordinary shares outstanding to increase and, as a result, EPS will decrease.

Question 7

Solution: Option **c** is correct.

The diluted EPS is calculated using the if-converted method when a company has convertible preferred stock outstanding. The if-converted method computes what EPS would have been if the convertible preferred securities had been converted at the beginning of the period.

Therefore the number of shares outstanding for diluted EPS calculation equals 540,000 shares (500,000 common shares outstanding + additional shares issued if preferred converted 20,000*2 = 40,000 shares). The number of shares outstanding for basic EPS calculation equals 500,000 common shares.

If such a conversion had taken place, the company would not have paid preferred dividends. Thus, under the if-converted method, the net income available to common shareholders to calculate diluted EPS does not need to subtract the preferred dividends.

Thus, Basic EPS = (Net income − Preferred dividends)/Weighted average number of shares outstanding = ($1,200,000 − $2∗20,000)/500,000 shares = $2.32.

Diluted EPS = (Net income − Preferred dividends)/(Weighted average number of shares outstanding + Additional shares issued if preferred converted) = ($1,200,000-0)/(500,000 shares + 40,000 shares if converted) = $2.22.

Question 8

Solution: Option **c** is correct.

Generally, diluted EPS is equal to or less than Basic EPS, but it's not necessarily true in all cases. For example,

When a company has convertible preferred stock outstanding,

$$\text{Diluted EPS} = \frac{\text{Net income} - \text{Preferred dividends}}{\begin{array}{c}\text{(Weighted average number of shares outstanding +} \\ \text{New common shares that would have} \\ \text{been issued at conversion)}\end{array}}$$

Both the nominator and denominator will increase when calculating diluted EPS. As a result, diluted EPS is not necessarily smaller than Basic EPS.

Question 9

Solution: Option **c** is correct.

Common-size statements facilitate comparison across companies and periods. A common size income statement restates each income statement line as a percentage of revenue.

Question 10

Solution: Option **a** is correct.

The gross profit = Revenue − Cost of goods sold = 100,000 − 30,000 = 70,000.

The gross profit margin = Gross profit/Revenue = 70,000/100,000 = 0.7.

The net profit = Revenue − Expenses = 100,000 − 30,000 − 28,000 − 21,000 − 1,000 = 20,000.

The net profit margin = Net profit/Revenue = 20,000/100,000 = 0.2.

Chapter 10

Understanding Balance Sheets

A balance sheet is a snapshot of a company's cumulative financial position at a particular point in time. It answers the question of "what is the company's financial position at the end of the period?". It is also referred to as Statement of Financial Position or Statement of Financial Condition.

10.1 Uses and Limitations of the Balance Sheet in Financial Analysis

The three limitations to balance sheets are assets being recorded at historical cost, the use of estimates, and the omission of valuable non-monetary assets.

Learning Objectives

- Describe the uses and limitations of the balance sheet in financial analysis.

Main Takeaways

Main Points

- Analysis of a company's balance sheet can provide insight into the economic resources the company controls.
- Differences in accounting methods can limit cross-sectional financial ratio analysis.
- Lack of homogeneity of a company's operating activities can limit comparability. For diversified companies operating in different industries,

using industry-specific ratios for different business lines can provide better comparisons.

- The balance sheet does not reflect those assets that cannot be expressed in monetary terms, such as skill, intelligence, honesty, and workers' loyalty.
- Some of the current assets are valued based on estimation, so the balance sheet cannot reflect the business's true financial position.

Main Terms

- **Carrying value:** Book value or carrying value refers to an asset's value according to its balance sheet account balance in accounting. The value is grounded on the asset's original cost, less any depreciation, amortization, or impairment costs made against the asset.
- **Homogeneity:** Composed of parts or elements that are all of the same kind, not heterogeneous.
- **Cross-sectional:** A type of observational study that analyzes data from a population, or a representative subset, at any point that uses cross-sectional data.

The purpose of the balance sheet is to provide information about the financial status of a business at a specific point in time. The statement shows what an entity owns (assets) and how much it owes (liabilities), as well as the amount invested in the business (equity). The balance sheet can be a helpful tool for users of financial statements. However, it has several limitations.

10.1.1 *Uses of Balance Sheet*

The balance sheet provides information about a company's financial condition at a given point. It offers valuable information about the assets that the company governs alongside how these assets are being financed.

The balance sheet can be a helpful tool for analysts when examining a company's capability to: make payments for its current operating engagements (liquidity position), fulfill future debt obligations, and distributions to stakeholders.

10.1.2 *Shortcomings of Balance Sheet*

The balance sheet elements are measured differently; certain assets and liabilities are reported at historical value, whereas others are reported at current market costs. The measurement method chosen can affect the figures that are recorded.

Items valued at current market cost provide information about the 'current' cost at the end of the fiscal period. However, these values can be significantly different after the balance sheet is prepared.

The balance sheet cannot reflect attributes of a company, such as management skills or reputations.

Finally, the balance sheet does not reflect intangible assets expressed in monetary terms, such as skill, intelligence, honesty, and workers' loyalty.

10.2 Assets, Liabilities, and Equity

The assets, liabilities, and shareholders' equity are the three main components of a balance sheet statement.

Learning Objectives

- Understand the balance sheet's accounting equation and describe the balance sheet elements: assets, liabilities, and equity.

Main Takeaways

Main Points

- The statement of financial position (or commonly known as the balance sheet or statement of financial condition) of an entity reflects information about what it owns (or controls), what it owes, and the stakeholders' claims at a specific point time.
- The balance sheet summarizes a business's assets, liabilities, and shareholders' equity.
- The balance sheet is organized based on this equation; Assets = Liabilities + Owners' Equity.

Main Terms

- **Assets:** Refers to what the company owns (or controls). In a more formal definition, assets are resources controlled by the company due to past events and from which future economic benefits are expected to flow to the entity.
- **Liabilities:** Refers to what the company owes. More formally, liabilities refer to an entity's obligations that arise from past events or the

settlement of which is expected to result in a future outflow of economic benefits.

- **Stockholders' equity:** Represents the residual interest in the firm's net assets (after the liabilities have been provided for).
- **Balance sheet:** Referred to as the "snapshot of a company's financial condition." A standard company balance sheet contains three parts: assets, liabilities, and ownership equity.
- **Inventory:** Includes goods that are ready for sale, raw material, and partially completed products, which will be sold when they are completed.
- **Working capital:** Also known as net working capital (NWC), is the difference between a company's current assets, such as cash, accounts receivable (customers' unpaid bills), and inventories of raw materials and finished goods and its current liabilities, such as accounts payable.

10.2.1 *Elements of the Balance Sheet*

The statement of financial position or statement of financial condition, more commonly referred to as a balance sheet, is a financial statement that reflects information about a corporation's assets, liabilities, and owners' equity, at a point in time. The balance sheet displays information about what a corporation holds and owes and the owners' claims to the corporation's assets.

Assets, liabilities, and equity are the three basic balance sheet elements. Assets are what a corporation holds or controls and from which future economic benefits are expected to flow.

On the other hand, Liabilities refer to everything that the corporation owes. They are obligated to pay an individual or an organization or claim of creditors on the assets.

Owners' equity or shareholders' equity is the owner's residual interest in the firm's assets after deducting the liabilities.

The relationship between the three elements can be expressed as a fundamental accounting equation in the form of Assets = Liabilities + Owners' Equity.

The equation $A = L + E$ can be summarized in the following way: the left side of the equation reflects the company's resources, and the right side reflects how those resources were financed. Assets, liabilities, and owners' equity are as defined above. Contributed capital refers to capital that the firm's owners contributed, and ending retained earnings refers to the end-of-period cumulative earnings retained by the firm.

The accounting equation shows that what a firm owns (its assets) must tally with what a firm owes (its liabilities and equity). A Sample Balance Sheet is shown below: Note from the example above that assets and liabilities are typically separated into current and non-current amounts. Recall that current amounts refer to probable inflows or outflows of economic resources expected to occur within 1 year or the operating cycle (whichever is longer). Non-current amounts refer to potential inflows or outflows of economic resources expected to occur later than 1 year or the operating cycle. A proper terminology you may wish to keep in mind is "working capital," which is the difference between currents assets and current liabilities.

Balance sheet information is as of a specific point in time. These exhibits are from the companies' annual financial statements, so the balance sheet information is the last day of their respective fiscal years. A sample balance sheet is shown in Figure 10.1.

Under current accounting standards, the balance sheet is a mixed model concerning measurement. Certain assets and liabilities in the balance sheet are measured grounded on historical cost, sometimes with adjustments. In contrast, others are measured grounded on a fair value, representing its current value as of the balance sheet date.

The measurement method chosen can affect the figures that are recorded. Even if the items correctly reflect the value at the time of reporting, they are likely to change after the reporting date. Finally, the value of a corporation is a function of many contributing attributes, including future cash flows expected to be generated by the company and current market conditions. Important attributes such as management skills or reputations etc.- will not be included in the balance sheet.

The balance sheet as of 31 December 20XX

Cash	200	Accounts Payable	300
Accounts Receivable	800	Wages Payable	400
Inventory	1000	Accrued Liabilities	500
Current Assets	2000	**Current Liabilities**	1200
Property, plant & equip.	1000	Bonds	1800
net	500	Owners' equity:	
Long-term Investments	500	Common Stock	500
Goodwill, net		Retained Earnings	500
Total Assets	4000	**Total Liabilities & Equity**	4000

Figure 10.1: Sample company balance sheet of the year ended 31 December 20XX.

References/Further Readings

Robinson, T., Henry, E., Pirie, W., Broihahn, M., & Cope, A. (2015). *International Financial Statement Analysis*, 3rd edn. Wiley, Chaps. 5, 9, 10, and 13.

Subramanyam, K. R. (2014). *Financial Statement Analysis*, 11th edn. McGraw Hill, Chaps. 3, 4, and 6.

10.3 Different Types of Assets and Liabilities and Their Measurement Bases

10.3.1 *Historical Cost versus Fair Value Accounting*

On a balance sheet, asset and liability values reported may be estimated based on fair value or historical cost.

Learning Objectives

- Understand the differences between historical cost versus fair value accounting.

Main Takeaways

Main Points

- Historical costs refer to recorded values from actual transactions that have taken place.
- Fair value provides information about an asset's most current economic value (or liability) grounded on market valuation or market-based assumptions.
- The balance sheet under current accounting standards is a mixed model concerning measurement. Some assets and liabilities in the balance sheet are valued at historical cost. In contrast, other assets and liabilities are valued at fair value, representing their current value as of the balance sheet date.

Main Terms

- **Historical cost:** The amount paid to purchase an asset, including any costs of acquisition and preparation regarding assets, and liabilities, the amount of proceeds received in exchange for issuing the liability.
- **Fair value:** The rational and unbiased amount at which an asset could be exchanged, or liability to be settled, between knowledgeable, willing parties in an arms-length transaction is called the fair value. A fair value

is also known as the price that would be received to sell an asset or paid to transfer a liability in an orderly transaction between different parties.

Two methods used to record an asset's price or value are fair value accounting and historical cost accounting. Historical cost estimates the value of the original cost of an asset, whereas fair value estimates the current market value of the asset.

(a) Historical Cost Method

As recorded in an entity's accounting records, historical cost is the original cost of an asset. Many of the transactions recorded in an organization's accounting records are stated at their historical cost. This cost principle clarifies the process, stating that one should record an asset, liability, or equity investment at its original acquisition cost only. One can easily prove historical cost by accessing the source purchase or trade documents. However, the historical cost has the disadvantage of not representing the actual fair value of an asset necessarily, which can likely diverge from its purchase cost over time. Yet, on some occasions, valuing assets at historical cost prevents overstating an asset's value when asset appreciation may result from volatile market conditions.

Though fair value is replacing it for some types of assets, such as marketable investments, historical cost is still a central concept for recording assets. The ongoing replacement of historical cost by a measure of fair value is grounded on the argument that historical cost presents an excessively conservative organizational picture.

(b) Fair Value Method

The practice of measuring assets and liabilities at their current market value is called fair value accounting. The fair value is when the asset could be sold or a liability settled for a fair value to both the buyer and the seller. It's a method that companies use to report their assets and liabilities at the estimated amount of money they would receive if they were to sell the assets or be alleviated of their liabilities. The ideal determination of fair value is grounded on prices offered in an active market, which is one in which there is a sufficiently high volume of transactions to provide ongoing pricing information.

Although both methods are widely adopted by entities when computing their income and financial positions, there is controversy over their superiority. Historical cost accounting quotes assets and liabilities at the initial price they were exchanged for at the transaction time. Fair value accounting reports the prevailing price in the market. Both methods impact financial statements, but the impact of fair value accounting is more extreme because of its potential volatility. Fair value accounting is considered superior since it reflects the market's current situation, whereas the latter is grounded in the past. Moreover, in relative terms, fair value accounting provides users with more recent financial information and visibility.[1]

10.3.2 *Different Types of Assets*

Assets are divided into various categories for accounting, taxation, and measuring an entity's value or financial health.

Learning Objectives

- Describe the different types of assets and their measurement bases.

Main Takeaways

Main Points

- Current Assets refer to probable inflows of economic resources expected to occur within 1 year or the operating cycle (whichever is longer), and non-current assets refer to potential inflows of economic resources expected to occur later than 1 year or the operating cycle.
- Cash and cash equivalents are cash or highly liquid short-term investments with a maturity of fewer than 90 days. They are reported at either fair value or amortized cost.
- Marketable securities include investments in debt or equity securities traded in a public market and whose value can be determined from price information in a public market.
- Trade receivables are debts owed to a corporation by its customers for goods or provisions of services. These goods and services have already been delivered or used but not yet paid.
- Inventories are recorded at the lower of cost or net realizable value. The entity must write down the inventory value and record an expense if the

[1] Jaijairam, P. (2012). Fair Value Accounting vs. Historical Cost Accounting. *Review of Business Information Systems (RBIS)*, *17*(1), 1–6. https://doi.org/10.19030/rbis.v17i1.7579.

net realizable value of a company's inventory falls below its carrying amount.

- IFRS provides companies with the choice to report PPE using either a historical cost model or a revaluation model. US GAAP permits only the historical cost model.
- Investment property refers to property not used in a company's regular operations. Under IFRS, investment properties need to be valued using the cost model or fair value model. US GAAP does not include a specific definition for an investment property.
- A company assesses whether the useful life for its intangible asset is finite or indefinite. An intangible asset with a limited useful lifespan is amortized on a methodical basis over the closest estimate of its useful life.
- An intangible asset with an indefinite useful life is not amortized. Instead, it is tested for impairment at least annually.
- Goodwill is not amortized; instead, it is tested for impairment annually.
- There are two ways for net changes in fair value to be recognized: profit or loss on the income statement or other comprehensive income (loss), which bypasses the income statement.

Main Terms

- **Amortized cost:** The historical cost (initial, recognized cost) of the asset adjusted for amortization and impairment.
- **Fair value:** Under IFRS and US GAAP, fair value is grounded on an existing price, the price received to sell an asset or paid to transfer a liability in an orderly transaction between two market participants on the date of the measurement.
- **Historical cost model of PPE:** Under the historical cost model, PPE is carried at amortized value (historical value after deducting accumulated depreciation or accumulated depletion, and less any impairment losses).
- **Revaluation model of PPE:** Under the revaluation model, the reported and carrying value for PPE is the fair value at the date of revaluation, deducting any accumulated depreciation.
- **Intangible assets:** Unlike other assets, intangible assets are not physical. Examples of intangible assets include goodwill, brand recognition, and intellectual property, such as patents, trademarks, and copyrights.

- **Carrying value:** The accounting measure of value in which an asset or company's value is grounded on the figures in the respective company's balance sheet is called the carrying value. For physical assets such as machinery or computer hardware, carrying cost is calculated by the difference between the original cost and accumulated depreciation).
- **Net realizable value (NRV):** The net realizable value (NRV) is the value of an asset that can be realized upon its sale. A reasonable estimate of the costs associated with the asset's eventual sale or disposal is deducted.
- **Impairment:** The impairment reduces the recoverable amount of a fixed asset (or goodwill) below its carrying amount. Accounts commonly recognize and record all of a company's assets' values. The current market typically determines the value of these assets.
- **Comprehensive income:** Is a financial performance statement that lists all profit and loss and other comprehensive income (OCI) of the entity over the specified period. Some items that belong to OCI includes unrealized gains or losses on hedge/derivative financial instruments or gain and losses on foreign currency transaction.

10.3.3 *Assets and Their Measurement Bases*

(a) Current Assets

Current assets are generally maintained for operating purposes. They include cash and items that are expected to be converted into cash (e.g., trade receivables), used up (e.g., office supplies, prepaid expenses), or sold (e.g., inventories) in the current operating cycle. Current assets provide information about the company's operating activities and operating capability as they consist of cash and cash equivalents, marketable securities, trade receivables, and inventory.

1. **Cash and cash equivalents:** They refer to demand deposits in the banks and are highly liquid securities with maturities of 90 days or less.
2. **Marketable securities:** These are assets that can be easily liquidated to cash. They are investments in equity or debt securities that can be easily bought or sold on public exchanges. Their values are derived from the current trading prices in the exchange. Supplementary information on these financial assets will usually be reported in the financial statements' notes.

3. **Accounts receivable or trade receivable:** Debts owed to a corporation by its customers for goods or provisions of services. The goods and services have already been delivered or used but not yet paid. These receivables are commonly valued at net realizable value. We obtain net realizable value by deducting an allowance for doubtful and uncollectible accounts from trade receivables. An allowance for doubtful accounts reflects a corporate's gauge on the percentage of receivables expected to be uncollectible. Additions to this allowance in a specific period are recorded as bad debt expenses; this allowance for doubtful accounts decreases the gross receivables.
4. **Inventories:** Inventories refer to goods held for sale as part of a company's operation. Inventories form a crucial component of operating assets and are valued based on lower acquisition costs or market. How inventories are valued is known as the lower-of-cost-or market-rule. Both IFRS and US GAAP prescribe somewhat comparable treatments. Specifically, IFRS requires inventory valuation based on lower-cost or net realizable value. Net realizable value is the expected selling price of the inventory in the market, less any selling costs. US GAAP requires inventory valuation based on lower of cost or market. The market is the current replacement cost of the inventory.
5. **Other current assets:** Assets that do not contain material amounts that need to be tracked separately as a single line item on the balance sheet. Other current assets comprise (i) prepaid expenses and (ii) deferred tax assets. Prepaid expenses are future expenses paid for a good or service in advance of receiving it. Deferred tax assets are income taxes incurred before the income tax expense is recognized on the income statement.

(b) Non-current Assets

The firm's assets are not held for resale but are used in the firm's operations. They are generally used for more than one period and thus long-lived. These can consist of property, plant, equipment, intangible assets, or goodwill.

1. **Property, plant, and equipment (PPE):** PPE are sometimes called fixed assets, are long-term, non-current, or long-lived assets that are tangibles. They may be held for use in production, use in normal operating activities, rental, etc., they are expected to be used for more than one period. The IFRS allows PPE to be reported with either the cost

model or the revaluation model, whereas The US GAAP only allows the cost principle to be applied to PPE.

a. Under the cost model, PPE is carried at cost, which is derived as historical cost less accumulated depreciation and impairment.
b. With the revaluation model, PPE is carried at a revalued amount derived as fair value at revaluation date minus subsequent accumulated depreciation & impairment, given that fair value can be measured reliably.

2. **Investment property:** It is a property that is entirely used to earn rental income, capital appreciation, or both. The IFRS allows investment property to be valued in either historical cost or its' fair value.
   a. Like PPE, valuing under cost model, investment property is carried at cost, which is derived as historical cost less accumulated depreciation and impairment.
   b. If a fair value model is chosen, an investment property will be valued at its fair value. Gains or losses from any change in the fair value of investment property are immediately reflected on the income statement once it arises.
3. **Intangible assets:** An intangible asset is defined as an identifiable asset without physical substance held for use in the production or supply of goods and services, rental to others, or administrative purposes. In general, accounting for an intangible asset depends on whether the asset was created internally, purchased externally, or obtained as part of business combinations. Examples of intangibles include license, computer software, patents, leasehold rights, brand names, etc. Some have a finite life, while others have infinite life. The cost of a finite-lived intangibles asset is amortized over its useful lifespan. Indefinite lived intangibles assets are not amortized but tested for impairment at least once a year. The impairment is recognized as a loss in the income statement. Intangibles assets are also considered identifiable or unidentifiable. Under IFRS, an identifiable intangible asset must be (i) capable of being separated from the firm or arising a contractual legal right, (ii) controlled by the firm, (ii) expected to provide future economic benefits, which must be probable and whose cost must be reliably measured. An unidentifiable intangible asset cannot be purchased separately and may have an indefinite life. Goodwill is an example of it.
4. **Goodwill:** Goodwill generally arises in a scenario involving an acquisition refers to the difference between the cost of an acquired firm and

the target the fair market value of its net assets. It represents the amount paid for the target's ability to earn excess profits not attributable to its tangible asset value. Both IFRS and US GAAP require that goodwill that arises from acquisitions be capitalized. Goodwill is usually tested for impairment annually. If the fair value is less than its carrying value, goodwill is considered impaired and written down to fair value. The charge is then reported to the income statement. Impairment losses are deducted from income in the current fiscal period and lead to reductions to current earnings and total assets. The amount of goodwill can be determined by determining the fair value of net assets acquired and comparing it with the purchase price. The following steps describe accounting standards' requirements for recognizing goodwill:

a. The total cost to purchase the target company (the acquiree) is determined.
b. The acquiree's identifiable assets are measured at fair value. The acquiree's liabilities and contingent liabilities are measured at fair value. The difference between the fair value of identifiable assets and the fair value of the liabilities and contingent liabilities equals the net identifiable assets acquired.
c. Goodwill arising from the purchase is the excess of a) the cost to purchase the target company over b) the net identifiable assets. A transaction will involve purchasing net identifiable assets with a value greater than the cost to purchase from time to time. Such transactions are called "bargain purchases." Everything gained from a bargain purchase is reflected in profit and loss in the period in which it arises.

5. **Financial assets:** By IFRS definition, a financial instrument is a contract that gives rise to a financial asset of one entity and a financial liability or equity instrument of another. Financial securities are valued with either amortized cost model or a fair value approach.

   a. 'Trading securities' is a term for debt and equity securities. These are short-term investments purchased to sell them for a higher profit in the near term, usually held less than three months. These are carried at fair market value on the balance sheet. All the unrealized or realized gains or losses are included as profit or loss in the income statement and reflected in retained earnings within owners' equity.
   b. 'Mark to market' is the action of adjusting the value of financial security to reflect the current fair value grounded on market prices.

c. 'Available-for-sale' assets are carried at fair market value, with any change between the fair value and carrying amount recognized as a component of other comprehensive income. They are classified as current assets if they intend to sell them away within a year. Otherwise, all available for sale securities are classified as long-term. However, this type of asset is no longer an option under IFRS after IFRS9 became effective in 2018. Nevertheless, this concept is still in the curriculum. IFRS still permits few equity securities to be valued at fair value with unrealized gains or losses reflected in other comprehensive income statements. These assets are now known as "Financial assets valued at fair value through other comprehensive income" or FVOCI.

d. 'Held-to-maturity' assets are securities that management has the intention and ability to hold to maturity. An investment in these assets can be classified as short and long-term depending on the expected maturity date. They are generally carried at cost and not sold before maturity unless under rare circumstances. These assets are reflected as an amortized cost on the balance sheet only if the entity plans to hold the financial asset until maturity.

Table 10.1 summarizes the accounting standards for different financial assets.

Table 10.1: Accounting for financial instruments.

Financial assets type	Balance sheet carrying value	Income statement	
		Unrealized gain/losses	Others
Held to maturity	Cost or Amortized cost	Not recognized in both net income or comprehensive statement	(i) Recognize realized gain/loss in net income (ii) Interest Income in net income
Available for sale	Fair market value	Not recognized in net income but recognized in comprehensive statement	(i) Recognize realized gain/loss in net income (ii) Interest Income in net income
Trading	Fair market value	Recognize in net income	(i) Recognize realized gain/loss in net income (ii) Interest Income in net income

Source: Adapted from Subramanyam, K. R. (2014). *Financial Statement Analysis*. Mc-Graw Hill.

10.3.4 *Different Types of Liabilities*

There are three types of liabilities: current, non-current, and contingent liabilities.

Learning Objectives

- Describe different types of liabilities and their measurement bases.

Main Takeaways

Main Points

- Current liabilities are obligations due within a year or within a business's normal operating cycle. Obligations settled beyond a year are referred to as non-current liabilities.
- Financial liabilities that mature within 1 year or the operating cycle, whichever is longer, appear in the balance sheet's current liability section.
- Accrued expenses have been recognized in the income statement but not yet paid as of the balance sheet date.
- Deferred income (also known as deferred revenue or unearned revenue) is income that arises when a company receives payment in advance of delivering the goods and services associated with the payment.
- Non-current liabilities are liabilities not expected to be settled or paid within 1 year or one operating cycle of the business, whichever is greater.
- Long-term financial liabilities and deferred tax liabilities are known as the Two typical types of non-current (long-term) liabilities
- Long-term financial liabilities include loans (i.e., borrowings from banks) and notes or bonds payable (i.e., fixed-income securities issued to investors). Liabilities such as bonds issued by a company are typically reported at amortized balance sheet costs.
- Deferred tax liabilities arise from temporary timing differences between a company's income reported for tax purposes and income reported for financial statement purposes.

Main Terms

- **Payables:** Trade payables refer to the amounts that a business owes its vendors for purchases of goods and services.
- **Accruals:** Revenues earned or expenses incurred, impacting a company's net income on the income statement, even though cash related to the transaction has not changed hands. Accruals affect the balance sheet so that they involve non-cash assets and liabilities.

- **Contingent liabilities:** Liabilities that may occur depending on an uncertain future event's outcome are contingent liabilities. If the contingency is likely and the liability can be reasonably estimated, the contingent liability is recorded. Unless both conditions are not met, the liability may be disclosed in the financial statements' footnote.
- **Deferred tax liabilities:** Taxes that are assessed or are due for the current period but have not yet been paid are called the deferred liabilities. It records that the company will pay more income tax in the future from a transaction during the current period, such as an installment sale receivable.

(a) Liabilities and Their Measurement Bases

Current Liabilities: Current liabilities are defined as probable outflows of economic resources that are due within a year or a business's normal operating cycle. Examples of current liabilities include accounts payables, notes payable, accrued expenses, and deferred income.

- **Trade payables or accounts payable:** The amounts that a firm needs to pay its suppliers from purchases of goods and services.
- **Notes payable:** A written agreement of a liability account that an entity owes to its creditors through a formal loan agreement are called the notes payables.
- **Accrued expenses:** That have been incurred at the end of an accounting period but to be paid by a company.
- **Deferred income:** Money received for goods or services has not yet been earned. It is recorded as a liability till delivery is made.

Non-Current Liabilities: Long-term liabilities, more commonly known as non-current liabilities, refer to the probable outflows of economic resources expected to occur later than 1 year or a regular business's operating cycle. Examples of long-term debt include bonds, deferred tax liabilities, long term loans. Long-term liabilities are an essential part of the financing of a company. A company can acquire immediate capital to fund capital assets or invest in new capital projects from long-term debt.

Long-term liabilities are essential in the determination of business solvency. If businesses cannot pay their long-term debts when approaching maturity, they have a high chance of facing a solvency crisis.

- **Long-term financial liabilities:** Examples of long-term financial liabilities include loans and notes or bonds payable. These are carried at their amortized cost in the balance sheet. Upon maturity, the bond's amortized cost or carrying amount will equal its face value.
- **Deferred tax liabilities:** Amount of income tax payable in future periods regarding temporary taxable differences. Temporary differences are defined as differences between the carrying amount of an asset (or liability) and its tax base, the amount at which the asset (or liability) is valued for tax purposes. Taxes that are assessed or are due for the current period but have not yet been paid are called the deferred liabilities.

Contingent Liability: Liabilities that may occur due to the outcome of a future event are called contingent liabilities. Therefore, contingent liabilities are potential liabilities reported as liabilities on the balance sheet and disclosed in the notes to the financial statements when probable they will incur a loss and when the loss can be reasonably estimated.

For example, a company is facing a lawsuit of $100,000. The company will incur liability if the lawsuit proves successful. However, if they lost the case, then no penalty would arise. A contingent liability is only recorded in accounting standards when the liability is probable (defined as more than 50% likely to happen). The amount of the resulting liability can be reasonably estimated.

References/Further Readings

Robinson, T., Henry, E., Pirie, W., Broihahn, M., & Cope, A. (2015). *International Financial Statement Analysis*, 3rd edn. Wiley, Chap 5.

Subramanyam, K. R. (2014). *Financial Statement Analysis*, 11th edn. McGraw Hill, Chaps. 3 and 4.

10.4 Long-Lived Assets — Capitalized Costs and Costs that are Expensed

Capitalizing versus expensing different costs during the accounting of long-lived assets is influential to its profitability, financial ratios, and trends.

Learning Objectives

- Understand the differences between capitalized costs and costs expensed and how it affects the financial statement and ratios.

Main Takeaways

Main Points

- Long-term assets are listed in the balance sheet at their carrying value, which is the unexpired portion of the asset's cost for the asset's remaining useful life.
- All long-term assets are subject to an annual impairment evaluation to determine if the carrying value exceeds the asset's fair value when the asset is deemed to have suffered an impairment and necessary adjustments are made.
- Capitalization means putting the asset on the balance sheet and recognizing the cost over several periods. This procedure contrasts with expensing the cost immediately in the income statement, which reduces profit in the current period.
- An expenditure expected to provide a future economic benefit over multiple accounting periods is capitalized. The expenditure is expensed if the future economic benefit is unlikely or uncertain.
- Management can exercise judgment regarding the capitalization decision of the following costs: (1) Interest cost incurred during asset construction, (2) Software development and R&D costs, and (3) Oil exploration costs — the full cost versus successful efforts method.
- Capitalizing or expensing has a direct impact on financial statements and ratios. Capitalization results in higher net income in the initial period of capitalization.
- A company's solvency can be better assessed when they include the capitalized interest in calculating interest coverage ratios.

Main Terms

- **Long-lived Assets:** Also known as long-term assets, refer to the firm's operating assets, which are not held for resale but are used in the firm's operations. They are generally used for more than one period and are thus long-lived. Examples include tangible fixed assets such as plants, machinery, land, buildings, natural resources, etc., and intangible assets such as computer software, patents, trademarks, and goodwill.
- **Amortization:** The practice of spreading an intangible asset's cost over that asset's useful life is called amortization. Intangible assets are not physical assets, *per se*.

- **Impairment:** Commonly used to describe a drastic reduction in the recoverable amount of a fixed asset. Impairment occurs when a change in legal or economic circumstances surrounding a company or a casualty loss from unforeseen devastation occurs.
- **Cash flow from investing activities (CFI):** Inflows or outflows of cash from a company's long-term investments are called the cash flow from investing activities, which involves long-term uses of cash. Investing activity includes purchasing or selling a fixed asset like property, plant, or equipment.
- **Cash flow from operating activities (CFO):** Inflows or outflows of cash generates from a company's ongoing, regular business activities.
- **Economic benefit:** Benefits that can be quantified in monetary terms are known as economic benefits. Profits, net cash flow, net income, or revenue are examples of economic benefits.

10.4.1 *Long-Lived Assets*

Long-lived assets are expected to generate economic benefits in the future (typically more than a year). Examples include long-lived tangible assets, long-lived intangible assets, long-lived financial assets.

Two main issues in accounting for a long-lived asset are determining its cost at acquisition and the allocation of cost to expense over time. The costs of most long-lived assets are capitalized and then allocated as expenses in the profit or loss (income) statement over time. They are expected to provide economic benefits. Two types of long-lived assets that are not allocated over time are land, which is not depreciated, and those intangible assets with indefinite useful lives.

10.4.2 *Intangible Assets*

The definition of intangible assets is an identifiable asset without physical substance held for use in the production or supply of goods or services, rental to others, or administrative purposes. In general, accounting for an intangible asset depends on whether the asset was created internally, purchased externally, or obtained as part of a business combination.

Licenses, computer software, patents, leasehold rights, brand names, copyrights, and goodwill are typical examples of intangible assets. Some of them have finite lives, while others have indefinite lives. The cost of a finite-lived intangible asset is amortized over its useful life. Indefinite-lived intangible assets are not amortized but tested for impairment at least annually. The impairment is recognized as a loss in the income statement.

Intangible assets need to be classified as either identifiable or unidentifiable. Under IFRS, an identifiable intangible asset must be:

- Expected to provide future economic benefits, which must be probable and whose cost must be reliably measurable.
- Controlled by the firm.
- Capable of being separated from the firm or arising from a contractual or legal right.

An unidentifiable intangible asset has an indefinite life that cannot be purchased separately. One example will be goodwill.

In general, goodwill is the difference between an acquired firm's cost and the fair market value of its net assets, and it always arises in a scenario involving an acquisition. It represents the amount paid for the target's ability to earn excess profits not attributable to its tangible asset value. Goodwill may be the reason for monopoly, customer satisfaction, better management, manufacturing efficiency, employee relations, etc.

Under most international accounting rules, goodwill can be recognized when acquired using the acquisition method. Details will be discussed in later sessions. The amount of goodwill can be determined by determining the fair value of net assets acquired and comparing it with the purchase price.

Goodwill is usually tested for impairment on an annual basis. If the fair value of goodwill is less than its carrying value, it will be considered impaired. The fair value with the charge being reported to the income statement instead.

10.4.3 *Allocation*

Allocation is the process of periodically expensing a deferred cost over the periods that the firm is expected to benefit from the asset. Tangible assets are subject to "depreciation" while intangible assets are subject to "amortization". Depreciation and amortization are charged in the income statement. Intangible assets such as goodwill or trademarks may seem to have an indefinite useful life, and as a result, they are not subject to amortization. Instead, they will be tested for impairment annually. We will look at depreciation methods in greater detail in a subsequent section.

10.4.4 *Capitalization and Impact on Financial Statements*

The Capitalization Decision: The purchase of long-term assets is a decision made through capital budgeting. In general, an entity would analyze the cash flows associated with acquiring, using, and disposing of the asset at the end of its useful life to include any cost savings when determining the net present value (NPV) of the investment at the internal hurdle rate. If the NPV is sufficiently positive, the company may proceed with the investment. A company may choose to make investments in some rare cases even if they cannot establish their NPV viability for strategic or other reasons.

Once the investment decision has been made, the next step is to determine which costs should be "capitalized" towards the asset's carrying value on the balance sheet and which costs should be expensed in the current period. This decision can be significant and controversial at the same time. Capitalization means putting the asset on the balance sheet and recognizing the cost over several periods. In contrast, expensing the cost immediately in the income statement reduces profit in the current period.

An expenditure expected to lead to future economic benefit over multiple accounting periods will be capitalized in a general way. If the future economic benefit is unlikely or uncertain, the expenditure is expensed. However, firms can apply this principle differently. Management can exercise judgment with regards to the capitalization decision of the following costs:

- Interest cost incurred during asset construction;
- Software development and R&D costs;
- Oil exploration costs — the full cost versus successful efforts method.

Generally, an analyst needs to make adjustments coordinated with his analysis and understanding of what should have been capitalized or expensed in the period.

10.4.5 *Impact on Financial Statements and Ratios*

Effect on Reported Income: Firms that capitalize costs and depreciate the asset over time tend to show a smoother reported income pattern. On the contrary, firms that expense costs show more significant variability in reported income.

Effect on Profitability: As long as a firm keeps growing and generating upward-sloping expenditure, the early years would show lower profitability because of the high depreciation costs. Although expensing results in lower profitability, it also lowers assets and equity. As a result, mature firms' profitability ratios could be higher than firms with lower expenses.

Effect on Shareholder's Equity: Capitalization results in higher net income at the beginning of capitalization, which leads to higher retained earnings, and hence shareholders' equity is higher initially.

Effect on CFO: Capitalized assets are typically reported in the cash flow from investing. In other cases, when a firm expense instead of capitalizing, the amount would instead affect cash flow from operations. As a result, CFO will be higher for a firm that capitalizes.

Effect on Leverage Ratios: Firms that expense their assets would show a higher leverage ratio measured by either debt to equity or debt to asset ratios due to low asset and equity base. The converse is true of firms that capitalize instead. (Financial ratios are discussed in Part E, Section 1: Financial Analysis Techniques.)

Table 10.2 summarizes the effect capitalizing versus expensing has on financial ratios.

10.4.6 *Capitalization of Interest*

The interest incurred during the construction of long-lived assets is known as the capitalized interest. Instead of being charged as interest expense on

Table 10.2: Summary table of capitalizing or expensing have on financial ratios.

	Capitalizing	Expensing
Income variability	Lower	Higher
Profitability — early years (ROA and ROE)	Higher	Lower
Profitability — later years (ROA and ROE)	Lower	Higher
Total cash flows	Same	Same
Cash flow from operations	Higher	Lower
Cash flow from investing	Lower	Higher
Leverage ratios (D/E and D/A)	Lower	Higher

the income sheet, this type of interest is included in the asset's initial cost on the balance sheet. The treatment of construction interest is indifferent under IFRS and US GAAP.

Interest cost is capitalized only when a firm is leveraged by debt. The interest rate used to capitalize interest is grounded on debt that is exclusively related to the asset's construction. If there is no specific borrowing rate, the weighted average interest rate will be used as a substitute. In general, capitalized interest is reported in the cash flow statement as an outflow from investing activities, while interest expense is reported as an outflow from operating activities.

Financial statements' impact is that capitalized interest decreases interest expense and increases net income. Also, interest coverage ratios would be overstated due to the lower interest expense.

Capitalized interest distorts the classification of cash flows. Capitalized interest is reported as CFI, not CFO. So, CFO is overstated, and CFI is understated.

The following adjustments are needed from an analyst to reverse the impact of capitalized interest:

- Interest Expense. Interest capitalized during the year should be added to interest expense.
- Depreciation. Amortization of interest capitalized should be deducted from depreciation.
- Cash flow. Interest capitalized should be added back to cash flow from investment and deducted from cash flow from operations.
- The interest coverage ratio should be calculated with interest expense adjusted to add back capitalized interest to avoid overstating it.

References/Further Readings

Robinson, T., Henry, E., Pirie, W., Broihahn, M., & Cope, A. (2015). *International Financial Statement Analysis*, 3rd edn. Wiley, Chap. 9.

Subramanyam, K.R. (2014). *Financial Statement Analysis*, 11th edn. McGraw Hill, Chap. 4, pp. 243–245.

10.5 Depreciation

Depreciation is a systematic allocation of the asset's cost over time, generally the asset's useful economic life.

Learning Objectives

- Understand the three main classes of depreciation methods and their impact on the financial statement.

Main Takeaways

Main Points

- Allocation is the process of periodically expensing a deferred cost over the periods that the firm is expected to benefit from the asset. Unlike tangible assets, which are subject to "depreciation," intangible assets are only subject to "amortization."
- Depreciation and amortization are charged to the income statement. Intangible assets, including goodwill or trademarks, may be considered an indefinite useful life and are not subject to amortization. Instead, they are tested for impairment on an annual basis.
- The three main classes of depreciation methods are straight-line method (SLM) depreciation, accelerated depreciation method, and units of production method.
- Accelerated depreciation methods lead to lower reported net income and equity and are generally considered more conservative than the SLM.
- Longer, useful life and higher expected residual lead to a lower depreciation rate relative to a shorter useful life and lower anticipated residual value.

Main Terms

- **SLM depreciation:** Based on a straightforward application of the matching principle. Given a constant asset and cash flows each year, a fixed amount of depreciation is charged annually. This amount is determined by distributing the cost of acquisition of the asset over its balance of useful economic life.
- **Accelerated depreciation method:** This approach increases the depreciation rate as the asset ages, grounded on the premise that the cashflows could be higher in earlier years and lower in later years as the asset gets older and requires more maintenance expenditure.
- **Units of production method:** The allocation of cost is associated with the actual usage in a given period. It assumes that depreciation will be higher in a given year with a greater activity volume.
- **Residual value:** Also known as salvage value, is the estimated value of a fixed asset at the end of its lease term or useful life.

- **Depreciable life:** The time over which an asset can be depreciated (= shown to lose value) in a company's accounts.
- **Carrying amount or value:** Equal to the asset's original cost minus any depreciating factors. The depreciating factors for an asset vary due to the asset's nature.

10.5.1 *Depreciation Methods and Calculation of Depreciation Expense*

There are three basic ways to measure depreciation. Nevertheless, regardless of the method applied, the asset's carrying value is not reduced below the estimated residual value.

Depreciation methods include (1) the SLM in which the cost of an asset is allocated to expense evenly over its useful life, (2) accelerated methods, in which the allocation of charge is more significant in earlier years, and (3) the units-of-production way, in which the share of cost corresponds to the actual use of an asset in a particular period. The amounts reported on the financial statements, including the charges for reported assets, operating, and net income, can be affected by the depreciation method's choice. The choice, in turn, is also influential for a variety of financial ratios, including fixed asset turnover, total asset turnover, operating profit margin, operating return on assets, and return on assets.

1. In the SLM, an equal amount of depreciation is assigned to each period. Depreciation expense is equal to the depreciable cost divided by the estimated useful life. The depreciable cost can be derived by taking the tangible asset's historical cost less estimated residual (salvage) value. If we put it into an equation, it will look like this:
   - Depreciation expense = (Historical cost of the asset – Estimated residual value)/Estimated useful life.
2. The accelerated method assigns an asset's cost to its useful life in a decreasing manner. Two common approaches in accelerated depreciation will be a double-declining balance (DDB) and the sum of years' digits. In the DDB approach, this method's application will cease when depreciation expense would cause the net book value to fall below the estimated salvage value, and only the difference is taken as depreciation expense.
   - Sum of the years digits = (Cost – Salvage value)(Years remaining)/(Sum of Years).

- Double Declining Balance (DDB) = 2 × (Cost − Accumulated depreciation)/(Assets life).

3. In the units-of-production method, a fixed amount of depreciation is assigned to each unit of output or service rendered by the asset. It determines the depreciation based on the utilization of the asset. With that said, a higher depreciation is being recorded in the years of greater use. The usage may be computed based on total units of output produced or service hours rendered. A limitation of this approach will be the decrease in depreciation expense recorded during low production times even though the asset is subjected to a reduction of its value due to economic forces.
   - In the form of an equation, Depreciation expense = (Depreciable cost∗ Production)/Estimated total productive capacity.

10.5.2 *Estimates Required for Depreciation Calculations*

Depreciable life or useful life refers to the total number of service units expected from an asset. The depreciable life can be valued based on total units of output expected to be produced, total hours of service to be rendered, or the number of years it is expected to be used. The longer the useful life, the lower the annual depreciation expense.

Decreasing a depreciable life of an asset will affect a company reporting statements in the following ways:

- A higher depreciation expense.
- Lower book value of the asset.
- Lower net income. The percentage effect on net income is usually more significant than the impact on assets and shareholders' equity.
- Lower shareholders' equity (due to lower retained earnings).

A shorter depreciable life tends to increase debt-to-equity ratio and asset turnovers while lowering profit margin, returns on assets, and returns on equity. Nevertheless, any depreciable life changes will not affect the cash flows, as depreciation is a non-cash item.

Salvage value, also known as residual or scrap value, refers to an asset's estimated worth at the end of its useful life.

Since salvage value is subtracted from an asset's historical cost to derived annual depreciation expenses for all the depreciation approaches, a higher salvage value will result in a lower annual depreciation.

Salvage value serves as a floor for net book value for depreciation methods such as units-of-production, double-declining-balance, and service hour depreciation.

These factors are interlinked with depreciation approaches to determine the depreciation expense. For example, the use of the SLM with shorter depreciation lives may lead to depreciation expenses similar to that obtained from the use of an accelerated method with longer lives.

10.5.3 *Impact on Financial Statements and Ratios*

Impact on Financial Statements: Accelerated depreciation methods lead to lower reported net income and equity and usually are considered more conservative than the SLM. While they also have a depressing effect on the net asset base, profitability ratios are often lower in this method because the numerator effect overrides the denominator effect.

The impact may remain continuingly for firms that maintain a stable or growing asset base with new assets being added, contributing to higher depreciation expense in their early stages. The accelerated depreciation method will cause a lower depreciation expense in later years only in a situation of declining asset bases.

Impact of Assumptions: Note that the depreciation expense amount can be affected by two key assumptions: useful life and salvage value. The usage of short useful life and lower salvage value would be more conservative and vice versa. The analyst must pay close attention to any change in these assumptions.

Impact on Taxes: The use of accelerated depreciation methods leads to higher depreciation expenses, lower net income, and taxes and improves cash flow. We refer to the impact of taxes as a depreciation tax shield. Such methods are widely used in many countries to stimulate individual and corporate investments.

Changes in Depreciation Methods, Assumptions: Companies are free to choose the method of depreciation applicable to new assets, all assets, or change the assumption of useful lives and salvage values. When the change applies only to new assets, companies do not need to restate past earnings. Nevertheless, when comparing performance over the years, the analyst must realize the impact of a lower depreciation expense in the future from a switch to SLM from, for example, the SYD (sum of year) method.

Generally, past periods' cumulative effect has to be reported separately when the change applies to all assets. This information should be carefully reviewed and used by the analyst for any comparative analysis.

Changes in asset lives or the salvage values do not require any special reporting because these are changes in accounting estimates. Still, they may result in lower depreciation expenses and higher reported earnings. The analyst must evaluate whether the change in assumptions is economically justifiable. Also, an adjustment should be made for any comparative analysis with past performance.

References/Further Readings

Robinson, T., Henry, E., Pirie, W., Broihahn, M., & Cope, A. (2015). *International Financial Statement Analysis*, 3rd edn. Wiley, Chap. 9.

Subramanyam, K.R. (2014). *Financial Statement Analysis*, 11th edn. McGraw Hill, Chap. 4, pp. 245–253.

10.6 Non-Current Liabilities (e.g., Debt)

Non-current (or long-term) liabilities refer to probable outflows of economic resources expected to occur later than 1 year or one operating cycle.

Learning Objectives

- Determine the initial recognition, initial measurement, and subsequent measurement of bonds

Main Takeaways

Main Points

- Bonds are a common source of financing from debt markets.
- Issuers record bond and bond-related transactions at issuance (when bonds are issued), subsequently (at the time of interest payment), and at retirement (when issuers call bonds).
- The sales proceeds of a bond issue are determined by discounted future cash payments using the market rate of interest at the time of issuance

(effective interest rate). The reported interest expense on bonds is based on the effective interest rate.

- Future cash payments on bonds usually include periodic interest payments (made at the stated interest rate or coupon rate) and the principal amount.
- If the market rate of interest is equal to the bonds' coupon rate, the bonds will be sold at par (i.e., at a price equal to the face value). On the other hand, if the market rate of interest is higher than the bonds' coupon rate, the bonds will bc sold at a discounted price. If the market rate of interest is lower than the bonds' coupon rate, the bonds will be sold at a premium.
- An issuer amortizes any issuance discount or premium on bonds over the bonds' lifetime.
- In general, the carrying amount of bonds is the amortized historical cost, which can be different from their fair value.

Main Terms

- **Stated (contractual, coupon) interest rate:** The interest to be paid in cash on the bond. It is stated on the bond certificate and is used to compute the interest payments paid in cash.
- **Market interest rate:** The rate available on investments in similar bonds at the moment and varies with economic conditions.
- **Effective interest rate:** The market interest rate on the day the bonds are sold (remains fixed through the life of the bond) and is used to compute the amount of interest Expense to recognize.
- **Book value:** Refers to an asset's value according to its balance sheet account balance. The value is grounded on the asset's original cost, less any depreciation, amortization, or impairment costs made against the asset.
- **Face value:** The amount of a debt obligation reported as payable in a debt document. The face value does not include any interest or dividend payments that may later be paid over the debt instrument's term.
- **Bond premium:** Occurs if the bond price has increased in the secondary market due to a fall in market interest rates. A bond sold at a premium to par has a market price higher than the face value.
- **Discounted bond:** A bond issued for less than its par (or face) value or is currently trading for less than its par value in the secondary market is called a discounted bond.

- **Zero-coupon bond:** Refers to debt security that does not pay interest but trades at a deep discount, rendering a profit at maturity when the bond is redeemed for its full face value.

10.6.1 *Measurement of Bonds*

Debt is classified into short-term (ST) and long-term (LT) categories.

General principles to keep in mind when evaluating a debt: In general, debt is reported at the book value of the principal amount due. The market value of debt depends on the prevailing market interest rate. It is determined as the present value of contracted principal and interest payments discounted at the market interest rate. Interest payments are paid at the initially contracted coupon rate on the book value of debt at intervals depending on the terms of the original debt arrangement.

Bonds are investment securities where an investor lends money to an entity for a time in exchange for periodic interest payments.

In general, the bonds obligate the issuing company to pay two types of future payments to bondholders: the bond's face value and periodic interest payments.

The face value of a bond, also known as the principal, stated value, maturity value, or par value, is the amount of cash a corporation has to pay to its bondholders once the bond reaches its maturity. On the other hand, the periodic interest payments are made grounded on the stated interest or coupon rate promised in the bond contract to be applied to the bond face value.

The market value is a bond's present value, which equals the principal payment's present value plus the present value of all periodic interest payments. It can be obtained by discounting all the future cash payments using the market rate of interest. A market rate of interest is when investors demand loaning their money.

When a coupon rate of a bond is offered at a higher rate than the current prevailing market interest rate, the bond is said to be issued at a premium as investors demand a higher yield and are willing to pay for it. A premium bond will always be priced higher than its par (face) value. Vice versa, when the coupon rate of a bond is offered at a lower rate than the current prevailing market interest, the bond is said to be selling at a discount. A discount bond will be priced lower than its par (face) value.

Just basing off in Figure 10.2, we can observe the following:

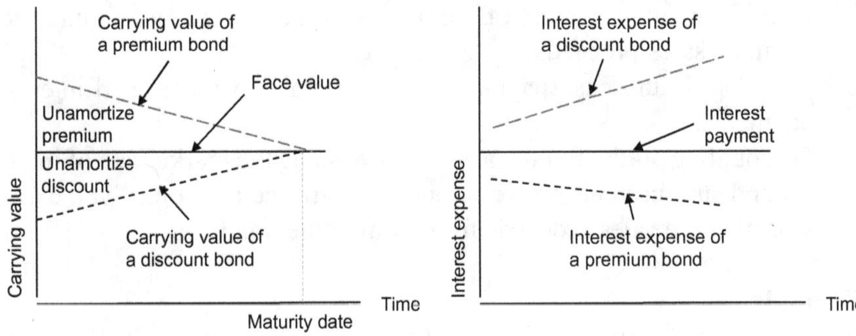

Figure 10.2: Graphical Illustration of the characteristics of premium bonds and discount bonds.

- The carrying value of a premium (discount) bond decreases (increases) towards face value.
- At maturity, both bonds' carrying value will have a value equal to the bond's face value.
- The interest expense of a discount (premium) bond increases (decreases) over time due to the increasing (decreasing) carrying value.

The effective interest rate or borrowing rate that the company incurs on the debt is the market rate at the issuance time. The effective interest rate is the discount rate equal to the sum of the present value of the two types of promised future cash payments to their selling price. For the issuing entity, interest expense recorded for the bonds in the reporting statements is grounded on its effective interest rate.

10.6.2 *Initial Recognition, Initial Measurement, and Subsequent Measurement of Bonds*

When a bond is issued, the entity's cash receipts or sales proceeds are reflected as a financing cash inflow on the issuer corporation's cash flows statement. Also, bonds payable usually are valued and recorded at the sales proceeds on the issuer entity's balance sheet at issuance, i.e., at the bond's face value subtracting any discount or premium.

To determine whether bonds are issued at face value, at a premium, or a discounted value, an analyst can use the three steps as follows.

1. Identify the main factors of the bond and the market rate required to compute sales proceeds;
2. Calculate future cash payments — principal repayment and interest payments;
3. Discounting all the future cash outflows using the market rate of interest and sum up their present value to determine the bonds' value and after that the sales proceeds from issuing the bonds.

Example:
XYZ issued $10 million of 5-year bonds, dated 1 January 2019, when bonds of comparable risk and terms are 3% per annum. The bonds pay coupons at 3% annually on 31 December. What are the bonds' sales proceeds when issued, and how was this shown in the financial statements?

Solution:
Step 1: Terms of Bond

Face value:	$10 million
Maturity:	5 years
Coupon rate:	3%
Frequency of interest payment:	annual
Coupon payment	$300,000 = 0.03 × $10,000,000
The market rate for bonds of similar terms:	3%

Step 2: Determine the cash flow and their timing.
Step 3: Determine the present value of the cash flow.
Steps 2 and 3 are shown below.

Date	Coupon payment	PV at market rate (3%)	Face value payment	PV at market rate (3%)	Total present value
31 Dec 2019	$300,000	$291,262			
31 Dec 2020	$300,000	$282,779			
31 Dec 2021	$300,000	$274,525			
31 Dec 2022	$300,000	$266,546			
31 Dec 2023	$300,000	$258,783	$10,000,000	$8,626,088	
Total		$1,373,912		$8,626,088	$10,000,000

The date is shown in column 1, and the timing of coupon payments and face value are shown in columns 2 and 4, respectively. The present value is shown in columns 3 and 5, and the discount rate is the market rate of bonds of similar terms.

The proceeds of the bonds at the time of sale are the total present value of future payments (the coupon payments and face value). There is no discount or premium as the bonds were issued at face value. The bond issue is reflected as a cash inflow and a long-term debt liability in the balance sheet. The issuance is reflected as an inflow in the statement of cash flows as a finance cash inflow of $10,000,000.

The price of bonds is often expressed as a percentage of face value. For example, the price of bonds issued at par, as in Example 1, is 100 (i.e., 100% of face value). In Example 2, in which bonds are issued at a discount, the price is 95.55 (i.e., 95.55% of face value).

Example:
XYZ issued $10 million of 5-year bonds, dated 1 January 2019, when bonds of comparable risk and terms are 4% per annum. The bonds pay coupons at 3% annually on 31 December. What are the bonds' sales proceeds when issued, and how was this shown in the financial statements?

Solution:
We repeat the process as with Example 1. However, similar bonds' market rate is 4% instead of 3%.

Step 1: Terms of Bond

Face value:	$10 million
Maturity:	5 years
Coupon rate:	3%
Frequency of interest payment:	annual
Coupon payment	$300,000 = 0.03 x $10,000,000
The market rate for bonds of similar terms:	4%

Step 2: Determine the cash flow and their timing.
Step 3: Determine the present value of the cash flow.
Steps 2 and 3 are shown below.

Date	Coupon payment	PV at market rate (4%)	Face value payment	PV at market rate (4%)	Total present value
31 Dec 2019	$300,000	$288,462			
31 Dec 2020	$300,000	$277,367			
31 Dec 2021	$300,000	$266,699			
31 Dec 2022	$300,000	$256,441			
31 Dec 2023	$300,000	$246,578	$10,000,000	$8,219,271	
Total		$1,335,547		$8,219,271	$9,554,818

The bond proceeds at the time of sale $9,554,818, and this is a discount of $445,182 from the face value of $10,000,000. There is no discount or premium as the bonds were issued at face value. The balance sheet reflects at the time of issuance of cash inflow and an increase in debt liability of $9,554,818. The issuance is reflected as an inflow in the statement of cash flows as a finance cash inflow of $9,554.818.

In Example 2, the bonds were issued at a discount to face value because the bonds' coupon rate of 3% was less than the market rate. Bonds are issued at a premium to face value when the bonds' coupon rate exceeds the market rate.

In general, bonds issued with a coupon rate of zero (zero-coupon bonds) are issued at a discount to face value. The value of zero-coupon bonds is grounded on the principal payment's present value only since there are no periodic interest payments.

For example, let us suppose a market interest rate of 6%, a $200,000 face value zero-coupon bond payable in 3 years will be issued at $167,496.85 (semi-annual compounding). The computation is carried out by pressing the following calculator keys: 200000 FV; 3I/Y; 6N; CPT PV. Or using Excel as =PV (3%, 6, 200000)

The journal entry (of the issuer) to record this issue will be:
Bank (balance sheet): $167,496.85 (debit)
Bond liability (balance sheet): $167,496.85 (credit).

At maturity, the total amount to be paid will be the principle of $200,000, including the interest payment of $32,503.15. The significant difference between a zero-coupon and a par value bond is that the interest of $32,503.15 is never reported as a cash flow from operations for a zero-coupon bond. The full $200,000 is reported as a cash flow from financing for the zero-coupon bond.

References/Further Readings

Robinson, T., Henry, E., Pirie, W., Broihahn, M., & Cope, A. (2015). *International Financial Statement Analysis*, 3rd edn. Wiley, Chap. 10.

Subramanyam, K. R. (2014). *Financial Statement Analysis*, 11th edn. McGraw Hill, Chap. 3, pp. 132–145.

10.7 Income Taxes

Changes in the income tax rate can affect income tax expense and the deferred tax asset and liability carrying amount in the change year.

Learning Objectives

- Describe the differences between accounting profit and taxable income and define deferred tax assets, deferred tax liabilities, taxes payable, and income tax expense.

Main Takeaways

Main Points

- Taxable income refers to the income used to determine the tax payable under the prevailing tax laws that are closer to accounting's modified cash basis. Reported income on the income statement is on an accrual basis. Thus there exist differences between reported income and taxable income. These differences may be temporary or permanent.
- Permanent differences originate in the current period and do not reverse in subsequent periods. Such differences may arise from income not subject to tax and expenses disallowed for tax purposes as defined by the Income Tax Act or any other tax regulation.
- A company's effective tax rate does not equal the firm's statutory tax rate due to the permanent differences. The effective tax rate is calculated as the tax expense figure divided by the pre-tax income.
- Temporary differences between reported (accounting) income taxable income are differences that arise in the current period and reverse in the subsequent period, representing income and expenses included in the one period's financial statements. However, it will only be taxed or deducted for tax purposes in another period (i.e., timing).
- A deferred tax liability or asset arises when an income or expense item is treated differently on financial statements and tax reporting. Differences are expected to reverse in the future.

- Deferred tax assets must be evaluated for their prospective recoverability. If it is probable that they will not be fully or partially recovered, the carrying amount should be reduced. The reduction is made by using a valuation allowance under US GAAP.
- The fundamental relationship is: Income tax expense = Current tax expense + Deferred tax expense. The difference between income tax expense and taxes payable is the deferred tax expense which results from changes in deferred tax assets and liabilities.

Main Terms

- **Permanent differences:** The differences in what is recognized on the accounting income statement and tax return. Differences between tax reporting and financial reporting will not be reversed in the future.
- **Temporary differences:** Are differences that are temporary and are expected to reverse in the future.
- **Income tax expense:** Expense resulting from current period pre-tax income; this includes taxes payable (from the tax return) and deferred income tax expense. It is reported in the income statement.
- **Current tax expense (or taxes payable):** Taxes due to the government as indicated in the tax return. It arises from both permanent and temporary differences.
- **Deferred tax expense:** Accrual of income tax expense expected to be paid (or recovered) in the future (the difference between taxes payable and income tax expense). Due to changes in deferred tax assets and liabilities under (US) SAAS 109. It arises from temporary differences only.
- **Deferred tax liability:** If the current tax expense is lower than income tax expense, the deferred tax liability is created, i.e., the tax liability is deferred to future years.
- **Deferred tax asset:** A deferred tax asset is created when the current tax expense is greater than the income tax expense. Balance sheet item results from a temporary excess of taxes payable over income taxes expense. It is expected to be recovered from future operations, and it is not created if the excess is a permanent difference.
- **Pre-tax income:** Income before income tax expense.
- **Carrying amount:** The amount at which the asset or liability is valued according to accounting principles is called the carrying amount.

10.7.1 *Main Terms and Basic Understanding*

The complexity in accounting for income taxes arises because the current period taxable income is computed using different rules than those used in accounting for pre-tax income.

Taxes are paid grounded on tax reporting, but from a financial reporting standpoint, the tax expense in the income statement (IS) is grounded on the matching principle and is computed on pre-tax accounting income. Deferred tax entries are put through the accounting books to match taxes on taxable income and taxes on pre-tax income for accounting purposes.

Deferred tax liabilities (credits) and deferred tax assets (debits or prepaid taxes) arise from the differences between the tax expense for tax and the accounting tax expense.

Here are some essential terms grounded on tax return:

1. **Taxable income:** Income subject to tax based on the tax code.
2. **Taxes payable:** Tax return liability resulting from current period taxable income. It is also known as the "current tax expense or benefit" under (US) SFAS 109.
3. **Income tax paid:** This refers to the actual cash flow for income taxes, including payments (refunds) for other years.
4. **Tax loss carried forward:** Tax return loss that can cause a reduction in taxable income in the future.
5. The amount attributed to that asset or liability for tax purposes is called the tax base of an asset or liability.

10.7.2 *The Disparity between Accounting Profit and Taxable Income*

The disparity between taxable income and accounting profit can happen for different reasons. Examples are:

- Expenses and revenue can be recognized in one fiscal period for tax purposes and in a different accounting period.
- Certain expenses or revenue can be recognized for accounting purposes but not recognized for tax, or conversely, be recognized for taxation and not recognized for accounting.
- The difference in asset and liabilities tax base and carrying amount.
- For income tax and accounting purposes, the deductibility of gains and losses of assets and liabilities can differ.

- Prior years' tax losses can be used to lower the taxable income in future years, subjected to tax rules, which will lead to differences between the accounting and taxable income (tax loss carryforward).
- The reported financial data adjustments from prior years may not be equally recognized for accounting and tax purposes or recognized in different periods.

10.7.3 *Temporary versus Permanent Differences*

The successful analysis of financial statements requires understanding periodic income tax expenses and the associated tax assets and liabilities.

Financial statements are prepared based on an accrual basis. Reported income on the income statement is on an accrual basis. This reported income can differ substantially from the taxable income. Taxable income refers to the income used to determine the tax payable under the prevailing tax laws that are closer to accounting's modified cash basis. Thus there exist differences between reported income and taxable income. These differences may be temporary or permanent.

10.7.4 *Permanent Differences*

Permanent differences are differences in what is recognized on the accounting income statement and tax return. Specifically, income and expenses recognized as income and expenditure on the income statement may not be recognized as taxable income or tax-deductible expense. For example, a tax-free bond gives rise to accounting income instead of taxable income since the interest coupons are exempt from tax. Such permanent differences will not be reversed in the future.

Permanent differences originate in the current period and do not reverse in subsequent periods. Such differences may arise from income not subject to tax and expenses disallowed for tax purposes as defined by the Income Tax Act or any other tax regulation. Because of the permanent differences, a company's effective tax rate does not equal its statutory tax rate. The effective tax rate is the tax expense figure divided by the pre-tax income.

$$\text{Effective tax rate} = \text{Income tax expense/Pretax income}$$

10.7.5 *Temporary Differences*

Temporary (or timing) differences are timing differences in recognition. For example, reported income uses straight-line depreciation, whereas tax reporting uses accelerated depreciation methods like DDB. Note that the total depreciation of an asset using the straight-line depreciation method and the accelerated depreciation method does not change the asset's useful life. The total depreciation of an asset is calculated by the initial cost minus salvage value. As a result, the reported depreciation expense for accounting and tax reporting purposes may differ over the asset's useful life. There is a difference only in the timing of the recognition. The total depreciation reported over time, however, is the same.

Temporary differences between reported (accounting) income and taxable income arising in the current period and will be reversed in the subsequent period. It represents income and expenses included in the one period's financial statements. However, the temporary difference will only be taxed or deducted for tax purposes in another fiscal period. A deferred tax liability or asset arises when an income or expense item is treated differently on financial statements and tax reporting. Differences are expected to reverse in the future. The fundamental relationship is:

$$\text{Income tax expense} = \text{Current tax expense} + \text{Deferred tax expense}$$

The income tax expense on the income statement is first derived by accounting for temporary differences between reported and taxable income and next by accounting for the impact of permanent differences under current tax expense.

Deferred tax liability is created, i.e., the tax liability is deferred to future years if the current tax expense is less than income tax expense. An example is the exchange rate gain on capital transactions and situations where tax depreciation is more generous than accounting depreciation charges.

When the current tax expense is higher than income tax expense, a deferred tax asset is created, e.g., the exchange rate loss on capital transactions and situations where tax depreciation is lower than accounting depreciation charges.

In summary, due to the presence of permanent and temporary differences, reported income might not equal taxable income. The income tax expense on the income statement may not equal the taxes payable. The difference between income tax expense and taxes payable is the deferred tax expense which results from changes in deferred tax assets and liabilities.

References/Further Readings

Robinson, T., Henry, E., Pirie, W., Broihahn, M., & Cope, A. (2015). *International Financial Statement Analysis*, 3rd edn. Wiley, Chap. 13.

Subramanyam, K.R. (2014). *Financial Statement Analysis*, 11th edn. McGraw Hill, Chap. 6, pp. 378–385.

10.8 Components of Shareholders' Equity

Equity is the owners' residual ownership interest in the company's assets after deducting all liabilities from the assets.

Learning Objectives

- Describe components of shareholder's equity and the statement of changes in equity.

Main Takeaways

Main Points

- Six contributing elements that make up the owners' equity segment of a balance sheet are contributed capital, preferred shares, treasury shares, retained earnings, accumulated other comprehensive income, and noncontrolling interest.
- The statement of changes in equity provides details about the rises or falls in each contributing element of a firm's equity over a given period.

Main Terms

- **Contributed capital (or common stock, or issued capital):** the total financing contributed to the entity by owners in return for capital shares.
- **Treasury shares:** Shares that have been repurchased by the company and held as treasury shares instead of being canceled.
- **Retained earnings:** Earned capital of a company, the aggregate amount of earnings in the company which has not been used for dividends.
- **Accumulated other comprehensive income (or other reserves):** Under US GAAP and IFRS, other comprehensive income is accumulated over time and separately reported from retained earnings but as a section of owner equity labeled as accumulated other comprehensive income.
- **Noncontrolling interest (or minority interest):** The equity interests of minority shareholders in the subsidiaries that have been consolidated but are not wholly-owned by the parent company.

10.8.1 *Equity*

Equity is the owners' residual ownership interest in a company's assets after deducting its liabilities. It provides information about the claim of the owner against the company. Funds directly invested by the owners or earnings that are reinvested over time, gain or loss items that are not recognized in the income statement can also be considered equity.

(a) Components of Equity

Six main components typically comprise total owners' equity. The first five components listed below comprise equity attributable to the parent company's owners. The sixth component is the equity attributable to noncontrolling interests.

1. **Capital contributed by owners (or common shares, or issued capital):** The total financing received from shareholders in return for capital shares. For each class of common shares distributed, the company must declare the number of shares approved, issued, and outstanding.
2. **Preferred shares:** Preferred shares allow holders to distinguish themselves from ordinary shares holders by possessing specific attributes or rights not enjoyed by common shares holders. The attributes include dividends distribution preference, liquidation priorities, etc.
3. **Treasury shares:** Shares that have been repurchased and held as treasury shares instead of being canceled. It Helps reduces owners' equity by the value of the acquisition cost and at the same time decreasing the number of outstanding shares.
4. **Retained earnings:** This is referred to as the company's earned capital, the collected amount of undistributed earnings recognized in its income statement.
5. **Accumulated other comprehensive income (or other reserves):** This refers to other comprehensive income that has not been reflected in retained earnings and recognized as part of net income.
6. **Minority interest:** Also referred to as noncontrolling interest. It represents ownership of less than 50% in the entity being reported in the parent company's consolidated statements.

Figures 10.3 and 10.4 show the following Exhibits A and B. It presents excerpts of the balance sheets of SAP Group and Apple Inc., respectively, with detailed line items for each company's equity section.

Exhibit A:SAP Group Consolidated Statement of Financial Position		
(in millions of Euros)		
Assets	2017	2016
Total current assets	11,930	11,564
Total non-current assets	30,567	32,713
Total assets	42,497	44,277
Total current liabilities	10,210	9,674
Total non-current liabilities	6,747	8,205
Total liabilities	16,957	17,880
Issued capital	1,229	1,229
Share premium	570	599
Retained earnings	24,794	22,302
Other components of equity	508	3,346
Treasury shares	-1,591	-1,099
Equity attributable to owners of parent	25,509	26,376
Non-controlling interests	31	21
Total equity	25,540	26,397
Total equity and liabilities	42,497	44,277

Figure 10.3: Exhibit A; An extract of SAP 2017 group annual report.

Source: SAP Group annual report 2017.

Exhibit B: Apple Inc. Consolidated Balance Sheet		
(in millions of $) (Number of Shares in thousands)		
Assets	30-Sep-17	30-Sep-16
Total current assets	128,645	106,869
All other assets	*246,674*	*214,817*
Total assets	375,319	321,686
Liabilities and shareholders' equity		
Total current liabilities	100,814	79,006
Total non-current liabilities	*140,458*	*114,431*
Total liabilities	241,272	193,438
Common stock and additional paid-in capital, $0.00001 par value: 12,600,000 shares authorized; 5,126,201 and 5,336,166 shares issued and outstanding, respectively	35,867	31,251
Retained earnings	98,330	96,364
Accumulated other comprehensive income/loss	-150	634
Assets		
Total shareholders' equity	134,047	128,249
Total liabilities and shareholders' equity	375,319	321,687

Figure 10.4: Exhibit B; An extract of SAP 2017 group annual report.

Source: Apple Inc. 2017 annual report.

SAP's balance sheet indicates that the company has €1,229 million issued capital. The financial statements' notes disclose that the company has issued 1,229 million no-par common stock with a nominal value of €1 per share. SAP's balance sheet also indicates that the company has €1,591 treasury shares, and the notes to the financial statements disclose that the company holds 35 million of its shares as treasury shares. The line item share premium of €570 million includes amounts from treasury share transactions (and certain other transactions). The amount of retained earnings, €24,794 million, represents the cumulative amount of earnings that the company has recognized in its income statements, net of dividends. SAP's €508 million of "Other components of equity" includes the company's accumulated other comprehensive income. The notes disclose that this is composed of €330 million gains on exchange differences in translation, €157 million gains on remeasuring available-for-sale financial assets, and €21 million gains on cash flow hedges.

Next, the balance sheet presents a subtotal for the amount of equity attributable to the parent company €25,509 million, followed by the amount of equity attributable to noncontrolling interests €31 million.

Total equity includes both equity attributable to the parent company and equity attributable to noncontrolling interests. The equity section of Apple's balance sheet consists of only three-line items: common stock retained earnings and accumulated other comprehensive income/(loss).

Although Apple's balance sheet shows no treasury stock, the company repurchases its shares but cancels the repurchased shares rather than holding the treasury shares. Apple's balance sheet shows that 5,126,201 thousand shares were issued and outstanding at the end of fiscal 2017, and 5,336,166 thousand shares were issued and outstanding at the end of fiscal 2016. Details on the change in shares outstanding are presented on the Statement of Shareholders' Equity in Exhibit B, which shows that in 2017 Apple repurchased 246,496 thousand shares of its previously issued common stock and issued 36,531 thousand shares to employees.

10.8.2 *The Statement of Owners' Equity*

The Statement of Changes in Owners' (Shareholders') Equity reports the amounts and sources of changes in stockholders' equity over a period. It provides detailed information about the movement in shares and other equity-related details such as earnings attributable to equity holders.

The statement reflects information such as changes in:

- Preferred shares
- Common shares
- Additional paid-in capital
- Retained earnings
- Treasury shares which are repurchased shares
- Employee stock option plan adjustments

The statement of changes in equity (or statement of shareholders' equity) presents information about the increases or decreases in a company's equity over a period. IFRS requires the following information in the statement of changes in equity:

1. total comprehensive income for the period;
2. the effects of any accounting changes that have been applied retrospectively to previous periods;
3. capital transactions with owners and distributions to owners;
4. reconciliation of the carrying amounts of each component of equity at the beginning and end of the fiscal year.

Table 10.3 depicts Exhibit C, which presents an excerpt from Apple's Consolidated Statements of Changes in Shareholders' Equity. The section shows only one of the years presented on the actual statement. It begins with the balance as of 24 September 2016 (i.e., the beginning of fiscal 2017). It presents the analysis of changes to 30 September 2017 in each component of equity shown on Apple's balance sheet. As noted above, the number of shares outstanding decreased from 5,336,166 thousand to 5,126,201 thousand as the company repurchased 246,496 thousand shares of its common stock and issued 36,531 thousand new shares, which reduced the dollar balance of Paid-in Capital and Retained earnings by \$913 million and \$581 million, respectively. The dollar balance in common stock also increased by \$4,909 million connected with share-based compensation. Retained earnings increased by \$48,351 million net income, minus \$12,803 million dividends, \$33,001 million for the share repurchase, and \$581 million adjustments in connection with the stock issuance.

For companies that pay dividends, the amount of dividends is shown separately as a deduction from retained earnings. The statement also

Table 10.3: Exhibit C: Excerpt from Apple Inc.'s consolidated statement of changes in shareholders' equity (in millions, except share amounts in thousands).

	Common stock and additional paid-in capital		Retained	Accumulated other comprehensive	Total shareholders'
	Shares	Amount	earnings	income/(Loss)	equity
Balances as of Sep 24, 2016	5,336,166	31,251	96,364	634	128,249
Net income			48,351		48,351
Other comprehensive Income/(Loss)			(12,803)		(12,803)
Repurchase of common stock	(246,496)		(33,001)		(33,001)
Share-based compensation		4,909			4,909
Common stock issued, net of shares withheld for employee taxes	36,531	(913)	(581)		(1,494)
Tax benefit from equity awards, including transfer pricing adjustments		620			620
Balances as of Sep 30, 2017	5,126,201	35,867	98,330	−150	134,047

details the $784 million change in Apple's Accumulated other comprehensive income. Note that the account provides a subtotal for total comprehensive income that includes net income and each component of other comprehensive income.

References/Further Readings

Robinson, T., Henry, E., Pirie, W., Broihahn, M., & Cope, A. (2015). *International Financial Statement Analysis,* 3rd edn. Wiley, Chap. 5.

Subramanyam, K. R. (2014). *Financial Statement Analysis*, 11th edn. McGraw Hill, Chap. 3, pp. 166–177.

10.9 Sample Questions

Question 1 (Assets, Liabilities, and Equity)
At the end of the previous year, the company's assets totaled $900,000, and its liabilities totaled $760,000. During the current year, the company's total assets increased by $60,000, and its total liabilities decreased by $30,000. At the end of the current year, stockholders' equity was:

(a) $230,000
(b) $220,000
(c) $34,000

Question 2 (Different Types of Assets and Liabilities and the Measurement Bases of Each)
On 30 June of the current year, the assets and liabilities of Phoenix, Inc. are as follows: Cash and cash equivalents $20,500; Accounts Receivable, $7,250; Supplies, $650; PPE, $12,000; Accounts Payable, $9,300. What is the amount of equity as of 1 July of the current year?

(a) $13,050
(b) $20,500
(c) $31,100

Question 3 (Long-Lived Assets — Capitalized Costs and Costs that are Expensed)
Which of the following is least correct?

(a) Capitalized costs mean adding the purchase cost of a good or service to an asset account rather than expensing the cost immediately.
(b) Costs are expensed (i.e., not capitalize) when benefits are immediate, or future benefits are too uncertain or immaterial.
(c) Costs of purchasing PPE is expensed immediately and is shown as an expense in the income statement.

Question 4 (Depreciation)
Mulan Enterprises pays $235,200 for equipment that will last 5 years and has a $52,500 residual value. Using the equipment in its operations for 5 years, the company expects to earn $85,500 annually after deducting all expenses except depreciation. Assuming straight-line depreciation, what are the depreciation expense and net (pre-tax) profit each year?

(a) Depreciation expense is $36540, and net profit is $85,500 every year
(b) Depreciation expense is $29940, and net profit is $48,960 every year
(c) Depreciation expense is $36540, and net profit is $48,960 every year

Question 5 (Non-Current Liabilities, e.g., Debt)
Suppose BreadTalk issues $100,000 of semi-annual 9% 5-year bonds when the market interest rate is 10%. What is the amount of sales proceeds BreadTalk receives initially?

(a) $96,138
(b) $100,000
(c) $98,145

Question 6 (Income Taxes)
Income tax expense reported on a company's income statement equals taxes payable, plus the net increase in:

(a) deferred tax assets, less the net increase in deferred tax liabilities.
(b) deferred tax liabilities, less the net increase in deferred tax assets.
(c) deferred tax liabilities, plus the net increase in deferred tax assets.

Question 7 (Components of Shareholders' Equity)
A company has paid-up capital of $30,000, Retained Earnings of $65,000, Treasury Shares of $18,000, and Ordinary Shares of $10,000. If the company does not have any accumulated other comprehensive income (loss), what is the total amount of shareholders' equity?

(a) $113,000
(b) $77,000
(c) $87,000

Question 8 (Components of Shareholders' Equity)
On 1 January of the current year, Bob's Lawn Care Service reported equity totaling $122,500. During the current year, total revenues were $96,000 while total expenses were $85,500. Nevertheless, Bob withdrew $20,000 from the company during the current year. No other changes in equity occurred during the year. If, on 31 December of the current year, total assets are $196,000, the difference in equity during the year was:

(a) A decrease of $9,500
(b) An increase of $9,500
(c) An increase of $30,500

Solutions

Question 1

Solution: Option **a** is correct.

At the end of the current year

Assets = Liabilities + Shareholder's equity

\$900,000 + \$60,000 = (\$760,000 – \$30,000) + Shareholder's equity

Shareholder's equity = \$230,000

Question 2

Solution: Option **c** is correct.

Assets	Liabilities
Cash and Cash equivalents \$20500	Accounts payable \$9300
Accounts receivable \$7250	Shareholder's Equity = 20500+7250+650+12000-9300=\$31100
Supplies \$650	
PPE \$12000	

Question 3

Solution: Option **c** is correct.

PPE is capitalized as an asset in the balance sheet when purchased and expensed over time as depreciation expense in which the company receives benefits from such costs

Question 4

Solution: Option **c** is correct.

Under straight line method, Deprecation expense = (\$235,200 – \$52,500)/ 5 years = \$36,540;

Net profit = \$85,500 – \$36,540 = \$48,960

Question 5

Solution: Option **a** is correct.

Face value = \$100,000
Stated interest rate = 9% therefore semiannual = 4.5%
Interest payment = 4.5%∗100,000 = \$4,500 per period
Bond life = 5 years therefore n = 10
Market interest rate = 10% therefore semiannual = 5%
Cash Proceeds = Present value of Face Value + Present value of annuity of Interest Payment=(\$100,000∗0.6139)+(4,500∗7.7217)= \$96,138

Question 6

Solution: Option **b** is correct.

Higher reported tax expense relative to taxes paid will increase the deferred tax liability, whereas lower reported tax expense relative to taxes increases the deferred tax asset.

Question 7

Solution: Option **b** is correct.

Note that Ordinary Shares are part of paid-up capital.
Total Shareholders' Equity
= Paid-up Capital + Retained Earnings – Treasury Shares
= \$30,000 + \$65,000 – \$18,000 = \$77,000

Question 8

Solution: Option **a** is correct.

Beginning shareholder's equity + Additional Share Capital + Net Income – Dividends = Ending Shareholder's Equity = 122500 + (–20000) + (96000–85500) – 0 =113000
Changes in Equity= 113000-122500= – 9500

Chapter 11

Understanding Cash Flow Statements

The cash flow statement is a financial document used to explain the change in a firm's cash account on the statement of financial position by declaring the firm's cash payments and receipts for a given accounting period. The statement categorizes cash receipts and cash payments during a given period into operating, investing, and financing activities.

11.1 Cash Flows from Operating, Investing, and Financing Activities

All companies engage themselves in operations, investment, and finance-related activities. Under IFRS and US GAAP, all these activities are classified under the cash flow statement.

Learning Objectives

- Identify cash flow activities from operations, investments, and finance to compare and categorize cash flow items into one of the three categories.

Main Takeaways

Main Points

- Cash flow activities are classified into three categories: operating, investing, and financing activities.

  1. Cash flows from operations (CFO) reflect flows associated with the primary, day-to-day business of the firm. There are two

methods to depict operating cash flow on a cash flow statement: the direct and indirect methods.

2. Cash flow from investing (CFI) results from activities corresponding to the purchase or sale of assets or the company's investments. Having a negative cash flow from investing might not be a bad sign if the management invests in its long-term health.
3. Cash flows from financing (CFF) reflect flows related to securing money for the company's use by issuing shares or borrowing. The cash flow statement's financing activity focuses on how a firm raises capital and pays it back to investors through capital markets.

- Not every significant activity of a company involves cash. Significant non-cash activities are either reported in a supplementary schedule or a separate piece of note to the financial statements.

Main Terms

- **Cash flows from operations (CFO):** Reflects revenue-generating and related activities of the firms are categorized under CFO.
- **Cash flow from investing (CFI):** Activities related to the purchase or sale of productive assets (physical assets and investments).
- **Cash flow from financing (CFF):** Represents both acquiring and dispensing of the ownership of funds and borrowings.
- **IFRS:** Refers to the International Financial Reporting Standards. It is the primary accounting standards system used outside of the US.
- **GAAP:** Refers to the Generally Accepted Accounting Principles. It is the standard framework of guidelines, conventions, and rules accountants are expected to follow in recording, summarizing, and preparing financial statements in any given jurisdiction.
- **Investing activities:** An activity that causes changes in non-current assets or involves a return on investment and actions where the money is put into something with the expectation of gain, usually over a longer-term.

11.1.1 *Introduction*

The cash flow statement illustrates the change in the firm's cash account on the statement of financial position by declaring both the cash payments and receipts for a given period. All the operating, investing, and financing activities are classified either as cash receipts or cash payments under the statement.

11.1.2 *Classifications of Cash Flows*

There are three types of activities that companies usually engage in: operating, investing, and financing activities. Following both IFRS and US GAAP standards, cash flows in the cash flow statement are categorized according to the following three types:

1. **Cash flow from operating activities:** Cash receipts or payments arising from the day-to-day activities of a business, for instance, cash flows from the sale of inventory, provisions of services, or other activities that are not of an investing nor financing nature. Cash payments and receipts derived from the trading or dealing in securities that are not for investment purposes are also classified.
2. **Cash flow from investing activities:** Represent the purchase or sale of productive assets (physical assets and investments). It includes cash flows relating to acquisitions and sale of long-term assets such as property, plant, and equipment, and investments in debt instruments and short-term marketable securities (equity or debt instruments) are also reflected under this classification.
3. **Cash flow from financing activities:** Represents acquiring and dispensing ownership funds and borrowings. The cash flows reflected under these classifications are those relating to the resources raised by the company from shareholders or creditors. Examples of inflows include proceeds of equity issuances, ST and LT borrowings. Examples of outflows include payment of cash dividends, repayment, etc.

11.1.3 *Classifications under IFRS and US GAAP*

Table 11.1 shows the Cash Flow Statements: Classifications of IFRS and US GAAP.

11.1.4 *Cash Flow from Operating Activities — Direct Method*

Cash flow from operating activities, also commonly referred to as cash flow from operations or operating cash flow, reflects flows related to a business's revenue-generating activities. There are two acceptable methods for presenting cash flow from operating activities; direct and indirect methods. Both approaches yield identical results; the difference lies only in the operating cash flow's reporting format. The presentation format for investing and financing cash flows is uniform, irrespective of the methodology used in presenting operating cash flows.

Table 11.1: Classifications of IFRS and US GAAP.

Topic	IFRS	US GAAP
Classification of cash flows:		
Interest received	Operating or investing	Operating
Interest paid	Operating or financing	Operating
Dividends received	Operating or investing	Operating
Dividends paid	Operating or financing	Financing
Bank overdrafts	Considered part of cash equivalents	Not considered part of cash and cash equivalent and classified as financing
Taxes paid	Generally operating, but a portion can be allocated to investing or financing if identified explicitly with these categories.	Operating
Format of statement	Direct or indirect, direct is encouraged	Direct or indirect; direct is encouraged. A reconciliation of net income to cash flow from operating activities must be provided regardless of its method.

Source: IAS 7, FASB ASC Topic 230 and "IFRS and USGAAP: Similarities and Differences," Price water house Coopers (November 2017), available at www.pwc.com.

The direct method will be depicted in this section, followed by the indirect method and the explanation of the later segments' differences.

The direct method shows the cash inflows and outflows categorized under cash flow from operating activities. It represents each cash inflow and outflow corresponding to its cash receipts and disbursements. In other words, any impact of accruals is eliminated under the direct method, and only cash receipts and cash payments are illustrated.

The principal argument in favor of the direct method is that information on the specific sources of operating cash receipts and payments is reflected under this method. On the contrary, only the net result of these payments and receipts is illustrated under the indirect method.

Table 11.2 illustrates a sample cash flow statement prepared under IFRS using the direct method.

Table 11.2: Sample operating cash flow statement under IFRS using the direct method.

	31-Dec-2020	31-Dec-2019
	$$	$$
Cash flow from operating activities		
Cash received from customers	25,900	23,478
Cash paid to suppliers and employees	−15,658	17,534
Dividend received	1,200	178
Net interest and other financial expenses paid	−5,426	−4,789
Taxes paid	−1,963	−750
Net cash from operating activities	**4,053**	**583**

11.1.5 *Indirect Method*

Under the indirect approach, only the net results of payments and receipts are provided. After adjusting the operating cash flows for non-cash and non-operating items and net changes in operating accruals, net income (the starting point of the indirect method) is reconciled. The main arguments in favor of the indirect method are as follows:

- The reasons for differences between operating cash flows and net income is illustrated under this method.
- The method replicates a forecasting approach which begins with forecasting future income, which is followed by deriving cash flows by adjusting for changes in balance sheet accounts which materialize due to the difference in the timing between cash accounting and accrual accounting.
- Adjustment of net income to operating cash flows is convenient and less expensive than reporting the gross operating cash payments and receipts, using the direct approach.

Table 11.3 depicts an example of deriving operating cash flows from the net income from a cash flow statement prepared as per the IFRS standards, using the indirect method.

11.1.6 *Purpose of Cash Flow Statements*

Cash flow statements help determine liquidity and identify the amount of capital that is free to capture the current market opportunities. Being one of the essential financial statements to be publicly released by public

Table 11.3: Sample operating cash flow statement under IFRS using the indirect method.

	31-Dec-2020	31-Dec-2019
	$$	$$
Cash flow from operating activities		
Net profit	3,457	4,256
Taxation	1,200	1,189
Net finance costs	536	245
Operating profit (continued and discontinued operations)	5,193	5,690
Depreciation, amortization and impairment	1,028	1,001
Changes in working capital	1,517	1,501
Inventories	245	657
Trade and other receivables	536	426
Trade payable and other current liabilities	736	418
Provision less payments	−275	−74
Elimination of profits and losses on disposals	54	−1,567
Non cash charges for share base compensation	167	195
Other adjustments	17	32
Cash flow from operating activities	**7,701**	**32**

enterprises, it is also a handy benchmark for investors when considering different organizations' capacity to adapt and capture new opportunities.

11.2 Cash Flow Statement Link to the Income Statement and the Balance Sheet

The preparation of a business's cash flow statement uses the information from both the income statement and the balance sheet.

Learning Objectives

- Describe how the cash flow statement is linked to both the income statement and the balance sheet.

Main Takeaways

Main Points

- The cash flow statement is linked to a company's income statement and comparative balance sheets and data in both the statements.

- Information on the cash flows statement is not "new" over and above the balance sheet and income statement. The Statement of Cash Flow (SCF) value derives from the way information has already been categorized.
- The SCF values are derived from (1) comparative statements of financial position, (2) current income statement, and (3) additional documentation.
- The cash flows statement ultimately shows the change in cash during an accounting period, which implies the difference in the beginning and ending balances of the cash asset in the balance sheet.
- A business's investing activities are generally associated with a balance sheet's fixed asset segments. Its financing activities are usually associated with the long-term debt and equity segments.

Main Terms

- **Indirect method:** Refers to cash flow statements, a format to present a statement, whereby under operating cash flow, it starts with net income followed by the necessary subtractions and additions, which results in operating cash flow.
- **Accounting irregularities:** An accounting term for a practice that does not reconcile to the ordinary laws, practices, and rules of the accounting profession, to purposefully deceive or defraud. Intentionally misstating amounts and other information in financial statements or omitting information required to be disclosed falls under Accounting irregularities. Accounting irregularities generally differ from unintentional mistakes or errors.

11.2.1 *Relationship between the Income Statement and Cash Flow Statement*

Fundamental knowledge of the relationship between cash flow statements, income statements, and balance sheets is essential to understand a business's financial health. It can also facilitate identifying any accounting irregularities.

The essential associations between the cash flow statement, income statement, and the balance sheet include the following:

1. The amount of cash and cash equivalents at the beginning and end of the balance sheet are associated with the cash flow statement. Explicitly, the statement of cash flows reflects the change in the

cash balance during the reporting period, as per the following equation:

(Cash balance at the beginning + Cash receipts from operating, investing as well as financing activities) – (Cash payments for operating, investing, and financing activities) = Cash balance at the end

Beginning Balance Sheet at 31 December 20X8	Statement of Cash Flows for Year Ended 31 December 20X9		Ending Balance Sheet at 31 December 20X9
Beginning cash	Plus: Cash receipts (from operating, investing, and financing activities)	Less: Cash payments (for operating investing, and financing activities)	Ending cash

2. The current assets and liabilities section of a balance sheet generally illustrates a business's operating activities and decisions. A change in a short-term asset or short-term liability on the balance sheet is due to the cash and the accrual differences for an operating transaction.

Beginning Balance Sheet at 31 December 20X8	Income Statement for Year Ended 31 December 20X9	Statement of Cash Flows for Year Ended 31 December 20X9	Ending Balance Sheet at 31 December 20X9
Beginning accounts receivable	Plus revenues	Minus: Cash collected from customers	Equals: Ending accounts receivable

3. The fixed asset section of a balance sheet is associated with investing activities. The balance sheet's equity and long-term debt sections correspond to the business's financing activities.

Understanding the interrelationships between the balance sheet and income statement and the cash flow statement helps evaluate the company's financial health and identify any misconduct or inconsistent accounting behaviors.

11.3 Preparation of Direct and Indirect Cash Flow Statement

A cash flow statement can be built in two ways. Both ways end up with the same answer, but differently.

Learning Objectives

- Describe the steps to prepare both a direct and an indirect cash flow statement, including how cash flows can be computed using income statement and balance sheet data.

Main Takeaways

Main Points

- Businesses can choose to use direct or indirect approaches to report their operating cash flow.
- An evaluation of a cash flow statement should involve assessing the sources, cash use, and the main drivers of cash flow within each activity category.
- Using the direct method to report their operating cash flow, the operating cash inflows are identified by its' provenance (for example, cash received from buyers and income from investments) and the operating cash outflows by use (for example, cash paid to suppliers and for interest).
- The indirect method reconciles net income to operating cash flow by making adjustments to net income for all non-cash items and the net changes in the operating working capital accounts.
- Cash flow from investing always uses the direct method to present information. Cash inflows include the sale of plant and equipment, property, sale of non-cash equivalent debt and equity securities of other firms (investments), and collection of principal on loans to other firms. Cash outflows include acquiring property, plant, and equipment, purchasing non-cash equivalent debt and equity securities of other firms (investments), and making loans to other firms.
- Cash flow from financing always uses the direct method to present information. Cash inflows include issuing the firm's stock, issuing bonds, mortgage notes, etc., and borrowing short or long-term debt. Cash outflows include payment of dividends, repurchase of the firm's stock, payment of the short- or long-term debt, the redemption of bonds.

Main Terms

- **Non-cash expense:** Expenses recorded in the income statement but do not involve an actual cash transaction.
- **Accumulated depreciation:** The sum of all recorded depreciation on an asset up to a specific date. The carrying value of an asset is its historical cost minus accumulated depreciation.
- **Book value:** The total amount of the company's worth if it winds up all of its assets and pays back all its liabilities. Book value can also refer to a particular asset's value on its balance sheet after depreciation on the asset has been accounted for.
- **Retained earnings (RE):** Refers to the amount of net income of a business left after the dividends are paid to its shareholders.

11.3.1 *Preparation of Cash Flow Statement*

The cash and cash equivalents account reported on the balance sheet statement at the beginning and end of an accounting period are directly associated with the cash balances at the beginning and end of a cash flow statement.

There are various reasons for the differences between net income and net operating cash flows.

- One of the many reasons is non-cash expenses, like depreciation of tangible assets and intangible assets amortization. Such expenses reduce net income but do not affect the net cash flows as they require zero cash outlays.
- The existing difference in the time between revenue expense recognition and materialization of the underlying cash flows is another point of difference.

The income statement can be converted from an accrual basis to a cash basis using two methods: direct or indirect methods. Companies can use either of the two methods to report their operating cash flow.

- With the direct method approach, under the operating activities category, it reports operating cash inflows by its' provenance (such as cash received from buyers, cash received from investment) and outflows by use (such as cash payments to suppliers and cash payments for interest).

  - Each item is adjusted to its' cash equivalent in the income statement.
  - Reflects operating cash payments along with cash receipts. A more significant amount of information on the cash flows can be read, and it is more straightforward to understand for an average reader.
- The indirect method approach essentially reconciles the accrual-based net income to net cash flow from operating activities by adjusting backward for non-cash and other items. The next step is to adjust for changes in working capital accounts.
  - It illustrates the difference between net income as well as operating cash flows.
  - A maximum number of companies use it.
- The alternative formats are direct and indirect in reporting the net cash flows from operating activities. Both methods will yield identical results of the same net amount for operating activities.
- Under IFRS and US GAAP, both direct and indirect methods are acceptable for financial reporting. The direct approach reveals more information on the organization. However, as many organizations prefer to disclose limited information, the indirect approach is mostly preferred.
- For both direct and indirect methods, presenting investing and financing activities are similar. The difference is only in the presentation of operating activities.

11.3.2 *The Direct Method*

Net cash flows from operations are reported in the statement of cash flows as significant classes of operating cash receipts and disbursements. All the income statement items are converted into cash equivalents under the direct method. The difference between the cash receipts and cash disbursements helps calculate the net operating cash flows.

Assume that Table 11.4 balance sheet and income statement are of a hypothetical company named ABC.

11.3.3 *The Direct Method*

- Cash receipts: \$252,000 reflects sales based on accrual. The cash collections are greater than accrual-basis sales as the receivables have decreased by \$7,000.

Table 11.4: Company ABC balance sheet and income statement.

Balance sheet		(in thousands)
	2019	2018
Cash	64	58
Receivables	50	57
Inventory	74	77
Prepaid Expense	6	4
Accounts Payable	60	70
Taxes Payable	10	5

Income statement	(in thousands)
	2019
Sales	252
Cost of goods sold	(106)
Gross Profit	146
Admin and selling expenses	(56)
Income before income taxes	90
Income tax expenses	(40)
Net income	50

Notes: Additional information:

- The cost of goods sold is related to accounts payables, whereas sales are related to receivables.
- Prepaid expenses and the depreciation of $6,000 are related to administrative and selling costs.

Sales: $252,000
Add decrease in receivables: $7,000
Cash receipts: $259,000

- Cash purchases: As the Inventory decreased by $3,000, goods purchased in previous years were considered the costs of goods sold. Accounts payable is added back to cash purchases since there is a decrease of $10,000 as an outflow of cash payments.

Costs of goods sold: $106,000
Less decrease in inventories: $3,000
Add decrease in accounts payable: $10,000
Cash purchases: $113,000

- Administrative and cash selling expenses: A non-cash charge of $6,000 related to depreciation is also included in the selling and administrative expenses. Additionally, prepaid expenses (assets) increased by $2,000, added to the administrative and selling expenses.

  Administrative and selling expenses: $56,000
  Less depreciation expense: $6,000
  Add increase in pre-paid expense: $2,000
  Administrative and selling expenses: $52,000

- Cash income taxes: income tax expense stated on the income statement is at $40,000. There is an increase in tax payable by $5,000, implying a share of the taxes yet to be paid. Hence:

  Income tax expense: $40,000
  Less increase in taxes payable: $5,000
  Income tax paid: $35,000

The direct method for presenting net cash flow from operating is shown in Table 11.5.

11.3.4 *The Indirect Method*

The calculation of net cash flow from operating activities using the indirect method starts with net income and adjusts backward for all non-cash and other items, followed by adjustments for working capital changes.

Using the following four-step process:

1. **Begin the process with net income.**
2. **Adding back all non-cash charges such as the depreciation of tangibles assets and amortization of intangibles.** Cash payment is

Table 11.5: Statement of operating cash flow using the direct method.

Statement of Cash Flows (Direct Method) (in thousands)	
Cash Flow from Operating Activities	
Cash received from customers	259
Cash paid to suppliers	(113)
Admin and selling expenses paid	(52)
Taxes paid	(35)
Cash disbursed for operating activities	(200)
Net cash provided by operating activities	59

incurred whenever fixed assets are bought, and such purchases are categorized as an investing activity during that point in time. Depreciation expense realized during the current period implies the paper allocation of the original purchase cost to the present period. This expense will not generate any cash outflow but will cause the expenses to increase. The depreciation needs to be added back to net income to derive the net CFO as it does not affect net cash flows.

3. **Subtract any gains and Add back losses from financing or investing activities.** Non-operating items appearing in the income statements are added/deducted, for instance, removing gains (or adding back losses) from assets' sale. It is to be noted that the gain or loss on the sale of investments or assets is effectively factored in by the amount of cash proceeds recorded under cash flow from investing activities. As such, gains or losses must be adjusted from net income when determining cash flows from operating activities using the indirect method to avoid double counting.
4. **Adjusting for changes in operating related accounts (current assets and current liabilities other than cash, short-term borrowings, and short-term investments).** Changes in operating asset and operating liabilities accounts–an increase or decrease in operating assets such as accounts receivables, inventory, prepaid expenses is deducted and added respectively. Increased or decreased operating liabilities such as accounts payable, accrued expenses are added and reduced.

Note that short-term borrowing is listed as a financing activity and short-term investments as an investing activity.

An illustration of a hypothetical company cash flow statement based on the indirect method is shown in Table 11.6.

Most businesses report cash flow using the indirect method. A key disadvantage of it will be the lack of information. This method mainly provides a reconciliation between net income and net cash flow from operations and makes it difficult to trace specific operating costs and cash flow elements.

11.3.5 *Conversion of Cash Flows from the Indirect to the Direct Method*

Although the majority of corporations widely uses the indirect method, a simple three-step procedure can be followed by an analyst to change it to the direct format:

Table 11.6: Sample illustration of a company full cash flow statement using the indirect approach.

Cash flow from operating activities		
Net income	3,350	
Adjustments for non-cash items:		
Depreciation	450	
Allowance for doubtful debts	40	
Fair value of biological assets	970	
Inventory write-down	500	
Fair value of derivative instruments	−240	
	5,070	
Change in working capital accounts		
Increase in trade and other receivables	−500	
Decrease in inventories	1,050	
Decrease in trades payables	−1,740	
	−1,190	
Net cash flow from operating activities		3,880
Cash flow from investing activities		
Acquisition of subsidiary XYZ, net of cash acquired	−550	
Purchase of property, plant and equipment	−350	
Proceeds from sale of equipment	20	
Interest received	200	
Dividends received	200	
		−480
Net cash used in investing activities		
Cash flow from financing activities		
Proceeds from issue of share capital	250	
Proceeds from long-term borrowings	250	
Payment of finance lease liabilities	−90	
Dividends paid	−1,200	
Net cash used in financing activities		−790
Net increase in cash and cash equivalents		2,610
Cash and cash equivalents at beginning of period		120
Cash and cash equivalents at end of period		2,730

Table 11.7: Summary table illustrating an indirect approach to calculating operating activities.

Start with Profit before tax
Non-cash Items:
+ Depreciation/amortization
Gain or Loss of Sales of Assets
+ Loss on the sale of long-term assets
− Gain on sale of long-term assets
Changes in non-cash Current Assets/Current Liabilities
+ Decreases in non-cash current assets
+ Increases in current liabilities
− Increases in non-cash current assets
− Decreases in current liabilities
Cash flow from interest/dividend should disclose separately
− Interest revenue
− Dividend revenue
− Interest expense
+ Interest received
+ Dividend received
− Interest paid
Cash flow from taxes should disclose separately
− Income tax paid

- Sum up all revenues as well as all expenses.
- Each non-cash item from aggregated revenues and expenses should be removed, breaking out the remaining items into appropriate cash flow items.
- Working capital changes need to be adjusted for converting accrual amounts into cash flow amounts.

To summarize, the indirect method for calculating the operating activities of a statement of cash flows for easy understanding is in Table 11.7.

References/Further Readings

Robinson, T., Henry, E., Pirie, W., Broihahn, M., & Cope, A. (2015). *International Financial Statement Analysis*, 3rd edn. Wiley, Chap. 6.

Subramanyam, K. R. (2014). *Financial Statement Analysis*, 11th edn. McGraw Hill, Chap 7.

11.4 Sample Questions

Question 1 (Cash Flows from Operating, Investing and Financing Activities)
Which of the following statement on cash flows from financing activities is correct?

(a) Include all cash inflows and cash outflows associated with a firm's lending activities.
(b) Include all cash inflows and cash outflows between a firm and its shareholders.
(c) Are always negative due to the payments of cash dividends and interest and principal on debt.

Question 2 (Cash Flows from Operating, Investing and Financing Activities)
Suppose a firm usually records expenses and revenue before receiving or making cash payments. Which of the following statements is incorrect?

(a) If revenues are decreasing, a net loss could result even though the firm reports a net cash inflow from operating activities.
(b) If revenues increase, net income could result even though the firm reports a net cash outflow from operating activities.
(c) Net income and net cash flows provided by operating activities will always agree.

Question 3 (Cash Flow Statement Link to the Income Statement and the Balance Sheet)
Which of the following statements on the link between a cash flow statement, income statement, and balance sheet is least accurate?

(a) The change of the beginning and ending balances of the cash asset in the balance sheet is equal to the total cash flow in the corresponding accounting period in the cash flow statement.

(b) Typically, the balance sheet's long-term asset category is associated with its investing activities. The balance sheet's equity and long-term debt category is related to the financing activities.
(c) The net operating cash flow derived from the direct and indirect methods is not equal.

Question 4 (Preparation of Direct and Indirect Cash Flow Statement)
Which of the following transactions affect cash?

(a) Conversion of debt to common stock
(b) Credit sales
(c) Sale of fixed assets at their book value

Question 5 (Preparation of Direct and Indirect Cash Flow Statement)
A firm spent $250,000 by purchasing equipment with an expected life of 10 years and zero residual value. The company sold the equipment for $94,000 after 6 years. The firm uses straight-line depreciation and the indirect method to calculate operating cash flows. Which of the following statement illustrates how the equipment's sale should be reported in the cash flow statement?

(a) $94,000 is recorded as a cash inflow from investing activities, and other categories of the statement are unaffected.
(b) $94,000 is recorded as a cash inflow from investing activities, and $6,000 is added to convert net income to net cash flow, which is provided by operating activities.
(c) $94,000 is recorded as a cash inflow from investing activities, and $6,000 is subtracted to convert net income to net cash flow, which is provided by operating activities.

Question 6 (Preparation of Direct and Indirect Cash Flow Statement)
A company issues new shares of $1 million and pays $200,000 in cash dividends during the year. Additionally, the company took advantage of falling interest rates to borrow $1.5 million and pay off existing loans of $2 million. The company bought 500 of another company's shares and paid $600,000. The net cash flow provided by financing activities is:

(a) An outflow of $200,000
(b) An outflow of $100,000
(c) An inflow of $300,000

Question 7 (Preparation of Direct and Indirect Cash Flow Statement)
Suppose a company prepares its cash flow statements as per the directions. If we assume that the company's inventory and accounts payable increase during the accounting period, what would be the effect of the changes on the cash flow calculations?

(a) The changes in each account are both added to net income.
(b) Add the increase in accounts payable to the cost of goods, and deduct the inventory increase from the cost of goods sold to estimate the cash paid to suppliers.
(c) Reduce the increase in accounts payable from the cost of goods sold, and add the rise in the inventory to the cost of goods sold to calculate the cash paid to suppliers.

Solutions

Question 1

Solution: Option **b** is correct.

Cash flows from financing activities include all cash inflows/outflows between a company and its shareholders. Cash flows associated with borrowing activities and lending activities are considered a part of the investing category.

Question 2

Solution: Option **c** is correct.

Accrual basis accounting is used to prepare financial statements. When performance obligation revenues are realized, only when incurred expenses are accounted for, while revenues can be recorded on credit even before cash is collected. Expenses can also be recorded before making cash payments. There is a difference between net income and net cash given by operating activities.

Question 3

Solution: Option **c** is correct.

The net operating cash flows using the direct and indirect methods are equal.

Question 4

Solution: Option **c** is correct.

Question 5

Solution: Option **b** is correct.

Sale of PPE=$94,000 is listed as a cash inflow from investing activities

According to the indirect methods to prepare cash flows from operating activities, adjustments related to PPE are the (1) depreciation expense for the period and (2) loss or gain on the sale of PPE

(1) Depreciation expense for the year = $250,000/10 years = $25,000 (straight-line method)

(2) Gain/loss on the sale of PPE = Selling price of PPE − Net Book Value of PPE = \$94,000 − (\$250,000−\$25,000∗6) = −6,000

The question only asks for the amount added to net income related to the sale of PPE (that is, losses on the sale of PPE \$6,000).

Question 6

Solution: Option **c** is correct.

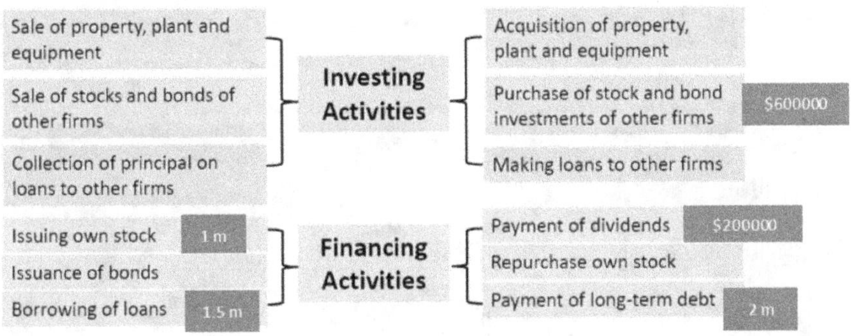

Net cash flow provided by financing activities = 1m + 1.5m − 2m − 0.2m = 0.3 million

Question 7

Solution: Option **c** is correct.

Inventory

BB Purchases	COGS
EB	

Accounts Payable

Payment for inventories	BB Purchases
	EB

Purchases

= Ending balance of Inventory + COGS − Beginning balance of inventory

= Increase in Inventory + COGS

Cash paid for inventories (suppliers)

= BB of accounts payable + Purchases − EB of accounts payable

= − Increase in accounts payable + Purchases

= − Increase in accounts payable + Increase in inventory + COGS

Part E: Financial Analysis and Evaluation

Chapter 12

Financial Analysis Techniques

12.1 Tools and Techniques Used in Financial Analysis

Financial analysis techniques effectively summarize data from financial reports and assess the financial position or performance.

Learning Objectives

- Illustrate the tools and techniques used during financial analysis.

Main Takeaways

Main Points

- Financial analysis techniques include ratio analysis and common-size financial statements, help summarize data from financial reports and assess the financial position or performance.
- Financial ratios and common-size financial statements eliminate the effect of size, enabling time series analysis and cross-sectional analysis with peer companies.
- In a common-size statement, all elements in the financial statement are shown as percentages of a common base amount.
- It is typical to select total assets as the common base in a balance sheet and select total sales as the common base in the income statement because sales impact almost all expense categories.

Main Terms

- **Ratio analysis:** A financial analysis technique that uses ratios to summarize financial reporting data.
- **Common-size analysis:** Restating financial statement items using a common denominator, allowing one to recognize trends and significant differences.

Financial analysis is useful for evaluating a firm's financial performance over a period and analyzing trends in the performance. Financial analysis is also handy in the valuation of equity securities in a firm, financial risk exposures assessment, and fulfilling the necessary due diligence when a prospective merger or acquisition occurs.

Some different tools and techniques are useful when assessing a firm's financial status. They are shown to be markedly helpful when comparing a firm's financial data over time (time-series analysis) and against peer companies' performance (cross-sectional study). They may include chart analysis, ratios analysis, and common-size financial statements.

12.1.1 *Financial Ratios*

Ratios compare values, and it compares one value with another. Ratios are appealing as they both are straightforward and convenient. Ratios can present a firm's profile, economic attributes, competitive strategies, and distinctive operating, financial, and investment attributes.

12.1.2 *Common-Size Analysis*

Primary figures hide related data that percentages often disclose. Common-size statements regulate income statements, balance sheets, and cash flow statement items for comparability between different-sized firms. They lessen all dollars to a percentage of a common base figure

- Common-size balance sheet denotes all balance sheet items as a percentage of total assets.

$$\text{Common-size BS ratios} = \frac{\text{Balance sheet account}}{\text{Total assets}}$$

- Common-size income statement denotes all income statement accounts as a percentage of sales. Common-size income statement ratios have an advantage in analyzing the trends of costs and profit margins.

$$\text{Common-size IS ratios} = \frac{\text{Income statement account}}{\text{Sales}}$$

- Analysts can choose common-size statement analysis for cash flow statements. Two recommended methods include the total cash inflows/total cash outflows method and the net revenue method percentage.

The above ratios can compare financial statements between different size firms or of the same firm over time.

- **Trend analysis** gives useful information on a firm's historical growth and performance or a forecasting and management tool for analysts and management.
- **Cross-sectional analysis** is also known as relative analysis. It compares one firm's metrics with the same metrics for another firm, allowing comparisons to be made regardless of whether the firms are of notably different sizes or financial data reported in other currencies.

12.1.3 *Graphs Charts*

Graphs aid in comparing financial structure and performance over time, underlining changes in notable aspects of a firm's operations. On top of that, graphs present analysts with a visual summary of risk trends in a firm. Graphs are also used efficiently to convey an analysts' overview of risk management and financial conditions.

12.1.4 *Regression Analysis*

Regression analyses facilitate the definition of relationships between variables that can affect forecast estimates. It can also help identify ratios of moving items contrary to their historical statistical relationships.

References/Further Readings

Robinson, T., Henry, E., Pirie, W., Broihahn, M., & Cope, A. (2015). *International Financial Statement Analysis*, 3rd edn. Wiley, Chaps. 1 and 7.

Subramanyam, K.R. (2014). *Financial Statement Analysis*, 11th edn. McGraw Hill, Chap.1, pp. 27–33.

12.2 Uses and Limitations

There are several limitations in the techniques mentioned in financial analysis. The outcome of financial techniques gives vital inputs into security valuation.

Learning Objectives

- Describe the uses and limitations of the tools and techniques used in financial analysis.

Main Takeaways

Main Points

- Common-size financial statement analysis also provides useful input to more advanced financial analysis tools such as asset composition analysis and assessing a firm's capital structure's riskiness.
- Ratio analysis is commonly adopted to assess an organization's performance, outlook, and risk profile. Such study may determine an organization's performance relative to the overall economy, industry, industry peers or evaluate an organization's performance over time.
- Analysts need to note that financial ratios measure historical performances and trends and continuously keep alongside new data, news, financials, and related reports for the firm under analysis.
- Depending on a firm's nature, the analyst needs to consider if it is best to do ratio analysis at an aggregate or segmental level.

Main Terms

- **Horizontal common-size analysis:** Horizontal analysis refers to the study of specific line items and comparing them to a similar line item in the previous or subsequent financial period.
- **Vertical common-size analysis:** Refers to analyzing specific line items with a base item within the same financial period.
- **The fiscal year ends:** Suggest completing a 12 month or 1-year accounting period.

12.2.1 *Uses and Limitations of the Tools and Techniques Used in Financial Analysis*

Ratio analysis allows the evaluation of a firm's historical performances, an assessment of its current financial position, and offers insights that can help project future results. Ratio analysis can be involved in (1) Equity valuation, (2) Credit rating, and (3) Predicting insolvency.

Limitations to ratio analysis include:

- Comparing companies may be challenging due to the heterogeneity or homogeneity of a company's operating activities.
- Occasionally, using various ratios during a ratio analysis may lead to an inconsistent outcome; not all ratios are needed for specific analyses. One should determine which particular ratios are most relevant to answering their questions.
- Different accounting methods can misstate ratios (e.g., inventory valuation, depreciation approach).
- The ratio must be interpreted with care. When comparing companies in an industry or the same company across different periods, an analyst should check that the companies are comparable. The financial ratios may not be directly comparable to others in the industry due to (1) Accounting methodology, (2) Operating philosophy, and (3) Business mix.

Common-size: Financial statement analysis enables easy analysis between firms or between periods of a given firm. Using common-size financial statements may occasionally help analysts spot trends that are not apparent from reading raw financial statements. Therefore, analysts can draw useful assumptions about attributes of an organization's operating performance, for instance, profitability margins, expense ratios, and the firm's distribution of resources in current and non-current assets over preceding periods.

The vertical common-size analysis highlights the constitution of the balance sheet. It provides an answer to questions such as what mix of assets the firm is holding, how it is financing, and how the firm's balance sheet composition compared to its peer companies, and explanations for any difference that exists.

Horizontal common-size analysis can highlight structural differences in a firm over time. An analysis of historical trends (historical analysis) can help to establish future expectations by assessing whether trends are likely to change direction or continue.

When firms whose financial performance is being compared differ notably for size or their financial information is reported in different currencies, net income comparison will not be needed. Financial ratio and common-size financial statements will be a preferred choice as they eliminate size as a limiting factor allowing for a more practical comparison.

Differences in a fiscal year-end and accounting standard can cause be a limitation to comparability. Such limitations can be overcome by using trailing twelve months of information and identifying where those differences impact comparability. This impact is best minimized by making adjustments where available.

References/Further Readings

Robinson, T., Henry, E., Pirie, W., Broihahn, M., & Cope, A. (2015). *International Financial Statement Analysis*, 3rd edn. Wiley, Chap. 7.

Subramanyam, K.R. (2014). *Financial Statement Analysis*, 11th edn. McGraw Hill, Chap.1, & pp. 27–39.

12.3 Evaluation of Companies Using Ratio Analysis

12.3.1 *Classification and Calculation of Financial Ratios*

Ratio analysis is a tool to evaluate a firm's reporting statements and relates them to risk, reward (profitability), solvency, and how well a firm operates.

Learning Objectives

- Classify, calculate, and interpret activity, liquidity, solvency, profitability, and valuation ratios.

Main Takeaways

Main Points

- Financial ratios may be categorized as Activity, Liquidity, Solvency, Profitability, and Valuation ratios.
- Ratios can also be jointly assessed to understand better how leverage and efficiency are linked to profitability.
- Activity ratios measure how effectively a firm operates day-to-day tasks, such as receivables collection and inventory management. Liquidity ratios measure the firm's ability to meet its short-term commitment. Solvency ratios measure a firm's ability to meet long-term commitment.

- Profitability ratios compute the firm's ability to generate profits from its assets.
- Valuation ratios measure the amount of an asset or flow (e.g., earnings) related to ownership of a specified claim (e.g., ownership or share of a business).
- Valuation ratios depict the relationship between a firm's market value or its equity (for example, the price per share) and other financial variables related to the firm's fundamentals (e.g., earnings per share).

Main Terms

- **Inventory turnover:** Assess the efficiency of a company's inventory management. A high ratio suggests that inventory is not stored up in warehouses or on shelves but instead has a fast turnover time from the time it was purchased to sale. A firm's accounting method's choice may affect the inventory turnover ratio.
- **Receivable turnovers:** Assess the company's credit policy's efficiency and illustrate the investment level needed in receivables to sustain the company's sales level. Only trade receivables are used in the calculation of this ratio. Other receivables from investment activities or loans shall not be used as they are not classified as regular operating transactions.
- **Receivable days:** Compute the average number of days receivables are outstanding before clients collection. Also known as the average credit days granted to customers.
- **Cash Ratio:** Being the most conservation measuring only actual cash and securities converted to cash quickly.
- **Operating cycle:** Compute the sum of the number of days it takes from selling inventory to the number of days until the resulting receivables are converted to cash.
- **Diluted EPS:** Includes the effect of all the company's securities whose conversion or exercise would result in a reduction of basic EPS; dilutive securities include convertible debt, convertible preferred, warrants, and options.
- **Dividend payout ratio:** Measures the earnings that a firm distributes out as dividends to their stakeholders in percentage terms.
- **Retention rate:** The retention rate, also known as the earnings retention rate, is a supplement of the dividend payout ratio (i.e., 1 − payout rate).

- **Sustainable growth rate:** It is measured as a function of a firm's profitability (ROE or return on equity) and its capability to finance the growth from internally generated funds (the retention rate). The sustainable growth rate is the retention rate multiplied by ROE times the retention rate.

(a) Activity Ratios

Activity ratios assess how effectively an organization executes everyday tasks, for instance, receivables collection or inventory management. Table 12.1 shows the computation for the majority of the activity ratios.

(b) Liquidity Ratios

Liquidity ratios assess an organization's potential to meet its short-term commitments and how fast assets are turned into cash. The listing in Table 12.2 shows the computation for most liquidity ratios.

Table 12.1: Summary of activity ratios.

Activity ratios	Ratio calculation
Inventory turnover	$\frac{\text{Cost of goods sold}}{\text{Average inventory}}$
Days of inventory on hands (DOH)	$\frac{\text{Number of days in the period}}{\text{Inventory turnover}}$
Receivables turnover	$\frac{\text{Revenue or revenue from credit sales}}{\text{Average receivables}}$
Days of sales outstanding (DSO)	$\frac{\text{Number of days}}{\text{Receivables turnover}}$
Payable turnover	$\frac{\text{Purchases}}{\text{Average payables}}$
Number of days of payables	$\frac{\text{Number of days in a period}}{\text{Payable turnover}}$
Working capital turnover	$\frac{\text{Revenue}}{\text{Average working capital}}$
Fixed assets turnover	$\frac{\text{Revenue}}{\text{Average fixed assets}}$
Total assets turnover	$\frac{\text{Revenue}}{\text{Average total assets}}$

Table 12.2: Summary of liquidity ratios.

Liquidity ratios	Ratio calculation
Current	$\frac{\text{Current assets}}{\text{Current liabilities}}$
Quick	$\frac{\text{Cash + Short term marketable securities + Receivables}}{\text{Current liabilities}}$
Cash	$\frac{\text{Cash + Short term marketable securities}}{\text{Current liabilities}}$
Defensive Interval	$\frac{\text{Cash + Short term marketable securities + Receivables}}{\text{Daily expenditures}}$
Cash conversion cycle	DOH + DSO − Number of days of payables

Table 12.3: Summary of solvency ratios.

Solvency ratios	Ratio calculation
Debt-to-assets	$\frac{\text{Total debt}}{\text{Total assets}}$
Debt-to-capital	$\frac{\text{Total debt}}{\text{Total debt + Total shareholder's equity}}$
Debt-to-equity	$\frac{\text{Total debt}}{\text{Total shareholders' equity}}$
Financial leverage	$\frac{\text{Average total assets}}{\text{Total shareholders' equity}}$
Coverage ratios	Ratio calculation
Interest coverage	$\frac{\text{EBIT}}{\text{Interest payments}}$
Fixed-charge coverage	$\frac{\text{EBIT + lease payments}}{\text{Interest payments + lease payments}}$

(c) Solvency Ratios

Solvency ratios assess an organization's potential to meet long-term commitments. Subcategories of solvency ratios are otherwise named "long-term debt" and "leverage" ratios. Table 12.3 summarizes the computation for solvency ratios.

Table 12.4: Summary of profitability ratios.

Return on sales ratios	Ratio calculation
Gross profit margin	Gross profit Revenue
Operating margin	Operating profit Revenue
Pretax profit	EBT (Earnings Before Taxes Revenue)
Net profit margin	Net Income Revenue
Return on investment ratios	**Ratio calculation**
Operating ROA	Operating income Average total assets
ROA	Net income Average total assets
Return on total capital	EBIT Debt + Equity
Return on common equity	Net income – Preferred dividends Average common equity

(d) Profitability Ratios

Profitability ratios assess an organization's potential to yield profits from its assets. The following listing in Table 12.4 illustrates the computation of those ratios.

(e) Valuation Ratios

Valuation ratios assess the size of an asset or flow (e.g., earnings) affiliated with the ownership of a specific claim (i.e., ownership or share of a business). Table 12.5 depicts most of the frequently used valuation ratios.

(f) Integrated Financial Ratio Analysis

Ratios can also be jointly assessed to understand how leverage and efficiency are linked to profitability. The data from one ratio class might help answer problems brought up by another category of ratios. The most detailed overall summary comes from integrating data from all sources.

Table 12.5: Summary of valuation ratios.

Valuation ratios	Ratio calculation
P/E	$\frac{\text{Price per share}}{\text{Earnings per share}}$
P/CF	$\frac{\text{Price per share}}{\text{Cash flow per share}}$
P/S	$\frac{\text{Price per share}}{\text{Sales per share}}$
P/BV	$\frac{\text{Price per share}}{\text{Book value per share}}$
Price per share	**Ratio calculation**
Basic EPS	$\frac{\text{Net income} - \text{Preferred dividends}}{\text{Weighted average number of ordinary shares outstanding}}$
Diluted EPS	$\frac{\text{Net income} - \text{Preferred dividends} + \text{After-tax interest on convertible debt}}{\text{Weighted average number of ordinary shares outstanding} + \text{number of common shares that would have been issued at conversion}}$
Cash flow per share	$\frac{\text{CFO} - \text{Preferred dividends}}{\text{Weighted average number of ordinary shares outstanding}}$
EBITDA per share	$\frac{\text{EBITDA}}{\text{The average number of common stock}}$
Dividends per share	$\frac{\text{Dividends paid}}{\text{Number of shares outstanding}}$
Dividend-related ratios	**Ratio calculation**
Dividend payout ratio	$\frac{\text{Common share dividends}}{\text{Net income attributable to common shares}}$
Retention rate (b)	$\frac{\text{Net income attributable to common shares} - \text{common share dividends}}{\text{Net income attributable to common shares}}$
Sustainable growth rate	b x ROE

12.3.2 *Relationships among Ratios*

Ratios compare values, compare one value with another, and assess a company's performance over time.

Learning Objectives

- Describe relationships among ratios and evaluate a company using ratio analysis.

Main Takeaways

Main Points

- Efficiency directly impacts liquidity (the firm's ability to meet its short-term obligations). Hence activity ratios help measure liquidity.
- The data from one ratio class helps answer problems raised by another class. The most detailed overall summary comes from integrating data from all sources.

Main Terms

- **Solvency:** A company can meet its long-term debts and other financial obligations. Solvency is one measure of a firm's financial health since it determines its ability to manage future operations.
- **ROA:** A measure of how profitable a company is relative to its total assets. ROA gives an analyst, investors, managers a concept of how efficient a firm's management is at using its assets to generate earnings. ROA is depicted as a percentage.
- **Asset utilization:** Asset utilization ratio calculates the total revenue earned for every dollar of assets a company owns. This ratio is frequently used to compare a company's efficiency over time.

Financial ratios compare values. It compares one value with another and allows one to examine a company's performance over time.

(a) Financial Ratio Relationships

It is advised to study an assortment of financial ratios and not just a single class of ratios or single ratio individually. Exploring a variety is useful in determining a firm's overall financial position and performance over a given time.

Example:

The following data on a firm is given for the year ended December 31, 2019, and December 31, 2020.

Ratios	31-Dec-2020	31-Dec-2019
Return on Equity	5.75%	4.12%
Return on Assets	3.17%	2.98%
Current ratio	2.1	1.5
Inventory turnover	35.8	31.7
Net profit margin	3.23%	1.56%
Debt-to-asset	56.23%	65.00%

Solution:
The data illustrates that, in general, there is an improvement in the firm's performance from 2019 to 2020. Improvements are shown in:

- Profitability increase; evidenced by a rise in the figures of the ROE, ROA, and net profit margin ratios.
- Liquidity increase; evidenced by a rise in current ratio.
- An increase in asset utilization; indicted by a rise in the inventory turnover ratio.
- Better solvency as indicated by the drop in the debt-to-assets ratio.

References/Further Readings

Robinson, T., Henry, E., Pirie, W., Broihahn, M., & Cope, A. (2015). *International Financial Statement Analysis*, 3rd edn. Wiley, Chap. 7.

Subramanyam, K.R. (2014). *Financial Statement Analysis*, 11th edn. McGraw Hill, Chap. 10.

12.4 Dupont Analysis of Return on Equity and Effects of Changes in Its Components

The breakdown of ROE enables investors to focus on the individual components to identify strengths and weaknesses.

Learning Objectives
- Demonstrate the application of DuPont analysis of return on equity and interpret effects of changes in its components.

Main Takeaways

Main Points

- DuPont analysis is a useful technique used to breakdown the different return drivers on equity (ROE).
- ROE can be computed by multiplying net profit margin, asset turnover, and financial leverage together. This breakdown is often known as DuPont analysis.
- Decomposing ROE is useful in determining the reasons for ROE changes over time for a given firm and differences in ROE for different firms over a given period.
- Decomposing also presents a firm's overall profitability, measured by ROE, as a function of its efficiency, operating profitability, taxes, and use of financial leverage.
- A 5 step DuPont consist of; ROE = [(operating profit margin) × (total asset turnover) − (interest expense rate)] × (financial leverage multiplier) × (tax retention rate).

Main Terms

- **DuPont analysis:** Method decomposing return on investment, e.g., return on equity, using the product of other financial ratios.

DuPont analysis is an approach used to break down ROE into its respective components, which expresses the fundamental ratio as the component ratios' product. The breakdown helps evaluate the basis of ROE changes for a given business over a period.

DuPont Model is generally known as the decomposition of ROE into constituent ratios to evaluate its impact.

Traditional DuPont equation:

- ROE = net income/common equity
- ROE = (net income/net sales) × (net sales/common equity). Therefore, ROE = (net profit margin) × (equity turnover). Therefore ROE = ROA × Leverage.
- ROE = (net income/net sales) × (net sales/total assets) × (total assets/common equity)

Each respective component will affect the general return to shareholders. An increase in asset turnover, profit margin, or leverage will cause the return to increase. The downside; when the firm suffers losses in any year, the asset turnover or financial leverage will multiply the loss effect.

$$\text{ROE} = \text{net profit margin} \times \text{assets turnover} \times \text{equity multiplier}$$

So, to increase its return on equity, a firm should eventually aim to be more:

- Profitable (higher net profit margin, e.g., pricing and expense control).
- Efficient (increase total asset turnover, e.g., asset use efficiency).
- Leveraged (increase its financial leverage ratio).

The extended DuPont model considers the above three components integrating the effect of taxes and interest based on the level of financial leverage.

- Rewriting in accounting terms:

ROE = [(operating profit margin) × (total asset turnover) − (interest expense rate)] × (financial leverage multiplier) × (tax retention rate)

$$ROE = \left[\left\{\frac{EBIT}{\text{Sales}}\right\} \times \left\{\frac{\text{Sales}}{\text{Assets}}\right\} - \left\{\frac{\text{Interest}}{\text{Assets}}\right\}\right] \times \left\{\frac{\text{Assets}}{\text{Equity}}\right\} \times \{1 - \text{Tax Rate}\}$$

$$ROE = \left[\left\{\begin{matrix}\text{Operating}\\ \text{Profit Margin}\end{matrix}\right\} \times \left\{\begin{matrix}\text{Assets}\\ \text{Turnover}\end{matrix}\right\} - \left\{\begin{matrix}\text{Interest}\\ \text{Expense Rate}\end{matrix}\right\}\right]$$
$$\times \left\{\begin{matrix}\text{Equity}\\ \text{Multiplier}\end{matrix}\right\} \times \left\{\begin{matrix}\text{Tax Retention}\\ \text{Rate}\end{matrix}\right\}$$

Higher financial leverage doesn't always increase ROE; higher financial leverage will increase interest expense rate, eliminating any benefits of higher leverage. This decomposition aids an analyst in understanding what happened to a firm's ROE and why it happened.

References/Further Readings

Subramanyam, K.R. (2014). *Financial Statement Analysis*, 11th edn. McGraw Hill, Chap. 8.

12.5 Sample Questions

Question 1 (Tools and Techniques Used in Financial Analysis)
Which of the following statement on tools and techniques used in financial analysis is least accurate?

(a) Financial analysis techniques, including common-size financial statements and ratio analysis, are useful in summarizing financial reporting information and assessing a corporation's performance and financial position.
(b) Common-size financial statements and financial ratios eliminate the effect of size, allowing comparisons of a company with peer companies and comparing a company's results over time.
(c) Comparison of a company's financial results to other peer companies for same period is called time series analysis.

Question 2 (Uses and Limitations)
Which of the following statement on uses and limitations of ratio analysis is least accurate?

(a) Ratio analysis is widely used to analyze a company's performance, outlook, and risk profile.
(b) Ratios and analyses performed on published financial statements will not be outdated. Analysts should always treat financial ratios as indicators of current performances.
(c) Although we distinguish among the different categories of ratios to emphasize various aspects of a firm's financial condition and performance, we must always remember that these building blocks are interrelated.

Question 3 (Calculation of Financial Ratios: Activity)
How efficiently a company performs day-to-day tasks, such as the collection of receivables and management of inventory, is answered when an analyst examines:

(a) Activity ratio
(b) Solvency ratio
(c) Profitability ratio

Question 4 (Calculation of Financial Ratios: Liquidity)
A company has current assets of $450,000, and a current ratio is 2.5. Assume that the company prepays $20,000 rent for nine months. The current ratio after this transaction is closest to:

(a) 2.39
(b) 2.61
(c) 2.5

Question 5 (Calculation of Financial Ratios: Liquidity)
How able is a company's to meet its short-term obligations is answered when an analyst examines the:

(a) Liquidity ratio
(b) Solvency ratio
(c) Profitability ratio

Question 6 (Calculation of Financial Ratios: Solvency)
Company X has net sales revenue of $436,000, cost of goods sold of $343,000, and net income of $3,000. If interest expense is $10,000 and income tax expense is $1,000, the times interest earned ratio is closest to:

(a) 1.4
(b) 0.33
(c) 1.3

Question 7 (Calculation of Financial Ratios: Solvency)
How able is a company to fulfill its long-term obligations is answered when an analyst examines the:

(a) Liquidity ratio
(b) Solvency ratio
(c) Profitability ratio

Question 8 (Calculation of Financial Ratios: Profitability)
Over 2 years, Premium Product's gross profit percentage went from 70.4% to 69.7%. Which of the following could not have been the cause of this change?

(a) Reduced selling prices
(b) Rising product cost as a percentage of sales
(c) An increase in selling price

Question 9 (Calculation of Financial Ratios: Profitability)
How able a company to generate profits from its resources (assets) are answered when an analyst examines the:

(a) Liquidity ratio
(b) Solvency ratio
(c) Profitability ratio

Question 10 (Calculation of Financial Ratios: Valuation)
If a company's P/E ratio is 12.5 and the company's stock price is $17.50 per share, then the company's EPS is:

(a) $0.71
(b) $1.40
(c) $5.00

Question 11 (Calculation of Financial Ratios: Valuation)
A share is trading at $20. The company has $64 million in earnings and 200 million outstanding shares. The Price/Earnings ratio for the company is closest to:

(a) 62.5
(b) 200
(c) 0.31

Question 12 (Dupont Analysis)
Your company achieves the same ROE in the financial years 2018 and 2019. Compare the differences in drivers of ROE in 2 years.

Your company	Profit Margin	Asset turnover	Financial leverage	ROE
Year 2018	0.046	1.61		13.3%
Year 2019		1.10	1.52	13.3%

Which year's profit margin is higher, and which year's financial leverage is higher?

(a) The profit margin was higher in 2018, and financial leverage was higher in 2019.
(b) The profit margin was lower in 2018, and financial leverage was higher in 2019.
(c) The profit margin was lower in 2018, and financial leverage was lower in 2019.

Question 13 (Dupont Analysis)
A decomposition of ROE for Company A's FY2018 and FY2019 is as follows:

Your company	Profit Margin	Asset turnover	Financial leverage
FY2018	7%	1.5	4
FY2019	13%	1.5	2

An analyst is most likely to conclude that:

(a) FY2019s ROE is higher than FY2018s, and one explanation consistent with data is that company A has made a strategic shift to a product mix with lower profit margins.
(b) FY2019s ROE is higher than FY2018s, and one explanation consistent with the data is that FY2018 may have purchased newer equipment to replace older, depreciated equipment.
(c) FY2018s ROE is slightly higher than FY2019s, and one explanation consistent with data is FY2018's high financial leverage.

Solutions

Question 1

Solution: Option **c** is correct.

The cross-sectional analysis compares companies during the same period. Time-series or trend analysis is comparing financial data across different periods.

Question 2

Solution: Option **b** is correct.

Ratios and analysis performed on published financial statements may be outdated because it is based on lagged audited financial statements.

Question 3

Solution: Option **b** is correct.

Question 4

Solution: Option **c** is correct.

The company prepays rent:
Dr. Prepaid Rent $20,000
Cr. cash $20,000
Prepaid rent and cash both belong to current assets. The sum of the two would not change.
The current ratio also would stay the same.

Question 5

Solution: Option **a** is correct.

Question 6

Solution: Option **a** is correct.

Times Interest Earned = Earnings before Interest and Taxes (EBIT)/ Interest Expense

= ($3,000+$10,000+$1,000)/$10,000
= 1.4

Question 7

Solution: Option **b** is correct.

Question 8

Solution: Option **c** is correct.

Gross Profit Margin = Gross profit/net sales
= (Net sales – Cost of goods sold)/net sales
Usually, we can think net sales = Selling Price of Goods * No. of Goods Sold
Cost of goods sold=Cost * No. of Goods Sold
Therefore, gross profit margin = (Selling price per unit − Cost per unit)/ Selling price per unit
An increase in selling price would probably increase gross profit margin

Question 9

Solution: Option **c** is correct.

Question 10

Solution: Option **b** is correct.

P/E ratio = Price/EPS
12.5 = $17.5/EPS
EPS =1.4

Question 11

Solution: Option **a** is correct.

Price = $20;
EPS = $64 million earnings/200 million outstanding shares = $0.32
P/E ratio = $20/$0.32=62.5

Question 12

Solution: Option **a** is correct.

Financial leverage in 2018 = 13.3%/1.61/0.046 = 1.80
Profit margin in 2019 = 13.3%/1.52/1.10 = 0.080

Question 13

Solution: Option **c** is correct.

ROE=Profit margin∗asset turnover∗financial leverage.
FY2018 has a slightly higher ROE due to the high financial leverage.
a is incorrect as FY2018 has slightly higher ROE and profit margin is higher in FY2019. **b** is incorrect. If Company A had purchased newer equipment to replace older, depreciated equipment, then its asset turnover ratio (computed as sales/assets) would have declined, assuming constant sales.

Chapter 13

Financial Reporting Quality and Evaluation

We review a theoretical framework for evaluating the quality of financial statements and summarizing potential issues that impact financial reports' quality.

13.1 Methods to Manage Earnings, Cash Flow and Balance Sheet Items

Investors need to be aware of how accounting approach choices can impact financial reporting.

Learning Objectives

- Illustrates the accounting methods (estimates and choices) that can manage earnings, cash flow, and balance sheet items.

Main Takeaways

Main Points

- In terms of allowance for doubtful accounts/loan loss reserves, typical concerns include additions to such allowances lower or higher than in the past, or does the collection experience justify any difference from historical provisioning.
- Under inventory cost methods, typical concerns may include whether the costing method produces fair reporting results or is reserves used for obsolescence in its inventory valuation.

- In light of goodwill, the firm needs an annual assessment of goodwill balances for impairment on a qualitative basis. The disclosures on goodwill testing suggest that the exercise was skewed to avoid impairment charges.

Main Terms

- **FIFO:** It is the acronym for first-in, first-out, which indicates that the oldest inventory items are recorded as sold first, which is the cost associated with the inventory that was purchased first is the cost expensed first.
- **LIFO:** Stands for last in, first out, and is an approach used for inventory accounting that reports the most recently produced items as sold first.
- **Weighted average cost:** Using a weighted average approach, we divide the cost of the goods available for sale by the number of units still on the shelf. This computation yields the weighted average cost per unit — an amount that can then be used to assign a cost to both ending inventory and the cost of goods sold.
- **Accrual accounting:** Assess a firm's performance and position by recognizing the economic situation regardless of when cash transactions occur, whereas cash accounting only records transactions when payment occurs.
- **Double declining method:** An accelerated depreciation method in which the asset value is depreciated twice the rate it is done in the straight-line method. Since the depreciation is done twice as fast, it is called accelerated depreciation.

Investors need to be aware that the accounting approach choice may impact a financial statement. The accounting approach chosen doesn't necessarily need to incorporate complex accounting regulations to notably affect the timing of revenue and the associated financial statements. The better the financial report's quality, the more relevant data, financial statements users have to evaluate the impact of accounting approaches.

Various accounting approaches will enable firm managers to show an impression of the firm's earnings, balance sheet, and cash flow items being better than they are.

13.1.1 *Cost Flow Assumptions*

Approaches of cost flow assumption can impact profitability. As an illustration, firms often assume that its' inventory is sold to clients on a first-in-first-out (FIFO) basis. Hence it would mean that leftover inventory depicts the recent date costs. Alternatively, one can also assume that inventory is sold to clients on a weighted-average cost method.

When prices change, the FIFO approach has a more exact representation of ending inventory value. Hence its balance sheet figure will be much more pertinent to investors. Using weighted-average cost, the balance sheet holds a mix of new and old costs. Also, the current costs will be depicted in the cost of sales, which enables the income statement to be more relatable than with the FIFO approach.

13.1.2 *Accrual Accounting versus Cash Basis Accounting*

Cash basis accounting depicts only all-cash transactions carried out by a firm, leaving a great deal of financial information concealed. On the contrary, accrual accounting strives to outline the impact of the firm's economic situation during a specified period.

Accrual accounting illustrates a more transparent summary of what unfolds over the reporting period than cash-based accounting. However, accrual accounting can entice firms to focus on financial values instead of managing the business.

13.1.3 *Depreciation Method*

Businesses may choose to depreciate long-lived assets using either (i) a straight-line method, reporting constant depreciation expense every year; (ii) an accelerated method, with a higher depreciation expense reported in the early years of an asset's life; or (iii) an activity-based depreciation, where it categorizes depreciation expense based on units of use or production. The salvage value of an asset also affects depreciation expense.

The decision on the depreciation approach can impact reported income.

13.1.4 *Goodwill*

Goodwill estimation relies on the assessment of future financial performance. To shy from writing down any form of goodwill, estimates may be biased upwards.

13.1.5 *The Preparation of the Statement of Cash Flows*

Firms can beautify the cash flow from operations (CFO) statements without genuinely improving them. For instance, management can intentionally prolong the accounts payable credit period to enhance its CFO. Moreover, in a situation where net income is notably higher than CFO, it is possibly due to management's use of an accounting approach to "artificially" increase net income. It is also likely to misclassify operating uses of cash into either the investing or financing segments of the statement to make CFO looks more superior than it is.

References/Further Readings

Robinson, T., Henry, E., Pirie, W., Broihahn, M., & Cope, A. (2015). *International Financial Statement Analysis*, 3rd edn. Wiley, Chaps. 11 and 17.

Subramanyam, K.R. (2014). *Financial Statement Analysis*, 11th edn. McGraw Hill, Chap. 11, pp. 106–131.

13.2 Accounting Warning Signs

Your company's financial reports provide important clues about your business's financial health. Some of these clues manifest as financial warning signs.

Learning Objectives

- Describe accounting warning signs and methods for detecting information manipulation in financial reports.

Main Takeaways

Main Points

- Financial manipulation can be either time-related or location-related.
- Less-than-high-quality financial reports may be issued for one of several reasons, including (a) to conceal poor performance, (b) to heightened the stock price, (c) to increase personal compensation, and (d) to avoid violation of debt covenants.
- The warning signs of data manipulation in reported statements are associated with the basic means of manipulation: biased revenue recognition and biased expense recognition.

- Investors and analysts can notice revenue, inventory signals, capitalization policies, deferred costs, the relationship between cash flow and net income, and other possible red flags for financial manipulation.

Main Terms

- **Timing bias:** Occurs when a company either accelerates or defers recognition.
- **Location bias:** Occurs when a company classifies an item incorrectly.
- **Financial manipulation** involves using creative accounting tricks, resulting in a company's financial statements reflecting performance wished by management rather than its actual performance.

13.2.1 *Financial Manipulation*

Some Potential Warning signs or red flags analysts need to take note of:

1. Revenue. Checking of revenue recognition policies and revenue relationship.
2. Inventories. Assessing the relationship of inventory.
3. The relationship between cash flow and net income.
4. Other red flags.

13.2.2 *Pay Attention to Revenue*

Revenue is the most commonly manipulated element. Few approaches to assess the quality of revenue:

1. **Examining accounting policies note for firm's revenue recognition policies:** Ensure the recognition of revenue of each deliverable matches with the recognition of the costs needed to make that deliverable.
2. **Looking at revenue relationships:** Analyse the firm's revenue growth with its peer competitors or its industry group. When the growth of the firm's revenues is accelerated than that of the peer/industry group, the outstanding performance needs to be justified. Potential justifications can include better management (or/and) better products/service quality.
3. **Comparison of accounts receivable with revenues over the years:** A rise in the ratio can suggest inadequate allowance for doubtful accounts or even fabricated sales.

13.2.3 *Inventories Signals*

1. **Compare inventory growth with peer and industry benchmarks:** When a firm drops the trend, it can easily indicate inventory obsolescence or lousy inventory management. The former meant that both the firm's profits and assets are overstated.
2. **Computation of inventory turnover ratio:** A deceleration in the ratio can mean inventory obsolesces.

13.2.4 *Pay Attention to the Relationship between Cash Flow and Net Income*

When cash flow to earnings is continuously lower than one, it might suggest heavy use of the accrual approach.

(a) Other Potential Warnings Signs

1. **Depreciation methods and useful lives:** Significant differences in the depreciation method and the firm's estimated useful life with its peers might signal a manipulation intent.
2. **Fourth-quarter surprises:** Companies attempt to avoid falsifying until the imminent. Manipulation usually occurs in the fourth-quarter results. Hence, an analyst needs to take precaution with companies that continuously exceed expectations' consensus results in the fourth quarter, presuming that there isn't any seasonality in the firm's business.
3. **Non-operating income or one-time sales included in revenue:** A firm can add an asset disposal amount to revenue to conceal a decrease in the revenue. Likewise, a firm can decrease its losses by categorizing some expenses as "non-recurring".

13.3 Earnings Quality of a Company

The quality of earnings refers to the proportion of income attributable to the core operating activities.

Learning Objectives

- Describe factors influencing earnings quality.

Main Takeaways

Main Points

- Reporting quality pertains to the data disclosed. High-quality reporting depicts the firm's economic reality during the reporting period and its financial condition at the end of the period.
- Earnings quality relates to the earnings and cash produced by a firm's actual economic activities and the resulting financial condition relative to current and future financial performance expectations. Quality earnings are regarded as sustainable, providing a sound platform for forecasts.
- High-quality earnings raise the firm's value more than low-quality earnings, and one assumes "high-quality earnings" equates with high reporting quality.
- Low-quality earnings are inadequate to cover the firm's capital cost and are derived from non-recurring, one-off activities. Furthermore, the term "low-quality earnings" is commonly used when the reported data does not clarify the firm's performance.

Main Terms

- **Mean reversion:** Used in finance suggesting asset prices with historical returns eventually reverting to the long-run mean or average level of the entire dataset.
- **Recurring Earnings:** The part of a business's revenue expected to continue in the future. As opposed to once-off sales and other situations that may recur but with great uncertainty.

Earnings quality range from high and sustainable to low and unsustainable. The majority of providers of resources incline towards high and sustainable earnings. High earnings quality raises a firm's value, while low earnings quality results in a decline in its value.

- High earnings quality must be persistent and sustainable.
- It is not how much money a company is making that counts. It's how it makes its money.

It's how repeatable a firm's earnings are. Companies that generate lots of sustainable cash from their operations have good earnings quality.

Several alternatives are used as indicators of earnings quality.

13.3.1 *Recurring Earnings*

Net income incorporates the effect of non-recurring items that are either transitory or random. Hence, net income is not considered a good future income indicator. Recurring pretax income from continuing operations suggests a firm's sustainable income. Therefore it should be the core of the analysis. Low-quality earnings are usually derived from non-recurring or one-off activities.

Separating the outcome of recurring operations from non-recurring items expedites forecasting future cash flows and earnings. Typically, analysts shall not include items that are non-recurring when forecasting the firm's future cash flows or earnings. However, it doesn't mean that all non-recurring item from the income statement needs is disregarded.

Management has a habitude of naming various items in the income statement as "non-recurring", particularly for those which decrease reported income. As an analysis intention, a vital issue is to identify if non-recurring items are really "non-recurring", regardless of their tags.

13.3.2 *Earnings Persistence and Related Measures of Accruals*

Accounting earnings involves two underlying components. A cash component presents both relevant and reliable information. An accrual component offers relevant information, but with reliability being significantly compromised. Because the accrual component is less reliable than cash, the accrual component of earnings is less persistent than the cash component.

(a) Beating Benchmarks
Earnings quality should be questioned if a firm frequently reports earnings that exactly meet or narrowly beat benchmarks.

13.4 Earnings Management

Earnings management refers to a firm's intentional use of accounting techniques to beautify its' financial reports.

Learning Objectives
- Understand earnings management and evaluate earnings quality.

Main Takeaways

Main Points

- Earnings management relates to the alteration of financial reports to mislead shareholders about a firm's performance or influence results dependent on reported accounting numbers.
- Earnings manipulation decreases the quality of earning and weakens the credibility of financial reporting.
- An analyst should note that relating to a firm's earnings is a mean reversion in earnings to evaluate earnings quality. Excessive earnings are not sustainable and tend to revert to normal levels over time.
- Another aspect pertains to the persistence and sustainability of a firm's earnings. More persistent and sustainable earnings are considered of higher quality.
- High-quality earnings raise the firm's value more than low-quality earnings, and one assumes "high-quality earnings" equates with high reporting quality.
- Low-quality earnings are inadequate to cover the firm's capital cost and are derived from non-recurring, one-off activities. Furthermore, the term "low-quality earnings" is commonly used when the presented data does not clarify the firm's performance.

Main Terms

- **Non-recurring:** Not occurring or happening again, not significantly often or periodically. An income or charge considered of a nature not likely to occur or happen again.
- **Earnings quality:** Also known as quality of earnings (QoE), in accounting, refers to the ability of reported earnings (income) to forecast a firm's future earnings.
- **Capitalization:** It is an accounting approach in which the cost is expensed over that asset's useful life, rather than being expensed in the period the cost was initially incurred.
- **Big bath accounting:** It is an earnings management technique where a one-time charge is taken against income to reduce the amount of assets, hence reducing expenses in the future. This write-off that eliminates or reduces the asset from the reporting statement leads to a lower net income for the year when the write-off is made.

13.4.1 *Earnings Management*

Earnings management is the intentional intervention by management during earnings determination. Management can exercise discretion over accounting numbers because accrual accounting, to a large extent, relies on the use of judgment and estimation. For example, firms can manipulate net income by recognizing revenue earlier or later. Earnings management reduces the quality of the accounting numbers.

Typical approaches adopted may include:

1. Classifying bad news into non-recurring items and good news into operating items.
2. Smoothing of income over time: deferring income recognition in good years as a buffer for the future or in the classification of income into recurring and extraordinary.
3. Use "big bath accounting" to report higher losses in bad years to show more robust recovery in upcoming years.
4. Adopting aggressive accounting practices.
5. Changing accounting practices and accounting estimates to manipulate or beautify earnings.

Analysts must be cautious of the discretionary nature of income statement elements allowing management to manage earnings by:

1. Manipulation of the timing of the occurrence of an item, and
2. Classifying the item as unusual, ordinary, or extraordinary.

Earnings manipulation decreases the quality of earning, which affects the analyst's ability to use the financial statements for analysis. An analyst should be aware that financial statements may sometimes be subjected to earnings management and, if it occurs, make adjustments for it.

13.4.2 *Evaluate Earnings*

An analyst should note several aspects relating to a firm's earnings to evaluate earnings quality. One aspect is mean reversion in earnings. Specifically, earnings at extreme levels are not sustainable and usually return to normal levels over time. This occurrence is called mean reversion. Mean reversion happens when the competitive marketplace corrects poor performance. Poor projects are discarded while capital is attracted to successful projects, increasing competition and lowering returns. They happen to have an inverse relationship between accruals and cash flow. When earnings mostly comprise accruals, the mean reversion will be even faster.

Another aspect pertains to the persistence and sustainability of a company's earnings. More persistent and sustainable earnings are known as higher quality. The accrual component of income is generally less sustainable or persistent than cash. Hence, interpreting a firm's accruals or deferrals is another alternative approach to evaluate earnings quality.

Example:
With the following information, interpret and comment on the earnings quality of following the same industry companies.

Accrual ratio	2020	2019
Company A	13.2%	16.8%
Company B	11.3%	9.5%

Note: The accrual ratio is a way to identify firms with accrual-derived earnings relative to their cash flow. The formula is given by (net income – free cash flow)/Total assets. The larger positive accrual ratio means that cash earnings are increasingly less than accrual earnings.

Solution:
Company B's higher-earning quality as its accrual ratio is lower for 2020 and 2019. However, Company A's earning's quality shows an upward trend while Company B's earning quality reflects a deteriorating trend.

An analyst should also be alert to red flags during financial statement analysis and accounting analysis. Red flags, in general, refer to items that can notify an analyst to carry out in-depth studies of financial reports better understand the performance of a company:

- Poor financial performance has a strong incentive to take up an aggressive accounting approach. The analyst needs to exercise caution when assessing such a company's statements.
- The significant divergence between reported income and cash flows or a higher proportion of non-cash items needs a comprehensive analysis to evaluate the causes.

- The significant divergence between reported income and taxable income shows a signal of aggressive tax practices that might adversely impact the future.
- Sudden and notable changes in items across periods, as well as the use of techniques (e.g., Big baths') through large one-time charges, will require thorough and more in-depth scrutiny.
- Indicators of issues include qualified financial reports, frequent changes in accounting policies and the form of accounting disclosure, unusual footnotes.
- Changes in the composition of boards and frequent management changes also require attention.

13.5 Indicators of Cash Flow Quality

Cash flow statements are unaffected by some of the financial reports' considerations based on the accrual approach.

Learning Objectives

- Describe indicators of cash flow quality.

Main Takeaways

Main Points

- Reported cash flows, interpreted as high quality, suggest that a firm's underlying economic performance was satisfactory. It also heightens the firm's value and acknowledges that the firm had high reporting quality (e.g., that the data computed and produced by the firm was a good indicator of economic reality).
- Cash flow can be characterized as "low quality" for two reasons: reported data correctly symbolize genuinely bad economic performance, or second, because the reported data misstates economic reality.
- OCF is often considered more difficult to manipulate than operating or net income.

Main Terms

- **Operating cash flow (OCF):** Measures cash generated by a company's regular business operations. OCF analyzes whether a firm can generate sufficient positive cash flow to grow or maintain its operations; otherwise, it may require external financing for capital expansion.

- **Corporate life cycle:** Or business life cycle is the progression of a business in phases over time and is most commonly divided into five stages: launch, growth, shake-out, maturity, and decline.
- **Earnings growth:** For investors, growth rates typically represent the compounded annualized rate of growth of a company's revenues, earnings,

13.5.1 *Cash Flow Quality*

OCF is the cash flow segment that is the most crucial for evaluating a firm's performance and valuation of a firm or its securities. Cash flow can be characterized as "low quality" for two reasons, first, because the reported data accurately symbolize bad economic performance (poor results quality), or second, because the reported information misstates economic reality (low reporting quality).

From an economic standpoint, the corporate life cycle and industry attributes impact cash flow and must be considered when assessing the cash flow statements. For instance, a start-up firm may hold negative operating and investing cash flows funded from borrowing or equity issuance (e.g., financing cash flows). However, an established firm will usually have positive OCF from which it funds essential investments or returns to capital providers (e.g., dividends, share repurchases, or debt repayments — all of which are financing cash flows).

Generally, a high-quality cash flow will include the below attributes:

- Positive OCF
- OCF derived from sustainable sources
- OCF adequately cover capital expenditures, dividends, and debt repayments
- OCF with somewhat low volatility (relative to industry participants)

The reported cash flows should be relevant and faithfully reflect the economic reality of a firm's activities. For instance, categorizing an investing inflow as a financing inflow would misstate the economic truth.

13.6 Indicators of Balance Sheet Quality

Three main categories of investment-quality measurements can assess a company's balance sheet's strength.

Learning Objectives
Describe indicators of balance sheet quality.

Main Takeaways

Main Points

- Measures of financial reporting quality include completeness, unbiased measurement, and clear presentation. Indicators of a healthy balance sheet include having an optimal amount of leverage, reasonable liquidity, and economically efficient asset allocation.
- A balance sheet's strength is evaluated using ratio analysis and common-size financial statements.

Main Terms

- **Absolute value:** Otherwise known as intrinsic value, refers to a business valuation approach that uses discounted cash flow (DCF) to value a firm's financial worth.
- **Purchase contract:** The purchase contract is the one that transmits the ownership of a good (movable or immovable) of one person (seller) to another (buyer).
- **Off balance sheet (OBS):** Term for items (asset and liabilities) that is not on a firm's balance sheet. Even though they are not written on the balance sheet, they are still assets and liabilities.
- **Goodwill:** An intangible asset arises when a buyer acquires an existing business. Goodwill represents assets that are not separately identifiable.
- **Impairment:** It is generally interpreted as a drastic decrease in a fixed asset's recoverable amount. Impairment usually happens when a change in economic or legal circumstances surrounding a firm or a casualty loss from an unforeseen situation is present.

An excellent financial reporting quality is determined by completeness, unbiased measurement, and clear presentation. High financial reporting standard (e.g., a healthy balance sheet) is determined by an adequate amount of leverage, decent liquidity, and economically successful asset allocation.

A fundamental criterion of financial reporting quality for the balance sheet is completeness. A balance sheet with a substantial value of off-balance-sheet debt would not have fulfilled the completeness aspect of financial reporting quality. Significant amounts of off-balance- sheet obligations can be a worrying affair for an analyst as an omission of these obligations could misstate a firm's leverage. Here is one example.

OBS financing attempts to borrow money so that liabilities and their associated interest expense are kept off the company's balance sheet and income statement, respectively. A classic example is leasing. In general, lessees prefer leases to be categorized under operating leases. They need not recognize the loan or assets on their balance sheet despite receiving all of the benefits of using the asset. Hence, operating leases reduce the reported leverage for lessees and increase profitability ratios.

Another vital criterion of the balance sheet's financial reporting quality is unbiased measurement. Unbiased measurement is critical for assets and liabilities when valuation is subjective as in:

- Understatement of impairment charges for inventory; can lead to an overstatement of balance sheet assets and overstatements of profits on the income statement.
- A firm's investments in another firm's equity or debt securities would preferably be based on observable market information. The valuation will be based entirely on management estimates for certain investments with no visible market information.

Lastly, clear presentation is also vital for a balance sheet's financial reporting standard. Although accounting policy states different attributes of what may be reported on the balance sheet, firms may hold their discretion.

13.7 Sources of Information about Risk

A firm's financial statements present valuable operating, financial, or other risk indicators.

Learning Objectives

- Describe sources of information about risks.

Main Takeaways

Main Points

- The management commentary, also known as the management discussion and analysis (MD&A), provides readers with information on the

financial statement useful in evaluating a firm's risk exposures and methods to tackling risk.
- The financial press is a useful source of data regarding risk, e.g., when a financial reporter discovers past financial reporting concerns that had not been known. An analyst should commence an investigation when a concern is identified.

Main Terms
- **Operating risk:** It is the level of uncertainty associated with the core operations.
- **Management commentary:** It is defined as: A narrative report that relates to financial statements that have been prepared following IFRSs.
- **Disclosure statement:** An official document that outlines the terms, conditions, risks, and rules of a financial transaction, such as a loan or an investment.

The financial statements present valuable indicators of operating or financial risk.

13.7.1 *Management Commentary*

The management commentary (MD&A) provides users with relevant data useful in evaluating the firm's risk exposures and leveraging risk strategies. The commentary allows users of the financial reports to understand better a firm's risk exposures, approaches to leveraging risks, and risk management effectiveness. The practice statement comprises of few aspects to be required to write in the commentary: (1) nature of the business; (2) objectives and strategies; (3) resources, risks, and relationships; (4) prospects and outcome; and (5) performance measures and indicators. The IFRS specifies that firms should only list the primary risks and not potential risks and uncertainties.

13.7.2 *Required Disclosure*

If a company fails to promptly make required disclosures like necessary financial reports and upper management changes, such failures might be a warning sign of financial reporting quality complications. Financial securities disclosures consist of data about risks, such as liquidity risk, credit risk, or market risks that emerge from a firm's financial securities and how they are managed.

13.7.3 *Financial Press*

The financial press might be another useful source for risk, such as; a financial reporter discovers reporting problems that were not found previously. An analyst should commence an additional investigation when the problem is identified. Information disclosed by an established financial news provider is more credible than information from less-established sources. Likewise, blogs or journals reported by financial journalists are less likely to be biased as compared to those reported by individuals with a product or service to sell.

13.7.4 *Auditor Opinion*

An auditor's opinion is not likely to be an analyst's primary source of information about a firm's risk. When it comes to reporting statements, a clean audit opinion suggests that the data was presented fairly in the financial statements and accordance with the accounting principles. As for internal controls, a clean audit opinion suggests that a firm maintains adequate internal controls over financial reporting. A negative or going-concern audit opinion of a financial report indicates a weakness in internal control is one clear warning sign for the analyst. However, an audit opinion relies on historical data and will not provide data on a timely enough basis to be a valuable source on risk.

References/Further Readings

Robinson, T., Henry, E., Pirie, W., Broihahn, M., & Cope, A. (2015). *International Financial Statement Analysis*, 3rd edn. Wiley, Chaps. 11 and 17.

Subramanyam, K.R. (2014). *Financial Statement Analysis*, 11th edn. McGraw Hill, Chap. 11, pp. 106–131.

13.8 Sample Questions

Question 1 (Methods to Manage Earnings, Cash Flow and Balance Sheet Items)
A company wishing to inflate (bias) revenue in the reporting period may choose to:

(a) Revenue is recognized before goods are shipped to customers.
(b) Engage in extensive rebate programs involving many estimates.
(c) Shift to a low-cost product strategy.

Question 2 (Methods to Manage Earnings, Cash Flow and Balance Sheet Items)
Typical tactics employed by management may include:

(a) Classify good news into operating items and terrible news into non-recurring items.
(b) Smooth income over time: deferring income recognition in good years as a buffer for the future or income classification into recurring and extraordinary.
(c) Both (a) and (b).

Question 3 (Methods to Manage Earnings, Cash Flow and Balance Sheet Items)
Accounting choices or areas that can affect financial reporting include:

(a) revenue recognition
(b) related-party transactions
(c) both (a) and (b)

Question 4 (Accounting Warning Signs)
Analysts must be wary of the discretionary nature of income statement items which allow management to manage earnings by:

(a) Manipulating the timing of the occurrence of the item
(b) Classification of the item as ordinary, unusual, or extraordinary
(c) Both (a) and (b)

Question 5 (Earnings Quality of a Company)

(a) Which of the following statement on a company's earnings quality is least accurate? Earnings that result from non-recurring activities are unsustainable. Unsustainable earnings are an example of lower-quality earnings.
(b) Financial reports span a quality continuum from high to low based on decision-usefulness and earnings quality.
(c) Earnings, and the decision usefulness of earnings, are only a function of the performance itself, not the measurement of performance.

Question 6 (Earnings Management)
Which of the following statement is least accurate on earnings management?

(a) More persistent and sustainable earnings are considered of higher quality. Management may tend to smooth earnings.
(b) The significant divergence between reported income and cash flows or a higher proportion of non-cash items should need the investor's detailed analysis to determine the causes.
(c) The three categories of ratio analysis: profitability, liquidity, and solvency, directly measure the risk or uncertainty of earnings and the cash flows, which analysts can entirely rely on to assess a company's earnings quality.

Solutions

Question 1

Solution: Option **c** is correct.

If a company wants to bias and inflate reported revenue, it may engage in specific revenue recognition policies requiring attention. Barter transactions can be challenging to value correctly. Rebate programs involve many estimates, which can significantly affect revenue recognition. Recognizing revenue immediately upon shipment of goods makes it easier to recognize revenue prematurely.

Question 2

Solution: Option **c** is correct.

Question 3

Solution: Option **c** is correct.

Question 4

Solution: Option **c** is correct.

Question 5

Solution: Option **c** is correct.

Earnings, and the decision usefulness of earnings, are only a function of the performance itself, as well as the measurement of performance.

Question 6

Solution: Option **c** is correct.

Profitability, liquidity, and solvency implicitly address whether the company is likely to continue operations. However, these ratios do not directly measure the risk or uncertainty of earnings and the cash flows, which will impact a company's survival.

Chapter 14

Applications of Financial Statement Analysis

14.1 Assessing Credit Quality

Credit analysis is the assessment of credit risk. Credit analysis can involve the credit risk of an obligor in a particular transaction and an obligor's overall creditworthiness.

Learning Objectives

- Describe the financial statement analysis's role in assessing a potential debt investment's credit quality.

Main Takeaways

Main Points

- Evaluation of a company's past performances addresses the reason behind its causes and performances alongside how it affects the company's strategy.
- Credit risk is the risk of loss caused by a counterparty's or debtor's failure to make due payment.
- Credit analysis is the assessment of credit risk. Credit analysis may involve the credit risk of an obligor in a specific transaction and an obligor's overall creditworthiness.
- Credit risk typically involves the estimation of a company's period-by-period cash flows. Return measures relate to the operating cash flow as

it symbolizes cash generated internally and makes it accessible to pay creditors.

- Credit analysis assesses credit-relevant factors, including leverage tolerance, operation stability, and margin stability.

Main Terms

- **Scale:** A firm's sensitiveness to adverse events, economic status, and other elements — such as market leadership, purchasing power with suppliers, and the accessibility to capital markets — might affect debt-paying capability.
- **Rating factors:** Factors taken into the account for an individual's credit score consist of one's history of payments, amounts owed, and length of credit history, new credit, and types of credit. Some factors stated weigh greater than others.
- **Creditworthiness:** The extent to which a person or company is considered suitable to receive financial credit, often based on their reliability in paying the money back in the past.

Credit risks occur due to the irresolution of a counterparty's ability to meet its obligations. Credit analysis is the assessment of credit risk. It emphasizes cash flow and debt-paying ability rather than accrual-income returns.

Moody's ratings focus mainly on four elements:

1. Company profile — Scale and diversification.

The profile indicates other attributes that mollify risk and are good indicators of market leadership, operational flexibility, purchasing power, etc.

This element relates to a company's sensitiveness to adverse events or economic status and others, such as accessing capital markets, affecting its debt-paying capability.

2. Financial policies — Tolerance for leverage.

Cash flow service availability to indebtedness is considered the most elementary credit stature measure. Various solvency ratios are used for that purpose.

3. Operational efficiency.

This element is similar to operating leverage. It relates to a company's cost structure. Since they can produce higher cash flow levels, a firm with low operating leverage (i.e., superior profit margins) can allow bigger debt loads. Since debt loads can be restructured, companies with lower costs can hold better prospects than companies with higher costs in light of financial stress/distress or forced reorganizations.

4. Margin stability.

Margin stability refers to the past volatility of profit margins. Margins with lower volatility would imply lower risk corresponding to economic status. Higher margin stability is related to lower credit risk.

14.2 Screening for Potential Equity Investments

Ratios assembled from market information and financial statement information are frequently used to screen for possible equity investments.

Learning Objectives

- Detail the use of financial statement analysis in screening for potential equity investments.

Main Takeaways

Main Points

- A security selection method involving financial ratios is applied regardless of the investor's top-down analysis or bottom-up analysis.
- Analyst modification to a firm's stated financial statements is occasionally necessary (e.g., differentiating firms that use an alternative accounting approach or assumptions). The modification comprises those associated with investments; inventory; property, plant, equipment; and goodwill.
- An analyst may wish to assess how the portfolio with a specific screen would have performed previously. For this purpose, the analyst uses a procedure known as "backtesting".

Main Terms

- **Screening:** Utilizes a set of rules to minimize possible investments to a smaller group with several desirable characteristics.
- **Growth investing:** It is a stock-buying method with primary attention on companies expected to grow at an above-average rate in contrast to their industry or the market.
- **Value orientated:** Related to value investing is an investment plan that entails picking stocks that seem to be trading for less than their intrinsic or book value.
- **Market orientated:** An investor using market orientation invests time researching current trends in a given market.
- **Back testing:** It is the process of applying a trading strategy or analytical method to historical data to see how accurately the strategy or method would have predicted actual results.

Financial ratios are used continuously to screen for possible equity investments by distinguishing organizations that satisfy specific standards. The analysis can support creating a portfolio or constructing a more in-depth analysis of potential investment targets.

A security selection approach incorporating financial ratios is applied regardless of the investor's top-down analysis or bottom-up analysis. A bottom-up manager searches for stocks company by company. They are the typical "stock pickers", who don't care if a stock is an airline or a drug-maker. Once any stock meets their standards, they accept it. This approach opposed that of a top-down manager. These managers take a bird's-eye view of the economy. The top-down analysis includes searching for appealing geographical sectors and industry sectors, from which the investor selects the most compelling investments.

Disregarding their philosophy, portfolio managers exploit ratios using financial statement data and market data to screen for possible equity investments.

Various studies were performed to establish the most competent accounting ratios for screening equity investments.

Backtesting is a procedure of experimenting with a trading approach on prior periods. Back-testing can help evaluate how a portfolio based on a screen would have performed formerly. It uses the portfolio selection principles to previous information and calculates the earned returns if a specific approach is applied. Nonetheless, backtesting may not deliver a reliable estimation of future performance because of various factors such as:

- Survivorship bias: When backtesting database remove firms that die off, the leftover firms collectively will appear to have achieved better results.
- Look-ahead bias: If repeated financial information is duplicated in the database, investors will have a conflict on what they would have known when they invested and the data used during the backtesting.
- Data-snooping bias occurs when the model is assembled based on prior findings and used to test it.

Reference/Further Reading

Robinson, T., Henry, E., Pirie, W., Broihahn, M., & Cope, A. (2015). *International Financial Statement Analysis*, 3rd edn. Wiley, Chap. 12.

14.3 Sample Questions

Question 1 (Assessing Credit Quality)
Which of the following on credit analysis is least accurate?

(a) Credit analysis is the evaluation of credit risk, which is the risk of loss caused by a counterparty's or debtor's failure to make a promised payment.
(b) In assessing an obligor's overall creditworthiness, one general approach is credit scoring, a statistical analysis of credit default determinants.
(c) Credit analysis usually focuses on accrual income rather than cash flow.

Question 2 (Assessing Credit Quality)
Which of the following is likely to be included in a company's credit scoring?

(a) Scale: A company's sensitivity to adverse events, adverse economic conditions, and other factors
(b) Business profile: A company's competitive position, the stability of revenues, product and geographic diversity, growth prospects, and the stability and volatility of cash flows.
(c) Financial policy: A company's financial risk tolerance and its capital structure.

Question 3 (Assessing Credit Quality)
Which of the following is most likely to be weighted higher than other rating factors in a company's credit scoring?

(a) Subfactors of scale: Total revenue & operating profit
(b) Subfactors of business profile: Competitive position & expected revenue stability
(c) Subfactors of Leverage and coverage: Debt/EBITDA, Retained cash flow/net debt & EBIT/Interest.

Question 4 (Assessing Credit Quality)
A credit analyst assesses the efficiency and leverage of two companies in the same industry based on certain sub-factors. The analyst calculates the following ratios:

	Company A	Company B
Debt/EBITDA	10	4
Retained cash flow/Net Debt	3%	9%
EBIT/Interest	5	8

If we base solely on the information given above, which company is more likely to have a higher rating?

(a) Company A is more likely to have a higher rating.
(b) Company B is more likely to have a higher rating.
(c) Company A and Company B will have an equal rating.

Question 5 (Assessing Credit Quality)
Credit analysts are likely to consider which of the following in making a rating recommendation?

(a) Business risk but not a financial risk
(b) Financial risk but not business risk
(c) Both business risk and financial risk

Question 6 (Screening for Potential Equity Investments)
Which of the following on screening for potential equity investments is least accurate?

(a) Top-down analysis involves identifying attractive geographical segments and industry segments from which the investor chooses the most attractive investments. Both business risk and financial risk.
(b) Fundamental to this type of analysis are decisions about which metrics to use as screens, the number of metrics to include, values of those metrics to use as cut-off points, and weighting to give each metric.
(c) Only financial ratios will be used in the screening process.

Question 7 (Screening for Potential Equity Investments)
Below is a hypothetical example of a simple stock screen based on the following criteria:

Stock Meeting Criterion
• Market Capitalization>$100 million
• P/E<20
• Total liabilities/Total Assets <0.8
• ROA>0

Which of the following statement on the stock selection criteria is least accurate?

(a) The second criterion selects stocks that appear relatively cheaply valued.
(b) The third criterion sets a limitation on financial leverage to control for financial risk.
(c) All criteria are entirely independent of each other, i.e., it is impossible for a stock that passes one test also pass another.

Question 8 (Screening for Potential Equity Investments)
What are the analysts' cautions to note when screening for potential equity investment?

(a) Unintentional selections can be made if criteria are not specified carefully.
(b) The inputs to ratio analysis are derived from financial statements, and companies may differ in the financial standards they apply.
(c) Both (a) and (b).

Solutions

Question 1

Solution: Option **c** is correct.

Credit analysis is concerned with how the ability to repay is sensitive to adverse events and poor economic conditions. As the repayment is generally in cash, credit analysis focuses on cash flow rather than accrual income. As such, credit analysis is related to a firm's operating cash flow that is cash generated internal to service repayment to creditors.

Question 2

Solution: Option **c** is correct.

Question 3

Solution: Option **c** is correct.

The debt level relative to earnings and cash flow is a critical factor in assessing creditworthiness. Higher levels of debt for a company typically result in higher risk in meeting interest and principal payments on its debt obligations.

Question 4

Solution: Option **b** is correct.

The leverage and coverage ratio are all in favor of Company B; based solely on these factors, Company B is more likely to have a higher rating.

Question 5

Solution: Option **c** is correct.

Both business risk and financial risk are considered by credit analysts when making a rating recommendation.

Question 6

Solution: Option **c** is correct.

Metrics for screening may include financial ratios and characteristics such as market capitalization or membership as component security in a specified index.

Question 7

Solution: Option **c** is correct.

Criteria are often not independent.

Question 8

Solution: Option **c** is correct.

Section 3: Financial Management

Part F: Finance Foundation

Chapter 15

Time Value of Money

15.1 Introduction and the Time of Value of Money

The concepts of the time value of money (TVM) underlie the valuation of securities and bonds. Cash flows from financial securities and investment projects occur in the future at various points in time. However, the same dollar received at different points does not have the same value today. Using the TVM, we can adjust the cash flows received in the future to their equivalent amounts today to make a comparison.

Learning Objectives

- Define the TVM and understand its use in Finance.

Main Takeaways

Main Points

- The TVM concept is based on the notion that a dollar received today is worth more than the same dollar received in the future.
- Using the TVM, we can compare cash flows received at different times by looking at their equivalent values today.
- If an investment is made, the investor expects to receive cash flows in the future. Whether the investor thinks the investment is worthwhile will depend on whether the sum of the future cash flows adjusted for the TVM exceeds the investment cost.
- The TVM is the reason why interest is needed. It compensates the lender for the use of the funds.

Main Terms

- **Present Value (PV):** the value of a sum of money to be received in the future, today.
- **Interest rate:** the cost that the lender charges the borrower for using money over one year.
- **Future Value (FV):** the value in the future that a sum of money today can grow to, assuming a specific interest rate or rate of return.

In everyday life, individuals have to make personal financial decisions. These decisions are about how much to spend and how much to save for the future. Individuals could also be saving with a goal in mind, for example, saving enough to make a down payment for the purchase of a house or saving for retirement. Whatever the case the individuals may not just put their money in a savings deposit but would consider investing the funds in stocks and bonds if they are saving for retirement. They would need to be able to understand which alternative suits their needs in terms of risk and return.

As most individuals do not have the cash to pay outright for big-ticket items like cars or houses, they would need to borrow money. In this case, the individuals would need to know which loans offer the best value.

Whether investing in our savings or taking a loan, the concepts of the TVM would help us evaluate the various options.

TVM concepts are also used to value financial securities like stocks and bonds and make capital budgeting decisions or decisions involving the investment of large sums of money.

TVM allows us to compare cash flows received at different points in time. The reason is that the same dollar amount at different points in time does not have the same value today. Hence we have to make adjustments to those cash flows to find their equivalent value today. Mastery of TVM concepts and techniques is essential for investment analysis.

This section discusses the methods to find the time value of different types of cash flows. Such cash flows could be single cash flows or multiple cash flows. Multiple cash flows that have a definite pattern are the annuity, the growing annuity, the perpetuity and the growing perpetuity.

15.2 Interest Rates

15.2.1 *Interpretation of Interest Rates*

The interest rate is a percentage of the amount of funds that the lender charges for its use. It is quoted on an annual basis.

Learning Objectives

- Understand the concept of an interest rate.

Main Takeaways

Main Points

- An interest rate is an additional amount in percentage terms that needs to be paid besides the principal of a loan.
- The difference between what an amount of money grows to after one year and the original amount is the interest. The interest rate is that difference divided by the original amount.
- The interest rate normally quoted, the nominal or stated rate, is an annual rate. The rate for a period shorter than a year is equal to the stated annual interest rate divided by the number of compounding periods per year.

Main Terms

- **Opportunity cost:** an opportunity cost of an investment is the value that investors forgo by choosing a particular investment rather than the next best alternative investment.
- **Real return:** when inflation is removed from the nominal rate, what results is the real rate of interest. The real return measures the increase in real terms of the value of an investment.
- **Nominal interest rate:** nominal interest rate refers to the stated rate or advertised rate of interest before the effect of inflation is removed. It can also refer to the interest rate charged on a loan before factoring in any fees or interest compounding.

We illustrate the concept of TVM with the following example. Suppose a bank offers you the following investment: Invest by depositing $1,000 today and be paid $1,040 in one year. This scheme gives you a return of \$40 over a year. We say that you earn an interest of \$40/\$1,000 or 4% in percentage terms.

The interest rate can also be thought of differently. If we divide \$1,040 by $(1 + r)$ where "r" is the interest rate, we end up with \$1,000, the original amount before interest was paid. Dividing by $(1 + r)$ is called discounting, and "r" is the discount rate. The terms interest rate and discount rate are often used interchangeably.

Another way to think of the interest rate is as an opportunity cost. If we spend the \$1,000 today, we forgo the opportunity to earn an extra \$40 if we deposit it in the bank. \$40 is the opportunity cost of consuming today instead of investing.

15.2.2 *Determinants of Interest Rates*

The interest rate consists of a few components which are essentially compensations for lack of liquidity or bearing risk.

Learning Objectives

- Understand and interpret various components of an interest rate.

Main Takeaways

Main Points

- All of the interest rate components are important in determining the rate for bond investments.
- The interest earned provides compensation for forgoing liquidity or bearing risk.

Main Terms

- **Liquidity:** refers to the ease with which an asset, or security, can be converted into cash. The cash amount should be at, or close to its fair market value.
- **Maturity:** the maturity of a loan or security is the date on which the principal must be repaid in full.
- **Risk-free rate:** the risk-free rate of return is the certain return on a security. The Treasury bill provides a risk-free return as the investor is certain that the T-bill's principal or face value will be repaid in full upon maturity since it is issued by the government. A T-bill's interest is implicit because a T-Bill is sold at a discount to its face value.

Interest rates are set in the marketplace by supply and demand forces. Individuals or entities with excess funds supply funds, and individuals or entities who need funds form the demand for funds. The interest rate can be thought of as a price such that the market for funds clear: the supply of funds is equal to the demand for funds.

An interest rate "*r*" is composed of a real risk-free interest rate plus a set of premiums that are the required returns or compensation for bearing various risks:

$$r = \text{Real risk-free interest rate} + \text{Inflation premium} + \text{Default risk premium} + \text{Liquidity premium} + \text{Maturity premium}$$

The real risk-free interest rate is the one-year interest rate for completely risk-free security; that is, there is no default risk or risk of non-payment and no inflation risk. The real rate of return is essentially compensation for someone to defer consumption or use of the funds today.

The inflation premium is compensation for the loss of purchasing power through inflation. Investors are well aware that the same dollar may buy different amounts of the same good at different times. Compared to the past, the amount purchased is usually less. This observation shows the effect of inflation or loss of purchasing power. The inflation premium is based on the market's expectation of how much inflation will be in the future. Typically, the inflation premium is added to the real risk-free rate to give the nominal return for a default-free bond, for example, a government bond.

The default risk premium compensates investors for the possibility that the borrower will not make the payments due on the security. In the case of bonds, the payments are the regular coupon interest and principal's repayment upon maturity.

The liquidity premium compensates investors for the loss arising from selling an investment quickly to get cash. The more liquid an investment, the faster it can be converted into cash at close to its fair value. For example, some investments are very liquid as there are many buyers and sellers in the market. However, the liquidity is much lower for a relatively small company bond. Because of the smaller market for the bond, any sale beyond a small quantity will impact the price negatively.

The maturity premium compensates investors because long-term bonds experience larger price changes than short-term bonds when the interest rate changes.

15.3 Future and Present Value of a Single Cash Flow

15.3.1 *Definitions and Calculations*

The future value (FV) of a sum is equal to its present value (PV) plus the interest earned by investing it.

Learning Objectives

- Calculate and interpret FV and PV for a single cash flow stream.

Main Takeaways

Main Points

- With simple interest, the interest amount remains the same throughout the period the investment is held, while the amount of interest increases exponentially when compound interest is used.
- An investment that is based on compound interest pays interest on the principal as well as the interest. The interest includes amounts that have been earned in previous periods.
- The market convention is that interest is paid on a compound basis.

Main Terms

- **Compound Interest:** compound interest is the interest paid on the principal and accumulated interest earned in previous periods.
- **Discounting:** discounting is the process of determining the present value of a payment or a series of payments that is to be received in the future.
- **Accrue:** To accrue means to accumulate over time.

You expect to earn interest when you deposit money in the bank. Suppose you deposit \$100 and the bank pays 5% interest a year. At at the end of one year, the amount will grow to \$105, consisting of \$5 interest and the original \$100 deposited. If you keep the money in the bank for another year, the bank deposit will grow to \$110.25 [new principal of \$105 plus interest of \$5.25 (\$105 × 0.05)].

Compounding describes the process through which the deposit grows. The deposit earns compound interest as opposed to simple interest where interest each year is paid on the original principal deposited. By contrast, in compound interest, the principal grows. The interest earned each year is added to the principal. Thus, the deposit does not only earns interest on the original principal but also on the accumulated interest, that is, earning interest on interest.

We refer to the deposit/investment made today as the **present value (PV_0)**. The amount it accrues to in the future is known as the **future value at time "*t*" (FV_t)**. If the rate of interest is "*r*" per period and the deposit is invested for "*t*" periods, we then have this relationship:

$$FV_t = PV_0 \times (1 + r)^t$$

The above equation enables us to compare cash flows at different points in time. We can find an equivalent cash flow at one point in time to a cash flow occurring at another point in time. So a person would be indifferent to getting \$100 today or \$110.25 in two years if he requires a return of 5% per year.

Here's an example applying this method. Suppose you are given the choice of \$100 today, \$106 next year, and \$110 in 2 years. Which would you prefer given an interest rate of 5%?

To answer this question, it may be useful to use a **timeline** to indicate the timing of cash flows.

Figure 15.1 shows a timeline showing the points in time when the cash flows occur. It is usual practice to reference today as time 0, one year from today as time 1, and so on. The cash flows from the question above are depicted in Figure 15.1.

We find the equivalent amounts of the three cash flows in 2 years to answer the question. The \$100 at time 0 will be worth \$110.25 in year. The \$106 at time 1 will grow to \$111.3, which is the highest of the 3 amounts at time 2.

Example: Future value of single cash flow

John wants to know if he invests \$10,000 today, whether the future value of this sum is sufficient to pay for his daughter's college tuition fees of \$50,000 in 15 years. The investment can earn a return of 12% per year.

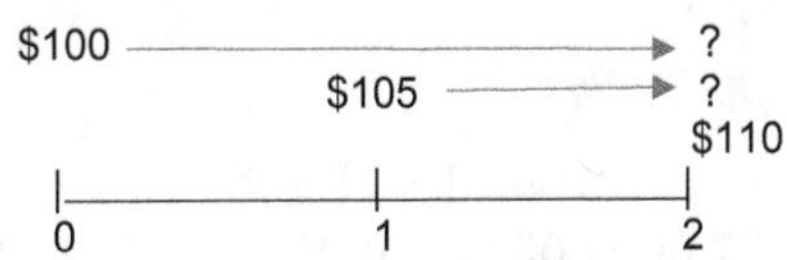

Figure 15.1: Timeline illustration of future value.

Solution:
PV = \$10,000, $t = 15$ years and $r = 12\%$.

The future value is given by:

$$FV_T = PV(1 + r)^T$$
$$FV_{15} = \$10{,}000\ (1 + 0.12)^{15} = \$54{,}735.66$$

(a) Finding the Present Value of a Single Cash Flow
The present value of a sum to be received in the future is just the future value's reciprocal. The process of finding the present value is called discounting.

To find the present value, we find the future value factor's reciprocal. Recall that the future value factor is $(1 + r)^t$. The present value factor would then be $1/(1 + r)^t$. Multiplying the future amount by the present value factor gives us the future sum's present value.

The process is shown below.

$$FV_t = PV(1 + r)^t$$
$$PV = FV_t \left[\frac{1}{(1+r)^t}\right]$$
$$PV = FV_t\,(1 + r)^{-t}$$

Example: Present value of single cash flow stream
Suppose when you retire in 30 years, you will get a lump sum of \$1,000,000. What is the present value of the retirement amount if the discount rate is 6%?

Solution
PV = X
FV_T = \$1,000,000
$r = 6\%$
$t = 30$

$$PV = FV_t(1 + r)^{-t}$$
$$PV = \$1{,}000{,}000\ (1 + 0.06)^{-6} = \$174{,}110.13$$

15.3.2 *Compounding Frequency*

The compounding frequency is the number of times a stated interest rate is assumed to be paid during a given year.

Learning Objectives

- Calculate and interpret the FV and PV given the stated frequency of compounding.

Main Takeaways

Main Points

- The frequency of interest payment (frequency of compounding) makes an essential difference between the accumulated amount and total interest earned.
- When the compounding frequency *(m)* increases, the accumulated amounts tend to a limit.
- The frequency could be yearly, half-yearly, quarterly, monthly, weekly, daily, or continuously (or not at all, until maturity).

Main Terms

- **Continuous compounding:** Continuously compounded interest assumes interest is compounded and added to the balance an infinite number of times a year.
- **Quarter:** Three consecutive months (1/4 of a year).

What happens to the investment if interest is paid more than once a year? The convention of paying interest once a year existed in the time before computers as we know them became available, perhaps 100 years ago. Interest computations were then calculated using adding machines. Hence it is understandable that banks would not pay interest more often because of the enormous computational task.

Today, many banks pay interest daily. Some may pay monthly. Whatever the case, this makes it difficult to compare what effectively the customer gets as all banks quote interest on an annual basis.

When interest is paid more than once a year, the effective rate will be higher than the quoted rate. Suppose the quoted interest is 4% a year. If the bank pays interest quarterly the amount that accumulates after one year is $(1 + r/2)^2 = (1 + 0.04/2)^2 = 1.0404$. The computation means that the effective rate is 4.04%, higher than the quoted rate.

With more than one compounding period per year, the future value formula is:

$$FV_t = PV\left(1+\frac{r}{m}\right)^{mt}$$

where r is the quoted annual interest rate, m is the number of compounding periods per year, and t the number of years. The rate for the period is found by dividing the quoted rate by the number of times interest is compounded, m, giving a periodic rate of r/m. The number of compounding periods is then equal to mt.

(a) Future Value Example with Compounding More than Once a Year

Suppose your bank pays you an annual interest of 6% compounded monthly on your savings deposit. How much will your savings deposit balance be after two years?

$$PV = \$1{,}000; \quad FV_t = X; \quad r/m = 0.06/12 = 0.005; \quad t = 2;$$
$$mt = 12 \times 2 = 24 \text{ compounding periods}$$

$$FV_t = PV\left(1+\frac{r}{m}\right)^{mt}. \quad FV_t = 1{,}000(1+0.005)^{24} = 1{,}127.16$$

At the end of 2 years, the balance will be $1,127.16. If interest were paid only once a year, the balance would be $1,123.60. The monthly compounding earned $3.56 more interest.

(b) Continuous Compounding

What happens if compounding is done continuously, that is, the number of compounding periods per year becomes infinite? In this case, if we use the future value is given by:

$$FV_t = PVe^{rt}$$

where e is the transcendental number and is approximately equal to 2.71828.

Suppose in our earlier example of the $1,000 savings deposit that earns a 6% annual interest, what would be the balance if there is continuous compounding of interest?

$$PV = \$1{,}000; \quad FV_t = X; \quad r = 0.06; \quad t = 2$$

$$FV_t = PVe^{rt}$$

$$FV_t = 1{,}000e^{0.005x24} = 1{,}127.50$$

With continuous compounding, the $1,000 savings grows to $1,127.50 in 2 years, compared with $1,127.16 with monthly compounding.

15.3.3 *Effective Annual Rate*

The Effective Annual Rate (EAR) is the interest rate that considers the number of times compounding occurs over a given period.

Learning Objectives

- Calculate and interpret the effective annual rate.

Main Takeaways

Main Points

- When interest compounds more than once a year, the effective interest rate (EAR) will be higher than the nominal or stated interest rate.
- The more frequent the compounding periods, the greater the EAR.
- The effective rate of interest is often used to compare investments with different compounding periods.

Main Terms

- **Annual percentage rate (APR):** this is the stated interest rate for a whole year. It is also known as the nominal rate.
- **Effective annual rate:** this is the APR adjusted for the number of compounding periods in a year. The larger the number of compounding periods, the greater the effective annual rate.
- **Compounding periods:** the length of time between the points at which interest is paid.
- **Nominal interest rate:** the nominal or stated rate is the interest rate assuming interest is paid once a year.

(a) Quoted versus Effective Rates

The interest rate quoted by a lender is known as the nominal rate or stated rate. It is also known as the annual percentage rate (APR), where interest is paid annually. However, what the borrower ends up paying is the *effective annual rate* (*EAR*).

The EAR takes into account how interest is computed. If interest is compounded more than once a year, the EAR will be higher than the APR. The EAR is given as:

$$\text{EAR} = (1 + \text{Periodic interest rate})^m - 1$$

Example: An effective annual rate

We use the savings deposit example where the annual interest is 6%, and interest is paid monthly.

The monthly interest rate is 6%/12 = 0.5%, and the number of compounding periods is 12.

$$\text{EAR} = (1.005)^{12} - 1 = 6.17\%.$$

15.4 Future Value and Present Value of a Series of Cash Flows

15.4.1 *Definitions and Calculations*

Just as we can calculate future and present values for single cash flows, we can calculate future and present values for multiple cash flows.

Learning Objectives

- Classify and calculate the FV and PV of multiple cash flows.

Main Takeaways

Main Points

- An annuity consists of a stream of equal cash flows occurring at regular intervals.
- The PV of multiple cash flows is found by discounting each cash flow to a specific point in time, usually the present time, and summing up the PVs of all the cash flows.
- If the multiple cash flows are of the same amount, the cash flows constitute an annuity. The PV can be found using the present value factor for an annuity.

Main Terms

- **Annuity:** a stream of equal regular cash flows over a fixed period.
- **Perpetuity:** an unending stream of equal regular cash flows.
- **Discounting:** discounting is the process of determining the present value of a payment or a stream of payments that is to be received in the future.

This section discusses different types of multiple cash flows and how to find their present and future valucs.

One set of cash flows consists of different cash flows with the common characteristic that the cash flows are of the same size and occur at regular time intervals. These series include:

- Annuity: It is a series of equal-sized cash flows occurring at regular time intervals, for example, a year. Annuities can be subdivided into the ordinary annuity and the annuity due.
- Perpetuity: It is similar to the annuity in terms of a series of equal-sized cash flows occurring at regular time intervals, except the cash flows continue forever.

The second set of cash flows consists of cash flows of different sizes that do not occur regularly.

15.4.2 *Ordinary Annuity*

An ordinary annuity consists of a series of equal cash flows occurring at fixed intervals. The first cash flow occurs at the end of the first period.

Learning Objectives

- Differentiate and calculate the FV and PV of an ordinary annuity.

Main Takeaways

Main Points

- Annuities are commonly used in payment schemes. Their predictability in terms of the amount and the timing of the payments helps the borrower plan her finances.

- An example of the annuity arrangement is the home loan, where the borrower makes monthly fixed payments.

Main Terms

- **Ordinary annuity:** consists of fixed cash flows at regular intervals, with the first cash flow occurring at the end of the first period.

A finite series of regular equal-sized cash flows is an annuity. For example, a series of 4 yearly cash flows of $100 each is an annuity. There are two types of annuities. The first cash flow comes at the end of the first period in the ordinary annuity. However, for an annuity due, the first cash flow comes at the beginning of the first period.

Annuities are found in many financial products. Many loans are structured with the repayment of the loan consisting of the same amount spread over a period.

(a) Future Value of an Ordinary Annuity

The FV of an ordinary annuity can be found from the following formula: C is the cash flow, t = number of periods, and r the interest rate for each period.

$$\mathrm{FV}_t = C\left[\frac{(1+r)^{t-1}}{r}\right]$$

The term in brackets is the future value annuity factor. To find the FV of an ordinary annuity, multiply the cash flow per period by the future value annuity factor.

Another way to find the future value of an annuity is to find the annuity's present value first. With the present value of the annuity as a single sum, compound it over t periods to get the annuity's future value.

Example (FV of an ordinary annuity)

Suppose you invest $30,000 a year for 20 years in your retirement account earns a 10% return. How much money would you have accumulated after 20 years? We solve this problem by using the future value annuity factor.

C = $30,000
r = 10%
t = 20

$$FV_t = 30{,}000\left[\frac{(1+0.1)^{20}-1}{0.1}\right] = 1{,}718{,}249.98$$

(b) The Present Value of an Ordinary Annuity

The present value of an ordinary annuity is found using the following formula:

$$PV = C\left[\frac{1-\frac{1}{(1+r)^t}}{r}\right]$$

where C = the annuity amount; r = interest rate per period; t = the number of annuity cash flows.

The PV of an ordinary annuity can be found easily by multiplying the annuity cash flow with the present value annuity factor (the term in brackets). Other ways to find the PV of an ordinary annuity include using a financial calculator or the spreadsheet's annuity function.

Example (PV of an ordinary annuity)

Your financial adviser is proposing a financial product that pays \$5,000 a year for ten years, with the first payment one year from now. Based on the product's risk, the financial adviser suggests that 10% should be the required rate of return. How much should you be willing to pay for this product?

To find the value of the financial product, we use the present value of an ordinary annuity formula with:

A = \$5,000
r = 10%
t = 10

$$PV = 5{,}000\left[\frac{1-\frac{1}{(1+0.1)^{10}}}{0.1}\right] = 30{,}722.84$$

With a required return of 10%, the financial product's value is \$30,722.84.

15.4.3 *Annuity Due*

An annuity due is an annuity where the first cash flow occurs at the beginning of the first period.

Learning Objectives

- Differentiate and calculate the TVM of an annuity due.

Main Takeaways

Main Points

- The difference between an annuity due and an ordinary annuity is in the cash flows' timing. Cash flows for the annuity due occur at the beginning of the period, while cash flows for the ordinary annuity come at the end of the period.
- As the cash flows of the annuity due come one period before the cash flows of the ordinary annuity, each of the cash flows of the annuity due earns one more period of interest. Hence the value of the annuity due is $(1 + r)$ times the value of the ordinary annuity.
- An example of an annuity due is leases or property rentals, where payment is at the beginning of each period, usually at the beginning of the month.

The cash flows of an ordinary annuity and an annuity due are shown in Figures 15.2 and 15.3. Notice that we can align the annuity due's cash flows to ordinary annuity cash flows by shifting forward each of the annuity due's cash flows by one period. Suppose we were to compare the

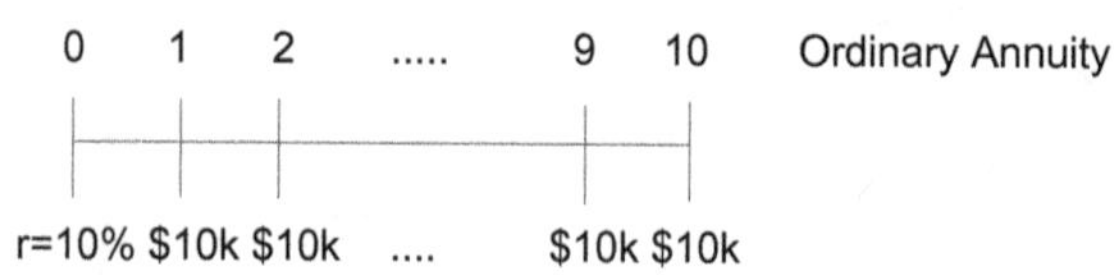

Figure 15.2: Timeline illustration of an ordinary annuity.

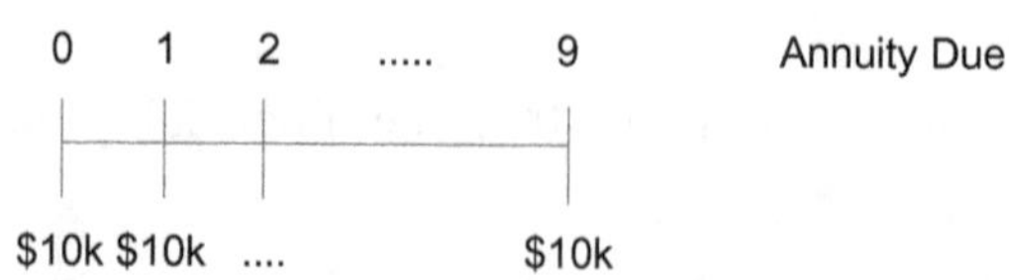

Figure 15.3: Timeline illustration of an annuity due.

values of these two annuities. In that case, the annuity due's cash flows coming one period before those of the ordinary annuity means that each cash flow of the annuity due would earn one period more interest than the corresponding cash flow of the ordinary annuity. Hence the value of the annuity due is (1 + r) times that of the ordinary annuity. The relationships are as follows:

PV of annuity due = PV of ordinary annuity × $(1 + r)$ and
FV of annuity due = FV of ordinary annuity × $(1 + r)$

15.4.4 *Perpetuity*

A perpetuity is a stream of equal cash flows that goes on forever.

Learning Objectives

- Calculate the PV of a perpetuity.

Main Takeaways

Main Points

- A perpetuity is similar to an annuity, except the cash flows continue indefinitely.
- An example of a perpetuity is the preferred stock, which like an ordinary stock, has no maturity. The preferred stock pays a fixed dividend and the dividend stream is a perpetuity.
- When valuing a company, perpetuities are used to find the present value at a point in time after which the company's projected cash flow stream grows at a low steady rate. The value obtained is called the company's terminal value.

Main Terms

- **Terminal Value:** terminal value (TV) is the value of a business or project due to cash flows beyond the forecast period.
- **Dividend:** pay-out to shareholders from a company's profits.
- **Preferred Stock:** preferred stocks are similar to a common stock except they pay a fixed dividend like a bond.

A perpetuity is quite similar to an ordinary annuity except that the cash flow series does not end. It continues indefinitely. An example of a

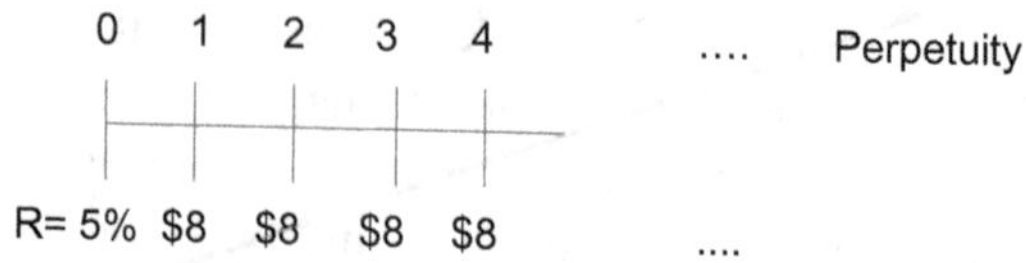

Figure 15.4: Timeline illustration of perpetuity.

perpetuity is a perpetual bond. This bond has no maturity, meaning that all an investor gets is the stream of interest payments from the bond. The timeline of a perpetuity is illustrated in Figure 15.4.

The present value, PV_0 of a perpetuity, is:

$$PV_0 = \frac{C}{r}$$

where C is the cash flow each period, and r is the rate of return per period.

The present value of the perpetuity is: $PV_0 = 8/0.05 = \$160$.

Example (present values of perpetuity and annuity)
Suppose you are offered the following investment. Pay \$X per year for ten years and receive \$1,000 a year thereafter, forever. If the discount rate is 10%, compute the value of X.

Solution

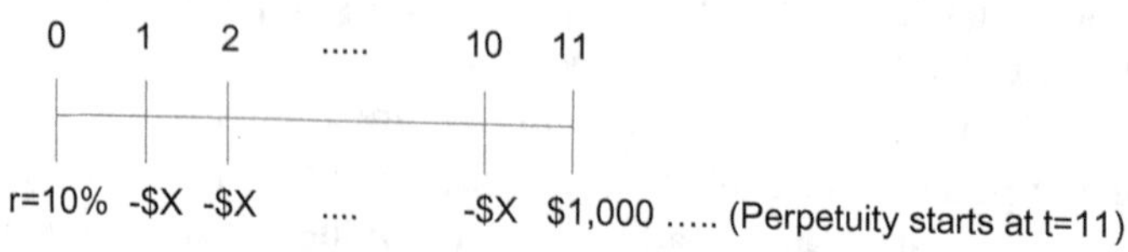

First, we draw the timeline to guide us in the computation.

Present value of the perpetuity of \$1,000 a year at time 10 = C/r = \$1,000/0.1 = \$10,000

Present value of perpetuity at time 0 = $10,000/(1 + 0.1)^{10}$ = \$3,855.43

We use the value of \$3,855.43 as the PV at time 0 of the 10-year annuity and solve for \$$X$ the annual payment, using the annuity formula.

$$PV = C\left[\frac{1-\frac{1}{(1+r)^t}}{r}\right]$$

$$3{,}855.43 = X\left[\frac{1-\frac{1}{(1+0.1)^{10}}}{0.1}\right]$$

Or $\$X = \$627.45$

15.4.5 *Growing Perpetuity*

A growing perpetuity is an infinite series of periodic cash flows that grow at a constant rate.

Learning Objectives

- Calculate the PV of a growing perpetuity.

Main Takeaways

Main Points

- The present value of a growing perpetuity can be found by dividing the cash flow at the end of the first period by the difference between the discount rate and the growth rate, provided the growth rate is lower than the discount rate.
- When the growth rate is higher than the discount rate, the growing perpetuity value is infinite.

Main Terms

- **Growth rate:** the rate of growth of the cash flows.

The growing perpetuity is a set of cash flows growing at a constant rate, with the cash flows stretching into the future forever. The timeline showing the cash flows is shown in Figure 15.5.

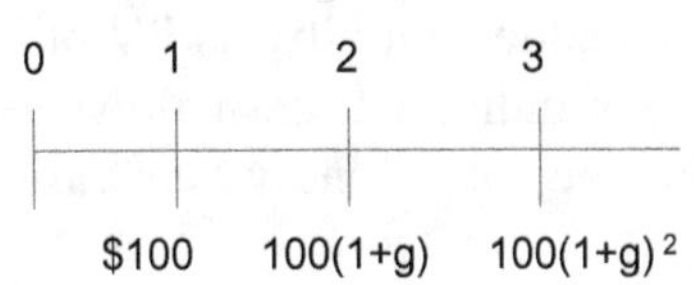

Figure 15.5: Timeline illustration of growing perpetuity.

$$PV_0 = \frac{C}{r-g}$$

We will use the growing perpetuity method to value shares of firms whose dividends grow at a constant rate.

Mr. Lee invested in the shares of Star Company. At the end of the first period, he received \$5,000. The dividends are expected to grow at a rate of 5% per year forever. If the required return for Star Company shares is 12%, what is Mr. Lee's investment in Star Company worth?

$$PV_0 = \frac{5{,}000}{12\% - 5\%} = 71{,}429$$

Mr. Lee's shares are worth a total of about \$71,429.

15.4.6 *Series of Unequal Cash Flows*

A series of equal cash flows is either an annuity or a perpetuity. Any other pattern can be classified as a series of unequal cash flows.

Learning Objectives

- Calculate and interpret the FV and PV of a series of unequal cash flows.

Main Takeaways

Main Points

- A series of unequal cash flows may have embedded annuities or a perpetuity of both.
- There is no formula to compute the PV or FV of a series of unequal cash flows.
- The method to find the PV or FV of a series of unequal cash flows is to sum the individual cash flows' PVs or FVs.
- Where there is an embedded annuity, its PV or FV can replace the PV or FV of the annuity's individual cash flows. Similarly, the PV of a perpetuity is used in place of the individual cash flows constituting the perpetuity.
- Examples of a series of unequal cash flows are the stream of common stock dividends or coupon payments from a floating-rate bond.

A series of cash flows is known as a series of uneven cash flows when the series is not an annuity or a perpetuity. However, it is possible to have embedded within the variable cash flows an annuity or a perpetuity, or both.

Since the series of cash flows consists of uneven cash flows, there is no single formula to find its present value or future value. Instead, we need to find the PV or FV by summing the individual cash flows' PVs or FVs. When the series of uneven cash flows has embedded annuities or a perpetuity, we can find the PV of the embedded annuity or perpetuity first. The PV found is the PV at the point in time one period before the start of the annuity or perpetuity.

(a) Future Value of Unequal Cash Flows

The future value of a series of unequal cash flows is found by compounding each cash flow to find the FV and summing up the FVs of all the cash flows.

15.5 Modeling Time Value Problems

15.5.1 *Use of Timeline to Aid Valuation*

A cash flow timeline shows a company's cash inflows and cash outflows and the business activity that caused them over a given period.

Learning Objectives

- Demonstrate the use of the timeline to solve TVM questions.

Main Takeaways

Main Points

- A timeline is a line used to show the amount and timing of cash flows. It helps to keep track of the cash flows in an investment project.
- The timeline is handy to track unequal cash flows.

A timeline plots on a line the amount and timing of cash flows. Equal and regular cash flows can be modeled as annuities or perpetuities if the cash flows continue indefinitely. When modeling cash flows using the spreadsheet, each cell along a row or down a column can represent the points in time.

Example:

You have an investment proposal to receive \$5,000 a year each year in perpetuity. The payments will start in 3 years. How much would you be willing to pay for this investment if alternative investments offer a return of 10%?

To solve this problem, first, draw a timeline.

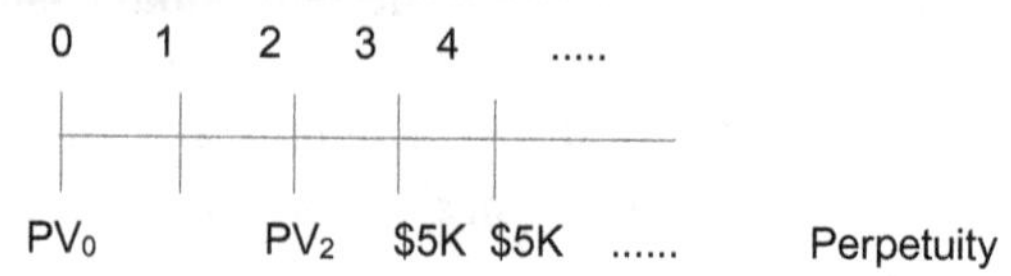

First, find the present value at time 2 (denoted as PV_2) of the perpetuity. Recall that the perpetuity's first cash flow starts one period from when we want to find the present value using the perpetuity formula.

$$PV_2 = \frac{C}{r}$$

We get:

$$PV_2 = \frac{5,000}{0.1} = 50,000$$

After we obtained the value of the perpetuity at $t = 2$, we need to discount this amount by two periods to get the value at $t = 0$. Using the PV formula:

$$PV = FV_t(1+r)^{-t} = \frac{50,000}{(1+0.1)^2} = 41,322.31$$

15.5.2 *Valuation of Bonds as PV of Bond Cash Flows*

The fair value of a bond is the sum of the present values of the bond's cash flows.

Learning Objectives

- Apply concepts learned in the TVM to value bonds.

Main Takeaways

Main Points

- When a bond's par value and interest payments are set, bond valuation helps investors figure out what rate of return would make a bond investment worth the cost.
- If the bond's market rate or required return is greater than the bond's coupon rate, the bond will be sold at a discount. If the required return is less than the bond's coupon rate, the bond will be sold at a premium.
- When calculating the present value of a bond, use the market rate as the discount rate.

Main Terms

- **Bond:** a bond is a debt instrument that pays interest in the form of regular coupon payments and repays the principal at maturity.
- **Par Value:** this is the face value or redemption value of a bond.
- **Maturity Date:** The maturity date is when the bond's principal amount is due.
- **Bond Yield:** this is the required return of the bond.
- **Zero-coupon Bond:** the interest earned on a zero-coupon bond is implicit as the bond is sold at a discount to its par value.

(a) Bond Valuation

We can apply the same methods of computing time value to stocks and bonds if they have similar cash flow patterns.

(b) What is a Bond?

A bond is a debt security issued by a firm. The security is a promise by the firm to make regular interest payments called coupon payments either annually or semi-annually. The firm also promises to repay the principal amount upon maturity which is the period of time until the bond matures.

The coupon amount is equal to a rate of interest called the coupon rate multiplied by the par value (also know as face value or redemption value). The par value is the principal, usually \$1,000, that needs to be repaid at the maturity of the bond

Suppose a bond pays a 7% coupon (paid annually) and matures in 10 years.

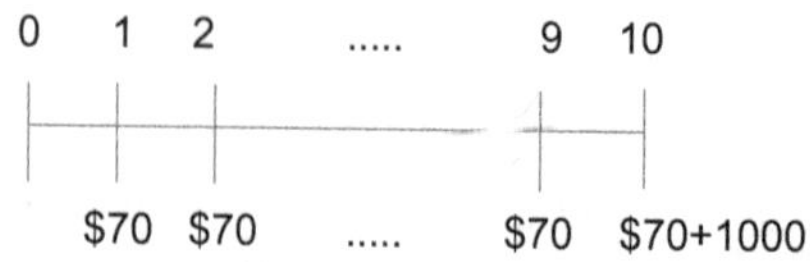

Figure 15.6: Timeline of 7% coupon paying bond (annually).

The cash flows of this bond are shown in Figure 15.6.

How do we compute the value of this bond? It depends on what rate of return we require at the time we bought the bond. We use our required rate of return to compute present value of the bond's cash flows to find its value.

Typically bonds are issued a price equal to the par value. To do this we need to set the coupon rate equal to the bond's required rate of return.

After the bond is issued, the return required by investors is likely to change with new information about the economy, the prospects for the firm, and other relevant information. Consequently the value of the bond would also change. How it changes depends on interest rate movements in the bond market. *Suppose after one year, the required return goes down to 6%.* What is the price of the bond now?

The bond's cash flows consist of a 9-year annuity plus the face value at time 9. The value is determined by the formula below, where "C" is the coupon interest, "r" is the bond's yield or required return, "C_T" is the face value, and "T" is the time to maturity for the bond

$$PV_0 = C\left[\frac{1-1/(1+r)^T}{r}\right]+\frac{C_T}{(1+r)^T}$$

$$PV_0 = C\left[\frac{1-1/(1+0.06)^9}{0.06}\right]+\frac{1000}{(1+0.06)^9}$$

The bond's cash flows' present value or the bond price is $1,068.02.

We also learn that when the required return increases, the bond price falls. In other words, the bond price and the bond yield are inversely related. The difference between the bond's yield and the coupon rate and its relationship to the difference between the bond price and the par value is as follows.

Bond yield > coupon rate → bond price < par value, bond sells at a discount
Bond yield = coupon rate → bond price = par value, bond sells at par
Bond yield < coupon rate → bond price > par value, bond sells at a premium

Note: In the bond market, bond prices are quoted as a percentage of the par value. If the price indicated is 106 and the bond has a par value of $1,000, then the bond price is $1,060.

(c) Bond Yield

A 4% coupon bond that matures in 10 years is trading at $900, below its par value of $1,000. This bond seems like a bargain. If you buy the bond today, you will get a coupon payment of $40 each year and, on top of that, have a capital appreciation of $100. But suppose new 10-year bonds paying a 5% coupon are being sold at par in the market. Now, which bond is the better deal?

The two bonds have the same maturity but different prices and coupon rates, The first bond pays a lower coupon rate of 4% but costs less at $900 versus the second bond which pays a higher coupon rate of 5% but costs $100 more at $1,000. How do we decide?

If two investments are similar and have the same risk, the one that gives the higher return is the better investment. We know that the second bond has a yield of 5% as it is sold at the par value.

For the 4% bond, we plug in the values of the bond price, the coupon and the maturity into the bond price equation and solve for "*r*".

$$900 = C\left[\frac{1-1/(1+r)^{10}}{r}\right] + \frac{1000}{(1+r)^{10}}$$

Using a financial calculator or the Excel program we obtain the value of $r = 5.315\%$. Since this is higher than the 5% yield from the 5% coupon bond, the 4% coupon bond that sells at $900 is the better deal.

15.5.3 *Valuation of Stocks Using a Growing Perpetuity*

Stocks can be valued using the principle of the TVM to find the *present value of* the cash flows that accrue to a stock.

Learning Objectives

- Apply concepts learned in TVM to value stocks.

Main Takeaways

Main Points

- Stocks can be valued in two ways. One is the price multiples approach where the price of the stock is related to some financial variable. The other is the discounted cash flow approach.
- The second approach makes an essential assumption that dividends grow at a constant rate "*g*". We value the stock using the growing perpetuity formula.
- The growth rate of dividends, "*g*", must always be lower than market rate "*r*" for this formula to work.

Main Terms

- **Intrinsic value:** an asset's inherent value based on an investor's assessment. Investors compare the intrinsic value to the stock's market price to assess whether a stock is overpriced or under-priced. A stock is overpriced according to the investor's reckoning if its market price exceeds the intrinsic value.

We can value stocks in two ways. One way is to use price multiples where we multiply the value of a financial variable with the multiple. For example, in the PE or price-to-earnings method we determine the appropriate PE ratio by taking the average PE of other similar firms. This average PE is multiplied with the firm's earnings to determine its price.

The second way is the discounted cash flow approach. This method states that the price we are willing to pay for a firm's shares depends on the cash flows that we expect to get from the firm in the future. We discuss this approach below:

The cash flows are dividends received from the firm as shown in Figure 15.7.

The value the stock is the present value of the dividends we will receive each year all the way into the distant future at time T plus the present value of the price of the stock then. To find the present value of

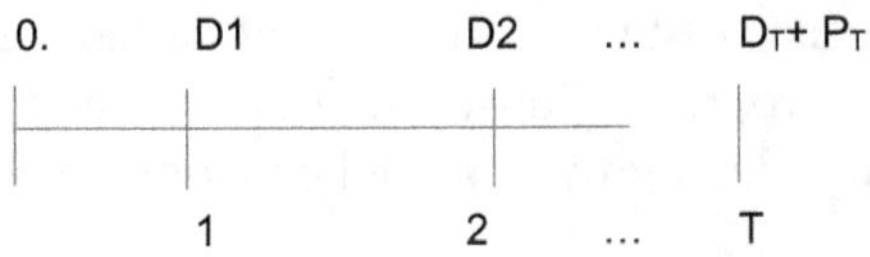

Figure 15.7: Timeline illustration of holding dividends.

this stream of dividends is not an easy task as we have to estimate the dividends paid out by the firm for a long period of time. However, if we make the assumption that dividends grow at a constant rate "*g*", then we can value the stock as a growing perpetuity:

$$\text{PV}_0 = \frac{D_1}{r-g}$$

where PV_0 = price of the stock, D_1 = dividend at time 1, r = required return for the stock, and g = growth rate of dividends.

Note that the formula is not valid if "*g*" is greater than "*r*". The formula can also be rewritten with the dividend D_0 that has just been received as the first cash flow.

$$\text{PV}_0 = \frac{D_1}{r-g} = \frac{D_0(1+g)}{r-g}$$

Our method of valuing stocks this way is known as the constant dividend growth model.

Example:

(i) The current dividend of \$3.00 is expected to grow at 5% indefinitely. If the required rate of return is 12%, value the share using the constant dividend growth model.

$$\text{PV}_0 = \frac{D_1}{r-g} = \frac{D_0(1+g)}{r-g} = \frac{3.00(1.05)}{0.12\text{-}0.05} = \$45$$

(ii) Determine the constant dividend growth rate that would justify a market price of \$50.

Our estimate of the stock price of \$45 is less than the market value of \$50.00. This price implies that the market forecasts a growth rate higher than the 5% we used, assuming that the model and the required return assumptions are appropriate. Substituting the values for all the variables into the constant dividend growth model equation, except for g we get:

$$50 = \frac{3.00(1+g)}{0.12 - g}$$

$$g = 0.0566$$

An expected dividend growth rate of 5.66% is required for the stock price to be correctly valued at the market price of $50.

15.5.4 *Two-Stage Valuation of Stock as a Series of Non-Constant Dividends Followed by a Growing Perpetuity*

The two-stage dividend discount model assumes that dividends grow at two different rates.

Learning Objectives

- Understand and calculate the value of a stock using the two-stage valuation method.

Main Takeaways

Main Points

- The constant dividend growth model cannot be used for companies that are currently experiencing fast growth. Instead, we use the two-stage dividend discount model.
- We do not expect a company to sustain the high growth experienced in the initial stage. Eventually, the company's growth will settle to a more sustainable rate in the second stage where the increase is in line with the economy's growth rate.

Main Terms

- **Non-constant growth:** abnormal growth rate over a finite length of time.
- **Dividend discount model:** The dividend discount model (DDM) is a quantitative method used for predicting the price of a company's stock. The model is based on the theory that its present-day price is worth the

sum of all of its future dividend payments when discounted back to its present value.

- **H model:** similar to the two-stage dividend discount model. It differs because the growth rate in the first stage transitions to the growth rate in the second stage. Rather than an abrupt drop in the growth rate from the first stage to the second stage, the first stage's growth rate declines at a constant rate till it reaches the growth rate in the second stage.
- **Terminal value:** captures thc value of the firm's cash flows beyond the terminal date. Usually, the TV is the present value of a perpetuity or a growing perpetuity where the growth rate is some long-term growth low rate close to the growth rate of a mature economy.

There are two versions of the two-stage dividend growth model. They differ in the transition from the high growth (abnormal growth) stage to the low growth (normal growth) stage.

The first version or the standard two-stage dividend growth model consists of a first stage with a high dividend growth rate, followed by a low dividend growth rate in the second stage. In the first stage, the company is growing very fast. The first stage could be a company in a new industry taking off or a company that has launched a new product that is taking the world by storm. However, as competitors start appearing and the product is no longer novel, growth slows to a much lower rate. As dividends are paid from the company's profits, the high dividend growth in the first stage reflects the high growth rate of sales, while the low dividend growth rate subsequently reflects the expected slow sales growth of a mature industry or product.

The second version of the two-stage dividend growth model, called the H-model, does not have an abrupt drop in the first model's dividend growth rate. The high dividend growth rate declines at a constant rate until it reaches the low dividend growth rate in the second stage.

For the first version of the two-stage dividend growth model, we cannot apply a formula to value the dividends in the first stage as either the growth rate of dividends is uneven or the growth rate exceeds the discount rate. So we find the PV of each dividend. In the second stage of the two-stage DDM, the growth rate is a fairly low sustainable rate. The present value of the cash flows from the second stage can be obtained by applying the growing perpetuity formula and discounting the value obtained to the present time. The value of the stock in two-stage DDM is given below:

$$V_0 = \Sigma \frac{D_t}{(1+r)^t} + \frac{V_t}{(1+r)^T}$$

where V_T is used as an estimate of P_T. The two-stage model assumes that the first t dividends grow at a high short-term growth rate, g_S:

$$D_t = D_0 (1 + g_s)^t$$

After time T, the annual dividend growth rate changes to a normal long-term rate, g_L. The dividend at time $n + 1$ is $D_{n+1} = D_n(1 + g_L) = D_0 (1 + g_S)n(1 + g_L)$, and this dividend continues to grow at g_L. V^T can be computed using the constant dividend growth model:

$$V_T = \frac{D_0(1+g_s)^T(1+g_L)}{(r-g_L)}$$

Example: Valuing stock using two-stage DDM
ABC Diagnostic is a biotech company that provides screening and diagnosis for blood disorders. The stock is trading at $15 per share. It is forecasted that the current dividend of $0.50 will grow by 10% per year during the next ten years. After that, the growth rate will decline to 4% and remain at that level indefinitely. The required return for the stock is 12%. Based on your calculation of the intrinsic value, should the stock be bought?

The calculations below show the first ten dividends, and their present values are discounted at 12%. The terminal value of the stock at $t = 10$ is

$$V_{10} = \frac{0.50(1+0.1)^{10}\ (1+0.04)}{(0.12-0.04)} = 16.86$$

The terminal stock value and its present value are also given. Where present value equals

$$V_0 = \Sigma \frac{D_t}{(1+r)^t} + \frac{V_n}{(1+r)^n}$$

The intrinsic value derived from the calculations is \$13.35. As this is below the market price of \$15, the stock should not be bought.

Time	Value	Calculation	D_t or V_t	Present Values $D_t/(1.071)_t$
1	D1	0.50(1.1)	0.5500	0.5093
2	D2	$0.50(1.1)^2$	0.6050	0.5187
3	D3	$0.50(1.1)^3$	0.6655	0.5283
4	D4	$0.50(1.1)^4$	0.7321	0.5381
5	D5	$0.50(1.1)^5$	0.8053	0.5480
6	D6	$0.50(1.1)^6$	0.8858	0.5582
7	D7	$0.50(1.1)^7$	0.9744	0.5685
8	D8	$0.50(1.1)^8$	1.0718	0.5791
9	D9	$0.50(1.1)^9$	1.1790	0.5898
10	D10	$0.50(1.1)^{10}$	1.2969	0.6007
10	V10	0.50(1.1)10(1.04)/(0.12 − 0.04)	16.8593	7.8091
TOTAL				13.3477

The two-stage DDM is useful as many companies initially grow fast, but the growth rate falls to a more sustainable level with more competition and a more mature market. For example, a company may achieve super-normal growth through possession of a patent or first-mover advantage. However, a company seldom continues to maintain its advantage over its competitors. Its growth soon settles to that of the overall economy.

(a) Two Stage Valuation: The H Model Method

The two-stage DDM model assumes a very high growth rate in the first stage followed by a much lower constant growth rate after that. The difference in growth rates may be quite large. Consequently, the abrupt drop from a high growth rate in one year to a very lower growth rate the following year may seem unrealistic. The H-model's innovation provides a gradual decline linearly from the high growth rate in the first stage to the low growth rate in the second stage. The value under the H-model is:

$$V_0 = \frac{D_0(1+g_L)+D_0H(g_s+g_L)}{(r-g_L)}$$

where, V_0 = value per share at $t = 0$; D_0 = current dividend; r = required rate of return on equity; H = half-life in years of the high-growth period (i.e., high-growth period = 2H years); g_S = initial high dividend growth rate in the short term; g_L = normal long-term dividend growth rate after Year 2H.

Example: Valuing a stock with the H model

Star Company is a successful snack company that sells the popular sugar-free No-Guilt Ice Cream. Its sales have been growing fast, but management expects that as competitors and newcomers develop similar ice creams, the growth will slow. Use the H-model to value the company based on the following data:

- Star's price is \$20.
- The current dividend is \$1.00.
- The current dividend growth rate is a relatively high figure of 10%. Growth is expected to decline at a constant rate over the next five years to a normal 4% after that.
- Using data from a financial services firm, Star's equity return is estimated at 12%.
  1. Use the H-model to estimate the intrinsic value of Star.
  2. Suppose Star did not have fast growth and instead grew at the normal rate from the beginning. Estimate the intrinsic value of Star in this case.
  3. Evaluate whether Star's shares appear to be fairly valued, overvalued, or undervalued.

Solution to 1

Using the H-model, we have:

$$V_0 = \frac{D_0(1+g_L) + D_0 H(g_s - g_L)}{(r - g_L)}$$

$$= \frac{1.00(1.04) + 1.00(5)(0.10 - 0.04)}{(0.12 - 0.04)} = 16.75$$

Solution to 2

If Star just grew at the normal rate initially, its estimated value would be the first component of the H-model estimate, \$13. Note that the faster initial growth assumption adds \$3.75 to its value.

Solution to 3

\$16.75 is approximately 16% lower than Star's current market price, which suggests that the shares are overvalued.

References/Further Readings

Ross, S., Westerfield, R., & Jordan, B. (2002). *Fundamentals of Corporate Finance*. 6th edn. McGraw — Hill Irwin, pp. 158–300.

15.6 Sample Questions

Question 1

You are given the option of receiving \$1,000 now or an annuity of \$85 per month for 12 months. Which of the following is correct?

(a) You cannot choose between the two without computing present values.
(b) You cannot choose between the two without computing future values.
(c) The choice you would make when comparing the future value of each would be the same as the choice you would make when comparing present values.

Question 2

You are comparing two investment options which cost the same. Both options will pay a total of \$10,000 over five years. Option 1 pays 5 annual payments of \$2,000 each. Option 2 pays \$6,000 in the first year, followed by four annual payments of \$1,000 each. Which one of the following statements is correct regarding the options?

(a) Both options are of equal value as they pay the same amount of \$10,000 over five years.
(b) Option 2 is the better choice of the two, given any positive rate of return.
(c) Option 2 is preferable because it is an annuity due.

Question 3

You have received two offers for a property you own. The first offer is for $390,000 today in cash. The second offer is the payment of $200,000 today and an additional $200,000 one year from today. Which is the better offer if the discount rate is 4%?

(a) You should accept the second offer as it has a higher net present value.
(b) You should accept the second offer because you will receive $10,000 more.
(c) You should accept the first offer because it has a higher future value.

Question 4

A bank lends you $1,000 for three months, after which time you must pay $1,030. What is the effective annual rate of this loan agreement?

(a) 3.0%
(b) 12.0%
(c) 12.6%

Question 5

John will retire in 6 years. He expects to receive $40,000 each year for three years, starting two years from now. The money received will earn a 10% return. How much money will he have in total at the time when he retires?

(a) $132,400
(b) $145,640
(c) $160,204

Question 6

You have a choice between receiving ten annual $50,000 retirement payments, starting one year from today, or receiving a lump sum today. If the money received can be invested at an annual rate of 8%, what lump sum amount would make you indifferent to getting the lump sum or the annuity?

(a) $313,344.40
(b) $335,504.07
(c) $362,344.40

Question 7

Robert thinks of buying an investment product that will fund his son's future university tuition costs, estimated at $45,000/year for four years, with the first payment due in 11 years. What is the likely amount Robert needs to pay for the investment product if it earns an expected annual return of 10%?

(a) $49,996
(b) $54,995
(c) $60,495

Question 8

A perpetual preferred stock pays a semi-annual dividend payment of $2.00 in one year. If the required annual rate of return is 8% compounded semi-annually, the stock's present value is closest to:

(a) $46.30
(b) $48.08
(c) $50.00

Question 9

ABC Company's dividend is assumed to grow at the same rate of 4% forever. The dividend is currently $2.00 per share. The investor's required return is 9%. What is the value of ABC Company's stock closest to?

(a) $40.00
(b) $41.60
(c) $43.60

Question 10

A stock is selling for $50. It has just paid a dividend of $4. If the stock's required return is 12%, what is its expected growth rate in dividends closest to?

(a) 3.7%
(b) 4.0%
(c) 8.0%

Solutions

Question 1

Solution: Option **c** is correct.

If one option's present value is greater than the other, the future value will also be greater than the other. To get the future value from the present value, we are compounding the present values at the same interest rate.

Question 2

Solution: Option **b** is correct

As a greater proportion of the $10,000 comes earlier in the second offer, this offer's present value is higher than the first offer since the discounting effect is less.

Question 3

Solution: Option **a** is correct

The second offer's present value is $188,679 compared to the first offer of $390,000 today.

Question 4

Solution: Option **c** is correct

The rate for 3 months is 3%. The effective annual rate = $(1.03)^4 - 1$ =0.126 or 12.6%.

Question 5

Solution: Option **c** is correct

The computations are as follows:

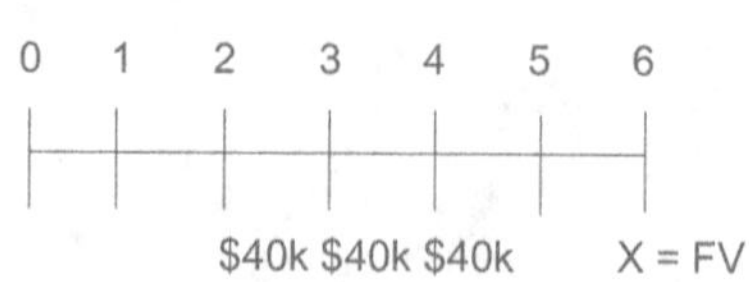

The annuity's future value at time four is found from the formula for an annuity's future value.

$$FV = C\left[\frac{(1+r)^t - 1}{r}\right]$$

FV_4 = \$132,400
FV of the annuity at time 6 = \$132,000 × $(1.1)^2$ = \$160,204

Question 6

Solution: Option **b** is correct

The computations are as follows:

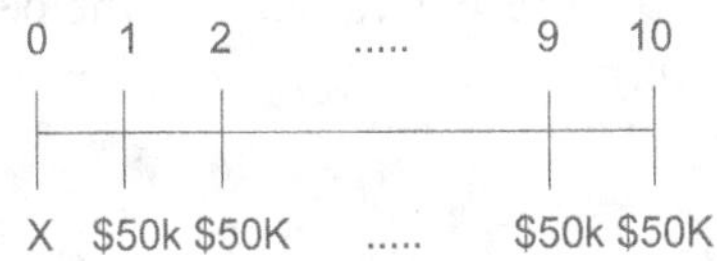

Using the formula for the present value of an annuity.

$$PV = C\left[1 - \frac{1}{\frac{(1+r)^t}{r}}\right]$$

$$PV = 50\left[1 - \frac{1}{\frac{(1+0.08)^{10}}{0.08}}\right] = 335{,}504.07$$

If a financial calculator is used, the inputs are
$n = 10$
$r = 8\%$
PMT = –50,000   PV computed = 335,504.07

Question 7

Solution: Option **b** is correct.

Find the present value (PV) of an ordinary annuity in Year 10 that represents the tuition costs:

$$PV = 45000\left[1 - \frac{1}{\frac{(1+0.1)^4}{0.1}}\right] = 142{,}644$$

Then, find the PV of the annuity in today's dollars (where FV is future value):

$$PV_0 = \frac{142,644}{(1+0.1)^{10}} = 54,995$$

Question 8

Solution: Option **b** is correct

The value of the perpetuity six months from now is calculated as:

PV = C/r, where PV is the present value, C is the perpetuity amount, and r is the semi-annual return.

PV = \$2.00/ (0.08/2)
PV = \$50

The value today is (where FV is future value)

$PV = FV_t\,(1 + r)^{-t}$
PV = \$50/(1 + 0.04)
PV = \$48.08

Question 9

Solution: Option **b** is correct

The value of the stock is found using the growing perpetuity formula. PV = $C/(r-g)$.

Note that the formula assumes the cash flow is at the end of the period. However, the dividend of \$2 is paid now. So the value for C should be \$2 × 1.04.

PV = (2 × 1.04)/(0.09 − 0.04) = \$41.60

Question 10

Solution: Option **a** is correct

Using the growing perpetuity formula of PV = $C/(r-g)$, we get

$$
\begin{aligned}
r &= C/\text{PV} + g \\
0.12 &= [4(1+g)/50] + g \\
6 &= 4 + 4g + 50g \\
g &= 2/54 \\
&= 3.7\%
\end{aligned}
$$

Chapter 16

Return and Risk Measures of Assets

16.1 Return and Risk

When people invest in assets, they expect a return on that asset because of the time value of money, a concept covered in an earlier section. However, an asset's returns is associated with a level of risk, usually measured by the variance of returns. In: asset correlation and covariance measure how and when these assets move with each other. A portfolio, which consists of two or more assets with imperfect correlation, allows investors to reduce risk without necessarily decreasing returns. For completeness, topics in Module 1A4 on Return and Risk Measures of Assets is repeated here as a preliminary to the discussion on computing the Weighted Average Cost of Capital.

Learning Objectives

- Calculate the expected return and variance of an investment portfolio.

Main Takeaways

Main Points

- The expected return is a weighted average return. It sums up the future possible returns multiplied by their associated probability of the return. Investors assess investments on the basis of their risk and expected return.
- The variance of return is a measure of the risk or uncertainty associated with the return. It is calculated by summing a weighted average of the squared deviations from the mean return.

- A portfolio comprises two or more assets and is uniquely determined by the proportion of assets in the portfolio.
- The portfolio's expected return is the weighted sum of the asset returns.
- The portfolio variance measures the dispersion of returns of a portfolio. Portfolio variance is calculated using the portfolio weights, the standard deviation of each security in the portfolio, and the correlation between securities in the portfolio.
- Combining assets in a portfolio allows some risk to be reduced through diversification. However, an amount of risk (called systematic or non-diversifiable risk) cannot be reduced as most assets are affected by common economic events.

Main Terms

- **Standard deviation:** It is a measure of the uncertainty associated with a return and is obtained by taking the square root of the variance. It measures the dispersion of the individual returns around the mean return.
- **Correlation:** A statistic that measures the degree to which two investments move with each other. It is measured by the correlation coefficient, which ranges from −1.0 to 1.0. A positive correlation means that as the price of one investment rises or falls, the other investment rises or falls with it to a degree based on the correlation's strength.
- **Diversification:** Refers to a strategy to reduce the overall risk by investing in multiple assets within a portfolio.

16.1.1 *Single Asset Expected Return*

Consider a single asset i. Suppose there are S possible states of the economy in the next period. If we let p_s be the probability of economic state s occurring and R_{is} be the return of asset i if state s occurs, then the expected return on asset i is

$$E(R_i) = \sum_{s=1}^{S} p_s R_{is} \tag{16.1}$$

The p_s weights correspond to the probabilities and $E(R_i)$ are the return we would earn on average if we could repeat the investment many times, drawing the return from the same probability distribution of returns each time.

16.1.2 *Single Asset Variance*

Also, for asset class i, the variance and standard deviation of its returns are, respectively,

$$\mathrm{VAR}(R_i) = \sigma_i^2 = \sum_{s=1}^{S} p_s \left(R_{is} - E(R_i)\right)^2 = E\left\{\left[R_{is} - E(R_i)\right]^2\right\} \quad (16.2)$$

and

$$SD(R_i) = \sigma_i = \sqrt{\mathrm{VAR}(R_i)} \quad (16.3)$$

16.1.3 *Portfolio of Assets*

Now, consider a portfolio of N assets. We can describe a portfolio by its constituent assets and by its portfolio weights, the fraction of the total investment in the portfolio held in each asset in the portfolio. The portfolio weight for asset class i is

$$w_i = \frac{\text{Value of investment } i}{\text{Total value of portfolio}} \quad (16.4)$$

Note that the portfolio weights add up to 1 so that they represent how we have divided our money between the different individual assets in the portfolio.

We can then find the expected portfolio return using one of two ways. One way is to first find the portfolio return in each state as follows:

$$R_{Ps} = \sum_{i=1}^{N} w_i R_{is} \quad (16.5)$$

Note that the portfolio return in state s is the weighted average of the returns on the portfolios' assets, where the weights correspond to the portfolio weights.

Then, find the expected portfolio return using the portfolio-equivalent of Equation (16.1) as follows:

$$E(R_P) = \sum_{s=1}^{S} p_s R_{Ps} \quad (16.6)$$

Note that the expected portfolio return is the weighted average of the possible portfolio returns, where the weights correspond to the respective probability of that return.

Another way is first to find the expected return using Equation (16.1) for each of the N assets in the portfolio. Then, the expected portfolio return is the weighted average of the expected returns of the investments within it, using the portfolio weights:

$$E(R_P) = \sum_{i=1}^{N} w_i E(R_i) \tag{16.7}$$

16.1.4 *Portfolio Expected Return*

Portfolio volatility can be found using one of two ways as well. One way is to use Equation (16.5) to find the portfolio return in each state before using the portfolio-equivalent of Equations (16.2) and (16.3) to find the portfolio volatility. However, it is more insightful to relate portfolio risk to the portfolio's constituent assets' risk.

Consider a two-asset portfolio. Since $R_p = w_1R_1 + w_2R_2$, and using the basic statistical property of the variance of a linear combination of two random variables, the variance of the two-asset portfolio is

$$\begin{aligned} \text{VAR}(R_P) = \text{VAR}(w_1R_1 + w_2R_2) = w_1^2\text{VAR}(R_1) + w_2^2\text{VAR}(R_2) \\ + 2w_1w_2\text{cov}(R_1,R_2) \end{aligned} \tag{16.8}$$

Equation (16.8) shows that the portfolio variance depends on the variance of the individual assets *and* the covariance between them.

The covariance measures the degree to which the returns of the two assets move together and is defined as

$$\text{COV}(R_1,R_2) = E\{[R_1 - E(R_1)][R_2 - E(R_2)]\} \tag{16.9}$$

Intuitively, if the returns on the two assets move together, their returns will be above or below average simultaneously, and the covariance will be positive. If the returns on the two assets move in opposite directions, the covariance will be negative. Covariance indicates the direction of the linear relationship between two variables. The correlation coefficient indicates both the direction and the strength of the linear relationship. The equation to compute the correlation coefficient is given next:

$$\text{CORR}(R_1,R_2) = \rho_{12} = \frac{\text{COV}(R_1,R_2)}{\text{SD}(R_1)\text{SD}(R_2)} \tag{16.10}$$

Note that the correlation between the two asset returns has the same sign as the covariance, so it has a similar interpretation. However, dividing the covariance by the volatilities of the assets ensures that correlation is always between −1 and +1, which allows us to gauge their relationship's strength. The closer the correlation is to +1, the more the closely the returns move together.

When the correlation (and thus the covariance) equals 0, the returns are uncorrelated. This means that the asset returns do not tend to move either together or in the opposite direction to each other. Finally, the closer the correlation is to −1, the more the returns tend to move in opposite directions.

16.1.5 *Portfolio Variance*

By making the subject of Equation (16.10) and substituting the expression for it in Equation (16.8), the portfolio variance becomes

$$\text{VAR}(R_p) = w_1^2\text{VAR}(R_1) + w_2^2\text{VAR}(R_2) + 2w_1w_2\text{SD}(R_1)\text{SD}(R_2)\rho_{12} \tag{16.11}$$

Note that if the assets' returns are perfectly positively correlated (i.e., $\rho_{12} = 1$, then the portfolio volatility is

$$\text{SD}(R_p) = w_1\text{SD}(R_1) + w_2\text{SD}(R_2) \tag{16.12}$$

Note that portfolio risk is a weighted average of the assets' risks if the two assets are perfectly positively correlated. However, if, with a positive amount invested in each asset, the relation becomes:

$$\text{SD}(R_p) < w_1\text{SD}(R_1) + w_2\text{SD}(R_2) \tag{16.13}$$

Since returns for any two assets are unlikely to be perfectly positively correlated, the relationship in (16.13) implies that portfolio risk is less than the weighted average of the risks of its components. However, from Equation (16.7), the portfolio expected return is still a weighted average of its constituent assets' expected returns. Combining less than perfectly correlated assets is the essence of diversification.

In the general case of an N-asset portfolio, the portfolio variance is given by

$$\mathrm{VAR}(R_p) = \sum_{i=1}^{N} \sum_{j=1}^{N} w_i w_j \mathrm{COV}(R_i, R_j) \tag{16.14}$$

Where R_i and R_j are the returns on assets i and j, respectively. Equation (16.14) says that the portfolio variance is equal to the weighted average of the covariances of the returns of all pairs of assets in the portfolio. The portfolio's overall variability depends on the total co-movement of the assets within it. From Equation (16.9), we note that the covariance of an asset's return with itself is its variance. Thus, for asset i:

$$\mathrm{COV}(R_i, R_j) = \mathrm{VAR}(R_i) \tag{16.15}$$

Using Equations (16.14) and (16.15), we will obtain Equation (16.8) for the special case where $N = 2$.

16.1.6 *Diversification*

Combining assets in a portfolio eliminates some of their risks through diversification. Independent risks can be diversified away in a large portfolio, whereas systematic or common risks are not. The amount of risk that remains depends on the degree of correlation, namely, to their exposure to the common risks. For example, there is a tendency for asset returns to be affected similarly by economic events.

Non-diversifiable risk, also called systematic risk, applies to a particular market or industry. It cannot be diversified away. Diversifiable risk is also called non-systematic risk, which applies to one particular investment unrelated to the market and can be diversified away. An example would be a strike at one specific company, or a company's factory had to shut down due to flooding.

The expected return of a diversified portfolio is the expected return of each of its underlying assets multiplied by the weight the investment receives. The variance of a diversified portfolio reduces with the number of assets and less than perfectly correlated asset returns. Figure 16.1 shows how the portfolio standard deviation of a portfolio of NYSE stocks reduces with the portfolio's number of securities. Also illustrated is the limit of diversification, where increasing the number of stocks within a portfolio does not reduce portfolio variance.

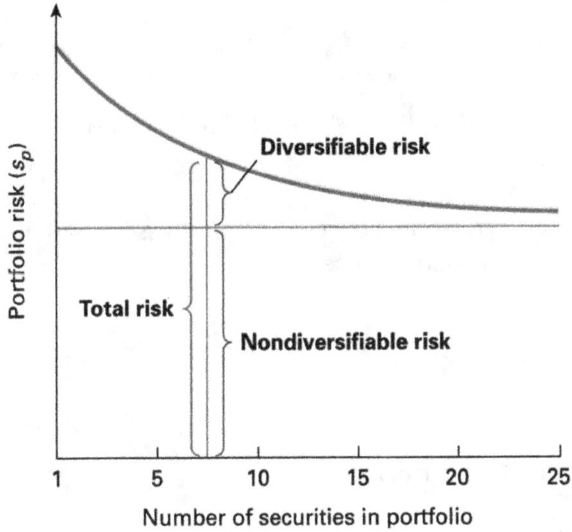

Figure 16.1: Graphical illustration of diversification.

Examples:
Use the following portfolio to answer Examples 1 and 2:

Asset	Weight (%)	Expected Return (%)	Expected Standard Variation (%)
A	40	8	20
B	60	3	10

Example 1:
Calculate the expected return of the portfolio

(a) 5.0%
(b) 6.0%
(c) 6.4%

Solution: Option **a** is correct.

A portfolio's expected return is the weighted average of the expected average of its components. Using Equation (16.5),

$$R_{Ps} = \sum_{i-1}^{N} w_i R_{is}$$

$$R_{ps} = 0.4 * 8\% + 0.6 * 3\% = 5.0\%$$

Example 2:
Given that the correlation between the two assets is 0.5, the standard deviation of the portfolio is closest to:

(a) 9.8%
(b) 10.2%
(c) 11.1%

Solution: Option **b** is correct.

Using Equation (16.11),

$$\mathrm{VAR}(R_p) = w_1^2 \mathrm{VAR}(R_1) + w_2^2 \mathrm{VAR}(R_2) + 2w_1 w_2 \mathrm{SD}(R_1)\mathrm{SD}(R_2)\rho_{12}$$

$$\mathrm{SD}(R_p) = \sqrt{w_1^2 \mathrm{VAR}(R_1) + w_2^2 \mathrm{VAR}(R_2) + 2w_1 w_2 \mathrm{SD}(R_1)\mathrm{SD}(R_2)\rho_{12}}$$

$$\mathrm{SD}(R_p) = \sqrt{0.4^2 0.2^2 + 0.6^2 0.1^2 + \mathbf{2}(0.4)(0.6)(0.2)(0.1)(0.5)}$$

$$\mathrm{SD}(R_p) = 0.102 = 10.2\%$$

Do note that the variance between Asset A and B is counted twice. Counting twice accounts for the variance between Asset A and B and the variance between B and A.

References/Further Readings

Bodie, Z., Kane, A., & Marcus, A.J. (2020). *Investments*, 12th edn. Mc-Graw Hill, pp. 119–158.

Brealey, R.A., Myers, S.C., & Allen, F. (2010). *Principles of Corporate Finance*, 10th edn. McGraw-Hill, pp. 156–184.

Ross, S., Westerfield, R., & Jordan, B. (2002). *Fundamentals of Corporate Finance*, 6th edn. McGraw-Irwin Hill, pp. 416–425.

Part G: Investing Decisions

Chapter 17

Cost of Capital

17.1 Weighted Average Cost of Capital

17.1.1 *Definitions and Calculations of WACC*

The weighted average cost of capital (WACC) is the return that the firm's assets must generate to satisfy its fund providers' required returns. The WACC is not a simple average of the different components of the firm's capital. It is weighted according to the proportions of the various capital components' market values.

Learning Objectives

- Calculate and interpret the WACC of a company.

Main Takeaways

Main Points

- The WACC is often used as a hurdle rate to evaluate investment opportunities.
- The WACC is calculated by summing over the different components of capital the product of the required return of the component and its weight, which is the proportion of the value of the component to the firm's total value.
- In calculating the WACC, the market values, rather than the book values of capital components should be used.
- For a project to be accepted, its returns should exceed the company's cost of capital.

Main Terms

- **Weighted average cost of capital:** This is the weighted average after-tax cost of a company's different capital components. The components are the company's common stock, preferred stock, and bonds. Each component's cost is the required return demanded by investors, while its weight in the WACC is the proportion of its market value to the total value.
- **Market value:** The value of an asset as determined in the market. For example, a company's market value is the product of the total number of its outstanding shares multiplied by the share price, that is, the market capitalization.
- **Book value:** The book value of an asset or a liability is the value of shareholders' equity shown on the company's balance sheet.

(a) How Cost of Capital Works

A company needs capital to fund the purchase of the assets necessary to run the business. The capital of the company is raised from different sources. These sources include common stock, preferred stock, and bonds. Each of these components has a cost: the required rate of return that investors demand from investing in that particular financial instrument. These required returns become the inputs to the computation of the WACC.

The cost of capital is not just the simple average of the components' required returns. Instead, each component's cost is weighted by the proportion of the total capital it accounts for. For example, suppose common stock accounts for 60% of the company's total capital. In that case, the cost of equity, the required return for common stock, is multiplied by 60% to contribute to the overall cost of capital. The same procedure is carried out with the other components of capital. However, for the cost of debt, it is further adjusted by a factor of $(1 - t)$, where t is the corporate tax rate — reducing by the tax rate reflects the fact that debt interest is an expense used to decrease the taxable profit. Hence the effective cost of debt is $r_d \times (1 - t)$, where r_d is the yield-to-maturity of the debt.

The WACC is the sum of each of the components' weighted costs with the cost of debt-adjusted further by $(1 - t)$. The formula for WACC is shown below:

$$\text{WACC} = W_d * r_d (1 - t) + W_p * r_p + W_e * r_e \tag{17.1}$$

where W_d is the proportion of debt that the company uses when it raises new funds; r_d is the before-tax marginal cost of debt; t is the company's marginal tax rate, W_p is the proportion of preferred stock the company uses when it raises new funds, r_p is the marginal cost of preferred stock, W_e is the proportion of equity that the company uses when it raises new funds, and r_e is the marginal cost of equity.

We examine how each components' cost can be estimated in the next sections.

17.2 Cost of Debt

17.2.1 *Definitions and Calculations*

The cost of debt is the yield to maturity (YTM) of the bond that the company has issued. Or it may be the interest rate of a bank loan.

Learning Objectives

- Define and calculate the cost of debt using the YTM approach and the debt-rating approach.

Main Takeaways

Main Points

- The debt component of capital can consist of short or long terms loans or bonds.
- The cost of debt tends to be lower than the cost of equity as debt is less risky than equity — debt holders get paid first before equity holders as debt interest is paid before dividends in normal circumstances. If the company goes into bankruptcy and is liquidated, debt holders get paid ahead of equity holders.
- Interest rates, Inflation, and other economic forces play a substantial role in the overall cost of capital.
- Fluctuations in the marketplace (i.e., market risk or systematic risks) can be unpredictable and can influence the overall risk and return for investors, impacting capital cost.

Main Terms

- **Cost of debt:** The effective interest rate a company pays on its debts. If the debt is in the form of a bond, the cost of debt is the YTM of the bond. The cost of debt that is calculated is the before-tax cost of debt. The effective cost of debt is the after-tax cost of debt as interest expense is tax-deductible, reducing taxable profit and taxes paid.

Hence the effective cost of debt or the after-tax cost of debt is much lower than the before-tax cost.

For the WACC debt component, we use the after-tax cost of debt, $r_d(1-t)$. The before-tax cost of debt, r_d, is the interest rate at which firms can issue new debt. The tax savings due to the tax-deductibility of interest results in a lower after-tax cost of debt which is computed as follows:

$$\text{After-tax cost of debt} = \text{interest rate on loan} - \text{tax savings}$$
$$= r_d - r_d(t) = r_d(1-t)$$

$$\text{The after-tax cost of debt} = r_d\,(1-t) \tag{17.2}$$

Example: Cost of debt
ABC Ltd. wants to issue new debt. Firms of similar risk are paying 8% on their debt. If the corporate tax rate is 40%, what is ABC's cost of debt?

The after-tax cost of debt is

$$r_d(1-t) = 0.8(1-0.4) = 4.8\%$$

17.2.2 *Yield to Maturity Approach*

The YTM is the annual return that an investor expects to earn on a bond if the investor purchases the bond today and holds it until maturity.

Learning Objectives
- Compute the cost of debt using the YTM approach.

Main Takeaways

Main Points
- The cost of debt is the YTM of the issued bond.
- The coupon rate should not be confused with the cost of debt. If the bond is trading at its par value, the coupon rate is the same as the YTM. However, if the bond is not trading at its par value, the cost of debt which is the YTM, is different from the coupon rate.
- If the YTM is greater than the coupon rate, the bond sells at a discount, that is, below the par value. Conversely, a YTM lower than the coupon rate results in the bond selling at a premium, that is, at a price higher than the par value.

Main Terms

- **Trading at par:** A bond trades at its par value if the bond price is the same as its face value.

The cost of debt is found by solving for the YTM (r_d) in the following equation:

$$P_0 = \frac{\text{PMT}_1}{(1+r_d)} + \cdots + \frac{\text{PMT}_n}{(1+r_d)^n} + \frac{\text{FV}}{(1+r_d)^n} = \left(\sum_{t=1}^{n} \frac{\text{PMT}_t}{(1+r_d)^t}\right) + \frac{\text{FV}}{(1+r_d)^n} \quad (17.3)$$

where P_0 is the current market price of the bond, PMT_t is the interest payment in period t, r_d is the YTM, n is the number of periods remaining to maturity, and FV is the maturity value of the bond.

The equation assumes that the bond pays an annual interest. However, suppose the bond pays interest on a semi-annual basis. In that case, the equation is adjusted by substituting $r_d/2$ for r_d, increasing the number of periods to $n \times 2$, and setting the regular payment in each period to half the annual coupon.

The YTM is computed on the assumption that the coupons received are reinvested at the YTM.

(a) Relationship Between Coupon and Yield

- If **YTM** = **coupon rate**, then **bond price** = **par value.**
- If **YTM** > **coupon rate**, then **bond price** < **par value.** Selling at a discount called a discount bond.
- If **YTM** < **coupon rate**, then **bond price** > **par value.** Selling at a premium called a premium bond.

Example: Computing YTM (r_d)

The Sonic Company issued a 10-year bond to raise funds for a new project. The bond has a face value of $1,000, with a 6% coupon rate paid semi-annually. The bond was issued at $1,030. Compute the company's after-tax cost of debt if it pays a marginal tax rate of 30%.

Using a financial calculator with the following parameters:

PV = 1030
FV = 1000
PMT = 1000 × 0.06/2 = 30
$n = 10 \times 2 = 20$

$$1030 = \left(\sum \frac{30}{(1+i)^t}\right) + \frac{1000}{(1+i)^{20}}$$

The before-tax cost of debt on a semi-annual basis is $i = 2.802\%$.
The before-tax cost of debt is $r_d = 2.802\% \times 2 = 5.604\%$.
The after-tax cost of debt is $r_d(1 - t) = 0.05604*(1 - 0.30) = 3.92\%$.

17.2.3 *Debt Rating Approach*

The other method for estimating the cost of debt is the debt-rating approach. Debt-rating agencies classify debt into different risk classes. If the company's debt is infrequently traded such that reliable, current market price data for its debt is unavailable, but it has a debt rating, then its cost of debt is similar to the yields of more actively traded bonds with the same rating and maturity.

Learning Objectives

- Describe the process for the debt rating approach.

Main Takeaways

Main Points

- Interpret the cost of debt using the debt rating approach.
- Identify the issues in estimating the cost of debt.

For a bond that is not actively traded such that current prices are not readily available, we use the debt rating approach. This method involves looking at the yields for actively traded bonds with the same rating and maturity. Bonds with the same rating should have similar yields.

Example: Estimating the YTM (r_d)

An analyst wants to determine the cost of debt to compute the WACC to evaluate the Lucky Company. Lucky's debt is thinly traded, and the analyst felt that using the bond's prices to estimate Lucky's cost of debt may not produce reliable results. Fortunately, Lucky's bonds were rated A when the bonds were first issued, and the company's financial situation had not changed much since. Lucky's bonds have a remaining maturity of 10 years. 10-year A-rated bonds are trading in the market to yield 6%.

If the marginal tax rate is 30%, the company's after-tax cost of debt is computed as follows:

$$r_d(1 - t) = 6\%*(1 - 0.3) = 4.2\%$$

Care should be taken when using this approach. Factors other than debt ratings can affect the yield. For example, some factors to consider are the seniority of the debt and the presence of call or put provisions. Appropriate adjustments to the yield need to be made to reflect the differences between the debt being assessed and the debt trading in the market.

(a) Issues in Estimating Cost of Debt

(1) Fixed-rate debt versus floating-rate debt
The debt we have been discussing is debt where the interest is a fixed amount paid each period. However, companies need not restrict themselves to raising funds using fixed-rate debt. Instead, they can issue floating-rate debt in which the coupon rate is not fixed but pegged to some index, for example, the prime rate or LIBOR. When the reference rate changes, the floating-rate bond's rate would change.

Does a floating rate pose problems in computing the cost of debt compared to a fixed-rate? The answer is no. Recall that in calculating the cost of debt, we use the YTM of the bond. The YTM is not the same as the coupon rate of the bond unless the bond is selling at the par value.

(2) Debt with option-like features
On top of using floating-rate debt, instead of fixed-rate debt, firms may add option-like features to the bond such that the YTM of the bond with the option-like feature will be different from that of a comparable bond without the feature.

Option-like features would include the call provision that allows the issuer to call or redeem the bond before maturity, if it chooses to do so. Issuers usually call the bonds when interest rates have fallen below the coupon rate. The other option-like feature is the put provision that confers to the bondholder the option to redeem the bond before maturity.

For bonds with option like features, their yields will be different from comparable bonds without the features. Compared to similar bonds without the feature, a bond with the call feature would require a higher YTM, whereas the yield for a bond with a put feature would be lower.

(3) Non-rated debt
For bonds that are not rated and traded, establishing the cost of debt poses a challenge. One approach is to look for firms in the same industry with traded or rated bonds. Comparing the ratios of the two firms would indicate the difference in risk between the two bonds. However, this is somewhat imprecise as financial ratios may not incorporate some factors that affect a bond's risk. Determining the risk of non-rated bonds requires extensive fundamental analysis of the firm, and the methods used are beyond the scope of this discussion.

(4) Leases
Instead of borrowing funds to buy an asset, the firm can lease the asset. A lease can act as a substitute for borrowing. If the company leases its assets, then the leases can be considered another capital component. Its cost should be included in the computation of the WACC. The method to determine the cost of leasing is beyond the curriculum's scope.

17.3 Cost of Equity

The cost of equity is the rate of return that a company's common shareholders require.

Learning Objectives

- Calculate and interpret the cost of equity capital using various approaches.

Main Takeaways

Main Points

- The cost of equity can be computed using the capital asset pricing model (CAPM) approach, the dividend pricing model approach, and the bond yield plus risk premium approach.
- The beta coefficient is the risk of a new project with the risk of markets as a whole.

Main Terms

- **Capital asset pricing model:** Describes the relationship between the expected return for an asset and its systematic risk.

The cost of equity (r_e) is the required rate of return on the firm's common stock. Estimating the cost of equity is a challenge because the future cash flows are uncertain in terms of the amount and timing.

17.3.1 *Capital Asset Pricing Model Approach*

The CAPM is used to calculate the expected rate of return of an asset. The model describes the relationship between the asset's expected return and its systematic risk. Please note that the underlying concepts of risk and expected returns are discussed earlier.

Learning Objectives

- Use the CAPM Equation to estimate the Cost of Equity.

Main Takeaways

Main Points

- The risk-free rate is the return on an asset with no default risk. The risk-free rate used in the CAPM model should be the rate of a risk-free asset whose maturity should be commensurate with the maturity of the asset for which we are determining the expected return using the CAPM model.
- The multifactor model employs more than one risk factor to explain an asset's expected return.

Main Terms

- **Market risk premium/Equity risk premium:** The additional return that investors demand for investing in a market portfolio relative to the risk-free rate.
- **Multifactor model:** Uses more than one risk factor to explain the expected return of an asset or portfolio.
- **Systematic risk:** This risk is also known as market risk. All securities are exposed to this risk that cannot be diversified away.
- **Capital asset pricing model:** This model states that the expected rate of return of an asset is composed of the risk-free rate plus a risk premium. The risk premium is equal to the market risk premium (the difference between the expected return on the market less the risk-free rate) multiplied by the asset's beta which measures the systematic risk of the asset relative to the market.

(a) The Capital Asset Pricing Model

The CAPM model shows the relationship between an asset's expected return and its risk, particularly its systematic risk.

$$E(R_i) = R_f + \beta_i\,(E(R_m) - R_f)$$

To compute the expected return, we need a risk-free rate, R_f, an estimate of the market risk premium, and the asset's systematic risk as measured by its beta, βi.

The values of the variables in the CAPM can be estimated as follows:

Step 1: For the risk-free rate, R_f, the yield of a Treasury bond such as the 10-year Treasury bond, is used. The 10-year Treasury bond is actively traded and is considered default-free since the government issues it.

Step 2: The stock's beta, βi, is estimated through a regression of the stock's return against the market's return. Various methods are used to adjust the value obtained, but a discussion of the methods is beyond the scope of the curriculum.

Step 3: The expected rate of return on the market, $E(R_m)$, is obtained by adding the risk-free rate to the market risk premium. One way to calculate the market risk premium is to use historical averages. Another method is to back out the market risk premium from the constant dividend growth model.

Example: Using CAPM to estimate the cost of equity

Suppose $R_f = 4\%$, $R_m = 12\%$, and Peach Company has a beta of 1.5.

Estimate the cost of equity for Peach Company.

Solution:

The required rate of return for Peach Company's stock using the CAPM is

$$R_e = 4\% + 1.5 \times (12\% - 4\%) = 16\%$$

An advantage of the CAPM approach is that it can be applied to companies that do not pay dividends, a requirement for the second approach discussed below. However, the CAPM approach's disadvantage is that the estimate of the cost of equity is highly sensitive to the values of the variables used in its computation.

17.3.2 *Dividend Discount Model Approach*

In the dividend discount model (DDM), the value of the firm's equity is none other than the sum of all the present values of its future dividend payments.

Learning Objectives
- Estimate cost of equity using the constant dividend growth model.

Main Takeaways

Main Points
- The equity risk premium needed for the CAPM can be estimated using the constant dividend growth model.
- The constant dividend growth model assumes dividends are expected to grow at a constant rate, g, which is less than the cost of equity.
- The sustainable growth rate (SGR) is the return on equity multiplied by the earnings retention ratio.

Main Terms
- **The constant dividend growth model**, commonly known as the Gordon growth model, is used to value stocks based on the net present value of future dividends that grow at a constant rate.
- **Sustainable growth rate:** The SGR is the maximum growth rate that a company can grow without having to tap external financing, whether in the form of additional equity or debt.
- **Earnings retention ratio:** the retention ratio is the proportion of earnings that the firm keeps as retained earnings to finance its growth. This ratio is equal to one less the payout ratio.

(a) Dividend Discount Model
The constant dividend growth model is based on the principle that the value of the company's share is the sum of the discounted dividends. The model further assumes that the dividends grow at a constant rate that is lower than the discount rate, that is, the dividends are similar to a growing perpetuity.

The model, also known as the Gordon Growth Model, determines the value of each share by the following formula:

$$P_0 = \frac{D_1}{r_e - g}$$

where P_0 is the price of the stock, D_1 is the dividends to be paid the next period, r_e is the required rate of return on the stock, and g is the expected growth rate of dividends (g is assumed to be less than r_e).

By rearranging the terms in the equation, the required rate of return on the stock is then

$$r_e = \frac{D_1}{P_0} + g$$

This model is useful to value the shares of relatively mature companies where the growth rate of dividends is low and relatively stable. It is not applicable for young companies where the growth rate could be higher than the required return on the stock or where the growth rate is not constant.

(b) Estimating Growth Rate (*g*)

The expected growth rate, g, can be estimated in two ways;

- Use the forecasted growth rate that is published by a financial data service (e.g., Bloomberg); or
- Use the product of the return on equity (ROE) and the retention rate

$$g = \text{ROE} \times \text{retention rate or}$$
$$g = \text{ROE} \times (1 - \text{payout rate})$$

In this formulation, the assumption is that the firm relies only on its retained earnings to fund its growth. The expected growth rate, also known as the sustainable growth rate, is the rate of growth that the firm can sustain without resorting to external financing.

(c) Estimating r_e Using the Constant Dividend Growth Model

Example:

Suppose the Peach Company's stock sells for $20 and the expected dividend next year is $1.50. If the expected ROE is 12%, and the company retains half of its earnings, what is its cost of equity?

Solution:

g = (ROE) (retention rate)

g = (0.12) (1 − 0.5) = 0.06 or 6%

r_e = (1.5/20) + 0.06 = 0.135 or 13.5%

17.3.3 *Factor Model Approach*

In the CAPM, the expected return on the stock depends mainly upon only one risk factor: the expected market return. Some researchers assert that the CAPM model's prediction of expected return can be improved by including other risk factors. Such a multifactor model comprises a set of systematic factors that can better explain the average returns of many risky assets.

Learning Objectives
- Describe the use of multifactor models.

Main Takeaways

Main Points
- The arbitrage pricing model (APM) relates expected returns to various systematic factors derived through factor analysis.
- Multi-factor models incorporate multiple risk factors that can be macroeconomic, fundamental, or statistical to analyze and explain asset prices.

Main Terms
- **Systematic risk:** The risk that is intrinsic to the marketplace.
- **Multifactor model:** The multi-factor model uses more than one risk factor to explain the expected return of an asset or portfolio.

(a) How Does the Factor Model Apply to Cost of Equity?

A multi-factor model is a financial model that uses multiple factors to determine the expected return of an asset. Unlike the CAPM, where the only source of risk is the market, the multi-factor model incorporates extra-market sources of risk that can arise from several macroeconomic sources.

This approach's advantage is that the systematic risks that affect security returns are explicit and not subsumed under a broad market factor. This approach allows different stocks to exhibit different sensitivities to the various factors.

The number and the identity of the factors are determined using historical returns data.

(b) The Arbitrage Pricing Model

The APM relates expected returns to systematic factors. The sensitivity of expected return to each factor is associated with a beta specific to the factor. The formulation of the model is somewhat similar to the CAPM except that in place of the market beta multiplied by the market risk premium, we have a set of factor-specific betas and their associated risk premia as shown in the equation below.

$$E(Ri) = R_f + \sum_{j=1}^{K} \beta_j (E(R_j) - R_f)$$

where R_f is the risk-free rate, bj is the beta specific to factor j, $E(R_j) - R_f$ is the risk premium per unit of factor j risk, and k is the number of factors.

Example: Using the APM to estimate the cost of equity
Suppose there are three factors in the multi-factor model. The values of the variables are shown below:

Risk free rate = 3%

$E(R_1) - R_f$ = 3%: Risk Premium for factor 1
$E(R_2) - R_f$ = 4%: Risk Premium for factor 2
$E(R_3) - R_f$ = 5%: Risk Premium for factor 3

Suppose the betas specific to each of these factors for the Pear Company are as follows:

$b_1 = 1.5$
$b_2 = 0.8$
$b_3 = 1.0$

Substituting into the APM,

$$\text{Cost of Equity} = 3\% + 1.5 \times 3\% + 0.8 \times 4\% + 1 \times 5\% = 15.7\%$$

(c) Comparison of the CAPM and the APM
As the CAPM has only one risk factor, it is a simpler model to estimate and use than the APM. However, the CAPM will underperform the APM as some companies may be sensitive to economic factors not well represented in the market index. For example, oil companies tend to have low CAPM betas as their risks stem from oil price movements.

The major drawback of the APM is that the model does not explicitly identify the factors driving expected returns.

(d) Other Multi-Factor Models

The failure of the APM to identify the risk factors in the model led to other models where the unidentified factors are replaced with macro-economic variables.

One of the multi-factor models that has gained prominence is the Fama and French (FF) three-factor model. This model uses firm characteristics as proxies for exposure to systematic risk. In this model, the return on security i, at time t, is given by

$$R_{it} = \alpha_i + \beta_{iM} R_{Mt} + \beta_{iSMB} SMB_t + \beta_{iHML} HML_t + e_{it}$$

where SMB is the Small minus Big (the return on a portfolio of s mall stocks less the return on a portfolio of large stocks) and HML is the High minus Low (the return on a high book-to-market-value portfolio of stocks less the return of a low book-to-market-value portfolio of stocks).

17.3.4 *Bond Yield Plus Risk Premium Approach*

The value of a company's cost of equity can be found by adding a risk premium to the YTM on its long-term debt.

Learning Objectives

- Describe the process for the bond yield plus risk premium approach.

Main Takeaways

Main Points

- The fundamental principle underlying this approach is that the riskier the cash flows, the higher the return to be associated with them. Bonds are safer than stocks as they receive priority of payment before shareholders.
- The risk premium compensates for the additional risk of equity compared with debt.
- The bond yield plus risk premium approach does not produce as accurate an estimate as the CAPM or discounted cash flow analysis.

Main Terms

- **Risk premium:** Captures the additional yield on a company's stock relative to its bond.

In the bond yield plus risk premium approach, a risk premium consisting of a few percentage points is added to the market yield on the firm's long-term debt.

This approach uses the notion that as equity is riskier than debt, the cost of the firm's equity should be higher than the yield on its bonds. Therefore, to find the cost of equity, a risk premium or the additional yield on a company's stock relative to its bonds is added to the before-tax cost of debt, r_d, as follows:

$$r_e = r_d + \text{Risk premium}$$

This risk premium is often estimated using historical spreads between bond yields and stock yields.

(a) Estimating r_e with Bond Yield Plus Risk Premium Method

Suppose the Peach Company has an issue of 10-year bonds yielding 5%. If the historical spread between stock yields and bond yields has been 4% on average, then the cost of equity for the Peach Company is 5% + 4% = 9%. Note that this estimate of the cost of equity is often different from the calculations based on other models, for example, the CAPM. This process reflects the difficulty in estimating the cost of equity.

17.3.5 *Country Risk Premium*

The country risk premium (CRP) is the additional premium demanded by investors to compensate them for the higher risk associated with investing in a foreign country.

Learning Objectives

- Understand CRP in the CAPM approach.

Main Takeaways

Main Points

- The CRP is generally higher for developing markets than developed nations.

- The CRP is the sovereign yield spread adjusted by the ratio of the volatility of the equity index to the bond index's volatility.
- There are three approaches to incorporating the CRP to the CAPM. The methods differ in terms of how the CRP is adjusted.

Main Terms

- **Sovereign yield spread:** The difference between the bond yields of two countries' government bonds with the same maturity. One of the two countries is usually the United States as its bonds are considered close to default free.

Investing in companies overseas adds another dimension to an investments's risk. Less developed countries pose an additional risk to the investor due to lower political or economic stability than developed countries. The cost of equity for companies in developing countries needs to incorporate a risk premium known as the CRP.

To determine the CRP, we first calculate the sovereign yield spread, which is the difference between the developing country's government bond yield less the developed country's government bond yield. This spread is then adjusted by the ratio of the volatility of the developing country's equity market to the volatility of its sovereign bond market as follows:

$$\text{Country risk premium} = \text{Soverign yield spread} \times \frac{\text{Annualized standard deviation of equity index}}{\text{Annualized standard deviation of sovereign bond market based on developed country's currency}}$$

A simple approach to incorporating the CRP is to add it to the cost of equity:

$$\text{Cost of equity} = \text{Risk-free rate} + \textit{Beta}\,(\text{Mature market risk premium}) + \text{Country risk premium}$$

The above method is somewhat simplistic as it assumes all firms have the same risk.

One way to differentiate between high-risk firms and low-risk firms is to scale the CRP according to the firm's beta. We assume that low-risk firms will be less exposed to country risk than high-risk firms. The cost of equity is then:

Cost of equity = Risk-free rate + *Beta* (Mature market risk premium + Country risk premium)

A more refined approach is to consider the CRP as another risk factor to which the firm is exposed. If the coefficient for this variable in the equation is lambda (l), then the cost of equity is represented as

Cost of equity = Risk-free Rate + *Beta* (Mature Market Premium) + l (Country Risk Premium)

17.4 Cost of Preferred Stock

The cost of preferred stock in the required return demanded by holders of preferred shares.

Learning Objectives

- Calculate and interpret the cost of non-callable, non-convertible preferred stocks.

Main Takeaways

Main Points

- Preferred stock dividends are paid out of *after-tax cash flows.*
- The preferred stock is a hybrid security as it has the features of debt in terms of fixed dividends and equity features as there is no return of the principal, unlike bonds.

Main Terms

- **Non-callable and non-convertible stock:** A non-callable, non-convertible preferred stock is a stock that receives dividends ahead of common shareholders. The company does not have the right to call or redeem the stock. Such preferred stock does not possess the right to be converted into common stock.
- **Perpetuity:** Security that pays a fixed amount regularly for an infinite amount of time.

17.4.1 *Non-Callable, Non-Convertible Preferred Stock*

The cost of preferred stock is the required return demanded by preferred stockholders who receive a fixed dividend and are paid ahead of common stockholders.

The stream of preferred dividends is a perpetuity. The preferred shares are valued as

$$P_p = \frac{D_p}{r_p}$$

We can use the constant dividend growth model to value the preferred stock by setting the growth rate, g, to zero.

Rearranging the above equation, the cost of preferred stock is

$$r_p = \frac{D_p}{P_p}$$

Note that unlike debt, there is no adjustment for taxes. The reason is that preferred dividends are paid from after-tax profits, whereas interest payments are an expense that reduces taxable profits.

Example:
Suppose Peach Company has preferred stock that pays a $2 dividend per share. The price of the stock is currently $40. What is Peach's cost of preferred stock?

Solution:

$$r_p = \$2/\$40 = 0.05 = 5\%$$

17.5 Tax on Cost of Capital

17.5.1 *Taxes on the Cost of Capital from Different Capital Sources*

Taxes can significantly impact a company's WACC.

Learning Objectives
- Discuss how taxes affect the cost of capital from different capital sources.

Main Takeaways

Main Points

- Taxes affect the cost of capital as both firms and investors must factor tax into their investment decisions.
- Taxes do not affect cost of common equity or cost of preferred stocks.
- Debt serves as a tax shield as interest expense can be used to reduced income and hence the amount of taxes paid.
- If interest cannot be deducted for tax purposes, the tax rate applied is zero so that the effective marginal cost of debt is equal to r_d.

Main Terms

- **Marginal cost of debt:** The marginal cost of debt capital is the interest rate demanded by investors, adjusted for taxes.

The marginal cost of debt financing is the cost of debt that factors in the tax deduction for debt interest. If interest cannot be deducted for tax purposes, the tax rate applied is zero so that the effective marginal cost of debt is equal to r_d. If interest can be deducted in full, the debt's tax-deductibility reduces the effective marginal cost of debt to $r_d(1 - t)$. Note that debt shields some of the income from tax as interest is tax-deductible. The amount of tax reduced is known as the tax shield.

Here is an illustration of the tax shield. For example, suppose a firm has \$100 million of debt. If the coupon rate is 5%, the interest payable is \$5 million a year. This interest expense reduces income by \$5 million. The tax savings would be \$5 million times the tax rate. The effective cost of the debt is $r_d \times (1 - t)$, where t is the applicable corporate tax rate. If the firm's marginal tax rate is 30%, then the effective cost of debt is \$5 million × (1 − 0.3) or \$3.5 million.

If the firm is unable to deduct the interest expense due to a limit of the amount that can be deducted, then $r_d \times (1 - t) = r_d$ since $t = 0$.

17.6 Weights of Components

17.6.1 *Market Value Weights*

The WACC is the sum of the cost of each capital component (equity, debt, preference shares, etc.) multiplied by its weight in the capital structure. The weights used are the target capital structure weights based on market values.

Learning Objectives

- Discuss why market value is preferred over book value for WACC.

Main Takeaways

Main Points

- The market values of equity, debt, and preferred stockshould incorporate the capital structure's target capital structure that is the capital structure after new financing is obtained. The current capital structure cannot be used unless capital is raised in the same proportions as the existing capital structure.
- Market values for the components are used because the market value of capital incorporates investors' required rates of return.
- In general, market value tends to be greater than book value because book value does not incorporate intangibles such as the future growth prospect.

Main Terms

- **Market value:** The market value of an asset is the quantity of the asset multiplied by the price. For a company, it is the total number of its outstanding shares multiplied by the price, or its market capitalization.
- **Book value:** The book value of a company is the total value of the assets less the total value of the equities as shown on the balance sheet of the company.

The weights in the WACC calculation should be based on the firm's target capital structure which consists of the proportions of the various components of capital that the firm expects to achieve over time. If no information is forthcoming about the target capital structure, the existing capital structure is used.

Example: WACC with market rates

The market values of a firm's capital are as follows:

Debt (Bonds)	\$30 million
Preferred stock	\$10 million
Common stock	\$60 million
Total capital	\$100 million

What is the firm's target capital structure based on its existing capital structure?

Solution:
The weights of each component are:

Debt	= 30/100 = 30%
Preferred stock	= 10/100 = 10%
common stock	= 60/100 = 60%

References/Further Readings

Bodie, Z., Kane, A., & Marcus, A.J., (2020). *Investments*,12th edn. McGraw-Hill Irwin, pp. 275–330.

Reilly, F., Leeds, S., & Brown, K. (2019). *Investment Analysis and Portfolio Management*, 11th edn. Cengage, pp. 209–248.

Ross, S., Westerfield, R., & Jordan, B. (2002). *Fundamentals of Corporate Finance*, 6th edn. McGraw-Hill Irwin, pp. 493–524.

17.7 Sample Questions

Question 1

If both the firm's corporate tax rate and the risk-free rate decrease, what is the impact on the WACC? (Consider the events independently and assume the firm's beta is greater than one.)

Tax rate decreases	Risk-free rate decreases
(a) Decrease WACC	Increase WACC
(b) Increase WACC	Increase WACC
(c) Increase WACC	Decrease WACC

Question 2

Compute the WACC given the following costs or the components and a corporate tax rate of 40%.

	Cost	Amount
Long-term debt	4%	$40 million
Preferred stock	5%	$10 million
Common stock	10%	$50 million

(a) 4.26%
(b) 6.46%
(c) 7.10%

Question 3
For computing the WACC, a tax adjustment is generally applied to the:

(a) Cost of debt
(b) Cost of common equity
(c) Cost of retained earnings

Question 4
The cost of equity can be estimated using three methods: CAPM method, constant dividend growth model method, and the bond yield plus risk premium approach. The data to estimate the cost of equity is:

Risk-free rate = 2%
Before tax cost of debt = 5%
Expected market return = 10%
Beta = 1.2
Current stock price = $40
Next year's dividend = $3
Dividend growth rate = 4%
Risk premium above debt = 6%

The average of the cost of equity from the three methods is closest to:

(a) 11%
(b) 11.4%
(c) 12%

Question 5
Compute the WACC based on the following data:

Cost of debt = 5%
Cost of preferred stock = 8%
Cost of equity = 12%
Number of bonds outstanding = 20,000
Face value of bonds = $1,000
Price of bonds = 105%

Number of preferred stocks = 1,000,000
Price of preferred stocks = \$15
Number of common shares = 100,000
Price of common share = \$200
Tax rate = 40%

(a) 7.55%
(b) 7.66%
(c) 8.30%

Question 6
The WACC for a firm may be dependent upon the firm's:

1. Growth rate of dividends
2. Debt-equity ratio
3. Risk-free rate

(a) I and II only
(b) II and III only
(c) I, II, and III

Question 7
The use of the current cost of capital to discount cash flows in capital budgeting is valid if:

(a) capital structure does not matter
(b) the company does not plan to issue more debt
(c) the risk of the project is comparable to the overall risk of the company

Question 8
When calculating the WACC, the capital structure weights do not depend on the:

(a) Market value of debt
(b) Market value of equity
(c) Book value of equity

Question 9

Peach Company will pay a dividend of $2.00 next year. It has a stock price of $40, a payout ratio of 40%, and an ROE of 10%. Using the constant dividend growth model, the cost of equity for the Peach Company is closest to:

(a) 9%
(b) 11%
(c) 13%

Question 10

You have been asked to compute the CRP for Country X, given the following data:

Country X's 10-year Treasury bond rate = 6%
US 10-year government bond yield = 3%
Standard deviation of Country X government bond index = 30%
Standard deviation of US Treasury bond index = 20%

Country X's CRP is closest to:

(a) 4.0%
(b) 4.5%
(c) 6.0%

Solutions

Question 1

Solution: Option **c** is correct.

The interest on debt reduces the firm's taxable income. A decrease in the tax rate would reduce the tax savings since the firm would be paying less in taxes due to the reduced tax rate. Thus the cost of debt would increase, resulting in a higher WACC. A decrease in the risk-free rate would reduce both the cost of equity and cost of debt, assuming the risk premiums for both components remain the same. WACC would be reduced accordingly.

Question 2

Solution: Option **b** is correct.

$$\text{WACC} = 4 \times (1 - 0.4) \times 40/100 + 5 \times 10/100 + 10 \times 50/100 = 4.26\%$$

Question 3

Solution: Option **a** is correct.

Interest is an expense that is deductible from taxable income. Hence, the cost of debt is lowered by the lower tax payable. Dividends are paid from profits after tax. Retained earnings are the after-tax profits that have not been paid out to shareholders. As both dividends and retained earnings derive from after-tax profits, there is no need for further tax adjustments.

Question 4

Solution: Option **b** is correct.

CAPM method:

$$r_e = 2\% + 1.2 \times (10\% - 2\%) = 11.6\%$$

Constant dividend growth model method:

$$r_e = \text{D1/P} + g = 3/40 + 4\% = 11.5\%$$

Bond yield plus risk premium method:

$$r_e = 5\% + 6\% = 11\%$$

Average of 3 methods: 11.6% + 11.5% + 11% = 11.37%

Question 5

Solution: Option **a** is correct.

Value of debt = 20,000 × \$1,000 × 1.05 = \$21 million

Value of preferred stock = 1,000,000 × \$15 = \$15 million

Value of common stock = 100,000 × \$200 = \$20 million

Total firm value = \$(21 + 15 + 20) million = \$56 million

WACC = (5% × 0.6 × 21/56) + (8% × 15/56) + (12% × 20/56) = 7.55%

Question 6

Solution: Option **c** is correct.

The growth rate of dividend is required for the constant dividend growth model, the debt-equity ratio is needed for the weights, and the risk-free rate for the CAPM model.

Question 7

Solution: Option **c** is correct.

The appropriate rate used to discount the project's cash flows must be the rate commensurate with the project's risk.

Question 8

Solution: Option **c** is correct.

The market values of the components of the firm's capital are used to compute the weights.

Question 9

Solution: Option **b** is correct.

Growth rate = (1 − pay-out ratio) × return on equity = (1 − 0.4) × 10% = 6%

$$r_e = (D1/P0) + g = 2/40 + 0.06 = 11\%$$

Question 10

Solution: Option **b** is correct.

Sovereign bond spread = 6% − 3% = 3%

Country X's CRP = 3% × 30/20 = 4.5%

Chapter 18

Capital Budgeting

18.1 Capital Budgeting Process

18.1.1 *Introduction and Capital Budgeting Process*

Capital budgeting is a process of evaluating whether a firm should invest in a project.

Learning Objectives

- Understand the capital budgeting process and its methods.

Main Takeaways

Main Points

- Capital budgeting is the process of determining whether a long-term investment should be made.
- Standard methods for capital budgeting include Net Present Value (NPV), Internal Rate of Return (IRR), Payback period, and Profitability index.
- The principles of capital budgeting can also be applied in other finance areas for decisions on leasing, mergers and acquisition, and security valuation.

Main Terms

- **Capital investments:** Investments in the long term, fixed assets such as new building, new machinery, new plants, research and development projects, etc.

- **Mutually exclusive:** If two projects are mutually exclusive, only one can be selected.
- **Modified IRR:** The modified internal rate of return (MIRR) is used when the assumption of the IRR that intermediate cash flows can be reinvested at the IRR is not valid. MIRR assumes intermediate cash flows can be reinvested at some rate of return, often the opportunity cost of funds. The method compounds all intermediate cash flows to the project's end date at the assumed rate. The sum of the compounded cash flows at the end date, together with the initial investment for the project, can then be used to determine the compounded rate of return, which is the MIRR.

Firms use capital budgeting methods to help them decide on their long-term investments. It is important that good investments are selected as large sums are invested and the outcomes could impact the success or failure of the firm.

Capital budgeting uses valuation tools that are quite similar to those used to value stocks and bonds. The methods are also useful in areas like mergers and acquisitions of other firms and leasing decisions regarding equipment or buildings.

The capital budgeting process begins with the generation of investment proposals or ideas, the evaluation of the project proposal based on cash flows, and the monitoring of the project. This module excludes the generation of investment ideas as it is outside the course's scope.

The project is launched after the investment proposal is accepted. The first step is to, develop the cash flows associated with the project. We discuss how this is done in a later section.

The next step uses various capital budgeting methods to evaluate the cash flows in order to decide whether the project should go ahead.

Once a project gets underway, the next phase is monitoring the project. This involves comparing the project's actual results with the results predicted by the investment proposal.

The last step involves the decision whether to continue with the project, whether any strategic changes or modifications to the strategy are needed. The decision could involve whether to reduce or increase the project's size. This step is outside the program's scope.

18.1.2 *Basic Principles of Capital Budgeting*

Capital budgeting relies on just a few fundamental principles that companies use to decide on investing in their capital projects.

Learning Objectives

- Describe the basic principles of capital budgeting for cash flow estimation.

Main Takeaways

Main Points

- Consider only after-tax cash flows based on opportunity costs.
- Conventional cash flows consist of a cash outflow at the beginning of the project and cash inflows subsequently. Nonconventional cash flows do not conform to the conventional cash flow pattern. For example, there could be cash outflows in the years following the start of the project. An extreme example is where the project has no cash inflows at all, only cash outflows.
- Decisions are based on incremental cash flows and not accounting income.
- Sunk costs are not considered.

Main Terms

- **Opportunity cost:** The difference in returns between an investment one makes and another that one chooses not to make.
- **Sunk cost:** A sunk cost is one that has already been incurred. Hence it should not be included in deciding whether to undertake a project or not.
- **Incremental cash flow:** An incremental cash flow is the additional cash flow that results from undertaking the project. This cash flow is the difference between the cash flow arising from the project less the corresponding cash flow if the project was not undertaken.
- **Externality:** An externality refers to the impact on the firm's cash flows apart from the project's cash flows. The cash flows in the other parts of the company could be affected positively or negatively. Externalities should be included in the capital budgeting decision.

(a) Basic Principles of Capital Budgeting

Use of Cash Flows: Decisions should be based on cash flows rather than accounting income. The cash flows in the capital budgeting decision are incremental cash flows, which are the additional cash flows that will occur if the project is undertaken.

Sunk costs are not incremental cash flows since these costs have already been incurred. Whether to take on a project or not would not affect the amount of sunk costs. As such, they should be excluded from the analysis. Common examples of sunk costs include fees paid for a market study on a new product or a survey on potential uses for a property. Just because a cost can be associated with a project does not mean it should be included in the capital budgeting decision. Costs in capital budgeting are the cost incurred if and only if the project is undertaken.

Externalities impact the firm's other cash flows due to the acceptance of a project. Positive externalities are the beneficial effects on the other areas of the firm arising from the project. On the other hand, negative externalities adversely impact other parts of the firm. One negative externality is cannibalization. Cannibalization occurs when a new project siphons sales from an existing product. For example, when a firm launches a low-sugar version of its breakfast cereals, sales for the existing cereals would be reduced as some health-conscious consumers switch to the low-sugar version.

The projects' cash flow patterns fall into two categories — conventional and non-conventional. A conventional cash flow pattern consists of a cash out-flow (negative sign) at the beginning of the project followed by a series of cash inflows (positive sign). Projects with conventional cash flow patterns have only one sign change. An unconventional cash flow pattern has more than one sign change or no sign change at all. An example of a project with unconventional cash flows would be a negative cash flow at the beginning of the project, followed by positive cash flows in the subsequent years except for the last year when the cash flow is negative. This pattern is typical of some mining projects. At the end of the project, costs are incurred to rehabilitate the environment at and around the mine. Such a cash flow pattern has two sign changes from negative to positive at the end of the first year and positive to negative at the end of the project period.

Opportunity Costs: Cash flows are based on opportunity costs: the alternative cash flows the firm forgoes when it takes on the project. Opportunity costs are part of the project cost. For example, a firm owns some office space that is currently unoccupied. If the new project were to utilize the space, some might think that the cost is zero since it already owns it. However, by taking on the project, the firm forgoes renting the space to someone else. The rent foregone is the opportunity cost of the space and should be included as part of project costs.

Timing of Cash Flows: As cash flows from the project occur over several years, when those cash flows occur is important. The same amount of cash flow received later is worth less than when it is received earlier, due to the time value of money. Capital budgeting decisions are made using discounted cash flows.

Taxes: Cash flows are analyzed on an after-tax basis. The reason for this is that the actual cost of an expense is not the amount that is paid. Instead, as expenses are tax-deductible, the actual cost of an expense is $(1 - t)$ times the actual expense, where "t" is the corporate tax rate. The reason is that $1 of expense reduces the taxable profit by $1, which implies that ($\$1 \times t$) less tax needs to be paid. An extra dollar of revenue does not accrue entirely to the firm. As taxes need to be paid, the after-tax cash flow of $1 of revenue is $\$1 \times (1 - t)$.

Financing Costs: Financing costs should not be included in the expenses of the project. The reason is that when we discount the cash flows to find their present values, we are implicitly incorporating the financing cost. Note that only when a project's expected return exceeds the required return will there be an increase in the firm's value.

18.1.3 *Capital Budgeting Project Classification*

Companies often classify capital budgeting projects into various categories so similar projects can be analyzed consistently.

Learning Objectives
- Explain how the different types of classification, particularly mutual exclusivity, capital rationing, and project sequencing, affect the evaluation and selection of capital budgeting projects.

Main Takeaways

Main Points
- Cash flow analysis in capital budgeting becomes more complicated when there are interactions between different projects.
- An integer programming approach solves a situation of capital rationing. In this case, the program chooses a combination of the projects that yields the highest NPV but stays within the capital budget or amount available for investment.

Main Terms

- **Capital rationing:** A situation where the company has more projects to invest in than the funds available. As such, the company may forgo some positive NPV projects.
- **Net present value:** The sum of the present values of all the cash flows for the project, whether they are cash inflows or cash outflows. The rate used to discount the cash flows is commensurate with the project's risk.
- **Shareholder value:** The value of the stake of a firm's equity owners. The change in the stock price reflects changes in shareholder value which could be due to management's strategy and actions.

(a) Types of Capital Budgeting Projects

Capital budgeting projects can be classified into four categories:

1. **Replacement projects:** Buying a new machine to replace an old one is not a complex decision. There is not much uncertainty regarding the project's cash flows unless drastically different technology is involved.
2. **Expansion projects:** There will be more uncertainty about the cash flows for such projects compared to replacement projects. The uncertainties involve the reception by new customers and the reactions of competitors trying to protect their market shares.
3. **New products and services:** Such projects are associated with the most uncertainty regarding market acceptance of the products or services. This accounts for the high failure rate of businesses launching new products.
4. **Regulatory, safety, and environmental projects:** Such projects are usually undertaken because of regulatory requirements. With climate change and clean air becoming big issues for many cities, companies have to invest in green technology which can be costly. Such projects often entail cash outflows and little, if any, cash inflows.

(b) Mutually Exclusive Projects and Capital Rationing

Independent versus Mutually Exclusive Projects: Independent projects are projects that are not related to each other. When a project is independent, the acceptance decision can be made without taking other projects into account.

When projects are mutually exclusive the acceptance of one project means the other projects cannot be accepted. For example, suppose two projects are acceptable if each were evaluated on its own. However, because both projects are mutually exclusive, the firm can only accept either one but not both. For example, a firm has a choice between building a cinema on a piece of land that it owns or a fitness club. Both are viable choices. But the firm can only choose one option as the projects are mutually exclusive.

Capital Rationing: A capital rationing situation occurs when a firm finds itself having more viable projects than the funds available to do so. A simple solution would be to rank the projects based on the profitability index. The projects that the firm chooses to undertake would start from the project with the highest profitability index, followed by the project with the next highest profitability index, and so on down the list until the funds are exhausted. However, this method may not be optimal. A better approach is a method called integer programming which chooses the combination of projects that do not exceed the available funds but delivers the highest total NPV.

18.2 Capital Budgeting Methods, Advantages and Disadvantages

18.2.1 *Capital Budgeting Methods*

Capital budgeting methods help us determine whether a project is worthwhile to invest.

Learning Objectives

- Calculate and interpret the results of using the NPV, IRR, Payback Period, and Profitability Index to evaluate a single capital project.

Main Takeaways

Main Points

- Capital budgeting methods analyze investment proposals by ranking them using different methods.
- The starting point is to identify the inputs to the capital budgeting decision.
- For each method, we need to understand its economic rationale and its strengths and limitations in practice.

- Always place a higher priority on capital budgeting projects that will increase a company's value.
- The test of a project's economic viability is when the present value of its cash inflows exceeds the present value of its cash outflows with the project's required rate of return used to discount the cash flows.

Main Terms

- **Hurdle rate:** The rate of return that a project must exceed for it to be accepted.
- **Discounted cash flow (DCF):** Discounts the cash flows of a project at its required rate of return and compares the sum of the present values of cash inflows to the sum of the present values of cash outflows. A project is accepted if the sum of the PV of cash inflows exceeds the sum of the PV of cash outflows.

There are several methods used to evaluate capital investments. The two most commonly used methods to decide whether a project should be accepted or rejected are the NPV and IRR methods. There are four other methods, namely the payback period, discounted payback period (DPP), average accounting rate of return (AAR), and profitability index (PI).

To decide on the investment merits of various projects we need the following inputs:

1. **Initial investment:** The initial investment is the cost of the project. The cost usually involves a large amount upfront, for example the purchase of land to build a new factory as well as the equipment needed to run it.
2. **Operating cash flows:** These are the cash flows that consist of revenue and cost items that recur each year during the project's life. These cash flows are obtained from the project's proforma income statement.
3. **Terminal cash flows:** These are cash flows that occur in the last year of the project. They could include the sale of the machine and the return of working capital.
4. **Discount rate:** This is the rate used to discount the cash flows to find their present values.
5. **Decision rule:** A rule that suggests which projects should be accepted or rejected.

18.2.2 *Payback Period Method*

The payback method measures the time required to recover the initial investment.

Learning Objectives
- Define and calculate an investment payback period.

Main Takeaways

Main Points
- Accept the project if the payback period is less than some cut-off period.
- All else equal, a shorter payback period is preferred to a more extended payback period.
- The drawbacks of the payback method are that it ignores the time value of money (TVM) and does not consider the cash flows beyond the payback period.
- When liquidity is an important consideration, the payback period is often used. In a sense, the payback considers investment risk as to the longer the project period, the greater the uncertainties regarding future cash flows.

Main Terms
- **Payback period:** The amount of time required to recover the funds spent on the investment.
- **Time value of money:** The TVM is based on the concept that a dollar received is worth more than the same dollar received in the future. The reason is that the dollar received today earns interest or a return when it is invested so that at a future date, the amount is more than the dollar to be received then.
- **Cumulative cash flow:** This is the sum of all cash flows related to the project from its inception.

(a) Payback Period
The payback period is the number of years it takes to recover a project's investment. The payback is based on cash flows. For example, if you invest $10 million in a project, how long will it be until you recover the entire original investment? The method involves adding the cash inflows until the sum is equal or just exceeds the project's initial investment.

Table 18.1: Sample extract of cash flows from Year 0 to Year 5.

Year	0	1	2	3	4	5
Cash Flow	−5,000	1,000	1,500	2,000	2,500	3,000
Cumulative		1,000	2,500	4500	7,000	10,000
Outstanding	5,000	4,000	2,500	500	0	

The time taken for this to occur is the payback period. Decision rule: Accept the project if the payback period is less than some cut-off period.

Example: Payback period computation

Table 18.1 depicts the cash flow of a company for 5 consecutive years. The company recovers 1,000 of the investment in the first year. In the second year, the company recovers another 1,500, for 2,500 recovered so far. We have 2,500 still unrecovered. In the third year, with the cash inflow of 2,000, only 500 remains to be recovered. You can see that the company recoups its original investment between Year 3 and Year 4. After 3 years, 500 is still unrecovered. As the Year 4 cash flow is 2,500, it would take 0.2 years (500/2500) after Year 3 to recover the investment fully. The result is a payback period of 3.2 years.

(b) Advantages and Disadvantages of the Payback Period Method

Table 18.2 shows the advantages and disadvantages of the payback period. A key advantage of the payback period is that it is easy to understand. Other capital budgeting methods may be harder to explain to those with little knowledge of finance. The project's risk is partially accounted for by the method's bias toward liquidity as earlier cash flows are emphasized over later cash flows in the recovery of the project's investment. A firm that has limited liquidity would tend to favor the payback period.

One main disadvantage of the payback period is that it ignores cash flows beyond the cut-off date. Ignoring such cash flows results in a bias towards short-term projects at the expense of longer-term projects, which may be more profitable. A second disadvantage is that a dollar of cash flow has the same weight regardless of when it is received. The TVM is not factored in the computations. Finally, how the cut-off period is established can be entirely arbitrary and not based on sound economic principles.

Table 18.2: Advantages and disadvantages of the payback period.

Advantages	Disadvantages
1. Easy to understand	1. Ignores time value of money
2. Adjusts for the uncertainty of later cash flows	2. Requires arbitrary cut-off period
3. Biased towards liquidity	3. Ignores cash flows beyond cut-off date
	4. Biased against long term projects

18.2.3 *Discounted Payback Period Method*

The DPP is a modified version of the payback period that accounts for the time value of money.

Learning Objectives

- Compute the DPP using discounted cash flows.

Main Takeaways

Main Points

- The DPP overcomes the objection that the payback period is deficient because it does not consider the time value of money. It improves on the payback period by using discounted cash flows in computing the discounted payback period.
- As the DPP uses discounted cash flows whereas the payback period does not, the DPP will be longer than the payback period for the same set of cash flows.
- The DPP accounts for TVM and liquidity risk within the discounted period, but cash flows after the DPP are ignored.
- DPP is used as a measure of liquidity similar to the payback period.

Main Terms

- **Discounted payback period:** The DPP is the time taken to recoup an investment based on discounted cash flows.

The DPP uses discounted cash flows, whereas the payback period does not. Since the discounted value of a cash flow is less than if the cash flow is not discounted, the DPP must be longer than the payback period for the same set of cash flows. Decision rule: Accept the project if the DPP is less than some cut-off period.

Table 18.3: Computations of discounted cash flows for Year 0 to Year 5.

Year	0	1	2	3	4	5
Cash flow (CF)	−5,000	1,000	1,500	2,000	2,500	3,000
Cumulative CF	−5,000	−4,000	−2,500	−500	2,000	5,000
Discounted CF	−5,000	909	1,239	1,503	1,708	1,863
Cumulative discounted CF	−5,000	−4,091	−2,852	−1,349	359	2,222

Example: Discounted payback period computation
We used the same cash flows when we calculated the payback period above to calculate the DPP. A 10% discount rate is used to find the present value. Table 18.3 illustrates the computed discounted cash flows for years 0 to 5.

The DPP occurs between the third and fourth year. It is 3 + [0 − (1,349)]/[359 − (−1,349)] = 3 + 1,349/1,708 = 3.79 years. By contrast the payback period is 3.2 years.

(a) Disadvantages of Discounted Payback Period Method
While the discounted payback improves on the payback period by taking into account the time value of money, the other drawbacks of the payback period remain. These drawbacks are the arbitrary cut-off period and not considering cash flows after the DPP.

18.2.4 *Net Present Value*

The NPV of a project is the present value of the cash inflows less the present value of the cash outflows.

Learning Objectives
- Calculate the NPV and interpret a series of NPV calculations.

Main Takeaways

Main Points
- When the project's NPV is positive, and the project is undertaken, shareholder value in the firm increases by the amount of the NPV.
- The rate used to discount the cash flows should be commensurate with the project's risk.
- The discount rate at which NPV equals 0 is called the IRR.

Main Terms

- **Discount rate:** the interest rate used to discount future cash flows to find the present value.
- **Internal rate of return:** The rate of return on an investment such that the NPV of all future cash flows is zero.

(a) Computing the Net Present Value

The NPV of a project is derived by subtracting the sum of the present values of the cash outflows from the sum of the present values of cash inflows. For a conventional project, the cash flow pattern is an initial cash outflow (the initial investment) followed by a series of cash inflows. In this case, the NPV is given by:

$$\text{NPV} = \Sigma \frac{\text{CF}_t}{(1+r)^t} - \text{initial investment}$$

where CF_t = after-tax cash inflow at time t and r = required rate of return for the investment.

However, if the project is not conventional, that is, there are cash outflows after the initial investment, the NPV is just the sum of the present values of all cash flows. NPV is given by:

$$\text{NPV} = \Sigma \frac{\text{CF}_t}{(1+r)^t}$$

where CF_t = after-tax cash flow at time t, from $t = 0$ to T and r = required rate of return for the investment.

The decision rule for the NPV method is: Accept the project if the NPV is greater than zero. Investing in a positive NPV project is expected to increase shareholder wealth while taking on a negative NPV project decreases shareholder wealth.

Example: NPV computation

Star Company is looking into the feasibility of investing $100 million in a project. The project will deliver after-tax cash flows of $25 million a year for 3 years and $30 million a year in the next 2 years. If the required rate of return is 12%, compute the NPV.

$$\text{NPV} = \frac{25}{1.12^1} + \frac{25}{1.12^2} + \frac{25}{1.12^3} + \frac{30}{1.12^4} + \frac{30}{1.12^5} - 100$$

$$\text{NPV} = 96.13 - 100 = -\$3.87 \text{ million}$$

Table 18.4: Advantages and disadvantages of NPV model.

Advantages	Disadvantages
1. Considers all cash flows	1. May be difficult to communicate the concept of NPV
2. Considers time value of money	
3. Takes risk into account	
4. Consistent with shareholder wealth maximization	

On a present value basis, the investment delivers a value of \$96.13 million. Against this, we have to consider the investment of \$100 million. The project's NPV is the difference between the investment value and the cost, which in this case is a negative \$3.87 million, or NPV = −\$3.87 million. Since the NPV is negative, the project should not be undertaken. If undertaken, it will reduce shareholder value by \$3.87 million.

(b) Advantages and Disadvantages of NPV Method
Table 18.4 shows the advantages and disadvantages of the NPV model.

18.2.5 *Internal Rate of Return*

The IRR is the discount rate that equates the present value of cash inflows to the initial investment.

Learning Objectives
- Define and calculate the IRR.

Main Takeaways

Main Points
- A firm should undertake a project when the project IRR exceeds the required rate of return.
- IRR assumes all cash in-flows are reinvested at the project's IRR.
- For non-conventional projects, projects with cash outflows occurring after the initial investment, multiple IRRs could arise.
- In an accept or reject decision regarding an independent project, IRR and NPV give consistent results. However, for mutually exclusive projects, IRR and NPV can give conflicting rankings.

Main Terms

- **Required rate of return:** This is the return that the project should earn that is consistent with its risk.
- **Internal rate of return:** The rate of return on an investment which causes the NPV of all cash flows to be zero.
- **Independent project:** For an independent project, the decision of whether to undertake the project or not just depends on whether it meets the acceptance criterion, for example, NPV greater than zero. The decision is made without the need to consider other alternative projects
- **Mutually exclusive projects:** Two projects are mutually exclusive if one project's acceptance means the rejection of the other project.

(a) Computing the Internal Rate of Return

The IRR is the discount rate that equates the sum of the present values of cash inflows to the sum of the present value of cash outflows.

$$\text{PV (inflows)} = \text{PV (outflows)}$$

As the NPV is the difference between the two quantities, the IRR is also the discount rate such that the NPV of the project is equal to zero:

$$\text{NPV} = \Sigma \frac{\text{CF}}{(1+\text{IRR})^{t}} - \text{Initial outlay} = 0$$

The IRR is calculated using a financial calculator or the financial function in a spreadsheet program, e.g., Excel.

The decision rule for IRR is: Accept the project only if IRR is greater than the required rate of return.

Example: IRR computation

We use the Star Company's cash flows in the NPV section to illustrate the IRR computation. The IRR is the discount rate that solves the following equation:

$$-100 + \frac{25}{(1+\text{IRR})^{1}} + \frac{25}{(1+\text{IRR})^{2}} + \frac{25}{(1+\text{IRR})^{3}} + \frac{30}{(1+\text{IRR})^{4}} + \frac{30}{(1+\text{IRR})^{5}} = 0$$

The IRR computed from the financial calculator, or the Excel spreadsheet is 10.485%. As this rate is lower than the required rate of return of 12%, the project should be rejected.

Table 18.5: Advantages and disadvantages of IRR model.

Advantages	Disadvantages
1. Closely related to NPV	1. A project may have multiple IRRs
2. Gives the same decisions as NPV for projects with conventional cash flows	2. May lead to incorrect decisions when comparing mutually exclusive projects
3. Easy to understand and communicate	

(b) Advantages and Disadvantages of IRR Method

Table 18.5 shows the advantages and disadvantages of the IRR model.

18.2.6 *Profitability Index*

The profitability index (PI) is a ratio of the PV of the cash inflows to the PV of the cash outflows.

Learning Objectives

- Calculate and interpret the Profitability Index.

Main Takeaways

Main Points

- The Profitability Index is closely related to the NPV.
- If the NPV is positive, the profitability index will be greater than one. A negative NPV corresponds to a profitability index that is less than 1.
- Investors should invest in the project only if the PI is greater than 1.
- A profitability index of 1 indicates that the project will break even.

Main Terms

- **Profitability index:** The PI is the present value of a project's cash inflows divided by the present value of the cash outflows.
- **Net present value:** The NPV of a project is the sum of the present values of cash inflows less the sum of the present values of the cash outflows.

The PI is the present value of a project's cash inflows divided by the present value of the cash outflows. If we are dealing with a conventional project, then the cash outflows are just the initial investment. Thus PI can be expressed as

$$PI = \frac{\text{PV of cash inflows}}{\text{PV of cash outflows}} = 1 + \frac{\text{NPV}}{\text{Initial Investment}}$$

The profitability index's decision rule is that the project will be accepted if the PI is greater than 1. The profitability index and the NPV are closely related as they both use the quantities PV of cash inflows and PV of cash outflows. PI uses a ratio of the two quantities, while NPV gives the difference between the two quantities. Thus NPV > 0 implies PI > 1, while NPV < 1 implies a PI < 1.

We can extend the relationship between PI and NPV to include IRR. NPV > 0 implies PI > 1 and IRR > required rate of return. NPV < 0 implies PI < 1 and IRR < required rate of return. When IRR = required rate of return, NPV = 0 and PI =1.

The PI indicates the value you get per dollar of investment. PI may be used as a quick way to choose the projects to invest when the firm faces capital rationing. We do this by selecting the highest PI project, going down the line with the project with the next highest PI, and continuing until the funds run out. Such a method of choosing the projects may not be optimal, though. A more sophisticated approach is the use of integer programming. However, this method is beyond the scope of our curriculum.

The PI method is sometimes known as the cost-benefit ratio and is often used by non-profit organizations.

Example: Profitability index computation

We use the Star Company cash flows to compute the PI. The PV of cash inflows is \$96.13 million, while the initial investment is \$100 million. Hence the PI is given by:

$$PI = \frac{\text{PV of cash inflows}}{\text{Initial investment}} = \frac{96.13}{100} = 0.9613$$

The PI can also be calculated as

$$PI = 1 + \frac{\text{NPV}}{\text{Initial investment}} = 1 + \frac{-3.87}{100} = 0.9613$$

Because PI < 1, the project should be rejected.

Table 18.6: Advantages and disadvantages of the PI model.

Advantages	Disadvantages
1. Closely related to NPV	1. May lead to incorrect decisions when comparing mutually exclusive projects
2. Easy to understand and communicate	
3. May be useful when available funds are limited (Capital Rationing)	

(a) Advantages and Disadvantages of Profitability Index

Table 18.6 shows the advantages and disadvantages of the PI model.

18.2.7 *NPV versus IRR Method*

NPV and IRR are two of the most widely used capital budgeting methods. Each approach has its distinct advantages and disadvantages.

Learning Objectives

- Explain the NPV profile and compare the NPV and IRR methods when evaluating independent and mutually exclusive projects. Describe the problems associated with IRR.

Main Takeaways

Main Points

- The NPV method measures the return of an investment in dollar amounts after subtracting the cost, while IRR gives the return on a percentage basis.
- When the NPV method is used, the project's main consideration is the amount of NPV generated, regardless of the investment cost. The project with a higher NPV will rank ahead of a project with a lower NPV. By contrast, the IRR measures an investment's attractiveness by its rate of return. Ranking projects by the IRR ignores the value brought in by each project.
- When projects are ranked using IRR and NPV, conflicts in the rankings may occur. Such conflicts result from differing project scale and cash flow timing.

From a theoretical perspective, the NPV method is the most sound. An implicit assumption in using the NPV method to evaluate projects is that the firm has sufficient funds to undertake all feasible projects. However, in a capital rationing situation where funds are limited, a project with a lower NPV may be chosen over a project with a higher NPV because the project's cost is taken into account, and the objective is to maximize the NPV of the group of projects within the budget constraint.

While the IRR measures profitability on a percentage basis, showing the return on each dollar invested, it fails to account for the value delivered by each project. A useful feature of the IRR is that it provides information on the safety margin that the NPV does not. The difference between the IRR and the required return for the project indicates how much the project's return can fall before the project becomes not viable, that is, negative NPV results.

Example: Ranking conflicts between NPV and IRR methods
Cash Flow Timing: We consider two projects with an initial investment of $3,000 each. The required rate of return is 10%. The cash flows associated with each project are shown below:

Year	Project A	Project B
0	–$3,000	–$3,000
1	1,000	0
2	1,000	0
3	1,000	0
4	1,000	0
5	1,000	7,000
NPV	$790.79	$1,346.45
IRR	19.86%	18.47%

When we examine the NPV and IRR for the two projects, we notice a conflict in the ranking. Based on IRR, Project A is preferred since it has a higher IRR than Project B. However, based on NPV, the order is reversed — Project B has a higher NPV than Project A. Such a reversal of ranking creates a dilemma for the decision-maker. Which project should be undertaken?

If Project A is chosen, it adds $790.79 to the firm's value. However, Project B will add $1,346.45 to firm value if it is selected. As the financial manager's objective is to maximize shareholders' wealth, Project B should be undertaken since it generates more value.

Project Scale: Besides cash flow timing differences, a conflict in rankings arises from project size differences. We illustrate this issue by considering two projects. The first project has an investment cost of $1 million, while the second project requires a $2 million investment. We can expect the larger project to yield a higher NPV. But the smaller project could conceivably have a higher IRR.

This conflict can be resolved because funding for the projects is not an issue. In this case, the project with the larger NPV should be accepted. However, another reason for using NPV is the assumption about the reinvestment rate for the cash inflows of the project. NPV assumes that those cash flows are reinvested at the required rate of return. This assumption is more reasonable than the reinvestment rate assumption in the IRR. IRR assumes that the cash inflows can be reinvested at the same rate of return as the IRR. Such an assumption is quite unrealistic as only the project itself could offer the return implicit in the IRR.

18.2.8 *Independent and Mutually Exclusive Projects (NPV versus IRR)*

A conflict in rankings between the NPV and IRR methods could arise in a situation of mutually exclusive projects.

Learning Objectives

- Understand and apply NPV and IRR concepts when evaluating an independent and mutually exclusive project.

Main Takeaways

Main Points

- Mutually exclusive projects can be ranked based on their NPV, but rankings based on other methods will not necessarily maximize the firm's value.
- An independent project is a project in which a decision about acceptance of one project does not affect the decision regarding the others.

- In the case of mutually exclusive projects, an NPV and IRR conflict may arise in which one project has the higher NPV, but the other has higher the IRR.
- As IRR has several limitations, mutually exclusive projects should be chosen by the NPV method.

Main Terms

- **Reinvestment rate:** The rate at which an investor can reinvest cash flows from an investment.

A possible conflict in the rankings given by NPV and IRR can be resolved by considering the cases of independent projects and mutually exclusive projects.

An independent project is one where the investment decision does not need to consider other projects. There is no conflict between NPV and IRR regarding the investment decision for a conventional project. Both methods will give the same result for the decision. However, the conflict between the two approaches can arise in mutually exclusive projects. This conflict is illustrated using the NPV profile in the next section.

18.2.9 *Net Present Value Profile* (*NPV versus IRR*)

The NPV profile of a project is a graph that plots the NPV of the project as the discount rate is changed.

Learning Objectives

- Understand the concept of NPV profile.

Main Takeaways

Main Points

- The discount rate that causes a project's NPV to be zero is the IRR. On the NPV profile of the project, this occurs when the graph intersects the horizontal axis.
- The discount rate at which the NPVs of 2 projects are equal is called the crossover rate.
- The NPV profile declines as the discount rate increases.

- An NPV profile with a steep slope indicates that the project's NPV is more sensitive to changes in discount rate than an NPV profile with a less steep slope.

Main Terms

- **Discount rate:** The interest rate used to discount the future cash flows of a project.

The NPV profile of a project is a graph that plots the NPV of the project as the discount rate is changed. The NPV profile slopes downwards as the NPV decreases with increasing discount rates. Figure 18.1 shows the NPV profiles of projects B and C.

The point where the NPV profile cuts the X-axis indicates the IRR of the project. The reason is that the IRR is the discount rate which results in the equality of the PV of the cash inflows and the PV of the cash outflows, that is, when NPV is equal to zero.

If projects are considered alone, for example, project B, the two methods will be consistent suggesting whether to accept or reject the project. Suppose the discount rate is r_1. According to NPV, we accept the project as NPV is positive. Looking at Figure 18.1, we see that IRR_B is greater than r_1. Hence, IRR will accept project B as well.

The crossover point is the point at which the two NPV profiles intersect. The discount rate at which this happens is known as the crossover

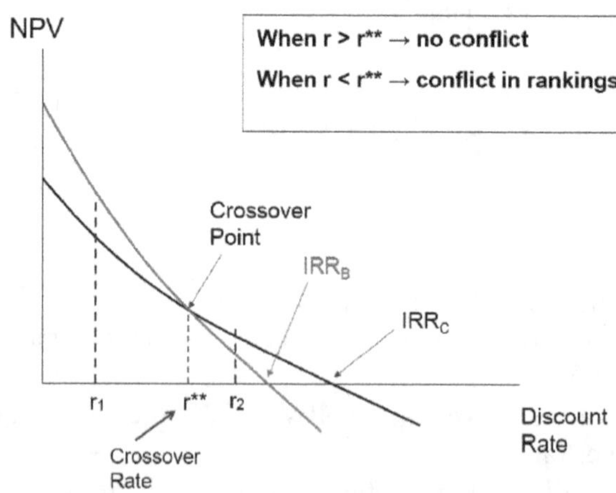

Figure 18.1: Illustration of NPV profile curve.

rate. If the discount rate is higher than the crossover rate, both NPV and IRR are consistent. For example, at r_2, both the NPV and IRR of project C are higher than the corresponding NPV and IRR for project B

The conflict between NPV and IRR rankings only arises when the crossover rate is higher than the discount. At r_1 NPV of project, B is higher than NPV of project C. So NPV would rank project B ahead of project C. However, as $IRR_C > IRR_B$, IRR would rank project C ahead of project B.

18.2.10 *Issues with IRR Method (NPV versus IRR)*

Some problems with the IRR method are the reinvestment rate assumption and the issue of multiple IRRs or no IRR at all.

Learning Objectives

- Describe the problems with the IRR method.

Main Takeaways

Main Points

- The IRR method assumes that all the cash inflows are reinvested at the IRR rate itself. This assumption is unrealistic, and a more reasonable assumption is that the reinvestment rate is equal to the project's required return.
- A non-conventional cash flow project has the possibility of multiple IRR or no IRR.
- When a project has all negative cash flows, there would be no IRR at all.
- One way to resolve the reinvestment rate assumption and the problem of multiple IRRs is to use the Modified IRR method, which results in only one value for the IRR.

Main Terms

- **Modified internal rate of return:** The MIRR overcomes the problem of the IRR reinvestment rate assumption and the possibility of multiple IRRs. The MIRR method assumes that the cash inflows are reinvested at the required rate of return, unlike the IRR method, which assumes the cash flows are reinvested at a rate equal to the IRR. For the multiple IRR problem, the MIRR method gives only one rate of return associated with the project.

- **Non-conventional project:** A conventional project involves a series of cash inflows following a cash outflow. All other patterns of cash flows are considered non-conventional cash flows. For example, the cash flows could be all negative. That is, they are all cash outflows. Alternatively, there could be cash outflows in the future.
- **Descartes rule of signs:** This rule states that the number of sign changes gives the number of real roots of an equation. The number of IRRs is the number of sign changes in the cash flows applying Descartes' rule to the IRR method.

(a) Reinvestment Rate Assumption

Implicit in the IRR method assumes that the firm's cash flows derived from the project can be reinvested at the same rate as the IRR. This assumption is not realistic unless those cash flows can be invested in another investment or project that gives the same returns as the current project. A more reasonable assumption is that the cash flows can be reinvested at the project's required rate of return. This assumption is more realistic as many investments offer similar returns as the project since they all have similar risks.

(b) Multiple IRR Problem

A problem with using the IRR is the possibility of multiple project IRRs. This can occur when the project has non-conventional cash flows. Conventional cash flows follow a pattern of a cash outflow or negative cash flow at time 0 followed by positive cash flows after that. The cash flow pattern is depicted as − + + + + + +. Nonconventional cash flow patterns occur when negative cash flows occur after the first cash flow.

Some examples of non-conventional cash flow patterns are: − + − + − + − − or − + + − − + + + + −.

A sample NPV profile illustrating a project with two IRRs (where NPV = 0) is shown in Figure 18.2.

The problem with multiple IRRs is the issue of which is the appropriate IRR to use to compare with the required return. The two IRRs are 100% and 200% in the diagram above. Suppose the required return is 150%. Should the project be accepted? If we choose 100% as the IRR's value to compare with the required return of 150%, we will reject the project. However, if 200% is chosen as IRR, then the project would be accepted since this rate is higher than the required rate of return.

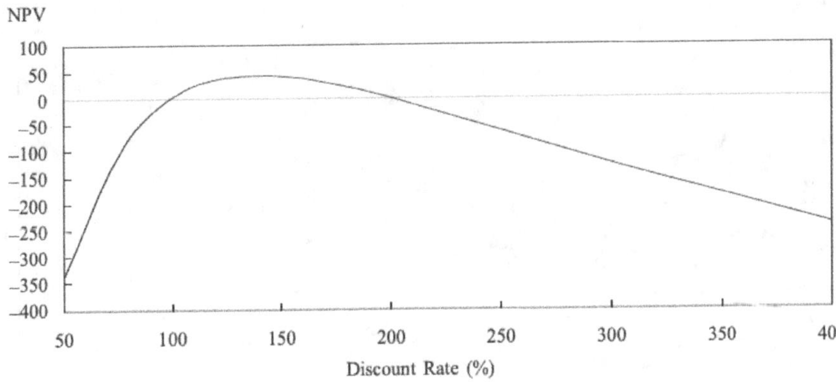

Figure 18.2: NPV profile of projected project with two IRRs.

When the project has non-conventional cash flows, the possibility of more than one IRR makes the IRR method problematic to use. As demonstrated above, the project could be accepted or rejected depending on which rate is taken as the valid IRR to compare with the required rate of return.

(c) No IRR Scenario

Another issue is that there may be no IRR at all. This can occur if the project cash flows are all negative. For example, suppose a company builds some recreational facility to help its employees maintain a healthy lifestyle. There are costs to maintain the facility besides the initial building cost. This results in a series of negative cash flows. If the cash flow all have the same sign, IRR cannot be found. Consequently, we cannot use IRR to compare two competing proposals to build the facility. However, with NPV, we would pick the proposal with the higher NPV even though both NPVs are negative. For example, the proposal with NPV = –\$500,000 would be picked over the proposal with NPV = –\$580,000.

A sample NPV profile with no IRR solution is shown in Figure 18.3.

For conventional projects where the cash flow pattern consists of a cash outflow followed by a series of cash inflow, there will only be one IRR. Why is that so? How do we know? One way is to plot the NPV profile and see how many times it crosses the horizontal axis.

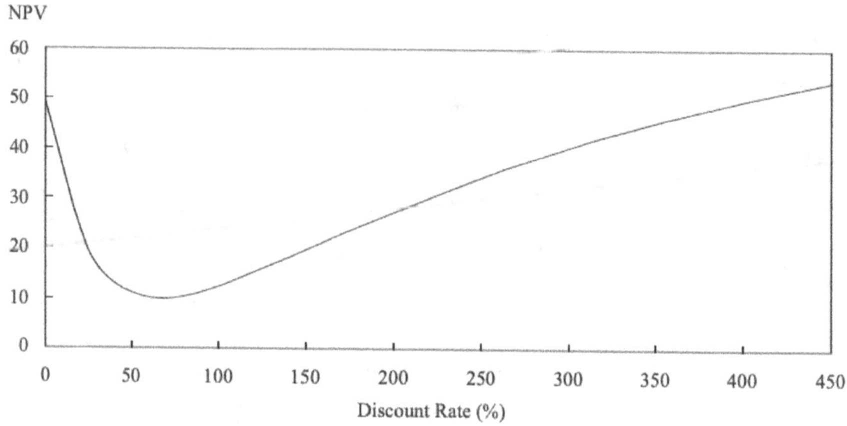

Figure 18.3: Graphical illustration of NPV profile with no IRR solution.

A more straightforward way is to use Descartes' Rule of Signs. Rene Descartes is a famous French mathematician and philosopher who lived in the 17th century and made many mathematical discoveries. The Rule states that the number of real roots of a polynomial equation depends on the number of sign changes. Solving for the IRR is similar to solving a polynomial equation.

We illustrate the rule of signs with the following examples:

Suppose the cash flows from the project have the following pattern: $-+++--+++-$, where the minus sign denotes a cash outflow and the plus sign a cash inflow. There are 4 sign changes: $-$ to +, + to 1, $-$ to + and + to $-$. The project will then have four IRRs.

There is no sign change for the project that just has a series of outflows, and therefore there will not be an IRR for the project.

18.2.11 *Common Capital Budgeting Pitfalls*

In making capital budgeting decisions, there are several common mistakes to avoid.

Learning Objectives

- Describe the common capital budgeting pitfalls.

Main Takeaways

Main Points

- Net income is not a cash flow.
- Ensure that the discount rate used is appropriate given the project's risk. A discount rate higher than what it should be would cause projects to be rejected when they should be accepted.
- When mutually exclusive projects are involved, NPV should be used. IRR may not lead to the correct decision.

Main Terms

- **Opportunity cost:** The differences in return between an investment one makes and another that one chooses not to make.
- **Earnings per share (EPS):** EPS is calculated as a company's profit divided by the outstanding number of shares of its common stock.
- **Return on equity (ROE):** ROE is computed by dividing net income by shareholders' equity. It is an accounting measure of the returns that accrue to the company's shareholders.

Although capital budgeting principles look reasonably straightforward, applying them in a real-world context can be challenging. Some common mistakes to avoid are compiled in Table 18.7.

(a) Capital Budgeting Templates Wrongly Used

A company may develop capital budgeting templates for ease of analysis and to have some standardization. However, improper use of the

Table 18.7: Common capital budgeting pitfalls.

Some common capital budgeting pitfalls
Capital budgeting templates are wrongly used
CEO's preferred projects
Investment decisions based on accounting measures like EPS, net income, or return on equity, but not cash flows
Using IRR to make investment decisions
Inappropriate risk-adjusted discount rate used

templates could result important information left out as the project in question in order to conform to the template.

(b) CEO's Preferred Projects

Pet projects are usually projects that have strong appeal for the CEO but may not seldom investment merit. Such projects may be undertaken going through the capital budgeting process.

(c) EPS, Net Income, or ROE

Sometimes projects show strong EPS, net income, or ROE. However, these are accounting measures and projects chosen on the basis of the accounting rate of return may not pass the NPV criterion.

(d) Inappropriate Use of Discount Rates

This error is often the result of not properly adjusting for the risk of the project. It could arise because the project involves new technology which have not been fully tested out or the project is situated in a foreign country and some risks are left out because of unfamiliarity with the environment in that foreign country.

18.2.12 *Estimation of Project Cash Flow*

Cash flow factors are the operational, financial, or investment activities that cause cash to enter or leave the organization

Learning Objectives

- Define and estimate relevant cash flows for capital investments

Main Takeaways

Main Points

- Cash flows factors can be used to calculate parameters to measure organizational performance.
- The cash flow analysis must account for all cash flow components, such as opportunity costs and depreciation and maintenance expense.
- In estimating a project's cash flows, the focus is on incremental cash flows.

- Cash flow comes in three forms, operating, investing, and financing.
- Positive cash flow indicates that a company's liquid assets are increasing. Companies with substantial financial flexibility fare better in downturns by avoiding financial distress costs.

Main Terms

- **Parameter:** A variable kept constant during an experiment, calculation, or similar.
- **Liquidity:** Availability of cash over the short term: the ability to service short-term debt.

The second step in the capital budgeting process involves estimating the cash flows related to the project.

The cash flows for projects involving a new product, service, or country are often difficult to estimate. However, the decision whether to accept a project rests with capital budgeting criteria like NPV or IRR which, in turn, rely on the accuracy of cash flows as they are the critical inputs in the capital budgeting method. Overoptimistic projections of cash flows lead to accepting projects that are hard to justify when they are implemented and unanticipated problems occur.

(a) The Appropriate Discount Rate for Capital Budgeting

The appropriate discount rate to use for discounting the cash flows should be commensurate with the project's risk. This rules out using the weighted average cost of capital (WACC) if the project does not have the same risk as the firm and will not be financed in the same proportion in terms of debt and equity as the overall firm.

18.2.13 *Relevant Cash Flows (Estimation of CFS)*

In capital budgeting problems, one needs to be careful about differentiating non relevant and relevant cash flows for inclusion of non-relevant cash flows may bias the decision to take on the project.

Learning Objectives

- Define and estimate relevant cash flows for capital investments

Main Takeaways

Main Points

- Operational cash flows are a measure of the amount of cash generated by a company's regular business operations.
- Financing cash flows are those originating from the issuance of debt or equity.
- Investment cash flows are cash generated or spent relating to investment activities.
- Free cash flow, a measure commonly used by analysts to assess a company's profitability, represents the cash a company generates after accounting for cash outflows to support operations and maintain its capital assets.

Main Terms

- **Sunk cost:** A sunk cost has already been incurred. You cannot change a sunk cost. On the other hand, today's decisions should be based on current and future cash flows and should not be affected by prior, or sunk, costs.
- **Opportunity cost:** The difference in return between an investment one makes and another that one chose not to make.

(a) Statement of Cash Flow in Financial Statement

A business's Statement of Cash Flows illustrates its calculated net cash flow. The net cash flow of a company over a period (typically a quarter or a full year) is equal to the change in cash balance over this period: It's positive if the cash balance increases (more cash becomes available); negative if the cash balance decreases. The total net cash flow is composed of several factors:

1. **Operational cash flows:** Cash received or expended due to the company's internal business activities. Operational cash flows include cash earnings plus changes to working capital. Over the medium term, this must be net positive if the company remains solvent.
2. **Investment cash flows:** Cash received from the sale of long-life assets or spent on capital expenditure, such as investments, acquisitions, and long-life assets.
3. **Financing cash flows:** Cash received from the issue of debt and equity or paid out as dividends, share repurchases, or debt repayments.

(b) Reasons for Relevant Cash Flow

In analyzing capital budgeting problems there are many cash flows to consider. However, not all cash flows are relevant to the project.

A test for whether a cash flow is relevant or not is the question of whether the cash flow arises as a result of the firm taking on the project.

Suppose the firm decides to manufacture and sell a new line of vacuum cleaners. It would produce them in a new factory to be built on land that it owns. Six months ago, the firm commissioned a feasibility study regarding how to use the land. What arc the relevant cash flows for this project?

The cash flows arising from the sale of the new vacuum cleaner and the cost to manufacture and sell them would be relevant costs. So would the cost of building the factory. Would the cost for the feasibility study be relevant?

If the firm uses the land to build the factory, it foregoes using it for other purposes. It could rent the land or even sell it if the firm does not want the land for itself. This means that the value of the land is a relevant cash flow and represents a cost for the project. This cost of foregoing other uses is known as opportunity cost. As the cost of the feasibility study was incurred in the previous year, it is a *sunk cost,* and was not incurred because of the project. It is relevant as far as the project is concerned.

The new vacuum cleaner line may result in the cannibalizing or loss of sales from the existing vacuum cleaners that the firm is currently selling. This side effect of the loss of existing sales should be factored in the project analysis.

18.2.14 *Computing Operational Cash Flow* (*Estimation of CFS*)

Operating cash flow includes all cash generated by a company's main business activities

Learning Objectives

- Define and compute operating cash flow (OCF).

Main Takeaways

Main Points

- Operational cash flows are a measure of the amount of cash generated by a company's regular business operations.

- There are two methods for depicting operating cash flow on a cash flow statement: the indirect and direct methods.
- Operating cash flow is crucial because it provides the analyst insight into the health of the company's core business or operations.
- The most common example of an operating expense that does not affect cash is depreciation.

Main Terms

- **Amortization:** The action or process of gradually writing off an asset's initial cost.
- **Depreciation:** Depreciation is an accounting method of allocating the cost of a tangible or physical asset over its useful life or life expectancy. Depreciation is a non-cash expense and ideally should not have any effect on the cash flows.
- **Net working capital:** Working capital, also known as net working capital (NWC), is the difference between a company's current assets and its current liabilities.

Example Step 1: Estimation of cash flow

To illustrate the cash flows arising from a project, we use the following example:

The Star Printing Press Company has received a new printing order. However, it is producing at full capacity. To accept the new order, the company would need to buy a new printing machine. The details relating to the order, the new machine, and other costs are shown below:

Year	1	2	3
Sales	$800,000	$880,000	$9,600,000

Variable cost = 80% of sales

The project requires an additional net working capital of $30,000, which is sufficient for the duration of the project.

Cost of new machine = $400,000

Life of machine = 3 years

Salvage value of the machine at the end of 3 years = $100,000

Depreciation is straight line to zero over 3 years

Cost savings from using new machine per year = $10,000

To estimate the cash flows, we group them into three sets.

(a) Initial Investment

These are the cash outflows that the firm needs to incur at the beginning of the project to get it started. The initial investment consists of:

Cost of new asset
+ Installation and delivery cost
– Investment tax credit (if any)
+ Additional working capital
Initial Investment

Should there be any installation and delivery costs, they should be added to the cost of the asset. The rationale is that the asset should be functional and any costs that are needed to ensure it is should be incorporated in the asset cost. The total cost is called the depreciable outlay on which depreciation is based.

Working capital consists of current assets such as cash, accounts receivable, and inventory that the firm needs for its operations. As the business scale of operations increases, there should be a corresponding increase in the working capital. For simplicity, the working capital level is increased at the beginning of the project. This increase in working capital is considered part of the initial investment.

For the example, the initial investment is:

Cost of the new machine	$400,000
+ Additional working capital	$30,000
Initial investment	$430,000

Example Step 2: Estimating operating cash flows

The operating cash flows refer to the net benefits received over the project's life. To compute these cash flows, we use the income statement framework. For example, the operating cash flows would be:

Year	**1**	**2**	**3**
Sales	800,000	880,000	960,000
Less Variable cost (80%)	(640,000)	(704,000)	(768,000)
Gross profit	160,000	176,000	192,000
Plus cost savings	10,000	10,000	10,000
EBITDA	170,000	186,000	202,000
Less Depreciation	(100,000)	(100,000)	(100,000)
EBIT	70,000	86,000	102,000

Less Tax @ 30%	(21,000)	(25,800)	(30,600)
NOPAT	91,000	111,800	132,600
OCF (NOPAT + Dep)	191,000	211,800	232,600

The operating cash flow is found by adding the depreciation expense to the net operating profit after tax (NOPAT). As depreciation is a non-cash expense it does not affect the cash flow.

18.2.15 *Computing Cash Flow from Asset (Estimation of CFS)*

Cash flow from assets is the total of all cash flows related to the project.

Learning Objectives
- Define and compute cash flow from the asset.

Main Takeaways

Main Points
- Cash flow from assets is computed by subtracting capital spending and additions to net working capital from your operating cash flow, and adding.
- A *negative cash flow from assets* should not be of concern as it indicates that the firm is investing.
- This measure does not account for the effect of financing. An increase in borrowing or the sale of stock can offset any negative cash flow from assets.

Main Terms
- **Salvage value:** The estimated value of an asset that the company expects to when it disposes the asset at the end of its useful life.

Example Step 3: Estimating terminal cash flow
At the end of the project we must consider a few cash flows besides the operating cash flow for that year. The other cash flows are:

1. Return of working capital;
2. Salvage value of the asset less any tax adjustment.

The tax adjustment is needed if the salvage value and book value are not equal. For our project both values are equal. So there is no need for any tax adjustment.

However, if there is a difference between the two values, the result is under- or over-depreciation of the machine and the consequently over- or under-payment of tax. Here's an example:

Cost of machine = \$10,000
Expected life = 5 years
Expected salvage value = \$2,000 at the end of its life
Sale of machine at end of life = \$1,000

Annual depreciation on straight-line basis of the machine = (\$10,000 − \$2,000)/5 = \$1,600

Total depreciation = \$1,600 × 5 = \$8,000.
Depreciation allowed based on correct salvage value = (\$10,000 − \$1,000) = \$9,000

Therefore firm under-depreciated machine by \$9,000 − \$8,000 = \$1,000

Taxes overpaid = \$1,000 × 30% = \$300

For the example, all three sets of cash flows are summarized in the table below:

Year	0	1	2	3
OCF		191,000	211,800	232,600
Cost of new machine	(400,000)			
Change in net working capital	(30,000)			30,000
Salvage value of machine				100,000
Less Tax on salvage value				(30,000)
CFFA	(430,000)	191,000	211,800	332,600

Reference/Further Reading

Ross, S., Westerfield, R., & Jordan, B. (2002). *Fundamentals of Corporate Finance*, 6th edn. McGraw-Hill Irwin, Chaps. 9 and 10.

18.3 Sample Questions

Question 1

Given the following cash flows for a capital project, calculate its payback period and DPP. The required rate of return is 10%.

Year	0	1	2	3
Cash flow	−30,000	15,000	15,000	15,000

The DPP is:

(a) 0.15 years longer than the payback period.
(b) 0.25 years longer than the payback period.
(c) 0.35 years longer than the payback period.

Question 2

If the required rate of return is 10% and the cash flows are shown below. The NPV and IRR are nearest to:

Year	0	1	2	3
Cash flow	−30,000	15,000	15,000	15,000

	NPV	IRR
(a)	$6,105	19.9%
(b)	$7,303	23.4%
(c)	$8,656	26.9%

Question 3

You purchase a perpetual bond that costs $1,000. It pays a tax-free coupon of $60 a year. If the required rate of return is 5%, compute the investment's profitability index.

(a) 1.05
(b) 1.06
(c) 1.20

Question 4
Which one of the following is an example of a sunk cost?

(a) $15,000 cost of market analysis done last year
(b) $3,000 lost sales because item was out of stock
(c) $10,000 non-refundable deposit if building if firm chooses to lease another building

Use the following data for Questions 5 and 6.
You are asked to evaluate the two projects below. Use a discount rate of 10%.

	Project A	Project B
Initial cost	$10,000	$15,000
Life	4 years	3 years
Cash inflows	$3,500/year	$6,000/year

Question 5
What is your decision if the projects are independent?

(a) accept Project A and reject Project B
(b) reject Project A and accept Project B
(c) accept both projects

Question 6
What is your decision if the projects are independent?

(a) accept Project A and reject Project B
(b) reject Project A and accept Project B
(c) reject both projects

Question 7
In estimating the incremental cash flows from a project, which is most likely to be excluded?

(a) interest costs
(b) externalities
(c) opportunity costs

Question 8

In evaluating two projects, the conflict in ranking between IRR and NPV will:

(a) Never occur
(b) Occur when the discount rate is higher than the cross-over rate of the two NPV profiles
(c) Occur when the discount rate is lower than the cross-over rate of the two NPV profiles

Question 9

You own a store selling gift items. In which of the following scenarios would you use NPV or IRR?

1. Opening another store
2. Deciding how many items to order for the coming Christmas holidays
3. Selling snacks in addition to the gift items

(a) I only
(b) I and II only
(c) I and III only

Question 10

IRR analysis may fail to give the same ranking as NPV analysis when

(a) The required rate of return is too high
(b) Projects are independent
(c) Projects are mutually exclusive

Solutions

Question 1

Solution: Option **c** is correct.

Year	0	1	2	3
Cash flow	−30,000	15,000	15,000	15,000
Cumulative	−30,000	−35,000	0	15,000
Discounted CF	−30,000	13,636.36	12,396.69	11,269.72
Cumulative DCF	−30,000	−16,363.64	−3,966.94	7,302.78

The cumulative cash flow offsets the initial investment in exactly 2 years from the table above. The payback period is 2 years. The DPP is between 2 and 3 years. The DPP is 2 + 3.966.94/3,966.94 + 7302.78 = 2.35 years. The DPP is 2.35 − 2.00 = 0.35 years longer than the payback period.

Question 2

Solution: Option **b** is correct.

$NPV = -30{,}000 + 15{,}000/1.1 + 15{,}000/(1.1)^2 + 15{,}000/(1.1)^3$
$NPV = -30{,}000 + 13{,}636.36 + 12{,}396.69 + 11{,}269.72$
$NPV = 7{,}302.78$

The IRR, found with a financial calculator, is 23.4%.

Question 3

Solution: Option **c** is correct.

The present value of future cash flows is PV = 60/0.05 =1,200

The profitability index is PI= PV/Investment = 1,200/1,000 =1.2

Question 4

Solution: Option **b** is correct.

Sunk cost refers to money that has already been spent and cannot be recovered.

Question 5

Solution: Option **c** is correct.

Using financial calculator, NPVs for both projects are:

A: $N = 4$, $I = 10$, PMT = 3,500; NPV = 3,713
B: $N = 3$, $I = 10$, PMT = 6,000; NPV = 2,703

For independent projects, accept all projects with positive NPV

Question 6

Solution: Option **a** is correct.

Accept the project with the higher NPV.

Question 7

Solution: Option **a** is correct.

The financing cost of the project is taken into account through the discounting process.

Question 8

Solution: Option **c** is correct.

The conflict in ranking occurs when the discount rate is lower than the cross-over rate. From the diagram showing graphs of the two NPV profiles we see that project C's IRR is higher than project B.

Question 9

Solution: Option **c** is correct.

Scenario I about opening another store requires capital budgeting evaluation. So does Scenario II which is starting a different line of business. Scenario II is an operational issue.

Question 10

Solution: Option **b** is correct.

Option **b** is correct. When projects are independent, NPV > 0, implies IRR > discount rate. So a project that is accepted by NPV will also be accepted by IRR. However, when projects are mutually exclusive, there may be a conflict in ranking so a Project accepted by NPV may not be accepted, so Option **c** is not the answer. Option **a** is not correct as it is vague how high the required return must be.

Part H: Working Capital Management

Chapter 19

Sources of Short-Term Liquidity

19.1 Primary and Secondary Sources

19.1.1 *Primary and Secondary Sources of Liquidity*

Primary and secondary sources are generally the two major sources of liquidity for a company. For a company, its sources of liquidity are all the resources that can be used to generate cash.

Learning Objectives

- Define the primary and secondary sources of liquidity.

Main Takeaways

Main Points

- Primary sources of liquidity are the cash the company holds, investments in very liquid short-term securities like certificates of deposit and money market securities, and the cash flow generated in the business.
- Secondary sources of liquidity include reducing the amount needed to service the debt obligations by negotiating with lenders to extend the maturity, cash flow generated from liquidating assets and filing for bankruptcy and reorganization. The last method allows the firm to stop payments to its creditors while reorganizing its business.
- A firm's liquidity position is affected by how the cash inflow or cash outflow is affected.

Main Terms

- **Liquidity management:** Liquidity management refers to the process a company uses to ensure it meets its short-term financial obligations.
- **Drag on liquidity:** A drag on liquidity results when the accounts receivable are collected slowly. The slow collection means that funds are needed to cover the cash flow that would have been available if accounts receivable are collected more efficiently.
- **Pull-on liquidity:** A pull on liquidity results when the firm is paying suppliers of goods or services too quickly. It could also result from the limited availability of trade credit. Pull-on liquidity implies that the firm needs funds to cover the period from the disbursements of cash to receipt of cash from sales.

Working capital management is the process of managing a firm's short-term assets and short-term liabilities to ensure that it has sufficient liquidity to meet its payments due. The payments consist of paying short-term liabilities like accounts payables and expenses incurred in the firm's operations. Besides managing the cash, the firm has to manage the other components of current assets like accounts receivable, inventory, and accounts payable.

To meet its liquidity needs, the firm can tap on two liquidity sources, namely the primary and the secondary sources. The primary sources of liquidity involve the company's normal operations, whereas the secondary financing sources do not.

(a) Primary Sources of Liquidity

Primary sources of liquidity represent resources that are readily accessible for the firm's use when needed. When using primary sources of liquidity, a company's normal operations are not expected to be impacted.

Primary sources include:

- Cash balances in bank accounts, cash collected from customers, and cash resulting from the sale or maturing of money market instruments held.
- Short-term funds consist of trade credit, lines of credit from the bank, and short-term investment portfolios.
- Cash flow management is the company's effectiveness in managing its cash. This involves the efficient use of its system for collection of

payments. It also involves consolidating their funds at different locations for firms with many sites. A large bank aids consolidation by having branches in many of the firms' locations to facilitate banking services. Further consolidation across the firm's many accounts means a lower cash balance needs to be maintained with one bank than the combined cash balances across the different banks when many banks are involved.

(b) Secondary Sources of Liquidity

Unlike primary sources of liquidity, using a secondary source may change the company's financial and operating positions.

Secondary sources include:

- Negotiating with the lenders to restructure the debt so it could be paid over a more extended period, resulting in lower current payments of interest and partial repayment principal where required.
- Selling assets to raise cash, for example, selling the buildings the firm occupies and leasing them back from the buildings' purchasers.
- Filing for bankruptcy protection and reorganization allows the firm to stop payment to its creditors while reorganizing its business temporarily.

Secondary sources should be used only after exhausting the primary sources' funds as tapping on secondary sources may send a negative signal regarding the firm's business prospects. As a last resort, the firm can file for bankruptcy protection as this temporarily suspends payments to its creditors. Such a move allows the firm to continue its business operations until a restructuring plan has been devised and approved.

(c) Factors that Impact a Company's Liquidity Position

Cash flow transactions (cash receipts and disbursements) significantly affect a company's liquidity position. We refer to these effects as drags and pulls on liquidity. A drag on liquidity is when the accounts receivable is collected too slowly. This means that when funds are needed for payments, the firm cannot count on the funds that would have been available if collections of accounts receivable had been more efficient. Consequently, the firm needs to provide funds to cover this gap between when payments have to be made and when the cash is received from customers.

Suppose accounts receivable are not collected in a timely fashion. With payments, the outflow of funds will result in a "drag" on liquidity duc to the decreased availability of funds.

Drags on liquidity include:

- Uncollected receivables.
- Obsolete inventory.
- Difficulty in accessing short term funds due to tight credit conditions.

If payments are made too early, a pull on liquidity will result as the cash balance will be drawn down before it is replenished from funds received through sales. Pulls on liquidity include:

- Making payments early.
- Reduced credit limits from suppliers.
- Limits on the amount available for short-term borrowing.
- Low liquidity position in the firm.

19.2 Evaluation of Short-Term Funding

19.2.1 *Operating Cycle and Cash Conversion Cycle*

The operating and cash conversion cycles (CCCs) are measures of liquidity that are used to gauge a company's operational and financial effectiveness.

Learning Objectives

- Calculate the firm's operating cycle (OC) and CCC and use those measures to assess the firm's effectiveness in managing its working capital.

Main Takeaways

Main Points

- The OC is the time taken between the receipt of the inventory and the receipt of cash from the goods' sale.
- The OC is the sum of two periods: days' sales in inventory and average collection period.
- The CCC measures the period between the payment for inventory bought and cash receipt from the sale of goods.

- CCC is the difference between the OC and the accounts payable period which is the average time the firm takes to pay its bills.

Main Terms

- **Inventory:** It is the term for the goods available for sale and raw materials used to produce goods available for sale.
- **Receivable:** A receivable or account receivable is the debt owed by a customer for goods sold or service provided that has not been paid for.
- **Payable:** A payable or account payable is the amount owed by a firm to a supplier for either goods bought or service provided.

Firms in an economy typically sell products or services. For simplicity, our discussion will focus on companies that deal with products, whether as manufacturers or retailers.

A manufacturer buys raw materials, converts them into a finished product, and then sells it. On the other hand, a retailer buys a finished product for resale. In either case, goods (raw materials or finished goods) are bought on credit and need to be repaid later, a period known as the **accounts payable period**. Meanwhile, time is needed before the raw material is transformed into a finished product and sold. For the retailer, the wholesaler's goods take some time to be sold. In either case, that period is known as the **inventory period**.

If the good is sold on credit, the time between the sale and when cash is collected is known as the **accounts receivable period**. The **OC** is the time interval beginning when a good is bought and received until the money is received from the sale of the good. It consists of the inventory period and the accounts receivable period. A graphical illustration of an OC is depicted in Figure 19.1.

The OC is calculated as follows:

$$\text{Operating cycle} = \text{Inventory period} + \text{Accounts receivable period}$$

where

$$\text{Inventory period} = \frac{365}{\text{Inventory turnover}}$$

$$\text{Accounts receivable period} = \frac{365}{\text{Accounts receivable turnover}}$$

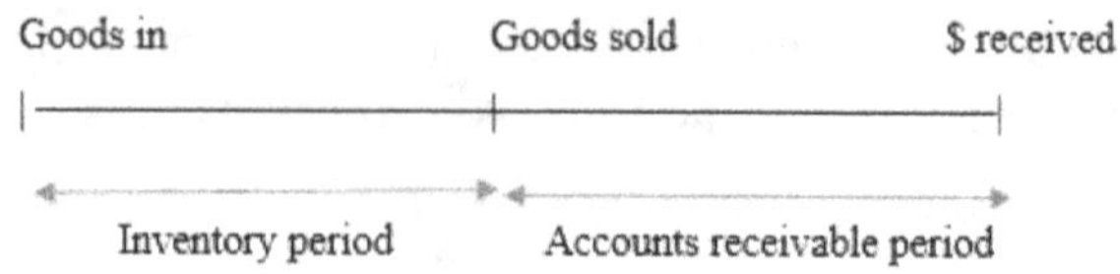

Figure 19.1: Graphical illustration of the OC.

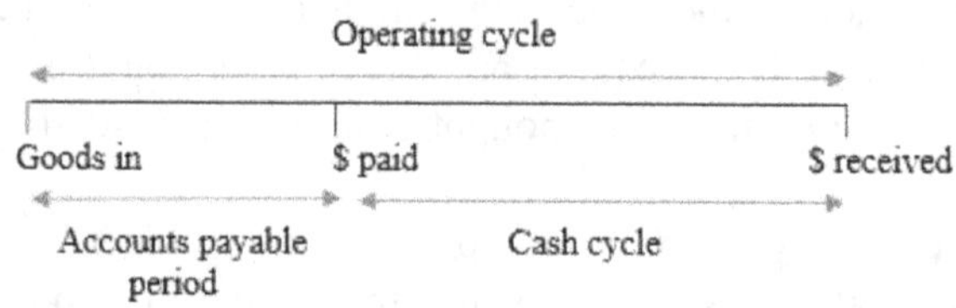

Figure 19.2: Graphical illustration of the cash cycle.

The **cash cycle** is the period between paying out cash for goods bought earlier from the suppliers and then receiving the cash from the customers.

The cash that is needed to cover this mismatch in the cash flows' timing is part of working capital. Refer to Figure 19.2 for an illustration of the cash cycle.

The cash cycle is calculated as follows:

$$\text{Cash cycle} = \text{Operating cycle} - \text{Accounts payable period}$$

where

$$\text{Accounts payable period} = \frac{365}{\text{Accounts payable turnover}}$$

Can the cash cycle be negative? Yes! If money is paid for the goods by the customers before the firm needs to pay its suppliers. Thus the firm does not need to start with a pool of cash to pay its creditors first. An example is a restaurant that collects cash from its diners but gets credit from its suppliers.

The diagram below shows the timing regarding the goods and the cash flows in a situation where the cash cycle is negative. Remember that

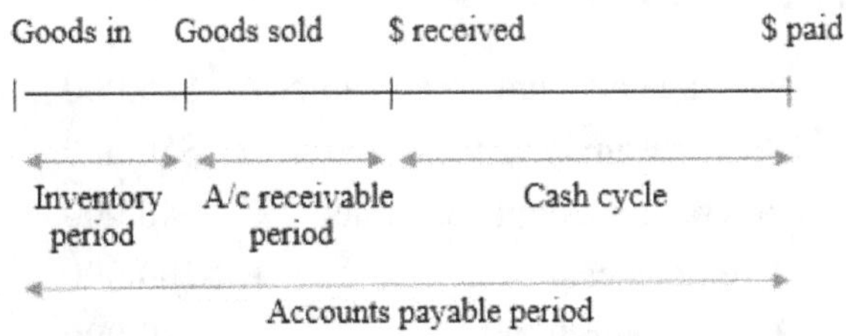

Figure 19.3: Graphical representation of a negative cash cycle.

the cash cycle is measured from the time cash is paid to the firm's creditors until cash is received from the customers (Figure 19.3).

When the cash flow sequence is reversed, where cash is received from customers first followed by payment to the creditors, a negative cash cycle is the result. What are the implications of such a situation for liquidity ratios like the current ratio?

$$\text{Current ratio} = \frac{\text{Current assets}}{\text{Current liabilities}}$$

The cash to pay its suppliers for a typical company comes from customers' payment of the accounts receivable. However, if the firm cannot sell what it manufactures or bought from the wholesaler or if customers who purchased the product are slow in paying or fail to pay, the firm will be in a difficult position to make payments to its suppliers. For this reason, firms need a much larger amount of current assets compared to their current liabilities, that is, have a current ratio much greater than one. The excess of the current assets versus the current liabilities serves as a buffer for the customers' delay in making payments.

However, for a firm with a negative cash cycle, its OC is much shorter than its accounts payable period. It can better manage its cash flows as its receipts from customers come before the payments due to its suppliers. It does not need to maintain the buffer of additional current assets versus the current liabilities, and its current ratio can be much lower than one.

Managing the cash cycle is part of the firm's overall cash management. In a later section on the cash budget, we show how the cash received from customers and the cash paid to the suppliers are combined with the other cash inflows and cash outflows of the firm.

Example:

Average accounts receivable:	$25,000
Average inventory:	$50,000
Average accounts payable:	40,000
Credit sales:	$300,000
Cost of goods sold:	$180,000
Total purchases:	$200,000

What are the OC and the cash cycle?

Solution:

Receivables Period: The receivables turnover rate is the number of times, on average, that the business collects on from its customers the credit extended to them. Receivables turnover = Credit sales/Average accounts receivable = 300,000/25,000 = 12 times.

Receivables period = 365 days/receivables turnover = 365/12 = 30.42 days. On average, customers take about 30.42 days to pay on credit extended to them. If the firm gives its customers a 30-day credit period, the receivables period of 30.42 days means that the customers are, on average, paying up promptly on their credit.

Inventory Period: The inventory turnover rate indicates the number of times that raw materials or goods come into the firm before they are sold to customers. Another way to look at it is the number of times during the year that a firm replaces its inventory. Inventory turnover is cost of goods sold/Average inventory = 180,000/50,000 = 3.6 times.

Inventory period = 365 days/Inventory turnover = 365/3.6 = 101.39 days. On average, the inventory stays on the shelf for 101.39 days before they are sold. If the firm is selling durable goods like TVs and furniture, an inventory period of this length may be quite reasonable. However, it would be a concern if the goods sold are sitting on the supermarket shelves for more than three months.

Payables Period: The accounts payable period is somewhat similar to the accounts receivable period except that we are dealing with the payments to the firm's suppliers. The computation of this period is as follows:

Accounts payable turnover = Total purchases/Average accounts payable
= 200,000/40,000 = 5 times

Payables period = 365/Accounts payable turnover = 365/5 = 73 days. On average, it takes 73 days to pay the suppliers. If suppliers give the firm 60 days to pay up, the company may want to expedite its payments. The firm needs to have a reputation for being prompt in its payments, especially for key suppliers. When supplies are constrained, for example, through disruptions in the supply chain, suppliers will ration the available stocks they have to their better customers. Those customers lower down the line in terms of their relationship with the supplier will have low priority to get the scarce stocks.

Operating Cycle: The OC is the period that stretches from the time inventory is bought to the time the firm receives money from the sale of that inventory. The OC comprises two periods, the inventory period and the accounts receivable period.

For the firm, the OC = Inventory period + Accounts receivable period = 101.39 + 30.42 = 131.81 days.

Cash Cycle: The cash cycle is equal to the OC less the accounts payable period. It is the number of days for which the firm must finance its inventory and receivables.

$$\begin{aligned}\text{Cash cycle} &= \text{OC} - \text{Accounts payable period}\\ &= \text{Inventory period} + \text{Receivables period} - \text{Payables period}\\ &= 101.39 + 30.42 - 73 = 131.81 - 73 = 58.81 \text{ days}\end{aligned}$$

In this example, the firm must pay for its inventory 58.81 days before it collects its customers' payment from the inventory that was sold. Shortening this cash cycle period would reduce the amount needed for working capital.

Reference/Further Reading

Ross, S., Westerfield, R., & Jordan, B. (2002). *Fundamentals of Corporate Finance*, 6th edn. McGraw-Hill Irwin, pp. 666–699.

19.3 Sample Questions

Question 1
Which of the following are primary sources of liquidity?

(a) Negotiating with lenders to restructure debt
(b) Cash balances in bank accounts
(c) Filing for bankruptcy protection and reorganization

Question 2
Which one of the following is a definition of the cash cycle?

(a) Inventory period plus the accounts receivable period
(b) OC minus the inventory period
(c) OC minus the accounts payable period

Use the following data to answer the next two questions:

	($)
Credit sales	500,000
Cost of goods sold	200,000
Accounts receivable	80,000
Inventory	50,000
Accounts payable	60,000

Question 3
The OC is closest to:

(a) 95 days.
(b) 146 days.
(c) 150 days.

Question 4
The cash cycle is closest to:

(a) 40 days.
(b) 44 days.
(c) 58 days.

Use the following data to answer the next two questions:

Accounts receivable turnover = 7 times
Accounts payable turnover = 4 times
Inventory: The firm practises just-in-time inventory management and carries a negligible amount of inventory
The firm gives its customers a credit period of 60 days.
The firm's suppliers give a credit period of 80 days on average.

Question 5
The OC is closest to:

(a) 50 days.
(b) 60 days.
(c) 80 days.

Question 6
The cash cycle is closest to:

(a) −40 days.
(b) 20 days.
(c) 40 days.

Solutions

Question 1

Solution: Option **b** is correct.

Cash balances in bank accounts are an example of a primary source of liquidity.

Answers **a** and **c** are incorrect. Both would impact the firm's normal operations, especially in the case of reorganization of the firm under bankruptcy protection.

Question 2

Solution: Option **c** is correct.

The CCC comprises the sum of the days' sales in inventory and accounts receivable period less the accounts payable period.

Question 3

Solution: Option **c** is correct.

Inventory period = 365/(200,000/50,000) = 91.3 days

Accounts receivables period = 365/(500,000/80,000) = 58.4 days

OC = 91.3 + 58.4 = 149.7 days

Question 4

Solution: Option **a** is correct.

Accounts payable period = 365/(200,000/60,000) = 109.5 days

Cash cycle = OC − Accounts payable period = 149.7 − 109.5 = 40.2 days

Question 5

Solution: Option **a** is correct

Inventory period = 0

Accounts receivables period = 365/7 = 52.1 days

OC = 0 + 52.1 days = 52.1 days

Question 6

Solution: Option **a** is correct

Accounts payable period = 365/4 = 91.3 days

Cash cycle = OC − accounts payable period
= 52.1 − 91.3 = −39.2 days

Part I: Corporate Risk Management

Chapter 20

Framework and Types of Corporate Risks

20.1 Hedging Strategies

20.1.1 *Definition of Hedging Strategies*

A hedging strategy is a plan of action that aims to minimize the risk of price changes that adversely affect the value of assets or liabilities.

Learning Objectives

- Define corporate risk management and understand various hedging strategies.

Main Takeaways

Main Points

- Hedging is a risk management strategy that aims to offset losses in investments from adverse price movements. The hedge is done by taking an opposite position in a related asset.
- Hedging comes at a cost. While risk is reduced, the return is also reduced.
- In Corporate Finance, risk management involves measuring, monitoring, and controlling of both the operational and financial risks. The firm's risk can be summarized by a measure called value at risk (VaR). Particular aspects of the firm can also be monitored through profit at risk (PaR) or margin at risk.

Main Terms

- **Value at risk (VaR):** Measures the financial risk in terms of the amount of loss that the firm will sustain over a specific period with a certain level of confidence.
- **Profit at risk (PaR):** Measures the risk of a decline in profitability of a portfolio of physical and financial assets over a period. It is a measure often used in the energy industry.
- **Hedge:** A hedge is an investment made to offset the risk of adverse price movements in an asset.

A company faces internal or external factors that can negatively affect its profitability or even survival. Corporate risk management consists of measures that a company employs to minimize such risks. Risk management is not just the risk specialists' concern, but every employee has a part to play. To prevent losses due to adverse circumstances, the company institutes internal controls on people and technologies. While such systems are relatively comprehensive, they cannot cover all eventualities. Every employee has to be sensitive to possible developments that may affect the firm adversely in their sphere of responsibilities.

To manage risk, a company needs to know how exposed it is to adverse price movements or events. One measure of the overall risk exposure is VaR. VaR measures how much loss the firm will sustain over a specified period (usually a day) if adverse events strike. This measure entails a level of statistical confidence, with the VaR value increasing with higher confidence levels. In contrast to the firm's overall loss, PaR measures the amount of profitability of a portfolio of physical and financial assets that adverse events can diminish.

(a) Types of Risks

The five main corporate risk types include Strategic Risk, Compliance Risk, Financial Risk, Reputation Risk, and Operational Risk.

1. Strategic risk is the impact on the company arising from the failure of strategic business decisions.
2. Compliance risk comprises the legal and financial penalties for failing to comply with external regulations and laws.
3. Financial risk is the risk of losses arising from the firm using too much leverage to fund its investments and operations.
4. Reputational risk refers to the potential for events that affect the public's regard for the firm. Examples of such events are the recall of

tainted products or a high-level executive's arrest over corruption charges. The impact of such events is that customers or businesses lose confidence in the company's integrity and reduce their business dealings with the company.

5. Operational risk is the prospect of loss resulting from any event that disrupts business processes.

(b) Hedging Strategies

A hedging strategy is a method that a firm uses to minimize its risks. Such risks would adversely affect its revenues or costs. For example, a significant risk to a commodity producer is the fall in price of the commodity. For other firms, the increase in price for the raw materials that go into the product and the inability to pass on the increased cost to the customer would result in lower profitability. To mitigate such risks, firms may use financial instruments.

Hedging strategies can be broadly classified as follows:

1. **Forward contract:** This is a contract between two parties for buying or selling an asset at a specified price and on a specified date. For example, an airline could engage in forward contracts for its fuel to lock in a price it pays for it.
2. **Futures contract:** This is a contract between two parties for buying or selling assets on terms set by the futures exchange. The terms specify the price, quantity, and expiration of the contract.
3. **Money market:** The money market is where financial instruments with maturities of less than 1 year are transacted.
4. **Natural hedge:** A natural hedge is a strategy used to reduce the risk in a company's operations. An example of a natural hedge is a company that sells its products in a foreign country. To mitigate foreign currency risk the company can locate its production facility in that country. Much of the production costs are in the same foreign currency as the revenues.
5. **Hedge fund:** There are so many different hedge fund strategies that the only common characteristic of hedge funds is that they are lightly regulated. The first hedge fund strategy, which was used in the 1950s, embodies the concept of hedging. The fund tries to profit by buying stocks it believes are undervalued but hedges its investments by short-selling stocks in the same industry that are overvalued. Using this method of the fund is not exposed to market risk, which affects all stocks. If the market falls, the fund will lose on stocks it has bought. This loss is offset by the gains from the stocks that it has shorted.

20.2 Decision to Hedge

Hedging aims to enable the firm to mitigate the adverse effects of changes in prices of either the product it sells or its costs.

Learning Objectives

- Understand the decisions to hedge.

Main Takeaways

Main Points

- Changes in interest rates, exchange rates, or other market factors can adversely affect the firm's profitability. In their hedging decisions, some managers try to incorporate their outlooks regarding how prices would move. However, injecting a personal view regarding market movements carries an element of risk as market movements are essentially unpredictable.
- When the firm hedges, it has to weigh the benefits of hedging against the costs of obtaining the protection from hedging.

Main Terms

- **Cash flow:** Cash flow consists of the cash generated from sales of goods or services and the cash outflows to pay for expenses and purchase of raw materials or goods for resale.
- **Commodity:** A basic good used in commerce that is interchangeable with other goods of the same type. Commodities are most often used as inputs in producing other goods or services. The quality of a given commodity may differ slightly, but it is essentially uniform across producers.

20.2.1 *Reasons for Hedging*

- To achieve stability in cash flows.
- To fix either the sale price or purchase price of a commodity.
- To reduce the risks of the firm's outstanding position in a commodity.

A company attempts to sell its goods or services at relatively constant prices as variability in prices can affect demand. To do this, the company tries to remove the variability in the company's costs. Having relatively stable prices helps the company in its planning process. Price stability enables the company to focus on its core business and make longer-term commitments. To achieve price stability, the company often resorts to hedging.

There are multiple factors to consider in the hedging decision. For anticipated one-off events, such as an anticipated contract or an acquisition, the firm needs to decide whether to hedge fully or partially. In the case of a partial hedge, the hedge amount may be based on the probability of success. The firm increases the amount to hedge as the degree of certainty of the commitment increases. Ongoing exposure to foreign currency risks occurs when the company imports raw materials from overseas sources and sells them in foreign markets. The firm may want to consider using natural hedges, such as netting the costs against the revenues in the same currency. Other considerations include the period to hedge projected exposures and whether hedging delays an economic reality that the company will be subjected to.

The nature of the industry and the company's appetite for risk feature in the decision whether to hedge or not. Users and producers of commodities often hedge to ensure relative certainty of the price they pay for the commodity's purchase or the price they receive selling the commodity. For example, an oil producer may want to hedge the oil price it produces. Hedging enables the company to have a degree of certainty regarding its cash flows to plan its expenditures on investments such as exploring new oil fields.

References/Further Readings

Maginn, J., Tuttle, D., McLeavey, D., & Pinto, J. (2007). *Managing Investment Portfolios A Dynamic Process*, 3rd edn. CFA Institute, pp. 579–596, 598–604.

Ross, S., Westerfield, R., & Jordan, B. (2002). *Fundamentals of Corporate Finance*, 6th edn. McGraw-Hill Irwin, pp. 803–831.

20.3 Sample Questions

Question 1

Which of the following best describes market risk?

(a) the risk of loss due to inefficient markets
(b) the risk of loss due to market failure
(c) the risk of loss due to events that affect the whole market

Question 2

VAR is a measure of:

(a) systematic risk
(b) the maximum loss a company can sustain during a year
(c) the loss the company can sustain within a period with a given probability

Question 3

Risk management

(a) helps the company to recruit competent staff
(b) enables the company to avoid bankruptcy
(c) helps prevent the company from passing up profitable investment opportunities

Solutions

Question 1

Solution: Option **c** is correct.

Market risk is the risk that affects all securities in the market. Option a is not correct as market inefficiency affects single securities. Market failure refers to the market's inability to allocate resources, goods, or services efficiency.

Question 2

Solution: Option **c** is correct

VAR is a measure of risk that affects the company and is therefore not systematic. VAR factors in the probability of the loss during a period, so option b is not correct.

Question 3

Solution: Option **c** is correct

Risk management may not be an inducement for people to join the firm. While risk management can reduce the probability of bankruptcy occurring, it is no guarantee that the company would not become bankrupt. A company could not invest in a good opportunity if its risk management is deficient, as the investment would be deemed too risky.

Section 4: Investment Management

Part J: Equity Markets

Chapter 21

Introduction to Equity

Equity market is one of the major capital markets where corporations' equity securities trade. When a business is in the start-up phase, the business owners use their capital and funds borrowed from their friends, relatives, and banks, along with venture capitalists' funds, to run the company. As the company grows and requires more capital, the owners will turn to the general public to issue shares to raise funds.

When shares are issued, the corporation receives funds, usually known as share capital funds. In return for providing the funds, investors (also called the shareholders) obtain rights such as:

1. Electing the Board of Directors;
2. Voting in the general body meetings;
3. Sharing of the profits;
4. Claim a share of the business's residual value in case of liquidation.

These shares sold to a shareholder are commonly known as common or ordinary shares of the business.

When one invests in equity securities, cash flow from ownership of the stock comes in three forms:

1. Periodic dividends paid by the company.
2. A share repurchase (or buyback) where the company pays shareholders the share's market value.
3. Capital gains or loss from selling the security in the market.

This section focuses on the analysis of equity securities and their valuation.

21.1 The Need for Analysis

A critical approach to equity investing is for investors to determine equity security value and support if the security provides attractive opportunities.

Learning Objectives

- Discuss and understand the need for equity analysis and the concept of value.

Main Takeaways

Main Points

- Analysts gather and process information to make significant investment decisions, namely, the buy and sell recommendations.
- Equity securities represent ownership claims in companies. These can include Common Stocks, which typically have dividends rights, and the company's voting matters.

Main Terms

- **Dividends:** Shareholders receive dividend payments, usually in cash.
- **Liquidation:** An event that usually occurs when a company is insolvent, meaning it cannot pay its obligations when they are due.
- **Intrinsic value:** Refers to an investor's perception of the implicit value of an asset, such as a company, stock, option, or real estate.
- **Cash flow:** The net amount of cash and cash-equivalents transferred in and out of the business.
- **Discount fate:** In valuation models, the future cash flows are to be discounted at the appropriate risk-adjusted discount rate to arrive at the value.

All investments face uncertainty. When an investment is uncertain, one does not know the future cash flows at the time of investing.

When uncertainty is quantified, the investors will develop some risk measures for the investment. These risk measures would provide some degree of uncertainty.

In the case of equity, the future cash flows for an investor come from:

- future dividends potentially paid by the firm;
- the future selling price of the shares if the investor wants to sell the same after some time;
- the amount that a shareholder will receive in any case that of company's liquidation.

All these three cash flows are uncertain. Thc company pays dividends from the profits based on the dividend policy, and until the company announces a dividend for any period, the dividend is not known. When the company is likely to liquidate, and the cash flows in case of liquidation are also uncertain. The shares' future selling price is also unforeseeable at the purchase time. Thus, an equity investment is highly uncertain, and we need to get some risk measures that will assist in establishing the likely cash flows to the shareholders.

The stream of dividends paid in the future will be subject to the future cash flows that the company can make. Similarly, the possibility of liquidation and liquidating dividends will also rely on future cash flows. Since the shareholders have the right to future cash flows, the future selling price will also depend on future cash flows. Therefore, it is essential to estimate the future cash flows that the shareholders will receive to assess the investment's return potential and riskiness.

In fundamental analysis, the analyst would analyze the external environment and firm-specific resources and capabilities to forecast the future cash flows that a firm can generate and assess these cash flows' riskiness. The discount rate is dependent on the riskiness of the cash flow. Once the future cash flows are estimated, these cash flows are discounted at the risk-adjusted rate to arrive at the shares' value. The value is then compared to the market price to see whether the shares are undervalued or overvalued. Buying opportunities are the cases when stocks are considered undervalued and selling opportunities when shares are considered overvalued. Thus, the primary purpose of fundamental analysis is the valuation of shares.

21.1.1 *Concept of Value*

Ways to express share value include:

- Par value
- Book value

- Replacement value
- Liquidation value
- Intrinsic value

Of these, only intrinsic value has a relationship to the assets' earning power, upon which the market prices shares. Thus, Security Analysis is the approach used to calculate the share's intrinsic value. The definition of intrinsic value is as follows:

Value = or value is the sum of discounted future cash flows

All companies own assets currently and will also purchase more assets in the future. Thus, future cash flows will come from the company's assets and from assets generated in the future whenever the assets are purchased. Therefore, the value is the sum of two components: value arising from the assets currently owned and the value from assets purchased in the future. Now, the assets to be purchased in the future depend on the company's growth opportunities. As such, one can write the current value as follows:

Value = Present value of cash flow from assets that are in place now
+ Present value of growth opportunities

Reference/Further Reading

Pinto, J.E., Henry, E., Robinson, T.R., & Stowe, J.D. (2010). *Equity Asset Valuation*, 2nd edn. John Wiley & Sons, Inc., pp. 1–6.

Chapter 22

Characteristics of Stocks

22.1 Dividends, Stock Splits, Repurchase

Apart from distributing capital to shareholders through cash dividends, some organizations use special dividends and share repurchases.

Learning Objectives

- Describe characteristics in regular cash dividends, stock splits, share repurchase.

Main Takeaways

Main Points

- A stock split increases the number of shares outstanding without changing the firm's market capitalization.
- A stock split does not affect the firm's market capitalization; it merely changes the outstanding shares. Hence, decreasing the price per share as the number of shares outstanding increases.
- A share repurchase happens when a company buys its stock from public shareholders, consequently reducing shares outstanding.
- The dilution or increase of the shares outstanding means that even if profits remain the same, the earnings per share decrease.

Main Terms

- **Market capitalization:** The total market value of the equity in a publicly-traded entity.

- **Stock split:** To issue a higher number of new shares to replace old shares and effectively increase the number of shares outstanding without changing its market capitalization.
- **Repurchase:** To buy back a company's shares. The issuing company pays public shareholders for their shares.
- **Earnings per share (EPS):** Calculated as (Net Income − Dividends on Preferred Stock)/Outstanding Shares.

22.1.1 *Dividends*

The dividend discount models attempt to value stocks by discounting expected future cash dividends.

We note that the focus is on future cash dividends. A firm may announce a *stock dividend* (also known as a *bonus issue of shares*). A stock dividend is a type of dividend where a firm distributes additional shares of its common stock to shareholders instead of cash.

The stock dividend does not dilute existing shareholders as the stock dividend is distributed proportionately to existing shareholders. The stock dividend divides the "pie" into "smaller pieces" and does not affect the pie's value. In this regard, stock dividends are not relevant for valuation.

22.1.2 *Stock Splits*

Stock splits and reverse stock splits are identical to stock dividends in that they have zero economic effect on the company or its shareholders. *A stock split* involves an increase in the number of shares outstanding with a consequent decrease in the share price as the split has no value consequences on the overall firm.

An example of a stock split is a three-for-two stock split in which each shareholder is issued two additional shares for three shares currently owned. A *reverse stock split* involves a decrease in the number of shares outstanding that will increase in the share price. In a two-for-three reverse stock splits, each shareholder would receive two new shares for every two old three shares held, thereby reducing the number of shares outstanding by a third.

22.1.3 *Share Repurchase*

Unlike stock dividends and stock splits, share repurchases (or buyback) are an alternative to cash dividend payments. A **share repurchase (or**

buyback) is when a company uses cash to buy back its shares and re-absorb them from public or private investors. Shares repurchased are then not considered for dividends, voting, or computing earnings per share. While a share repurchase is akin to payment of cash dividends, other considerations by firms choosing to repurchase shares include:

1. Signaling management's belief that their shares are undervalued (or, more generally, to support share prices).
2. Increasing flexibility in timing and quantum of cash to shareholders compared with the distribution of cash.
3. Improving tax efficiency where tax rates on dividends exceed tax rates on capital gains.
4. Increasing the firm's ability to reduce dilution resulting from the exercise of employee stock options.

22.2 Dividend Payment Chronology

A dividend chronology depicts the timeline for a series of events that occur after a firm decides to pay dividends to its shareholders.

Learning Objectives

- Discuss dividend payment chronology.

Main Takeaways

Main Points

- The main dates in the dividend timeline are the declaration date, ex-dividend date, holder-of-record date, and payment date.
- The pay-out of regular cash dividends to common shareholders follows a fairly standard timeline after the company's board of directors' votes to pay the dividend.

Main Terms

- **Ex-dividend date:** The first day on which a new stock purchase will not be entitled to the dividend.
- **Holder of record date:** Holder-of-record date or the record date. The company determines it as the business day on which a shareholder listed in the company's records is deemed to have ownership of its shares to decide who can and who cannot receive a dividend when paid.

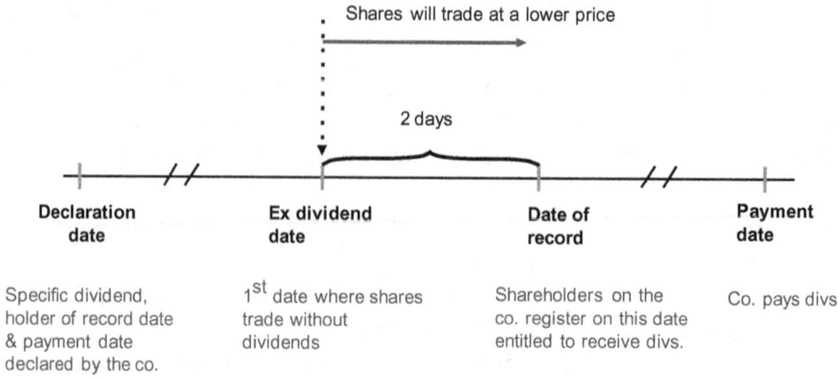

Figure 22.1: Dividend payment chronology.

The pay-out of regular cash dividends to common shareholders follows a fairly standard timeline once the company's board of directors' votes to pay the dividend. Figure 22.1 shows a timeline for dividend payment.

1. The **declaration** date. The day on which the company issues a statement declaring a specific dividend.
2. Next comes the **ex-dividend** date (or ex-date). The first date that a share trades without (i.e., "ex") the dividend.
3. Next is the **holder of record** date (also called the owner-of-record date, shareholder-of-record date, record date, date of record, or book closure date). This date is usually one or two business days later. Importantly, this is the date that a shareholder listed on the company's books will be deemed to have ownership of the shares for purposes of receiving the upcoming dividend.
4. Lastly comes the **payment** date (or payable date) when the company transfers by mail or electronically the shareholders' dividend payment.

Example:
Company A declares \$0.50 per share dividend on March 1, the ex-dividend date is March 21, and the date-of-record is March 23. The dividend payment date is March 28.

Clarin bought 2,000 shares on March 21, and Damian sold 1,000 shares on March 22. Will they receive dividends on March 28?

Solution:
As Clarin bought the shares ex-dividend on March 21, she will not receive the dividend on March 28.

Damian sold the shares on March 22 and remains on the company register to receive the dividend.

The likely impact on the share price, since buyers of a company's shares on the ex-dividend date, are not entitled to the upcoming dividend payment, all else being equal, the share price ex-dividend date decreases by the amount of the foregone dividend.

22.3 Sample Questions

Question 1
XYZ's share closing price was $5 on the day before the ex-dividend date, and the upcoming dividend is $0.25. All else remaining unchanged, the shares should start the trading day at _____ on the ex-dividend date.

(a) $4.75
(b) $5.00
(c) $5.25

Question 2
If an investor purchases shares before the company's ex-dividend date, which of the following statements is accurate?

(a) The investor will receive the dividend when the company pays it.
(b) The investor will not receive the dividend when the company pays it.
(c) The investor will receive a portion of the dividend when paid by the company.

Question 3
QPay, Inc. made the following dividend declaration:

"The Board of Directors of QPay, Inc. has declared a regular quarterly dividend of $0.20 per share payable June 10, 2020 (a Wednesday) to all stockholders-of-record as of the close of business on May 21, 2020 (a Thursday)."

Assuming a two-day settlement for QPay stock and no holidays in the weeks surrounding the record and payment dates, determine the ex-dividend date.

(a) Monday, May 18, 2020
(b) Tuesday, May 19, 2020
(c) Wednesday, May 20, 2020

Solutions

Question 1

Solution: Option **a** is correct.

On the ex-dividend date, all else remaining unchanged, one should subtract the upcoming dividend value of $0.25 from the previous day's closing price. The reason for doing so is because the buyer of the share on the ex-dividend date will not be eligible for that next dividend payment.

Question 2

Solution: Option **a** is correct.

If a buyer purchases shares before the ex-dividend date, the shares' buyer will receive the dividend. If the buyer buys the shares on or after the ex-dividend date, the buyer will not be paid the upcoming dividend.

Question 3

Solution: Option **b** is correct

With a two-day settlement, the ex-dividend date would be two days before the holder-of-record date, which would be Tuesday, May 19, 2020. If an investor bought QPay on Monday, May 18, 2020, they would settle for it before Thursday, May 21, 2020 and would be the holder-of-record at the close of trading on that date. Hence they would receive the dividend. As such, the shares will go ex-dividend on Tuesday, May 19. Wednesday May 20 is within the ex-dividend period but is not the day the share goes ex-dividend.

Chapter 23

Fundamentals Analysis of Equity

The fundamental analysis usually follows a top-down method that requires an economic analysis followed by an analysis of the industry and the company analysis. Fundamental analysis can take on either; a top-down approach or a bottom-up approach. The bottom-up approach begins by looking at a company first.

In a top-down approach, one takes the following steps:

1. Assessing the economic outlook.
2. Conducting the industry analysis.
3. Performing the company analysis.
4. Identifying inputs needed to forecast future cash flows.
5. Forecasting future cash flows.
6. Selecting an appropriate valuation model.
7. Estimating the appropriate discount rate.
8. Applying the valuation model to forecast future cash flows.
9. Calculating the value per share.
10. Making the appropriate recommendations.

23.1 Industry Analysis

23.1.1 *Strategic Analysis*

Strategic analysis is a process that involves researching an organization's business environment within which it operates. On the other hand, an organization's strategy is articulated across many organizational levels, including corporate and business, and functional units. For example, an approach like differentiation while being cost-effective has underpinned a global airline's success over several decades.

Learning Objectives

- Explain the principles of strategic analysis of an industry.

Main Takeaways

Main Points

- Industry analysis facilitates understanding a company's business and its business environment, allowing one to identify active equity investment opportunities.
- Industries differ in their market structure resulting in differing competitive environments. Recall that the competitiveness level within an industry is closely related to industries' profitability and the companies within them.
- A crucial component of industry analysis involves strategic analysis to look at the level of competition within an industry and then consider the implications of the corporate strategy environment.

Main Terms

- **Strategic analysis:** Formulate strategic plans for the organization's decision-making and smooth working.
- **Corporate strategy:** The highest-level plans of an organization define the corporate goal and direction.
- **Business strategy:** Actions and directions that a business takes to be competitive in its industry.

For a thorough analysis of a company, an analyst must understand its context. Ultimately, industry analysis facilitates understanding a company's business and its business environment, allowing one to identify active investment opportunities.

Industries differ in their market structure resulting in differing competitive environments. Recall that the competitiveness within an industry is closely related to industries' profitability and the companies within them (see Module 1A1 Chapter 3 Market Structure). Some industries are highly competitive, with companies having difficulties earning returns above their cost of capital. In contrast, others have unique characteristics that allow a larger number of industry participants to make healthy profits.

This observation is one reason why industry analysis is vital to analyzing a company.

In industry analysis, one should also think of the attributes that could change in the future. For example, while the airline business in the US had been highly competitive, the level of competitiveness may have moderated perhaps in the selected market within the US given the significant consolidation within the industry.

An important component of industry analysis involves strategic analysis to look at the level of competition within an industry and then consider the implications of the environment for corporate and business strategy. Michael Porter's "five forces" framework underpins a strategic analysis. Internal managers of the company and outside analysts use Porter's framework. Porter (2008) identified the following five considerations of the intensity of competition in an industry:

1. The threat of entry to the industry considers barriers to entry or how difficult it would be for new competitors to enter the industry. Sectors that are easy to join will generally be more competitive than industries with high entry barriers.
2. Suppliers' power allows them to raise prices or limit inputs to a company. Suppliers of rare or limited parts often retain considerable pricing power.
3. The power of buyers can impact competition's intensity by exercising suppliers' authority regarding prices.
4. The threat of substitutes can negatively affect demand if customers choose other satisfying needs.
5. The rivalry among existing competitors is a function of the industry's competitive structure.

An analyst should address the above points, especially in evaluating the threat of new entrants and the level of competition in an industry, thereby providing a good base for the industry's study and interpretation.

23.1.2 *Barriers to Entry*

A barrier to entry is a fixed cost that must be incurred by a new entrant, regardless of production or sales activities, into a market that incumbents do not have or have not had to incur.

Learning Objectives

- Describe the effects of barriers to entry.

Main Takeaways

Main Points

- All else being the same, a company's ability to sustain economic profits depends on the level of entry barriers in the industry it operates.
- The height of entry barriers to potential entrants is an important determinant of the economic profit achieved within an industry.

Main Terms

- **Pricing power:** Defines the effect of a change in a product price based on the quantity demanded of that product.
- **Economic profits:** An economic profit or loss is the difference between the revenue received from the sale of an output and the costs of all inputs used and any opportunity costs. Deducting opportunity costs and explicit costs from revenues earned to give the economic profit.
- **Economy of scale:** Are cost advantages when companies achieve efficiency (usually producing to size to benefit from the quantity produced).

All else being the same, a company's ability to sustain economic profits depends on the level of entry barriers in the industry it operates in. One of the main elements defining competition within an industry is how competitors can challenge the incumbents. If new entrants can enter without much effort, the industry will likely be highly competitive. Such an environment would see high returns on invested capital quickly competed away by new entrants who are eager for their share of the economic profits. Incumbent companies in industries with low entry barriers have minimal pricing power. Any price increases that raise the companies' returns on capital will draw new entrants to the industry.

When barriers to entry protect incumbents, there is a lower threat of new entrants, and incumbents may enjoy a more-friendly competitive environment. These entry barriers can often lead to greater pricing power because potential competitors would find it hard to enter the industry and undercut incumbents' prices. Of course, high entry barriers do not always promise pricing power because incumbents may compete fiercely with each other.

Theoretically, any firm should enter and exit a market, and if free entry and exit exist, profits always should be nominal. In reality, however, industries possess characteristics that protect firms' high profit levels and inhibit other rivals from entering the market. These are barriers to entry that advantage the incumbents relative to new entrants.

Examples of entry barriers include economies of scale, steep learning curve, access to distribution channels, and access to capital. Some companies can differentiate and gain customer loyalty, invest in research to develop patents, and develop processes such that it is costly for its customers to switch. Regulatory and unique tax benefits are other examples.

To summarize, the height of entry barriers to potential entrants is a critical determinant of the economic profit achieved within an industry, translating to that growth's profit growth and duration. Industry profitability moderates if entry barriers are low, entry threat is high.

While high entry barriers can lead to better pricing and less competitive industry conditions, barriers to entry do not guarantee success. High entry barriers do not necessarily lead to good pricing power and attractive industry economics. Barriers to entry can also change over time.

23.1.3 *Industry Concentration and Capacity*

Concentration within an industry can be defined as the degree to which a small number of firms make up for the market's total production.

Learning Objectives

- Define the relation of industry concentration and industry capacity to industry analysis.

Main Takeaways

Main Points

- Although not always, industry concentration is most common, a sign that the industry may have pricing power and rational competition. However, industry fragmentation is a much better signal that the industry is competitive and pricing power is limited.
- Tight or limited capacity gives participants higher pricing power, whereas overcapacity often leads to price cuts along with an immensely competitive environment as the surplus in supply chases demand.

- An analyst should not only just focus on current capacity conditions but also focus on future capacity. An in-depth analysis will allow the analyst to recognize its duration for suppliers to react to demand changes.

Main Terms

- **Fragmented industry:** A composition of many companies within the same industry that compete, but there is no single or small group of companies that dominate the industry.
- **Absolute market share:** The market share of a company is calculated by dividing its sales by the total sales in its market. The result is presented in percentage points, showing the percentage of a market that a company represents.

(a) Industry Concentration

Concentrated industries with a comparatively small number of players often experience comparably lower price competition. Yet, there are exceptions, and one should not merely presume that concentrated industries always have pricing power or that fragmented sectors do not.

A fragmented industry is one with many companies where not a single or small group of companies dominate. Such industries tend to be highly price competitive. The reasons being:

1. A large number of companies makes coordination difficult because there are too many competitors for each industry member to monitor effectively.
2. Each player has such a small piece of the market that even a small gain in market share can make a meaningful difference to its profitability, which increases the incentive of each company to undercut prices and attempt to steal market share.
3. Many players encourage industry members to think independently rather than as members of a group, leading to aggressive competitive behavior.

Although not always, industry concentration is most common, a sign that the industry may have pricing power and rational competition. However, industry fragmentation is a much better signal that the industry is competitive and pricing power is limited.

Essential exceptions exist in concentrated industries with weak pricing power and fragmented industries yet with strong pricing power. The level of industry concentration is just a guideline. An example of such exceptions might be markets dominated by a few large grocery chains without any pricing power that need to confront low customer switching costs and the sale of commoditized products that lack differentiation.

(b) Industry Capacity

The effect of industry capacity (the maximum amount of goods or services that can be supplied in a given period) on pricing power is relatively straightforward: Under tight or limited capacity, participants possess increased pricing power with demand for the goods or service exceeding supply. In an overcapacity situation, prices are reduced in an immensely competitive environment with excess supply chasing demand.

In looking at industry capacity, an analyst should consider the current capacity conditions and future capacity levels. Important questions include the time it takes for demand and supply to reach equilibrium and if the strained supply conditions are sustainable.

In general, it takes a longer time to shift physical capacity than to move financial or human capital to new uses.

23.2 Industry Life Cycle

23.2.1 *Industry Life Cycle and Limitations*

The industry life cycle introduces an industry or business's progression through four stages based on the characteristics commonly exhibited in each phase.

Learning Objectives

- Describe the stages and limitations of the industry life cycle concept.

Main Takeaways

Main Points

- An industry's position in its life cycle has a significant influence on its competitive dynamics, so it is vital to keep the positioning in mind when performing a strategic analysis of an industry.
- The economic and industry analysis will provide opportunities and threats for companies in the same industry.
- The decline phase concludes the industry life cycle. A decline phase happens when the industry or business is incapable of sustaining growth.

Main Terms

- **Shakeout period:** During this stage, the growth rate of revenue, cash flows, and profit start slowing down as the industry approaches maturity.
- **Product differentiation:** A marketing strategy that strives to distinguish a company's products or services from the competition.
- **Cyclical industries:** A type of industry sensitive to the business cycle, such that revenues are generally higher in periods of economic prosperity and expansion and lower in periods of economic downturn and contraction.

(a) Economic Cycle

The economy always moves in cycles. We start with the lowest point at the bottom of the economic cycle. Economic growth uses the gross domestic product (GDP) growth measure. When the economy recovers, the economic activity increases. Then, growth will moderate until it reaches the highest point at which it will be called the economic boom. Then the economy will slide, with economic activities slowing down and heading towards the bottom again. In economic analysis, it is essential to identify which part of the economic cycle the economy is in and how long it will take to move in the future.

(b) Industry Life Cycle

All industry growth will follow a cycle with phases as follows:

1. Pioneer phase/embryonic;
2. Growth phase;
3. Shakeout phase;
4. Maturity phase;
5. Decline stage.

Figure 23.1 shows the different stages of the industry life cycle. The growth rate, resource requirements, level of competition, and risk are depicted where appropriate at each stage.

Slowing growth, intense competition due to a slower expanding pie, and declining profitability characterize the shakeout stage. As compared with earlier life cycle analysis, this phase is concerned when an industry transitions from the growth phase to maturity.

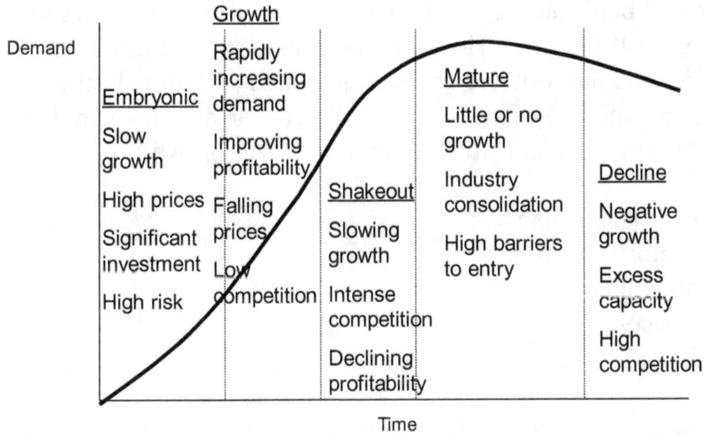

Figure 23.1: Industry life cycle.

It is crucial to identify the life cycle phase that the industry is currently in and how long it will be in that phase.

Industries and Economic Cycle: All industries do not react to changes in the economic cycle in the same way. Depending on the impact of the economic cycle, we can classify the industries:

- **Growth industries:** Even in poor economic conditions, revenues will increase
- **Defensive industries:** The impact of the economy on future cash flow is minimal. If the economic growth decreases, the revenues may not fall much, while if economic growth increases, the future cash flow may not increase much.
- **Cyclical industries:** The performance of these industries depends on economic circumstances. In favorable economic circumstances, the revenues will be higher, and in weak economic cases, revenues will be lower.

(c) Limitations of Industry Life Cycle Analysis

An industry's growth does not always follow an anticipated pattern as multiple external elements (regulatory, social, technological, or demographic changes) may significantly change the pattern's model. Furthermore, companies' performance within the industries does not always mirror that of the overall industry. There can be successful companies in declining industries and unprofitable companies in high-growth industries. Limiting factors may include changes in the following areas, which are also factors that determine secular (or longer-term) industry growth:

- Technological changes;
- Regulatory changes;
- Demographics;
- Macroeconomic;
- Social.

Another limitation of the model specifies that not all companies in the industry encounter similar performance. An analyst must recognize the likely winners while avoiding potential losers. A highly profitable organization can survive in a competitive sector with below-average profitability and vice versa.

23.3 Industry Growth Factors

23.3.1 *Factors that Influence Industry Growth*

These external factors influence the industry's profitability, growth, and risks.

Learning Objectives
- Describe macroeconomics, technological, demographics, government, and social influence on industry growth.

Main Takeaways

Main Points
- Demographics refers to changes in the dynamics of whole population size, distribution of age, and gender.
- Government influences on an industry's revenues and profitability are extensive and significant. By setting up tax rates and regulations for corporations and individuals, governments influence profits and incomes, which successively affect personal and corporate spending.
- Societal changes, the way people work and spend their money, relish their leisure time, and conduct other aspects of their lives can significantly impact different industries' revenue.

Main Terms

- **Cyclical trend:** The changes in economic activity caused by the business cycle.
- **Structural trend:** Enduring changes in the composition or magnitude of economic activity.

(a) Macroeconomic Influences

Cyclical or structural trends may have a consequential impact on the demand for the industry's products or services. Changes in interest rates, credit availability, gross domestic product, and inflation may impact an industry's revenue and profitability.

(b) Technological Influences

Advancement in technologies creates new and improved products that can thoroughly change the industry, allowing changes to how other industries that use the products conduct their operations.

(c) Demographic Influences

Changes in demographic characteristics, population size, distribution of age and gender, and other demographic factors may significantly impact economic growth and the types and amount of goods and services demanded.

(d) Governmental Influences

Governments have a notable influence on industries with their ability to govern tax rates or their standing as major purchasers of goods and services across various sectors. Governments may exercise their influence indirectly by authorizing other self-regulatory or regulatory organizations to administer the affairs of the industry.

(e) Social Influences

Societal changes that involve human behavior, such as how people work, expenditure habits, relishing of their leisure time, may have a significant impact on the sales revenue of industries.

References/Further Readings

Bodie, Z., Kane, A., & Marcus, A.J. (2020). *Investments*, 12th edn. McGraw Hill, pp. 545–560.

Pinto, J.E., Henry, E., Robinson, T.R., & Stowe, J.D. (2010). *Equity Asset Valuation*, 2nd edn. John Wiley & Sons, Inc., pp. 7–35.

23.4 Sample Questions

Question 1
We expect price wars to be absent in the following lifecycle phases?

(a) Growth
(b) Shake-out
(c) Mature

Question 2
Plotting the life-cycle model for an industry as a curve, the variables on the *y* and *x*-axes are:

(a) Price and time
(b) Demand and time
(c) Demand and stages of the life cycle

Question 3
The most likely characteristics in a concentrated industry:

(a) Infrequent, tacit coordination
(b) Industry members attempting to gain market share
(c) Industry members attempting to avoid price competition

Question 4
Which of the following life-cycle phases is typically characterized by high prices?

(a) Mature
(b) Growth
(c) Embryonic

Question 5

Results of an industry analysis would be most useful in a company's decision on its:

(a) Dividend policy
(b) Business strategy
(c) Management of corporate expenses

Solutions

Question 1

Solution: Option **a** is correct.

The growth phase is not likely to experience price wars because expanding industry demand allows companies to grow even without increasing market share. When industry growth is stagnant when the life cycle is at the shake-out or mature stages, companies may only grow by increasing market share, making them more likely to engage in price competition.

Question 2

Solution: Option **b** is correct.

The industry life-cycle model shows how demand evolves through time as the industry passes from the embryonic stage to the decline stage.

Question 3

Solution: Option **c** is correct.

The relatively few industry members will most likely try to avoid price competition. Of course, if the pie is not growing, it may resort to such measures to gain market share.

Question 4

Solution: Option **c** is correct.

The embryonic stage is characterized by slow growth and high prices. This stage is when the firm is trying to gain acceptance of its products or services, yet it cannot benefit from scale due to its small volume.

Question 5

Solution: Option **b** is correct.

Determining a company's business strategy requires understanding its competitive environment from analyzing its operating industry.

Chapter 24

Company Analysis

24.1 Overview of a Company Analysis

24.1.1 *What is a Company Analysis?*

A company analysis includes a breakdown of its financial statement, products and services, and competitive strategy. Detailed company analysis occurs after the analyst has understood the company's external environment and includes answering questions about how the company will respond to the threats and opportunities presented by the external environment.

This section discusses how several critical external factors and interactions affect its prospects. The essential factors to be addressed are competition, pricing power, market share stability, and sensitivity to the business cycle.

Learning Objectives

- Define the factors of company analysis and its relationship to an industry analysis.

Main Takeaways

Main Points

- Company analysis occurs after the analyst has understood the company's external environment and includes answering questions about how the company will respond to the threats and opportunities presented by the external environment.

- Several important external factors and interactions affect the company's prospects. The key elements include market share stability, competition, pricing power, market share stability, and sensitivity to the business cycle.
- Demand for a company's products fluctuates. Some products' demand is sensitive to changes in general business conditions, while others are less so.

Main Terms

- **Competitive strategy:** A long-term action plan of a company that to gain a competitive advantage over its rivals after evaluating their strengths, weaknesses, opportunities, and threats in the industry and compare it with its own.

(a) Market Share Stability

A useful starting point is the market share stability that indicates competition within an industry. Market shares that are highly variable likely indicate a highly competitive industry in which firms have little pricing power. More stable market shares likely indicate less intense competition in the industry. While market share stability is useful as an indicator of competition, we can also better understand what contributes to the stability in carrying out the analysis. Factors that affect market share stability include:

1. Barriers to entry,
2. New products introductions and innovations, and
3. Switching costs that customers face when changing from one firm's products to another.

An example of the impact on market share stability by new product introductions and innovation is the smartphone introduction and the enormous changes in the winner's and losers' fortune. Switching costs that customers face include the time and expense of learning how to use a competitor's product. Switching costs tend to be higher for specialized or differentiated products. High switching costs contribute to market share stability and pricing power. In the medical field, the high switching costs for orthopedic devices coupled with slow innovation resulted in a situation where there was little benefit for patients to switch. The orthopedic devices market is a stable one.

(b) Assessing the Level of Industry Competition

We have discussed how competition affects the industry and a company. We must be clear that not all companies will be affected by the level of industry competition. Some companies may indeed be exceptional, where their business model allows them to be more resilient to competitive pressure. Some have argued that the budget airline model developed by Southwest Airlines has made it resilient to the competitive pressures within the US airlinc industry.

Regardless, it is always necessary to understand the industry's competitive pressures. Most companies are affected to a smaller or larger extent by the competitive pressure within an industry. It usually takes an exceptional company to do well, especially in a highly competitive industry. As discussed in Section 3, Industry Analysis, several vital questions are crucial to helping the analyst evaluate new entrants' threat and the level of competition faced by a company.

The main questions are:

1. What barriers to entry are difficult or easy for a new competitor to challenge incumbents?
2. How concentrated is the industry — do a small number of competitors control a large share of the market, or are there many players with a small market share?
3. What are capacity levels — based on existing investment, how many of the goods or services can be delivered in a given time frame?

An analyst can analyze a companies' historical profit margins within an industry. If the industry has benefited from high economic profits, then a company's future profitability may be affected by the following scenarios:

Scenario 1:

- The entry of new competitors if high barriers to entry cease to exist or weakened significantly leading to:
    - Increase in competition resulting from the new entrants.
    - They are competing away high returns on capital if new entrants can capture their share of economic profits.
    - Lesser pricing power because price increases that raise returns on capital attract new competitors to the industry.

Scenario 2:

- Barriers to entry continue to remain healthy, leading to:
  - Continuing low threat of new entrants into the industry.
  - A continuing benign competitive environment as potential competitors find it difficult to enter the industry and undercut incumbents' prices.
- We must continue to be vigilant as high barriers do not guarantee pricing power because incumbents may fiercely compete against each other.

(c) Pricing Power

We recall that pricing power is an economic term that describes that effect of a change in price on the quantity demanded (see Module 1A1 Part A Section 3 Market Structure). We note that pricing power is in most cases when we have high barriers to entry and a low level of competition. A paradox would then be a situation with a high entry barrier with concurrent poor pricing power. Conditions giving rise to this paradox:

1. Where price is a sizeable component of the customer's purchase decision and the buyer's motive is to reduce operating costs.
2. On the other hand, the producing industries have high exit barriers, which means they are prone to over-capacity.
3. Exacerbating the situation is the difficulty in repositioning capital elsewhere from a weakened unprofitable problem, like finding a buyer to facilitate the exit.

We have discussed fragmented industries that are highly competitive and compared these with concentrated industries. Here, we add to the discussion on concentrated industries where leading industry members are large; therefore, they have more to lose and less to gain by destructive price behavior. The fortune of large companies and their industry are closely intertwined. Generally, we observe that pricing power and rational competition characterize concentrated sectors. Industry fragmentation is a strong signal that the industry is competitive with limited pricing power.

We discussed the effect of capacity on pricing power before. With capacity fixed in the short-term, capacity utilization indicates shorter-term price movement. However, while capacity remains set in the short term, it is variable long-term. Long-term pricing benefits can vary depending on how long it takes to put the new capacity in place. Examining the oil market, we had the impression that capacity remains fixed, and at one time, analysts were discussing peak oil. In the longer term, one needs to think more about the energy rather than the oil market that is disrupted by fracking, renewables, etc.

(d) Factors that Affect Sensitivity to Business Cycles

A cyclical company is likely to undergo broader-than-average fluctuations in demand, with low demand during economic contraction and high demand during economic expansion and subjected to greater-than-average profit volatility linked to increased operating leverage. In comparison, non-cyclical companies produce goods or services where demand remains relatively constant throughout the business cycle.

Describing a company as defensive or cyclical enables the investor to have a fundamental knowledge of how the company is likely to perform in different circumstances. The stock of a cyclical company will likely be more volatile than the stock of a non-cyclical company; an investor may use these definitions during the process of portfolio construction.

One constraint of the cyclical/non-cyclical classification; business-cycle responsiveness is a continuous spectrum rather than an "either/or" matter, so placement of organization into either one of the two fundamental groups is relatively arbitrary. Another limitation would be the processing of business cycle stages; different regions or countries of the world progress the business cycle's variant stages at other times.

Reference/Further Reading

Pinto, J.E., Henry, E., Robinson, T.R., & Stowe, J.D. (2010). *Equity Asset Valuation*, 2nd edn. John Wiley & Sons, Inc., pp. 7–35.

24.2 Sample Questions

Question 1

A cyclical company is most likely to:

(a) Have low operating leverage.
(b) Sell relatively inexpensive products.
(c) Experience wider-than-average fluctuations in demand.

Question 2

A company that is sensitive to the business cycle would most likely:

(a) Not have growth opportunities.
(b) Experience below-average fluctuation in demand.
(c) Sell products that the customer can purchase later if necessary.

Question 3

Which of the following industry characteristics is generally least likely to produce high returns on capital?

(a) High barriers to entry.
(b) High degree of concentration.
(c) Short lead time to build new plants.

Question 4

An industry with high barriers to entry along with weak pricing power most likely has:

(a) High barriers to exit.
(b) Stable market shares.
(c) Significant numbers of issued patents.

Question 5

Companies operating in an industry with stable market share most likely has the following characteristic?

(a) Low costs of switching.
(b) Low barriers to entry.
(c) Slow pace of product innovation.

Solutions

Question 1

Solution: Option **c** is correct.

Cyclical companies experience low product demand during periods of economic contraction and high product demand during economic expansion periods. As a result, these companies experience more significant product demand fluctuations than the average company.

Question 2

Solution: Option **c** is correct.

Products where customers can exercise greater discretion or flexibility when purchasing are more sensitive to the business cycle. Consumer products class as consumer durables and consumer staples.

Question 3

Solution: Option **c** is correct.

Demand increases are quickly satisfied if one can increase industry capacity rapidly. However, such situations can also lead to overcapacity and hence reduced profitability.

Question 4

Solution: Option **a** is correct.

While one source of the high barrier to entry in an industry may be the requirement for substantial physical and financial investment, weak pricing power will make it challenging to find a buyer to facilitate an incumbent's exit from the industry.

Question 5

Solution: Option **c** is correct.

A slow pace of product innovation often means that customers prefer to stay with supplies and suppliers they know, implying stable market shares.

Chapter 25

Equity Valuation Models

25.1 Fundamental Issues

25.1.1 *Intrinsic Value versus Market Price*

Intrinsic value can be defined as an estimate of a company's actual true value, regardless of market value.

Learning Objectives

- Differentiate the difference between intrinsic value and price.

Main Takeaways

Main Points

- Market value is the firm's existing value as reflected by its stock price. The market value may be significantly lower or higher than the intrinsic value.
- After carrying out a firm's analysis, an analyst may come to one of three conclusions when comparing his estimates of value with the market price: that the security is undervalued, fairly valued, or overvalued.
- Valuation models are used to calculate intrinsic value.
- The conclusion of mispricing should consider confidence in the valuation model and the input data.

Main Terms

- **Intrinsic value:** Refers to an investor's perception of the inherent value of an asset, such as a company, stock, option, or real estate (synonym: fundamental value).
- **Market capitalization:** Refers to the total dollar market value of a company's outstanding shares.
- **Catalyst:** This can precipitate a change in stock investing trends.

The market value is the firm's securities' current value as reflected by the firm's stock price. The market value may be significantly lower or higher than the intrinsic value. After carrying out a firm's analysis, an analyst may come to one of three conclusions when comparing his estimates of value with the market price: that the security is undervalued, fairly valued, or overvalued.

In a simple illustration, let us say that a security market is $100. If the analyst estimates that the intrinsic value to be $80, a rational conclusion is that the security is overvalued. If the analyst's estimate is close to $100, the deduction may be that the security is fairly valued. If the estimate is $130, an over-valued conclusion may be considered rational.

By estimating the value, the analyst presumes that the market price is not naturally the best estimate of intrinsic value. If the market price is lower than the estimated value, the analyst concludes that the security is undervalued. If the estimated value equals the market price, the security is fairly valued. If the market price is higher than the estimated value, the security is overvalued.

There is an essential difference between market value and intrinsic value, though both ways help in its valuation. Intrinsic value estimates a company's actual true value, regardless of market value.

Market value is the firm's value calculated from its current stock price and rarely reflects its actual current value. Market value, in simple terms, is an estimate of how much the market values the company or how much it would cost to buy it.

(a) Calculation of Intrinsic Value

To calculate the intrinsic value, we apply valuation models, following these three steps:

1. Forecasting of future cash flows;
2. Estimating the appropriate discount rate;
3. Discounting of future cash flows and summing up the cash flows.

(b) Mispricing of Intrinsic Value

After estimating the intrinsic value of an asset's price, the difference between this estimated value and the market price is termed perceived mispricing.

In carrying out a valuation of an asset, one may encounter situations that range from relatively high confidence to relatively low confidence in the valuation model and the inputs. In a case when confidence is relatively low, one might require a substantial divergence between the estimated value estimate and the market price before acting on apparent mispricing.

For example, suppose the estimated value was $10, and the market price was $10.50 (or a 5% difference) in a situation on relative uncertainty in the company's earnings growth. In that case, the analyst might more reasonably conclude that the security is fairly valued rather than undervalued.

Also, confidence in the convergence of the market price to the intrinsic value over the investment time horizon has to be taken into account before one acts on apparent mispricing or makes a buy, sell, or hold recommendation. The ability to benefit from identifying a mispriced security depends on the market price converging to the estimated intrinsic value. Notably, one or more catalysts should be determined to drive such convergence over the investment time horizon. Catalysts can include product market share and prices or even the earnings next quarter.

Both investors and analysts need to treat market prices with respect in their search to identify mispricing and attractive investments. Estimates of intrinsic value need to be rechecked, particularly the models and inputs used. For example, one might wish to check the earnings growth rate required to produce the valuation model's market price. Lastly, one must keep in mind that mispricing may be more likely in securities neglected by analysts and why such mispricing can be persistent.

25.2 Price Multiples

25.2.1 *Overview of Price Multiples*

Price multiples are ratios of a stock's market price to some measure of fundamental value per share.

Learning Objectives

- Explain the rationale for using price multiples to value equity, how it relates to fundamentals.

Main Takeaways

Main Points

- Analysts and investors use price multiples to increase insight into a firm's valuation as part of the process of evaluating a firm for prospective investment.
- Commonly used price multiples include price-to-sales (P/S) ratios, price-to-book value (P/BV) ratios, and price-to-earnings (P/E) ratios.
- Price multiples are crucial in providing a static and forward glance at a stock's valuation. The multiples enable comparison between future (forecasted) and present valuation multiples of a firm's historical values and peers.
- Price multiples allow investors to determine if a stock is under, fairly, or overvalued.

Main Terms

- **Price multiple:** It refers to a ratio that compares the share price with some money flow or value to evaluate its relative worth.
- **Overvaluation:** An overvalued stock has a current price that is not justified by its earnings outlook, known as profit projections, or its price-earnings (P/E) ratio.
- **Terminal growth rate:** It refers to the constant rate that a company is expected to grow. This growth rate starts at the end of the last forecasted cash flow period in a discounted cash flow model and goes into infinity.

A multiple is computed generally as "what you get" divided by "what you pay (for what you get)." So the term price multiple compares the share price with a measure of value to evaluate the relative worth of a company's stock. Practitioners use price multiple ratios in the following ways:

1. As a screening mechanism, identify candidates to buy if the ratio falls below some specified value and identify shares to sell if the ratio exceeds a specified value.
2. Pick attractively valued stocks: Use the appropriate ratios to examine a group or sector of stocks and select attractively valued shares as those with *relatively* low ratios.

Some price multiples commonly used by analysts are as follows:

- **Price-to-earnings ratio (P/E):** Stock price per share divided by earnings per share. Arguably, the most commonly used price multiple suggests that having a low P/E multiple is related to higher returns in the future.
- **Price-to-book value ratio (P/BV):** Stock price per share divided by book value per share. Evidence suggests P/B multiples are inversely related to higher returns in the future.
- **Price-to-sales ratio (P/S):** Stock price per share divided by sales. While evidence suggests that a low P/S multiple is the most useful multiple for predicting future returns, predicting future profit margin built into price expectations is often challenging.

The following sections will discuss in-depth calculations of the individual ratios.

(a) Use of Price Multiples in Valuation

We can use Price Multiples in two different ways:

- Method of comparable;
- Method of fundamentals.

In the method of comparable, the steps are as follows.
You wish to analyze ABC Company.

1. If a group of "comparable" companies exists, that will provide one alternative. Otherwise, you may need to identify one company, say Company XYZ, similar to Company ABC in terms of fundamentals such as sales, asset size, earnings, operating ratios, and asset utilization ratios.
2. Identify the most appropriate variable in the pricing of stocks: earnings, book value, or sales.
3. Find the variable for Company XYZ or the group of companies from the latest accounting statement.
4. Calculate the price multiple for Company XYZ using the market price for Company XYZ or the group of companies. Compute the average for the group, making due considerations for outliers.
5. Since Company ABC and Company XYZ are similar, the price multiple should also be identical. In case there are differences in fundamentals, the price multiple for Company XYZ should be adjusted to

obtain the price multiple for Company ABC. The same holds for the case that a group of companies replaces company XYZ.

6. From the accounting statements for Company ABC, find the variable's value.
7. Multiply the adjusted price multiple and the variable's value to get the company ABC's value per share.

Since the value of Company, ABC is made relative to Company XYZ's value or a group of "comparable" companies; these models are called ***relative valuation*** models.

Problems with relative valuation models are:

- Finding truly comparable companies is very difficult.
- Adjusting the price multiples for differences in fundamentals is difficult.
- Since we use Company XYZ's market price, if the shares of Company XYZ are not fairly valued, this error carries over to Company ABC. Using a group of companies moderates this issue.

(b) Relation to Fundamentals

In Finance, the central and conceptually sound model of valuation is the present value model, or more specifically, we call them the discounted cash flow model. Practitioners often use price multiples independently of present value models. While we do not include cash flow forecasts or discounting to present value when carrying out price multiple valuations, the price multiple is often related to fundamentals (like growth and risk) through a discounted cash flow model. The Gordon growth model is sometimes used to demonstrate the relationship between a price multiple and fundamentals. The relationship obtains using simple algebraic operations.

Understanding the relationship between a price multiple and fundamental allows the analyst to understand why price multiples can be different within a group of comparable companies and make subjective changes when appropriate. For example, we say that a firm with a lower P/E is undervalued than a firm with a higher P/E. However, if the higher P/E firm is expected to experience higher earnings growth, a subjective adjustment is necessary.

Furthermore, the expressions developed between the price multiple and fundamentals can be interpreted as the *justified* value of a multiple — that is, the *value justified* by (based on) fundamentals or a set of cash flow predictions. These expressions are an alternative way of presenting intrinsic-value estimates.

So in the method of using fundamentals (as opposed to the technique of using comparable), price multiples are calculated using the fundamentals of the company itself. The price multiple thus calculated can be compared to the market price multiple to see whether the stock is undervalued or overvalued.

(c) Price to Earnings Multiple (P/E)

We calculate the price to earnings multiple as P/E = price per share/EPS.

There are problems associated with calculating P/E. Which Earnings to use? Past earnings or future earnings?

If we use past earnings, P/E is called Lagging P/E, and if we use estimated future earnings, P/E is called the Leading P/E.

$$\text{Lagging P/E ratio} = P_0/E_0$$
$$\text{Leading P/E ratio} = P_0/E_1$$

When we use P/E for valuation purposes, accounting adjustments are necessary:

1. Since valuation uses earnings from continuing operations, non-recurring items should be removed in earnings calculations.
2. Business cycle fluctuations should be avoided. When a company is in a cyclical industry, *normalized* earnings should be used to calculate P/E.
3. If the method of comparables is used, the changes in accounting methods among the two (or more) companies must be reconciled.
4. Adjustments also may be necessary to take into account the dilution. Some analysts provide both basic EPS and diluted EPS, taking into account possible dilution due to warrants and executive stock options.

For a company that is in the terminal growth stage, we can calculate P/E using the Dividend discount formula as:

$$P_0/E_0 = (1-b)\,(1+g)/(r_e - g)$$
$$P_0/E_1 = (1-b)/(r_e - g)$$

where b is the retention ratio, and g is the sustainable growth rate.

Thus, P/E depends on the dividend payout ratio, cost of equity, and the growth rate (the fundamentals). A company that has a higher growth rate should have a higher P/E keeping the cost of equity and dividend payout ratio constant.

P/E can be used for:

- Valuation of securities using comparable;
- To screen stocks for investment;
- To calculate terminal values in DCF models.

(d) Price-to-Book Value Multiple (P/BV)

Book value multiple provides the ratio of price per share to the book value of equity per share. The investors are willing to pay the price, whereas the book value is what the investors have paid in the past. If a company has good growth prospects, the price to book value should be more than one. If the company's prospects are not good, the ratio can be less than one. Thus, this ratio provides an idea of how well the company is expected to perform in the future. It is given by:

$$\text{P/BV} = \text{Price per share/Book value of equity per share}$$

Usually, the book value at the beginning of the year is used to calculate the P/BV.

Using the constant growth dividend model, P/BV can be calculated as:

$$\text{P/BV} = (\text{ROE} - g)/(r_e - g)$$

The numerator is the actual return provided to the shareholders' net of growth, and the denominator is the required return net of growth. Thus, if ROE > r_e, P/BV will be greater than one, and if ROE < r_e, P/BV will be less than one.

P/BV depends on ROE. If a company has a higher ROE, it should also have a higher P/BV. P/BV is used for the following purposes:

Uses of P/BV:

1. **Valuation:** Usually, P/BV is not used for valuation using comparable. The reason is that there may be different usage of assets by various companies. Even if both have the same assets and one firm has better

utilization of assets, it will have a higher ROE and higher P/BV. Thus, P/BV will have to be adjusted for differences in fundamentals if one wants to use P/BV for valuation.

2. **Stock screening:** If there are two stocks with similar fundamentals and if the stock with a higher ROE has a lower P/BV, it may be under-valued relative to the other company.
3. **Formulating investment strategies:** Low P/BV stocks generally provide positive abnormal returns and, hence, they may be better investments.

(e) Price to Sales Multiple (P/S)

We calculate the Sales multiple as Price per Share/Sales per Share.

If we use the constant growth dividend model, we can write P/S as:

$$P/S = \frac{\Pi \times (1-b)(1+g)}{(r_e - g)}$$

where Π is the net profit margin; thus, P/S is a function of the net profit margin. A company that has a higher net profit margin should have a higher P/S.

Uses of P/S:

1. **Valuation:** Usually, P/S is not used for valuation using comparable. The reasons are that there may be different levels of cost control in various companies. Even if both have the same assets and one firm has better control of costs, it will have a higher profit margin and higher P/S. Thus, P/S will have to be adjusted for differences in fundamentals if one wants to use P/S for valuation.
2. **Stock screening:** If there are two stocks with similar fundamentals and if the stock has a higher profit margin and has a lower P/S, it may be undervalued relative to the other company.
3. **Formulating pricing strategies:** When a company plans to change its pricing strategy, its sales are likely to change. If a pricing strategy change positively impacts the share price, the pricing strategy is implemented. We examine the price impact of the strategy change by calculating the P/S ratio before and after strategy change.

25.2.2 *Enterprise Value Multiples*

One can use enterprise multiples (for example, the company's enterprise value (EV) divided by its EBITDA) in place of price multiples to calculate companies' value. These multiples are deemed appropriate for corporate events like mergers and acquisitions, where the price of the acquisition includes the value of debt that needs to be paid off.

Learning Objectives

- Describe EV multiples and their use in estimating equity value.

Main Takeaways

Main Points

- Enterprise multiples in general and the EV/EBITDA multiple, in particular, is a ratio used to determine a company's value.
- One often views the EV as the acquisition cost. It is most commonly known as the sum of market capitalization and market value of preferred stock plus the market value of debt minus cash equivalents and short-term investments.
- Alternatives to using EBITDA in EV multiples include free cash flow to firm (FCFF), earnings before interest and taxes (EBIT), and operating income.

Main Terms

- **Enterprise value:** A measure of a firm's total value, often used as a more comprehensive preference to equity market capitalization. EV includes the market capitalization of a firm and short and long-term debt along with any cash on the company's balance sheet in its calculations.
- **EBITDA:** The acronym for earnings before interest, taxes, depreciation, and amortization, is a measure of a company's overall financial performance and commonly used as an alternative to the net income in some standings.
- **Capital expenditure:** It is what a firm spends to buy, maintain or improve its fixed assets.

The term Enterprise value multiples compare the EV to its fundamental value. Among several variables for this relation's denominator, two feasible selections are earnings before interest, taxes, depreciation, amortization (EBITDA), and operating income. The numerator of the relation,

EV, is most commonly defined as the sum of market capitalization and market value of preferred stock plus the market value of debt less cash and investments (cash equivalents and short-term investments).

One can also interpret EV as the cost of a takeover: As in a buyout, the acquiring company assumes the acquired company's debt and receives its cash. Since we are looking at the firm's value, EV is most useful when comparing companies with significant capital structure differences.

Alternatives to using EBITDA in EV multiples include free cash flow to firm (FCFF) discussed in Section 25.5, earnings before interest and taxes (EBIT), and operating income.

(a) EV/EBITDA

EBITDA (earnings before interest, taxes, depreciation, and amortization) is viewed as a source of means to pay off the company's financial stakeholders (lenders, shareholders, the government, etc.). EV/EBITDA is arguably the most conventional EV multiple. Over the past few years, the EV/EBITDA ratio for S&P 500 companies averaged 13. As a general benchmark, an EV/EBITDA value of below ten is generally interpreted as healthy by analysts. However, such a numerical standard is not considered a sound practice as the numerical value of multiples changes with market conditions.

One essential advantage of using the EV/EBITDA is that EBITDA is mostly positive even when net income is negative; EV/EBITDA can be derived when a price-to-earnings (P/E) multiple may not be readily accessible.

(b) EV/FCFF

We discuss the definition and use of free cash flow to firm (FCFF) in Section 25.5. Using FCFF as the denominator in the EV multiple has its proponents as FCFF is unencumbered and reflective of the cash flows that a firm has to work with. On the other hand, EBITDA is considered more reflective of a firm's performance as it does not include capital expenditures made at the discretion of management.

(c) EV/EBIT and EV/Operating Income

Although we often use EBIT and operating income interchangeably, we note that operating income does not include non-operating income, non-operating expenses, and other income.

We sometimes use EV/EBIT and EV/Operating income as alternatives to EV/EBITDA. EBIT and Operating income are more meaningful metrics because of their relation to cash flow than EBITDA. Some propose using EBIT and operating income for capital-intensive industries, such as oil and gas, mining, and infrastructure. On the other hand, some have argued using EBITDA for long gestation projects does not overly penalize firms who invest in such projects. Those who favor EBITDA view capital investment as discretionary and should be excluded when focusing on firm performance.

References/Further Readings

Damordaran, A. (2012). *Investment Valuation Tools and Techniques for Determining the Value of Any Asset*, 3rd edn. John Wiley & Sons, pp. 453–541.

Pinto, J.E., Henry, E., Robinson, T.R., & Stowe, J.D. (2010). *Equity Asset Valuation*, 2nd edn. John Wiley & Sons, Inc., pp. 257–311, 320–331.

25.3 Asset-Based Valuation

25.3.1 *Overview of Asset-Based Valuation Model*

The asset-based valuation model is often adjusted to calculate a company's net asset value based on the market value of its assets and liabilities.

Learning Objectives

- Understand the use of asset-based valuation model and its use in estimating the value

Main Takeaways

Main Points

- Asset-based valuation models estimate value based on the estimated market(fair) value of a company's assets and liabilities.
- One would use asset-based valuations in conjunction with multiple models to value private firms or supplement public firms' valuation.
- If a company has significant intangibles, alternative valuation approaches are preferred.
- In a hyperinflationary economic condition, asset valuations may be of limited use.

Main Terms

- **Hyper-inflationary:** An economic term to depict excessive, rapid, and out-of-control price increases in an economy. While inflation is a measure of the pace of rising prices for goods and services, hyperinflation is rapidly growing inflation.
- **Assets:** An economic resource that an individual, corporation, or country owns or controls to expect to provide a future benefit.
- **Liabilities:** Something a person or company owes, usually a sum of money.

Asset-based valuation models estimate value based on the estimated market (fair) value of a company's assets and liabilities. These models, thus, work well for companies that do not have a high proportion of intangible assets and do not have a high proportion of current assets and liabilities. The process of valuation of such companies starts with the balance sheet. However, for most companies, balance sheet values are different from the market (fair) values, and the market (fair) values can be difficult and time-consuming to determine.

Asset-based valuation models are often used together with multiple models to value private companies. Increasing use of asset-based models to supplement discounted cash flow and multiple models is expected with public companies increasingly reporting or disclosing fair values. Important factors to note when carrying out an asset-based valuation include:

- Hard to analyze companies using asset-based valuation models is those with significant property, plant, and equipment that do not have readily determinable market (fair) values.
- Asset and liability fair values can differ substantially from values carried on the balance sheet.
- Financial statements do not report all intangible assets. Intangible assets, such as the value from synergies or the value of a good business reputation, are unlikely to be shown on the books. Given that we do not include valuable intangibles in an asset-based analysis, this will lead to an underestimate. If a company has significant intangibles, alternative valuation approaches are preferred.
- A hyperinflationary environment makes asset values may be more challenging to estimate.

- An entity's value can be much higher when assets are disposed of piece by piece, and the future income of assets is considered explicitly.

Example: Non-public company

A small enterprise owns a row of shophouses where its traditional Chinese medical (TCM) clinic operates. The real estate is collateral for a loan of \$5 million. How may asset-based valuation be used to value this business?

Solution:

You will first appraise the land and building value, reducing the appraised value by the loan of \$5 million. Also, the TCM business will need to be valued. This appraisal will include any used value of the business's equipment and intangible value, for example, reputation and location.

Large companies' assets can be so extensive that the effort to transition from book value to market value piece-by-piece will be too demanding. Considering the task's difficulty, one would consider using the asset-based valuation approach only when one can readily estimate its market value. A second consideration is that the intangible assets are a relatively small proportion of the company's assets as intangible assets are typically challenging to value. Typical companies amenable to asset-based valuation include financial companies, natural resource companies, and formerly going-concerns in liquidation. In other companies, asset-based valuation of tangible assets estimates a baseline or minimum value.

Example: An airline

With the slow-down in travel, airlines are losing billions of dollars and will stop paying dividends. Using most valuation metrics, the airlines will have a negative value. How would a competitor use an asset-based valuation model to value another airline as a potential acquisition?

Solution:

An airline's assets may be of value to a competitor, such as landing rights, leases of airport facilities, ground equipment, and airplanes. Apart from the losses incurred in storage charges, maintenance, and redundant staff, these may be valued separately.

25.4 Dividend Discount Model

25.4.1 *Overview of the Dividend Discount Model*

The dividend discount model (DDM) is a method of valuing a company's stock price based on the theory that its stock is worth the sum of all of its future dividend payments, discounted back to its present value.

Learning Objectives

- Calculate a company's intrinsic value using constant growth and multistage DDM.

Main Takeaways

Main Points

- Dividend Discount Models are commonly used to value equity securities.
- Dividend growth depends on the stage of growth that the company is in.
- The easier way of integrating growth into a value is to make it endogenous, i.e., associating more closely with its actions to create and sustain that growth.
- Assuming constant return on equity (ROE), the earnings growth rate is equal to the retention ratio multiplied by ROE.
- If ROE is allowed to change, increasing return on equity will generate a spurt in the growth rate in the period of improvement; a decline in the return on equity will create a more than a proportional drop in the growth rate.

Main Terms

- **Dividend:** A means of distributing profits by a corporation to its shareholders.
- **Return on equity (ROE):** A measure of financial performance calculated by dividing net income by shareholders' equity.
- **Retention ratio or *b*:** It is the fraction of net income retained by the firm to grow the business.
- **Payout ratio or (1–*b*):** It is the fraction of net income paid to shareholders as dividends.

(a) General Dividend Discount Model

Dividend Discount Models are commonly used to value equity securities. The general DDM is as follows:

$$V_0 = \sum_{t=0}^{\infty} \frac{D_t}{(1+r_e)^t}$$

where V_0 is the value of security at time, 0, D_t is the dividend at time, t, and r_e is the required return of the equity security.

We will need to forecast future dividends to apply this model.

(b) Dividends and Growth Stages

Dividend growth depends on the stage of growth that the company is in. Previously discussed, we saw that industries could either be in a pioneer stage, growth stage, maturity stage, or decline stage. Conditional on the company's stage, its risk levels, investment needs, and dividend policy will change. Therefore, it is crucial to know its growth stage before the dividend can be forecast. Table 25.1 provides details of dividend policy, investment needs, and risk for various growth stages.

During the early stages of any industry, one can expect very few companies, and the revenue of these companies is likely to increase at a very high rate. Since the company is growing, the amount of dividends paid will be low due to the high investments required for business advancement. After some time, depending on the entry barriers and competition, the growth rate will decrease to *a terminal growth rate* sustained over an extended period.

The sustainable low growth period is called the *terminal growth stage*. With slower growth, investments will decline to a lower amount while the amount of dividends paid will be higher. Companies will only see a steady low to no growth in revenue and profit in this terminal growth stage. The company's risk level will be increased when it has high growth

Table 25.1: Different growth stages.

Growth stage	Investment needs	Dividend policy	Risk level
High growth stage	Very high	Nothing to low dividend	High
Terminal growth stage	Moderate	Moderate	Moderate
Steady/terminal growth stage	Low	High payout	Low

prospects, and the risk will decrease when in terminal growth and no growth stage.

Companies can be in different stages of growth. We can construct different models to cater to the company in different growth stages. Hence, there is a single-stage model where the company is growing at a steady growth rate for an indefinite period. A two-stage model shows the company with high growth, but this growth will dip to continued low growth after a specific time. The three-stage model is when the company is in the high growth stage but, over time, is expected to arrive at the terminal growth stage, and then it will remain in a slow, steady growth stage for a long time.

(c) Estimating Growth

Fundamental Determinants of Growth: The easier way of integrating growth into a value is to make it endogenous, i.e., associating more closely with its actions to create and sustain that growth. We consider the relationship between fundamentals and growth in equity income.

Growth in Equity Earnings: When estimating cash flows to equity, we usually start with net income estimates. We present the fundamentals that determine the expected growth in net income. To establish this, note that:

$$g_t = \frac{(NI_t - NI_{t-1})}{NI_{t-1}}$$

where g_t is the growth in net income and NI_t is the net income in year t.

Take note that ROE in period t is written as NI in period t divided by the Book value of equity in period t–1. Given the rationale of return on equity, the net income in year t–1 can be written as:

$$NI_{t-1} = \text{Book value of equity}_{t-2} \times \text{ROE}_{t-1}$$

where ROE_{t-1}= Return on equity in year t–1.

We can spell out the net income in year t as NI_t = (Book value of equity$_{t-2}$ + Retained earnings$_{t-1}$) × ROE_t.

Assuming that the return on equity is unchanged (i.e., $\text{ROE}_t = \text{ROE}_{t-1} = \text{ROE}$):

$$\begin{aligned} g_t &= \text{Retained earnings}_{t-1}/NI_t \times \text{ROE} \\ &= \text{Retention ratio} \times \text{ROE} \\ &= b \times \text{ROE} \end{aligned}$$

where b is commonly known as retention ratio, and the payout ratio is 1 minus the retention ratio.

Assuming a constant pay-out ratio then g_t is also the dividend growth rate.

(d) Effects of Changing ROE

If we relax the assumption that return on equity is unchanged, we introduce a new growth factor — the effect of changing return on equity on existing investments over time. Hence, the additional growth is written as a function of the change in the return on equity:

$$\text{Addition to expected growth rate} = (\text{ROE}_t - \text{ROE}_{t-1})/\text{ROE}_{t-1}$$

where ROE_t is the return on equity in period t.

It is an addition to the fundamental growth rate derived from the multiplying return on equity and the return ratio.

While increasing return on equity will generate a spurt in the growth rate in the period of improvement, a decline in the return on equity will create a more than a proportional drop in the growth rate in the decline period.

It is worth distinguishing between returns on equity on new investments and returns on equity on existing investments. The additional growth that we are estimating comes from new investments but by changing the return on existing investments.

25.4.2 *Constant Growth Dividend Discount Model*

It assumes that a company's dividends will continue to rise at a constant growth rate indefinitely.

Learning Objectives

- Calculate the intrinsic value of a company using a constant growth model.

Main Takeaways

Main Points

- The Gordon (constant) growth DDM assumes dividends grow indefinitely at a constant rate.
- Based on constant growth, you can use that assumption to figure out what a fair price is to pay for the stock today based on those future dividend payments.
- The Gordon (constant) growth DDM is useful in valuing the equity of dividend-paying companies insensitive to the business cycle and in a mature growth phase.

Main Terms

- **Business cycle:** It is identified as having four distinct phases: peak, trough, contraction, and expansion. Business cycle fluctuations occur around a long-term growth trend and are usually measured by considering the real gross domestic product's growth rate.
- **Intrinsic value:** It refers to an investor's perception of the inherent value of an asset, such as a company, stock, option, or real estate.

As discussed earlier, the dividend amount is dependent on the stage of growth the company is in, and in different stages, the earnings and dividends are likely to have a different growth rate. This section will consider different DDMs based on the estimated growth in dividends. To facilitate understanding of the various models, we will start with a company with no growth.

(a) Valuation Model for No Growth Companies

When a company has no growth at all, the dividend payout ratio will be 100%, or all earnings will be paid out as dividends, and the amount of dividend will be the same at all future periods. Thus, if E_0 is the current earnings, future earnings will also be E_0 as there is no growth, and dividends in each period will be E_0.

Perpetuity with E_0 as the payment every year and hence the value of this company is given by:

$$V_0 = E_0/r_e$$

Note that this is also the value of assets that are currently in place.

Return from investing in stock comes in two forms: dividend payment and capital appreciation. Thus, the stock return is written as:

$$r_e = \text{dividend yield} + \text{capital gains yield}$$

where

$$\text{Dividend yield} = D_1/P_{0,}$$

and

$$\text{Capital gains yield} = (P_1 - P_0)/P_0$$

When a company has no growth, capital gains yield is zero, and all return comes in the form of dividend yield.

(b) Valuation Model for Constant Growth Companies

When a company's expected dividends and earnings grow at a constant rate of g percent every year for an indefinite time, the company is said to be in a terminal growth stage or constant growth stage. Important to note, this model assumes that the dividend payout ratio will stay constant over time. When a company has terminal growth, the value is given by

$$V_0 = \frac{D_1}{(r_e - g)} = \frac{D_0(1+g)}{(r_e - g)}$$

One should be careful in using the above formula for valuation. Given the current earnings and dividends, you need to use the second version that uses D_0. Given an expected future dividend, you should use the first version that uses D_1.

25.4.3 *Estimating Terminal Growth*

The terminal growth rate estimates a company's growth in expected future cash flows beyond a projection period.

Learning Objectives

- Define and estimate the terminal value with the terminal growth formula.

Main Takeaways

Main Points

- Since we cannot forecast cash flows forever, we generally impose closure in discounted cash flow valuation by stopping our cash flow sometime in the future and then computing a terminal value that reflects the firm's value at that point.
- You can find the terminal value in one of two ways. One uses a multiple to earnings, revenues, or book value to evaluate the value in the terminal year. The other assumes that the firm's cash flows will grow at a constant rate forever.
- In a Discounted Cash Flow Model of which the Dividend Discount Model is a special case, the terminal value usually makes up the largest proportion of value for a company (more than the forecast period).

Main Terms

- **Sustainable growth:** The rate at which a firm can grow without sourcing external finance or the rate that a firm can grow using only funds raised from operations.
- **Terminal value:** The firm's net present value of its cash flows beyond the forecast period.
- **Reinvestment rate:** The return an investor expects to make after reinvesting the cash flows earned from a previous investment.
- **Return on capital:** Apart from using the value of ownership interests in a company, it also includes the total value of debts owed by the company in the form of loans and bonds.

Recall that the general DDM is given by

$$V_0 = \sum_{t=0}^{\infty} \frac{D_t}{\left(1+r_e\right)^t}$$

Since we cannot forecast cash flows forever, we generally impose closure in discounted cash flow valuation by stopping our cash flow sometime in the future and then computing a terminal value that reflects the firm's value at that point.

You can find the terminal value in one of two ways. Both approaches value the firm as an ongoing concern at the terminal value estimation.

One uses a multiple to earnings, revenues, or book value to evaluate the value in the terminal year. The other assumes that the firm's cash flows will grow at a constant rate forever — a stable growth rate. With stable growth, the terminal value can be estimated using a perpetual growth model. Finding Terminal value is essential in using multistage DDM to find the intrinsic value.

Capital gains yield will be g, the same growth rate as the growth rate in earnings and dividends. Since r_e = capital gains yield + dividend yield, $r_e > g$. The constant growth rate means the future price will also increase every year by g percent.

The value of growth is as follows: Value if there is no growth is given by E_0/r_e.

Thus, the value of growth $= V = \frac{D_1}{(r_e - g)} - \frac{E_0}{r_e}$

Also, note that there may be differences for terminal growth situations and no growth situation with a higher re for terminal growth in practice. Thus, you need to adjust the r_e according to the growth situation.

Also, note that there may be differences for terminal growth situations and no growth situation with a higher re for terminal growth in practice. Thus, you need to adjust the r_e according to the growth situation.

(a) Estimation of Terminal Growth Rate Using Fundamentals

A company's fundamental decisions determine earnings growth on its profit margins, product lines, leverage, and dividend policy. If we assume that a company continues to have a constant profit margin, constant leverage, and constant dividend policy, we can write the growth rate as

$$g = b * \text{ROE}$$

where b is the retention rate = (1 − dividend pay-out rate) and ROE is the return on equity.

Using the Dupont equation:

$$\text{ROE} = \text{Net Profit Margin } (P) * \text{Total Asset Turnover } (A) * \text{Equity Multiplier } (T)$$

We write the growth rate, g as $g = P\,R\,A\,T$.

We can find the optimal sustainable growth that the firm can maintain for a level of optimal P, R, A, and T. Furthermore, should the company grow at a rate higher than this optimal sustainable rate, the company will soon face a cash flow problem. In this case, the company will need to:

- go for external financing through either debt or equity;
- prune away the marginal activities and concentrate only on highly profitable activities;
- outsource some or all production at a possibly lower cost;
- Merge with a cash cow growing at a rate lower than the optimal growth rate.

If a company has a growth rate lower than the optimal growth rate, it can:

- distribute the excess cash to the shareholders in the form of increased dividends or buying back shares,
- purchase a company that has growth.

In a Discounted Cash Flow Model of which the Dividend Discount Model is a special case, the terminal value usually makes up the largest proportion of value for a company (more than the forecast period). This result can be easily explained by the time horizon that extends to infinity which is usually assumed in the DCF model. The forecast period in many cases does not extend beyond 5–10 years. One must take due care when deciding on the terminal growth rate in DCF models.

Example:
SAM Limited had earnings of \$15 million in 2018. It has 5 million shares outstanding. It retained \$6 million, and its equity at the beginning of 2018 was \$60 million.

The earnings are expected to grow at a sustainable growth rate for a long time. The risk-free rate is estimated as 4%, and the market risk premium is estimated as 7%. The beta for SAM is estimated as 1.1. Evaluate the value per share for SAM. What is the value of growth?

Earnings	= \$15 million	
Number of shares outstanding	= 5 million	
EPS	= 15/5	= \$3
Retention ratio b	= 6/15	= 40%

Dividend pay-out ratio	= 1–40%	= 60%
Dividend	= 3 * 60%	= \$1.80
ROE = Earnings/Equity	= 15/60	= 25%
$g = b * \text{ROE}$	= 40% * 25%	= 10%
$r_e = rf + \beta$ (market risk premium)	= 4% + 1.1 * 7%	= 11.7%

$$V = D_0 (1 + g)/(r_e - g) = 1.80 * 1.1/(0.117 - 0.1) = \$116.47$$

If there is no growth at all, value is given by $E_0/r_e = 3/0.117 = \$25.64$. Value of growth = 116.47 − 25.64 = \$90.83.

(b) Characteristics of Stable Growth Firms

Companies assume stable growth firms' characteristics when they transition from high growth to stable growth. A firm in stable growth differs from that same firm in high growth in several areas. Usually, a stable growth firm will have moderate risk, lower to zero economic (or excess) returns, and need to invest less than one in the high growth stage. This section will consider how to transition each of these variables.

Equity Risk: High growth firms have higher exposure to market risk (and have higher beta) than stable growth firms. Among many reasons, high growth firms may be niche players selling discretionary products. Another reason may be that such firms have high operating leverage. For instance, new technology or social media firms have high betas. Over time, as the market and technology mature, such firms are likely to have reduced market risk exposure while their beta converges to the market average.

One option is to set the beta in stable growth to one for all firms. Another is to allow room for small differences to exist even in stable growth, with companies in more volatile businesses having higher betas than those in stable businesses.

In cases where firms already have beta well below one, like firms in the commodity business or consumer staples, betas can be assumed to be at such levels if they remain in the existing business. However, if longer-term growth is assumed on expansion in other businesses, then the beta should be adjusted upward toward one.

Debt Ratios and Cost of Debt: High growth firms generally use less debt than stable growth firms as firms mature, their debt capacity increases. Different debt capacities will change the debt ratio we use to determine the capital cost during the firms' valuation. When valuing equity, changing the debt ratio will alter both the cost of equity and the expected cash flows. Whether one should adjust the debt ratio for a firm to a more sustainable level in stable growth requires understanding the incumbent managers' view on debt and how much influence the stockholders have in the firms. Suppose managers are willing to change their financing policy and stockholders retain some influence. In that case, it is rational to expect the debt ratio to move to a higher level in stable growth. It is safer to leave the debt ratio at existing levels if not.

We should remember that as a firm's earnings and cash flows increase, the perceived default risk in the firm will also change. The reason is that firm that makes losses when new is likely to have a low credit rating, but its rating is expected to improve if it can achieve growth and profitability over time. One should adjust the firm's rating and cost of debt on improved revenue and operating income to be consistent. Stable growth firms that have scaled this growth path to stable growth warrant at least an investment grade (Baa or better) rating.

Practically, one can estimate what debt ratio and cost of debt to use in stable growth from looking at the financial leverage of larger and more mature firms in the industry.

Reinvestment and Retention Ratios: Stable growth firms tend to reinvest less than high growth firms, and we must capture the effects of lower growth on reinvestment and ensure that the firm reinvests enough to sustain its stable growth rate in the terminal phase. The actual adjustment will vary depending on whether we are discounting dividends, free cash flows to equity, or free cash flows to the firm.

In the DDM, the expected growth in earnings (or on a per-share basis) is a function of the retention ratio and the return on equity.

In the free cash flow to equity (FCFE) model, we focus on net income growth, where the expected growth rate is a function of the equity reinvestment rate and the return on equity.

Lastly, looking at FCFF, we estimated that the expected growth in operating income as a function of the return on capital (ROC) in stable growth and the reinvestment rate:

$$\text{Expected growth rate} = \text{Reinvestment rate} \times \text{Return on capital}$$

During stable growth

$$\text{Reinvestment rate} = \text{Stable growth rate/ROC}$$

25.4.4 *Two-Stage Dividend Discount Model*

The two-stage DDM comprises two parts and assumes that dividends will go through two growth stages.

Learning Objectives

- Compute and interpret the Intrinsic Value using the two-stage DDM.

Main Takeaways

Main Points

- The two-stage DDM estimates the value as the sum of the present values of dividends over a short-term period of high growth and the present value of the terminal value at the end of high growth. The terminal value is estimated using the Gordon growth model.
- The two-stage model is frequently used to evaluate the intrinsic value of a stock issued by a company that is undergoing above-normal growth (being elevated and hence unsustainable), subsequently reducing to stable growth.
- The three-stage model incorporates an initial period of very aggressive or paltry growth followed by incremental increase or decrease that eventually stabilizes at a more moderate growth rate that is assumed to continue for the company's life.

Main Terms

- **Intrinsic Value:** It refers to an investor's perception of the inherent value of an asset, such as a company, stock, option, or real estate.

In the two-stage model, the firm's earnings will grow at a high rate of $g+$ percent for a specified period, say, n years, and then it will grow at a sustainable growth rate of g percent from year $n+1$ onwards.

We carry out the valuation in the following manner. If you buy the stock now and sell at the end of n years when the terminal growth starts, you would receive dividends for the first n years, and at the end of n years, you will receive the price at which the stock will be selling. The terminal growth starts at the end of year n, the value (called the store's terminal value) is computed using the constant growth model (called the terminal value for the stock). Thus, the current value will be the present value of dividends you will get for the first n years and the terminal value at the end of *n* years calculated using the constant growth model. Thus, value is given by

$$V_0 = \sum_{t=1}^{n} \frac{D_0\left(1+g^+\right)^t}{\left(1+r_e\right)^t} + \frac{1}{\left(r_e - g\right)^n}\left(\frac{D_{n+1}}{r_e - g}\right)$$

The two-stage model is frequently used to evaluate the intrinsic value of a stock issued by a company that is undergoing above-normal growth (that is elevated and hence unsustainable), subsequently reducing to stable growth. Many firms between the growth and mature stages are modeled using a two-stage model.

Example:
SDDM Limited had earnings of $15 million in 2018 and has 5 million shares outstanding.

The earnings are expected to grow at 10% a year for the next 3 years, after which the growth rate will be the sustainable growth rate of 4%. The dividend payout ratio is 60% and will continue to remain constant. The risk-free rate is estimated at 3%, and the market risk premium is estimated at 5%. The beta for SDDM is estimated as 1.2. Estimate the value per share for SDDM.

Earnings	= $15 million	
Number of shares outstanding	= 5 million	
EPS	= 15/5	= $3
Dividend pay-out ratio	= 1–40%	= 60%
Dividend	= 3 * 60%	= $1.80

$r_e = r_f + \beta$ (market risk premium) = 3% + 1.2 * 5% = 9.0%

Year	Dividend	Present value factor	PV of dividend
1	1.80 * 1.1 = 1.98	1/1.09 = 0.9174	1.8165
2	1.98 * 1.1 = 2.18	$(1/1.09)^2$ = 0.8417	1.8332
3	2.18 * 1.1 = 2.40	$(1/1.09)^3$ = 0.7722	1.8500
4	2.40 * 1.04 = 2.49		

Terminal value @ $D_4 = D_4/(r_e - g) = 2.4916/(0.09 - 0.04) = \$49.83$
Present value of terminal value = $49.83/(1.09)^3 = \$26.94$
Present value of dividends = 1.8165 + 1.8332 + 1.8500= \$5.50
Initial value = 26.94 + 5.50 = \$32.44.

(a) Problems with the Two-Stage Model

- The earnings growth does not usually drop from a high rate to terminal rate overnight, which is unreasonable to assume. The growth rate is likely to reach the terminal growth rate over time. In such cases, we use an H-model that models declining growth overtime.
- The dividend payout ratio and risk are assumed to remain the same in the two stages, which may not be appropriate.

25.4.5 *Three-Stage Dividend Discount Model*

We will only briefly discuss the three-stage model here as the three-stage model is a simple extension of the two-stage case.

In the case of the three-stage model, assumptions are as follows:

Stage 1: High growth stage — Company will grow at a rate of *g*+ for *n* years
Stage 2: Transition stage — The growth rate will decrease linearly from *g*+ to *g* over *m* years
Stage 3: Terminal growth stage — Company will grow at the terminal growth rate *g*

Value is given by

V_0 = present value of dividends during the high growth stage + present value of dividends during transition stage + present value of terminal value when terminal growth starts, which is calculated using the terminal growth stage formula.

(a) Dividend Models and Market Expectations

In dividend models, the most important variable is the terminal growth rate *g*. If there is a small error in the estimate of *g*, there will be a substantial value error. One can infer the growth rate used in market price and then consider whether the growth rate implied in the market price is possible. We can infer from:

$$g = r_e - D_1/P_0$$
$$g = (P_0\, r_e - D_0)/(P_0 + D_0)$$

Example:
SDDM Limited had earnings of $15 million in 2018. It has 5 million shares outstanding. It retained $6 million, and its equity at the beginning of 2018 was $60 million.

The earnings are expected to grow at the terminal growth rate for a long time. The risk-free rate is estimated at 3%, and the market risk premium is estimated at 5%. The beta for SDDM is estimated as 1.2. The SDDM share price is $60. What is the implied growth rate for SDDM?

Earnings	= $15 million	
Number of shares outstanding	= 5 million	
EPS	= 15/5	= $3
Retention ratio *b*	= 6/15	= 40%
Dividend pay-out ratio	= 1–40%	= 60%
Dividend	= 3 ∗ 60%	= $1.80

$$r_e = r_f + \beta\,(\text{market risk premium}) = 4\% + 1.2 * 5\% = 9.0\%$$
$$g = ((P_0\, r_e - D_0)/(P_0 + D_0) = (60{*}0.09 - 1.80)/(60 + 1.80) = 5.825\%$$

Assuming that the terminal growth rate is 4%, it is likely that a growth rate of 5.825% is not achievable in the long run, and the stock is probably overvalued.

References/Further Readings

Damordaran, A. (2012). *Investment Valuation Tools and Techniques for Determining the Value of Any Asset*, 3rd edn. John Wiley & Sons, pp. 282–286, 304–350.

Pinto, J.E., Henry, E., Robinson, T.R., & Stowe, J.D. (2010). *Equity Asset Valuation*, 2nd edn. John Wiley & Sons, Inc., Chap. 3.

25.5 Free Cash Flow Valuation

25.5.1 *Overview of Free Cash Flow to Firm*

We use free cash flow to the firm (FCFF) to value the firm as a whole, while we use FCFE to value the company's shares.

Learning Objectives

- Calculate the value per share using the FCFF.

Main Takeaways

Main Points

- FCFF indicates the amount of cash flow from operations available for distribution after working capital, depreciation expenses, taxes, and investments are accounted for and paid.
- A positive FCFF value suggests that the firm has cash remaining after expenses and a negative value that the firm has not generated sufficient revenue to cover its expenses and investment activities.
- Free cash flow is one of the most important financial indicators of a company's stock value.
- The FCFF is appropriate for an acquisition where one requires a firm's value.

Main Terms

- **Working capital:** Capital of a business used in its day-to-day trading operations and calculated as the current assets minus the current liabilities.
- **Free cash flows:** Cash flows from operations no longer required to be kept in the firm and distributed to investors.
- **CapEx:** Capital expenditures, commonly known as CapEx, are funds used by a company to acquire, upgrade, and maintain physical assets such as property, buildings, an industrial plant, technology, or equipment. CapEx is often used to undertake new projects or investments by the firm.

(a) Introduction to Free Cash Flow

Free cash flows are cash flows from operations no longer required to be kept in the company and available to be distributed to investors. Operating cash flows must be retained in the business for additional investment requirements. Once provision has been made for it, the remaining cash flow is no longer required to be retained and distributed.

Depending on the group of investors that supplied capital and in return to whom the cash flow will be distributed, free cash flow can be either FCFE or FCFF.

A positive FCFF value suggests that the firm has cash remaining after expenses and a negative value that the firm has not generated sufficient revenue to cover its expenses and investment activities. Free cash flow is one of the most important financial indicators of a company's stock value.

(b) Calculation of Operating Cash Flow

Operating cash flow is different from net profit because of two reasons: First, Net profit uses the accrual concept whereby income and expenses are recognized as soon as they happen irrespective of whether cash is received/paid or not. Such items are included as inventories, accounts receivables, and accounts payables. Thus, to correct this, the change in net working capital will have to be adjusted against profit to get the cash flow. Second, the adjustment is for the presence of non-cash expenses such as depreciation and amortization. These are expenses already made, but they are written off over a period.

When they are written off, the profit for that period will decrease, but there will be no cash outflow during that period. Thus, one needs to adjust for non-cash expenses. Both adjustments will result in the following relationship between cash flow and operating profit. Operating profit is also called EBIT.

Operating cash flow = EBIT − Increase in net working capital + non-cash expenses.

An increase in net working capital is calculated as:

Increase in net working capital = (Increase in inventory + increase in accounts receivables + increase in other current assets) − (Increase in accounts payables + increase in other current liabilities).

Note that in valuation, we do not include changes in cash, marketable securities, and notes payables as these are at the discretion of the management and do not arise due mainly through operations.

(c) FCFF Models

FCFF is the free cash flow to the firm and is calculated as FCFF = EBIT (1−T) − (Capital investment − Depreciation) − Additional investment in working capital.

Or

FCFE = NI − (Capital investment − Depreciation) − Increase in net working capital + (Additional borrowings − Loan repayments).

Or

FCFF = Operating cash flow − Additional investments.

FCFF is the cash flow that can be distributed to all capital providers without obstructing the business's operations. Since it is the cash flow before distribution to all capital providers, FCFF models value the whole company and not the shares directly. We can use FCFF models to value the shares with some modifications that will be discussed later.

Since FCFF uses the cash flow before distribution to all capital providers, the appropriate discount rate is the weighted average cost of capital.

FCFF models can also be single-stage, two-stage, or three-stage models similar to the dividend model depending upon the stage of growth in which the company is.

Single-Stage FCFF Model: In a single-stage FCFF model, we assume that FCFF will grow at a constant rate of g percent a year for a long time. Under the assumption that EBIT margin is constant and working capital as a percentage of sales is constant, then the assumed growth rate in FCFF is equal to the sustainable growth rate as the capital investment is offset by depreciation.

Similar to the single-stage dividend model, the single-stage FCFF model is as follows:

$$V_{F,0} = \frac{FCFF_1}{(WACC - g)} = \frac{FCFF_0(1+g)}{(WACC - g)}$$

As noted earlier, the FCFF model provides the firm's value as a whole. To calculate the value of shares, we need to modify the model.

If V_D is the market value of debt, calculated by multiplying the number of bonds outstanding by the number of bonds outstanding, the Value of equity will be given by

$$V_{E,0} = V_{F,0} - V_{D,0}$$

$V_{E,0}$ gives the value of total equity. To find the value per share, we need to divide by the number of shares outstanding, or the value per share V_0 is given by

$$V_0 = V_{E,0}/N$$

Example:

SAFF Limited had revenues of $120 million in 2018. Its EBIT margin is 20%. Working capital as a percentage of sales is 30%. The revenues are expected to grow at a constant rate of 10% every year. Its debt has a market value of $800 million. The company has a target capital structure of 40% debt. Its cost of debt before tax is 8%, and the cost of equity is estimated at 14%. The number of shares outstanding is 50 million. Calculate the value per share using the FCFF model. The tax rate is 20%. Assume that capital investment will be offset by depreciation.

FCFF = EBIT(1–T) – (Capital investment – Depreciation) – Additional working capital investment

Revenue in 2018	= $120 million	
EBIT in 2018	= 120 ∗ 20%	= $24 million
Capital investment	= depreciation	
Working Capital in 2018	= 30% ∗ 120	= $36 million
Revenue in 2019	= 120 ∗ 1.1	= $132 million
EBIT in 2019	= 132 ∗ 20%	= $26.4 million
Working Capital in 2019	= 132 ∗ 30%	= $39.6 million

Additional investment in working capital at end of 2018= 39.6 – 36 = $3.6 million

FCFF in 2019 = 26.4 ∗ 0.8 – 3.6 = $21.12 – 3.6 = $17.52 million

We can calculate the FCFF only for 2019 as the amount of working capital at the beginning of the year 2018 is not known.

Weighted average cost of capital = 8% ∗ (1–0.2) ∗ 0.4 + 14% ∗ 0.6 = 10.96%

$$V_F = 17.52/(10.96\% - 10\%) = \$1825 \text{ million}$$

$$V_E = 1825 - 800 = \$1{,}025 \text{ million}$$

Value per share = 1025/50 = \$20.50

Two-Stage FCFF Model: In the two-stage FCFF model, we assume that the EBIT will grow at a high rate of g_h for n years, and after n years, FCFF will grow at g percent every year. Assuming depreciation is offset by capital investments during the terminal growth stage, working capital as a percent of sales is constant during the terminal growth period. EBIT margin remains constant; FCFF growth rate g will be the same as the sustainable growth rate. The value of the firm is then given by:

$$V_{F,0} = \sum_{t=1}^{n} \frac{FCFF_0 (1+g_h)^t}{(1+WACC)^t} + \frac{1}{(1+WACC)^n}\left(\frac{FCFF_{n+1}}{WACC-g}\right)$$

Three-Stage FCFF Model: In the three-stage FCFF model, we assume that during the stage of high growth, revenues will increase at a rate of g_h for n years, followed by a linear decline during the transition stage for m years to reach the terminal growth of g from year n+m+1. The value of the firm is then given by:

$$V_{F,0} = \text{PV (FCFF during high growth stage)} + \text{PV (FCFF during transition stage)} + \text{PV (Terminal value)}$$

When to use FCFF Model: The FCFF model is appropriate when:

1. FCFF can be estimated and is expected to be positive sometime soon.
2. The company does not have any clear capital structure policy or is in the process of paying down debt like a casino operation.
3. Value of the firm is required as in an acquisition.

25.5.2 *Free Cash Flow to Equity*

FCFE is the amount of cash a business generates available to be potentially distributed to shareholders.

Learning Objectives

- Calculate the value per share using FCFE.

Main Takeaways

Main Points

- The difference between FCFF and FCFE is interest expense and their impact on taxes. Assuming a company has some debt, its FCFF will be higher than FCFE by the after-tax cost of debt amount.
- Like FCFF, the FCFE can be negative. If FCFE is negative, it is a sign that the firm will need to raise or earn new equity, not necessarily immediately.
- FCFF is chosen rather than FCFE because the company to be valued does not have a clear capital structure policy.

Main Terms

- **Working capital:** The capital of a business used in its day-to-day trading operations, calculated as the current assets minus the current liabilities.
- **Free cash flows:** Cash flows from operations that are no longer necessary to be kept in the company and distributed to investors.

(a) FCFE Models

The difference between FCFF and FCFE is interest expense and their impact on taxes. Assuming a company has some debt, its FCFF will be higher than FCFE by the after-tax cost of debt amount.

Like FCFF, the FCFE can be negative. If FCFE is negative, it is a sign that the firm will need to raise or earn new equity, not necessarily immediately.

FCFE is the free cash flow to the equity holders and is calculated as:

FCFE = NI − (Capital investment − Depreciation) − Additional investment in working capital + (Additional borrowings − Loan repayments)

If a company follows a target capital structure of debt ratio of # and uses this structure to finance its additional needs,

FCFE = NI − (1–) (Capital investment − Depreciation) − (1–) Additional investment in working capital

Or

FCFE = Operating cash flow − Additional investments − Debt cash flow
FCFE = FCFF − Debt cash flow

FCFE is the cash flow available to be distributed to equity holders without obstructing the business's operations. Since it is the cash flow before distribution to equity holders, FCFE models are used to value the shares directly.

Since FCFE uses the cash flow before distribution to equity holders, the appropriate discount rate is the cost of equity.

FCFE model can also be single-stage, two-stage, or three-stage models similar to the dividend model depending upon the stage of growth in which the company is in.

Single-Stage FCFE Model: With the single-stage FCFE model, we assume that FCFE will grow at a constant rate of g percent a year for a long time. Taking that the NI margin is constant and working capital as a percentage of sales is constant. The assumed growth rate in FCFE is equal to the sustainable growth rate as depreciation will offset the capital investment. Similar to the single-stage dividend model, the single-stage FCFF model is as follows:

$$V_0 = \frac{FCFE_1}{(r_e - g)} = \frac{FCFE_0(1+g)}{r_e - g}$$

As noted earlier, the FCFE model provides the value of the shares.

Example:

SAFE Limited had revenues of $120 million in 2018. Its Net Income margin is 12%.

Working capital as a percentage of sales is 30%. The revenues are expected to grow at a constant rate of 10% every year. The company has a target capital structure of 40% debt.

Its cost of debt before tax is 8%, and the cost of equity is estimated at 14%. The number of shares outstanding is 50 million. Calculate the value per share using the FCFE model. The tax rate is 20%. Assume that capital investment will be offset by depreciation.

FCFF = NI − (1–) (Capital investment − depreciation) − (1–) Additional investment in working capital

Revenue in 2018	= \$120 million	
NI in 2018 = 120 ∗ 12%	= \$14.4 million	
Capital investment	= depreciation	
Working Capital in 2018	= 30% ∗ 120	= \$36 million
Revenue in 2019	= 120 ∗ 1.1	= \$132 million
NI in 2019 = 132 ∗ 12%	= \$15.84 million	
Working Capital in 2019	= 132 ∗ 30%	= \$39.6 million

Additional investment in working capital at end of 2018 = 39.6 − 36 = \$3.6 million

$$\text{FCFE in 2019} = 15.84 - (1 - 0.4) * 3.6 = \$13.68 \text{ million}$$

$$\text{FCFE per Share} = 13.68/50 = \$0.2736$$

Note that we can calculate the FCFE only for 2019 as the amount of working capital at the beginning of the year 2018 is not known.

$$\text{Cost of equity} = 14\%$$

$$V_0 = 0.2736/(0.14 - 0.10) = \$6.84$$

Two-Stage FCFE Model: With a two-stage FCFE model, we assume that the net income will grow at a high rate of g_h for n years, and after n years, FCFE will grow at g percent every year. We assume that capital investments offset depreciation during the terminal growth stage. Working capital as a percentage of sales is constant during the terminal growth period, and Net profit margin stays constant; FCFE growth rate g will equal the sustainable growth rate. The value of the firm is then given by:

Three-Stage FCFE Model: With a three-stage FCFE model, during the stage of high growth, it is assumed that net income will increase at a rate of g_h for n years, followed by a linear decrease during the transition stage for m years to reach the terminal growth of g from year n+m+1. The value of the firm is then given by

$$V_0 = \sum_{t=1}^{n} \frac{FCFE_0(1+g_h)^t}{(1+r_e)} + \frac{1}{(1+r_e)^n}\left(\frac{FCFE_{n+1}}{r_e - g}\right)$$

V_0= PV (FCFE during high growth stage) + PV (FCFE during transition stage) + PV (Terminal value)

When to use FCFE Model: FCFE model is relevant when:

1. FCFE can be estimated and is expected to be positive soon.
2. The company has a clear capital structure policy of the target debt ratio.
3. The company may or may not pay dividends but does not have a clear dividend policy.

FCFF is chosen rather than FCFE is the company being valued does not have a clear capital structure policy.

References/Further Readings

Damordaran, A. (2012). *Investment Valuation Tools and Techniques for Determining the Value of Any Asset*, 3rd edn. John Wiley & Sons, pp. 351–379.

Pinto, J.E., Henry, E., Robinson, T.R., & Stowe, J.D. (2010). *Equity Asset Valuation*, 2nd edn. John Wiley & Sons, Inc., Chap. 4.

25.6 Sample Questions

Question 1

After a careful analysis, Amalgamate Limited stock's intrinsic value was estimated to be in the range of €17.85 to €21.45. The current market price of the stock is €24.35. This stock is most likely:

(a) Overvalued
(b) Undervalued
(c) Fairly valued

Question 2
An analyst gathers the following information about two companies:

	Bravo	Delta
Current price per share	\$57.32	\$18.93
Last year's EPS	\$3.82	\$1.35
Current year estimated EPS	\$4.75	\$1.40

Which of the following statements is most accurate?

(a) Delta has the higher trailing P/E multiple and lower current estimated P/E multiple.
(b) Bravo has the higher trailing P/E multiple and lower current estimated P/E multiple.
(c) Bravo has the higher trailing P/E multiple and higher current estimated P/E multiple.

Question 3
The Remington Corporation just paid a dividend of \$1.75 per share. Suppose the required rate of return is 12.3% per year, and dividends are expected to grow indefinitely at a constant rate of 9.2% per year. In that case, the intrinsic value of the Remington Corporation stock is closest to:

(a) \$15.54
(b) \$56.45
(c) \$61.65

Question 4
An analyst gathers or estimates the following information about a stock:

Current price per share	€22.56
Current annual dividend per share	€1.60
The annual dividend growth rate for Years 1–4	9.00%
The annual dividend growth rate for Years 5+	4.00%
Required rate of return	12%

Based on a DDM, the stock is most likely:

(a) Undervalued
(b) Fairly valued
(c) Overvalued

Question 5
Asset-based valuation models are best suited to companies where the capital structure does not have a high proportion of:

(a) Debt
(b) Intangible assets
(c) Current assets and liabilities

Question 6
Which of the following is most likely a reason for using asset-based valuation?

(a) The analyst is valuing a privately held company.
(b) The company has a relatively high level of intangible assets.
(c) The market values of assets and liabilities are different from the balance sheet values.

The information provided below is used for Questions 7 and 8

Formula Provided:

$$\text{Operating cash flow} = \text{EBIT} - \text{Increase in net working capital} + \text{Non-cash expenses}$$

An increase in net working capital is calculated as:

Increase in net working capital = (Increase in inventory + Increase in accounts receivables + Increase in other current assets) − (Increase in accounts payables + Increase in other current liabilities).

Note that in valuation, we do not include changes in cash, marketable securities, and notes payables as these are at the discretion of the management and do not arise due mainly through operations.

Calculation of FCFF and FCFE:
Since FCFF is the operating cash flow after making additional investments, FCFF can be written as:

FCFF = EBIT (1–T) + Non-cash expenses − Increase in net working capital − Capital investment

FCFE = NI − (Capital investment − Depreciation) − Increase in net working capital + (Additional borrowings − Loan repayments)

We assume that the company has a target debt ratio, and its finances its additional investment needs using this target debt ratio δ. Then, FCFE can be written as:

FCFE = NI − (1− δ) (Capital investment − Depreciation) − (1 − δ) increase in net working capital

Consider the financial statements of ABC Corporation for the year 2019.

Income Statement (in $'000)	
Net sales	19,000
Materials	6,000
Wages	2,000
Overhead	1,500
Depreciation	1,500
Cost of goods sold	11,000
Gross profit	8,000
Selling expenses	2,000
Administrative expenses	1,000
EBIT	5,000
Interest	1,000
EBT	4,000
Tax (20%)	800
Net Profit	3,200

Balance Sheet

	2018	2019
Cash	1,500	1,300
Receivables	2,000	2,300
Inventory	4,000	4,500
Other C.A.	1,000	800
Total current assets	8,500	8,900
Gross fixed assets	20,000	24,000
Accumulated depreciation	5,000	6,500
Net fixed assets	15,000	17,500
Total assets	23,500	26,400
A/C payables	2,200	2,600
Notes payables	1,300	2,000
Other current liabilities	500	300
Total current liabilities	4,000	4,900
LT debt	6,000	6,000
Equity	10,000	10,000
Retained earnings	3,500	5,500
Total liabilities and equity	23,500	26,400

Question 7
The operation cash flow of ABC in 2019 is:

(a) \$3,200
(b) \$4,300
(c) \$4,700

Question 8
The FCFF and FCFE of ABC in 2019 are respectively:

(a) \$1,100, \$1,000
(b) \$1,100, \$1,500
(c) \$1,900, \$1,500

Solutions

Question 1

Solution: Option **a** is correct.

The current market price of Amalgamate stock exceeds the upper bound of the analyst's estimate of the intrinsic value of the stock.

Question 2

Solution: Option **b** is correct.

$$\text{P/E} = \text{Current price/EPS}$$

and

$$\text{Estimated P/E} = \text{Current price/Estimated EPS.}$$

$$\text{Alpha P/E} = \$57.32/\$3.82 = 15.01$$

$$\text{Alpha estimated P/E} = \$57.32/4.75 = 12.07$$

$$\text{Delta P/E} = \$18.93/\$1.35 = 14.02$$

$$\text{Delta estimated P/E} = \$18.93/\$1.40 = 13.52$$

Question 3

Solution: Option **c** is correct.

$P_0 = D_1/(r - g) = 1.75(1.092)/(0.123 - 0.092) = \$61.65.$

Question 4

Solution: Option **a** is correct.

The current price of €22.56 is less than the intrinsic value (V_0) of €24.64; therefore, the stock appears to be currently undervalued. According to the two-stage DDM:

$$V_0 = \Sigma \frac{D_0(1+g_s)^t}{(1+r)^t} + \frac{V_n}{(1+r)^t} \text{ and } V_n = \frac{D_{n+1}}{r - g_{\text{L}}}$$

$$D_{N+1} = D_0(1 + g_s)^n(1 + g_L)$$

$D_1 = €1.60 \times 1.09 = €1.744$

$D_2 = €1.60 \times (1.09)^2 = €1.901$

$D_3 = €1.60 \times (1.09)^3 = €2.072$

$D_4 = €1.60 \times (1.09)^4 = €2.259$

$D_5 = [€1.60 \times (1.09)^4](1.04) = €2.349$

$V_4 = €2.349/(0.12 - 0.04) = €29.363$

$$V_0 = \frac{1.744}{(1.12)^1} + \frac{1.901}{(1.12)^2} + \frac{2.072}{(1.12)^3} + \frac{2.259}{(1.12)^4} + \frac{29.363}{(1.12)^4}$$
$$= 24.64, \text{which is greater than } 22.56$$

Question 5

Solution: Option **b** is correct.

Intangible assets are hard to value. Therefore, asset-based valuation models work best for companies that do not have a high proportion of intangible assets.

Question 6

Solution: Option **a** is correct.

Asset-based valuations are most often used when an analyst is valuing private enterprises. Both B and C are considerations in asset-based valuations but are more likely to be reasons to avoid that valuation model rather than reasons to use it.

Question 7

Solution: Option **b** is correct

Net profit = **$3,200**
Non-cash expenses = Depreciation = **$1,500**
Change in receivables = (2300-2000) = $300;
Change in inventory = (4500-4000) = $500;

Change in other current assets = (800–1000) = ($200);
Change in accounts payables = (2600 − 2200) = $400;
Change in other current liabilities = (300 − 500) = ($200).
Change in working capital = Δ Receivables + Δ Inventory + Δ Other CA − Δ A/C payables − Δ Other CL
Change in working capital = 300 + 500 − 200 − 400 + 200 = **+$400**.
There is a $400 increase in working capital which is a cash outflow.

Operating cash flow = 3200 + 1500 − 400 = $4,300

Note that change in notes payables is not taken into account as this change is not due to operations but is at the management's discretion.

Question 8

Solution: Option **a** is correct

FCFF = EBIT (1–T) + Depreciation − Increase in net working capital − capital investment
EBIT = $5000;
Depreciation = $1,500;
Increase in net working capital = $400 (Calculated in the example);
Capital investment = Change in gross fixed assets
= 24,000 − 20,000 = $4,000;
T = 20%
FCFF = 5000 (1–20%) + 1500 − 400 − 4000
= **$1,100**

FCFE = NI − (Capital investment − Depreciation) − Increase in net working capital + (Additional borrowings − Loan repayments)
Other borrowings − Loan repayments
= Change in short term debt + Change in notes payables + Change in long-term debt
= 0 + 700 + 0 = $700
FCFE = 3200 − (4000 − 1500) − 400 + 700 = **$1,000**

Part K: Fixed Income

Chapter 26

Characteristics of Bonds

26.1 Features

26.1.1 *Basic Features of Fixed Income Instruments*

A fixed income security is an investment that provides a return in the form of fixed periodic interest payments and the return of principal at maturity.

Learning Objectives

- Describe the various features and terminologies associated with a bond.

Main Takeaways

Main Points

- The terms of a bond describe the amount and timing of the cash flows from the bond and the rights and obligations of the issuer and the bondholders.
- A fixed income security provides investors with fixed periodic interest payments and the principal's return at maturity.

Main Terms

- **Par value:** The principal amount to be repaid at the end of the bond's life.
- **Coupon rate:** The promised annual interest rate payable on the bond.
- **Maturity:** The time until the par value is repaid.

- **Bond indenture:** The legal contract between the issuer and bondholders describing the rights and obligations of the issuer and the bondholders.
- **Bond provisions:** The special arrangements regarding the redemption of the principal.
- **Bond covenants:** The promises to be fulfilled by the bond issuer.
- **Credit rating:** An indicator of an issuer's creditworthiness. A higher credit rating implies a lower risk of the bond's default when the issuer fails to make either coupon interest or principal payments.
- **Bond trustee:** This is a firm to whom the bond issuer remits the annual or semi-annual payments to be distributed to the bondholders. On behalf of the bondholders, the trustee monitors that the bond issuer fulfills its obligations under the terms of the bond covenants. Any infringement will be reported to the bondholders.

Fixed income securities, or bonds as they are commonly known, are long-term IOUs issued by corporations, governments or sovereigns, and supranational organizations like the World Bank. The typical bond pays a fixed interest or coupon amount periodically, typically every six months. Hence the name fixed income. We explore the various features associated with a bond.

(a) Par Value

Par value is also known as the face value or redemption value. It is the principal amount to be repaid at the end of the bond's life. The par value for most bonds is $1,000.

(b) Coupon Rate

The coupon rate is the promised annual interest rate payable on the bond. This rate is sometimes known as the nominal interest rate. The coupon rate may be a fixed or variable (floating) rate. The coupon amount is the coupon rate multiplied by the par value.

Floating Rate Bonds are called *floating rate notes (FRNs) or floaters*. The coupon rate is not fixed but reset periodically. The coupon rate is equal to a reference rate plus a margin, for example, (LIBOR + 2%). For a long time, the most common reference rate was the London Interbank Offer Rate (LIBOR). However, because of a scandal involving the LIBOR manipulation, it will be superseded by its successor, the Secured Overnight Financing Rate (SOFR).

Other Bond Rate Structures: Other structures include the *step-up coupon rate,* where the coupon rate is increased over time. Another structure is the *deferred coupon,* where the coupon is not paid in the first few years of the bond's life but is deferred till a later date. The deferred coupon structure is popular with infrastructure projects which take a considerable time to complete. Only upon completing the infrastructure project would the project deliver cash flows to service the loan.

Zero Coupon Bonds: Some bonds do not pay interest at all. These bonds are known *as zero coupon bonds.* The bondholder's interest is implicit in the difference between the face value and the price, set at a discount to the principal or face value.

Inverse Floaters: Are bonds whose coupon rate moves in the opposite direction of the reference rate. Thus the coupon rate = K − L × reference rate, where K is a fixed rate and L is some multiplier known as the coupon leverage.

Credit-Linked Coupon Bonds: Have coupon rates that would change if the bond's credit rating changes. For example, if the credit rating of the bond declines, that is, its risk increases, then investors would require a higher yield to compensate for the higher risk. In this case, the coupon rate would be adjusted upwards.

Another coupon structure is that *of the payment-in-kind (PIK)* bonds. Such bonds pay interest in the form of additional bonds.

Finally, *index-linked bonds* have the coupon payment linked to some index. An important index-linked bond is an inflation-linked bond, for example, the US Treasury Inflation Protected Security (TIPS). The coupon payment is based on the principal, which is adjusted by the inflation index.

(c) Maturity

Maturity is the time until the par or face value is repaid. It is usually denoted in years. If the bond has no stated maturity date, it is known as *a perpetual bond.*

Bonds with maturities of one year or less are known as *money market securities*. Bonds with maturities longer than a year are known as *capital market securities.* Short-term bonds with maturities less than ten years are often called *notes.*

(d) Bond Indenture

The bond indenture is also known as the *trust deed*. It is the legal contract that prescribes the issuer's obligations and the bondholders' rights. Some of the items in the indenture include as follows.

(1) Collaterals

These are the assets or guarantees that serve as *security* if the loan is unpaid. Other creditors or bondholders whose claims are not backed by these collaterals will not be paid out of these collaterals' proceeds.

- A *collateral trust bond* is one where the collateral is in financial assets, while an *equipment trust bond* is a bond with physical assets serving as the collateral. For example, the collateral backing *equipment trust bonds* could be planes and construction equipment.
- Other forms of collateral include mortgages and accounts receivable.

(2) Repayment of principal arrangements

There are various arrangements regarding the principal's repayment.

A *bullet bond* is a bond where the principal is repaid in full at maturity.

For a fully amortized bond, the bond's equal annual payments result in the bond's principal amount being fully repaid by the bond's maturity. Each annual payment comprises the interest and the principal payment components. In the *partially amortized bond,* the bond's annual payments are insufficient to fully repay the principal amount by maturity.

Table 26.1 shows the payment schedules for each of the three amortization arrangements: bullet, fully amortized, and partially amortized bonds.

(3) Bond provisions

These are arrangements that give rise to the possibility of part or full repayment of the principal before maturity. A fuller discussion is in the next section.

(4) Bond covenants

They describe the issuer's promises concerning the actions regarding the bond.

Table 26.1: Payment schedules for the bullet, fully amortized and partially amortized bonds.

Bullet Bond (Interest = 10%)				
Year	Investor cash flows	Interest payment	Principal payment	Outstanding principal at the end of the year
0	−1,000.00			1,000.00
1	100.00	100.00	0.00	1,000.00
2	100.00	100.00	0.00	1,000.00
3	1,100.00	100.00	1,000.00	0.00
Fully Amortized Bond (Interest = 10%)				
Year	Investor cash flows	Interest payment	Principal payment	Outstanding principal at the end of the year
0	−1,000.00			
1	402.11	100.00	302.11	697.89
2	402.11	69.79	332.32	365.55
3	402.11	36.56	365.55	0
Partially Amortized Bond (Interest = 6%)				
Year	Investor cash flows	Interest payment	Principal payment	Outstanding principal at the end of the year
0	−1,000.00			
1	201.92	60.00	141.92	858.08
2	201.92	51.48	150.43	707.65
3	201.92	42.46	159.46	548.19

Affirmative covenants consist of actions the issuer promises to take. Examples are promises to pay interest and principal on a timely basis, paying taxes when they come due, maintaining properties in good condition, and submitting periodic reports to the trustee.

Negative covenants consist of actions the issuer is prohibited from undertaking. Such restrictions include the issuance of more debt beyond a stated debt ratio, the disposal of assets, payments of large dividends, the type of investments the firm can undertake, and mergers and acquisitions unless the terms of the old bonds are carried over to the new entity. A significant negative covenant is a *negative pledge*. This pledge prohibits the issuance of new debt which ranks above or is senior to the existing debt.

(e) Currency Denomination

This describes the currency in which the bond's cash flows are paid.

If a bond is denominated in the currency of the country in which the issuer is domiciled or registered, it is known as a *domestic bond.* An example is a Singapore company issuing a Singapore dollar-denominated bond.

Should a foreign entity decide to issue a bond in another country, in the currency of that country, the bond is known as a *foreign bond.* An example is Toyota Motors issuing a Singapore dollar bond in Singapore.

Should any entity issue a bond in a currency outside the country of that currency, then the bond is known as a *euro bond.* An example is Toyota Motors issuing a US dollar bond outside the US. US authorities would not regulate the Toyota Motors euro bond since it is not issued in the US. For this reason, the issuance process can be much faster. The euro bond market is mostly institutional, that is, the participants are mainly financial institutions and large corporations.

Some bonds involve more than one currency. *Dual currency bonds* pay the coupons in one currency and the principal in another.

Currency option bonds give the bondholder the right to choose the currency in which the coupon or the principal is paid.

(f) Legal Entity

A company usually issues a bond in its own name. However, it may choose to issue a bond under a separate entity which it sets up and owns.

The alternative arrangement creates a separate entity known as a *Special Purpose Vehicle (SPV)* or *Special Purpose Entity (SPE)* to issue the bond. In this case, the assets which back the bond are held by the SPV. The bonds issued by the SPV may have a higher credit rating than the company that is behind the bond issue. The reason is that the SPV holds the assets backing the bond, and the firm's other bondholders have no claim on them. With a higher credit rating for the SPV, the company can reduce the coupon rate or cost that the SPV bond entails.

(g) Bond Identification

A bond is identified by the issuer's name, the coupon rate, and the date of issue. For example, a Toyota Motors bond would be identified as such: Toyota Motors 3.5s of 1/4/30, which means a Toyota Motors bond paying a 3.5% coupon and maturing on 1/4/30.

(h) Bond Price

In the market, bond prices are quoted as percentages of the par value. Under this convention, the par value is 100. A price of 95 means the bond price is 95% × $1,000 or $950 if the par value is $1,000.

26.1.2 *Contingency Provisions: Call, Put, Sinking Fund and Convertible Provisions*

Contingency provisions are sometimes included in the bond indenture. These provisions alter the bond's risk profile and consequently the required return compared to similar bonds without the provisions.

Learning Objectives

- Describe the call, put and sinking fund provisions, and discuss the implications of the presence of these provisions on the bond's returns.

Main Takeaways

Main Points

- Contingency provisions are arrangements that give rise to the possibility of early repayment of the principal in part or in full.
- The call provision allows the issuer to redeem the bonds before maturity.
- The put provision allows the bondholder to sell the bonds back to the issuer before maturity.
- A fall in interest rates gives the issuer an incentive to call the bonds, while a rise in interest rates provides the bondholder with an incentive to sell the bonds back to the issuer.
- When interest rates fall and the issuer redeems the bond, it can then issue new bonds that pay a lower coupon interest. Similarly, when interest rates rise, the bondholder may want to sell the bonds back to the issuer and use the proceeds to invest in bonds that pay higher coupon interest than the earlier bond.
- The sinking fund provision does not confer a right but rather an obligation on the issuer to redeem a portion of the bonds periodically before maturity.
- The convertible feature allows the bondholder to convert the bonds into stock. The feature increases the convertible bond's value when the stock price rises.
- As each provision gives an advantage to one party, the issuer or the bondholder, the bond's required return is adjusted to reflect this,

compared to the return of a comparable bond without the provision. If the provision disadvantages the bondholder, the required return will be higher than a similar bond without the provision.

Main Terms

- **Call provision:** Allows the issuer to redeem the bond issue before the bond's maturity.
- **Put provision:** Allows the bondholder to sell the bonds back to the issuer before the bond's maturity.
- **Sinking fund provision:** Requires the issuer to redeem a portion of the bond issue periodically before the bond's maturity.
- **Convertible provision:** Allows the bond to be converted into the company's shares.

Contingency provisions are sometimes included in the bond indenture. The call provision gives the issuer the option to buy back the bonds from bondholders, while the put provision provides the bondholder with the option to sell the bonds back to the issuer. The sinking fund provision provides an orderly way to reduce the size of bonds outstanding. Finally, the convertible provision allows the bondholder to convert the bonds into shares.

(a) Call Provision

A call provision gives the issuer the right to redeem the bond before maturity. When a bond with a call provision is first issued, it is usually protected from being called for a period known as the call protection or lock-out period. There are different styles or ways in which the call can be exercised. The American style allows the issuer to call at any time after the call protection period, while the European style allows the bond to be called only on the call date. A Bermuda-style call allows the bond to be callable only on dates specified in a call schedule.

(b) Put Provision

A put provision gives the bondholder the right to ask for the bond to be redeemed before maturity. Like the call provision, the bond will also have a period during which the bond cannot be put or sold back to the issuer. A one-time put bond allows the bondholder only one opportunity to exercise the put option before maturity. In contrast, a multiple put bond gives the bondholder multiple opportunities to sell the bond back to the issuer.

(c) Sinking Fund Provision

The sinking fund provision requires the issuer to buy back a portion of the bonds. The bond's outstanding size at maturity is significantly reduced compared to the original issue's size. This reduces the risk of the issuer not repaying the outstanding principal.

(d) Convertible Provision

The convertible provision gives the bondholder the option to convert the bond into shares. The number of shares each bond can be converted into is known as the *conversion ratio*. Alternatively, the price at which each share can be bought using the bond is known as the *conversion price*. The conversion ratio is the bond's par value divided by the conversion price. Note that we only need to know either the conversion ratio or the conversion price. Knowing one of them allows us to calculate the other easily.

Contingent convertible bonds, known as "Cocos", are bonds converted into the issuer's shares when the company's equity value falls below a certain amount. Banks issue such bonds to maintain their Tier 1 capital adequacy ratio which shows the proportion of the bank's capital to the loans. A higher capital adequacy ratio means a bigger cushion against losses due to bad loans.

Implications of Contingency Provisions: The bond issuer has the incentive to exercise the call option when interest rates have fallen such that the required return for the bond is less than the coupon rate. There are two ways to view this situation. The first is that a fall in the required return results in the rise of the bond price. The issuer is paying a lower call price than the market price by calling the bond. The second view is that by calling the bond, the issuer can now issue new bonds that pay a lower coupon rate than the old bonds. A bond with a call provision denies the bondholder from enjoying a higher coupon rate than what could be obtained in the market when interest rates have fallen. Consequently, to compensate for this disadvantage, the issuer would have to offer a higher return or yield in the form of a higher coupon rate for a callable bond than a comparable bond without the call provision.

The two parties involved in the bond issue are the issuer and the bondholder. What one party gains, the other party loses. In other words, it is a zero-sum game. Thus, we can view the put provision as giving us the call provision's mirror image. Using the call provision as a reference, the bondholder would have an incentive to exercise the put provision if the required return becomes higher than the coupon rate when interest rates rise. An increase in the bond's required return would cause the bond price to decrease. If the bond price goes below the par value and the bondholder exercises the put provision, the bondholder would then be selling the bond at a higher price, the par value, than the current bond price. Alternatively, the funds obtained by selling the bond back to the issuer could be used to buy new bonds that pay a higher coupon than the old bond. The put provision confers an advantage for the bondholder with regard to changes in the interest rate. Consequently, the issuer would issue putable bonds with a lower coupon rate than comparable bonds without the put provision.

The sinking fund provision requires the issuer to reduce the size of the outstanding bonds over time. This reduction makes it more likely that the issuer would redeem the remaining bonds at maturity than if the issuer had to redeem a much larger amount of bonds if there were no sinking fund provision. As bonds with a sinking fund provision have a lower risk of default, their required return would be lower than comparable bonds without the sinking fund provision.

26.2 Types of Bonds

There are many types of bond issuers. They range from countries, state governments, and corporations.

Learning Objectives

- Describe the features of sovereign, municipal, and corporate bonds and Euro and foreign bonds and money market instruments and differentiate the risks of different types of bonds.

Main Takeaways

Main Points

- The term bond is used to describe debt instruments with maturities exceeding one year.
- Debt instruments with maturities of less than one year are known as money market instruments.
- The issuers' credit ratings largely determine, all else equal, the risks of bonds. Within a country, the sovereign bond has the lowest risk.
- Whether municipal bonds have higher or lower risks than corporate bonds depends on their credit standing, unless the municipality's finances are linked closely to those of the sovereign government.

Main Terms

- **Sovereign bond:** A bond issued by the government of a country.
- **Municipal bond:** A bond issued by a municipality. A municipality is a subdivision, for example, a city or town, of a country and has a local government to cater to the local needs.
- **Corporate bond:** A bond issued by a corporate entity.
- **Money market instrument:** A debt instrument with a maturity of less than a year issued to meet short-term financing needs.
- **Off-the-run:** Off-the-run treasuries are Treasury bonds and notes issued before the more recently issued, on-the-run, bond or note of a particular maturity.
- **Promissory note:** A financial instrument that contains a written promise by one party (the note's issuer or maker) to pay another party (the note's payee) a definite sum of money, either on-demand or at a specified future date

Bonds with maturities of more than one year are known as capital market instruments or securities. Bonds with maturities less than a year are known as money market instruments or securities.

As the US bond market is the most active globally, we will discuss the various types of bonds issued in the US. The sovereign bonds issued in the US are securities issued by the US Treasury. US Treasury Bonds and Treasury Bills are considered very safe securities and are bought not only by US entities but also by foreign governments. US Treasury securities form quite a large portion of various countries' reserves.

26.2.1 *Sovereign, Municipal, Corporate and Euro and Foreign Bonds*

Sovereign Bonds: In the US, the US Treasury issues bonds that are considered default free since they are backed by the full faith and credit of the US government. Such securities have low returns or yields, reflecting their *risk-free* nature. Long-term US Treasury bonds are issued with a maturity of 10 years. Such bonds' yields serve as benchmarks for bonds with higher risk, where the higher risk is compensated for by an extra amount of return or yield known as the risk premium.

US Treasury bonds are issued in minimum denominations of multiples of $1,000. Such bonds trade in very active secondary markets. The liquidity of treasury bonds is denoted in the following order of liquidity. *Benchmark* securities are the most recently issued securities and are most liquid. They are followed by *on-the-run* securities that have been recently issued. The less liquid securities are the older securities known as *off-the-run* securities.

(i) Treasury Strips: Besides trading whole Treasury notes and bonds, the components of these Treasury securities components, namely the interest payments and the principal repayment, can be traded separately. When a Treasury bond is decomposed into two parts, the result is the creation of "Separate Trading of Registered Interest and Principal Securities" or STRIPS. The periodic interest payments are known as the Interest Only (IO) security, while the principal payment is known as Principal Only (PO) security. POs are essentially zero coupon bonds and are useful for immunizing against interest rate risk, that is, to ensure that interest rate risk does not affect the anticipated value of the bond that will be used to pay off liabilities. Figure 26.1 shows the cash flows from a STRIP.

Municipal Bonds: Municipal bonds (munis) are bonds issued by state or local governments. In the US, interest from munis is not taxed at the federal level. It allows municipal governments to finance their projects at lower cost. The tax exemption makes it attractive to investors as they require lower yields on munis compared to taxable bonds with equivalent risk.

A comparison of municipal bond rates with taxable corporate bond rates cannot be done directly. We have to adjust the return of one or the other. The formula to adjust for taxes is simple:

$i_a = i_b * (1 - t)$ where a and b stand for after tax and before tax, respectively.

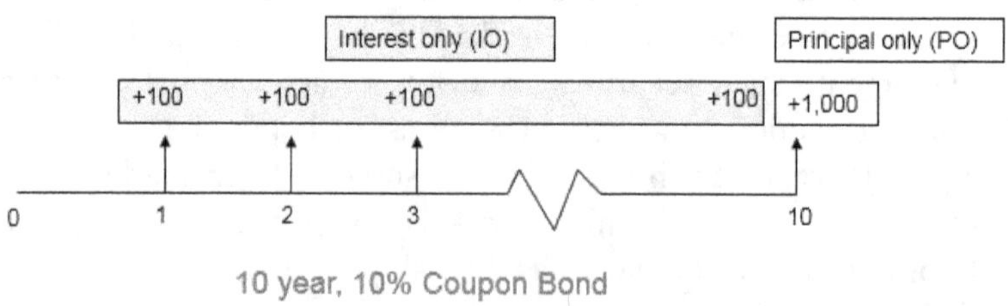

Figure 26.1: Treasury STRIP.

Take a 5% muni bond. The coupon rate appears rather low compared to a 6.5% corporate bond of equivalent risk. To make a comparison, both bond rates must be put on the same tax basis. For an investor paying tax at 30 the after-tax corporate bond rate $i_a = 6.5\% * (1 - 0.3) = 4.55\%$. The investor is able to obtain a higher after-tax interest rate with the muni rather than the corporate bond.

I. *General obligation (GO)* bonds are munis backed by the municipality's full taxing power.
II. *Revenue bonds* are raised to finance projects whose revenues are used only to repay such bonds. Such bonds are riskier than GOs as general tax revenues cannot be used to make payments on revenue bonds.

Corporate Bonds: Corporations raise funds for long-term capital needs by issuing corporate bonds. Such bonds can be quite risky if they are used to finance risky projects. The risk of the bond is assessed by one or more rating agencies. The minimum denomination is $1,000 on publicly traded bonds. For a *mortgage bond*, specific assets are set aside as collateral which make repayment of the bonds more secure. In the event of non-payment of interest or principal, the trustee has the right sell to sell the assets to recover money for the bondholders. *Debentures* have no specific assets pledged as collateral. Hence, they are riskier than mortgage bonds and have to pay higher yields. Subordinated debentures are even riskier since they are paid after the debentures.

Euro and Foreign Bonds: *Eurobonds* are bonds that are denominated in a local currency of a country but issued outside the same country. An example of a Eurobond is a bond denominated in US dollars but issued outside the US. One reason for the popularity of Eurobonds is that they circumvent regulation since they are issued in a foreign country.

Foreign bonds are bonds issued by foreign firms in the domestic currency. For example, Samurai bonds are yen-denominated bonds issued by foreign borrowers in Japan. Colorful names have been given to such bonds issued in various countries: Australia (koala), China (panda), India (masala), Korea (kimchi), Spain (matador), UK (bulldog), and the US (yankee).

26.2.2 *Money Market Instruments*

US Treasury Bills: US T-bills are short-term obligations of the US government issued to finance government spending needs. Typical maturities are 1, 3, 6, and 12 months. T-bills are considered default free, and the 1-year T-Bill rate is often used as a short-term risk-free rate.

Commercial Paper: Commercial paper is short-term *debt with maturity of less than a year*. It is usually issued by corporations and financial institutions with low default risk since it is an unsecured loan. Commercial paper is not very liquid and investors buy them because of the higher yield than government securities with similar maturity.

Negotiable Certificates of Deposit: A negotiable certificate of deposit (CD) is a short-term bearer security. It signifies ownership of of a time deposit at a bank from which the bearer can redeem the CD at maturity. Large CDs are negotiable instruments; that is, the ownership can be transferred. Their maturities have a similar range as T-Bills.

Banker's Acceptance (BA): The BA or draft is often used in international trade. The seller writes either a time draft or a sight draft. If the buyer of the goods or services accepts it, he undertakes to pay the amount on the draft. A *sight draft* is a claim that is payable when presented to the purchaser. A *time draft* is a claim that is payable at a future date shown on the draft.

If the seller is uncertain about the buyer's credit standing, the seller will only ship the goods if a third party guarantees the payment. A BA is a time draft where a bank guarantees payment by the buyer.

The time draft can be sold as a discount instrument, if:

- Seller proves that the goods have been shipped, and
- Documentation is presented to the buyer.

If the seller of the goods is not in urgent need of the funds, she will wait until maturity to receive payment. However, if the seller cannot wait, she can discount (sell at a discount) the note with the bank and receive the discounted face amount immediately.

BAs are bearer instruments with maturities of less than a year. The yields of BAs are very close to T-bill yields because the default risk is relatively low.

26.2.3 *Repurchase Agreements*

In a repurchase agreement contract, one party agrees to sell some securities to the other party with a promise to repurchase the securities at a specified price at a later date. The security used in the repurchase agreement is usually the T-bill. Hence, we can consider a repurchase agreement as a collateralized loan with T-bills serving as the loan's collateral.

In a reverse repurchase agreement (reverse repo) the obligation of each is opposite to that of the repo. In fact, where one party views the agreement as a repo, the other party would view it as a reverse repo. Repos generally have short-term maturities from 1 to 2 weeks.

Reference/Further Reading

Fabozzi, F.J. (2007). *Fixed Income Analysis*, 2nd edn. John Wiley & Sons, Inc., pp. 1–16, 37–73.

26.3 Sample Questions

Question 1
Which of the following is not true about a zero-coupon bond?

(a) Discount bond
(b) Par bond
(c) Deferred-coupon bond

Question 2
An example of a negative covenant is the requirement:

(a) To maintain and ensure fixed assets are in good condition
(b) To pay taxes when they come due
(c) That assets are not disposed of unless newer assets replace them

Question 3
An example of a domestic bond is a bond issued by

(a) Toyota Motors in Japan, denominated in US dollars; and sold in the US
(b) A Citibank subsidiary incorporated in Singapore, denominated in Singapore dollars and sold in Singapore
(c) Delta Airlines from the US, denominated in US dollars and sold in Europe

Question 4
A bond issued by British Airways in the UK, denominated in US dollars, and sold to an institutional investor in Germany, is most likely an example of a:

(a) Euro bond
(b) Global bond
(c) Domestic bond

Question 5
The structure that requires the largest repayment of principal at maturity is that of a

(a) Bullet bond
(b) Fully amortized bond
(c) Callable bond

Question 6
A bond with an embedded option that results in it being sold at a lower price than an otherwise similar bond without the option is likely a:

(a) Putable bond
(b) Callable bond
(c) Convertible bond

Question 7
The risk introduced by the call feature in a bond is best described as:

(a) Interest rate risk
(b) Reinvestment rate risk
(c) Liquidity risk

Question 8

The put provision of a putable bond

(a) Limits the risk to the bondholder
(b) Does not materially affect the risk of either the issuer or the bondholder
(c) Limits the risk to the bondholder only when interest rates fall

Question 9

For two bonds with similar characteristics, a sovereign bond and a non-sovereign bond, the sovereign bond is likely to trade at a yield that is:

(a) Lower
(b) Higher
(c) Lower than sovereign bonds when demand for sovereign bonds is low

Solutions

Question 1

Solution: Option **b** is correct.

Options (a) and (c) describe a zero coupon bond's attributes. As the zero-coupon bond does not make any coupon payment, the only return source is capital gain. Therefore the bond must sell at a discount or below the par value. Similarly, as there is no payment of intermediate cash flows, and the only payment is the face value, the zero coupon bond can be thought of as having a deferred coupon, in a sense, with the coupon being the par value. A par bond is a bond whose price is the par value which does not describe the zero coupon bond since it sells at a discount.

Question 2

Solution: Option **c** is correct.

A negative covenant requires the issuer not to do certain things. (a) and (b) are positive covenants.

Question 3

Solution: Option **b** is correct.

A domestic bond is issued by a local entity in the local currency and sold locally. (a) describes a foreign bond, while (c) describes a euro bond.

Question 4

Solution: Option **a** is correct.

A euro bond is a bond issued in a currency outside the currency's country.

Question 5

Solution: Option **a** is correct.

A bullet bond has just one payment: the repayment of the face value at maturity. The fully amortized bond pays the same amount each period, including the bond's maturity. This amortized payment consists of both interest and partial principal repayment. The purpose of a sinking fund is to reduce the outstanding amount to be repaid at maturity instead of the full amount of the face value.

Question 6

Solution: Option **b** is correct.

It is easier to change the perspective to looking at the bond yield. A lower price implies a higher yield. A higher yield than a comparable bond without the embedded option means the option disadvantages the bondholder. This is consistent with a callable bond. Answers (a) and (c) are advantages for the bondholder. The bondholder can exercise the put option when interest rates fall below the coupon rate. The convertible provision makes the bond more attractive as its value can be very high if the stock price increases substantially. Hence, both the put and convertible feature would result in a lowering of the required yield implying the bond would sell at a higher price.

Question 7

Solution: Option **b** is correct.

A bond is more likely to be called when interest rates fall below the coupon rate as the issuer can then refinance the bond at a lower coupon rate. This means the bondholder will be reinvesting the proceeds from the redemption of the bond at a lower coupon rate. Interest rate risk is about the price change with a change in interest rates. Interest rate risk and liquidity risk are not inherent to callable bonds but all bonds.

Question 8

Solution: Option **a** is correct.

The put provision limits the bondholder's risk from an increase in interest rates. A higher interest rate implies a lower price. As the bondholder can sell the bond back to the issuer at the par value with a put provision, the par value is the floor or lowest value for the putable bond. (c) is not the answer, as a fall in interest rates increases the bond value.

Question 9

Solution: Option **b** is correct.

Non-sovereign bonds have a higher risk than sovereign bonds and should have a higher required yield.

Chapter 27

Valuation of Bonds

27.1 Bond Pricing

The price of a bond is the present discounted value of the future cash flow stream generated by the bond.

Learning Objectives

- Explain how a bond can be priced using the yield to maturity or a series of spot rates to discount the cash flows and how to price bonds bought in-between coupon payment dates.

Main Takeaways

Main Points

- The price of a bond is the present value of the cash flows consisting of coupon and principal payments. The bond's yield to maturity is the discount rate that equates the bond price to the present value of the cash flows.
- The present value of the cash flows can be computed using spot rates as discount rates for the individual cash flows.
- If a bond is bought between coupon dates, an adjustment must be made for the accrued interest.
- The bond's full price or dirty price is the present value of the cash flows received.
- The flat price or clean price is the full price less the accrued interest.

Main Terms

- **Yield:** It refers to the yield to maturity or the return that accrues to the bond if it is held to maturity, assuming that coupon payments are reinvested at the yield to maturity.
- **Spot rate:** The return of a zero-coupon bond.
- **Accrued interest:** Interest earned but not received.
- **Full price or dirty price:** This is computed as the present value of the cash flows received, including the accrued interest.
- **Flat price clean price:** This is equal to the full price less the accrued interest.

A typical rate used to discount the bond's cash flows is the bond's yield to maturity. Another method uses spot rates to discount the cash flows.

A complication arises when bonds are bought or sold between coupon payment dates. The buyer has to compensate the seller for the accrued interest. The accrued interest is interest earned by the seller but will be received by the buyer.

27.1.1 *Bond Valuation Using the Yield to Maturity*

Principles of Valuation: An asset's value is equal to the sum of the present values of its expected cash flows. There are three steps to value a bond:

1. Estimate the expected cash flows;
2. Establish the appropriate discount rate(s);
3. Compute the present value of the expected cash flows.

Estimate Expected Cash Flows: Cash flows are the coupon and principal payments. It is relatively simple to estimate the expected cash flows of *plain vanilla bonds* such as *non-callable Treasury securities* and *option-free bonds* because of the high degree of certainty regarding the promised payments. The reason is these securities are practically default-free and there are no options to potentially change the pattern of cash flows. However, bonds with embedded options are more challenging.

Establish the Appropriate Discount Rate(s): The starting point in this step is the yield of a default-free bond. The yield of an "on-the-run" Treasury security with the same cash flows is used. Depending on the default risk of the bond, an appropriate yield premium is added to the Treasury security yield.

Compute the Present Value of the Expected Cash Flows: The bond's cash flows consist of the coupon payments and the repayment of principal. If bonds usually pay interest annually the coupon amount is the coupon rate multiplied by the par value. A zero-coupon bond has only one payment — the repayment of principal.

The bond's valuation is similar to finding the present value of a series of cash flows using the yield to maturity as the discount rate.

$$PV = \frac{PMT}{(1+r)^1} + \frac{PMT}{(1+r)^2} + \cdots + \frac{PMT + FV}{(1+r)^N}$$

or

$$\text{The price of bond} = \text{Annual coupon payment} \times \left[\frac{1-\frac{1}{(1+r)^n}}{r}\right] + \frac{\text{Par value}}{(1+r)^n}$$

Valuing Semi-Annual-Coupon Bonds: In practice, most of the bonds pay interest semi-annually. The formula used to calculate the present value of a semi-annual-coupon bond is similar to that of the annual-coupon bonds except the coupon payments are half those of the annual-coupon bonds.

$$\text{Price of bond} = \text{Semi-annual coupon payment} \times \left[\frac{1-\frac{1}{(1+r/2)^{n\times 2}}}{r}\right] + \frac{\text{Par value}}{(1+r/2)^{n\times 2}}$$

Valuing Zero-Coupon Bonds: As there is only one cash flow for the zero-coupon bond — the principal repayment or par value, its value is just the present value of the principal. The formula to be used is:

$$\text{Price} = \frac{\text{Par value}}{(1+r/2)^{n\times 2}}$$

where r is the annual discount rate, and n is the number of years to maturity.

27.1.2 *Bond Valuation Using the Spot Rate*

Spot Rates: Treasury securities spot rates are the yields of zero-coupon Treasury bonds. We use these yields to value default-free cash flows.

Valuing a Bond Using Spot Rates: Instead of discounting all the bond's cash flows by a single rate, we can discount each cash flow by the appropriate spot rate. (Recall that a spot rate is a yield to maturity for a zero-coupon bond.)

For example, we are given a 3-year 5% coupon bond and the following spot rates.

Time to maturity	Spot rate
1 year	2%
2 years	3%
3 years	4%

The value of the bond is given by

$$P_B = \frac{5}{(1+0.02)} + \frac{5}{(1+0.03)^2} + \frac{5+100}{(1+0.04)^2} = 102.96$$

27.1.3 *Bond Valuation between Coupon Payments*

A bond is seldom purchased on the coupon payment date. If a bond is purchased between two coupon payment dates, part of the first coupon that is received by the buyer consists of interest earned by the seller, or the accrued interest. An example of this is shown in Figure 27.1.

At the time of purchase, the price paid by the buyer includes the accrued interest. This price is known as the full price or dirty price which is just the present value of the bond cash flows.

Bond investors would like to know the true cost of the bond they bought. As the Full Price includes the accrued interest that the buyer pays the seller first but recovers it later, this accrued interest is deducted from the full price to give the clean price or flat price or simply the price. The clean price is the price that is quoted in the market.

$$\text{Clean Price} = \text{Full Price} - \text{Accrued Interest}$$

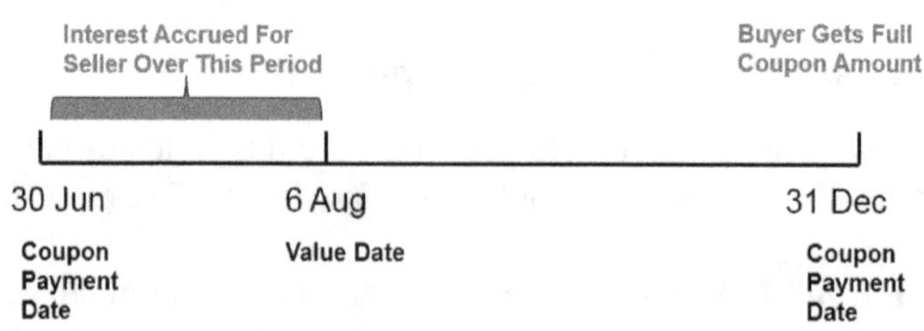

Figure 27.1: Accrued interest.

Accrued interest is calculated using the formula

$$\text{Accrued interest} = t/T \times \text{PMT}$$

where t is the number of days from the last coupon payment to the settlement date, T is the number of days in the coupon period, and PMT is the coupon payment per period.

In computing the accrued interest, various conventions relate to the computation of t and T in the formula. Two popular conventions are Actual/Actual and 30/360, which describe the number of days in the month/the number of days in the year.

Example:
Suppose the last coupon was paid on 30 June. The settlement date of the bond was 6 August. The semi-annual coupon payment is \$20. Then the accrued interest is calculated as follows:

Case 1: Actual/Actual (A/A) convention.

$t = 31 + 6 = 37$ days (since there are 31 days in July)

$T = 31 + 31 + 30 + 31 + 30 + 31 = 184$ days (the number of days in each month starting from July)

Accrued interest would be $(37/184) \times \$20 = \$4.02$, and this would be subtracted from the full price or "dirty price" to determine the clean price or quoted price.

Case 2: 30/360 (convention commonly used for corporate bonds).

$t = 30 + 6 = 36$ days (even though there are 31 days in July, it is 30 days by convention)

$T = 30 \times 6 = 180$ days (the number of days in each month is set at 30)

Accrued interest would be $(36/180) \times \$20 = \$4.00$, and this would be subtracted from the full price or "dirty price" to determine the clean price or quoted price.

Computing the bond price when the bond was bought on a date between coupon payments appears complicated because the periods over which we discount each cash flow do not correspond to the periods for coupon payments. However, this can be easily resolved. First, observe that the full price is nothing other than the present value of the cash flows from the bond:

$$PV^{Full} = \frac{PMT}{(1+r)^{1-t/T}} + \frac{PMT}{(1+r)^{2-t/T}} + \cdots + \frac{PMT + FV}{(1+r)^{N-t/T}}$$

The above formula can be simplified as follows:

$$PV^{Full} = \left[\frac{PMT}{(1+r)^{1-t/T}} + \frac{PMT}{(1+r)^{2-t/T}} + \cdots + \frac{PMT + FV}{(1+r)^{N-t/T}}\right] \times (1+r)^{t/T}$$

27.2 Relationship among Bond's Yield, Price, and Coupon Rate

The yield or return of a bond depends on the risk and the features of a bond. The relationship between yield, coupon rate, and the price is explored in this section.

Learning Objectives

- Describe the relationship between yield and price and the relationship between yield, coupon rate, and price.

Main Takeaways

Main Points

- The bond price is inversely related to its yield.
- When the bond is first issued, the coupon rate is usually set equal to the yield. This results in the price being equal to the par value.
- The bond sells at a discount (premium) if the yield is higher (lower) than the coupon rate.
- The bond sells at par when its yield is equal to the coupon rate.

Main Terms

- **Yield:** It refers to the yield to maturity or the return that accrues to the bond if it is held to maturity, assuming that coupon payments are reinvested at the yield to maturity.
- **Discount:** A bond sells at a discount when its price is less than the par value. The discount arises when the yield is higher than the coupon rate.

- **Premium:** A bond sells a premium when the price is higher than the par value. The premium is the result of the bond yield falling below the coupon rate.
- **Par:** The bond sells at par when its price is 100 or the same as the par value.

27.2.1 *Bond Price and Bond Yield*

We know that present value is inversely related to the discount rate from the time value of money. Thus, the price would be inversely related to the yield for a bond since the price is the present value of the bond's cash flows.

Figure 27.2 shows the graph of the bond price against the yield. It slopes downwards to the right, indicating that price falls when yield increases. However, the relationship is not linear. The graph is a convex curve. When the yield is low, any increase in yield results in a much larger fall in price than when the yield is high. We will come back to this point when we discuss bond risk.

27.2.2 *Yield to Maturity and Coupon Rate*

When a bond is first issued, the coupon rate is usually set equal to the bond's required yield. This results in the bond price being equal to the par value.

After the bond has been issued, the required yield will change because of changes in interest rates in the market. This change in yield causes the price to change.

Suppose we have a 30-year bond with a 10% coupon rate issued at the par value, which implies a yield of 10%. Suppose yield drops to 7% right after. The price of the bond would go to 137.2. If the yield does not change

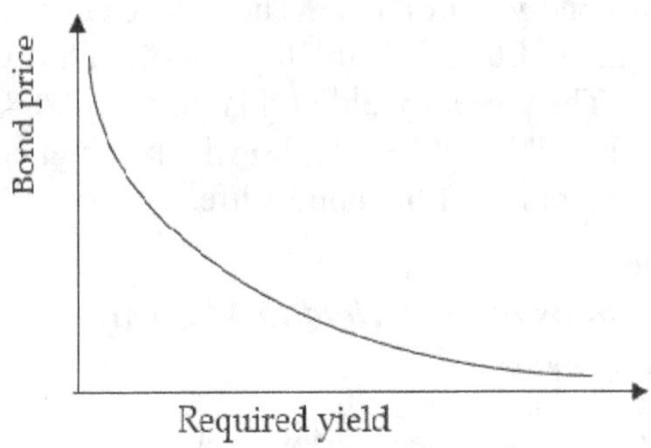

Figure 27.2: Bond price versus bond yield.

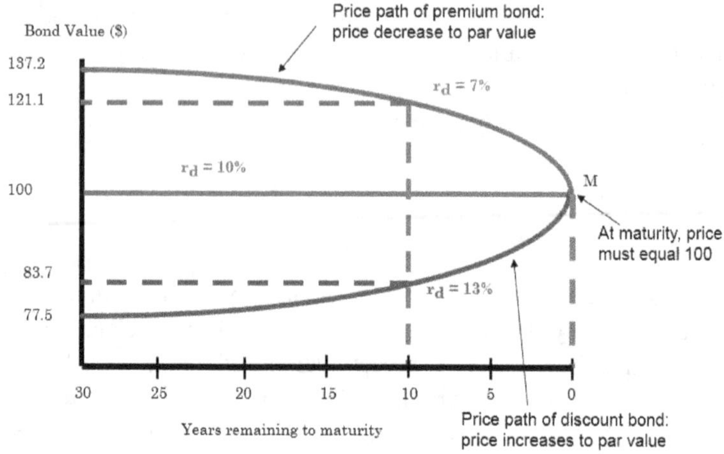

Figure 27.3: Price path of bond over time if yield is constant.

any further until the bond's maturity, Figure 27.3 shows the price path with prices declining to 100 at maturity. Figure 27.3 also shows the path if the yield rose to 13% and remained at that rate until maturity. In this case, the price would fall immediately and increase over time till it reaches the par value at maturity.

Figure 27.3 illustrates some interesting points about the bond's return. Like most assets, the bond's return consists of two components — the income component and the capital gain component. The current yield is the income component and is measured by the coupon divided by the price. The capital gain yield is calculated by the percentage change in consecutive bond prices.

When the yield rises to 13% at the start, the bond price falls to 77.5. The current yield is (10% × 100)/77.5 = 12.9%. The current yield is less than the required bond yield of 13%. The balance of 0.1% comes in the form of a capital gain of 0.1%. With 10 years of maturity left, the bond's price is now 83.7. The current yield at this time is 10/88.7 = 11.3%. The capital gain yield is 1.7% (13% − 11.3%) which is higher than the capital gain yield at the beginning of the bond's life.

27.2.3 *Relationships among Yield to Maturity, Coupon Rate, and Bond Price*

From Figure 27.3, we can see various relationships among the bond variables.

Table 27.1: Relationships among bond's yield, coupon rate, and price.

Bond selling at	Relationship
Par	Coupon rate = current yield = yield to maturity
Discount	Coupon rate < current yield < yield to maturity
Premium	Coupon rate > current yield > yield to maturity

If the yield is higher than the coupon rate, the bond will sell at a discount. (Yield rises to 13%, and price falls to 77.5). Conversely, if the yield falls below the coupon rate, the bond price will be higher than the par value, or the bond sells at a premium.

When the bond is selling at a discount, we notice that the current yield is higher than the coupon rate. For the bond priced at 77.5, the current yield of 12.9% is higher than the coupon rate of 10%. However, both the coupon rate and current yield are lower than the bond's yield of 13%. All these relationships can be summarized in Table 27.1.

27.3 Yield Measures

Unlike equity and other assets, there are many return or yield measures for fixed income instruments.

27.3.1 *Yields on Fixed Rate Bonds, Floating Rate Bonds, and Money Market Instruments*

There are many bond yield measures. Each gives an aspect of the return from the bond.

Learning Objectives

- Describe the yield measures of different fixed income instruments.

Main Takeaways

Main Points

- The current yield indicates the bond's income return as it focuses on the regular coupon payment.
- Yield to call, yield to put, yield to sinker, yield to worst, and cash flow yield, are the returns to the bond contingent on specific actions by the issuer or the bondholder.

- Yield to maturity is a measure of the total return of the bond.
- The holding period yield is a measure of the return to the bond, assuming various reinvestment rates for the coupons received before maturity.

Main Terms

- **Yield to maturity:** It refers to the bond's return if it is held to maturity and coupon payments received are reinvested at the yield to maturity.
- **Interest rate risk:** The risk of a change in the bond price resulting from a change in the bond yield.
- **Reinvestment rate risk:** The risk that coupon payments received in the future cannot be reinvested at the same rate as the yield to maturity.

(a) Traditional Yield Measures

These yield measures include:

a. **Nominal Yield:** This is the stated yield of a bond, that is, the coupon rate.
b. **Current Yield:** Some other terms for the current yield are flat yield, interest yield, and running yield. Current yield = Coupon/Price. It indicates the income component of the return from a bond.
c. **Yield to Maturity:** This is sometimes known as the redemption yield. It will be discussed below.
d. **Yield to Call:** The yield to call is the yield to maturity with the date when the bond can first be called, right after the call protection period, replacing the maturity date. The yield to call is also known as the yield to first call.
e. **Yield to Put:** This is the yield of the bond computed with the maturity assumed to be the date when the bond can first be put.
f. **Yield to Worst:** The yield to worst is, for a call, the lowest of the yields to call calculated for different call dates.
g. **Cash Flow Yield:** The cash flow yield is associated with bonds having embedded options. For mortgage-backed securities, it is known as mortgage yield. This is the monthly compounded discount rate that equates bond price with the net present value of all future cash flows.

All of the above yield measures are expressed as a percentage return rather than a dollar return. Among these, the most popular measure is the Yield to Maturity.

Yield to Maturity: The yield to maturity is found by equating the present value of a bond's cash flows to its market price and finding the interest rate that results in the equality (in this sense, it is similar to the internal rate of return). Without a financial calculator or the Excel spreadsheet program, the yield to maturity can be found through an iterative process of using different discount rates and calculating the present value, a somewhat cumbersome process.

While the current yield measures the income component of the bond's return, the yield to maturity gives the total return for the bond. The computation of the yield to maturity assumes that interim coupon payments are reinvested at the yield to maturity, and that the investor will hold the bond until maturity. If both assumptions are not met, the investor will not realize the yield to maturity stated at the time of purchase.

If either of the two assumptions do not hold the bond may yield a lower return than the yield to maturity. For example, if the bond is not held to maturity, the investor faces the risk of selling the bond for less than the purchase price. This is known as interest rate risk. Further, the investor faces the risk that future interest rates are less than the yield to maturity at the time of purchase. This is reinvestment risk. Bond risks will be discussed in a later section.

Holding Period Yield: The yield to maturity assumes that intermediate coupons are reinvested at an interest rate equal to the YTM. However, an investor may feel that this is unrealistic. Instead, she could explicitly incorporate the forecast of available reinvestment rates throughout the holding period of the bond. The yield that results is known as the holding period yield.

To calculate the holding period yield, compound all cash flows at the relevant rate up to end of the holding period and sum them up. The holding period yield is given by [Sum of all cash flows at the end of the holding period/Bond Price]$^{1/n}$ − 1.

We illustrate the holding period yield's computation using an example of a 3-year, 5% coupon bond with YTM equal to 7% and a price of 94.75. Suppose intermediate cash flows can be invested at 4%. The cash flows are shown in Table 27.2.

The holding period yield is:

$$94.75 \times (1 + r)^3 = 115.608 \quad \text{or} \quad r = 6.857\%$$

Bond-Equivalent Yield: In the bond market the annualized yield is just double the semi-annual yield to maturity. This yield is known as the

Table 27.2: Future value of reinvested cash flow.

Cash flow	Years to maturity	FV
5	2	5.408
5	1	5.2
5	0	102
Total		**115.608**

bond-equivalent yield. For example, if a semi-annual-coupon bond has a 4% semi-annual yield to maturity, its bond-equivalent yield is 8%.

Floating Rate Note (FRN) Yield: The interest received by an FRN is similar to the coupon interest for a bond. The main difference is that interest is not fixed but floating, as shown below:

$$\text{FRN interest} = \text{Reference rate} + \text{Quoted margin}$$

Just as a bond has a required return called the yield to maturity, the equivalent for an FRN is called the discount margin. The quoted margin is set equal to the discount margin when the FRN is first issued. However, the required or discount margin will change if credit or other considerations change. The FRN yield is used like any discount rate to calculate the present value of the FRN as follows:

$$PV = \frac{\frac{(\text{Index}+\text{QM})\times \text{FV}}{m}}{\left(1+\frac{\text{Index}+\text{DM}}{m}\right)^1} + \frac{\frac{(\text{Index}+\text{QM})\times \text{FV}}{m}}{\left(1+\frac{\text{Index}+\text{DM}}{m}\right)^2} + \cdots + \frac{\frac{(\text{Index}+\text{QM})\times \text{FV}}{m} + \text{FV}}{\left(1+\frac{\text{Index}+\text{DM}}{m}\right)^N}$$

where QM is the quoted margin, DM is the discount margin, m is the number of periods in a year.

Money Market Yield: In the money market, yields are calculated somewhat differently from bond yields. One reason is that money market securities have no coupon payments; that is, they are sold at a discount.

Discount Yield: Even though money market securities have maturities that are less than a year, the discount yield is quoted on an annual basis, assuming a 360-day year as a percentage of the face value. The discount yield is calculated as follows:

$$i_{dy} = \frac{(P_f - P_0)}{P_f} \times \frac{360}{h}$$

where P_f is the face value of the security, P_0 is the discount price of the security, and h is the number of days until maturity.

27.3.2 *The Term Structure of Interest Rates*

The term structure depicts the relationship between maturity and yields for bonds identical in all respects, except maturity.

Learning Objectives

- Describe the different shapes of the yield curve and explain the various term structure theories. Discuss how the different components of the yield curve can explain the yield curve's shape.

Main Takeaways

Main Points

- The yield curve can take many shapes — upward sloping, flat, downward sloping, and humped-shape.
- The term structure theories attempt to explain the yield curve's shape based on expectations, liquidity preference, and segmented markets.
- The yield curve can be decomposed into three components — the real interest rate, inflation premium, and interest rate risk premium.

Main Terms

- **Yield curve:** A graph of spot rates.
- **Treasury yield curve:** A graph consisting of Treasury spot rates. The Treasury yield curve is used as a benchmark for other yield curves, consisting of risk premiums added to the Treasury yield curve.
- **Real rate:** The rate of return to compensate for deferment of use of the funds either for consumption or investment.
- **Inflation premium:** The extra return that compensates for the loss of purchasing power.
- **Interest rate risk premium:** The extra return that compensates for interest rate risk. Long maturity bonds have higher interest rate risk than short-maturity bonds.

The term structure shows the relationship between bond yield and maturity, for bonds with the same rating, liquidity, and hopefully the same coupon (or differential tax effects may be present). The graph showing the relationship is known as the yield curve. It can take various shapes, with the most common being the upward sloping yield curve. (Meaning longer-term bonds promise higher nominal yields). The Treasury yield curve serves as a benchmark for other yield curves as Treasury securities are default-free.

(a) Yield Curve Shapes

The yield curve observed in the market is usually upward sloping, where higher yields are associated with longer maturity. However, the yield curve can be downward sloping and is sometimes known as an inverted yield curve, where long-maturity yields are lower than short-maturity yields. Other shapes are the flat yield curve, with the yield being the same for all maturities, and the humped yield curve, which is seldom observed. Figure 27.4 shows the various shapes of yield curves.

(b) Theories of the Term Structure

Theories of the term structure of interest rates explain how the yield curve is determined and how the yield curve changes. The three main theories of term structure are discussed below.

(1) Pure expectations theory

The *pure expectations theory* or *unbiased expectations theory* states that the forward rate is the unbiased predictor of the future spot rate. The

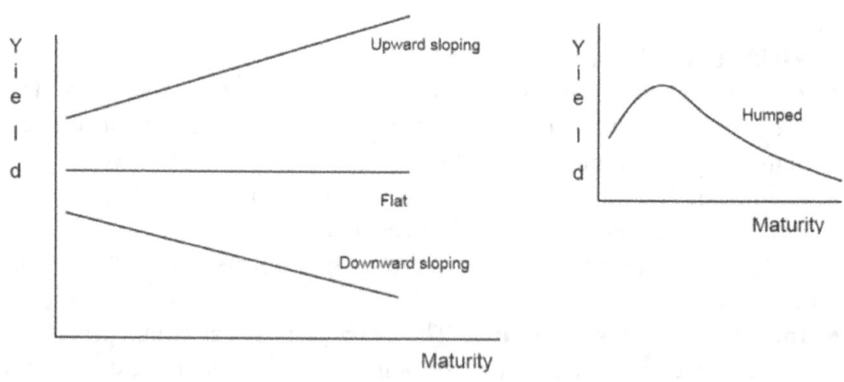

Figure 27.4: Yield curve shapes.

forward rate is the interest rate agreed today for a loan that will only be transacted in the future. It can be shown that the long-term interest rate is the geometric average of 1-year forward rates. If the pure expectations theory holds, then the geometric average of the current and expected future short-term rates gives us the long-term interest rate is. A simple arbitrage proof can be used to show this when interest rates are known with certainty under perfect markets:

Suppose the expected 1-year forward rates are 7%, 8%, and 9% for the next 3 years, respectively, and the 3-year rate is 6%, how could one make money from this relationship?

The average of the short-term 1-year rates is 8%, but the 3-year rate is only 6%. One could borrow any given amount, such as $5,000 for the full 3 years and invest that money 1 year at a time, or roll over the investment each year, for 3 years. The interest on the loan is 6%, but the average rate of return is 8%. This presents an arbitrage opportunity, and traders exploiting this opportunity would force the average of the 1-year rates to converge to the 3-year rate.

(2) Liquidity preference theory

Suppose investors prefer shorter maturities to longer ones. In that case, they will require a premium to invest over a more extended period all at once, compared to investing for the short term and rolling over the investment. For example, instead of investing for 10 years at a go, one could invest year by year, that is, when the investment matures at the end of 1 year, reinvest or roll over the investment for another year, continuing the process until the end of 10 years. In other words, the long-term rate *cannot* be the average of the expected short-term rates.

The liquidity preference theory builds on the pure expectations theory by adding a liquidity premium to compensate for uncertainty about the future interest rates. In essence, the longer the maturity, the higher the liquidity premium required by investors. However, theory does not show what the size of the liquidity premiums ought to be, except that they increase with maturity.

(3) Market segmentation theory

The market segmentation theory is also known as the preferred habitat theory. As the name suggests, some investors may prefer to invest in bonds of a particular maturity. Given the different preferences of investors, there could be a few distinct maturity segments. Investors in each segment will not venture out of their preferred habitat, even if favorable rates may be found in a different maturity segment. However, this is rather extreme and it is possible that large enough differences in yields will entice investors to switch out from their preferred maturity segments.

The reason for investors to prefer certain segments is that due to the nature of their business, some institutions may naturally have liabilities of a distinct maturity, e.g., life insurers prefer to invest long term since payouts on their insurance policies, for example life insurance policies, occur a long time after the policies were purchased.

One implication of this theory is that there is no reason to construct a term structure as there is no relationship between long-term rates and expected future short-term rates. However, this view about term structure is rather extreme as it suggests that opportunities to take advantage of securities' mispricing will not be exploited. For example, if the 15-year bond rate is much higher than warranted by expectations, one could buy the 15-year bond and short a 14-year bond.

(c) Components of the Yield Curve

The interest rate that we see in the market is known as the *nominal interest rate*. It is the compensation for lending out money. But what is the investor compensated for? Well, it is compensation for deferring the use of the funds for a start. For example, if I lend you money, you can use the money to buy things and enjoy them while I have to wait. This rate of compensation is known as the *real rate of interest*.

But that's not all. When I receive the money later in the future, the amount of goods or services that I can buy may change because they could have gone up in price. This purchasing power change is inflation, and the lender would want compensation for any loss in purchasing power. In other words, he demands compensation for the *rate of inflation* or an *inflation premium*.

Every interest rate contains the real rate of interest regardless of maturity. When the real interest rates rise, all interest rates will go up. (The real interest rate will increase when more people want to consume today rather than save and consume next year. So they may be willing to pay more to borrow money to enable them to consume today). So the real rate of interest doesn't determine the shape of the yield curve.

However, the shape of the yield curve is determined by future inflation expectations. For example, if I expect inflation to be higher in the future, I will demand a higher inflation premium when I lend money. The reason is that I expect that the money I receive in the future from the loan will buy much less than today.

The third component of the nominal interest rate is the *interest rate risk premium*. The prices of long-term bonds change much more than short-term bonds because of the discounting effect. (Recall that the longer the period, the greater the impact on the present value of the cash flows to be received in the future.) Hence, we would expect the interest rate risk premium to be higher if the maturity is more extended than if it is short.

The yield curves shown in Figure 27.5 incorporate the three components of the nominal interest rate: the real rate of interest, the inflation premium, and the interest rate risk premium. We can see that the inflation premium mainly determines the yield curve's shape.

27.3.3 *Yield Spread Measures*

The yield spread is the difference in yields between two bonds. It is a key metric that bond investors use for comparing bonds with different risks or maturities.

Learning Objectives

- Explain the different yield spread measures.

Main Takeaways

Main Points

- A yield spread is a difference between the yields of two bonds. It is customary to use the government bond yield as the default-free yield.
- The nominal spread measures the credit or default risk premium of a bond. It is found by taking the difference in yields between the bond and a government bond of the same maturity. It is also known as the G-spread.
- Unlike the nominal spread, which is the difference in yields for a particular maturity, the Z-spread measures the constant difference over the whole yield curve.
- The I-spread or interpolated spread most commonly uses the swap rate as the benchmark yield.
- The option-adjusted spread (OAS) is the yield spread applicable for a bond with an embedded option. The nominal spread cannot be used for such a bond as the maturity is uncertain because the embedded option

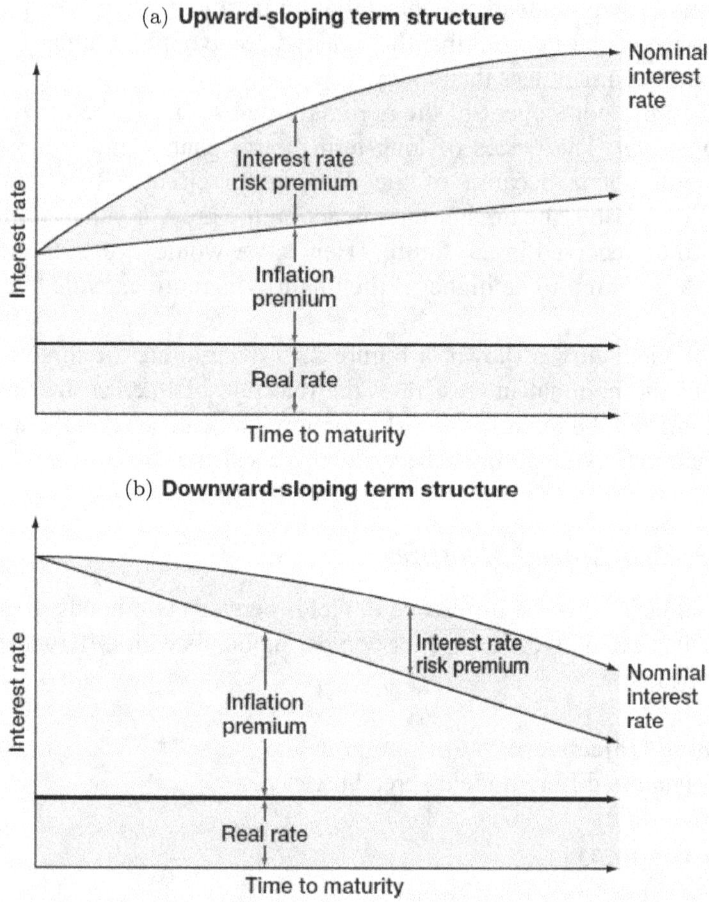

Figure 27.5: Term structure of interest rates.

Source: Ross, S.A., Westerfield, R.W., Jordan, B.D., Lim, J., & Tan, R. (2016). *Fundamentals of Corporate Finance*, 2nd edn. McGraw Hill.

can be exercised. For example, a callable bond can be called before the bond's maturity.

Main Terms

- **Nominal spread:** This is the difference in yields between a non-Treasury bond and a Treasury bond with the same maturity. It is also known, less commonly, as the G-spread.

- **Z-spread:** This is the constant spread over the government yield curve, also known as the zero-volatility spread.
- **I-spread:** This is a constant spread over the yield curve found by linear interpolation. Usually, that linearly interpolated yield curve uses the swap rate curve as the benchmark curve.
- **Option-adjusted spread (OAS):** The OAS is the Z-spread plus the option cost in basis points for a callable bond. For a putable bond, the OAS is the Z-spread less the option cost in basis points.

Besides the Treasury yield curve, we can construct yield curves for bonds that are not default-free: risky bonds. The difference between the yield of the risky bonds and Treasury bonds is the yield spread.

(a) Nominal Spread

The nominal spread is the difference between the yield for a non-Treasury bond and a comparable-maturity Treasury security. This spread is a measure of the premium for additional risks related to credit, optionality (the risk associated with any embedded option), and liquidity The nominal spread assumes that the yield curve is flat, that is, the same rate, which is the yield to maturity, is used to discount all cash flows. Further, this measure does not account for the term structure of the spot rates, embedded options, and change in future interest rate volatility.

(b) Zero-Volatility Spread

The Zero-Volatility Spread or Z-spread is a measure of the spread that the investor will realize over the entire Treasury spot rate curve if the bond is held to maturity (see Figure 27.6). While the nominal spread is a spread at one maturity on the Treasury yield curve, the Z-spread is a spread over the entire spot rate curve. It represents a spread to compensate for the non-Treasury security's various risks.

(c) I-spread

The I-spread is a spread over a linearly interpolated yield curve. While the underlying yields could be government yields, the more common linearly interpolated yield curve used as the benchmark is the swap rate curve. The I-spread is commonly used for the fixed leg of a floating-for-fixed interest rate swap.

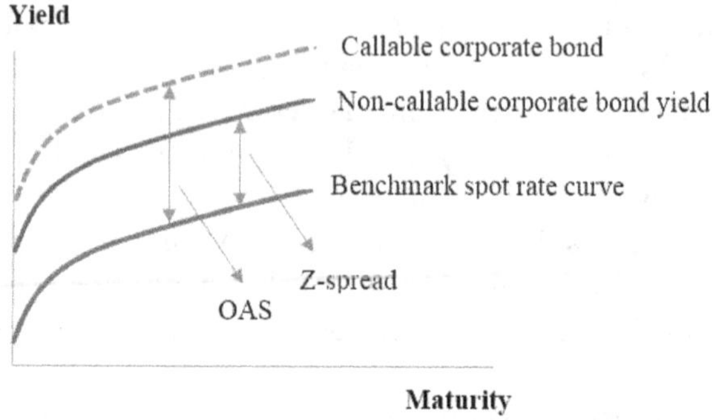

Figure 27.6: Yield curves showing Z-spread and OAS for a callable bond.

(d) Option-Adjusted Spread

The future cash flows of a bond can change with changes in interest rates and the presence of embedded options. However, this is not factored in the Z-spread as it assumes no interest rate volatility.

The Option-Adjusted Spread (OAS) adjusts the Z-spread to account for the embedded option. If the embedded option is a call, we expect the callable bond to have a higher yield than a non-callable bond. Hence,

For a callable bond, OAS = Z-spread + Option cost in basis points.
For a putable bond, OAS = Z-spread − Option cost in basis points.

For a callable bond, the option cost is the additional spread that the issuer needs to pay for the call feature. Hence if the Z-spread is 3%, the OAS 3.75%, then the option cost is an additional yield of 0.75%. This relationship between the Z-spread and the OAS is shown in Figure 27.6.

27.3.4 *Spot Rate and Forward Rate*

A spot rate is the yield-to-maturity on a zero-coupon bond, whereas the forward rate is the interest rate expected in the future.

Learning Objectives

- Compute spot rates using the bootstrapping approach and compute forward rates from spot rates.

Main Takeaways

Main Points

- Forward rates can be computed from spot rates.
- The forward rate is a rate for a loan/investment that will be transacted in the future.
- The spot rate can be considered a geometric mean of a series of 1-year forward rates.

Main Terms

- **Spot rate:** The rate of return for a zero-coupon bond.
- **Forward rate:** The interest rate for a future period that is agreed upon today.

A spot price is a price quoted today if the asset's transaction were to take place today. A forward price is quoted today for a transaction in the future. The spot rate and forward rate have similar meanings for the loans market. A spot rate is the rate quoted today for a loan taken out today, while the forward rate is the rate agreed today for a loan that will be made in the future.

(a) Spot Rate

A spot rate is the rate of return for a zero-coupon bond. To derive the Treasury yield curve, we use spot rates. However, the US Treasury issues coupon-paying bonds and not zero-coupon bonds. Spot rates can be obtained when the coupon paying bond is stripped into the interest-only and principal-only components. The spot rate is the yield to maturity of the principal-only component.

Another way to derive spot rates is to use the bootstrapping approach. This method derives the spot rates from the prices of coupon-bearing bonds. We illustrate this method with a 2-year coupon paying bond. The value of the bond is given by:

$$PV = \frac{PMT}{(1+r)^1} + \frac{PMT + FV}{(1+r)^2} \quad \text{where } r = \text{YTM}$$

The value of the bond can also be found by using spot rates to discount the cash flows:

$$PV = \frac{PMT}{(1+r_1)^1} + \frac{PMT + FV}{(1+r_2)^2} \quad \text{where } r_1 \text{ and } r_2 = \text{1-year and 2-year spot rates}$$

The yield to maturity of the coupon bond is known. We also see the value of the 1-year spot rate. Thus, we can solve for the 2-year spot rate from the two equations. Longer maturity spot rates can be obtained by the same process, iteratively.

Here's a numerical example to illustrate the bootstrapping method. The data for the example is as follows:

> 2-year 4% annual coupon bond: Price = 96.38, Yield = 6%.
> 3-year 5% annual coupon bond: Price = 92.01, Yield = 7%.
> 1-year spot rate = 3.5%.

For the 2-year bond, we have

$$PV = \frac{4}{(1+0.06)} + \frac{4+100}{(1+0.06)^2} = 96.38$$

$$PV = \frac{4}{(1+0.035)} + \frac{4+100}{(1+r_2)^2} = 96.38, \text{ where } r_2 \text{ is the 2-year spot rate.}$$

From the above, we obtain $r_2 = 6.026\%$.

$$PV = \frac{4}{(1+0.035)} + \frac{4+100}{(1+r_2)^2} = 96.38$$

We continue with the 3-year bond.

$$PV = \frac{5}{(1+0.035)} + \frac{5}{(1+0.06026)^2} + \frac{5+100}{(1+r_3)^3} = 92.01$$

We obtain $r_3 = 8.27\%$.

(b) Forward Rate

A forward rate can be computed from the existing term structure. Using arbitrage arguments, given a set of long-term spot rates, one can find the set of individual *1-year forward* rates.

We illustrate a forward rate computation below and use the following notation: r_{0n} is the spot rate for the maturity of n years, and f_{n1} is the 1-year forward rate for year n. Time 0 in the diagram below indicates today, while time n is n years from today.

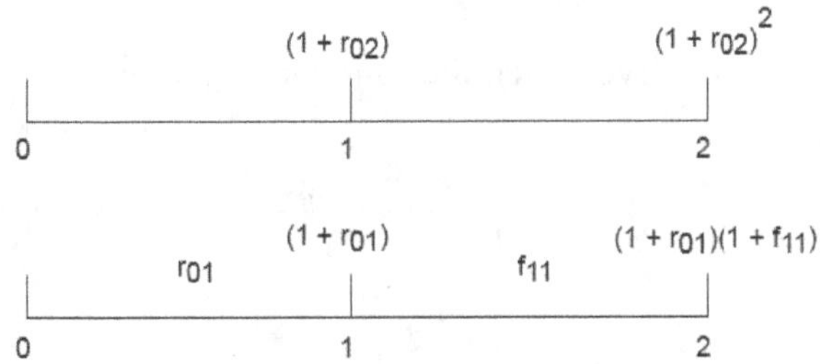

Figure 27.7: Forward rate computation.

Suppose we want to invest for 2 years. There are two ways to go about it. Commit to invest for 2 years and earn the 2-year rate, or invest for 1 year at the 1-year spot rate and reinvest (or rollover) the proceeds at the 1-year forward rate 1 year from today. This is illustrated in Figure 27.7.

(c) Par Curve and Forward Rate Curve

Par Curve: The par curve is derived from the yields to maturity of bonds of different maturities where each bond sells at the par value. Essentially this involves solving for the coupon payment in the equation below:

$$100 = PV = \frac{PMT}{(1+r_1)^1} + \frac{PMT}{(1+r_2)^2} + \cdots + \frac{PMT+100}{(1+r_N)^N}$$

Here's an example of how the curve can be derived. Suppose we have the following spot rates: $r_1 = 6\%$, $r_2 = 7.04\%$.

$$100 = \frac{PMT+100}{(1+0.06)^1} \text{ or PMT} = 6\text{, i.e. YTM is } 6\%$$

The 2-year par rate is given by

$$100 = \frac{PMT}{(1+0.06)^1} + \frac{PMT+100}{(1+0.0704)^2} \text{ or PMT} = 7\text{, i.e., YTM is } 7\%$$

Given the spot rates for years 3, 4, 5, and so on, we can derive the par curve over the same maturity range as the spot curve.

Forward Rate Curve: In the previous section, we discussed the derivation of forward rates. We can use the 1-year forward rate at each maturity to form the forward rate curve.

Example:
Derive the forward curve, given the following spot rates:

Year	Spot rate
1	8%
2	9%
3	10%

The following diagram depicts the timeline, spot, and forward rates, which will help us compute the forward rates.

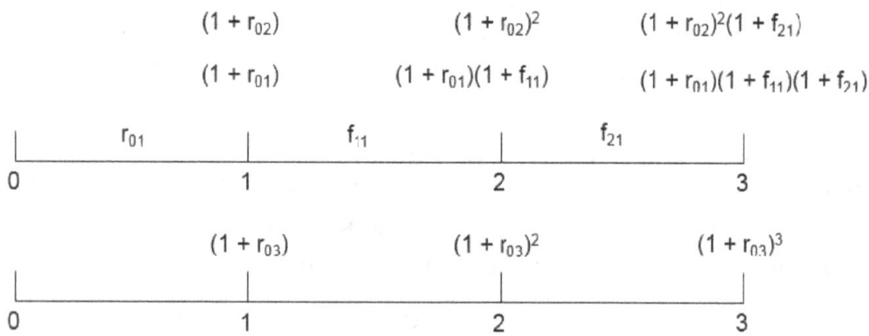

The forward rate for 1 year beginning at time 0 is also the 1-year spot rate. The diagram above shows the future value of an investment of 1 made today, that is, at time 0. Referring to the future values at time 2, we see that the value can be obtained by investing at the 2-year spot rate (r_{02}) for 2 years or investing at the 1-year spot rate (r_{01}) and rolling over the investment at the end of the year at time 1 and investing at the 1-year forward rate (f_{11}) starting at time 1. For no arbitrage, both methods should give the same amount. Hence

$$(1 + r_{02})^2 = (1 + r_{01})(1 + f_{11})$$
$$(1 + 0.09)^2 = (1 + 0.08)\,(1 + f_{11}) \quad \text{or} \quad f_{11} = 10\%$$

We can continue to compute the 1-year forward rate at time 2 (f_{21}).

$$(1 + r_{03})^3 = (1 + r_{02})^2(1 + f_{21})$$
$$(1 + 0.10)^3 = (1 + 0.09)^2(1 + f_{21}) \quad \text{or} \quad f_{21} = 12\%$$

The series of forward rates ($f_{01}, f_{11}, f_{21}, \ldots$) that we derive can be plotted to give us the forward yield curve.

References/Further Readings

Bodie, Z., Kane, A., & Marcus, A.J. (2020). *Investments*, 12th edn. McGraw-Hill Irwin, Chaps.14 & 15.

Fabozzi, F.J. (2007). *Fixed Income Analysis*, 2nd edn. John Wiley & Sons, Inc., pp. 119–146.

Leeds, S.J., Brown, K.C., & Reilly, F.K. (2019). *Investment Analysis and Portfolio Management*, 11th edn. Cengage, pp. 421–464.

27.4 Sample Questions

Question 1
ABC bond trades at 115. This is a

(a) Discount bond
(b) Par bond
(c) Premium bond

Question 2
A bond has a 5.5% coupon rate. Interest is paid annually. Its maturity is 3 years, par value is $1,000, and the required rate of return is 5%. The price of the bond value is closest to:

(a) $986.50
(b) $1,013.60
(c) $1,026.40

Question 3
A 2-year bond has a 5% coupon rate with interest paid annually. The 1-year and 2-year spot rates are 3% and 4%, respectively. As a percentage of the par value, the price of the bond is closest to:

(a) 101.93
(b) 102.75
(c) 105.81

Question 4
The clean price is

(a) Dirty price × $(1 + r)$
(b) Dirty price + accrued interest
(c) Dirty price − accrued interest

Use the following information for the next three questions:

Annual coupon	6%
Coupon payment frequency	Semi-annual
Interest payment date	8 March and 8 September
Maturity date	8 September 2020
Day count convention	Actual/Actual
Annual yield to maturity	4%
Bond purchase settlement date	5 May 2020

Question 5
The accrued interest per 100 of par value for the bond on the settlement date of 5 May 2020 is closest to:

(a) 0.94
(b) 0.96
(c) 0.97

Question 6
On the settlement date of 5 May 2020, the full price that the bond will be closest to:

(a) 105.37
(b) 106.32
(c) 107.25

Question 7
The flat price for the bond on 5 May 2020 is closest to:

(a) 103.36
(b) 103.78
(c) 104.41

Use the following information for the next two questions:

Bond	Price	Coupon rate	Time-to-maturity
A	102.59	6%	4 years
B	100.00	5%	3 years
C	97.12	4%	2 years

Question 8
Which bond has the yield to maturity equal to the coupon rate?

(a) Bond A
(b) Bond B
(c) Bond C

Question 9
Which bond has the highest yield to maturity, assuming the bonds pay an annual coupon?

(a) Bond A
(b) Bond B
(c) Bond C

Use the following information for the next four questions:
Bond A has 6 years until maturity. It has a 5% coupon with interest paid semi-annually. It trades at 102, and is callable in 3 years, according to the schedule:

End of Year	Call Price
3	103
4	102
5	101
6	100

Question 10
The bond's annual YTM is closest to:

(a) 4.62%
(b) 4.88%
(c) 5.127%

Question 11
The bond's annual yield-to-first-call is closest to:

(a) 4.62%
(b) 4.98%
(c) 5.36%

Question 12
Which theory states that if future short-term rates are expected to be lower than current short-term rates, the yield curve will be downward sloping?

(a) Liquidity preference theory
(b) Market segmentation theory
(c) Expectations theory

Question 13
Which of the following combinations will result in a sharply decreasing yield curve?

(a) Increasing expected short rates and increasing liquidity premiums
(b) Decreasing expected short rates and increasing liquidity premiums
(c) Decreasing expected short rates and decreasing liquidity premiums

Question 14
The yield spread of a specific bond over the standard swap rate in that currency of the same maturity is best described as the:

(a) I-spread
(b) Z-spread
(c) G-spread

Question 15
An option-adjusted spread (OAS) on a callable bond is the Z-spread:

(a) Minus the value of the embedded call option expressed in bps per year
(b) Minus the standard swap rate in that currency of the same tenor
(c) Plus the value of the embedded call option expressed in bps per year

Question 16

A yield curve constructed from a sequence of yields-to-maturity on zero-coupon bonds is the:

(a) Z spread
(b) Spot curve
(c) Forward curve

Question 17

Which of the following statements describing a par curve is correct?

(a) A par curve is obtained from a spot curve
(b) All bonds on a par curve are assumed to have different credit risk
(c) A par curve is a sequence of forward rates such that each bond is priced at par value

Solutions

Question 1

Solution: Option **c** is correct.

A premium bond trades above the par value.
Note: Bond prices are quoted as a percentage of the par value which would be 100.

Question 2

Solution: Option **b** is correct.

$$P = \frac{55}{(1+0.05)} + \frac{55}{(1+0.05)^2} + \frac{55+1000}{(1+0.05)^3} = 1013.60$$

Question 3

Solution: Option **a** is correct.

$$\text{P} = \frac{5}{(1+0.03)} + \frac{5+100}{(1+0.4)^2} = 101.93$$

Question 4

Solution: Option **c** is correct.

The dirty price is the present value of the bond buyer's cash flows. However, part of the buyer's first coupon was earned by the seller and needs to be paid to the seller. Hence, the bond's clean price or value is the present value of the bond's cash flows reduced by the accrued interest.

Question 5

Solution: Option **a** is correct.

$t = 23 + 30 + 5 = 58$; $T = 23 + 30 + 31 + 30 + 31 + 31 + 8 = 184$

Accrued interest = $t/T \times \text{PMT} = 58/184 \times 3 = 0.946$

Question 6

Solution: Option **a** is correct.

$$\text{PV Full} = \left[\frac{\text{PMT}}{(1+r)^1} + \frac{\text{PMT}}{(1+r)^2} + \cdots + \frac{\text{PMT}+\text{FV}}{(1+r)^N}\right] \times (1+r)^{t/T}$$

$$\text{PV Full} = \left[\frac{3}{(1+0.02)^1} + \frac{3}{(1+0.02)^2} + \cdots + \frac{3+100}{(1+0.02)^5}\right] \times (1+0.02)^{58/182}$$

PV Full = 105.37

Question 7

Solution: Option **c** is correct.

Flat price = Full Price − Accrued interest = 105.37 − 0.946 = 104.42

Question 8

Solution: Option **b** is correct.

When the yield to maturity is equal to the coupon rate, the price will be the par value or 100.

Question 9

Solution: Option **c** is correct.

Bond B's YTM is 5% as it sells at par. Bond A's YTM (calculated) is 5.265%, while Bond C's YTM (calculated) is 5.561%.

Question 10

Solution: Option **a** is correct.

$$102 = \frac{2.5}{(1+r)} + \frac{2.5}{(1+r)^2} + \cdots + \frac{2.5+100}{(1+r)^{12}}$$

$$r = 0.0231,\ \text{YTM} = 0.0231 \times 2 = 0.0462$$

Question 11

Solution: Option **c** is correct.

$$102 = \frac{2.5}{(1+r)} + \frac{2.5}{(1+r)^2} + \cdots + \frac{2.5+103}{(1+r)^6}$$

$$r = 0.0268,\ \text{YTM} = 0.0268 \times 2 = 0.0536$$

Question 12

Solution: Option **c** is correct.

As the spot rate is a geometric average of the forward rates, declining forward rates imply declining spot rates. The expectations theory states that the best predictor of the future 1-year spot rates is the 1-year forward rates.

Question 13

Solution: Option **c** is correct.

A sharply decreasing yield curve is the result of decreasing short rates. Decreases in the liquidity premiums would also make the yield curve steeper.

Question 14

Solution: Option **a** is correct.

The I spread is the spread over some interpolated yield curve, in this case, the swap rate curve. The Z-spread is the zero volatility spread or spread over the spot Treasury rate curve. The G spread is the spread over the government bond yields.

Question 15

Solution: Option **c** is correct.

The OAS represents the spread above the spot curve. It is calculated by either adding or subtracting the option cost in basis points. If the bond is callable, the option cost is added, so the yield is higher than a comparable non-callable bond.

Question 16

Solution: Option **b** is correct.

This is the definition of the spot curve.

Question 17

Solution: Option **a** is correct.

Statement (b) is incorrect as the bonds are assumed to be of the same risk. Statement (a) is correct as we use the spot rates to discount the coupons, while for a bond of a particular maturity, the coupon rate is chosen such that the bond is priced at the par value. Statement (c) is incorrect as forward rates are not used.

Chapter 28

Bond Risk

28.1 Types of Bond Risk

When the general interest rates change, bonds' required yields will change. Changes in the yield to maturity will result in changes in the bond price. This is interest rate risk which will be discussed in the following sections. Various other risks affect a bond; this section will explore some of them.

Learning Objectives

- Describe the various types of bond risk apart from interest rate risk.

Main Takeaways

Main Points

- Although interest rate risk is the main focus for bond investors, other risks stem from transacting and holding bonds.

Main Terms

- **Liquidity risk:** The risk that the bond would be sold below its fair value.
- **Marking-to-market:** A process of valuing assets at their current price.
- **Exchange rate risk:** The risk of losses due to unfavorable exchange rate movements.
- **Inflation risk:** The risk of loss of purchasing power due to inflation.

- **Volatility risk:** Changes in the volatility of interest rates affect the value of the embedded option in the bond and, consequently, the bond's value.
- **Event risk:** The risk of events like natural disasters or regulatory changes that affect the issuer's finances and hence the bond's value.
- **Sovereign risk:** The risk of actions by a sovereign entity that changes the bond's value.
- **Haircut:** This is the amount deducted from an asset's value for various purposes. The amount deducted is usually in percentage terms.

28.1.1 *Liquidity Risk*

Liquidity risk refers to the risk that the bond would be sold below its indicated value. The bid-ask spread measures this risk.

There is no liquidity risk for a bond held to maturity if there is no marking of the position to market prices. However, even if the bond is held to maturity, a marking-to-market requirement could result in a change in portfolio values arising from liquidity risk. In general, less liquid issues have greater variations in sellers' bid prices.

Marking-to-market requires the availability of prices. There are three levels listed in order of decreasing availability of prices or quotes:

- Level 1 – mark the position to market prices.
- Level 2 – mark the position to bid-ask quotes.
- Level 3 – mark the position to model values.

28.1.2 *Exchange Rate Risk*

A bond that is denominated in a foreign currency brings another dimension of risk for the bond investor. In this case, the bond suffers a decline in value due to a decrease in the value of the foreign currency.

28.1.3 *Inflation Risk*

While inflation is factored in the yields that investors require, the coupon rate for a non-floating rate bond is fixed once the bond is issued. Subsequent changes to the inflation rate, which cause actual inflation to differ from what was expected when the bond was first issued, would result in purchasing power risk. Changes in inflation or purchasing power are generally not provided for in bonds except inflation-indexed bonds like the Treasury Inflation Protection Security or TIPS.

28.1.4 *Volatility Risk*

For a bond with an embedded option, a change in the expected yield volatility will cause the bond price to change. The direction of the price change depends on whether the bond is callable or putable. The relationships between the value of a bond with an embedded option and the value of a straight bond are shown below:

$$\text{Callable bond price} = \text{straight bond price} - \text{embedded option price}$$

$$\text{Putable bond price} = \text{straight bond price} + \text{embedded option price}$$

Note that for the callable bond, a lower price than the straight bond implies a higher yield than the straight bond. When the interest rate becomes more volatile, the embedded option increases in value. This causes the callable bond to fall in price and the required yield to increase. For the putable bond, higher interest rate volatility also increases its price.

28.1.5 *Event Risk*

Event risk is the risk that the issuer is unable to pay due to events like:

- **Natural disasters:** This affects various companies exposed to the risk.
- **Takeover or restructuring:** LBOs like the RJR Nabisco deal resulted in increases in yields for the whole sector.
- **Regulatory changes:** Regulated entities like investment companies, depository institutions, insurance companies, and pension funds could be affected by regulatory rulings regarding the shares they can hold for certain companies.

28.1.6 *Sovereign Risk*

Sovereign risk is the risk that pertains to debt issued by sovereign governments. A government may be unable to pay due to its economic difficulties. The sovereign bonds may be restructured as a result and would often involve a substantial haircut; for example, two old bonds would be exchanged for a new bond, resulting in a 50% haircut.

A default of a sovereign bond can also occur because the government has repudiated its debt. Seeking legal means to enforce payments is almost impossible. It is difficult to sue a government, and enforcement of a court ruling would also be difficult against a sovereign entity. An investor should note the jurisdiction from which the sovereign bonds are issued. A foreign sovereign bond issued in London, for example, would be governed by British law. Such a bond may not allow changes to the terms of the bond by the issuer arbitrarily since the sovereign entity cannot change British law.

Reference/Further Reading

Fabozzi, F.J. (2007). *Fixed Income Analysis*, 2nd edn. John Wiley & Sons, Inc., pp. 17–36.

28.2 Relationship between Interest Rate Risk and Coupon, Maturity, and Level of Yield

Interest rate risk refers to the change in the bond price when its yield changes, and how the price changes are affected by differences in the coupon, maturity, and yield level.

Learning Objectives

- Explain the relationship between the change in the bond price and the size of the coupon, the length of the maturity, and the bond yield level.

Main Takeaways

Main Points

- All else equal, when the yield changes, the percentage price change is larger for low coupon than high coupon bonds.
- When the yield changes, the percentage price change is larger for long-maturity than short-maturity bonds. And the percentage price change is larger when the yield level is low than when the yield level is high.
- When the yield changes, the price changes are not symmetric. For the same yield change, the percentage price increase resulting from a decrease in yield is larger than the percentage price decrease resulting from a yield increase of the same amount.

Main Terms

- **Yield level:** This is the level of the yield before it changes.
- **Credit risk:** Credit risk is the possibility of a loss resulting from a borrower's failure to repay a loan or meet contractual obligations.

The relationship between the percentage price change of a bond when the yield, coupon, and maturity changes can be examined by looking at Figure 28.1. The percentage change in the prices for the same yield change for four bonds, A, B, C, and D, are shown. These bonds have the same bond rating or credit risk. Lastly, the yield rises from 10% to 11%.

28.2.1 *Percentage Price Change and Maturity*

Bonds A and B in Table 28.1 have the same coupon rate and credit risk. Bond B's percentage price change is larger than that for Bond A. So, all else equal, bonds with long maturity have higher interest rate risk or experience larger percentage price changes than bonds with short maturity when the yield changes.

28.2.2 *Percentage Price Change and Coupon Rate*

In Table 28.1, Bonds B and C have the same maturity and credit risk. With the lower coupon rate, Bond C experiences a much higher percentage price change than Bond B, when the yield changes. Note that we compare the percentage price changes and not absolute price changes. Bond C has a smaller absolute price change than Bond C. However, because of the much lower price of Bond C, its percentage price change is greater than Bond B.

Table 28.1: Percentage bond price change for different maturities and coupon rates.

Bond	Coupon	Term	10%	11%	Change	%
Effects of Maturity						
A	8%	5	$92.28	$88.69	−$3.59	−3.89%
B	8%	30	$81.07	$73.83	−$7.24	-8.93%
Effects of Coupon						
B	8%	30	$81.07	$73.83	−$7.24	−$8.93%
C	0%	30	$5.35	$4.03	−$1.32	−$24.7%
Effects of Maturity and Coupon						
B	8%	30	$81.07	$73.83	−$7.24	−$8.93%
D	0%	15	$23.14	$20.06	−$3.08	−$13.3%

28.2.3 *Percentage Price Change When Maturity and Coupon Rate Differ*

The last pair of bonds in Table 28.1, Bonds B and D, have different maturities and coupon rates. In this instance, our simple rules of longer maturity or lower coupon rate implying higher interest rate risk cannot be applied. Based on the maturity alone, we would say Bond B is riskier. However, based on the coupon rate, Bond D is riskier. One way to resolve which bond is more risky is by computing the actual percentage price changes.

In the next section, we discuss the bond's duration. Duration is measured in years, like maturity. However, we can say unequivocally that a bond with a longer duration would have a higher interest rate risk than a bond with a shorter duration. The reason is that the duration measure takes into account both the maturity of the bond and its coupon rate.

28.3 Duration Measures

Duration measures are some of the most important measures of bonds' interest rate risks.

Learning Objectives

- Compute and interpret the different measures of duration.

Main Takeaways

Main Points

- The Macaulay duration, or duration for short, measures the bond's interest rate risk. It is measured in years.
- The longer the bond's duration, the greater the percentage price change when the yield changes.
- Macaulay duration compares the percentage price change to the percentage yield change.
- Modified duration is obtained by dividing the Macaulay duration by $(1 + r)$. To find the percentage price change when yield changes, multiply the modified duration by the amount of yield change and not the percentage yield change.
- If the bond has an embedded option, the effective duration is used. The reason is that the bond's yield to maturity is not appropriate as the optionality feature could shorten the bond's maturity. For example, the bond could be called or put before its maturity. Effective duration measures the change in bond price with respect to a change in the benchmark yield.

- To find the absolute amount of bond price change when the yield changes, we use the money duration measure. Money duration is just a modified duration multiplied by the bond price.
- The amount of bond price change when the yield change is one basis point is given by PVBP or price value of a basis point. PVBP also goes by the name of Dollar Value of one basis point or DV01.

Main Terms

- **Macaulay duration:** This is the weighted average maturity of the bond. It measures the bond price's interest rate risk or sensitivity to changes in the yield. It is the price elasticity of the bond with respect to the yield. It is measured in years.
- **Modified duration:** This is the Macaulay duration divided by $(1 + r)$, where r is the bond yield.
- **Effective duration:** This is similar to the modified duration except that the change in the bond's price is measured with respect to a change in the yield of some benchmark yield and not its own yield.
- **Money duration:** It is obtained by multiplying the modified duration by the bond price. It measures the price change in terms of a dollar amount.
- **Price value of a basis point (PVBP):** It is also known as the dollar value of a basis point (DV01). This is the bond price in dollars resulting from a change in the yield of 1 basis point.
- **Key rate duration:** This measures how the bond price changes at a specific maturity on the yield curve.

28.3.1 *Macaulay Duration, Modified Duration, and Effective Duration*

Duration measures the sensitivity of the bond price to changes in the yield. The duration measure is used for hedging changes in bond prices due to interest rate changes.

Macaulay Duration: The Macaulay duration is calculated as follows:

$$D = \sum_{t=1}^{T} t * \frac{\mathrm{CF}_t/(1+r)^t}{\mathrm{Price}}$$

where CF_t is the bond's cash flow at time t.

Recall that the price of a bond is the present value of its cash flows, i.e.,

$$P = \sum_{t=1}^{T} \frac{\text{CF}_t}{(1 + \text{r})^t}$$

So the Macaulay duration is a weighted average maturity of the time to receipt of each cash flow. This becomes clear when we think of a coupon bond as a portfolio of zero-coupon bonds. This portfolio's maturity is nothing other than the weighted average of the maturity of each zero-coupon bond.

Example:
Consider a 3-year coupon bond. This bond consists of a portfolio of four zero-coupon bonds, namely, the three coupon payments and the face value. The weighted average maturity of this "portfolio" or its duration is

$$D = 1\times\frac{\frac{\text{PMT}}{(1+r)^1}}{\text{P}} + 2\times\frac{\frac{\text{PMT}}{(1+r)^2}}{\text{P}} + 3\times\frac{\frac{\text{PMT}}{(1+r)^3}}{\text{P}} + 3\times\frac{\frac{\text{FV}}{(1+r)^3}}{\text{P}}$$

For a small change in interest rates, duration is adequate for estimating the percentage price change. However, when the interest rate changes substantially, for example following a rate decrease announcement by the Fed, the percentage price change predicted by duration grossly underestimates the price change. This is due to the convex shape of the price-yield curve is convex, as explained below.

Bond prices are more sensitive to interest rate changes when bond yields are low than when yields are high. This is illustrated by the diagram in Figure 28.1.

Price changes of bonds based on duration are symmetric with respect to changes in the interest rate in both directions. An examination of the diagram below indicates that this is not true. Duration alone does not fully capture the bond price change when interest rates change. An adjustment for "convexity" needs to be made to improve the approximation provided by duration. How this is done will be discussed in a later section on convexity.

Looking at Figure 28.2, we see that the error in the bond price change predicted by duration is due to the bond price-yield curve's curvature.

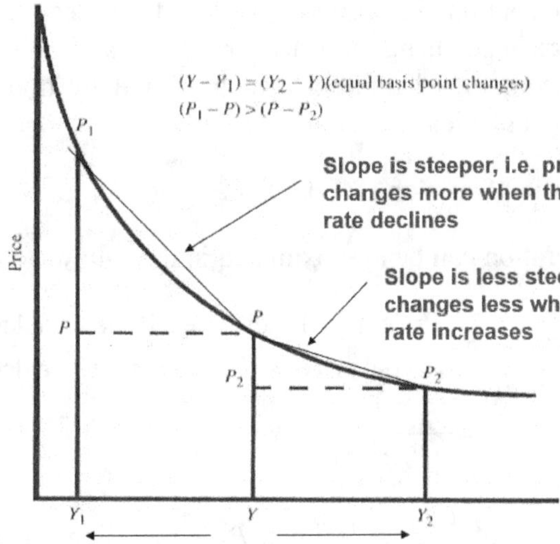

Figure 28.1: Duration — Slope of price-yield curve.

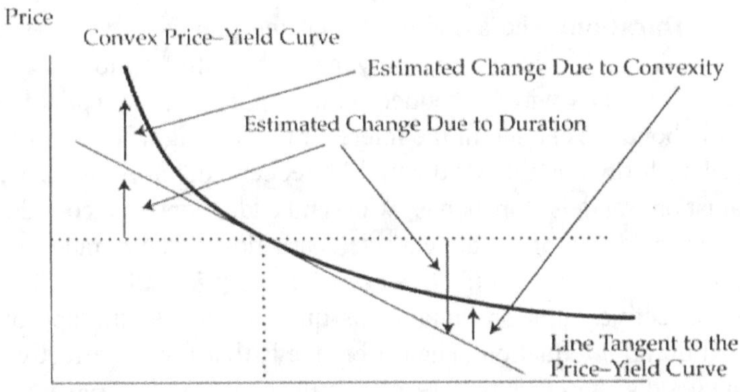

Figure 28.2: Duration and convexity — Slope of price-yield curve.

The degree of curvature is called convexity. Greater convexity leads to more significant price prediction errors. These errors can be quite significant for large interest rate changes.

Modified Duration: While the Macaulay duration, as an elasticity concept, measures the percentage change in price with the percentage change in the bond's yield to maturity, modified duration gives us the percentage change in the price for a unit change in the yield. More specifically, it is the approximate percentage change in price for a 100 basis point change in interest rates. The modified duration can be found by dividing the Macaulay duration by (1+ yield to maturity).

$$\text{Modified Duration (MD)} = \text{Duration}/(1+r)$$

The modified duration can be approximated in the following manner:

$$\text{Approx. Modified Duration} = \frac{(\text{Price if yields decline} - \text{Price if yields rise})/2}{(\text{Initial price})\ x\ (\text{Change in yield in decimals})}$$
$$= \frac{(P_{-} - P_{+})/2}{(P_0\ x\ \Delta r)}$$

where Δr is the change in yield in decimal; P_0 is the initial price of the bond; $P-$ is the new price of the bond if yields decline by Δr; and $P+$ is the new price of the bond if yields increase by Δr.

Effective Duration: The assumption that the bond's cash flows do not change when yield changes is only applicable for option-free bonds. However, for bonds with embedded options, for example, callable bonds or putable bonds, a change in the interest rate may significantly affect the expected cash flow as the bond could be redeemed before maturity.

Valuation models for bonds with embedded options consider how changes in yield will affect the expected cash flows. The duration measure that is derived is called the **effective duration** or **option-adjusted duration**.

The effective duration equation is quite similar to the approximate modified duration equation. The difference is that for the effective duration, the yield's change is with respect to the benchmark curve and not the bond's yield as in the approximate modified duration measure.

$$\text{Effective duration} = \frac{(P_{-} - P_{+})/2}{P_0 x\ \Delta\text{curve}}$$

28.3.2 *Money Duration and Price Value of a Basis Point*

Money duration is obtained by multiplying the modified duration by the bond price. The result is the bond price change with a 100 basis point change in the yield.

$$\text{Money Duration} = \text{Modified duration X } P_0$$

The Price Value of a Basis Point (PVBP) is also known as the Dollar Value of 1 basis point change ($DV0_1$). PVBP is similar to money duration except that the yield change is one basis point. Using the same notation in the computation of modified duration, PVBP is computed as

$$\text{PVBP} = (P_- - P_+)/2$$

28.3.3 *Portfolio Duration and Its Limitations*

A portfolio's duration is the weighted average of the durations of the bonds in the portfolio. The weight for each bond is the proportion of the portfolio that the bond comprises. Similar to individual bonds, the portfolio duration can be used to estimate the sensitivity of a portfolio to changes in interest rates provided the interest rate change is small.

The formula for portfolio duration is as follows:

$$\text{Portfolio Duration} = w_1D_1 + w_2D_2 + w_3D_3 + w_4D_4 + \cdots + w_nD_n$$

where w_i is the market value of bond *i*/market value of the portfolio, D_i is the duration of bond *I*, and *n* is the number of bonds in the portfolio.

28.3.4 *Summary of Duration Measures*

Linking the Different Duration Measures: The many duration measures may seem confusing at first. Let's see how they fit together. We start with the bond price equation and differentiate it with respect to (1+*r*). This allows us to find the bond price change given a change in *r* the bond yield.

$$P_0 = C/(1+r) + C/(1+r)^2 \cdots (C+F)/(1+r)^n$$

$$dP_0/d(1+r) = 1/d(1+r)\,[C/(1+r) + C/(1+r)^2 \cdots (C+F)/(1+r)^n]$$

After incorporating the price and some manipulation of the equation, we end up with

$$D = -\frac{\frac{\partial P_0}{P_0}}{\frac{\partial(1+r)}{(1+r)}} \approx -\frac{\Delta P_0/P_0}{\Delta r/(1+r)}$$

From the above equation, the percentage change in price is given by

$\Delta P_0/P_0 = -\ D/(1+r) \times \Delta r$ using duration, D
$\Delta P_0/P_0 = -\ \text{MD} \times \Delta r$ using modified duration, $\text{MD} = D/(1+r)$
$\Delta P_0 = -\ \text{MD} \times P_0 \times \Delta r$
$\Delta P_0 = -\ \text{Money}D \times \Delta r$ using money duration, $\text{MoneyD} = \text{MD} \times P_0$

The Modified Duration Equation: We present a simple explanation of how the approximate modified duration equation is derived.

$$\text{Approximate modified duration} = \frac{(P_- - P_+)/2}{P_0 x \Delta r}$$

Recall that duration is the first derivative of the bond pricing equation. This means that the price-yield curve slope is a measure of duration. How do we measure the slope?

Figure 28.1 gives us a clue.

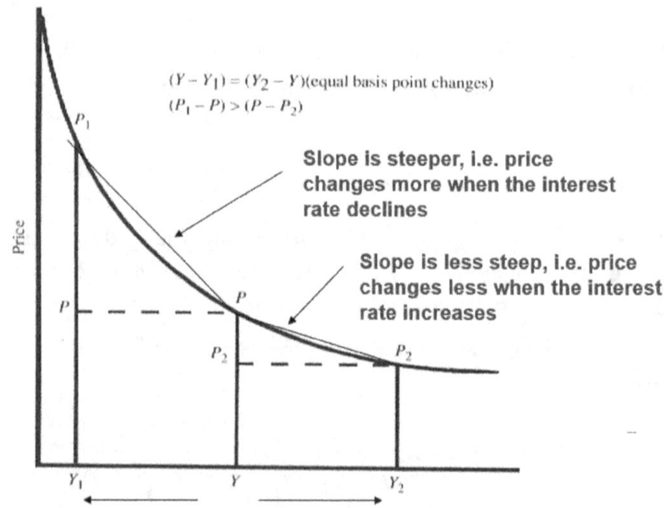

Reproduction of **Figure 28.1**: Duration: Slope of price-yield curve.

We approximate the slope of the tangent to the curve at P by taking the average of the slopes of the lines P_1P and PP_2.

Slope of line $P_1P = (P_1 - P)/(Y_1 - Y) = (P_1 - P)/\Delta r$
Slope of line $PP_2 = (P - P_2)/(Y_2 - Y) = (P - P_2)/\Delta r$

Average of the slopes $= [(P_1 - P)/\Delta r + (P - P_2)/\Delta r)]/2$
$= (P_1 - P_2)/2\Delta r$
$= (P- - P+)/2\Delta r$ where $P- = P_1$ and $P+ = P_2$

Since Modified Duration = Duration/P_0

Then MD = $[(P_- - P_+)/2\Delta r]/ P_0$ or

$$\text{MD} = \frac{(P_- - P_+)/2}{(P_0 \; x \; \Delta r)}$$

Yield Curve Assumption: The Macaulay duration measure is found by differentiating the bond price equation with respect to the interest rate. Notice that the bond price is the present value of the cash flows from the bond, which is found by discounting the cash flows using a single discount rate, the yield to maturity. This means that we are assuming a flat yield curve since spot rates for different maturities are equal. Further, the interest rate change is uniform across the term structure. In other words, we are also assuming a parallel shift in the yield curve, as demonstrated in Figure 28.3.

The two assumptions regarding a flat yield curve and a parallel shift in the yield curve mean that duration may not be suitable in the presence of steep yield curves and non-uniform changes over the

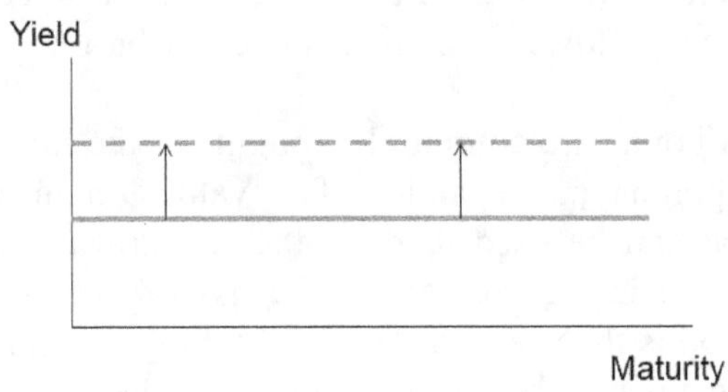

Figure 28.3: Parallel shift in flat yield curve.

maturity spectrum. To overcome these limitations in using duration to approximate price changes when yields change, we use the method of key rate durations.

Key Rate Duration: The duration measures we discussed earlier assume that the yield curve shifts in a parallel manner. Key rate durations overcome the assumption of a parallel shift by looking at the bond's sensitivity to changes in the yield curve at different maturities. For example, key rates could be at the 3-month, 1-year, 3-year, 5-year, 10-year, and other maturity points. Key rate durations enable us to see the sensitivity of a portfolio to changes in the yield curve's shape.

To compute key rate durations, we can do the following:

- Hold all yields constant and change the yield for a particular maturity of the yield curve by, say, one basis point.
- Determine the change in the value of the bond or portfolio.
- The sensitivity of the change in value to a particular change in the yield is called the key rate duration.

One key rate duration model, the Ho-Lee model, uses 11 key maturities of a Treasury spot rate curve to derive the key rate durations.

Uses of Duration Measures: Duration is often used to manage the risk that investment funds are insufficient to meet future liabilities. For example, pension funds need to make payments to retired employees. At the same time, insurance companies have to make payments for endowment policies that mature or life policies which the policyholder may want to cash out when she retires. These companies need to invest the cash flows from pension contributions and insurance premiums.

Long-term bonds are commonly bought for the investment portfolios as the coupon payments, and the face value at maturity are specific cash flows that can be used to meet the withdrawals. How does the portfolio hedge or immunize against the risk of interest rate changes? A simple method is the use of duration matching. Essentially, the duration of the assets is matched to the duration of the liabilities. There are other immunization methods, some involving dynamic rather than passive hedging programs, but these are beyond the scope of this program.

28.4 Convexity Measures

Convexity is a measure of the non-linear relationship between bond prices and bond yields.

Learning Objectives

- Compute and interpret the different measures of convexity

Main Takeaways

Main Points

- The convexity measure is used to supplement the duration measure to determine the bond's price change from a yield change.
- The convexity measure corrects for the error of using a linear measure like duration to approximate a change that is not linear, as shown in the curvature of the price-yield curve.
- Effective convexity is used for bonds with embedded options instead of the standard convexity measure for the same reason that effective duration is used in place of the Macaulay duration.

Main Terms

- **Approximate convexity:** This measure is used to correct the error caused by the curvature of the price-yield curve when using the duration measure to approximate the bond's price change resulting from a change in the yield.
- **Effective convexity:** Like effective duration, effective convexity uses the change in the benchmark yield in computing the convexity measure.

Because the price-yield curve is convex, the duration is suitable for measuring the effect of yield changes on the bond price only if the yield changes are small. Essentially we are approximating a curve with a straight line, namely the tangent to the curve.

We need to account for the curvature of the price yield-curve for larger yield changes. We can use the convexity measure for larger yield changes, which can be derived by taking the second derivative of the bond price with respect to the yield.

$$\text{Convexity} = \frac{1}{P_0} \times \frac{d^2 P}{dr^2}$$

$$\text{Convexity} = \frac{1}{P_0 \times (1+r)^2} \sum_{t=1}^{T} \left[\frac{CF_t}{(1+r)^t} (t^2 + t) \right]$$

The correction for convexity is given by

$$\frac{\Delta P}{P} \approx -MD * \Delta r + \frac{1}{2}[\text{Convexity} \times (\Delta r)^2]$$

We can find a measure of the approximate by looking at the slope of two lines P_1P and PP_2, in Figure 28.1.

We start with a straight line consisting of two segments. In this case, the slopes of both segments are the same. If we rotate clockwise the left segment of the line less than 90° then the two segments form an angle.

We can approximate the curvature for the price-yield curve by considering the difference in the slopes of the two lines P_1P and PP_2, in Figure 28.1. Also, note that the greater the difference in slopes, the more acute the angle, which connotes larger convexity.

$$\begin{aligned}\text{Difference in the slopes } &= [(P_1 - P)/\Delta r - (P - P_2)/\Delta r)] \\ &= [(P_1 - P_2) - 2P_0]\,/2\Delta r \\ &= [(P- - P+) - 2P_0]/2\Delta r\end{aligned}$$

where $P_- = P_1$; and $P+ = P_2$.

Note that the slopes' difference measures the rate of change in the slopes or the rate of change in duration. Dividing this rate of change by the change in interest rate would give us an approximate convexity measure as shown below:

$$\text{ApproxCon} = \frac{\frac{(P_- + P_+) - 2P_0}{P_0}}{(\Delta r)^2}$$

The effective convexity is

$$\text{EffCon} = \frac{\frac{(P_- + P_+) - 2P_0}{P_0}}{(\Delta \text{Curve})^2}$$

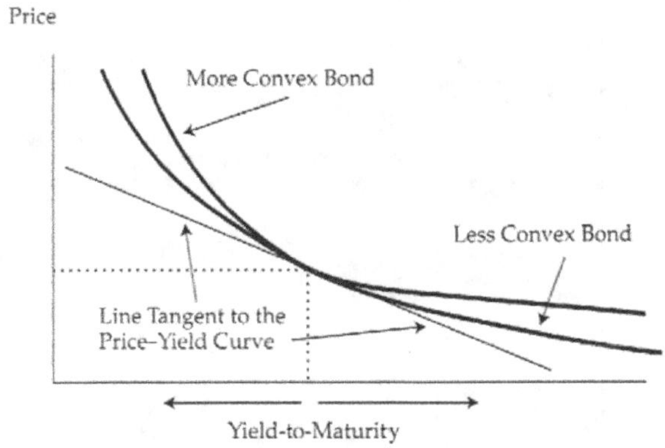

Figure 28.4: Convexity and impact on bond price when yields change.

28.4.1 *Investors Want More Convexity*

The price gain when the yield falls is more than the price loss when the yield rises. The more convex the price-yield curve, the greater the gain versus the loss. This is shown in Figure 28.4.

28.4.2 *Convexity of a Callable Bond*

When the bond yield falls below the coupon rate, the issuer has an incentive to call the bond. The bond price would increase when the yield falls for a non-callable bond. However, the call feature moderates the bond price increase for a callable bond.

Looking at Figure 28.5, we note that the callable bond's price yield curve's convexity moves from positive to zero and then to negative as the yield falls.

28.4.3 *Convexity of a Bond with Put Feature*

The holder of a putable bond has a position which is the mirror image of the position of the issuer of the callable bond. When yields rise above the coupon rate, the bondholder has an incentive to exercise the embedded put option.

As Figure 28.6 shows, the bond price decrease is moderated by the put feature. Further, the positive convexity of the bond increases with yield increases.

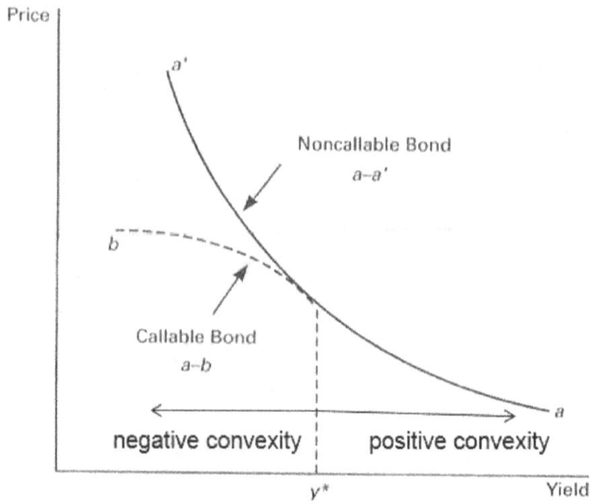

Figure 28.5: Convexity of a callable bond.

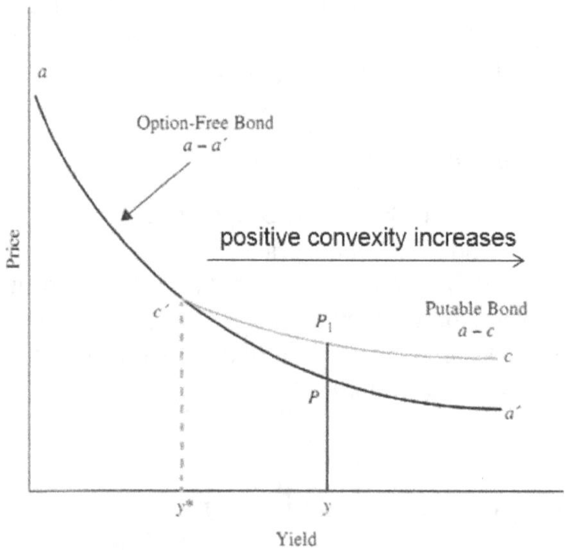

Figure 28.6: Convexity of a putable bond.

References/Further Readings

Bodie, Z., Kane, A., & Marcus, A. J. (2020). *Investments*, 12th edn. McGraw-Hill Irwin, pp. 495–512.

Leeds, S. J., Brown, K. C., & Reilly, F. K. (2019). *Investment Analysis and Portfolio Management*, 11th edn. Cengage, pp. 465–477.

28.5 Sample Questions

Question 1

Tom is a bond fund manager. His fund invests in foreign emerging market bonds. These bonds have high yields, but such bonds' demand is relatively low. Which of the following best describes the risks faced by the fund?

(a) Liquidity risk, volatility risk
(b) Sovereign, inflation risk
(c) Exchange-rate risk, liquidity risk

Question 2

When interest rates fall, which bond will experience the most price increase?

(a) Fixed-rate bond
(b) Floating-rate bond
(c) Inverse floating-rate bond

Question 3

All else equal, an increase in the coupon rate of a bond will increase interest rate risk, and an increase in the maturity of the bond will increase interest rate risk. The statement is correct with regard to:

(a) Only one effect
(b) Both effects
(c) Neither of the effects

Question 4

As a measure of interest rate risk, the Macaulay duration is most accurate when the yield curve is

(a) Upward sloping
(b) Downward sloping
(c) Flat

Question 5

Which of the following statements about duration is correct? A bond's:

(a) Modified duration is a measure of curve duration
(b) Macaulay duration is a measure that is meaningful for all bonds
(c) Modified duration cannot be larger than its Macaulay duration

Question 6

From the interest rate risk perspective, an embedded put option:

(a) Reduces the effective duration of the bond
(b) Increases the effective duration of the bond
(c) Decreases the convexity of the bond

Question 7

A pension fund has calculated its liabilities as follows: $400 million if the interest rate is 4%, $360 million under the current interest rate of 4.5%, and $330 million if the interest rate is 5%. What is the effective duration of the fund's liabilities?

(a) 9.72
(b) 17.50
(c) 19.44

Question 8

A bond has a modified duration of 7 and convexity of 60. If its yield to maturity decreases by 30 bps, the expected percentage price change is closest to:

(a) 1.98%
(b) 2.13%
(c) 2.33%

Question 9

With no accrued interest, which annual coupon bond has the greatest money duration?

Bond	Time to Maturity	Price	Coupon	YTM	Mod. Dur
A	5 years	91.34	3.0%	5.0%	4.48
B	7 years	88.63	3.5%	5.5%	5.95
C	9 years	86.40	4.00%	6.0%	7.19

(a) Bond A
(b) Bond B
(c) Bond C

Question 10

A bond with 6 years remaining till maturity has a 4% annual coupon. The bond is priced at 90.17 at a given yield to maturity of 6%. What is the estimated PVBP closest to?

(a) 0.045
(b) 0.048
(c) 0.052

Question 11

One problem in measuring the duration of a bond portfolio as a weighted average of the Macaulay durations of the individual bonds in the portfolio is:

(a) The assumption of a flat yield curve
(b) The presence of bonds with embedded options
(c) The assumption of a parallel shift in the yield curve

Solutions

Question 1

Solution: Option **c** is correct.

As the bonds are foreign, exchange rate risk is involved in transacting the bonds as the fund is dealing with a foreign currency. The low demand for the bonds means high liquidity risk when bonds have to be sold. There is no mention of inflation as a problem and no mention that the bonds are sovereign, so inflation risk and sovereign risk are not an issue. There is no mention that the bonds have embedded options, so volatility risk is not applicable.

Question 2

Solution: Option **c** is correct.

The floating rate bond's coupon falls when the interest rate falls. Hence its price hovers around the par value. Between the fixed-rate bond and the inverse floater, the inverse floater's price will increase more since the coupon increases with a fall in the interest rate, whereas the fixed-rate bond's coupon is unchanged. Note it is assumed the risk is the same for all three bonds, so the discount rate is the same for both bonds.

Question 3

Solution: Option **a** is correct.

An increase in the coupon rate decreases interest rate risk, but an increase in maturity increases interest rate risk. So the statement is correct for one effect.

Question 4

Solution: Option **c** is correct.

The Macaulay duration assumes that the yield curve is flat as the rate used to discount the cash flows in each period is the same. It also assumes the same quantum of yield change applies across all maturities; that is, the yield curve shifts in a parallel manner. If the yield curve is not flat, the same quantum of interest rate change will represent different amounts of the percentage change in the yield depending on the yield level. For an upward sloping yield curve, the percentage change in yield is lower for longer maturity than shorter maturity. The reverse is valid for the downward sloping yield curve. Whether the yield curve is upward or downward sloping, the fact is that the changes in the value of the coupons at each maturity will be different from those computed using the Macaulay duration.

Question 5

Solution: Option **c** is correct.

Modified duration is the Macaulay duration divided by $(1 + r)$. The modified duration will be lower for positive yields than the Macaulay duration. Option (a) is not correct as the modified duration is based on the bond's own yield rather than the benchmark curve yield. Option (b) is not correct as the Macaulay duration cannot be used for bonds with embedded options.

Question 6

Solution: Option **a** is correct.

The put option allows the bondholder to sell the bond back to the issuer. When interest rates rise, the bondholder has the incentive to exercise the put option as the price she gets for the bond is higher than its market price. The lower effective duration reflects the shorter maturity due to the put option. Option (c) is not correct as the bond's convexity will increase when interest rates rise.

Question 7

Solution: Option **c** is correct.

$$\text{EffD} \approx \frac{(P- - P+)/2}{\frac{P_0}{\Delta curve}}$$

P− = 400
P+ = 330
EffD ≈ (400 − 330)/2 × .005 × 360 = 19.44

Question 8

Solution: Option **b** is correct.

The percentage price change is calculated as follows:

$$\frac{\Delta P}{P} \approx -MD * \Delta r + \frac{1}{2}[Convexity \times (\Delta r)^2]$$

$$\Delta P/P \approx -7 \times 0.003 + 0.5 \times 60 \times (0.003)2 = 0.02127$$

Question 9

Solution: Option **c** is correct.

MoneyD (A) = 4.48 × 91.34 = 409.20

MoneyD (B) = 5.95 × 88.63 = 527.35

MoneyD (C) = 7.19 × 86.40 = 621.22

Question 10

Solution: Option **a** is correct.

$$P- = \frac{4}{(1+0.0599)} + \frac{4}{(1+0.0599)2} + \frac{4+100}{(1+0.0599)6} = 90.21$$

$$P+ = \frac{4}{(1+0.0601)} + \frac{4}{(1+0.0601)2} + \frac{4+100}{(1+0.0601)6} = 90.21$$

$$\begin{aligned} \text{PVBP} &= (90.21 - 90.12)/2 \\ &= 0.045 \end{aligned}$$

Question 11

Solution: Option **b** is correct.

The Macaulay duration is not appropriate if bonds have embedded options as the bonds may not be held to maturity as assumed in the Macaulay duration measure. Options (a) and (c) are not the answer as the Macaulay duration measure makes those assumptions.

Chapter 29

Credit Analysis

29.1 Credit Risk

Credit risk is the possibility of a loss resulting from a borrower's failure to repay a loan or meet contractual obligations. Methods of credit evaluation differ for various bonds and by the borrower's size.

Learning Objectives

- Describe the nature of credit risk and the associated measures.

Main Takeaways

Main Points

- Credit risk is the risk due to non-payment or partial payment of the bond's obligations on time.
- Credit risk can be decomposed into the default probability of the bond and its loss severity.
- Combining default probability and loss severity produces the expected loss measure.

Main Terms

- **Default probability:** The probability of the issuer failing to make the coupon payment or the bond's principal repayment.
- **Loss severity:** This is also known as the loss given default. The amount of loss the bondholder will experience once the bond has defaulted.
- **Expected loss:** The loss severity multiplied the default probability.

- **Bid-ask spread:** A bid-ask spread for an asset is the difference in price between the ask price and the bid price.

As a lender, non-payment of the debt obligations is the greatest concern. Therefore credit risk analysis is of primary importance to fixed income securities holders. Understanding of credit risk and credit analysis is useful for bankers who give out loans as well as those applying for loans. As the interest spread on loans can be quite thin, it is crucial that the bank does not suffer from bad loans. On the other hand, understanding the credit decision process would help the borrower increase his chances of success when seeking a loan.

There are several aspects of credit risk. Default risk is the one that most investors would associate with credit risk. However, others include spread risk, which incorporates downgrade risk and liquidity risk.

29.1.1 *Default Risk*

Default risk is the risk that the issuer fails to make full and timely coupon and principal payments. We can assess the risk by looking at its two components. The first, default probability, measures the likelihood that the issuer would default on its payments. The second, loss severity, also known as loss given default, looks at the recovery rate.

When the company goes into liquidation, the liquidators try to sell the parts of the company that can be sold off as viable businesses. The assets that are left in the company would then be sold off at low values or even as scrap. The total amount recovered from the sale of the businesses and the remaining assets is divided by the assets' book value to give the recovery rate.

The loss severity is computed as follows:

$$\text{Loss severity} = (1 - \text{recovery rate})$$

The expected loss that bondholders would experience is calculated as:

$$\begin{aligned}\text{Expected loss} &= \text{default probability} \times \text{loss severity}\\ &= \text{default probability} \times (1 - \text{recovery rate})\end{aligned}$$

In general, companies with good credit ratings experience high recovery rates. Hence, analysts often focus only on the default probability.

29.1.2 *Spread Risk*

Another aspect of bond risk is the risk that the bond's credit spread would widen. Credit spread is measured as the difference between the bond's yield and the yield of a government bond with the same maturity. The widening of the spread can result from the deterioration in the issuer's creditworthiness or an increase in market liquidity risk.

29.1.3 *Downgrade Risk*

Also known as credit migration risk measures the risk that bonds are downgraded due to deterioration in creditworthiness. When a bond is downgraded, there could be some negative consequences. Suppose the bond was downgraded from an investment grade rating (BBB and above) to a non-investment grade (BB and below). In that case, the bonds' demand could be reduced as some bond funds or other investment funds like pension funds have prohibitions against investing in non-investment grade bonds. Banks holding non-investment grade bonds have to increase their capital or reserves as bank capital adequacy ratios factor in the bank's loans and investments' riskiness.

29.1.4 *Market Liquidity Risk*

It incorporates the liquidity risk of a bond measured by the bid-ask spread. This spread tends to widen when less credit is available, or credit is more expensive for the bond dealers.

29.2 Seniority Structure

Seniority refers to the creditors' precedence in getting paid when a firm becomes bankrupt.

Learning Objectives
- Describe the differences in seniority for different creditors of the firm.

Main Takeaways

Main Points
- There is an order of precedence regarding who gets paid first when a firm goes into liquidation.

- The creditor at the top of the order gets paid first in full before the next creditor gets paid. If the amount available to the creditor is insufficient for them to receive the amount due in full, their partial repayment is all they get. Subsequent creditors get nothing.
- The relative ranking of a creditor in the list of creditors largely decides the credit risk of their debt.

Main Terms

- **Seniority:** The ranking of the debt in terms of precedence for payment when a firm goes into liquidation. The higher the debt's seniority, the earlier the debt gets paid.
- **Secured debt:** Debt is secured when assets serve as security for the debt. The amount realized from the liquidation of secured assets is used to pay the secured debt holders before the non-secured creditors.
- **Recourse:** The debt holder's right to seek full payment for the debt from the issuer if the liquidation of the secured asset does not yield enough funds to repay the debt in full.

The claims to the funds realized from the liquidation of the firm are paid according to the following order:

1. Senior debt with no recourse:
    - This debt is not on the company's balance sheet but resides within a special purpose vehicle (SPV) or special purpose entity (SPE). The firm sets up the SPV as a separate entity with its assets and liabilities. An example is an airline that sets up an SPV consisting of airplanes as assets financed in part by the SPV's bonds. Should the airline file for bankruptcy, the planes and the SPV are not considered part of the bankruptcy proceedings. Hence, in this sense, the SPV's debt ranks higher than the company's debt.
2. Secured debt with recourse:
    - Assets secure this debt. For example, an airline could sell debt secured by the planes placed in a trust account. If the assets that are sold off result in insufficient funds to pay this class of debt holders, these creditors can have recourse to the company's other assets.
3. Bank loans:
    - This is the first level of unsecured debt, consisting of lines of credit with banks.

4. Derivative obligations:
   - The obligations could arise from swap arrangements.
5. Senior unsecured debt:
   - Unsecured debt consists of many debt issues. Some of those issues are designated as senior by virtue of having been issued earlier through other arrangements. Debt issues with the same seniority are ranked equally or are said to have a "pari passu" ranking.
6. Trade obligations
   - These obligations arise from the credit given by suppliers of goods or services to the firm.
7. Senior subordinated debt:
   - These are debt that is ranked below the senior debt.
8. Subordinated debt:
   - These debt rank below the senior subordinated debt.
9. Convertible bond.
10. Income bond.
11. Preferred stock.
12. Common stock.

The order of precedence or seniority of the claims is inversely related to the claims' required return. Those debts at the top of the order earn low returns while shareholders who are paid last or are the residual claimants would have the highest required returns.

29.3 Rating Systems

A bond rating signifies the relative default risk of a bond. A bond with a high rating is considered less risky than a bond with a low rating.

Learning Objectives

- Describe the differences in ratings given to bonds and the implications in terms of required yields.

Main Takeaways

Main Points

- Bonds with high ratings have a lower risk than bonds with low ratings.
- Bonds with similar ratings should command similar yields.
- Bonds whose creditworthiness is deemed to have deteriorated are subject to a downgrade in ratings. Bonds whose creditworthiness have improved could have their ratings upgraded.

Main Terms

- **Rating:** This is a system of ranking bonds in terms of their default risks. Bond ranking agencies perform ratings.
- **Unrated:** This describes a bond that has not gone through a rating process.
- **Notch:** A broad rating, for example, A could be further subdivided into one of three notches, namely, A+, A, and A–.

Most bonds are rated in terms of default risk by at least one of the major rating agencies, typically *Moody's, Standard and Poor's*, and *Fitch*. Many institutions can hold only limited amounts of unrated or low-rated debt, so a favorable rating lowers the interest yield required and increases the number of potential buyers. *Junk bonds* are bonds rated below Baa by Moody's or BBB by S&P. Bonds rated Baa or BBB, and above are termed *investment-grade* bonds. Rating agencies evaluate a bond from various perspectives. At the industry level, the prospects for the industry as well as the issuer's competitive position is the first step. At the firm level, liquidity, profitability, debt capacity, and (since Sarbanes-Oxley) corporate governance are analyzed. Together, the various factors indicate the firm's ability to pay.

Issuers pay the bond rating agency to rate the bonds. The reason is that investors are uncertain about the risks of unrated bond issues unless the issuer is a well-known entity, for example, the government. Investors are unwilling to expend the effort to analyze the credit risk of unrated bonds and thus have less interest in such bonds compared to rated bonds. Further, given the uncertainty, investors tend to demand higher required yields than what the issuer thinks is justified. Another reason why investors favor rated bonds, besides knowing what yield it should command given its rating, is that the rating agencies monitor the issuer's financial circumstances and change the rating for a bond issue if the creditworthiness of the company changes.

29.3.1 *Rating Agencies Systems*

The chart in Table 29.1 shows the different rating systems from the rating agencies.

29.3.2 *Issuer versus Issue Ratings*

A distinction must be made between the credit rating for a firm and the credit rating for its bond issues. The issuer rating is given to the holding

Table 29.1: Different rating systems.

Moody's	S&P	Fitch	Definitions
Aaa	AAA	AAA	Prime Maximum Safety
Aa1	AA+	AA+	High Grade High Quality
Aa2	AA	AA	
Aa3	AA−	AA−	
A1	A+	A+	Upper Medium Grade
A2	A	A	
A3	A-	A-	
Baal	BBB+	BBB+	Lower Medium Grade
Baa2	BBB	BBB	
Baa3	BBB−	BBB−	
Ba1	BB+	BB+	Non-investment Grade
Ba2	BB	BB	Speculative
Ba3	BB−	BB−	
B1	B+	B+	Highly Speculative
B2	B	B	
B3	B−	B−	
Caal	CCC+	CCC	Substantial Risk
Caa2	CCC	—	In Poor Standing
Caa3	CCC−	—	
Ca	—	—	Extremely Speculative
C	—	—	May be in Default
—	—	DDD	Default
—	—	DD	
—	D	D	
—	—	—	

Notes: Moody's: Moody's Investor Service
S&P: Standard & Poor's Corporation

company of a group of companies and is based on the group's overall creditworthiness. The credit rating provided would apply to senior unsecured debt.

The issue rating could differ from the issuer rating because of specific considerations: how the bond issue ranks in the company structure. For example, the issue could be senior secured debt.

Rating agencies usually distinguish between the issuer and the issue rankings through the use of notches. A notch is a finer gradation within the broad class of the rating. For example, the firm could have a rating of A, but the issue could bear a rating of A+.

29.4 Credit Analysis — The 4 C's

The 4 C's is a systematic way of analyzing credit risk using quantitative and qualitative factors. The four factors are capacity, collateral, covenants, and character.

Learning Objectives

- Describe the attributes of the four factors of credit analysis.

Main Takeaways

Main Points

- A combination of the four factors assesses credit risk.
- Some of the factors go beyond the quantitative measures and use qualitative measures that give a more nuanced picture of the firm's creditworthiness.

Main Terms

- **Capacity:** Assesses the ability of the firm to service the debt.
- **Collateral:** The amount and quality of the asset backing the debt.
- **Covenants:** Refer to the requirements that the firm performs specific actions and prohibitions of the firm from taking other actions.
- **Character:** This factor assesses the record of management's actions concerning strategies and their execution as well as their treatment of bondholders.

29.4.1 *Capacity*

A simple rule regarding the granting of credit is the borrower's ability to repay the loan. The ability to service the debt may be assessed by looking at the industry's particulars. Some industries are more capital intensive and need to borrow more. The business's cash flow stability is essential as repayment of the debt is less affected by the business cycle. Another consideration is proper risk management and the judicious use of leverage.

29.4.2 *Collateral*

Collateral is the asset pledged by the firm to assure debt holders of the firm's ability to pay. In the event of default, the collateral pledged is disposed to settle any outstanding payment obligations.

Another issue relating to collateral is that firms selling services often have little collateral to back their borrowing, so the stability of the revenues is an important consideration. Much of the firm's value resides in the intangibles, namely goodwill, and patents. Intangible assets are not that suitable as collateral because of the difficulty of valuing the intangible assets and their illiquidity.

29.4.3 *Covenants*

Covenants are promises made by the issuer. They are important in constraining the activities of the company (negative covenants) and mandating action on the part of management (positive covenants). Stringent covenants may constrain the company's actions too much. In contrast, loose covenants may invite trouble for the creditors as it is unrealistic to appeal to humans' noble nature to "do the right thing".

29.4.4 *Character*

The quality of management and corporate governance ranks at the top of our list. A strong management capability means that the businesses and projects the company embarks on have been well-thought-out with proper due diligence undertaken. The quality of management is shown in how the company deals with setbacks and how it overcomes challenges. Good management enables the company to deliver cash flows and fulfill its debt obligations.

The other aspect of management is integrity. While corporate governance structures provide some checks and balances on the way management does its work, in the end, it is the character of people in management that determines whether the company cuts corners and engages in questionable practices. The integrity of management also means that the stakeholders' interests are taken into account in the decisions management makes.

Reference/Further Reading

Fabozzi, F.J. (2007). *Fixed Income Analysis*, 2nd edn. John Wiley & Sons, Inc., Chap. 15.

29.5 Sample Questions

Question 1
A bond's creditworthiness improvement is best characterized as:

(a) Credit migration risk
(b) Credit delta risk
(c) Credit convexity risk

Question 2
Companies JFK and LMN have similar financial and operating characteristics. JFK has less debt outstanding than LMN. Therefore, JFK's bonds are more likely to have _____ compared to LMN's bonds:

(a) Lower market liquidity risk
(b) Higher market liquidity risk
(c) Higher or lower market liquidity risk depending on the yield

Question 3
In the event of default, senior unsecured debt claims will most likely rank:

(a) Below that of senior subordinated debt holders
(b) Above that of subordinated holders
(c) Below that of bank loans

Question 4
In the event of default, the recovery rate of which of the following bonds would most likely be highest?

(a) Senior unsecured debt
(b) Senior subordinated debt
(c) Convertible bond

Question 5
To determine the capacity of a company, it would be most appropriate to analyze the:

(a) Company's strategy
(b) Growth prospects of the industry
(c) The size of the company in relation to its competitors

Question 6
Which of the three companies below has the lowest credit risk?

(a) A real estate developer
(b) A furniture maker
(c) A supermarket chain

Question 7
An investment-grade bond is best described as having a rating of

(a) A and above
(b) BBB and above
(c) BB and above

Solutions

Question 1

Solution: Option **a** is correct.

A change in creditworthiness or default risk will result in a change in the bond rating, that is, credit migration. Delta is a measure used in options, while convexity refers to the change in the bond's duration with respect to the yield.

Question 2

Solution: Option **a** is correct.

Among other factors, liquidity is the function of the quantity of the security available for trading.

Question 3

Solution: Option **c** is correct.

Senior unsecured debt ranks above both the senior subordinated debt and subordinated debt but below bank loans.

Question 4

Solution: Option **a** is correct.

The recovery rate of a bond depends on its seniority. The more senior the bond, the higher the priority of receiving payments from liquidation proceeds. Senior unsecured debt ranks above both senior subordinated debt and convertible bonds.

Question 5

Solution: Option **b** is correct.

Better growth prospects mean the firm would have more cash flows to service it. The company's strategy is used to assess management's ability which is part of the character factor. A large size may suggest a greater ability to pay. However, that is not necessary so as the larger firm may have a much higher debt level than the smaller firm.

Question 6

Solution: Option **c** is correct.

The supermarket chain is defensive; that is, it is relatively immune to the business cycle. The real estate industry and the furniture industry tend to be cyclical. When the economy is not doing well, people are less likely to take on mortgages or change their furniture.

Question 7

Solution: Option **b** is correct.

Investment grade bonds have a rating of BBB and above. Answer (a) is not correct as it excludes BBB bonds.

Chapter 30

Asset-Backed Securities

Asset-backed securities (ABS) are backed by a pool of debt securities such as mortgages, car loans, and credit card receivables. The pool of securities would receive regular payments from individuals who have to make monthly payments on their mortgages, car loans, or credit card loans.

30.1 Securitization

Securitization is a process of liquifying illiquid assets by issuing securities with those assets as collateral.

Learning Objectives

- Explain the securitization process and discuss the benefits of securitization.

Main Takeaways

Main Points

- Securitization transforms an asset into claims and thus creates liquidity for the asset.
- ABS are securities backed by a pool of loans or other assets. Borrowers make regular loan repayments consisting of interest and part repayment of principal. The payments on the loans are then passed on to the security holders.

- Some borrowers may choose to pay up their loans before the agreed loan period. They are said to prepay their loans.
- ABS are similar to bonds in that security holders receive regular payments similar to coupon payments, but the payments are not fixed.
- The payments that accrue to security holders depend on how the special entity is structured.
- Pass-through security holders receive pro-rated amounts of what is paid into the pool minus expenses.
- In a collateralized mortgage obligation structure, the payments to security holders are organized into tranches, with certain individual tranches getting paid first while other tranches get paid later.

Main Terms

- **Securitization:** A process of creating securities out of a pool of assets.
- **Asset-backed security:** Security backed by a pool of assets, typically loans.
- **Pass-through security:** Security where payments made to the pool of assets are passed on or paid on a pro-rated basis to security holders.
- **Tranching:** A process of arranging payments to security holders based on tranches that are paid sequentially.
- **Collateralized mortgage obligation:** Security backed by mortgages as collateral.

30.1.1 *Securitization Process*

Securitization is a process of liquefying assets. For example it would take quite a while for a home loan to be paid up. However, if the loans were combined and sold off, the bank would have the funds to issue more home loans. Typically home loans are sold to an entity which raises funds by selling securities or claims that are backed by the home loans. To do this, a special purpose vehicle (SPV) is set up as a fund incorporated for the purpose of buying the loans. The securities sold by the SPV are known as ABS, the assets being home loans in this case.

Transaction Structure: The securities are arranged into several tranches or classes in a securitization structure. Different tranches have different priorities in receiving payments. So the pool's overall risk is redistributed such that some tranches bear higher risks while others have lower risks.

The risk faced by the tranches could involve the different exposures to losses from defaulted loans, with some tranches designated to absorb those losses first. The tranches are arranged into senior and subordinate tranches, with the subordinate tranches bearing the credit losses first. The safer, senior tranches earn lower returns than the subordinate tranches. Note that the overall risk of the pool is not reduced by tranching. Instead, the risk is redistributed across the different tranches. This arrangement is known as **credit tranching**.

Another risk associated with loans is the prepayment risk. This risk stems from mortgage holders or those with loans prepaying on their debt. Like credit tranching, certain tranches absorb the prepayment risk before other tranches. Such an arrangement is called **time tranching**.

The collateral for asset-backed security could consist of various amortizing assets, for example auto loans, home loans or non-amortizing assets such as credit card receivables.

For collateral such as home loans, the principal repayments of these amortizing assets are distributed to the security holders. Where the collateral consists of non-amortizing assets, there would be a lockout period when principal repayments are not distributed to the security holders but reinvested in new assets. It is only after the lockout period that principal repayments are distributed.

When amortizing assets are securitized, there is no change in the composition of the collateral over the securities' life. However, for non-amortizing assets, the composition of the collateral changes. Regarding the funds received from the loans, interest is distributed to the security holders. However, the principal repayments can be either paid out to security holders or reinvested by purchasing additional loans.

30.1.2 *Benefits of Securitization*

There are many benefits to securitization:

- Securitization allows firms to sell their assets to special purpose entities, thus providing liquidity to the assets they hold. These special purpose entities issue securities against the pool of assets held in the entity.
- Securitization gives investors direct exposure to the underlying asset risks instead of going through an intermediary. For example, a Real Estate Investment Trust holds income-producing properties whose

rentals are passed on to the shareholders. By contrast, investing in a property company gives indirect exposure to property. The investor is exposed to the risks of various property sectors. Besides, if the property company also engages in property development, the risks are different from owning a property.
- For banks, securitization allows them to take mortgages off their books and enabling them to give out new loans.
- Securities have more liquidity than their underlying assets.
- If the assets are accounts receivable, securitization provides another funding alternative.

30.2 Residential Mortgage-Backed Securities

Residential mortgage-backed securities (RMBS) are securities backed by home loans.

Learning Objectives

- Describe the characteristics of RMBS and explain the different structures used in creating mortgage-backed securities.

Main Takeaways

Main Points

- A financial institution sells residential mortgages to a Special Purpose Entity (SPE). The SPE issues securities backed by the pool of mortgages.
- For pass-through securities, the mortgage payments less the SPE expenses are passed through to the investors on a pro-rata basis.
- Mortgage pools are subject to prepayment risk. Prepayment risk is the risk that homeowners pay up their home loans before maturity.
- Prepayments can result from liquidity needs. For example, a homeowner may sell the existing property to buy another property or because the homeowner is moving elsewhere.
- A much more significant concern stems from homeowners refinancing their loans when interest rates fall.
- When homeowners prepay, they exercise the embedded call option in the home loan. Investors lose out when homeowners prepay as the prepaid loan value is lower than the loan value if there were no prepayment options.

- Tranching is a way to redistribute the prepayment risk. The total risk of the pool of mortgages is not affected by tranching.
- Non-senior tranches that bear the risks first have higher expected returns than senior tranches, which are affected only after the non-senior tranches have no more capacity to absorb the prepayments.
- Later tranches benefit from having a maturity longer than the pool's average maturity.

Main Terms

- **Special purpose entity:** A firm set up to buy mortgages from financial institutions, using funds raised by selling securities to investors.
- **Pro-rata:** In a pro-rata arrangement, the amount received by an investor is proportional to the amount of the pool owned by the investor. If the investor owns 10% of the pool, she will receive 10% of what is paid out by the pool.
- **Pass-through security:** The cash flow received by pass-through securities is the amount received by the pool less expenses incurred by the entity.
- **Tranching:** A method of redistributing risks. The mortgage securities are grouped into tranches such that the investors bear the risks according to the tranche they occupy. Early tranches bear the prepayment risks first before subsequent tranches are affected.

The first type of ABS developed is a residential mortgage-backed security. In the US, institutions like the Federal Home Loan Mortgage Corporation (Freddie Mac) and the Federal National Mortgage Association (Fannie Mae) were created to increase home loans. Banks that gave home loans did not keep those loans on their books. Instead, they sold them to institutions like Freddie Mac and Fannie Mae so they could give out more loans. Freddie Mac and Fannie Mae formed pools from the loans they bought and sold mortgage-backed securities, which various funds, like pension funds, buy.

30.2.1 *Pass-Through Securities*

With the simple pass-through security, the pool organizer passes through all mortgage payments made by the homeowners, including prepayments, to the holders of the pass-through securities on a pro-rata basis (see Figure 30.1). The monthly payments are not fixed. How much is paid depends on how many homeowners pay off their mortgages early.

Figure 30.1: Pass-through securities.

Prepayment Risk: Prepayment risk is the risk that homeowners choose to repay their home loans early. This creates uncertainty regarding the maturity of loans. The most common reason for prepayment is falling interest rates. Homeowners reduce their mortgage payments by prepaying their loans and switching to new loans at lower interest rates. However, if interest rates were to rise, some home owners may change their plans for prepaying early and postpone prepayments. Prepaying of loans results in the shortening of the maturity of the pool, creating a risk for the investor known as contraction risk. When homeowners defer prepayments they create extension risk for the investor.

In normal times, homeowners sell their properties for a few reasons unrelated to the prevailing mortgage rates. These homeowners could be selling their present property to buy a bigger or smaller property. Or they could be relocating to another part of the country. Homeowners may also sell their properties if they need to raise funds for other purposes, while others do so because of their businesses' failure.

Whatever the reason for prepayments, the changes in prepayment rates unrelated to interest rate changes are much smaller than changes in prepayment rates due to declines in interest rates.

30.2.2 *Collateralized Mortgage Obligations*

CMOs are created by repackaging payments on pass-throughs. The CMO's innovation stems from offering different classes or 'tranches' with varying degrees of prepayment protection. The simplest form of a CMO is a sequential pay CMO (see below).

CMOs can be considered as having both the relative uncertainty in maturity of a pass-through and the relative certainty in maturity of a bond. With a sequential pay CMO, separate classes are created with different prepayment protection levels. Suppose a sequential pay CMO is structured to have three classes of securities, A, B, and C. Class A CMO holders receive all the initial principal payments including all prepayments first. Class B holders receive principal payments only after all the Class A

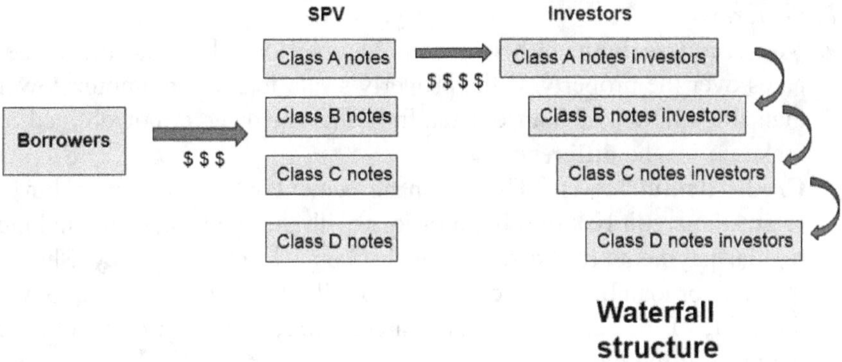

Figure 30.2: An illustration of tranching and the waterfall structure.

holders have been paid off. Likewise, Class C CMO holders are paid only after the early classes have been paid. As such their prepayments risk is lowest among all the classes. This system of paying one class off before the next class is paid is known as the waterfall structure, where cash flows cascade from one level to the next. The multiple classes allow investors to choose the prepayment risk level they are willing to accept (see Figure 30.2).

30.3 Other Asset-Backed Securities

Besides residential mortgages, other types of loans have been securitized. Among them are commercial mortgages, bank loans, credit card receivables, and auto loans.

Learning Objectives

- Describe the characteristics of other ABS.

Main Takeaways

Main Points

- Mortgages of income-producing commercial properties back commercial mortgage-backed securities. These are non-recourse mortgages.
- Collateralized Debt Obligations (CDOs) have debt other than mortgages as collateral. The collateral could be emerging market bonds, bank loans, and credit default swaps.

Main Terms

- **Non-recourse loan:** When a non-recourse loan defaults, the lender takes over the property. If the property's sale fetches an amount lower than the amount of loan outstanding, the borrower is not obliged to make up for the difference.
- **Credit default swap:** This is an agreement where the swap buyer swaps the credit risk of a bond or loan with the swap seller by making regular payments to the seller, much like an insurance policy. Should the bond or loan be defaulted, the swap seller has to pay the swap buyer the value of the security and any interests due from that date until the maturity of the loan.

30.3.1 *Commercial Mortgage-Backed Securities*

Commercial mortgage-backed securities are quite similar to CMOs. As the name suggests, these securities are backed by commercial mortgages on income-producing properties rather than residential mortgages. The commercial properties include apartment buildings, office buildings, shopping malls, and industrial buildings.

Commercial mortgages are generally non-recourse loans which are loans secured by the property. If the borrower defaults, the lender cannot go after the borrower for further compensation. Compared with a loan with recourse, the lender of a non-recourse loan would give the loan a lower loan-to-value ratio and a higher debt service coverage ratio requirement. If the borrower cannot meet the credit standards, the lender would require some form of credit enhancement, perhaps a third-party guarantee.

In the CMBS structure, interest is paid to all tranches. Losses from loan defaults are borne by the lowest priority tranche, which is also known variously as the "first-loss piece", "residual tranche", and "equity tranche". Further, investors in CMBS are protected against early prepayments. This is done at the CMBS structure level through sequential-pay tranches by credit rating. Higher-rated tranches receive payments first, while the lower-rated tranches absorb principal losses.

If it is done at the loan level, several call protection methods are used. In the prepayment lockout method, the loan agreement does not allow prepayments over a specified period. Another method is to impose prepayment penalty points. If the prepayment is to refinance the loan at a lower interest rate, there could be the imposition of a yield maintenance charge or make-whole charge. The last method is called defeasance, which involves the borrower paying funds to a servicer to invest in a portfolio that replicates cash flows that would exist in the absence of prepayments.

30.3.2 *Credit Card Receivables Asset-Backed Securities*

In a credit card receivables ABS, the collateral is the credit card loans that the banks have sold to the pool. Unlike mortgages, credit card loans are non-amortizing as there is no requirement for the credit card holder to pay regular amounts. The reason is that, unlike mortgages, the amount of the loan comes from the credit card holder not paying off the credit balance. The amount can increase if the credit card holder charges more to her card and does not pay the full amount due on those charges.

The cash flows from the credit card receivables include finance charges, fees, and principal repayments. During lock-out periods, investors only receive the finance charges and fees but not the principal repayments, which are reinvested. Such principal repayments are distributed to the investors only after the lock-out period.

30.3.3 *Collateralized Debt Obligations*

A CDO is a security backed by a diversified debt obligation pool. It is known by different names depending on the type of debt in the pool, such as:

- **Collateralized Bond Obligation (CBO):** The pool consists of high yield and emerging market bonds.
- **Collateralized Loan Obligation (CLO):** The pool consists of bank loans.
- **Structured Finance:** The pool consists of ABS, RMBS, CMBS, and other CDOs.
- **Synthetic CDO:** The pool consists of credit default swaps.

In a CDO, there are several bond tranches and an equity tranche. Each bond tranche has a promised yield. The returns from the pool are paid to the bondholders first. Any excess after satisfying the bondholders would be paid to the equity holders. An asset manager manages the portfolio of assets.

The tranches in a CDO include senior tranches, mezzanine tranches, and subordinate/equity tranches. The senior and mezzanine tranches are rated while the subordinate/equity tranches are unrated.

The CDO market has grown as institutions seek to liquify some of their assets. At the same time, there is a growing demand from pension funds and other institutions seeking such securities to diversify their portfolios from bonds and equities and earn higher yields.

Reference/Further Reading

Fabozzi, F.J. (2007). *Fixed Income Analysis*, 2nd edn. John Wiley & Sons, Inc., Chaps. 10 & 11.

30.4 Sample Questions

Question 1

Banks securitize their loans because the bank:

(a) Would earn higher profits than if the bank were to hold on to the loans
(b) Would be able to lend from the funds made available
(c) Can maintain ownership of the loans

Question 2

In a securitization, a SPV is responsible for

(a) Going after delinquent loans
(b) Approving which borrowers the bank can lend to
(c) Issuing the asset-backed securities

Question 3

Time tranching allows the investor to choose between:

(a) Extension and contraction risk
(b) Senior bonds and subordinated bonds
(c) Sinking fund and no sinking fund

Question 4

For a mortgage pass-through security, which of the following risks most likely increases as interest rates decline?

(a) Liquidity
(b) Extension
(c) Contraction

Question 5

For CMBS, credit risk is important if the mortgage loans backing the securities

(a) Are non-recourse
(b) Have call protection
(c) Have floating interest rates

Question 6

Which of the following best describes the cash flows that owners of a credit card receivable ABS receive during the lock-out period?

(a) No cash flow
(b) Only principal payments collected
(c) Only finance charges collected and fees

Solutions

Question 1

Solution: Option **b** is correct.

Securitization frees up the funds locked in the loans allowing the bank to make new loans. Option (a) is not the answer. Securitization is a different revenue model for the bank as the revenue is no longer the interest spread (the difference between the loan rate charged to borrowers and the deposit rate paid to depositors) but fees earned from originating the loan and servicing the loan. Option (c) is also not the answer. In securitization, the loans are sold to some other entity, so the bank no longer owns the loans.

Question 2

Solution: Option **c** is correct.

The SPV issues securities against the collateral or loans they hold. Option (a) is a service that the bank provides, while Option (b), the decision of which applicant gets the loan, depends on the bank's credit assessments.

Question 3

Solution: Option **a** is correct.

Time tranching allows for the redistribution of prepayment risk. Using sequential tranching, principal repayments are paid to one tranche and then a second tranche. Choosing an earlier or junior tranche means buying the shorter maturity securities than the longer maturity of the senior tranche. When interest rates fall, more homeowners will prepay. Hence, the junior tranche's maturity is reduced; that is, the tranche faces contraction risk. On the other hand, higher prevailing interest rates may discourage prepayments, and consequently, the tranche's maturity becomes longer than expected; that is, the tranche faces extension risk. (c) is not the answer as the sinking fund arrangement applies to corporate bond issues.

Question 4

Solution: Option **c** is correct.

When interest rates decline, homeowners are more likely to prepay their housing loans. This results in contraction of the average maturity;

contraction risk increases. Option (a) is not the answer as there appears to be no direct relationship between an interest rate decline and the securities' liquidity. Option (b) is not the answer as extension risk results from fewer homeowners prepaying than expected which is not the case when interest rates decline.

Question 5

Solution: Option **a** is correct.

If the loans are non-recourse, the borrower's creditworthiness is essential as the lender cannot go after the borrower's other assets. Option (b) is not correct as call protection is not relevant for mortgage-backed securities. The level of interest rates has implications for prepayments. The connection with credit risk is less direct, so Option (c) is not the answer.

Question 6

Solution: Option **c** is correct.

Finance charges and fees are paid out during the lock-out period. Principal repayments are reinvested and only distributed to investors after the lock-out period.

Part L: Derivatives

Chapter 31

Forward Contracts

31.1 Characteristics

31.1.1 *Introduction to Forward Contracts*

A forward contract is an agreement made today between two parties, known as counterparties, to buy or sell an asset, known as the "underlying", at an agreed price at a future date, known as the expiration date.

Learning Objectives

- Describe the risks of holding a forward contract.

Main Takeaways

Main Points

- The buyer in the forward contract has an obligation to pay the forward price and take delivery of the asset.
- The forward contract seller has an obligation to deliver the asset and receive the forward price.
- The terms of the contract are tailored to the parties' needs. This makes the forward contract a very flexible financial instrument.
- As these contract terms are highly customized, forward contracts have low liquidity, unlike standardized futures contracts.
- There is no secondary market that trades in forward contracts.
- Forward contracts face high risks of non-performance. The counterparty that faces losses if it performs according to the terms of the contract has an incentive to renege.

- The counterparties to a forward contract do not have to do anything after initiating the contract until the expiration date.

Main Terms

- **Counterparty:** The party with whom an investor had made a contract.
- **Counterparty risk:** The risk of the other party not fulfilling the terms of the contract, that is, non-performance. Non-performance tends to occur when a counterparty makes a large loss if it goes ahead to fulfill the contract's terms at the expiration date.
- **Settlement:** Occurs at the contract's expiration when the seller delivers the asset and the buyer pays the forward price.
- **Cash settlement:** When delivery of the asset is not feasible, e.g., delivery of the S&P 500 Index, the counterparties settle in cash.

A forward contract is an agreement made today between two counterparties, to buy or sell an asset at an agreed price at a future date. As there are only two parties involved, the terms of the contract can be tailored to each party's needs. This makes the forward contract much more flexible compared to the futures contract, whose contract terms are standardized by the futures exchange in which the futures contract trades.

The forward contract specifies the underlying asset's characteristics, the method and place of delivery, and the settlement process. With a highly customized contract, it is difficult to get a third party to take over the contract if one of the counterparties is not able to carry on with contract. This means that forward contracts are fairly illiquid and consequently there is no secondary market that trades in such financial instruments.

An advantage for the forward contract is that neither counterparty needs to do anything before expiration when the settlement process occurs. Some contracts involve assets where delivery may not feasible, for example, if the forward contract involves a stock index. Under these circumstances, the contract is settled in cash. For example, if the asset's price is lower than the forward price, the buyer will pay the seller the difference, and vice versa.

Besides low liquidity, forward contracts are beset by the risk of non-performance, that is, counterparty risk. Should one counterparty to the forward contract fail to perform according to the terms of the contract, the other counterparty's only recourse is to sue or initiate a legal process to compel performance by the defaulting party.

31.2 Valuation

31.2.1 *Value of a Forward Contract*

A forward contract's value is the difference between the spot price of the underlying asset at the expiration date and the contract price.

Learning Objectives

- Compute the value of a forward contract.

Main Takeaways

Main Points

- The forward price of the asset and the current spot price is related in the following manner:

$$F_0(T) = S_0 \times (1 + r)^T$$

- If the asset produces a known income with a yield, y, and the carrying cost for the investment in percentage terms is c then the above equation can be modified to:

$$F_0(T) = S_0 \times (1+R)^T \quad \text{where } R = r + y - c$$

- The valuation model incorporating carrying cost is known as the cost-of-carry model.
- The forward price, established when the contract is initiated, is the price agreed to by the two parties that produce a zero value at the start.

Main Terms

- **Cost-of-carry:** It refers to the cost to hold the asset until it is sold. The cost could include financial cost and storage cost if the asset is a physical asset.
- **Forward price:** The price at which a seller delivers an underlying asset, financial derivative, or currency to the buyer of a forward contract at a predetermined date.

- **Yield:** The earnings generated and realized on an investment over a particular period. It is expressed as a percentage based on the invested amount, current market value, or face value of the security.
- **Expiration date:** The last day that a derivatives contract, such as options or futures, is valid.
- **Riskless rate:** The theoretical rate of return of an investment with zero risks. In other words, this rate represents the interest an investor would expect from a risk-free investment over a specified period.

The value of a forward contract is computed by first agreeing to the forward price at the initiation of the contract. The forward price of the asset can be established using arbitrage arguments. Suppose the asset does not produce any income or have any carrying cost. If S_0 denotes the asset's spot price and $F_0(T)$ the forward price, which is the contract price, an investor can buy the asset at a price of S_0 today and sell it at the expiration date for $F_0(T)$. The investor's transaction is a riskless investment and should earn the riskless rate of return, r. Thus

$$F_0(T) = S_0 \times (1+r)^T$$

If the asset produces a known income, apart from the riskless rate, with a yield y, and the carrying cost for the investment in percentage terms is c, then the above equation can be modified to:

$$F_0(T) = S_0 \times (1+R)^T \quad \text{where } R = r + y - c$$

The valuation model incorporating carrying cost is known as the cost-of-carry model.

31.3 Sample Questions

Question 1

Forward contracts are popular with investors because

(a) There are only two parties to the contract
(b) There is no need for either counterparty to take action before the contract expires
(c) The terms of the contract can be customized

Question 2
The biggest risk for a forward contract is

(a) Lack of liquidity
(b) Non-performance
(c) Short period before the contract expires

Question 3
Forward contracts

(a) Allow a counterparty to transfer the position to another party
(b) Can be canceled at any time before expiration
(c) Do not require any investment upfront

Question 4
Forward contracts

(a) Cannot be valued because we do not know the future price
(b) Can be valued as the average of the spot price today and the forward price
(c) Can be valued by the cost-of-carry model

Solutions

Question 1

Solution: Option **c** is correct.

The forward contract's main attraction is that the terms that go into the contract are up to the counterparties to negotiate. Thus, the contract terms meet the needs of the counterparties. (a) is not the answer as most contracts in business are between two parties. (b) is not the answer as no action taken before expiration increases the risk of non-performance.

Question 2

Solution: Option **b** is correct.

Lack of liquidity (option a) is a risk faced by the counterparties, and the forward contract cannot be terminated before expiration. However, the bigger risk is non-performance which can result from one counterparty facing large losses if it were to go ahead with fulfilling the terms of the contract at expiration. Option (c) is not the answer as forward contracts have long expiration periods.

Question 3

Solution: Option **c** is correct.

Both Options (a) and (b) are not allowed for a forward contract. At the forward contract initiation, neither counterparty needs to put up good faith deposits.

Question 4

Solution: Option **c** is correct.

The forward contract is valued using the cost-of-carry model. An investor can acquire the asset at the forward price through the forward contract. The forward contract seller can buy the asset today and store it, incurring finance and other costs. The asset is then delivered at expiration to the buyer of the forward contract. For no-arbitrage, the forward price will be the current spot price S_0 compounded at a rate equal to the risk-free rate plus any income yield less any holding cost as given in the equation:

$$F_0(T) = S_0 \times (1 + R)^T, \text{ where } R = r + y - c.$$

Option (b) is not the answer. It is not the average of the two prices. However, the forward and current spot prices can be used to determine the rate of return.

Chapter 32
Futures Contracts

32.1 Characteristics

32.1.1 *Introduction to Futures*

A futures contract is a contract that trades on a futures exchange. It is a standardized agreement to buy or sell physical commodities or financial instruments for future delivery at a specified price on a specified date, known as the expiration date.

Learning Objectives
- Describe the features of a futures contract.

Main Takeaways

Main Points
- Futures contracts are quite similar to forward contracts as both call for the delivery of an asset at an agreed-upon price at a future date.
- The specifications of a futures contract are standardized.
- The futures exchange imposes rules regarding how trading is done.
- Margins are required to ensure that the counterparties have sufficient funds to meet losses.
- Counterparty risk is minimized by the clearinghouse becoming the counterparty for every trade.
- The mark-to-market process reduces the risk of non-performance.
- Like forward contracts, some futures contracts do not involve the asset's delivery but are cash-settled.

Main Terms

- **Clearing house:** A well-capitalized institution set up by the futures exchange to guarantee a contract's performance. The clearinghouse is inserted between the buyer and the seller. It becomes the seller to the buyer and the buyer to the seller of the futures contract.
- **Margins:** They are also known as good faith deposits. The counterparties post these to ensure there are enough funds to meet losses.
- **Initial margin:** The counterparty's deposit at the initiation of a futures contract.
- **Maintenance margin:** The minimum amount of margin required.
- **Margin call:** A call triggered when the margin falls below the maintenance margin level. The investor has to top-up the margin to the initial margin level, or the contract will be closed out.
- **Marking to market:** The investor's account is updated at the end of each day with the day's settlement price.
- **Variation margin:** The margin that needs to be posted if the margin balance falls below the maintenance margin. The amount is what is required to bring the margin back to the initial margin level.
- **Open interest:** The number of futures contracts outstanding. It is computed by adding either all outstanding long futures contracts or all the outstanding short futures contracts.

Futures contracts are quite similar to forward contracts as both call for the delivery of an asset at an agreed price at a future date. However, many differences stem from the fact that futures contracts are traded on a futures exchange with rules and regulations governing how the trading should occur.

Unlike forward contracts, the specifications of a futures contract are standardized.

The contract terms specify:

- the type of asset traded;
- the contract size or the quantity of the asset traded per contract;
- the expiration date when the exchange of asset and the price to be paid occur;
- the margins that need to be posted;
- the method of delivery of the asset.

Here is an example of contract specifications using wheat futures. For wheat traded on the Chicago Mercantile Exchange (CME), the grade and quality are specified as #2 Soft Red Winter wheat. The contract quantity for wheat is 5,000 bushels.

Futures exchanges specify the contract's expiration by the delivery month, which for CME wheat futures are the months of March, May, July, September, and December. The last day of trading is the 15th day of the contract month, and settlement is on the second business day following the last trading day of the delivery month.

A futures contract's key feature is minimizing counterparty risk by various measures. The first is the insertion of the clearinghouse into the contract. The futures contract is first initiated between a buyer and a seller. However, the buyer's counterparty is not the seller but the clearinghouse. The seller's counterparty is also the clearinghouse.

The risk of non-performance is reduced by the mark-to-market process and the presence of the clearinghouse.

- If the account balance falls below the maintenance margin, a margin call is triggered. The investor would need to top up the balance to the initial margin level. The amount that is required is known as the variation margin. The investor can withdraw a maximum amount of funds not greater than the amount by which the account balance exceeds the initial margin.

The futures contract's liquidity can be assessed by the open interest, which shows either the total of all long futures contracts or the total of all short futures contracts. When a futures contract is opened for trading, it takes time for the open interest to build up. The open interest size depends on traders' interest in using the futures contract. Open interest tends to be reduced when the futures contract nears expiration.

32.2 Forward Contracts versus Futures Contracts

Futures and forwards are financial contracts that are very similar, but there exist a few significant differences.

Learning Objectives

- Describe the differences between a futures contract and a forward contract and how the futures contract overcomes the forward contract's liquidity and non-performance issues.

Main Takeaways

Main Points

- Futures contracts trade on an exchange, unlike forward contracts which are traded over-the-counter.
- The futures contract specifications are standardized, whereas the forward contract terms are customized.
- Counterparties in a forward contract do not have to do anything before expiration. Futures contracts impose trading requirements like margins and marking to market. If the investor's account balance falls below the maintenance margin, an additional margin needs to be posted, or the contract is closed out.
- A futures contract position can be closed out any time before expiration by taking an opposite position in the futures contract. For example, if an investor has a long position, she has bought the futures contract, she closes out her position by going short in the futures market. That is, she sells the futures contract.
- Futures contract terms are standardized; futures contracts trade in the secondary market and provide liquidity for the contracts. There is no secondary market for forwards contracts as the contract terms are customized.
- Futures contracts overcome the non-performance issue of forward contracts through margins, which help ensure sufficient funds to meet losses. If margin calls are not met, the futures position is closed out, preventing further increases in losses. By contrast, the counterparties to a forward contract do not have to post any good faith deposit to ensure fulfillment of the contract terms at expiration.
- The marking-to-market process ensures that futures contract account balances are kept up to date to make margin calls on time. There is no mechanism in forward contracts to monitor the positions' value before expiration.

Main Terms

- **Liquidity:** The ease with which the investor can find a counterparty to take over her position at a price close to the contract's fair value. The presence of many buyers and sellers increases the liquidity of a contract.
- **Short:** It refers to a trading technique in which an investor sells security with plans to buy it later.

- **Secondary market:** The market where investors buy and sell securities they already own. Most people typically think of it as the "stock market," though stocks are also sold on the primary market when they are first issued.

Futures contracts are similar to forward contracts in that both are agreements about the purchase and sale of an asset at a future date. The price for transacting the asset is agreed upon beforehand. Both types of contracts are useful for hedging purposes, limiting the loss in an investment. However, there are many differences.

The differences between the two types of contracts stem mainly from how they are traded — futures contracts trade on an exchange, whereas forward contracts are traded over the counter. How these contracts trade has implications for the risks of these financial instruments.

The futures exchanges on which futures contracts trade have rules and regulations for futures trading as there are many market participants. Without the rules and regulations, the market will be disorganized and there will be low trust in the market process. By contrast, forward contracts are between two private parties free to decide about the nature of the contract mutually. We discuss some of the differences below.

32.2.1 *Specifications*

The terms of a futures contract are standardized. Standardization makes the contracts fungible; that is, there is no differentiation between contracts for a specific asset with the same delivery month. Hence a secondary market is possible, providing liquidity to the contract. By contrast, the terms of a forward contract are somewhat unique as they are crafted to meet the counterparties' specific needs. The result is that no secondary market can develop, and there is hardly any liquidity for forward contracts.

32.2.2 *Clearing House*

The presence of a clearinghouse that stands between the counterparties gives each counterparty assurance that there is little non-performance risk whatever happens to the other counterparty. This assurance of performance enhances traders' confidence to trade the futures contract.

Having the clearance house as the counterparty removes the risk of non-performance for the futures contract. Performance in forward contracts depends both on the ability and the willingness of the counterparties to fulfill their respective obligations. If fulfilling the forward contract obligations means incurring large losses for a counterparty, it may not have the resources to bear such losses. Alternatively, potential large losses would give the losing counterparty an incentive to renege on the contract.

32.2.3 *Rules and Regulations*

The rules and regulations that govern the trading of futures contracts help to minimize disputes between traders and the risk of non-performance. The basis for the contract's settlement when it expires is spelled out, so there is hardly any room for dispute.

There is no margin and mark-to-market mechanism for forward contracts. The absence of such tools allows losses for one counterparty to build up. If the losses are large enough, then the losing counterparty would either have an incentive to renege on the contract or be in no position financially to fulfill the contract's terms.

The combination of the clearinghouse, standardized contracts, and rules relating to settlement, margins, and mark-to-market results in confidence in the trading process and enhances the futures contracts' liquidity. Further, a trader who wants to close out her position can go into the market to initiate an opposite position to her current position. For example, suppose the trader is long a futures contract. In that case, she can go to the market and short the same futures contract to offset the earlier position, eliminating any previous position obligations. The differences between the forward and futures contracts cannot be starker.

Reference/Further Reading

Bodie, Z., Kane, A., & Marcus, A.J. (2020). *Investments*, 12th edn. McGraw-Hill Irwin, pp. 749–762.

32.3 Sample Questions

Question 1
Futures contracts differ from forward contracts because

(a) Futures contracts have more credit risk.
(b) Futures contracts have more liquidity risk.
(c) None of the above

Question 2
Which of the following statements is true?

(a) Futures contracts are traded over-the-counter.
(b) A forward contract can be terminated at any time.
(c) A forward contract has more counterparty risk than a futures contract.

Question 3
Which of the following statements is false?

(a) The terms of a forward contract are more flexible than a futures contract.
(b) Forward contracts involve no money at the initiation of the contract.
(c) Forward contracts require good faith deposits.

Question 4
If the initial margin is $6,000, the maintenance margin $4,000, and the trader's margin is $4,500, how much must the trader deposit?

(a) Nothing
(b) $1,500
(c) $2,000

Solutions

Question 1

Solution: Option **c** is correct.

The clearinghouse's presence minimizes the non-performance of futures contracts as it is the counterparty to all contracts. The standardization of contracts and the assurance of performance enhance liquidity for the futures contracts.

Question 2

Solution: Option **c** is correct.

The clearinghouse's presence minimizes counterparty risk for a futures contract as it is the counterparty for all contracts. Futures contracts are traded on an exchange. Forward contracts cannot be terminated before expiration.

Question 3

Solution: Option **c** is correct.

Forward contracts are not standardized like futures contracts. Its terms are negotiable between the counterparties. Forward contracts unlike, futures contracts, do not require the posting of margins.

Question 4

Solution: Option **a** is correct.

The margin call is activated if the margin balance falls below the maintenance margin.

Chapter 33

Options

33.1 Characteristics and Types

33.1.1 *Introduction to Calls and Puts*

A call is the right to buy, and a put is the option to sell the underlying stock at a predetermined exercise price until a fixed expiry date.

Learning Objectives

- Understand the different characteristics and types of options.

Main Takeaways

Main Points

- An option gives the right but not the obligation for the option holder to either buy or sell the asset.
- The choice given to the option holder is significant as the option holder would not want to buy or sell the asset if she ends up with losses. Contrast this to a forward contract where the counterparty has no choice but to buy or sell the asset that she has contracted, even if she incurs losses doing so.
- A call option buyer would exercise the option only if the stock price is higher than the exercise price.
- Options have limited life, and options traded on an options exchange often have short expiration periods.

Main Terms

- **Option buyer:** The buyer of the option.
- **Option writer:** Seller of the option. Writing an option means selling the option.
- **Exercise price:** The price that the call buyer needs to pay the call writer for an asset if she so wishes or the price the put buyer will get when she chooses to sell the asset to the put writer. The exercise price is set by the exchange when it lists the option for trading. For options that are not listed, over-the-counter options, the exercise price is agreed upon by the buyer and seller of the option.
- **Exercise:** The act of the option buyer exercising her right as stated in the contract. When a call is exercised, the call buyer tenders the call together with the exercise price and receives the asset. If a put is exercised, the put buyer tenders the put together with the asset and receives the exercise price.
- **American option:** Can be exercised at any time before expiration.
- **European option:** Can only be exercised at the expiration date.

We can combine an option with the underlying asset to modify the payoffs from owning the asset alone. Calls and puts can also be combined to achieve certain cash flow patterns over the price range for the underlying asset. To make it easier to understand, we use the common stock as the underlying asset. There are two types of options — a call and a put.

A call is a contract that gives the buyer the right, but not the obligation, to buy an asset at a fixed price, known as the exercise price or strike price, on or before a future date, known as the expiration date.

A put contract is similar to a call contract. The difference is that the put buyer has the right, but not the obligation, to sell the asset at the exercise price on or before the expiration date.

33.1.2 *Simple Combinations — Covered Put and Straddle*

A covered put position is created by buying (or owning) stock and buying an at-the-money put.

A straddle is created by buying both an at-the-money call and an at-the-money put.

Learning Objectives

- Explain the usefulness of simple option combinations.

Main Takeaways

Main Points

- A covered put is a strategy that involves buying a put to limit the losses in a long stock position.
- The maximum loss that results from the combination of a long stock and a long put is the put price.
- A straddle allows the investor to gain from wide swings in the stock price.

Main Terms

- **Covered:** An option is covered when the option position's investor has the underlying stock. Having the stock allows the put buyer to have the share ready to exercise the put if she wishes, resulting in a covered put position. In a covered call position, the call writer has the stock to deliver should the call buyer want to exercise her call.
- **Straddle:** An option position consisting of a long call and a long put on the same stock, at the same exercise price and expiration date.
- **Breakeven price:** The price that results in zero profit for the strategy or combination position.
- **Long position:** Benefits from an increase in the underlying asset price. Be careful about applying this definition to an option as an option is not an asset, but buying an option is buying a right to do buy or sell the asset. A long option benefits the option buyer from an increase in the asset's price only if it is a call but not if it is a put.
- **Short position:** Benefits from a decrease in the underlying asset price.

(a) Covered Put

The covered put position can best be explained using profit diagrams. A profit diagram is a graph where one axis indicates the stock price while the other axis indicates the position's profit.

In Figure 33.1, the profit diagram on the left shows the long position of a stock bought at $10. The position's profit is given by (Stock price − $10). If the stock price is $0, then the profit is ($0 − $10) = − $10 or a loss of $10.

The diagram on the right shows the long put position. If the stock price is higher than $10, the put will not be exercised, resulting in a loss equivalent to the put price. However, if the stock price were to fall below $10, then exercising the put would result in a profit of $10 less than the

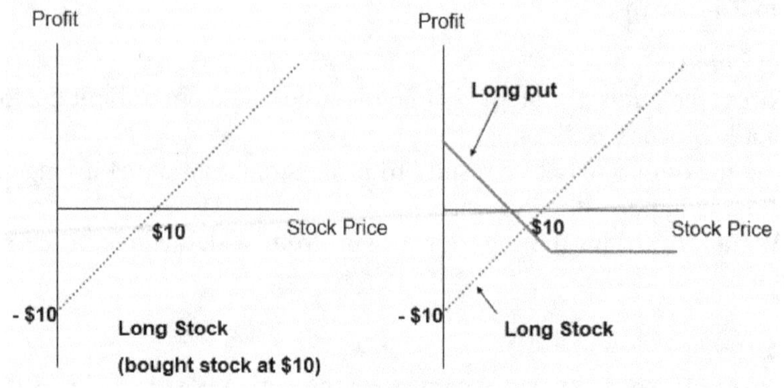

Figure 33.1: Profit diagrams for long stock and long put.

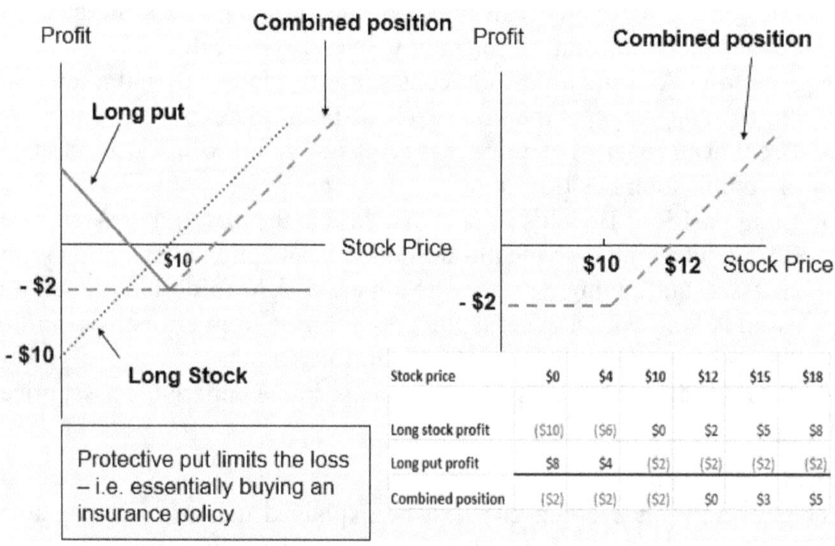

Stock price	$0	$4	$10	$12	$15	$18
Long stock profit	($10)	($6)	$0	$2	$5	$8
Long put profit	$8	$4	($2)	($2)	($2)	($2)
Combined position	($2)	($2)	($2)	$0	$3	$5

Figure 33.2: Profit diagrams for combined long stock and long put.

stock price and the put price. For example, if the stock price is $4, the put's profit would be $10 − $4 − $2 = $2. Note that the put's breakeven price is a stock price of $8. At this stock price, the put buyer makes $2 from exercising the put. However, this amount is offset by the price of $2 paid for the put.

In Figure 33.2, we combine the long stock position with the long put position in the left-hand side profit diagram. The combined position is shown in the profit diagram on the right. The table below the diagram shows how we can compute the combined position's profit. However much the stock price falls below \$10, the investor loses a maximum of \$2 or the put price. On the other hand, the upside for the position is not affected. The breakeven price for the protective put position is \$12.

(b) Long Straddle

A long straddle position consists of a long call and a long put at the same exercise price. Figure 33.3 shows the profit diagrams for a long call and a long put. We discussed the profit diagram of a long put position in the section above on the protected put. A long call is worth exercising if the stock price is higher than the exercise price. However, the call will show a profit only if the stock price is higher than the breakeven price, which is the sum of the exercise price plus the call price. For any stock price below the exercise price, the long call position shows a loss equal to the call price, as it is not worthwhile for the call buyer to exercise the option.

In Figure 33.4, we combine the long call and long put positions. The profit diagram on the right shows the combined position. We can see that

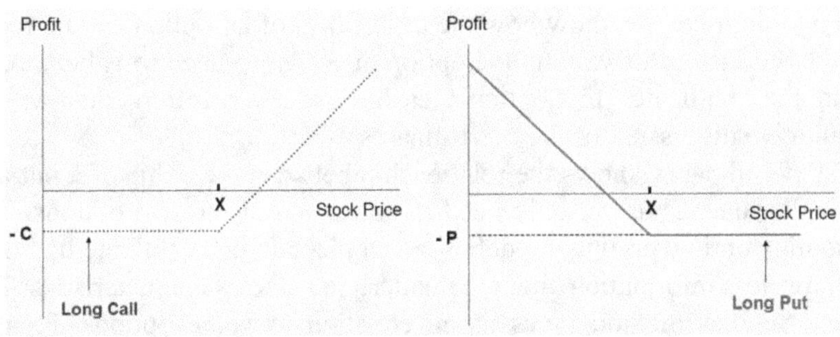

Figure 33.3: Profit diagrams for long call and long put.

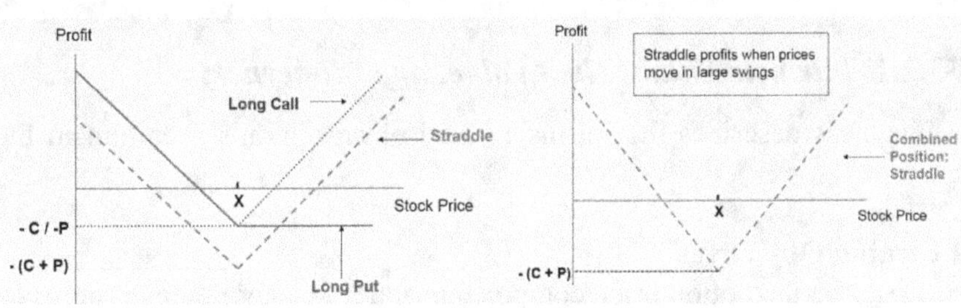

Figure 33.4: Profit diagrams for the long straddle.

the investor who holds a long straddle will make a profit only if the stock price is either very low or very high. The breakeven prices are $(X - C - P)$ and $(X + C + P)$.

The straddle is a useful strategy or combination if the investor is uncertain whether the stock price will decrease significantly or increase a lot from the current stock price. An example illustrating the use of a long straddle is if the investor is betting on an election's outcome, say the presidential election. If one candidate wins, the stock market will react very favorably as the candidate is seen to be pro-business. However, should the other candidate win, it would be unfavorable for the stock market as this candidate has pledged to increase corporate taxes and tighten the regulation of companies. Since the election outcome is a toss-up, the investor would profit regardless of which candidate wins the election.

33.2 Valuation of Options

There are various ways to value an option. We develop some simple notions first by decomposing an option price into the intrinsic value and the time value. Then we use arbitrage arguments to determine bounds on the option price. We show how the cash flows of an option can be replicated. So, instead of valuing the option directly, we need to value a portfolio that replicates the option's cash flows. We follow this with a qualitative discussion of the determinants of option value.

Put-call parity shows the relationship between the value of a put and the call value. Thus we only need to value one of the two options. The binomial option pricing model is a simple but powerful method that requires less information about the underlying stock's characteristics. The Black-Scholes method gives us an equation to value options. Finally, given the option's price, we can back-out the implied volatility of stock returns or the stock return volatility implicit in the option price.

33.2.1 *Intrinsic Value, Time Value, and Moneyness*

Moneyness describes the intrinsic value of an option's premium in the market.

Learning Objectives

- Describe the option price components and how they relate to the stock price.

Main Takeaways

Main Points

- The option price consists of two components: intrinsic value and time value.
- Time value is the difference between the option price and the intrinsic value.
- The time value of an option decays over time.
- Moneyness indicates whether it is worthwhile to exercise an option.
- In-the-money, at-the-money, and out-of-the-money are commonly used terms that refer to an option's *moneyness,* an insight into the intrinsic value of a derivatives contract.

Main Terms

- **Intrinsic value:** The value of the option upon immediate exercise.
- **Time value:** Measures the optionality of the option and the insurance aspect of the option.
- **In-the-money:** An option is in-the-money when the intrinsic value is positive.
- **At-the-money:** An option is at-the-money when the intrinsic value is zero, and the stock price is equal to the exercise price.
- **Out-of-the-money:** An option is out-of-the-money when the intrinsic value is zero, but the stock price is not equal to the exercise price.

(a) Intrinsic Value

The intrinsic value is the value of the option upon immediate exercise. For a call, we denote as Max $[0, S - X]$, which means you take the maximum of the quantities within the brackets. What this maximum function (Max) does is that it rules out negative values. In practical terms, it means that the holder of the option will only exercise the option if $(S - X)$ is greater than zero, that is, S is greater than X.

When the intrinsic value is positive, the stock price is greater than the exercise price, and we say that the call is "in-the-money". If the stock price is much greater than the exercise price, the call is considered "deep-in-the-money". Very deep-in-the-money calls behave like stocks in the sense that the quantum of price change for the call is quite close to the quantum of the price change for the stock.

For a put, the intrinsic value is denoted as Max $[0, X - S]$; that is, a put will not be exercised if the stock price is higher than the exercise price. Intuitively, it does not make sense to sell the stock at the exercise price when it can fetch a higher price in the market. Regarding the moneyness of the put, the same terms can be applied. A put is in-the-money when the stock price is less than the exercise price.

(b) Time Value

An option's time value is not to be confused with the time value of money, although the time to expiration affects the time value. All else equal, the longer the time to expiration, the higher the option's time value.

An option's time value is defined as the difference between the price of the option and the intrinsic value. If an option is exercised before expiration, the time value is extinguished. That the time value is lost must be considered when the investor plans to exercise an option early.

While time to expiration affects the option's time value, the more significant determinant of time value is volatility. This will be discussed in the next section on determinants of option value. The nature of the time value will be explained in Figure 33.5.

In the first graph in Figure 33.5, starting from the top left corner, the intrinsic value is 0 when the stock price is lower than the exercise price. However, once the stock price increases beyond the exercise price, the intrinsic value rises dollar for dollar as the stock price increases, as depicted by the 45-degree slope of the graph.

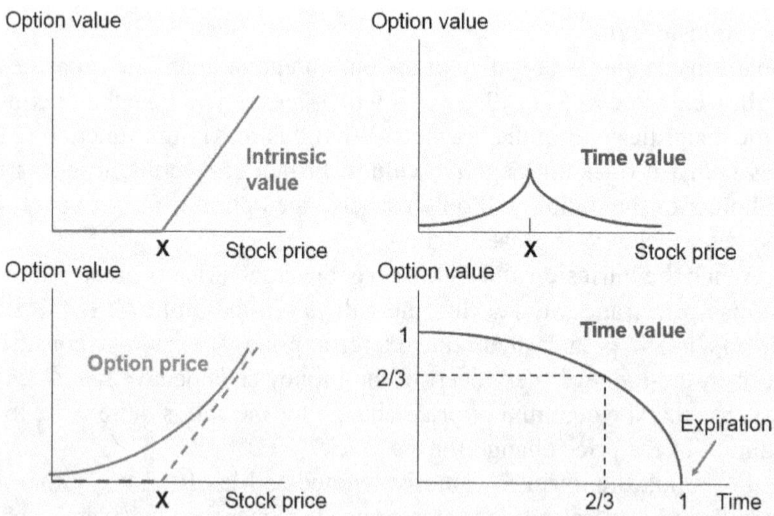

Figure 33.5: Intrinsic value, time value, and option price for a call.

The graph on the top right corner shows that the time value is almost zero when the stock price is either very low or very high, that is, the call is very deep out-of-the-money or very deep-in-the-money. The reason is that when the call is out-of-the-money, an investor buying a call is hoping to make money when the call becomes in-the-money. When the stock price is very low, the probability of the stock price going above the exercise price is very slim. In this case, an investor would pay very little for this bet. However, as the stock price approaches the exercise price, the probability that the call will end up in-the-money increases. The time value rises and reaches its maximum value when the stock price is equal to the exercise price.

When the call is in-the-money, why would someone buy a call rather than the stock itself? If the stock price were to fall, the value of a long position would fall by the same amount. Should the stock price fall by a large amount it would mean a considerable loss in the long position. However, for an investor who holds a call, her loss is limited to the price she paid for the call, regardless of how much the stock price falls. This limit to losses suggests that the time value reflects an "insurance" feature. If the stock price is very much higher than the exercise price, the likelihood the stock would fall by a substantial amount to end up being lower than the exercise price would be rather slim. An investor buying such a call would not pay much for this "insurance" feature. Hence the time value is minimal. However, as the stock price falls and approaches the exercise price, the call becomes much more valuable with the time value reaching a maximum when the stock price is equal to the exercise price.

The third graph, bottom right corner, shows how the time value decays over time. The time value decay is slow when the option is first issued. However, when the option nears expiration, there is rapid decay in the time value. As an approximation, the option loses two-thirds of its time value in the last one-third of its life. This observation implies that investors need to be aware that time value decay affects option returns negatively, with the effect being more significant near expiration.

The last graph in the lower-left corner combines value of the intrinsic and time values to give the call value. The time value of the option at each stock price is the vertical distance between the option price and the intrinsic value. Note that the time value reaches a maximum when the option is at-the-money. Investors are attracted to options where the stock price is close to the exercise price. The price of such options can go either way from being in-the-money to out-of-the-money, and vice versa. With a larger pool of investors, such options tend to be more liquid than options which are more out-of-the-money, or more in-the-money.

33.2.2 *Arbitrage, Replication and Risk Neutrality*

The concepts of arbitrage, replication, and risk neutrality are essential to comprehend the pricing of derivatives.

Learning Objectives

- Use arbitrage arguments to derive restrictions on the option price and discuss how replicating the cash flows of an option with other assets creates a risk-free and risk-neutral investment and pricing.

Main Takeaways

Main Points

- Arbitrage is based on the law of one price.
- Arbitrage profit is defined as a strategy with zero or positive cash flow today, and non-negative cash flows in the future.

Main Terms

- **Arbitrage:** The act of trying to profit from price discrepancies.
- **Replication:** The process of creating a portfolio that mimics the price behavior of a financial instrument we are interested in pricing.
- **Risk neutrality:** The assumption that risk does not matter. This assumption applies to options as they are essentially one-sided bets where the investor benefits from the upside but does not suffer from the downside.

Arbitrage is based on the law of one price; similar assets should sell for the same price. Arbitrage involves the simultaneous buying of one asset and the selling of another asset. If both assets have the same value but different prices, then arbitrage profit is possible. This is done by buying the cheaper asset and selling the more expensive one. Essentially arbitrage profit arises from a transaction that involves zero or positive cash flow today followed by non-negative cash flows in the future.

Replication is an important concept in Finance. Essentially, it involves creating an asset or financial instrument that gives the same payoffs as an asset or financial instrument we are trying to value. In option pricing, the option can be priced using a replicating portfolio whose price behavior

Table 33.1: Cash flows of long call, today and at future date.

Today		At future date	
		S < X	S > X
Action	Buy call	Do nothing	Exercise
Cash flow	+ C	0	(S − X) > 0

mimics that of the option. We will use the replication strategy in the discussion on put-call parity and the Black Scholes option pricing model.

Risk neutrality means that the investor is indifferent to risk. This seems puzzling as investors tend to be risk-averse. Two investments may have the same expected return. However, investors would favor the one with the lower risk. This conundrum can be easily resolved if we note that we are not dealing with the typical asset but are dealing with options where the downside risk does not matter. Further, as we will show later, we can create a portfolio consisting of an option and some other security such that the payoffs in the future are certain. In this case, the portfolio is riskless and should earn a risk-free return.

In the following sub-sections, we use arbitrage arguments to establish bounds or restrictions on option prices and explain how to profit from price discrepancies. While we cannot say what the price of an option is, we can at least narrow the range of possible values. For our purposes, only calls will be discussed.

(a) Call Price should be Greater or Equal to Zero; C > 0

It is obvious that a call should not have a negative price.

We show that this is true by proving that the opposite relationship cannot hold; otherwise, we can profit through arbitrage.

If $C < 0$ and we buy a call, we will be paid C today, a positive cash flow. Subsequently, in the future, if it is worthwhile to exercise the call this will result in a positive cash flow. If it is not worthwhile, we do nothing. These actions are summarized in Table 33.1.

(b) Call Price should be Less Than Stock Price; C < S

It is quite obvious that the right to buy an asset should not be worth more than the asset itself. Suppose it was not true, that is, $C > S$. We can make a profit by buying the stock at a lower price and selling the higher-priced call, resulting in a profit of (C − S) today. In future, should the call be exercised, give the call holder the stock and receive X. should the call not be exercised, we end up with the stock which has some value. Table 33.2 illustrates the actions and the corresponding cash flows.

Table 33.2: Cash flows of long stock and short call, today and at future date.

Action today	Cash flow today	At future date	
		S < X	S > X
Buy stock	− S	0	S − X
Sell call	+ C	0	− (S − X)
	C − S > 0	0	0

(c) Call Price should be Greater or Equal to Its Intrinsic Value; C ≥ Max [0, S − X]

Arbitrage profits can be made if the restriction is violated. For example, if the call is less than its intrinsic value, buy the call and exercise immediately. An arbitrage profit of [(S − X) − C], which is positive, is realized (see Table 33.3).

Table 33.3: Cash flows of long call and short stock today.

Action today	Cash flow
Buy call	− C
Exercise call	–X
Sell stock	+S
Net result	(S − X) − C > 0

(d) For Calls with Same Exercise Price, Price of Call with Longer Expiration should be Greater or Equal to Price of Call with Shorter Expiration: C(T2) ≥ C(T1) where (T2 > T1)

If this restriction is violated, that is C(T1) > C(T2), we can make an arbitrage profit of C(T1) − C(T2) by buying C(T2) and selling C(T1). If C(T1) is exercised, then exercise C(T2) by paying X and receiving one share. Give the one share to the buyer of C(T1) and receive X. In other words, exercising C(T2) when C(T1) is exercised results in offsetting transactions. However, if C(T1) is not exercised, we are left with C(T2), which has some value. Table 33.4 illustrates the actions and corresponding cash flows.

Table 33.4: Cash flows of long call with longer expiration date and short call with shorter expiration date, today and at future date.

Action today	Cash flow	At future date (t1)	
		S < X	S > X
Buy C(T2)	− C(T2)	> 0	S − X
Sell C(T1)	+ C(T1)	0	− (S − X)
	C(T1) − C(T2) > 0	> 0	0

(e) Price of Call with Lower Exercise Price should be Greater than Price of Call with Higher Exercise Price; C(X1) ≥ C(X2) if X2 > X1

Using a similar method to the earlier cases we can make arbitrage profits if the restriction is violated, C(X1), which was bought, will not be exercised if it is out-of-the-money. However, when the stock price is greater than X1, exercising the call results in a profit (S1 − X1). The buyer of call C(X2) will not exercise the call if the stock price is less than X2. However, the buyer of call C(X2) will exercise the call if the stock price is greater than X2. As we sold call C(X2) we have to deliver the stock to the buyer of the call when it is exercised. We obtain the stock by exercising call C(X1). This results in a cash flow of (X2 − X1) which is positive since X2 is greater than X1. The results are shown in Table 33.5.

Table 33.5: Cash flows of long call with lower exercise price and short call with higher exercise price, today and at future date.

Action today	Cash flow	At future date		
		S ≤ X	X1 < S ≤ X2	S > X
Buy call with lower X	− C(X1)	0	S − X1	S − X1
Sell call with higher X	+ C(X2)	0	0	− (S− X2)
	> 0	0	> 0	X2− X1 > 0

(f) For a Stock that Pays no Dividends the Call Price should be Greater or Equal to the Difference between the Stock Price and the Present Value of the Exercise Price; $C \geq \text{Max}[0, S - Xe^{-rt}]$

Again, arbitrage profits are possible if the restriction is violated. This is done by the following: Buy a call, invest the present value of the exercise price, Xe^{-rt}, and sell the stock. X is multiplied by e^{-rt} to find the continuous-time equivalent of $X(1+r)t$. The results are shown in Table 33.6. (*Note*: We buy the stock at a price of S_T at the expiration date and return the stock that we shorted earlier.)

Table 33.6: Cash flows of a long call, long bond, and short stock, today and at a future date.

Action today	Cash flow	At future date	
		$S_T \leq X$	$S_T > X$
Buy call	$-C$	0	$S_T - X$
Invest Xe^{-rt}	$-Xe^{-rt}$	X	X
Sell stock	S	$-S_T$	$-S_T$
	$(S - Xe^{-rt}) - C > 0$	$X - S_T > 0$	0

(g) Applying Restrictions on Option Price

From the restrictions shown in restrictions 1, 2 and 3, we see that the $C > 0$, $C < S$ and $C > (S - X)$. This is shown graphically in Figure 33.6.

Applying the restriction in point f above, then the lower bound is shifted to the left to the line $C > (S - X)$.

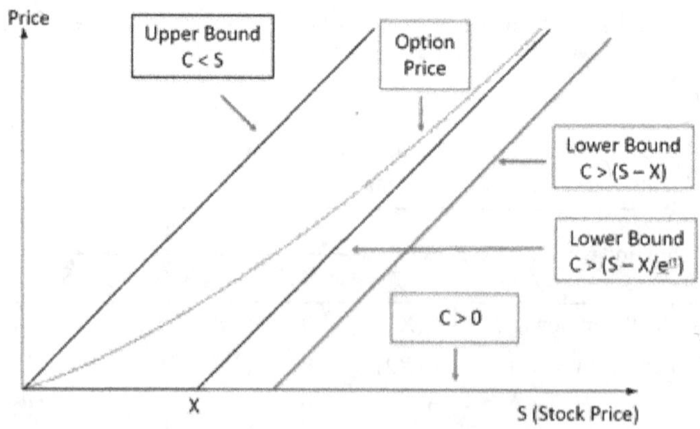

Figure 33.6: Restrictions on option price.

33.2.3 *Determinants of Option Value*

Pricing an option requires advanced mathematics like stochastic calculus. However, we can gain some qualitative insights by looking at the determinants of option value.

Learning Objectives

- Explain how the different variables affect the option value.

Main Takeaways

Main Points

- The value of an option depends on five key variables: the stock price, the exercise price of the option, the time to expiration, the risk-free rate, and the volatility of the underlying stock's returns.
- There is no disagreement about the values of the first four variables among investors.
- Investors have different expectations of what the future volatility of the stock's return would be.
- An investor who expects volatility to increase would buy an option, while an investor would sell the option if she expects that volatility will decrease.
- Dividends affect calls negatively but puts positively.

Main Terms

- **Volatility:** Expected volatility of the stock's return. It is the critical determinant in the value of an option.
- **Exercise price:** The price per share at which the owner of a traded option is entitled to buy or sell the underlying security.
- **Risk-free rate:** The theoretical rate of return of an investment with zero risks.

What are the variables that affect the value of an option? We looked at some of them when we discussed the option price restrictions. There are five key variables. They are the stock price, the exercise price, the time to expiration, the risk-free rate, and the stock returns volatility. These variables are the same as those found in the Black-Scholes option pricing equation, which we will discuss later. A sixth variable is dividends. On the ex-dividend date, the stock price will fall by an amount equal to the dividend, as investors who buy the stock are not entitled to receive the dividend paid to the seller of the stock.

The determinants of an option value are discussed below:

1. **Stock price:** The higher the stock price, the more valuable the call as it becomes less out-of-the-money or more in-the-money with increases in the stock price. For the put, the reverse is true. The put becomes more valuable with decreases in the stock price.
2. **Exercise price:** A lower exercise price benefits the call but works against the put. For a call, a lower exercise price means that the stock can potentially be acquired at a lower price. However a lower exercise price works against the put as exercising the means selling the stock at a low price.
3. **Time to expiration:** There are two effects associated with time to expiration. The first is the present value effect. A longer time to expiration decreases the exercise price's present value. This is the present value effect. As an option gives the right but not the obligation to exercise, a longer time to expiration increases the chance that an out-of-the-money option becomes an in-the-money option. This is known as the optionality effect.

   The present value effect and the optionality effect are both beneficial to the call holder. However, for the put holder, an increase in the time to expiration gives rise to two opposing effects. Like the call, the put benefits from a longer time to expiration. However, increasing the time to expiration reduces the present value of the exercise price. These two opposing effects make it difficult to judge the net effect of an increase in the time to expiration for a put. Which effect is greater depends on two things — whether interest rates are high or not and whether the option is near-the-money as opposed to being deep out-of-the-money. All else equal, a high interest rate would make the present value effect stronger. Similarly, the optionality effect would be greater for near-the-money options.
4. **Risk-free rate:** An increase in the risk-free rate, makes the call more valuable. The reason is that the present value of the exercise price decreases with increases in the risk-free rate. This benefits the call option investor as it would cost less, in present value terms, to acquire the stock should the option be exercised. The opposite is the case for puts as a higher risk-free rate reduces the present value of the exercise price.

5. **The volatility of return of the stock:** Like time to expiration, higher volatility is positive for both calls and puts. The reason is the one-sided bet nature of the option. If the option is in the investor's favor, that is, intrinsic value is positive, the investor has an incentive to exercise it. However, when the option is out-of-the-money, the investor cannot be forced to exercise. This is unlike positions in stocks, forward and futures contracts where potential gains and losses are symmetrical. This asymmetry means that for the investor, volatility is a plus. The higher the volatility, the higher the potential for gain. Higher volatility does not bring a corresponding potential for losses as the investor's loss is limited to the price paid for the option.
6. **Dividends:** The payment of a dividend hurts the value of a call but has a positive effect on a put. The reason is that when a stock goes ex-dividend, the stock price will fall. This fall in the stock price will not result in an adjustment of the exercise price unless the dividend is more than ten percent. However, adjustments are made for corporate actions like stock splits, mergers, take-overs, spin-offs, and special distributions of cash and stock.

   The stock price drops by the amount of dividend on the ex-date. However, option prices often incorporate the expected dividend way ahead of its announcement. The reason is that dividends are adjusted for in option pricing models. This will be discussed later.

   When a stock pays a dividend, the holder of an in-the-money call must decide whether to exercise early. The decision involves the trade-off between the dividend amount and the time value of the option that will be lost should exercise occur. If the dividend amount is lower than the option's time value, then the call should not be exercised.

Table 33.7 summarizes the effect of an increase in each variable on call and put values.

Table 33.7: Determinants of option value.

Variable	Effect of an increase in the variable on Call	Put
Underlying asset current price	(+)	(−)
Exercise price	(−)	(+)
Time to expiration	(+)	(+)/(−)
Risk-free rate	(+)	(−)
Volatility of underlying asset	(+)	(+)
Dividends	(−)	(+)

33.2.4 *Put-Call Parity*

The put-call parity relationship shows how the price of a European call is related to the price of a European put with the same exercise price.

Learning Objectives

- Discuss how the prices of a European call and a European put are related.

Main Takeaways

Main Points

- The put-call parity shows how a European put's cash flows can be replicated by a position consisting of a long European call plus the present value of the exercise price and less the stock price.
- The put-call parity relationship is based on the no-arbitrage argument.
- This relationship also demonstrates the replication method.

Main Terms

- **Put-call parity:** The relationship between European put and call options on the same stock and the same exercise price.
- **Long-put:** It refers to buying a put option, typically anticipating a decline in the underlying asset.
- **Face value:** The face value for bonds is often referred to as "par value" or simply "par".

In Section 13.1, on the protective put, that the combination of the holding both the stock and the put results in a graph that looks like that for a call. This insight will be used to prove the put-call parity relationship.

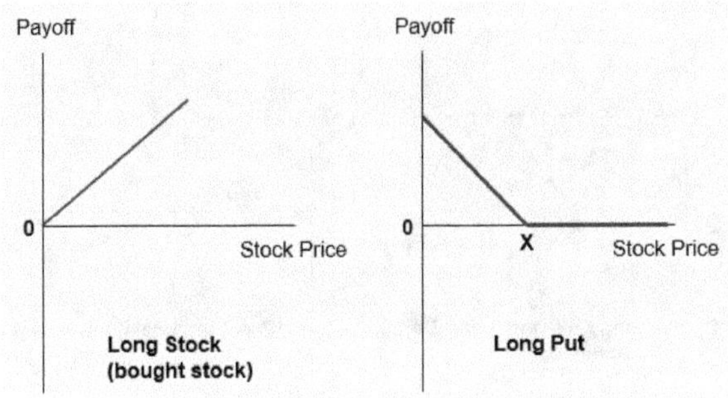

Figure 33.7: Payoff diagrams for long stock and long put.

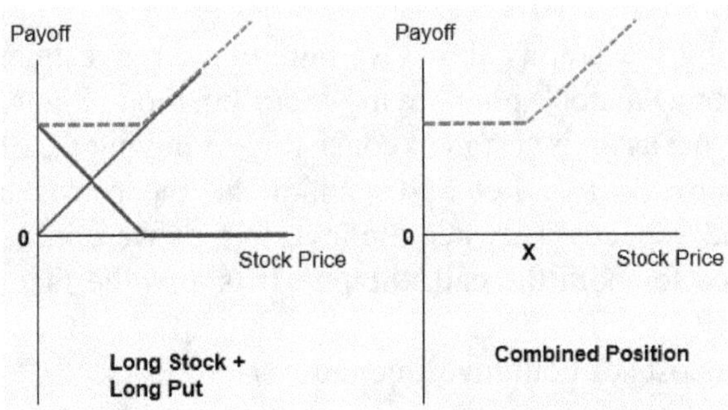

Figure 33.8: Payoff diagrams for combined long stock and long put.

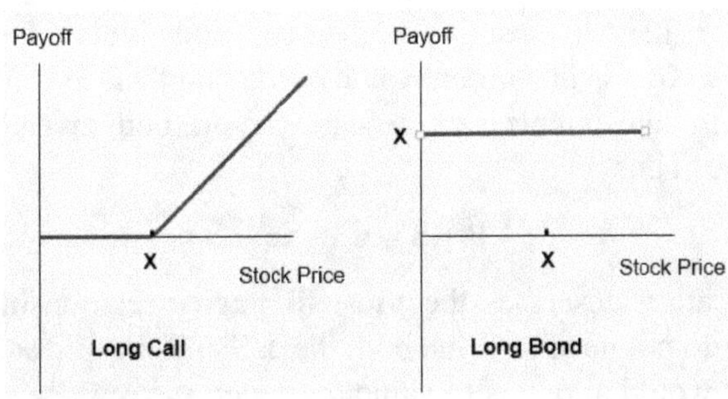

Figure 33.9: Payoff diagrams for long call and long bond.

The payoffs for a long stock and a long-put position are shown in Figures 33.7 and 33.8.

The payoffs for a long call plus long position in riskless bonds with a face value of X are shown in Figure 33.9.

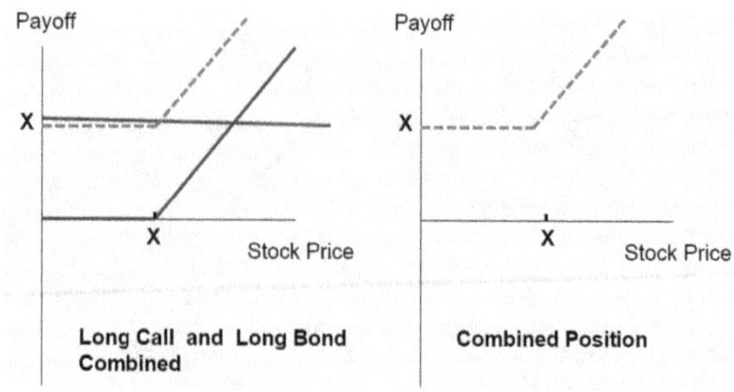

Figure 33.10: Payoff diagrams for combined long call and long bond.

Comparing the graphs above we note that an investment consisting of buying (long) a stock plus buying a put position (Figure 33.8) gives the same payoff as an investment consisting of buying a call plus buying a bond (Figure 33.10). Let S, C, and P be the prices of the stock, call, and put, respectively, when the investments were initiated. X is the exercise price for both the call, the put. It is also the face value of the bond.

Then the costs of both investments are as follows:

$$\text{Stock plus put: } P + S$$

$$\text{Call plus bond: } C + Xe^{-rt},$$

where r is the riskless interest rate for the bond, and t is the time to expiration of the options. Xe^{-rt} is the present value of the bond's face value X.

Since both investments give the same payoff, both investments should cost the same. Thus

$$P + S = C + Xe^{-rt}$$

This equation describes the **put-call parity** relationship. With this equation we do not need to value both the call and the put, as knowing the value of one would allow us to value the other.

33.2.5 *Binomial Option Pricing*

The binomial option pricing model is an option valuation method that uses an iterative procedure, allowing for the specification of nodes, or points in time, during the period between the valuation date and the option's expiration date.

Learning Objectives

- Explain how the Binomial Option Pricing Model can price an option.

Main Takeaways

Main Points

- The Binomial Option Pricing Model is based on the assumption that the stock price in the next period or interval of time can have only two values.
- By increasing the number of time intervals for a year, the result is an extensive binomial tree whose ending nodes would correspond to possible prices for the stock.
- At any node, the option's value depends on the two possible values at the end of the period.
- The option's value can be found by solving each node's value recursively starting from the final stock prices, a process known as backward induction.
- The size of the upward and downward moves depends on the stock's volatility.

Main Terms

- **Node:** Corresponds to the beginning or end of a period.
- **Binomial tree:** A lattice-like representation of the possible values that the option can take at each node.
- **Backward induction:** A method to solve recursively backward the option's value starting from the nodes before the last nodes.
- **Hedge ratio:** The ratio of the number of shares to one call such that the combination is riskless.

The Binomial Option Pricing model uses the binomial tree to model the evolution of stock and option prices. Starting at the first node for the stock binomial tree, the price can either go up or down, resulting in two nodes. From these two nodes, four nodes result. Continuing the process we eventually end up with a lattice-like diagram called the binomial tree. The final endpoints of the branches represent possible values of the underlying stock.

Corresponding to the binomial tree for the stock we have a similar binomial tree for the option. The value of the option at each node depends on the values of the following nodes. Working backward through the binomial tree, a process called backward induction, we can compute the value of the option at the starting point. This process is shown in the following sections.

(a) A Simple One-Period Binomial Option Pricing Model

Suppose the stock price is \$100, and the stock price could either go up 20% or down 10%. The stock's payoffs are either \$120 or \$90 in 1 year. If a call has an exercise price of \$110 and the risk-free interest rate is 4% per annum, what is the call price?

Let's look at the payoffs at the end of 1 year of two investments. The first investment consists of buying one call, while the second consists of buying one share and borrowing \$86.54.

For the call, the payoff will be 0 if the stock price is \$90 since the stock price is below the exercise price of \$110. If the stock price is \$120, the call's payoff is (\$120 − \$110) = \$10. This is shown in Table 33.8.

Table 33.8: Cash flows from buying 1 call.

Action today	Cashflow	At future date	
		S_T = \$90	S_T = \$120
Buy 1 Call	–C	\$0	\$10

We have the following payoffs for the portfolio of 1 share and borrowing \$86.54. For the one share of stock, the payoff is the stock price, that is, either \$90 or \$120. The loan of \$86.54 needs to be repaid with interest. This amounts to \$86.54 × (1.04) = \$90. If the stock price is \$90, our portfolio's payoff is \$0 since the payoff to the stock of \$90 is used to repay the loan. However, if the stock price is \$120, the portfolio's payoff is the value of the stock at \$120 minus the \$90 loan repayment, giving a net amount of \$30. This is shown in Table 33.9.

Table 33.9: Cash lows from buying 1 share and borrowing \$46.30.

Action today	Cashflow	At future date	
		S_T = \$90	S_T = \$120
Buy 1 share	\$100	\$90	\$120
Borrow \$86.54	+\$86.54	–\$90	–\$90
Portfolio	–\$13.46	\$0	\$30

Comparing the payoffs in Tables 33.8 and 33.9, we note that the portfolio's payoffs are three times the payoffs of the call for each stock price in 1 year. Hence, the stock and loan portfolio's value must be three times the value of the call. The cost of the portfolio is \$13.46.

Hence the value of the call is given by

$$3C = \$13.46 \quad \text{or} \quad C = \$4.49$$

The above shows that we can replicate the option's payoffs by an investment consisting of buying one share of the stock and borrowing. (Show that by buying 1/3 of a share and borrowing \$28.85, you can replicate the payoffs to the one call above.) We have developed an important concept used in option pricing formulas.

Here's an alternative view of the above transactions. If you buy one share and sell three calls, what would be the portfolio's payoff given that the stock price can be either \$90 or \$120 in 1 year?

Table 33.10: Payoffs to a portfolio of long 1 share and short 3 calls.

Action today	Cash flow	At future date	
		$S_T = \$90$	$S_T = \$120$
Buy 1 share	–\$100	\$90	\$120
Sell 3 calls	+3C	\$0	–\$30
Portfolio	–\$100 +3C	\$90	\$90

Table 33.10 shows that the portfolio will yield a payoff of \$90 in 1 year regardless of the stock price. As there is no uncertainty about the portfolio's value, the portfolio is essentially riskless. As a riskless portfolio should earn the riskless return rate, we can price the portfolio as the present value of \$90, which is 90/(1.04) = \$86.54. The cost of the portfolio is \$100 – 3C. For the investor, this represents a cash flow of –(\$100 – 3C) or –\$100 + 3C, as shown in Table 33.10.

$$\$100 - 3C = \$86.54 \quad \text{or} \quad C = \$13.46/3 = \$4.49$$

This concept of a riskless portfolio, or riskless hedge, to price the call is handy. There is no need to know the option or the stock's beta or expected return. The final stock price does not affect the payoff, so the stock's risk and return characteristics are not required in this method.

What is needed in this method is the hedge ratio or the number of shares to one call. To determine the hedge ratio, we take the ratio of the value of the range of the option's values to the value of the range of the stock values. For the example above, the range of the option's values is

10 (10 − 0). The range is 30 (120 − 90) for the stock, giving a hedge ratio of 10/30 or 1/3.

If we denote the value of the stock when it goes up as uS_0 and the value of the stock when it goes down as dS_0, and the corresponding values of the call as Cu and Cd, respectively, then the hedge ratio is given by

$$h = \frac{C_u - C_d}{uS_0 - dS_0}$$

(b) Refining the One-Period Binomial Option Pricing Model

The simple example above shows two possible stock prices after a year. This scenario is unrealistic as the possible stock prices are many more than two. We can refine the process by dividing the year into two six-month periods. In this case, over six months, the amount the stock would move would be half that for a year. At each node, the stock price can either go up 10% or down 5%.

Starting at the price of 100, the possible prices in 6 months would be 100 × 1.1 = 110 and 100 × 0.95 = 95. From the prices of 110 and 95, we carry on the process. From the node with a stock price of 110, the following two nodes would be 110 × 1.1 = 121 and 100 × 0.95 = 104.50. Note that the stock price of 104.50 can be derived in a second way.

From the node with a stock price of 95 the up-branch results in a price of 95 × 1.1 = 104.50.

From the same node with a price of 95, the down-branch gives a value of 95 × 0.95 = 90.25. This process gives rise to the binomial trees for the stock prices and the corresponding call prices, as shown in Figure 33.11.

Notice that the number of possible prices increases to three with the additional period introduced. Further, the range of possible prices

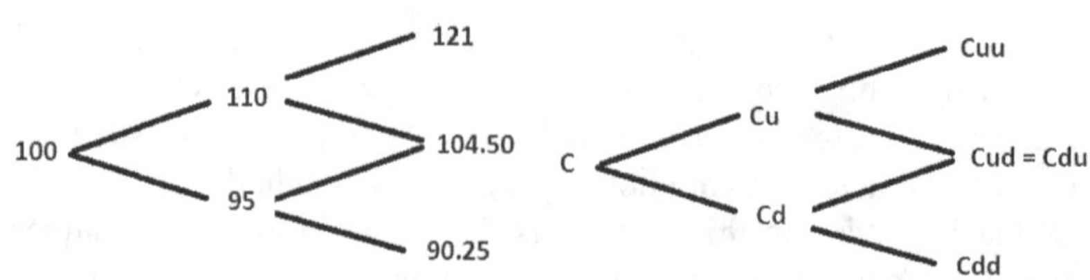

Figure 33.11: Two-period binomial trees.

widens. If we move to a 3-period binomial tree, there will be four possible prices. The number of possible prices is one more than the number of periods.

What are the values of Cuu, Cud, and Cdd? Given the exercise price of 110, Cuu is 121 − 110 = 11. Cud and Cdd are both zero since the corresponding stock prices of 104.50 and 90.25 are below the exercise price of 110.

What is the value of Cu? We have to solve for the hedge ratio first. Recall that the hedge ratio is the range of call prices to the range of stock prices. The hedge ratio is:

$h = (Cuu - Cud)/(uS_0 - dS_0) = (21 - 0)/(121 - 104.50) = 2/3$. In other words, a portfolio that is long two shares at \$110 and short three calls is a riskless investment as shown in Table 33.11.

Table 33.11: Payoffs to a portfolio of long 2 shares and short 3 calls.

Action today	Cash flow	At future date	
		$S_T = \$104.50$	$S_T = \$121$
Buy 2 shares	–\$220	\$209	\$242
Sell 3 calls	+3C	\$0	–\$33
Portfolio	–\$220 +3C	\$209	\$209

The portfolio which is long 2 shares and short 3 calls has the same value of \$209 in 6-months' time, regardless of the price of the stock. This means the value of the portfolio is the present value of \$209.

The 6-month interest rate is 4%/2 = 2%. Hence:

$$\$220 - 3C = \$209/(1.02) \quad \text{or} \quad 3C = \$220 - 204.90 = \$15.10$$

$$C = \$15.10/3 \quad \text{or} \quad C = \$5.03$$

Figure 33.12 extends the model to four periods of 3 months each. The up and down changes in price would be 20%/4 = 5%, and 10%/4 = 2.5%, respectively. Notice that there are now five prices with the differences between two adjacent prices getting smaller than the binomial models with fewer periods. Thus, by reducing each period's length, we get more periods during the year and more prices in the range of stock prices at the end of the year. The result is that the possible prices would resemble the prices that could occur in the real world more closely.

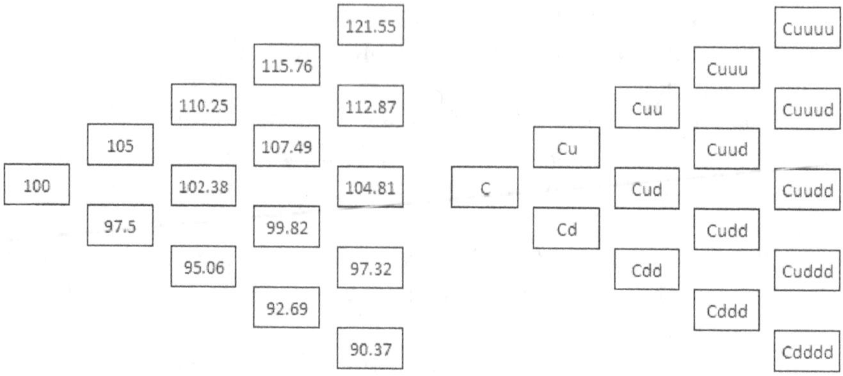

Figure 33.12: Four-period binomial trees.

(c) Applying the Binomial Option Pricing Model in the Real World

The binomial option pricing model is somewhat similar to a coin toss experiment. When you toss a coin, it can land up either head or tail. What is the probability of getting four heads in a row? If getting a head is equivalent to an up move in the stock, then the probability of the stock price being \$121.55 in the fourth period is much smaller than the price of \$112.87. The reason is that there is only one path that will lead to the price of \$121.55. However, for the price of \$112.87, there are four possible paths: uuud, uudu, uduu, and duuu. This observation suggests that the probability of getting a price at the extreme ends will be much smaller than getting a price that is in the middle of the range, which somewhat mirrors how stock prices will evolve.

Suppose we have two stocks with different return volatilities. In that case, the stock with the higher return volatility will end up with a wider range of prices than the stock with the lower return volatility.

This means that we need to incorporate the volatility of return into the values of u and d. To do this we set $u = \exp(\sigma\sqrt{\Delta t})$ and $d = \exp(-\sigma\sqrt{\Delta t})$. Notice that the values of u and d depend on the volatility of the stock's return, denoted by σ, the standard deviation of the stock's return, as well as Δt, the length of each sub-period.

Table 33.12 shows the values of u and d as the number of sub-periods increase and Figure 33.13 the corresponding probability distributions. From Figure 33.13, we can see that as the number of sub-periods increases, the probability distribution looks more and more like what we expect the probability distribution of possible stock prices to be.

Table 33.12: Values of u and d as the number of sub-periods increase.

Subperiods, n	$\Delta t = T/n$	$u = \exp(\sigma\sqrt{\Delta t})$	$d = \exp(-\sigma\sqrt{\Delta t})$
3	.333	$\exp(0.173) = 1.189$	$\exp(-0.173) = 0.841$
6	.167	$\exp(0.123) = 1.130$	$\exp(-0.095) = 0.885$
20	.015	$\exp(0.067) = 1.069$	$\exp(-0.067) = 0.935$

Source: Zvi Bodie, Alex Kane & Alan Marcus (2014). *Investments*, 10th edn. McGraw-Hill.

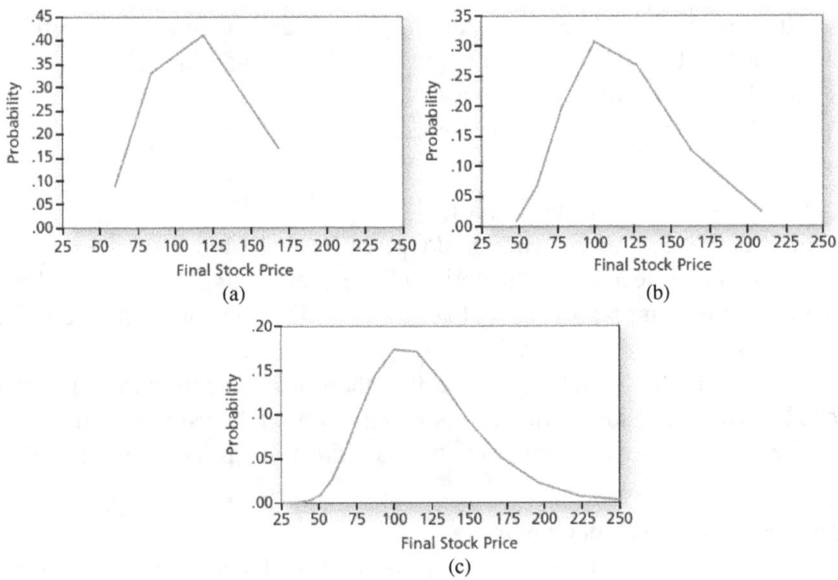

Figure 33.13: Probability distributions for final stock price.

Source: Zvi Bodie, Alex Kane & Alan Marcus (2014). *Investments*, 10th edn. McGraw-Hill.

33.2.6 *Black–Scholes Option Pricing and Implied Volatility*

One of the significant achievements of modern Finance is the Black–Scholes (BS) Option Pricing Model. The BS model is useful for us to understand what drives option pricing.

Learning Objectives

- Discuss the BS option pricing model's assumptions and explain the significance of the implied volatility of an option.

Main Takeaways

Main Points

- The BS option model is based on the idea of a riskless hedge that is maintained through the option's life.
- Implied volatility can be more accurate than historical volatility when dealing with upcoming events, such as quarterly earnings reports and dividend declarations.

Main Terms

- **Riskless hedge:** The combination of stock and option in proportions according to the hedge ratio such that the combination is riskless.
- **Implied volatility:** An estimate of the future return variability of the stock underlying the options contract.

(a) Black–Scholes Model Basics

From Section 3.2, on the Binomial Option Pricing Model, we see that an option can be priced using the notion of a riskless hedge. In essence, if we have a correct number of shares to one call option, the correct hedge ratio, the call's hedged position will be riskless. As the stock price changes, we can adjust the hedge ratio (h) such that the portfolio consisting of 1 call and h shares remains riskless. This is the BS model's essence, where the hedge ratio is adjusted continuously when the stock price changes.

(b) The Black–Scholes Formula

We will not go into the derivation of the BS model. Rather, we present the BS equation and discuss the equation's variables. According to the model, the call price is determined as follows:

$$C(S_0, t) = S_0\, N(d_1) - Xe^{-r(T-t)}\, N(d_2)$$

where $C(S_0, t)$ is the call option value at time t, S_0 is the stock price at time 0, X is the exercise price, $(T - t)$ is the time to expiration in years, T is the expiration date, r is the risk-free rate, σ = underlying volatility of the asset's return, $N(d1)$ is the standard normal cumulative distribution function where

$$d_1 = \frac{\ln \frac{S_0}{X} + (r + \frac{\sigma^2}{2})(T - t)}{\sigma \sqrt{T - t}}$$

N(d2) is the standard normal cumulative distribution function where

$$d_2 = d_1 - \sigma\sqrt{T-t} \text{ or}$$

$$d_2 = \frac{\ln\frac{S_0}{X} + (r - \frac{\sigma^2}{2})(T-t)}{\sigma\sqrt{T-t}}$$

(c) Assumptions of the Black–Scholes Option Pricing Model

The assumptions underlying the BS model are:

- Stock price moves according to the geometric Brownian motion.
- No transaction costs or taxes.
- All securities are perfectly divisible.
- The underlying stock is dividend-free.
- No arbitrage opportunity in the market.
- Trading occurs in continuous time.
- Borrowing and lending occur at a risk-free rate.
- The risk-free rate is assumed to be constant.
- The volatility of returns is assumed to be constant.

The BS model assumptions highlight the situations where Black–Scholes may not work well. Not all assumptions are critical. We highlight some of the important ones.

The geometric Brownian motion assumption implies that stock returns are log normally distributed. When markets are relatively calm, this assumption does not matter. However, the market occasionally experiences jumps in prices. Further, actual returns in the market seem to conform to the Stable distribution, which has fatter tails than the normal distribution, implying that the probability of extreme returns is higher than predicted under the normal distribution with its thinner tails.

Transaction costs and taxes are frictions in the market that may cause actual prices to deviate from true equilibrium prices.

The most critical assumption is the constant volatility of returns. Volatility is a key driver of changes in option value. But volatility changes when news cause investors to change their expectations about the future course of the market, which would change what they think future volatility would be. The market consensus about expected volatility is embedded in the option price. Implied volatility is the value of volatility that equates the BS equation value to the option's market price. Looking at the implied volatility, for example, the VIX, which gives the implied volatility of the S&P500 option index, we observe that the constant volatility assumption would not hold in volatile markets.

(d) Adjustment for Dividends

We can relax the various BS model to make the model more realistic, in particular, the assumption about no dividends. However, as the payment of dividends payment is quite common how can we adjust the model to incorporate dividends?

For short-term options, we subtract the present value of the expected dividends paid during the life of the option from the current value of the stock.

For long-term options, we adjust the risk-free rate by the dividend yield. If the dividend yield is q, then $d1$ and $d2$ in the call and put option price formulas are adjusted as follows:

$$C = S_0 e^{-qT} N(d_1) - X e^{-rT} N(d_2)$$

and

$$P = X e^{-rT} N(-d_2) - S_0 e^{-qt} N(-d_1)$$

where

$$d_1 = \frac{\ln \frac{S_0}{X} + (r - q + \frac{\sigma^2}{2})T}{\sigma \sqrt{T}}$$

$$d_2 = \frac{\ln \frac{S_0}{X} + (r - q - \frac{\sigma^2}{2})T}{\sigma \sqrt{T}}$$

(e) Option Implied Volatility

Recall that there are five determinants of the option price: the stock price, the exercise price, the time to expiration, the risk-free rate, and the volatility of the stock's returns. At any time, there is generally no disagreement among market participants regarding the first four determinants.

What market participants disagree about is the stock's expected volatility. Recall also that the higher the volatility of returns, the higher the option's value. So, if a trader thinks that the volatility ought to be higher than the consensus view, she would buy the option. Taking a step further, options trading is nothing other than the buying or selling volatility. You purchase something, hoping to make a profit if the price goes up.

What is the consensus view regarding volatility? We have a way of determining this from option prices. As traders incorporate their views regarding volatility when they buy or sell options, the option price would therefore encapsulate the consensus view about volatility.

If we believe that an option model captures the option pricing process accurately, we can use the model together with the values of the first four determinants to solve for the stock volatility. The value of the volatility that we derive is called the **implied volatility**, which is the volatility implied by the option price and the values of the other determinants of option value.

Implied volatility is a useful tool for the options trader as she can determine how far her views deviate from the consensus. A popular implied volatility indicator is the VIX. The VIX is a financial instrument that trades on the Chicago Board Options Exchange (CBOE) and is the implied volatility of the S&P 500 Index option. This instrument gives the trader a more direct way to trade her expectations about the equity market's future volatility.

33.3 Option Greeks

33.3.1 *Introduction to Option Greeks*

Option Greeks refer to the partial derivatives of the option pricing equation. Traders use different Greek values, such as delta, theta, and others, to assess options risk and manage option portfolios.

Learning Objectives

- Describe the characteristics of the Option Greeks.

Main Takeaways

Main Points

- The option Greeks measure the option price's sensitivity to changes in the variables found in the BS equation.
- They measure the change in the value of the option to changes in the variables that determine an option's value.

- The most common Greeks include the Delta, Gamma, Theta, and Vega — which are the first partial derivatives of the options pricing model.
- Delta is the most used option Greek. It measures the option price's sensitivity to changes in the stock price. It is used for hedging purposes.
- Gamma measures the rate of change in delta.

Main Terms

- **Delta:** Measures the option value's sensitivity to changes in the stock price.
- **Gamma:** Measures the sensitivity of delta to changes in the stock price. It is the second partial derivative of the option value with respect to the stock price.
- **Vega:** Measures the option value's sensitivity to changes in the volatility of the stock returns.
- **Rho:** Measures the option value's sensitivity to changes in the risk-free rate.
- **Theta:** Measures the option value's sensitivity to changes in the time to expiration.

The sensitivity of the BS option price to changes in its variables are measured by the Greeks which are essentially partial derivatives of the (Bk-S) equation. Partial derivatives are used as there is more than one independent variable in the equation. In Table 33.13, we list the

Table 33.13: Option Greeks and the effect on call and put options of changes in the value of the Greek.

Measure	Symbol	Effect on Call with an increase in the measure	Effect on Put with an increase in the measure
Delta	$\frac{\partial V}{\partial S}$	Increase	Decrease
Gamma	$\frac{\partial^2 V}{\partial S^2}$	Increases if S < X Decreases if S > X	Increases if S < X Decreases if S > X
Vega	$\frac{\partial V}{\partial \sigma}$	Increase	Increase
Rho	$\frac{\partial V}{\partial r}$	Increase	Decrease
Theta	$\frac{\partial V}{\partial t}$	Increase	Increase

commonly used Greeks, their symbols, and the effects of changes for call and put value, denoted by "V", when the variable changes.

(a) Application of the Greeks

The discussion below limits the application of the Greeks to call options. For puts the effect of changes in the variable is the opposite for puts, compared to calls, for the risk-free and stock price variables.

(1) Delta

The responsiveness of the option price to changes in the underlying stock price is measured by delta. Call option deltas have values between 0 and +1 (put deltas vary between 0 and −1).

- A deep out-of-the-money call, whose price is very unresponsive to changes in the stock price, has a delta close to 0.
- An at-the-money call has a delta close to 0.5.
- A deep-in-the-money call has a delta close to 1.

Figure 33.14 shows three delta curves with different times to expiration. As the call's expiration draws closer, the delta curve gets steeper. It approaches the value of 0 for out-of-the-money calls and 1 for in-the-money calls.

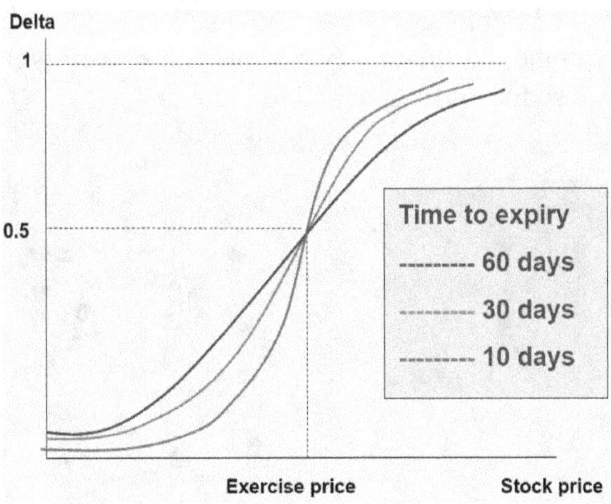

Figure 33.14: Call option delta curves.

Delta reveals the riskiness of an option position. The higher the delta value, the greater the exposure of the position to changes in the stock price. Delta is used for hedging using options. The value of delta tells us the number of calls to hedge one share to create a delta-neutral position. For example, if the delta is 0.4, we need 1/0.4 or 2.5 calls to hedge the risk of changes to the stock position.

(2) Gamma

The second partial derivative of the Black-Scholes equation with respect to the stock price measures how delta changes for a small change in the stock price. There are two observations regarding gamma.

- Gamma is always positive
  - When the stock price increases, the quantum of the call price gains is always more than the quantum of the call price loss resulting from a fall in the stock price of the same size, as price gains are associated with increasing delta.
  - Gamma reaches a maximum when the option is at-the-money.
  - As the stock price moves away from the exercise price, gamma decreases in value in both directions.
- Gamma changes with time
  - The nearer the option to expiration, the greater the divergence in gamma value between at-the-money options and both in-the-money and out-of-the-money options. The shape of the gamma curve is more peaked (leptokurtic). (see Figure 33.15).
  - Near expiration at-the-money options can be very volatile as delta can move suddenly from near 0 to close to 1.

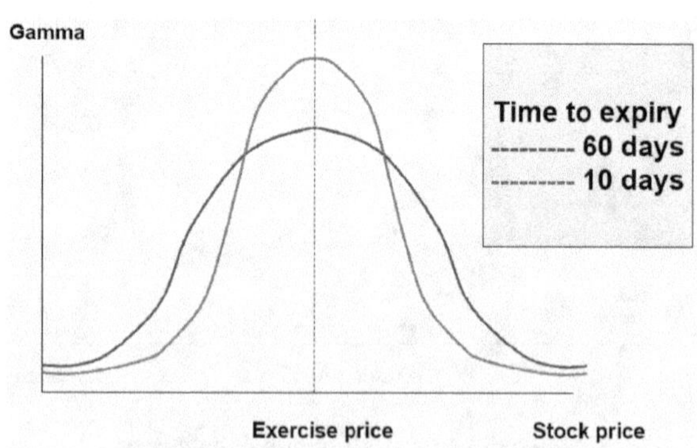

Figure 33.15: Call option gamma curves.

(3) Vega
The sensitivity of the option price to changes in the volatility of the returns of the underlying asset is measured by vega. Vega has the most effect on at-the-money-options. Vega increases with time to expiration. In uncertain markets where volatility can change quickly, vega becomes more important.

Volatility benefits holders of both calls and puts. This means that a long call or long put is long vega.

(4) Rho
The sensitivity of the option price to changes in the risk-free interest rate is measured by rho. A long call or a short put is long rho. An increase in the risk-free rate reduces the present value of the exercise price. This benefits the call holder and the put seller. Since changes in the risk-free rate changes are much less than changes in volatility, much less attention is paid to this measure.

(5) Theta
When the time to expiration increases, the value of a call increases while the change in the put's value is indeterminate. For the put, there are two factors that produce opposite effects. As discussed in the determinants of option pricing in an earlier section, when time to expiration increases, put value decreases because of the present value effect but it increases because of the optionality effect.

Theta measures the option price sensitivity as the time to expiration decreases. It is given as a negative number. The theta value is highest for at-the-money options but lower for both in-the-money and out-of-the-money options.

33.3.2 *Hedging Using Delta and Gamma*

Delta-gamma hedging is an options strategy that combines both delta and gamma hedges to mitigate the risk of changes in the underlying asset and delta itself.

Learning Objectives

- Explain how delta and gamma can be used in hedging using options.

Main Takeaways

Main Points

- The delta of an option tells us how many option contracts we need to hedge one share of stock.
- Delta is used to convert an options position into an equivalent futures position.
- Gamma is used to adjust the hedged position as the stock price changes.
- Delta hedging aims to reduce the risk associated with price movements in the underlying asset by offsetting long or short positions.
- Gamma hedging attempts to reduce or eliminate the risk created by changes in an option's delta.

Main Terms

- **Delta:** Measures the option value's sensitivity to changes in the stock price.
- **Gamma:** Measures the sensitivity of delta to changes in the stock price. It is the second derivative of the option value with respect to the stock price.
- **Perfect hedge:** A position undertaken by an investor that would eliminate the risk of an existing position or a position that eliminates all market risk from a portfolio.

(a) Understanding Delta–Gamma Hedging

In an earlier section, we discussed a protective put whereby we buy one put to hedge against the fall in the price of one share and hold the position until maturity. We are limiting the losses from a stock price decline for the protective put but preserving the upside. At any one time, the change in the value of the stock is not matched by the change in the option's value.

In delta hedging, the idea is that any change in the stock value due to changes in the stock price is matched by the change in the value of the option. Recall what delta measures. It measures the change in the option value against the change in the stock price, *all other factors constant*. This is important as the option value can change when the other factors or determinants of the option value change. Among the factors, the most important is the change in volatility with news arrival. This means that delta hedging does not produce the perfect hedge.

Delta is the first partial derivative of the option price equation. It is a good measure to work with for small stock price changes. When the stock price changes more, we need to augment delta with gamma, which measures delta change as the stock price changes. Here's how it works. Suppose the delta is 0.666. To hedge the stock's value you have to short 1/0.666 or about 1.5 options. The stock price falls, and the option delta is 0.5. This change now calls for a short position of 2 options. However, suppose gamma adjustment results in a change in the delta of 0.5; the gamma adjusted delta will be 0.45. So the number of options needed will be 1/0.45 or approximately 2.22 options instead of 2 options if no gamma adjustment was used.

Reference/Further Reading

Bodie, Z., Kane, A., & Marcus, A.J. (2020). *Investments*, 12th edn. McGraw-Hill Irwin, Chap. 21, pp. 659–679.

33.4 Sample Questions

Question 1
Which of the following could be viewed as holding a put?

(a) Renting a building with an option to buy it
(b) A program in which farmers can sell their output to the government at a guaranteed price
(c) Selling a call option

Question 2
Which of the following statements is true?

(a) A call option on a futures contract gives the buyer the right to buy a futures contract.
(b) The law of one price states that the price of an asset cannot change.
(c) If there are no dividends on a stock, an American call will sell for more than a European call.

Question 3

You are given the stock price, the risk-free rate, and the price of a European put option on the stock. The European call option value computed using the put-call parity turns out to be lower than the call's market price. Ignoring transactions costs, you would trade in the following manner:

(a) Buy the call and the risk-free bonds; sell the put and stock
(b) Buy the stock and the risk-free bonds; sell the put and the call
(c) Buy the put and the stock; sell the risk-free bonds and the call

The following table shows option prices for a stock priced at 108 in December.

Assume the options are American unless otherwise stated. Use the table for the next four questions.

	Exercise price	Jan	Mar	May
Call	105	3.60	4.30	5.10
Call	110	0.70	1.50	2.25
Put	105	0.80	1.55	2.30
Put	110	2.70	3.55	4.30

Question 4

The intrinsic value of the January call with an exercise price of 105 is

(a) 0.00
(b) 3.00
(c) 3.60

Question 5

The time value of the March put with an exercise price of 110 is

(a) 0.00
(b) 1.55
(c) 2.00

Question 6

The maximum value of the May call with an exercise price of 110 is

(a) 2.25
(b) 5.10
(c) 108

Question 7

The lower bound for the May European call with an exercise price of 105 is

(a) 3.00
(b) 3.60
(c) None of the above

Question 8

The effect of an increase in volatility on a call/put's price is

(a) Lower price due to potential higher losses
(b) Higher price due to potential higher gains
(c) Volatility does not affect the option price

Question 9

The values of u and d in the binomial option pricing model are:

(a) The return on the stock if it goes up or goes down, respectively
(b) The probabilities of the stock going up and down, respectively
(c) The proportion by which the stock price increases or decreases when the stock price goes up or down, respectively

Question 10

If the binomial model is extended to multiple periods over an option's life, what adjustments must be made?

(a) For each period, the up and down factors must be increased
(b) For each period the up and down factors and the risk-free rate must be decreased
(c) The initial stock price must be proportionately reduced

Question 11

Which of the following is not an assumption of the Black-Scholes model?

(a) Stock returns are normally distributed
(b) Constant volatility in stock returns
(c) None of the above

Question 12

Which of the following will make the American call more valuable than the European call?

(a) The volatility of stock returns is high
(b) The option is deep-in-the-money
(c) Cash dividend is made before option expiration

Question 13

An investor bought two European options on the same stock. Put A and Put B have exercise prices of 30 and 35, respectively. Both options are European 1-year put options.

Determine which statement is true about these options' moneyness, based on a particular stock price.

(a) If Put A is in-the-money, then Put B is in-the-money.
(b) If Put A is at-the-money, then Put B is out-of-the-money.
(c) If Put A is out-of-the-money, then Put B is out-of-the-money.

Question 14

Which of the following strategies is best for hedging an oil producer's risk?

(i) Buy a call on the price of oil
(ii) Sell a forward contract on the price of oil
(iii) Buy a put on the price of oil

(a) I
(b) II and III
(c) None of the strategies

Solutions

Question 1

Solution: Option **b** is correct

Having a put limits the amount of losses to the put price when the asset price falls. The put allows the holder to sell the asset at the exercise price, which is guaranteed.

Question 2

Solution: Option **a** is correct.

A call gives the holder the right to buy an asset at the exercise price. The asset could be another financial instrument, which is a futures contract.

Question 3

Solution: Option **c** is correct.

The put-call parity is: P + S = C + Xe-rt. As the computed call price is lower than the market price, we would buy the cheaper combination and sell the more expensive combination, i.e., buy (C + Xe-rt) and sell (P + S).

Question 4

Solution: Option **b** is correct.

The intrinsic value is given by Max[0, S − X] = 108 − 105 = 3

Question 5

Solution: Option **b** is correct.

The intrinsic value is Max[0, X − S] = 0. The time value is given by option price less intrinsic value = 1.55 − 0 = 1.55.

Question 6

Solution: Option **c** is correct.

The call cannot sell for more than the stock price.

Question 7

Solution: Option **a** is correct.

The lower bound is the intrinsic value = 108 − 105 = 3.

Question 8

Solution: Option **b** is correct.

Volatility increases the option's potential gains, but losses are limited to the price of the option.

Question 9

Solution: Option **c** is correct.

The stock price at a node is multiplied by either u or d to obtain the next period's up or down prices, respectively.

Question 10

Solution: Option **b** is correct.

As each period gets shorter, the up and down factors and the risk-free rate must be adjusted downwards accordingly. The initial price should not be adjusted downwards as we are starting from that price.

Question 11

Solution: Option **a** is correct.

Stock returns are assumed to be log normally distributed.

Question 12

Solution: Option **c** is correct.

Since the exercise price is not adjusted for dividend payments, a dividend payment lowers the stock price and the intrinsic value of the call. The European call cannot be exercised ahead of the anticipated fall in the stock price due to the dividend. However, as American options can be exercised before expiration, the American call will be exercised earlier. This opportunity for early exercise makes the American call more valuable than the European call.

Question 13

Solution: Option **a** is correct.

Put A has a lower exercise price than Put B. If Put A is in the money, that is, it is profitable to exercise, then Put B with a higher exercise price should be in-the-money, too, since the put holder can sell at a higher price. Answer (c) is not correct as the stock price could be between 30 and 35. In this case, Put A will be out-of-the-money since the exercise price is lower than the stock price. For Put B, as its exercise price is higher than the stock price, it is in-the-money.

Question 14

Solution: Option **b** is correct.

The oil producer will lose money if the oil price drops. Strategies II and III benefit from a fall in the oil price. The gains from either strategy will offset the losses the oil producer suffers by selling the oil at a lower price.

Chapter 34
Swaps

34.1 Characteristics of Swaps

34.1.1 *Introduction to Swaps*

A swap contract involves exchanging two sets of cash flows over a period.

Learning Objectives

- Describe the characteristics of a swap.

Main Takeaways

Main Points

- Swaps are traded over the counter, so there are no fixed terms. The terms are all negotiable between the counterparties.
- Swaps have the advantage over traded derivatives as those cannot be customized and often have short expiration periods.
- The exchange of cash flows is based on the swap's notional principal amount. While the notional principal and the cash flows can be huge, the exchange is for the difference between the two sets of cash flows and tends to be much smaller.
- The most common type of swap is the interest rate swap.

Main Terms

- **Notional principal:** The amount on which the exchange of cash flows is based.
- **Leg:** Each set of cash flows is known as a leg.

- **Netting:** A process of one party paying the net difference between the two sets of cash flows.
- **Plain vanilla swap:** A swap that consists of only two sets of cash flows that are exchanged.
- **Floating interest rate:** An interest rate that moves up and down with the rest of the market or index.
- **Maturity:** Refers to the end of a finite period of a contract at which time all outstanding obligations of the parties to the contract have to be settled. For the principal is repaid at that time.
- **Hedge:** It is an investment position intended to offset potential losses or gains that a companion investment may incur.

In carrying out their business activities, companies often encounter risks they wish to reduce. For example, some companies borrow large amounts and pay a floating interest rate. The floating interest rate results in variable interest amounts which make it harder for the company to plan its cash flows. An airline may need to hedge against fuel price increases as fuel is a critical operating cost. Those involved in the fund management industry may need to hedge against falls in the value of their portfolio holdings.

Companies can use the derivatives markets to hedge their risks. If they use derivatives traded on an exchange, the drawback is that those instruments cannot be customized. Further, if the company wants to hedge over the long term, it needs to keep rolling over the exchange-traded derivatives. This rolling over is inefficient and calls for actively managing the hedge, which can be costly. Further, margins are involved, which means tying up capital.

Swaps offer a better solution as they can be customized to meet the needs of the counterparty looking to hedge its risks. Further, the contract period can be very long, extending over many years. Another plus factor is that there is no need to post margins and have marking-to-market requirements, unlike futures contracts.

When a company needs to hedge its risks using swaps, it approaches a major investment bank which becomes the counterparty to the swap. As the investment bank has many clients, it will find counterparties for the swap it has taken on or else offset the risks within its extensive portfolio of swaps.

Swap counterparties agree on a notional principal amount on which the swap is based. Usually, the amount is proposed by a client of the investment bank.

Let's use an interest rate swap (IRS), which involves exchanging fixed interest payments for floating-rate interest payments, to illustrate the swap process.

The swap is based on a notional principal of \$100 million, a fixed rate of 5%, and a floating rate of LIBOR + 2%. The exchange of cash flows on a semi-annual basis is:

$$\text{Fixed-rate cash flow} = \$100 \text{ million} \times 5\%/2 = \$2.5 \text{ million}$$

If LIBOR is 2.5%, then LIBOR + 2% = 4.5%,

$$\text{Floating rate cash flow} = \$100 \text{ million} \times 4.5\%/2 = \$2.25 \text{ million}$$

$$\begin{aligned} \text{Net cash flow} &= \text{Fixed rate cash flow} - \text{Floating rate cash flow} \\ &= \$2.5 \text{ million} - \$2.25 \text{ million} = \$250{,}000 \end{aligned}$$

If the client has entered into the swap on the fixed-rate leg, the net cash flow paid by the client is \$250,000. Notice that the cash flow amount is a tiny fraction of the notional principal. This process of paying or receiving the net amount is called netting.

(a) The Different Types of Swaps

As swaps can be customized, there is no need to exchange the cash flows based on one variable. However, we will stick to plain vanilla swaps for our purposes, which involve exchanging one set of cash flows for another set. Besides the IRS, there are other swaps. We describe some of them below:

Currency swaps: Currency swaps are somewhat similar to the IRS. However, there are two main differences:

- The principal amount in the different currencies is exchanged at the beginning. At the swap's maturity, the principals are swapped back or returned to their respective counterparties.
- The interest payments are not made in one currency but the swap's currencies.

Here's an example of a currency swap. A Japanese manufacturer wants to set up a factory in the US It needs to borrow \$50 million to build and equip the factory. As the Japanese company is relatively unknown in the US, its US dollar borrowing cost is relatively high. However, the Japanese company is established in Japan, and it can borrow at much lower interest rates there. So the Japanese company borrows the equivalent of $50 million in Japanese yen and engages in a currency swap.

Assume that the dollar-yen exchange rate at the swap initiation is $1 = 100 yen. The Japanese company would receive $50 million and pays 5 billion yen.

Before the swap's maturity, the Japanese company would pay the US dollar interest rate while the counterparty would pay the Japanese yen interest rate. At maturity, the Japanese company would "return" or pay back $50 million while the counterparty would "return" the 5 billion yen.

Commodity swap: A commodity swap is a contract in which at least one set of cash flows is determined by the commodity price or commodity price index. Commodity swaps often do not involve the physical exchange of commodities.

An example of a commodity swap is an airline trying to hedge its fuel cost. The airline would like to hedge long-term, perhaps for 2 or 3 years. In this case, oil options and futures are not feasible. Instead, the airline enters into a swap and makes fixed periodic payments, usually every 6 months. In return, it receives variable payments based on an oil price index.

Essentially, the airline has locked into a fixed price for its fuel, which is the price on which its fixed periodic payment is based. Every 6 months, it pays the fixed payment for the fuel for the swap's fixed leg. In turn, it receives the variable payment, which it uses to pay for the purchase of fuel at the spot price. If the spot price rises, it gets a higher amount from the swap's variable leg to cover the cost of fuel it has to buy. However, if the price falls, the lower fuel cost is offset by the lower amount it receives from the swap.

Equity swap: Like the commodity swap, the swap's fixed leg pays a fixed amount and receives a variable amount based on the level of a stock index. The amount exchanged is based on a fixed percentage of the notional principal agreed between the counterparties.

34.2 Valuation of Swaps

34.2.1 *Swap Valuation Method*

Valuation of a swap contract is a process of determining a fair value of a swap, in other words, the present value of its expected cash flows.

Learning Objectives

- Describe how a swap can be valued.

Main Takeaways

Main Points

- A swap's value is measured by comparing the present values of the two sets of cash flows.
- At the swap initiation, the present values of the two sets of cash flows are equal.
- The terms regarding the exchange of cash flows are established at the initiation.

Main Terms

- **Initiation:** The date when the swap comes into existence and the swap's terms are established.
- **Fair value:** A broad measure of an asset's worth and is not the same as market value, which refers to an asset's price in the marketplace.
- **LIBOR:** Stands for the London Interbank Offered Rate which serves as a globally accepted key benchmark interest rate that indicates borrowing costs between banks. The rate is calculated and published each day by the Intercontinental Exchange (ICE).
- **Discount factor:** DF(T) is the factor by which a future cash flow must be multiplied to obtain the present value.
- **Premium:** An interest rate swap in which the counterparties agree to an interest rate that differs from the prevailing market rates.
- **Credit risk:** The possibility of a loss resulting from a borrower's failure to repay a loan or meet contractual obligations.

We will use the interest rate swap as an example of how to value a swap. In the interest rate swap, one set of cash flows consists of fixed-rate interest payments while the other set of cash flows consists of floating-rate interest payments.

The swap is priced at its initiation, which means that we set the terms of the swap such that the values of the two sets of cash flows, or legs, are equal. After the swap has been priced, subsequent changes in the floating rate due to changes in the reference rate, e.g., LIBOR, will result in the swap's value changing over time.

Here is a simple example of how we can price a 2-year interest rate swap with a notional amount of $100 million. Suppose the fixed-rate leg consists of four semi-annual payments. The floating-rate leg consists of four semi-annual payments at LIBOR. Let L_1, L_2, L_3 and L_4 be the forward LIBOR rate for periods 1 to 4, respectively. The cash flows for the floating leg are shown in Table 34.1.

In Table 34.1, the LIBOR forward rates can be obtained from Bloomberg or other financial data providers. It can also be calculated from the LIBOR yield curve's spot rates, assuming the pure expectations theory of interest rate holds, a topic that is discussed in Chapter 27 on Valuation of Bonds. The floating rate payments are based on the forward, or expected rates, at the swap initiation and are what the investor expects to get. Of course, after the swap is initiated, interest rates will change. How they change will determine the discount factors used to find the present values of the floating rate payments.

The discount factor for period 1 is 1/(1 + 0.015) = 0.9852. The discount factor for cash flows received at the end of period 2 is [1/(1 + 0.015)] × [1/(1 + 0.01625)] = 0.9695. In other words, the long-term spot rate is just the geometric average of the forward rates.

Table 34.1: Floating rate swap cash flows.

Six-month period	Annual LIBOR	Semi-annual LIBOR	Actual floating rate payment	Floating rate forward	PV of floating rate payment
Number	Forward rate	Forward rate	At end period	Discount factor	At end of period
1	3.00%	1.500%	$1,500,000	0.9852	$1,477,800
2	3.25%	1.625%	$1,625,000	0.9695	$1,575,438
3	3.50%	1.750%	$1,750,000	0.9528	$1,667,400
4	3.75%	1.875%	$1,875,000	0.9353	$1,753,688
			Sum of Discount Factors	**3.8428**	
				PV of Floating Rate Payments	**$6,474,325**

The present values of both legs' cash flows should be equal at the swap initiation. The fixed leg's cash flows consist of four payments of \$100 million × $R/2$ every 6 months, where R is the annual fixed-rate payable for the fixed leg. This is an annuity, and its present value is \$100 million × $R/2$ × (sum of discount factors for four periods). So,

PV of payments for fixed-rate = PV of payments for floating-rate
\$100 million × $R/2 \times 3.8428$ = \$6,474,325
Or $R = 3.37\%$

Once the rate is fixed at 3.37%, any change in LIBOR would change the value of the stream of fixed payments. When LIBOR increases, it reduces the fixed leg's value whereas that value increases should LIBOR decrease.

To reflect higher credit risk, a premium is added to LIBOR for the floating rate. Computing the fixed-rate follows the same procedure in the example.

Conceptually we can start with a fixed rate of say 5% for the fixed leg. As the present values of the payments for both for both rates should be the same, we can solve for the premium to be added to LIBOR. The premium computed would be incorporated as a part of the swap's terms.

References/Further Readings

Bodie, Z., Kane, A., & Marcus, A.J. (2020). *Investments*, 12th edn. McGraw-Hill Irwin, pp. 777–798.

Chance, Don M., & Brooks, Robert (2016). *An Introduction to Derivatives and Risk Management*, 10th edn. Cengage Learning.

34.3 Sample Questions

Question 1

Lee Inc. is a counterparty to a swap transaction with notional principal of \$1 million. It pays a fixed rate of 4% and receives a floating rate of LIBOR + 1%. If LIBOR is 4.5%, Lee Inc.'s cash flow is nearest to:

(a) \$2,500
(b) \$7,500
(c) \$15,000

Question 2
An investor wants to terminate an interest rate swap. Which method will likely result in the investor facing increased default risk?

(a) Receiving a payment from the original counterparty to terminate the swap
(b) Initiating a matching swap with another counterparty
(c) Transferring the obligations under the swap to another counterparty

Question 3
Which of the following swaps would least likely have netting of payments?

(a) Interest rate swap
(b) Equity swap
(c) Currency swap

Question 4
The swap where the payments are least likely to be known until the end of the period is

(a) Interest rate swap
(b) Equity swap
(c) Currency swap

Solutions

Question 1

Solution: Option **a** is correct.

Floating rate = 4.5% + 1% = 5.5%. Amount received is (5.5% – 4%) × 0.5 × $1,000,000 = $7,500

Question 2

Solution: Option **b** is correct.

The matching swap results in another counterparty, so the default risk increases.

Question 3

Solution: Option **c** is correct.

The currency swap involves two currencies. So the payments are likely to be on a gross basis.

Question 4

Solution: Option **b** is correct.

Both the interest rate swap and the currency swap are based on interest payments known at the beginning of the period. However, the payments that need to be made for the equity swap depend on the equity index's performance, which is known only at the end of the period.

Chapter 35

Hedging Using Derivatives

35.1 Hedging Fundamentals

35.1.1 *Hedging*

Hedging involves using a financial instrument or another asset to offset the risk of an asset's adverse price movements.

Learning Objectives

- Describe the process of hedging and discuss the factors that can lead to ineffective hedges.

Main Takeaways

Main Points

- Hedging is done using derivatives such as forwards, futures, options, and swaps.
- A long position in the asset is hedged by a short position in the derivative and vice versa.
- Where hedging is not possible using a derivative based on the asset, cross hedging is used. Cross hedging involves another asset or derivative based on this other asset which is positively correlated with the price movement of the asset we want to hedge.

Main Terms

- **Long position:** Position benefits from the rise in the asset's price or derivative underlying the position.

- **Short position:** Benefits from the fall in the asset's price or derivative underlying the position.
- **Cross hedge:** The practice of using another asset or its derivative to hedge an asset's risk.

The mitigation of risks is one of the benefits of using derivatives to hedge the various risks in a firm's business operations. For example, a firm that produces raw materials faces the risk of decline in the prices of minerals it extracts. For the users of the raw materials, for example a manufacturer, an increase in raw material prices mean reduced profit margins if it cannot pass on the increase in costs to its customers. This section focuses on how such risks can be hedged.

The principle behind hedging is to take a long position in an instrument whose price movement is the opposite to the price movement of an asset we want to hedge. Alternatively, we can hedge a long position in an asset by taking a short position in an instrument that tracks the asset's price. A long position benefits from a rise in the asset price, while a short position gains from a fall.

An example to illustrate hedging is that of an airline that needs to buy jet fuel. If the airline worries that jet fuel prices will rise in the future, it will use hedging to mitigate the increased cost of its jet fuel purchases. It can engage in long forward contracts.

35.2 Instruments for Hedging

Hedging techniques generally involve the use of financial instruments known as derivatives.

Learning Objectives

- Discuss how different types of risks can be hedged by forward and futures contracts, options, and swaps.

Main Takeaways

Main Points

- The losses and gains are symmetrical, ignoring transaction costs and margins, for forward, futures, and swaps, but not options.
- Margins are required for futures and options but not forwards and swaps.

Main Terms

- **CDS:** A credit default swap (**CDS**) is a financial derivative or contract that allows an investor to "swap" or offset their credit risk with that of another investor.
- **Basis point:** Otherwise known as bps or "pips", is a unit of measure used in finance to describe the percentage change in a financial instrument's value or rate. One basis point is equivalent to 0.01% (1/100th of a percent) or 0.0001 in decimal form.
- **Downside risk:** A security's potential to suffer a decline in value if the market conditions change or the amount of loss that could be sustained due to the drop.
- **Spot rate:** The price quoted for immediate settlement on a commodity, security, or currency. The spot rate is also referred to as the "spot price".

A hedge can be constructed from many types of financial instruments, including forward and futures contracts, swaps, options, and many types of over-the-counter and derivative products.

35.2.1 *Hedging with Forwards*

The forward contract is often used to lock-in a price. For example, a major expense for a biscuit manufacturer is the price of flour. When the flour price increases, the biscuit manufacturer may pass on the higher flour cost to its customers if it wants to maintain its profit margin. However, the more expensive biscuits may now cause customers to switch to other brands. However, through hedging, the biscuit manufacturer can maintain its biscuits prices.

Figure 35.1 illustrates how the forward contract fixes the flour price at $40 for a 50 kilogram bag. The spot/forward graph shows the profit or loss that the biscuit manufacturer would experience as the flour price changes in the spot/forward market. Suppose the flour price is $60 at the forward contract's expiration date. The biscuit manufacturer would then be making a $20 loss at this higher flour price as it is $20 higher than the $40 which it based its production cost. However, this loss is offset by the profit of $20 from its forward position.

Suppose the flour price went down to $30. The biscuit manufacturer would lose $10 on its forward position. This negates the $10 lower cost for flour. Thus, if biscuit manufacturer had not hedged, it would have benefited from the lower flour price. It would appear that the biscuit

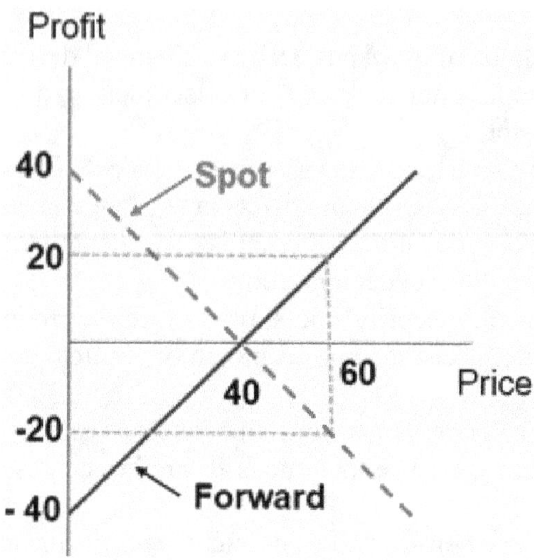

Figure 35.1: Hedging with forward contract.

manufacturer would be better off not hedging. However, do not be too quick to come to this conclusion as it is made on 20–20 hindsight. Commodity prices are difficult to predict and the firm is better off hedging than face the uncertainty of flour prices.

35.2.2 *Hedging with Futures*

Hedging with futures contracts is quite similar to hedging with forward contracts. The differences lie in the futures contracts. These have been discussed in Section 11.2. We highlight some differences as they pertain to implementing the hedging process.

The first difference is that forward contracts cover the whole duration over the period when the risk needs to be hedged. The duration could be for several years. However, some futures contracts expire in less than a year. This means that the futures contract needs to be rolled over, that is, a new contract is initiated just before the old contract expires. The roll-over process itself entails risk. If the hedged position that needs to be closed out results in a loss, cash payment must be made.

The second difference is the issue of margins and mark-to-market requirements. Futures contracts require the posting of the initial margin. Further, like the possible cash payments needed when the contract is closed out, a losing position in the futures contract calls for more cash payments. This stands in contrast to a forward position where nothing needs to be done until the expiration date.

The third difference stems from the clearinghouse serving as the futures contract counterparty. This difference drastically reduces the risk of non-performance or default by the counterparty for futures contracts compared to the higher risk of default by the counterparty in a forward contract.

The last difference lies in the fact that some futures contracts allow the seller to choose the grade of the commodity to deliver, which usually ends with the cheapest grade being delivered. Thus, the futures contract buyer does not have certainty regarding the particular grade of the commodity they get.

35.2.3 *Hedging with Options*

In Section 13.1, we showed how a long put position could be combined with a long position in a stock to form the protective put, limiting its downside risk. This section shows how currency options can be used to limit the downside risk arising from a depreciation of a currency.

Currency options, like most currency-related products, are mainly traded over-the-counter. Exchange-traded instruments exist but remain in the minority. They are traded on the NASDAQ OMX in the United States.

A currency option has as its underlying asset a currency. The price of a currency or its exchange rate is quoted as a currency pair, for example, EURUSD. The first currency, EUR, is known as the base currency or the asset to be priced. The second currency, USD in this case, is known as the quote or counter currency. The quote or counter currency is used to price one unit of the asset. Thus, an exchange rate of 1.2 for the EURUSD means that one euro's price is US$1.2.

As most international transactions are quoted in US dollars, this is why we price assets, whether physical or financial, in US dollar terms. The exchange rate EURUSD is known as a direct quote. If the quote is the amount of foreign currency for each US dollar, e.g., USDEUR, we are using an indirect quote. Note that the value of USDEUR is the reciprocal of EURUSD.

When firms or investors buy a currency, they don't take possession of the currency notes, unlike our transactions at the money changers. Instead, the purchased currency is left as a deposit in the bank or institution that sold it. This foreign currency deposit earns interest much like any other bank deposit. Hence, we can think of the currency deposit as similar to a stock that pays a dividend. The interest rate from the deposit would be equivalent to the stock's dividend yield. Consequently, we can apply the modified Black-Scholes theory to price currency options.

When we buy or sell a currency, the transaction can be looked at in two ways. Let's focus on the exchange of currencies using the EURUSD currency pair. If I buy EUR, I would receive EUR and pay in USD. This same transaction can be viewed in another way. As I give USD to the other party and receive EUR in return, it is as though I sold USD to the other party who paid for it with EUR.

Example:
In the context of options, buying a call with EUR as the underlying asset is the same as selling a put with the USD as the underlying asset for the EUUSD currency pair.

To understand this, note these relationships:

- Buying a call is having the option to buy the underlying asset.
- If the underlying asset is EUR, we buy EUR with USD.
- So, we are buying a call option on EURUSD.
- Buying EUR with USD is the same as selling USD and receiving EUR.
- The option to sell USD for EUR is similar to having a put option with USD as the underlying asset of USDEUR.
- So, a put option on EURUSD is a call option on USDEUR.

Hedging a currency exposure with currency options is not much different from hedging an asset using an option on the asset. The only thing to note is that since we are dealing with a currency pair, ensure that the notional that is matched is the foreign currency notional.

For example, suppose we have to pay EUR1 million in 6 months for equipment purchased. If the spot rate of EURUSD today is 1.25, and we want to pay just US$1.25 million in 6 months, we can lock-in the rate of 1.25 by buying a call option on EURUSD at an exercise price of 1.25 based on a notional 1 million units of EUR. If the EURUSD rate rises to 1.5, we would have to pay US$1.5 million to obtain the EUR1 million. However, the additional amount of US$0.25 million will be offset by the profit from the option position of US$0.25 × 1 million = US$0.25 million.

Suppose we hedge the currency exposure using USD as the notional. So, we buy a put option on the USD at the exercise price of 1/1.25 or EUR 0.8. (Note: a rise in the price of EUR is the same as a fall in USD's price. When the price of EUR rises to US$1.5, USD falls to EUR 0.666667. The US$1.25 million earmarked to pay the EUR1 million would only buy EUR (1,250,000 × 0.666667) or EUR833,337. For the put position, the gain per USD is EUR (0.1333333) from the drop-in price of EUR to EUR0.666667 from EUR0.8. The price drop resulted in a gain of EUR0.1333333. This translates to a gain of EUR (1,250,000 × 0.133333) or EUR166,667. EUR833,337 + EUR166,667 = EUR1,000,000 is the amount needed to pay for the equipment.

35.2.4 *Hedging with Swaps*

In Section 14, the mechanics of an interest rate swap was discussed. Here we discuss the use of swaps not to hedge interest-rate risk, but the risk of default on bonds, the credit default swap.

A credit derivative is a derivative whose value depends on credit risk. Credit derivatives come in the form of CDSs. They are used by bond portfolio managers who wish to hedge the risk of default by the issuers of debt securities they hold.

Conceptually, the CDS is like an insurance policy. The buyer of the CDS makes regular payments to the CDS seller much like what we do when we purchase a motor insurance policy from the insurance company to provide protection over a period of time. When the car is involved in an accident and suffers damage, the insurance company steps in to repair and restore the car to its condition before the accident. Similarly, should the issuer of the bond default on its payments, that is, when a credit event occurs, the CDS seller covers the losses sustained from the fall in bond value.

35.3 Sample Questions

Question 1
Which of the following strategies would profit from a bull market?

(a) A protective put
(b) Selling the equity index forward
(c) A covered call

Question 2
Which of the following strategies has the most significant potential loss?

(a) Selling a call
(b) Holding a put
(c) Having a long position in the stock

Question 3
Using a futures contract where the asset being hedged and the underlying asset are not the same is known as a

(a) Neutral hedge
(b) Cross hedge
(c) Basis hedge

Solutions

Question 1

Solution: Choice **a** is correct.

A protective put position has limited downside risk, but upside gains are not limited. Selling forward the equity index means paying a cash settlement consisting of the difference between the index's level against the agreed forward level, which is lower. A covered call is where a call is sold against stock held. In this case, the covered call holder does not benefit from the increase in the stock price as she has to deliver the stock when the call is exercised.

Question 2

Solution: Option **a** is correct.

Selling a call has unlimited downside risk as the stock price can rise to very high levels. Thus when the call is exercised, the call's seller has to buy the stock at a high price to fulfill the requirement to deliver the stock. The loss of holding a put is the put price. For a long stock position, the maximum loss is the stock price.

Question 3

Solution: Option **b** is correct.

A cross hedge is defined as using another asset different from the asset being hedged for the hedging process.

Part M: Portfolio Management

Chapter 36

Portfolio Analysis

This reading serves to give a summary of portfolios and their properties. Portfolios are generally less risky than single asset investments due to the diversification effect removing diversifiable risk. We then introduce the concept of risk aversion, in which investors with differing risk appetites have different utility functions. Next, we describe the Capital Allocation Line ("CAL") and its derivation. We combine the above concepts to derive the optimal portfolio for investors. Finally, we conclude with an explanation and use of the Capital Asset Pricing Model ("CAPM") and the Security Market Line ("SML").

36.1 Return and Risk Measures of Assets

36.1.1 *Return and Risk*

When people invest in assets, they expect a return on that asset because of the time value of money, a concept covered in an earlier section. However, the assets' returns also have varying levels of volatility, usually measured as the variance. Asset correlation and covariance measure how and when these assets move with each other. A portfolio, which consists of two or more assets that are not perfectly correlated, allows investors to reduce risk without necessarily decreasing returns.

Learning Objectives

- Calculate the expected return and variance of an investment portfolio.

Main Takeaways

Main Points

- The expected return is a concept that helps investors assess the value of a potential investment based on different future outcomes and a probability for each outcome.
- The variance of return is a measure of risk inherent when investing in an asset or portfolio and is calculated by summing a weighted average of the squared deviations from the mean return.
- A portfolio comprises two or more assets and is uniquely determined by the proportion of assets in the portfolio.
- The portfolio's expected return is the weighted sum of the asset returns.
- The portfolio variance measures the dispersion of returns of a portfolio. Portfolio variance is calculated using the portfolio weights and the standard deviation of each security in the portfolio, and the correlation between securities in the portfolio.
- Combining assets in a portfolio allow some risk to be reduced through diversification. However, an amount of risk (called systematic or non-diversifiable risk) cannot be reduced as most assets are affected by common economic events.

Main Terms

- **Standard deviation:** This deviation of an investment is obtained by taking the variance's square root. Compared to the variance, the standard deviation tells you that you can expect an investment's return to be one standard deviation above or below the average rate of return in a given year.
- **Correlation:** a statistic that measures the degree that two investments move with each other. It is measured by the correlation coefficient, which ranges from –1.0 to 1.0. A positive correlation means that as the price of one investment rises or falls, the other investment rises or falls with it to a degree based on the correlation's strength.
- **Diversification:** It refers to a strategy to reduce the risk of overall investment by investing in multiple assets within a portfolio.

(a) Single Asset Expected Return

Consider a single asset i. Suppose there are S possible states of the economy in the next period. If we let p be the probability of economic states occurring and R_{is} be the return of asset i if state s occurs, then the expected return on asset i is

$$E(R_i) = \sum_{s=1}^{S} p_s R_{is} \tag{36.1}$$

The p_s weights correspond to the probabilities and $E(R_i)$ are the return we would earn on average if we could repeat the investment many times, drawing the return from the same probability distribution of returns each time.

(b) Single Asset Variance

Also, for asset class i, the variance and standard deviation of its returns are, respectively:

$$\text{VAR}(R_i) = \sigma_i^2 = \sum_{s=1}^{S} p_s \left(R_{is} - E(R_i)\right)^2 = E\left\{\left[R_{is} - E(R_i)\right]^2\right\} \tag{36.2}$$

and

$$\text{SD}(R_i) = \sigma_i = \sqrt{\text{VAR}(R_i)} \tag{36.3}$$

(c) Portfolio of Assets

Now, consider a portfolio of N assets. We can describe a portfolio by its constituent assets and by its portfolio weights, the fraction of the total investment in the portfolio held in each asset in the portfolio. The portfolio weight for asset class i is

$$w_i = \frac{\text{Value of investment } i}{\text{Total value of portfolio}}. \tag{36.4}$$

Note that the portfolio weights add up to 1 to represent how we have divided our money between the different individual assets in the portfolio.

We can then find the expected portfolio return using one of two ways. One way is to first find the portfolio return in each state as follows:

$$R_{Ps} = \sum_{i=1}^{N} w_i R_{is} \tag{36.5}$$

Notice that the portfolio return in states is the weighted average of the portfolios' returns, where the weights correspond to the portfolio weights.

Then, find the expected portfolio return using the portfolio-equivalent of Equation (36.1) as follows:

$$E(R_P) = \sum_{s=1}^{S} p_s R_{Ps} \tag{36.6}$$

Notice that the expected portfolio return is the weighted average of the possible portfolio returns, where the weights correspond to the probabilities.

Another way is first to find the expected return using Equation (36.1) for each of the N assets in the portfolio. Then, the expected portfolio return is the weighted average of the expected returns of the investments within it, using the portfolio weights:

$$E(R_P) = \sum_{i=1}^{N} w_i E(R_i) \tag{36.7}$$

(d) Portfolio Expected Return

Portfolio volatility can be found using one of two ways as well. One way is to use Equation (36.5) to find the portfolio return in each state before using the portfolio-equivalent of Equations (36.2) and (36.3) to find the portfolio volatility. However, it is more insightful to relate portfolio risk to the portfolio's constituent assets' risk.

Consider a two-asset portfolio. Since $R_p = w_1R_1 + w_2R_2$, and using the basic statistical property of the variance of a linear combination of two random variables, the variance of the two-asset portfolio is

$$\begin{aligned} \text{VAR}(R_P) &= \text{VAR}(w_1R_1 + w_2R_2) \\ &= w_1^2\text{Var}(R_1) + \text{w}_2^2\text{Var}(R_2) + 2w_1w_2\text{COV}(R_1, R_2) \end{aligned} \tag{36.8}$$

Equation (36.8) shows that the portfolio variance depends on the variance of the individual assets and the covariance between them.

The covariance measures the degree to which the returns of the two assets move together and is defined as

$$\text{COV}(R_1, R_2) = \text{E}\{[R_1 - E(R_1)][R_2 - E(R_2)]\} \tag{36.9}$$

Intuitively, if the returns on the two assets move together, their returns will be above or below average simultaneously, and the covariance will be positive. If the returns on the two assets move in opposite directions, one will tend to be above average when the other is below average, and the covariance will be negative. Covariance indicates the direction of the linear relationship between two variables. The correlation coefficient indicates both the direction and the strength of the linear relationship. The equation to compute the correlation coefficient is given next:

$$\mathrm{CORR}(R_1,R_2)=\rho_{12}=\frac{\mathrm{COV}(R_1,R_2)}{\mathrm{SD}(R_1)\mathrm{SD}(R_2)} \tag{36.10}$$

Notice that the correlation between the two asset returns has the same sign as their covariance, so it has a similar interpretation. However, dividing by the volatilities ensures that correlation is always between –1 and +1, which allows us to gauge their relationship's strength. The closer the correlation is to +1, the more the returns move together. When the correlation (and thus the covariance) equals 0, the returns are uncorrelated. In that case, they do not tend to move either together or oppose each other. Finally, the closer the correlation is to –1, the more the returns tend to move in opposite directions.

(e) Portfolio Variance

By making the subject of Equation (36.10) and substituting the expression for it in Equation (36.8), the portfolio variance becomes

$$\mathrm{VAR}(R_p)=w_1^2\mathrm{VAR}(R_1)+\mathrm{w}_2^2\mathrm{VAR}(R_2)+2w_1w_2\mathrm{SD}(R_1)\mathrm{SD}(R_2)\rho_{12} \tag{36.11}$$

Notice that if the assets' returns are perfectly positively correlated (i.e., $\rho_{12}=1$, then the portfolio volatility is

$$\mathrm{SD}(R_p)=w_1\mathrm{SD}(R_1)+w_2\mathrm{SD}(R_2) \tag{36.12}$$

Notice that portfolio risk is a weighted average of the assets' risks if the two assets are perfectly positively correlated. However, if, with a positive amount invested in each asset, the relation becomes:

$$\mathrm{SD}(R_p)<w_1\mathrm{SD}(R_1)+w_2\mathrm{SD}(R_2) \tag{36.13}$$

Since returns for any two assets are unlikely to be perfectly positively correlated, relation (36.13) implies that portfolio risk is less than the weighted average of its constituent assets' risks. However, from Equation (36.7), the portfolio expected return is still a weighted average of its constituent assets' expected returns. The reduction in portfolio risk is the essence of diversification.

In the general case of an N-asset portfolio, the portfolio variance is given by

$$\mathrm{VAR}(R_p) = \sum_{i=1}^{N}\sum_{j=1}^{N} w_i w_j \mathrm{COV}(R_i, R_j) \tag{36.14}$$

where and are the returns on assets i and j, respectively. Equation (36.14) says that the portfolio variance is equal to the covariances' weighted average of the returns of all pairs of assets in the portfolio. The portfolio's overall variability depends on the total co-movement of the assets within it. From Equation (36.9), we notice that the covariance of an asset's return with itself is its variance. Thus, for asset i:

$$\mathrm{COV}(R_i, R_j) = \mathrm{VAR}(R_i) \tag{36.15}$$

Using Equations (36.14) and (36.15), we will obtain Equation (36.8) for the particular case where $N = 2$.

(f) Diversification

Combining assets in a portfolio eliminate some of their risks through diversification. Independent risks are diversified away in a large portfolio, whereas common risks are not. The amount of risk that will remain depends on the degree to which the assets are exposed to common risks. The tendency for asset returns to move together is affected by economic events.

Non-diversifiable risk, also called systematic risk, applies to a particular market or industry. It cannot be diversified away. Diversifiable risk is also called non-systematic risk, which applies to one specific investment unrelated to the market and can be diversified. An example would be a strike at one particular company or a company's factory that had to shut down due to flooding.

The expected return of a diversified portfolio is the expected return of each of its underlying assets multiplied by the weight the investment receives. The variance of a diversified portfolio reduces with the number

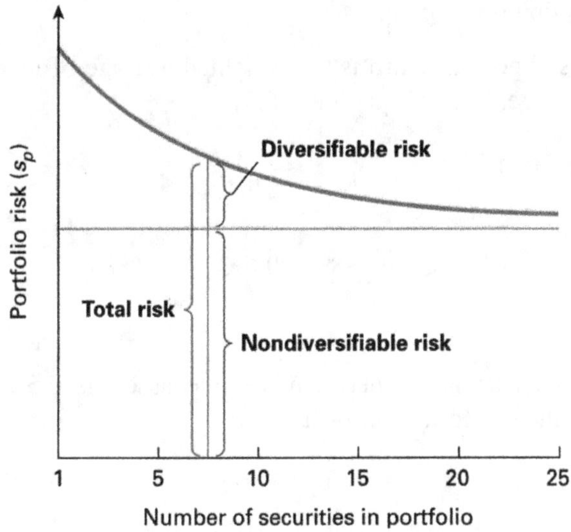

Figure 36.1: Portfolio risk and the number of securities in portfolio.

of assets and less than perfectly correlated asset returns. Figure 36.1 shows how the portfolio standard deviation of a portfolio of NYSE stocks reduces with the portfolio's number of securities. Also illustrated is the limit of diversification, where increasing the number of stocks within a portfolio does not reduce portfolio variance.

Examples:
Use the following portfolio to answer Questions 1 and 2:

Asset	Weight (%)	Expected return (%)	Expected standard variation (%)
A	40	8	20
B	60	3	10

Example 1:
Calculate the expected return of the portfolio

(a) 5.0%
(b) 6.0%
(c) 6.4%

Solution: Option **a** is correct.

A portfolio's expected return is the weighted average of its components' expected average. Using Equation (36.5),

$$R_{Ps} = \sum_{i=1}^{N} w_i R_{is}$$

$$R_{Ps} = 0.4*8\% + 0.6*3\% = 5.0\%$$

Example 2:
Given that the correlation between the two assets is 0.5, the standard deviation of the portfolio is closest to:

(a) 10.1%
(b) 10.2%
(c) 11.5%

Solution: Option **b** is correct.

Using Equation (36.11),

$$\text{Var}(R_p) = \text{w}_1^2\text{Var}(R_1) + \text{w}_2^2\text{Var}(R_2) + 2w_1w_2\text{SD}(R_1)\text{SD}(R_2)\rho_{12}$$

$$\text{SD}(R_p) = \sqrt{w_1^2\text{var}(R_1) + w_2^2\text{var}(R_2) + 2w_1w_2\text{SD}(R_1)\text{SD}(R_2)\rho_{12}}$$

$$\text{SD}(R_p) = \sqrt{0.4^2 0.2^2 + 0.6^2 0.1^2 + 2(0.4)(0.6)(0.2)(0.1)(0.5)}$$

$$\text{SD}(R_p) = 0.102 = 10.2\%$$

Note: the variance between Assets A and B is counted twice. We are counting the variance between Assets A and B and the variance between B and A.

References/Further Readings

Bodie, Z., Kane, A., & Marcus, A.J. (2020). *Investments*, 12th edn. Mc-Graw Hill, pp. 119–158.

Brealey, R.A., Myers, S.C., & Allen, F. (2010). *Principles of Corporate Finance*, 10th edn. McGraw-Hill, pp. 156–184.

Ross, S., Westerfield, R., & Jordan, B. (2002). *Fundamentals of Corporate Finance*, 6th edn. McGraw-Irwin Hill, pp. 416–425.

36.2 Risk Aversion and the Efficient Frontier

Most (if not all) investors can be said to be risk-averse, meaning when two portfolios have the same returns, it is assumed that investors will choose the one with lower risk. Here, we can also see how multiple risky assets with imperfect correlation can create multiple portfolios based on their weightage to create an efficient frontier.

Learning Objectives

- Understand the concepts of risk aversion, utility, and the efficient frontier.

Main Takeaways

Main Points

- Risk aversion is the concept whereby investors favor price stability over price volatility. If given the option between two investments with the same expected returns but different standard deviations, the investor will choose the lower standard deviation.
- The utility is a numerical expression of the total enjoyment an investor can derive from an investment or asset.
- Graphically, higher risk aversion results in a steeper indifference curve on the expected returns against the risk (standard deviation) diagram.
- The higher utility is derived from increasing expected returns or decreasing price volatility. Graphically, the indifference curves shift in the "north-west" for increasing utility.
- By adjusting the weightage of 2 risky assets with a correlation coefficient of <1 in a portfolio, it is possible to create multiple portfolios with different expected returns and variances.
- The Efficient Frontier is the optimal set of portfolios with the highest expected return for any given risk or vice versa. If a portfolio only has 2 assets, every weightage combination will result in a portfolio on the efficient frontier.
- The Minimum Variance Portfolio is the portfolio of assets with the lowest price volatility on the efficient frontier

36.2.1 *The Utility Function and Indifference Curves*

A numerical risk aversion can be measured in an interview or questionnaire in which the investor expresses preferences among sets of choices involving risky and certain returns. Empirically, an investor who is averse to risk penalizes the expected return by a certain percentage to account for the risk involved. We assume that each investor can assign a utility score to compete for portfolios based on those portfolios' expected return and risk. One function that is employed by finance theorist and by the CFA institute assigns a portfolio with expected return E(r) and variance of return σ^2 the following utility score:

$$U = E(r) - \frac{1}{2}A\sigma^2 \tag{36.16}$$

where U is the utility value, and A is an index of the investors' risk aversion.

Note that the higher A, the higher an investor's dislike of risk, and If $A > 0$, we say an investor is risk-averse.

The function relates to the notion that utility will increase with expected returns but falls with volatility. If we assume that returns are normally distributed, then the standard deviation is the appropriate risk measure.

The graph in Figure 36.2 shows the utility function for varying risk aversion measures on the expected return — standard deviation plane. Each curve is an indifference curve, i.e., each point on that curve has the same utility.

For a risk-averse investor, the utility function is always sloping upwards as an investment with a higher degree of riskiness (as represented by standard deviation) must be compensated with a higher expected return. As an investor's risk aversion (A) increases, the utility function's slope becomes steeper as the investor requires a higher return per unit of standard deviation.

The next graph in Figure 36.3 shows plots of the same utility value. The plot can be interpreted as plots of one specific investor, with A being fixed. What is plotted is then the expected return — return standard deviation combination for fixed U. Arrow points toward the "north–west" direction for increasing values of U. Greater utility comes from increasing return and decreasing volatility.

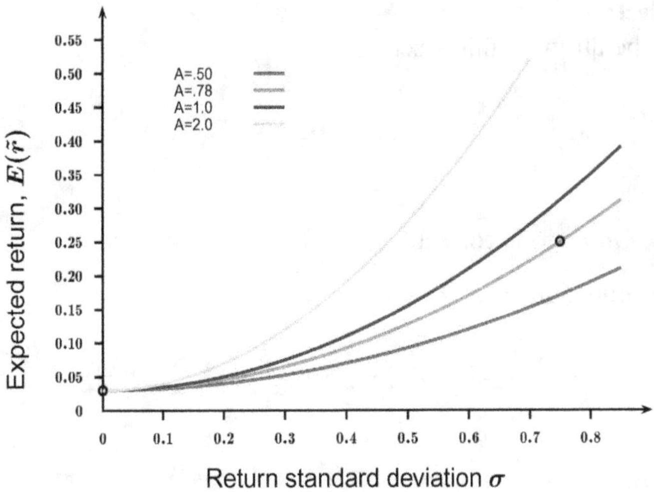

Figure 36.2: Utility function of varying measure of risk aversion on the expected return.

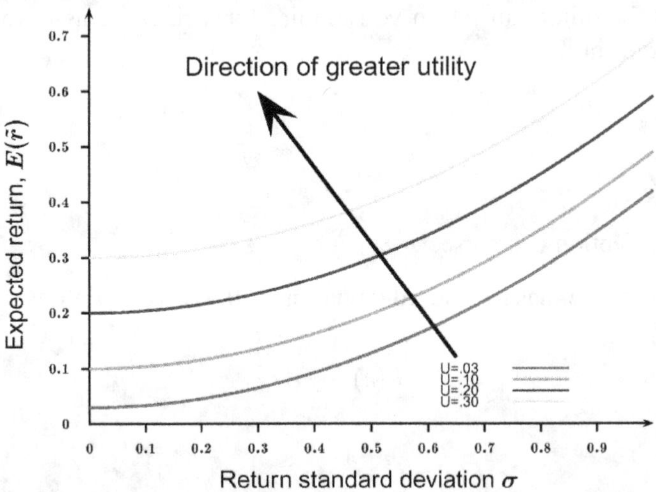

Figure 36.3: Direction of greater utility, with fixed risk aversion.

Examples:

Use the following statement for Questions 1 and 2. Assuming that you are given an asset with an expected return of 12% and a standard deviation of 10%, you have a risk aversion coefficient of 4.

Example 1:
What is the utility of this asset?

(a) −0.80
(b) 0.10
(c) −18.80

Solution: Option **b** is correct.

By using Equation (36.16),

$$U = E(r) - \frac{1}{2}A\sigma^2$$

$$U = 0.12 - \frac{1}{2}(4)(0.1)^2 = 0.10$$

Example 2:
What is the minimum return you require for a risk-free asset to achieve the same utility?

(a) 8.8%
(b) 11%
(c) 10%

Solution: Option **c** is correct.

A risk-free asset has a standard deviation of 0. By using Equation (36.16),

$$U = E(r) - \frac{1}{2}A\sigma^2$$

$$E(r) = U + \frac{1}{2}A\sigma^2$$

$$E(r) = 0.1 + \frac{1}{2}(4)(0)^2 = 10\%$$

36.2.2 *The Efficient Frontier*

Consider an investor who can only invest in two risky assets. If the two assets are perfectly positively correlated (=1), the graph of the portfolio's

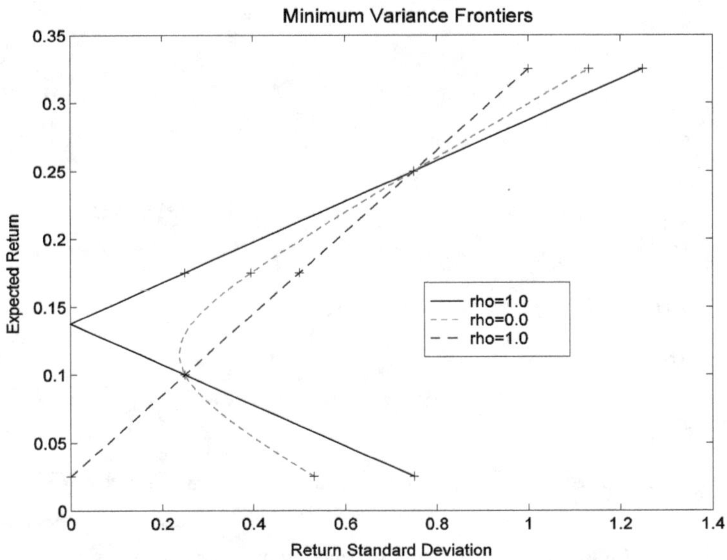

Figure 36.4: Minimum variance frontiers.

expected return against portfolio volatility for the set of possible portfolios is a straight line. When the correlation is less than 1, the portfolios' volatility is reduced due to diversification. The curve bends to the left, as shown in Figure 36.4. The reduction in risk (and the bending of the curve) becomes greater as the correlation decreases.

We next discuss efficient and inefficient portfolios. A portfolio is inefficient whenever it is possible to find another portfolio that provides a better tradeoff between expected return and volatility. An efficient portfolio offers the highest expected return for its given volatility level. While we can rule out inefficient portfolios as inferior investment choices, we cannot easily rank the efficient ones — investors will choose among them based on their preferences for return versus risk.

36.2.3 *The Minimum Variance Frontier for Two Assets*

Assume we can only trade in two risky assets, B and C. The correlation between the returns of B and C, $\rho_{\text{BC}} = 0.5$.

Asset	E(r)	σ
B	10%	20%
C	15%	30%

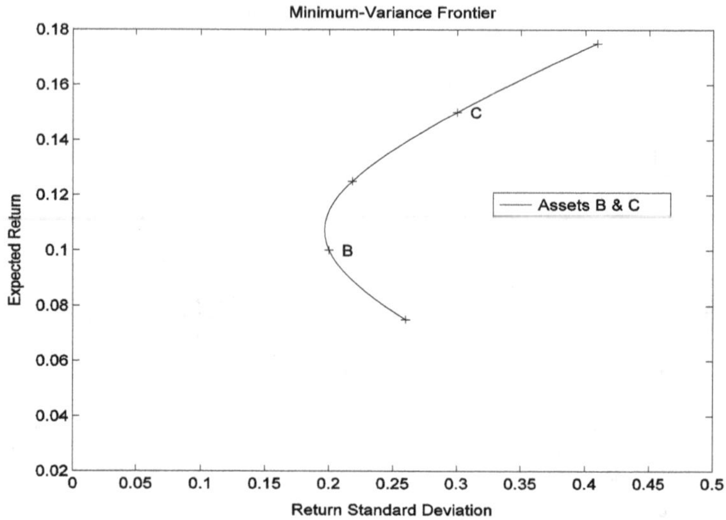

Figure 36.5: Minimum variance frontier for two assets.

The expected return — standard deviation plot is shown in Figure 36.5. Since we have only two risk assets, the minimum variance frontier (MVF) or efficient frontier for B&C is also the plot with varying weights in asset A and asset B.

36.2.4 *The Minimum Variance Frontier for More Risky Assets*

Consider the optimal portfolio problem with three assets:

Asset	E(r)	σ
A	5%	10%
B	10%	20%
C	15%	30%

Correlations			
Assets	A	B	C
A	1.0	0.0	0.5
B	0.0	1.0	0.5
C	0.5	0.5	1.0

What does the MVF look like now?

If we combine A and B, B and C, or A and C, we get the following possible portfolio combinations:

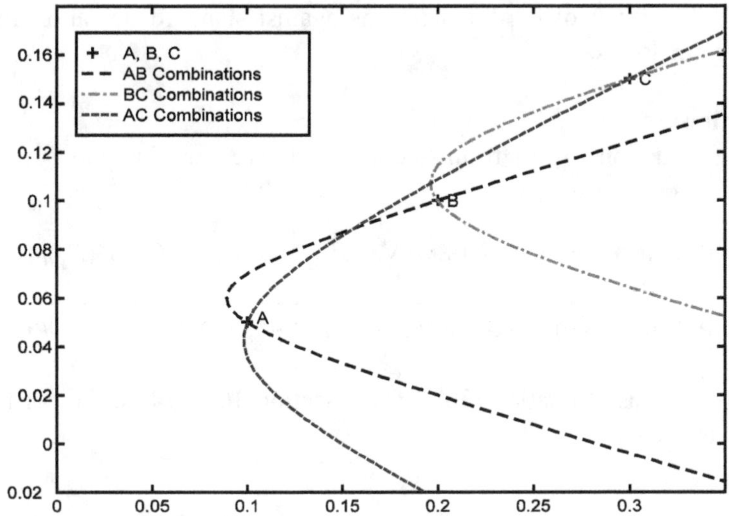

Figure 36.6: Minimum variance frontier for combinations of A, B, and C.

However, there are still "better" portfolios. With three assets, the MVF likely includes combinations of all three assets, A, B, and C (see Figure 36.6).

Example:
Assuming that you are an investor interested in creating a portfolio from the following two assets:

	Security A	Security B
Expected return	8%	15%
Standard deviation	10%	20%
Correlation between the two assets: 0.5		

Fill in the following table for the following five portfolios with different weights in A and B:

Portfolio	Weightage A	Weightage B	Standard deviation	Expected return
1	20%	80%		
2	40%	60%		
3	60%	40%		
4	80%	20%		
5	100%	0%		

Plot a graph of expected returns against standard deviation for the above portfolios.

Solution:
Using Equation (36.8) from Section 36.1, we can find the portfolio's standard deviation.

$$\mathrm{Var}(R_p) = w_1^2\mathrm{Var}(R_1) + w_2^2\mathrm{Var}(R_2) + 2w_1w_2\mathrm{SD}(R_1)\mathrm{SD}(R_2)\rho_{12}$$

$$\mathrm{SD}(R_p) = \sqrt{w_1^2\mathrm{Var}(R_1) + w_2^2\mathrm{Var}(R_2) + 2w_1w_2\mathrm{SD}(R_1)\mathrm{SD}(R_2)\rho_{12}}$$

We can use Equation (36.7) from Section 36.1 to find the portfolio's expected returns.

$$E(R_P) = \sum_{i=1}^{N} w_i E(R_i)s$$

Portfolio	Weightage A (%)	Weightage B (%)	Standard deviation (%)	Expected return (%)
1	20	80	16.6	13.6
2	40	60	13.6	12.2
3	60	40	11.1	10.8
4	80	20	9.8	9.4
5	100	0	10.0	8.0

The graph is shown in Figure 36.7.

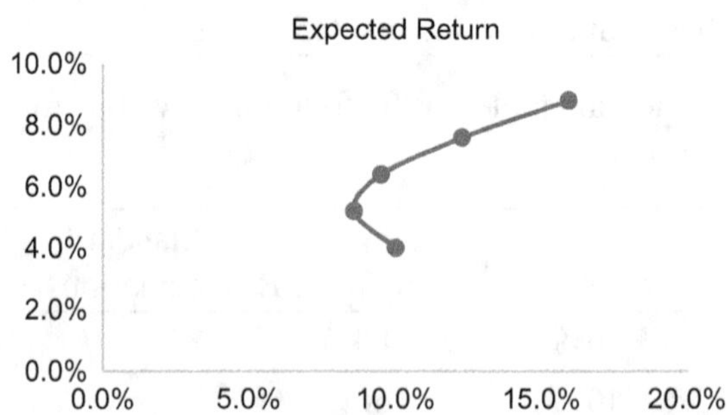

Figure 36.7: Plot of graph expected returns against standard deviation.

This example shows that diversification allows a portfolio to have a standard deviation that is even lower than the lowest standard deviation in its constituent assets, so long as the correlation between the assets is <1. Portfolio risk reduction is unlike portfolio expected returns, which can only be between its constituent assets. Diversification thus affects risk more than returns.

References/Further Readings

Brealey, R.A., Myers, S.C., & Allen, F. (2010). *Principles of Corporate Finance*, 10th edn. McGraw-Hill, pp. 185–199.

Bodie, Z., Kane, A., & Marcus, A.J. (2020). *Investments*, 12th edn. Mc-Graw Hill, pp. 159–165.

36.3 Optimal Portfolio Selection

Adding a risk-free asset to the portfolio can form a CAL, providing a portfolio for every risk profile. Adding the risk-free asset allows the formation of an optimal portfolio for any investor, regardless of how risk-averse.

Learning Objectives

- Understand the process of finding the optimal portfolio for an investor with a known risk-aversion.

Main Takeaways

Main Points

- The CAL is a set of portfolios involving risky assets and risk-free assets.
- The Sharpe ratio is the average expected returns above the risk-free returns per unit of risk.
- The optimal CAL for one risky asset and the risk-free asset is simply the line connecting both assets.
- The optimal CAL for multiple risky assets and the risk-free asset is the tangential point between the CAL and the efficient frontier, resulting in the highest Sharpe ratio possible in the given scenario.
- The optimal portfolio for an investor with a known risk-aversion is the point where the utility curve is tangent to the optimal CAL. The optimal CAL is the case where utility for the investor is highest.

36.3.1 *Capital Allocation Line*

The CAL is a line that plots returns of all possible combinations of risky and risk-free assets against risk. We shall first examine a scenario with one risky asset and a risk-free asset before considering a case with multiple risky assets and a risk-free asset.

36.3.2 *One Risky Asset with One Risk-Free Asset*

Consider an arbitrary risky asset with expected returns and a risk-free investment like a US Treasury bill with a return. If we invest a fraction *w* of our money in the risky portfolio, A while leaving the remaining in the risk-free asset, the expected return on this portfolio can be written as follows:

$$E(R_p) = (1 - w)r_f + wE(R_A) \tag{36.17}$$

Because the risk-free rate is fixed and does not move with (or against) the risky portfolio, its volatility and covariance with the risky portfolio are both zero. Thus, the volatility of the portfolio that combines the risky portfolio with the risk-free asset can be written as follows:

$$\mathrm{SD}(R_p) = \sqrt{w^2\mathrm{SD}(R_A)} = w\mathrm{SD}(R_A) \tag{36.18}$$

The volatility is only a fraction of the risky portfolio's volatility, based on the amount we invest in it. By making w the subject of Equation (36.18) and substituting the expression for it in Equation (36.17), we get the expected return-risk relation that describes the set of possible investments that combine the risky portfolio with the risk-free asset:

$$E(R_p) = r_f + \left[\frac{E(R_A) - r_f}{\mathrm{SD}(R_A)}\right]\mathrm{SD}(R_p) \tag{36.19}$$

The relation given by Equation (36.19) is called the CAL. Note from Equation (36.19) that the expected return is a linear function of the volatility.

The risky portfolio combinations with the risk-free asset are represented graphically in Figure 36.8 by a straight line that links the risk-free asset and passes through the risky portfolio.

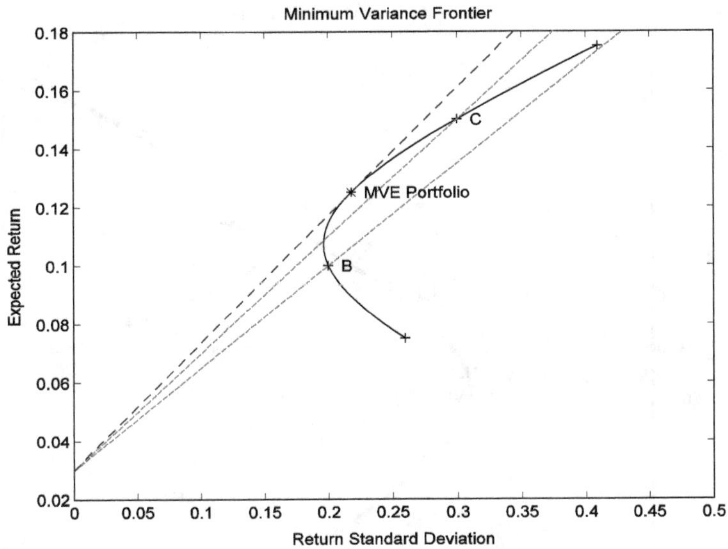

Figure 36.8: Minimum variance frontier for one/two risky asset(s) with one risk-free asset.

36.3.3 *Two or More Risky Assets with the Risk-Free Asset*

Consider including either B, C, or both B and C and the risk-free asset in our portfolio.

Combining the risk-free asset with asset B or C yields two possible CALs as shown in Figure 36.8: However, there is a combination of B and C that is superior. That combination is the tangential point between the CAL and the MVF (or efficient frontier). This combination of B and C is called the mean-variance efficient (MVE) portfolio. The CAL plot between the risk-free asset with risky assets is the line that provides the optimal feasible tradeoff.

The optimal weight turns out to be $w_B = 0.5$ which yields $E(r_{MVE}) = 0.125$ and $\sigma_{MVE} = 0.2179$. The Sharpe ratio compares to the individual Sharpe ratios of Asset B and Asset C where $SR_B = 0.35$ and $SR_C = 0.40$

The Sharpe ratio of the MVE is higher than that of B and C independently. The following graph in Figure 36.9 shows a case when we have three risky assets.

The optimal risky portfolio to combine with the risk-free asset will be the one with the highest Sharpe ratio, where the line with the risk-free asset is tangent to the efficient frontier of risky assets. As this tangent portfolio has the highest Sharpe ratio of any risky portfolio in the

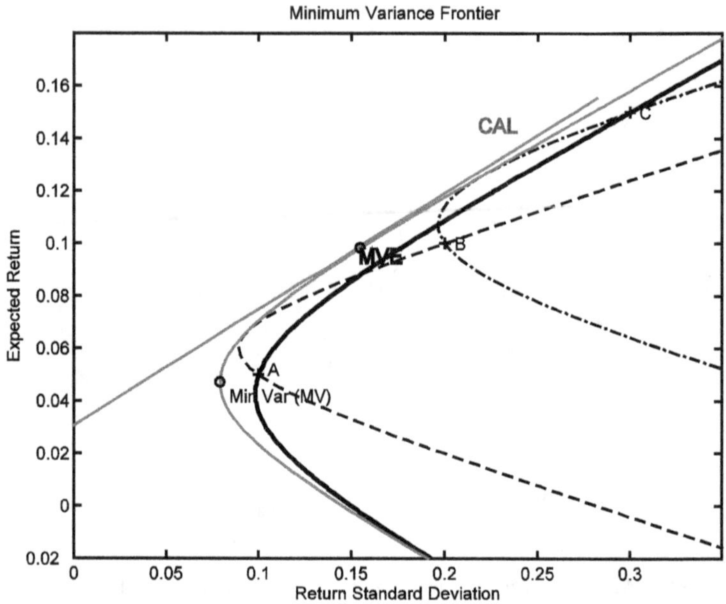

Figure 36.9: Minimum variance frontier for three risky assets.

economy, combining the risk-free asset with the tangent portfolio provides the best risk-return tradeoff available to an investor, and all other portfolios will lie below this line.

Notice that all efficient portfolios are combinations of risk-free investments once we consider a risk-free asset. The tangent portfolio and the efficient frontier are essentially a straight line (called the CAL). Furthermore, the optimal portfolio of risky assets no longer depends on an investor's risk aversion — every investor should invest in the tangent portfolio independent of their taste for risk; hence, we refer to this tangential point as the market portfolio. The investor's preferences will only determine how much to invest in the market portfolio versus the risk-free asset. Conservative investors will invest a small amount in the market portfolio, choosing a portfolio on the line near the risk-free asset. Aggressive investors will invest more, selecting a portfolio that is near the market portfolio or even beyond it by borrowing at the risk-free rate.

The CAL, as shown in Figure 36.10, shows all risk-return combinations possible for one risky-asset and the risk-free return. The slope measures the extra return you get from investing in the risky asset per unit of risk and is also called the reward-to-variability ratio or Sharpe ratio and is widely used to measure portfolio performance.

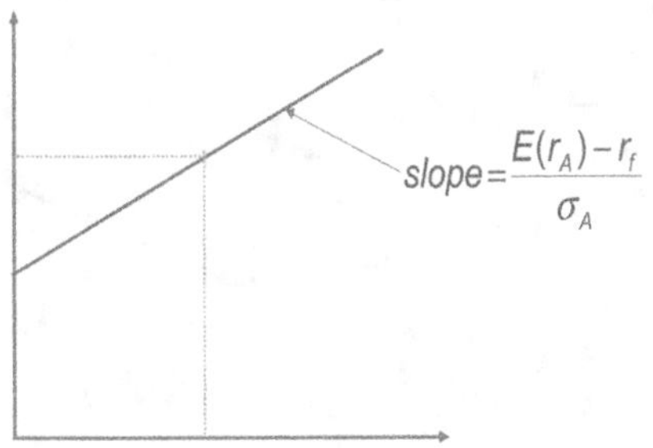

Figure 36.10: CAL and Sharpe ratio.

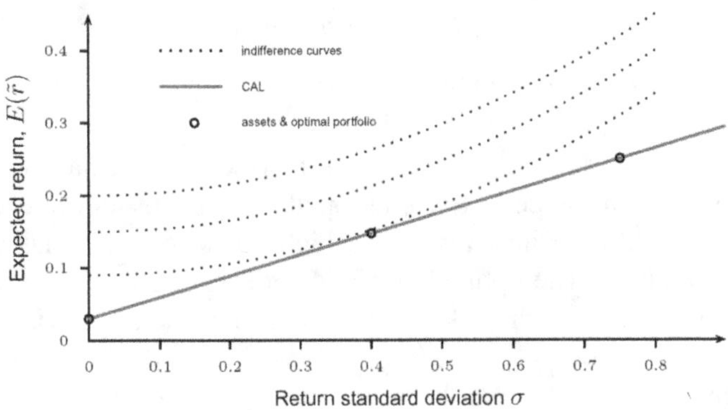

Figure 36.11: Graph of CAL and indifference curves.

$$\text{Sharpe ratio} = \left[\frac{E(R_p) - r_f}{\text{SD}(R_p)}\right] \tag{36.20}$$

36.3.4 *Combining the Indifference Curves with the CAL*

In choosing a risk-return combination along the CAL, we need to look at the utility function. Graphically in Figure 36.11, we solve the following problem: First, we consider an individual. This individual will select the CAL point tangential to the utility curve that provides her with the highest utility, which is feasible. This point is defined by the proportion of investment in the risk-free and risky asset.

Figure 36.12 shows that different levels of risk aversion lead to other choices. An investor with higher risk adversity has a steeper indifference curve, represented by the blue curve. The optimum portfolio for such an

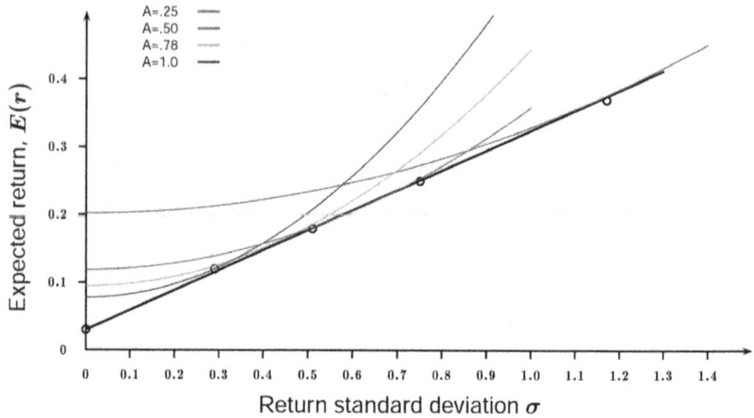

Figure 36.12: Graphs with different levels of risk aversion.

investor will have a higher weightage of the risk-free asset, as indicated by the lower risk and expected returns on the point the indifference curve touches the CAL. An investor with a higher risk tolerance has a gentler indifference curve. The optimal portfolio for such an investor will have a higher concentration of the risky asset, as shown by the curve with A = 0.25.

Example:
Calculate the Sharpe ratio of the CAL for the following risky asset and risk-free asset:

Asset	Expected return (%)	Standard deviation (%)
Risky	10	20
Safe	3	0

(a) 0.35
(b) 0.40
(c) 0.45

Solution:
Option **a** is correct.

Using the formula (36.20)

$$\text{Sharpe ratio} = \frac{E(R_p) - r_f}{\text{SD}(R_p)}$$

$$\text{Sharpe ratio} = \frac{10\% - 3\%}{20\%} = 0.35$$

References/Further Readings

Bodie, Z., Kane, A., & Marcus, A.J. (2020). *Investments*, 12th edn. Mc-Graw Hill, pp. 166–217.

36.4 Capital Asset Pricing

The CAL that uses the market portfolio is the optimal risky portfolio known as the capital market line.

Learning Objectives

- Understand the Capital Market Line (CML) and the Security Market Line (SML). Calculate a portfolio's beta.

Main Takeaways

Main Points

- The CML is the CAL where the risky asset is the market portfolio, which is also the tangential portfolio on the efficient frontier constructed from the set of all available risky assets.
- A beta coefficient for an individual asset or portfolio of assets measures how stock or portfolio value changes than a benchmark, like the S&P 500. A value of 1 suggests that it fluctuates as much as the index and in the same direction.
- A beta coefficient of less than 1 suggests a portfolio that fluctuates less than the benchmark. A negative beta is an indication that a portfolio moves in the opposite direction of its benchmark.
- The Capital Asset Pricing Model is the formula relating the non-diversifiable risk of an investment and expected return.
- The SML is the graphical representation of the Capital Asset Pricing Model.

Main Terms

- **Normalized variable:** In statistics, a normalized variable is calculated using a ratio of itself and some benchmark figure. Normalized figures tend to be smaller than the original values.

36.4.1 *Capital Market Line*

A CAL includes all possible combinations of the risk-free asset and an investor's optimal risky portfolio. The capital market line is a particular case of the CAL, where the risky portfolio is the market portfolio. The risk-free asset is a debt security with no default risk, no inflation risk, no liquidity risk, no interest rate risk, and no risk of any other kind. US Treasury bills are used as a proxy of the risk-free return, R_f.

The S&P 500 is a proxy of the market portfolio, the optimal risky portfolio. Therefore, the expected return on the risky portfolio is the expected market return, expressed as $E(R_m)$. The capital market line is shown in the graph below. Graphically, the market portfolio is the point on the Markowitz efficient frontier where a line from the risk-free asset is tangent to the Markowitz efficient frontier. When plotted together, the CML's point is tangent to the Markowitz efficient frontier is the optimal combination of risky assets, based on market prices and market capitalizations. The optimal risky portfolio is the market portfolio (see Figure 36.13).

We can express $E(R_p)$ in terms of σ_p. Like Equation (36.19), the market portfolio becomes the risky asset, with an expected $E(R_m)$ and standard deviation of σ_m. The equation for this specific CAL is also known as the CML:

$$E(R_p) = r_f + \left[\frac{E(R_m) - r_f}{\text{SD}(R_m)}\right]\text{SD}(R_p) \tag{36.21}$$

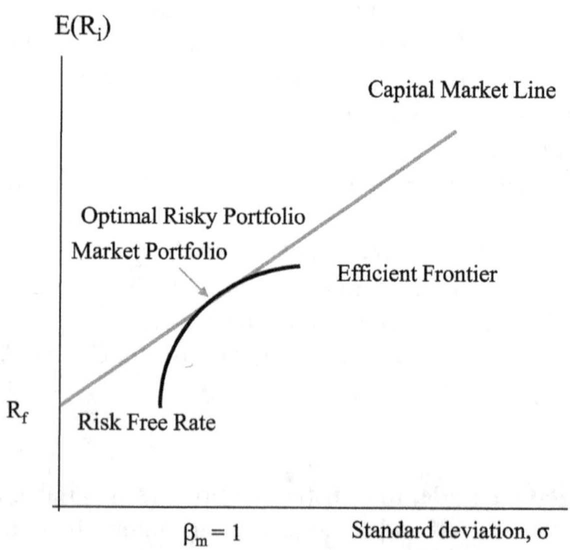

Figure 36.13: Markowitz efficient frontier and the optimal risky portfolio.

where r_f is the risk-free asset and the y-intercept on the graph

$$\left[\frac{E(R_m)-r_f}{SD(R_m)}\right].$$

The Sharpe ratio and the line's slope pass through R_f and R_m.

(a) Calculate and Interpret Beta, β

The sensitivity of the return of an asset to the market index return is the asset's beta. Beta is the covariance of the asset's return divided by the market return variance and is calculated as follows:

$$\beta_i = \frac{\text{Covariance of Asset } i\text{'s return with the market return}}{\text{Variance of the market return}} = \frac{\text{COV}_{im}}{\sigma_m^2} \quad (36.22)$$

We can use the definition of the correlation between the returns on asset i with the returns on the market index:

$$\rho_{im} = \frac{\text{COV}_{im}}{\sigma_i \sigma_m}$$

$$\text{COV}_{im} = \rho_{im}\sigma_i\sigma_m$$

Substituting for COV_{im} in the equation for B_i, we can also calculate beta as

$$\beta_i = \frac{\rho_{im}\sigma_i\sigma_m}{\sigma_m^2} = \rho_{im}\frac{\sigma_i}{\sigma_m} \quad (36.23)$$

It is important to note that beta tracks the portfolio's non-diversifiable risk and assumes that it has fully diversified company-specific risk.

36.4.2 *Security Market Line*

Now that we have the beta, we can plot another line like the CML. However, in this one, the x-axis will be the asset's or portfolio's covariance to the market portfolio (see Figure 36.14).

The equation of the SML is

$$E(R_i) = r_f + \left[\frac{E(R_m)-r_f}{\sigma_m^2}\right]\text{COV}_{i,m} \quad (36.24)$$

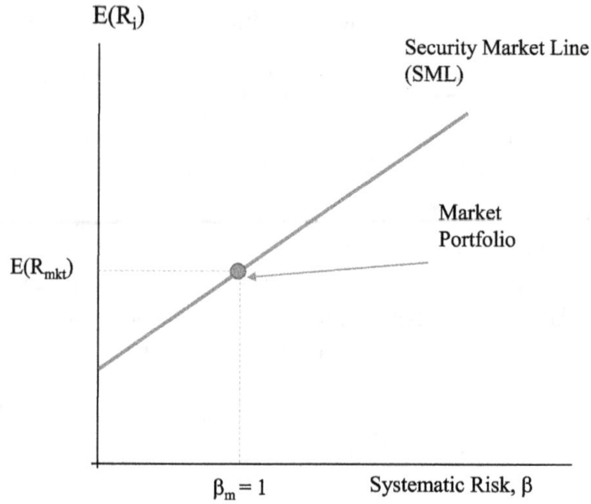

Figure 36.14: SML and market portfolio.

which can be rearranged and stated as

$$E(R_i) = r_f + \frac{cov_{i,m}}{\sigma_m^2}[E(R_m) - r_f]$$

By using Equation (36.23) which defines, we arrive at the CAPM equation:

$$E(R_i) = r_f + \beta_i[E(R_m) - r_f] \tag{36.25}$$

where r_f is the risk-free asset and the y-intercept on the graph, β is the beta of the portfolio i, and $[E(R_m - r_f)]$ is the market risk premium.

Example:
An analyst acquired the following information:

Portfolio	Expected returns (%)	Standard deviation (%)	Correlation (portfolio, market)
A	10	20	0.4
B	16	25	0.5
C	12	20	0.6

Which portfolio has the highest beta?

(a) A
(b) B
(c) C

Solution:
Option **b** is correct.

Recall Equation (36.23)

$$\beta i = \frac{\rho_{im}\,\sigma_i\,\sigma_m}{\sigma_m^2} \qquad (36.23)$$

The market's standard deviation is irrelevant as it is the same for each portfolio. Thus, the portfolio with the highest beta is the one with the highest which is B.

Reference/Further Reading

Bodie, Z., Kane, A., & Marcus, A.J. (2020). *Investments*, 12th edns. Mc-Graw Hill, pp. 275–277, 280–285.

36.5 Sample Questions

Question 1
Which of the following is an example of non-diversifiable risk for a random Company X?

(a) Corporate theft from a rival company
(b) A pandemic sweeping across the nation
(c) CEO of Company X goes missing

Use the following information for Questions 2 to 3:
A portfolio is constructed by purchasing 100 shares each for the following two stocks. The correlation coefficient between the two assets is –0.2:

Stock	Price on purchase	Expected return	Standard deviation
Alpha	3	10%	4%
Omega	8	20%	10%

Question 2
Calculate the standard deviation of the portfolio:

(a) 7.2%
(b) 3.8%
(c) 14.5%

Question 3
You are then given a risk-free asset with an expected return of 1%. What is the Sharpe ratio of the CAL between the risk-free asset and this portfolio?

(a) 0.51
(b) 3.10
(c) 2.25

Question 4
Asset Y's utility (expected return: 10%, standard deviation: 10%) is _______ for an investor with a risk aversion index of 3 than it is for an investor with a risk aversion of 5.

(a) Higher
(b) Lower
(c) Equal

Question 5
According to the capital asset pricing model, which of the following asset betas is most likely to have an expected return lower than the risk-free rate?

(a) 0.1
(b) −0.5
(c) 0

Solutions

Question 1

Solution: Option **b** is correct

Non-diversifiable risk, or market risk, refers to risks that affect all firms in an industry or geography. Options A and C are risks that affect only Company X and are not the answer. Option B Is a risk that will impact every firm in the nation and is thus a market risk.

Question 2

Solution: Option **a** is correct

The weightage of the asset in a portfolio is calculated using Equation (36.4)

$$w_i = \frac{\text{Value of investment } i}{\text{Total value of portfolio}}$$

$$w_{\text{Alpha}} = \frac{3*100}{3*100 + 8*100} = 27.3\%$$

By using Equation (36.11), we find the portfolio standard deviation.

$$\text{VAR}(R_p) = w_1^2\text{VAR}(R_1) + w_2^2\text{VAR}(R_2) + 2w_1w_2\text{SD}(R_1)\text{SD}(R_2)\rho_{12}$$

$$\text{SD}(R_p) = \sqrt{w_1^2\text{VAR}(R_1) + w_2^2\text{VAR}(R_2) + 2w_1w_2\text{SD}(R_1)\text{SD}(R_2)\rho_{12}}$$

$$\text{SD}(R_p) = \sqrt{0.27^2 0.04^2 + 0.73^2 0.10^2 + 2(0.27)(0.73)(0.04)(0.10)(-0.2)}$$

$$\text{SD}(R_p) = 7.2\%$$

Question 3

Solution: Choice **c** is correct.
Using Equation (36.20),

$$\text{Sharpe ratio} = \frac{E(Rp) - r_f)}{\text{SD}(R_p)}$$

$$\text{Sharpe ratio} = \frac{17.3\% - 1\%}{7.2\%} = 2.25$$

Question 4

Solution: Option **a** is correct.

Using Equation (36.16),

$$U = E(r) - \frac{1}{2} A\sigma^2$$

$$U_3 = 0.10 - \frac{1}{2} * 3 * 0.10^2 = 0.085$$

$$U_5 = 0.10 - \frac{1}{2} * 5 * 0.10^2 = 0.075$$

Question 5

Solution: Option **b** is correct.

Using the CAPM Equation (36.25), if an asset's beta is negative, the expected return will be less than the risk-free rates. Examples of assets with negative betas include insurance.

$$E(R_i) = r_f + \beta_i[\mathrm{E}(R_m) - r_f]$$

Chapter 37

Alternative Investments

37.1 Traditional and Alternative Investments

37.1.1 *Differences between Traditional and Alternative Investments*

Alternative investments include private equity (PE) or venture capital (VC), hedge funds, art and antiques, commodities, derivatives contracts. Real estate is also often classified as an alternative investment.

Learning Objectives
- Differentiate between traditional and alternative investments.

Main Takeaways

Main Points
- An alternative investment is a financial asset that does not fall into one of the conventional equity/income/cash categories.
- Alternative investments tend to be somewhat illiquid due to their lack of traditional markets and limited activities on both sides of the deal.
- Certain alternative investments lack an efficient market mechanism and may subject their valuation to speculations, creating uncertainties. Risks of alternative investments increase due to the absence of ready valuation information.
- There are two primary investment strategies, active (alpha seeking) and passive (buy and hold).

Main Terms

- **Absolute returns:** It refers to the amount of funds investment has earned. Also referred to as the total return, the absolute return measures the gain or loss experienced by an asset or portfolio independent of any benchmark or other standard.
- **Passive management:** Replicates a specific benchmark or index to match its performance.
- **Active management:** Active management portfolios strive for superior returns but take more significant risks and entail more considerable fees.
- **Cyclical stocks:** Volatile stocks that tend to follow trends in the economy

Alternative investments have gained popularity since the mid-1990s. This popularity was led by institutions such as endowments and pension funds, and high-net-worth individuals. There are several alternative investments such as hedge funds, PE, real estate, commodities, precious metals, and collectibles that are perceived to provide diversification and return opportunities. This section will consider the nature of alternative investments and the difference between alternative investments and traditional investments.

(a) What are Alternative Investments?

In most cases, alternative assets are perceived as different from traditional investments like stocks and bonds; they expand investors' investment opportunities. The expansion of the investment opportunity set means that additional assets are created, providing more risk-return opportunities.

Alternative investments include investments in such assets as real estate and commodities. Alternative investments also include non-traditional approaches to investing within special vehicles, such as PE funds, hedge funds, and some exchange-traded funds (ETFs). These funds may give the manager flexibility to use derivatives and leverage, make investments in illiquid assets, and take short positions. The assets in which these vehicles invest can include traditional assets (stocks, bonds, and cash) and other assets. Even though many assets can qualify as alternative assets, we will consider the following as alternative assets:

- Real estate investments and other real assets;
- Hedge funds;

- Private equity;
- Complex structured products.

The best-known alternative asset classes are hedge funds and PE. PE is investing in companies before issuing securities publicly or taking a company private. Investors own real estate property or securities issued by real estate companies such as real estate investment trusts (REITs). Other real assets include timberland, precious metals, and even art and other collectibles. This section will only discuss hedge funds, PE, and real estate investments. Complex structured products involve technical requirements beyond the coverage of the CFtP certification.

The Yale endowment's outstanding performance highlighted the benefits of investing in alternative assets. The Yale Model was developed by David Swensen and Dean Takahashi and is described in Swensen's book Pioneering Portfolio Management.[1] Revolutionary at the time was Swensen's recognition that liquidity is not a bad thing to be avoided but rather a good thing to be sought out. Thus, the Yale Model is characterized by relatively heavy exposure to asset classes such as PE compared to more traditional portfolios.

This investing — allocating only a small amount of traditional US equities and bonds and more to alternative investments — is followed by many larger endowments and foundations and is also known as the "Endowment Model" (investing).

(b) Nature of Alternative Investments

Alternative investments can be illiquid and transacted in inefficient markets. An illiquid market is one in which it will be challenging to sell the asset due to expenses, lack of interested buyers, or other reasons. In an inefficient market, investors with superior information can achieve abnormal returns. Hedge funds are often illiquid with redemption restrictions, along with an initial "lock-up" period for new investors.

Alternative investments provide different risk-return trade-offs than traditional investments such as equity or bonds. Further, diversification results from investing in alternatives as the correlation between the return on alternative assets and traditional assets are low.

---

[1] Swensen, D.F. (2000). *Pioneering Portfolio Management: An Unconventional Approach to Institutional Investment.* Free Press, U.S.

Other distinctive characteristics of alternative investments are listed below:

1. Subject to little investor protection regulation, but with restricted sale requirement to unqualified investors.
2. Lower transparency — increased risks in alternative investment due to lack of information, making monitoring and fund valuation difficult.
3. Higher fees — costs of purchase and sale may be relatively high.
4. The minimum investment is significantly larger compared with mutual funds or unit trusts.
5. Analysis using published data are subjected to biases, leading to estimates of higher returns and lower volatility.

(c) Traditional versus Alternative Investments

Defining what an alternative investment is can sometimes be subjective. In the equity asset class, we commonly define PE as an alternative investment, but other equity securities issued by firms are traditional investments. So, why the difference? We would conclude that PE is not listed on the stock exchanges, while traditional equity securities are listed. We now have more insights that traditional equity securities are priced and transacted frequently than private securities.

However, the lines between traditional and alternative assets are not always distinct and universal. For example, hedge fund-like returns are now available in publicly traded "liquid alternative" mutual funds called collective investment trusts (CITs). However, not all hedge fund strategies are available due to regulatory leverage and illiquidity.

Due to the several ways an investor can gain exposure to the real estate asset class, real estate investment can be traditional and alternative. Physical real estate is an alternative investment, while real estate may be accessed through publicly listed investment pools, such as REITs. However, REIT value can differ from the value of the underlying real assets for several reasons, including marketing expertise, trading of assets, and innovative technology and processes.

Other characteristics that distinguish alternative from traditional investments include:

1. Regulatory factors that influence the nature of an investment. For example, hedge funds are often less regulated than mutual funds.

2. Trading strategies where cash flows can be drastically altered compared to a passive one. The trading strategy in a fixed-income arbitrage hedge fund is drastically different from passive investment in a government bond.
3. Compensation structures that include the fee structures used to compensate and reward managers and financial arrangements that may expose managers to the investment's financial risk may have implications for agency costs and conflicts of interest.
4. Information asymmetries refer to the extent to which market participants possess different data and knowledge. In traditional investments, most securities are regulated and must disclose important information to the public.
5. Trading restriction refers to the inability to contract efficiently, resulting in investors not diversifying adequately. Narrow manager specialization, investment size requirements, and redemption restrictions in some alternative investments exacerbate the sub-optimal allocation limitations for investors.

(d) The Appeal of Alternative Investments

Having defined what alternative investments are from various perspectives, we introduce how and why people pursue alternative investing.

Adding Value through Active Management: Active management refers to buying and selling securities to pursue superior risk and return combinations. Alternative investment analysis typically focuses on evaluating active managers and their active management systems since most alternative investments are actively managed. Active management is the converse of passive investing.

Active management is an essential characteristic of almost all alternative investments. Unlike traditional investing, in which the focus is increasingly on passive portfolio management, alternative investing analyzes a fund or other investment's ability to generate attractive returns through active management.

Achieving Absolute Returns: There are two significant standards against which to evaluate returns in alternative investments: absolute and relative. An absolute return standard means that returns are to be assessed relative to zero, a fixed rate, or a riskless rate. Therefore, they are independent of performance in equity markets, debt markets, or any other markets.

Thus, an absolute return strategy seeks attractive absolute returns — returns unaffected by market directions. An example of an absolute return investment fund is an equity market-neutral hedge fund with equal-size long and short positions in stocks that the manager perceives as being undervalued and overvalued, respectively.

Pursuing Arbitrage and Return Enhancement: The term arbitrage is often used to represent efforts to earn superior returns even when risk is not eliminated. The long and short positions are not in identical assets or are not held over the same time intervals. Because investment professionals use the term arbitrage more loosely, these investment programs can contain active risk and generate relative returns.

An obvious goal of virtually any investor is to earn a superior combination of risk and return. Suppose the primary objective of including an investment product in a portfolio is the superior average returns that it is believed to offer. In that case, that product is often referred to as a return enhancer.

Reduced Risk through Diversification: A primary goal of alternative investing is to reduce risk through diversification. One of the distinguishing features of most alternative investments is their lack of correlation with the major traditional asset classes of public equities and public fixed-income assets. A portfolio containing various alternative assets may reduce risk without a proportionate reduction in expected return. A correlation matrix for traditional and alternative asset returns (2010–2019) is provided in Figure 37.1.

Alternative investments generally have a low correlation with the stock and bond markets that comprise the core of most sizable portfolios. Alternative investments are either driven by different forces than the stock or bond markets or are caused by the same forces but in different directions.

Now, alternative investments do invest in traditional assets. The difference is that non-conventional strategies are used in many cases, resulting in radical outcomes, unlike those managed conventionally, like passive and actively managed strategies adopted by mutual funds or unit trusts. In some cases, alternative investments provide high longer-term returns for investors who can invest for the longer term and bear liquidity risk.

Avoiding Obsolescence: Lastly, savvy investors like Yale have enjoyed a first-mover advantage among endowment funds and benefited from PE

Historical Correlation[1]: January 2010 - December 2019

Click Asset Class to Highlight RESET

	Positive	Negative
High	0.7-1.0	(0.7)-(1.0)
Moderate	0.4-0.7	(0.4)-(0.7)
Low	0.0-0.4	(0.0)-(0.4)

	Investment Grade Bonds	Cash	Commodities	Currencies	Equity Market Neutral	Event Driven	Global	Hedge Funds	International Equity	Long/Short Equity	Managed Futures	REITs	S&P 500*
Investment Grade Bonds	1.00												
Cash	0.11	1.00											
Commodities	(0.25)	0.07	1.00										
Currencies	(0.00)	(0.08)	(0.54)	1.00									
Equity Market Neutral	(0.03)	(0.04)	0.37	(0.64)	1.00								
Event Driven	(0.22)	(0.03)	0.57	(0.39)	0.41	1.00							
Global	(0.17)	0.01	0.61	(0.58)	0.47	0.80	1.00						
Hedge Funds	(0.02)	(0.03)	0.51	(0.42)	0.51	0.88	0.83	1.00					
International Equity	(0.11)	(0.00)	0.58	(0.66)	0.53	0.77	0.96	0.81	1.00				
Long/Short Equity	(0.18)	(0.03)	0.52	(0.49)	0.56	0.84	0.90	0.91	0.86	1.00			
Managed Futures	0.42	0.02	(0.07)	0.02	0.11	0.11	0.16	0.47	0.13	0.23	1.00		
REITs	0.30	0.02	0.25	(0.31)	0.28	0.46	0.65	0.54	0.58	0.56	0.29	1.00	
S&P 500*	(0.22)	(0.00)	0.57	(0.46)	0.40	0.77	0.97	0.79	0.85	0.87	0.16	0.65	1.00

Figure 37.1: Historical correlation: January 2010–December 2019.

Source: Calculated by Guggenheim Investments using Bloomberg.com, Barclays.com, and Standardandpoors.com.

investments that facilitated access to top-tier managers who were able to invest in attractively priced opportunities.

(e) Summary

There are several alternative investments, and they differ in characteristics, limitations, and trade-offs between expected return and risks. Most alternative investments lack transparency. For example, we would be hard-pressed to know a hedge funds' portfolio holding, even a limited fund partner, and performance in some PE are hard to track. In real estate, the valuation of assets can be stale. The other problem is the lack of liquidity — like investments in some public and private projects with long gestation periods. While this lack of liquidity is not a significant issue with longer-term investors, concerns remain, especially in times of significant financial stress and tight liquidity, like the recession in 2008–2009.

Reference/Further Reading

Anson, M.J.P., Black, K.H., Kazemi, H., & Chambers, D.R. (2015). *Alternative Investments*, 3rd edn. John Wiley & Sons Inc., pp. 3–21.

37.2 Hedge Funds

37.2.1 *Overview of Hedge Funds*

Hedge funds are alternative investments using pooled funds that employ different strategies to earn active return, or alpha, for their investors.

Learning Objectives

- Distinguish types of hedge funds and various strategies used.

Main Takeaways

Main Points

- Hedge funds, as compared to publicly traded mutual funds, are less regulated. The lower regulation is that private investment vehicles are not open to the general public.
- Profits in hedge funds can be generated from long positions and short positions, all in equal measure.
- Hedge funds employ a variety of strategies to generate alpha. Hedge fund strategies include long-short equity, market neutral, volatility arbitrage, and merger arbitrage.
- These funds may be managed aggressively or use derivatives and leverage to generate higher returns.
- Hedge funds concentrate on absolute performance.
- Hedge fund return may be skewed, making the assessment of management skills difficult.

Main Terms

- **Leverage:** Results from using borrowed capital as a funding source when investing in expanding the firm's asset base and generating returns on risk capital.
- **Active Return:** It refers to the returns produced by an investment portfolio due to active management decisions made by the portfolio manager that cannot be explained by the portfolio's exposure to returns or risks in the portfolio's investment benchmark.

- **Arbitrage:** The simultaneous purchase and sale of an asset to profit from a difference in the asset's price between markets.
- **Short Sell:** Happens when an investor borrows a stock, sells the stock, and then repurchases the stock to return it to the lender. Short sellers are betting that the stock they sell will drop in price.
- **Skewness:** It describes a distribution where the normal bell-shaped distribution is not symmetrical. A negative skew (i.e., a left-leaning bell) indicates more negative observations or downside exposure, while a positive skew (or a right-leaning bell) shows a positive bias.
- **Kurtosis:** A term used to describe the condition where the outlying observations occur more frequently or less frequently than the normal distribution.

The traditional mutual fund manager's performance is based on how the fund performed relative to a benchmark. However, many investors are more interested in absolute performance than relative performance. One of the essential alternative investments is hedge funds concentrating on absolute performance. In this section, hedge funds nature, the difference between hedge funds and traditional funds, the strategies used by hedge funds, and hedge funds' historical performance will be discussed.

(a) What are Hedge Funds?

Traditional investment strategies typically involve the purchase of money market, bond, or equity securities at a price deemed attractive by the individual or the portfolio manager and selling (or taking profit) at a higher price. However, many additional instruments and strategies have evolved that involve more complex strategies than the straight buy/hold/sell approach, and these strategies collectively are called "alternative investments". Hedge funds are a subset of this universe of alternative investments.

Hedge funds are heterogeneous in their strategies, mandates, and structures used to manage the funds. Generally, hedge funds offer the opportunity for attractive, consistent returns with less onerous constraints on liquidity than, for example, PE. Some hedge funds invest in arcane areas of the market or utilize quantitative strategies that are difficult to understand. Many invest in familiar listed securities and use strategies that are not overly complex. Hedge funds also have no limitations on the markets they invest in geographically or by asset-classes.

Hedge funds have evolved with few legislative or regulatory constraints, and over the years, they have moved in many directions. While being heterogeneous, hedge funds have certain characteristics in common:

- They continue to be private investment vehicles.
- They are not offered for sale to the public and are therefore exempt from many regulatory (e.g., SEC) requirements.
- The hedge funds are given more latitude because they are designed for sophisticated investors.
- Despite the broad exemption, they must satisfy specific disclosure requirements in offering their securities as well as anti-fraud and money laundering provisions.
- They are prohibited from advertising or broadly marketing their products.
- They have broad discretion over what they invest in and how.

Hedge funds are free to take both long and short positions, to concentrate assets in a small number of holdings, and to use leverage to any degree they choose. They can invest in a wide array of markets using virtually any investment strategy. On the other hand, hedge funds have specialized expertise and a prudent to limit themselves to a small number of markets and strategies. Lastly, hedge funds are open only to institutional investors and accredited investors as measured by income and net worth.

(b) Entry and Exit Conditions

Hedge funds virtually all require what most would consider a high account minimum. Hedge funds also limit when investors can get in or get out. Hedge funds open to new investors only at specified intervals, such as once every quarter. A hedge fund may permanently close to new investors after reaching a target amount. Investors can redeem their interests only by selling them back to the fund in the US, while a few offshore funds may be traded in stock exchanges. Many funds also impose an initial lock-out period, typically 1 year in length. Withdrawals may require some notice period.

Because of hedge funds' high investment minimums and somewhat limited liquidity, hedge fund investors' universe is essentially limited to two groups: High net-worth families and institutional investors.

(c) Fee Structure

The fee structure is different between hedge funds and traditional mutual funds. Traditional management fees are calculated as a percentage of the assets under management. The fee is charged regardless of how well or how poorly the investment performs. Hedge fund managers charge an asset-based management fee, too, typically 1–2% per year. The real motivation lies in the annual performance fees, which generally are 20% of the profits. This incentive fee is usually paid quarterly but sometimes annually. This incentive fee has to be earned. Sometimes, hedge funds specify a hurdle rate — a level of return that must be achieved before profit participation begins to kick in.

Often, the Treasury bill rate or Libor is used as the hurdle rate. Another standard provision is for a "high-water mark". The high-water mark stipulates that if managers incur net losses in a given year, they must recoup those losses before earning their performance fee the following year. This provision is essential as most hedge fund strategies are most successful when applied to a smaller account base. Sophisticated investors also prefer a fee-based structure like this.

(d) Hedge Fund Tools

Hedge Funds use various strategies, providing a range of risk-return combinations that range from non-leveraged hedge styles to highly leveraged directional approaches. Also, hedge funds use a host of tools and techniques. Major tools used are:

- Leverage;
- Short selling;
- Hedging;
- Arbitrage.

Leverage: While undertaking leverage, the belief is that return from the position will exceed borrowed funds' cost. Managers use leverage to put on new, favorable positions without taking off other positions prematurely. Since leverage increases risk, the manager may target small spreads and use leverage to magnify these discrepancies' returns.

Short Selling: Short selling means selling a security that you do not own. The collateral consists of other securities or Treasury Bills. Proceeds from a short sale earn interest until the position is closed. Different strategies use short selling in various fashions. The trading technique aims to drive profit, acting as a hedge against market declines. The only condition is that securities must be available to short sell.

Hedging: Hedging means taking a secondary position to counterbalance a known risk involved with a primary position. Hedging can be done by taking positions in specifically related securities for specific risks or purchasing index options for market risks. These positions are taken to offset changes in economic conditions other than the core investment idea, such as a change in the overall level of stock market prices, a change in interest rates, or a change in the exchange rate.

Arbitrage: Arbitrage involves the simultaneous purchase and sale of a related or similar security to profit from a pricing imbalance. Hedge fund strategies are typically risk arbitrage strategies. In these strategies, the hedge fund managers expect the pricing imbalance to be in one direction and form their arbitrage strategy based on this belief. However, if the price imbalance does not correct itself or moves in the other direction, hedge funds can face losses.

Instruments Used by Hedge Funds: Many hedge fund strategies use, in addition to stocks and bonds, instruments avoided by traditional investment funds such as

- Futures;
- Options;
- Asset-backed securities;
- Bank debt;
- Trade claims of companies with low credit or in bankruptcy proceedings.

(e) Crucial Differences between Hedge Funds and Traditional Funds

The following table summarizes the main differences between traditional funds and hedge funds.

	Hedge funds	Traditional funds (mutual funds)
Risk	The potential loss of invested capital.	Deviation/tracking error from a benchmark.
Return	Aim to deliver absolute returns, depends on the skill of hedge fund managers, mandated to beat the cash rate regardless of how well/bad the market is performing, low correlation with market activity, and non-linear returns-(optionality).	Aim to deliver relative returns, depends on the asset class's performance, relative return targets, highly correlated to returns of standard asset classes.
Investment strategies	Flexible, use long & short, leveraged, dynamic trading strategies, choose among various asset classes.	Limited, long-only, restricted use of leverage, buy-and-hold.
Fees	Pegged to performance, watermark feature, make up for previous losses before getting paid.	Pegged to assets under management (AUM), i.e., management fees.
Life span & size	Averaging about 5 years, very few survive > 10 years.	Comparatively longer life span.
Liquidity	Liquidity restrictions and initial lock-up periods.	Good liquidity.
Investment size	Usually, a large minimum initial investment.	Small minimum initial investment size.
Regulation	Less regulated, less mandated disclosure, limited risk exposure transparency, restrictions in marketing funds publicly.	Highly regulated, restricted use of short selling and leverage, high disclosure and transparency, can market fund publicly.

(f) Strategies Used by Hedge Funds

While hedge funds are heterogeneous, hedge fund strategies can be classified into two main categories: Directional and non-directional.

Directional strategies are easy to understand. They bet that one sector or another will outperform other market sectors. In contrast, non-directional strategies are usually designed to exploit temporary misalignments in security valuation. For example, a fund buys shares in Bank A and sells shares in Bank B in Singapore. Economic prospects drive banks' prospects in Singapore, so this is a bet on Bank A and Bank B's relative performance.

A further refinement categorizes strategies as relative value arbitrage, event-driven equity hedge (EH), and global macro.

We also have sub-categories of strategies as follows:

Relative value arbitrage:
- Fixed-income arbitrage;
- Convertible arbitrage;
- Equity market neutral.

Event-driven:
- Merger (risk) arbitrage;
- Distressed securities;
- Event-driven and special situations.

Equity hedge:
- Directional;
- Sector funds;
- Emerging market funds;
- Short selling.

Macro investing:
- Discretionary;
- Systematic.

Various strategies have very different risk/reward characteristics. Some are aggressive (discretionary macro investing), and some are conservative (equity market neutral, EMN). Thus, risk, as well as returns, are different. Figure 37.2 summarizes the categories of strategy and indicates roughly the exposure to market risk and where the strategy falls in terms of directional or non-directional bets.

We next describe the broad categories and sub-categories' rudiments by the different types of strategy.

(g) Relative Value Arbitrage

These funds seek to profit from temporary anomalies between related securities, for example, securities with a similar capital structure within the same industrial sector, by being simultaneously long and short.

Fixed-Income Arbitrage: Fixed-income arbitrageurs take long and short positions in similar fixed-income securities and their derivatives.

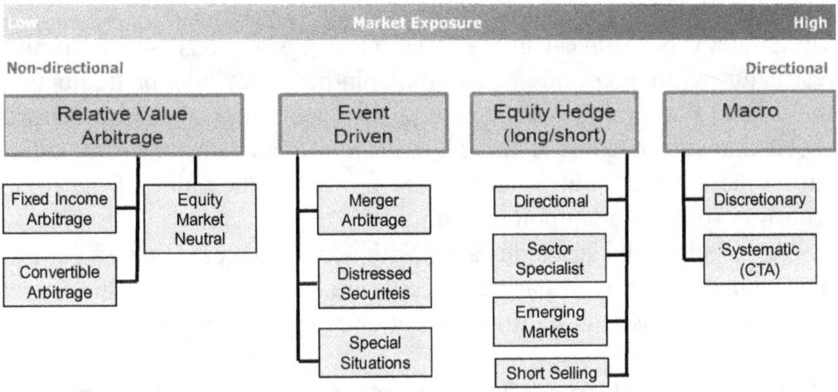

Figure 37.2: Categories of strategies.

The value of these instruments is mathematically or historically interrelated. However, that relationship is temporarily out of sync. The arbitrageurs realize a profit when the relationship between the securities behaves as they expect. Often spread relationships identified are only a few basis points from where they should be. High leverage is required to make a significant amount of money on such a trade.

Convertible Arbitrage: This strategy seeks to profit from the price relationship between convertible bonds and underlying common stocks. Convertible arbitrageurs extract arbitrage profits from these complex pricing relationships by buying convertible bonds and short selling the underlying stock. Generally, convertible bonds decline less rapidly than the stock in a falling equity market and mirror the stock price more closely in a rising market.

(h) Equity Market Neutral

An EMN strategy involves constructing portfolios that consist of approximately offsetting long and short equity positions. EMN specialists use sophisticated quantitative and qualitative models to select stocks while controlling exposure to systematic risk by balancing long and short exposure to various market factors.

Different long and short positions from the models are screened for elements that the models may miss before the positions are put on. Positions are re-evaluated and re-balanced regularly.

(i) Event-Driven

The strategy is to invest in corporate change situations — bankruptcy, restructuring, merger and acquisition, spin-off, asset sale, or liquidation. Significant corporate events create profit opportunities because the proposed changes' outcome is uncertain. Profits are made by correctly anticipating these events' outcomes and the impact on the value of the firm's securities towards and upon resolution.

As event-driven strategies are positioned to take advantage of corporate events' valuation disparities, returns are less dependent on the overall market conditions than traditional debt or equity approaches.

Merger (Risk) Arbitrage: The core strategy is leveraging opportunities such as mergers or a hostile takeover. The method involves buying shares of the target and short selling the acquirer's shares in some situations. Targets will usually sell at a discount relative to value after a merger because of the risk that the merger may not be completed. The fund will make profits if it correctly anticipates the outcome and captures the spread between the target's current market price and the price to which it will appreciate if the deal is completed.

The merger arbitrage is event-driven and not market-driven, and hence it has a low correlation with the market. It will depend on the overall volume of merger activity rather than market direction.

Distressed Securities: The strategy is to invest in companies that are experiencing financial or operational difficulties. The company may be in default, under bankruptcy protection, in distress, or heading towards such a condition. Distressed securities specialists hope to buy the distressed firm's securities at a low price, with profits gained when the firm comes out of distress resulting in the recovery of security prices. These specialists can tolerate long periods of illiquidity while looking for an exit catalyst for their holdings. In some cases, a specialist may sell existing holding for other firm securities if this action provides a more significant upside. Specialists can play an active role in the distress/bankruptcy restructuring process.

(j) Equity Hedge

The strategy is to combine long holdings of equities with short sales of stock or stock index derivatives. EH portfolios can be adjusted to long bias (net long) or short bias (net short) depending on market conditions. Leverage can be used to boost profits.

Theoretically, EH specialists can make money in both up and down markets because they retain the flexibility to go both long and short.

Emerging markets are a category of hedge funds (especially in the US) that specialize in such markets. The short-selling specialist focuses solely on selling overvalued securities and diversifying long-only investors.

Directional: This EH category is the generic ones that change their bets depending on market outlook — being long when markets are expected to perform well and vice versa.

Sector Funds: These fund managers confine their investment universe to a specific industry or a segment of the economy or other groupings that share a common product, market, or theme.

(k) Macro Investing

Macro investing hedge funds include discretionary and systematic funds. Discretionary funds can take advantage of extreme price valuations produced by extraordinary sets of macro conditions because they have the flexibility to move large amounts of capital into a variety of different investment positions in a timely fashion.

Macro investors look for the extraordinary sets of macro conditions that occasionally occur and make a particular investment approach very effective while those conditions persist. While representing a small percentage of hedge funds in numbers, individual macro managers have the largest asset size under management in the industry.

The systematic strategy (referred to as Commodity Trading Advisors, CTAs) and sometimes as Managed Futures); involves professional fund managers who invest in the global futures and options markets. Many CTAs adopt medium to long-term trend-following, trying to profit from up and down trends in various markets. As compared with other Macro strategies, CTAs have longer investment time horizons but more frequent adjustments. Underlying the trend-following approach is the concept of portfolio insurance, where periodic adjustments can be made to asset weights to allow downside protection while allowing for some investment upside.

(l) Fund of Hedge Funds

Investors can invest in a fund of hedge funds that invest in several different hedge funds — as few as 5 or 6 or as many as 20 or more. So a fund of funds is a one-stop-shop whose professional manager does the rest for you. Compare with the amount required to invest in an individual fund, the amount needed for the fund of funds is generally less. Further investors are provided diversification as many funds of funds invest in different hedge fund securities. Fees are higher. Investors pay fees to investee funds indirectly. They also pay a management fee of about 1–2% of assets under the management. On the other hand, investors pay for the expertise whereby individual funds are selected for investing and regular monitoring of the invested funds.

(m) Analyzing Hedge Fund Returns

One of the crucial value propositions is investing in managers who are skillful in managing their investment funds for hedge funds investors. Now, we can simplify the manager's investment skills demonstrating: (1) prowess — the manager's ability to identify and capitalize on situations that have a higher reward at lower risk than perceived by the market, and (2) risk management — the manager's ability to cut losses and let winners run.

Hedge fund managers manage their risk by: (1) closing positions outright to limit the downside but capping the upside, and (2) buying protection — using derivatives to transfer risk to another party, but incurring hedging cost and again limiting the upside.

Hedge managers trade and risk manage their positions with a wide array of strategies and instruments and synthesizing payoff in the process. Hedge fund returns can be positively or negatively skew (long tail in the probability density function) compared with the normal distribution) in mutual fund manager returns. Hedge fund returns can also exhibit leptokurtosis (or fat-tails).

Fat Tails and Skewness: Traditional performance measures use CAPM-based risk-adjusted measures discussed in Chapter 38. One common measure used is the Sharpe Ratio. Four researchers from Yale have shown that you can increase the Sharpe ratio of a portfolio of assets by selling calls and putting options on the underlying. The resulting portfolio distribution is also negatively skewed. We need to move beyond performance measures based on the underlying return distribution is normal. We have introduced the Sortino ratio again in Chapter 38. Another useful performance measure is the Omega measure.[2]

(n) Hedge Fund Assessment and Monitoring

Hedge funds being a sophisticated investment that is not always transparent requires a thorough assessment before investing and regular monitoring as market conditions change regularly, and managers often need to take action. Hedge fund management is an area where hedge fund managers' skills are paramount. In money management, support processes and resources also matter. We discuss these factors below.

The Fund Strategy: We need to know the details as the description of strategies is highly subjective. Details will involve sample trades to understand reward and risk trade-offs of the strategies employed. If the fund switches strategies, we need to know why. Going forward, we need to know if the strategies used are scalable. Lastly, we need to confirm if returns are consistent with the strategies described, area of risk concentration, illiquid positions held, and also to compare with close competitors.

The Fund Itself: We need to know essential information about a hedge, including fund domicile and legal structure of the fund, regulation exemptions, location of the fund's asset, and persons responsible for transfers. The fund's prime broker is essential, given the Lehman Brothers debacle. In terms of key personnel, the board of directors, significant clients, and if any client is receiving preferential terms. Other essential information is the subscription and redemption policy and fees and expenses, and how the funds' positions are valued.

The Management Team: As the manager's skill and expertise are crucial, information like expertise and background must be assessed. Compensation for key personnel and the fund's vulnerability to a particular manager's departure is also essential. Other information to assess motivation include the key partners and their contributions to the fund and if there is a potential conflict of interest like managers managing several funds simultaneously.

---

[2]Keating, & Shadwick (2002). A Universal Performance Measure. *Journal of Performance Measure*, 6(3).

The Infrastructure: In addition to the manager's skills, a hedge fund will need resources to support its operations. The resources include front office analytics, middle office risk management systems, back-office accounting and executions systems, how the various systems communicate and reconcile with one another, and critical updates shared to clients. There should be adequate backup and recovery processes in case of disaster.

The Process: The work processes for making investment decisions have to be detailed and safeguards to prevent unauthorized trading. An independent risk management system should exist in the hedge fund, with clear risk limits and a line of reporting from the unit to top management. The reconciliation process for trade and accounting decisions both internally and with the prime brokers must be well designed. Lastly, the fund's cash balances as a buffer must be rationalized.

References/Further Readings

Anson, M.J.P., Black, K.H., Kazemi, H., & Chambers, D.R. (2015). *Alternative Investments*, 3rd edn., John Wiley & Sons Inc., pp. 16–21.

Lhabitant, F.S. (2006). *Handbook of Hedge Funds*. John Wiley & Sons Inc.

37.3 Private Equity

37.3.1 *Introduction*

PE is an alternative investment class and consists of capital that is not listed on a public exchange.

Learning Objectives

- Define PE and assess stages of the VC process.

Main Takeaways

Main Points

- PE is composed of funds and investors that directly invest in private companies or engage in public companies' buyouts, resulting in public equity's delisting.
- PE can take various forms, from complex leveraged buyouts to VC.
- Most PE firms are open to accredited investors or those who are deemed as high-net-worth.

- Private securities are often regarded as highly illiquid. However, investors in the private markets expect to be compensated with higher returns for the additional limitations.
- VC financing is funding provided to companies and entrepreneurs. It can be provided at different stages of their evolution.

Main Terms

- **Venture capital:** A form of PE and a type of financing that investors provide to start-up companies and small businesses that are believed to have long-term growth potential.
- **Leveraged buyout (LBO):** The acquisition of another company using a significant amount of borrowed money to meet the acquisition cost.
- **Liquidity:** It refers to the ease with which an asset, or security, can be converted into ready cash without affecting its market price.

PE describes any type of funding for a privately held business. These businesses can be large and small. We will use PE and VC interchangeably to refer to the same activity in our context. Specifically, VC/PE is involved in financing:

- Start-ups firms (VC in the narrow sense);
- Mid-stage firms (growth capital);
- Matured companies (leveraged buyouts);
- Decline companies (distressed securities).

This section focuses on start-up and growth capital to a lesser extent.

(a) What is Venture Capital?

In the narrow sense, VC refers to risk capital for start-ups, embryonic companies that have just begun developing new products, services, or markets. However, in the broader sense, VC refers to risk capital for any form of business, from "seed capital" for start-ups, to funding leveraged buyouts and turnarounds. PE provides funding to start-ups in exchange for equity because they expect or hope that their shares will skyrocket in value.

(b) Debt and Equity Investment

Typically, PE firms invest in subordinated debt and equity.

Subordinated Debt: Subordinated debt is a semi-secured investment in the company (through a debenture) ranking below the secured lenders (chartered banks, trust companies, etc.) that often require periodic repayment. In the case of default, creditors with subordinated debt wouldn't get paid out until after the senior debt holders were paid in full. Subordinated debt is, therefore, riskier than unsubordinated debt.

Equity Investment: Equity investments are common or convertible preferred shares in the company that is repaid when the company is sold or goes public. A single deal can now involve common equity, convertible preferred equity, and subordinated debt.

PE's return will be based on the capital appreciation of its investment over the time it is held. The greater its growth and appreciation, the more profitable the investment.

Angel Investors: Angels are a specific venture capitalist (in the narrow sense). They generally are individuals in a community who invest in local businesses. They are generally less formal and less public in their approach to investing. Small businesses seeking more modest equity investment, informal investors known as angels often fill the gap between "love money" (money from friends and relatives) and formal PE. Angels play an important role in providing investment capital to small and medium-sized businesses.

Angels are accredited investors, meaning that they are somewhat wealthy and usually invest in start-ups. Companies typically seek angels as their first source of funding after friends and family. They are an excellent source of money as they usually ask for lower equity stakes in the company and dare to risk investing in companies at stages that are judged to be too early by the PEs. Angels also offer more chance of secure financing than PEs and are dedicated to their resources and time to grow.

(c) Generic Investment Process

Figure 37.3 provides the generic process for a PE investment. The diagram highlights critical functions that are carried out and important milestones. For brevity, only some of the processes are described in detail.

Deal Sourcing: Investors spend time and effort to find "good" investments. The characteristics of attractive deals include uniqueness

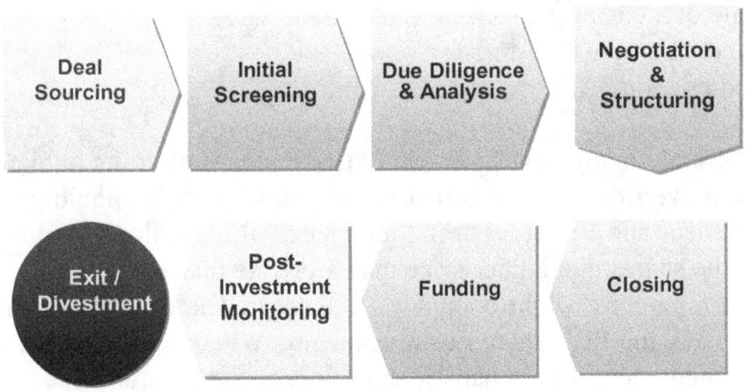

Figure 37.3: Generic investment process for private equity.

(of product or service), management (indicates experience and competence), potential profits, and value upon exit.

Deal Negotiation: Theoretically, the deal structure provisions are designed to control agency costs in the investor-entrepreneur relationship. Both the entrepreneur and PEs have to bear in mind that the negotiation will set the tone for their possible future working relationship. One important contention is while entrepreneurs are unwilling to give up portions of their company, PEs find that taking a small stake in a company is usually not helpful to their investment objectives.

PEs usually base their calculation on how much the entire company is worth by the percentage of their holdings. Using their investments and considering the upside and downside risk, additional funds needed, and exit strategy, they can derive how much they are willing to pay for a stake in the start-up.

Exit Strategy for PE: PEs are not in the business of owning or operating companies. Thus, they are not interested in owning a minority or majority share of the venture. They are more concerned about building up the start-up in a period and cashing in their position by selling their share in the companies; turning their ownership into cash is their only form of reward.

There are five ways PEs can cash in:

1. Going public;
2. Repurchase by entrepreneur;

3. Sale of a business to a third party (trade sale);
4. Finding a new investor;
5. Liquidation.

There are many advantages and disadvantages of going public; however, the overriding factor is that going public provides liquidity for the entrepreneur and PEs to cash in their shares. It also allows the company to sell the shares at a higher price than a private placement.

In a repurchase of the company, the entrepreneur can negotiate a price to buy back the PE's share of the company. Without sufficient cash, the entrepreneur can go for a bank loan to finance the repurchase.

When selling the entire business to a larger company, the PE and entrepreneur can liquidate their whole business position. The relationship between the PE and entrepreneur is also dissolved through the sale. There are a few ways to sell the business:

- Selling stock for cash, notes, or stock.
- Selling assets for cash, notes, or stock.

In a sale to a third party, the acquirer might sometimes require the entrepreneur to stay with the business long enough to let them know about the company and prepare a management team to run the business during the transition period. In another type of sale, the buy-sell agreement requires that the PE or entrepreneur buy out the other party's share on the same terms and conditions offered by a third-party acquirer if either party refuses to sell out.

The entrepreneur may sometimes find an investor willing to take over ownership of the PE's business position. In other situations, another PE might be interested in purchasing the current PE shares, and the new PE may loan money to the entrepreneur to buy out the current PE. The new PE is typically a medium-investor whose focus is on third or fourth-round financing where the business conditions are more stable.

The whole business is liquidated in the last exit strategy if it performs poorly. Selling the valuable assets — land, building, equipment, and others — might be easier than finding a buyer for the whole company. In a typical situation, entrepreneurs would find it more profitable to liquidate their assets than to find a buyer who might buy the business's book value at a considerable discount. However, when book value is worth more than the offer price, it is better to liquidate the assets than to sell out the business to a third party.

(d) Valuation of Investee Companies

One of the more critical aspects of the VC process is its valuation. Various valuation methods can be used to price the transaction, with the most common methods being comparable companies using multiple scenarios.

Analysis of private firms can be very complex. For example, lack of comparable private firms and adjustments required using listed companies. Other issues include:

- Differences in the development stage of the company and comparables.
- Lack of financial history of the company, its growth rate, and its profitability.
- The amount of influence that the venture capitalist can exercise.
- The amount of future dilution expected if additional VC financing is required.

Industry multiples typically create a basis for the valuation process. The commonly used multiples are based on revenue and earnings. These multiples are influenced by the attractiveness of the market in which the company operates, competition among other investors to be part of this financing, the stage of the company's development, and how other relevant or comparable public companies are valued.

	Pessimistic	Expected	Optimistic
Probability of Outcome	30%	50%	20%
Revenue in Year 6	$10,000,000	$25,000,000	S40,000,000
Profit Margin	5%	8%	10%
Price/Earnings Ratio at Sale	6	10	15
Company Valuation	$3,000,000	S20,000,000	$60,000,000
Weighted Valuation		S22,000,000	
Annual Required Rate of Return		45%	
Current Valuation		$2,500,000	

Assume that a company is seeking $1 million in VC financing. Three possible outcomes or scenarios — pessimistic, expected, and optimistic — represent different growth and profitability expectations. This company's revenues are expected to be $25 million in 6 years, with a net income margin of 8% in the expected scenario. At a price/earnings ratio of 10, its value is $20 million.

These calculations are repeated for the optimistic and pessimistic cases. Multiply the company value for each outcome with the probability of the outcome, and adding gives the weighted value of the company. Using similar figures stated above, the company's weighted average value is $22.9 million. With the venture capitalist expected to exit from this investment in 6 years and with an annual rate of return of 45%, the company's present value after financing is $2.5 million. The venture capitalist ends up with about 40% ownership for a $1 million investment based on that value.

(e) Due Diligence

This section will touch on the due diligence process when investing in PE. The need to carry out due diligence is first discussed, followed by several parts of the due diligence process. However, as this process involves a whole range of sub-processes, the discussion is not exhaustive.

(f) Need for Due Diligence

To begin, we will first define due diligence as follows:

"Due diligence is a detailed investigation of the business, property, and affairs of a company and is part of the process undertaken by potential investors and partners to analyze and assess the desirability, value, and potential of a business opportunity".

Due diligence is somewhat different than that carried out in an initial public offering (IPOs). Private companies seeking funds are not bound by law to provide the same information level. PE investors need to go through information gathering to make better investment decisions.

(g) The Screening Process

The screening process is usually the first among the many steps required for due diligence. PE investors typically trust sources that they are familiar with and have confidence in, and these include their network of lawyers, portfolio companies, and other respected contacts. Next, business plans that include the business concept, the target market, product offering, distribution channel, level of competition, the management team, and the financials and the amount to be raised are evaluated.

PE investors are also interested to know the quality of the existing investors in the company. A negative signal is if existing investors are unwilling to continue their business investment. Other relevant factors include the quality of customers (existence of impressive customers or partners), frequency of the deal being transmitted to other investors, compatibility with PE's investment strategy, and portfolio compatibility.

(h) Due Diligence Management

In the second process, investors always take a close look at the company's people. Typically, there are two primary assessment methods: the direct (where the investors interact directly with the entrepreneurs) and the indirect way (where investors talk to those who have had past experiences with the entrepreneurs).

At the most basic level, every company's success lies in the hands of the people running it. Thus, the management team's ability in all aspects (from management skills to technical knowledge, etc.) will largely determine the company's success or failure, other things being equal. PE investors focus on management teams because they understand that their investment rests heavily on the many decisions that the management teams make.

(i) Legal Due Diligence

For legal considerations, PE investors will need to know the business's form, e.g., company, partnership, limited liability partnership, etc. The business form is pertinent due to liability and taxation purposes. Additionally, there is also a need to review intellectual property (IP) protection. On IP, it is generally defined as a commercially valuable product of the human intellect that can be protected through patents, copyrights, trademarks, etc.

Some of the critical intellectual property issues include whether the company has ownership of its intellectual property and whether it can exploit or use its intellectual property following its business plan without infringing upon third parties' intellectual property rights. IP is vital for biotech companies since most biotech companies' value is directly associated with their intellectual property value.

On top of IP, other legal considerations will include issues like:

- whether non-competition agreements cover the key employees of the company,
- the nature of security to be used for the investment (e.g., common stock, preferred stock, convertible preferred stock, etc.),
- cost of entry, barriers of entry for competitors, and
- dilution issues as well as board representation issues.

(j) Financial Due Diligence

PE investors prefer to access any historical financial information that companies have compiled. Such financial information will then provide PE investors with vital data to monitor their burn rate. PEs will usually request balance sheets, income statements, and cash flow for companies that are already 1–2 years in operations. Should companies not provide such information, it will be a vital signal that the company's management team is not serious about using the financials to guide the company. However, even when financial statements are provided, PEs will also ensure the validity and accuracy of the information such that they are free of material problems.

Other financial due diligence undertaken by PEs include the source of financing for the company to date, the amount of funding required by the company, the utilization plans for funds raised, the lists for future rounds of financing, and the possibility of finding prospective financers. Finally, investors are expected to conduct their valuation to understand their risk exposure.

References/Further Readings

Anson, M.J.P., Black, K.H., Kazemi, H., & Chambers, D.R. (2015). *Alternative Investments*, 3rd edn., John Wiley & Sons Inc., pp. 613–682.

Anson, M.J.P., Fabozzi, F.J., & Jones, F.J. (2011). *The Handbook of Traditional and Alternative Investment Vehicles*. John Wiley & Sons, Inc., pp. 361–429.

37.4 Real Estate Investments

37.4.1 *Physical Real Estate, Funds and REITs*

There are many ways to invest in real estate: investing in the physical building via a real estate fund, a listed real estate operating company, or buying a listed REIT.

Learning Objectives

- Understand real estate investing and investing in REITs.

Main Takeaways

Main Points

- Investors can gain exposure to real estate directly or via divided claims, publicly traded or private, and debt or equity.

- A REIT is a company that owns, operates, and invests in real estate. REITs trade on stock exchanges. Due to their low betas and low market volatility, there is a limited investment risk for its returns, giving a favorable tradeoff or a high return-to-risk ratio. Furthermore, it provides diversification with its uniqueness.
- REITs distribute dividend income to their investors regularly. Real estate funds see capital appreciation as returns.
- Real estate managers make decisions that can significantly impact returns earned.

Main Terms

- **Security investments:** Financial instruments that can be purchased and held as investments. Held for investment is opposed to trading, i.e., for a short-term purchase or sale. Some of these financial instruments include fixed income or equity assets.

(a) What is Real Estate?

Real estate can be broadly categorized as residential and non-residential.

Residential real estate includes:

- **Residential homes:** The single-family homes to house residents.
- **Multi-family:** These include condominiums and apartments.

Non-residential real estate includes:

- **Shopping malls:** Properties that consist of shops and retailers.
- **Office buildings:** Properties used primarily for offices and work purposes.
- **Warehouses:** Properties for storage of goods.
- **Industrial buildings:** Properties where products are made/transformed.
- **Raw land:** Empty land without a facility yet.

(b) Difference between Real Estate and Security Investments

- Real estate provides a favorable return-to-risk ratio due to its low betas and low market volatility, which brings a limited investment risk for its returns. The return comes from property rental and leasing. Two main risks are the depreciation of the real estate and vacancies in the properties.

- Compared to security investments which can be bought/sold quickly, the real estate market is inefficient as it cannot be traded easily. However, higher gains can be derived from this type of investment.
- Some real estate investments can bring about tax benefits that can increase returns, such as tax incentives from the government.
- Real estate managers make decisions that can significantly impact returns earned.
  These include the price of rentals and leases, which depends on how well the properties are managed.
- There is a low correlation between stock returns and real estate markets based on studies. Adding real estate provides diversification to the portfolio.

(c) Basic Forms of Real Estate Investing

Investors can gain exposure to real estate directly or via divided claims, publicly traded or private, and debt or equity. The four quadrants describe the different forms of real estate investing as shown in Table 37.1.

Every form of real estate investment has its expected returns, set of risks, market structures, legal structures, and regulations. Comparatively, private real estate investments typically involve more considerable sums of investments due to real estate property's indivisibility nature. This lumpiness means that there is lower liquidity. Publicly traded real estate investment allows the real estate property to be undivided, but ownership or claim on the property to be divided. This division provides higher liquidity and investors to diversify by buying interests in many properties, rather than just one.

PE real estate investment requires property management expertise for owning or hiring property managers. REOCs and REITs have real estate

Table 37.1: The four quadrants.

	Equity	Debt
Private	Direct investment into real estate, either through sole ownership, joint venture, limited partnership, or other forms of pooled funds.	Mortgages
Publicly traded	Through the purchase of shares of real estate operating companies (REOCs) and shares of REITs	Mortgage-backed securities (residential and commercial)

managed professionally, and investors need not manage their shares of the REOCs and REITs.

A higher rate of return is required by equity investors, as they bear more risk than debt investors (i.e., lenders). Lenders have a right to claim cash flows and proceeds before equity investors. When the amount of debt increases, financial leverage increases, and debt and equity investors' risk increases. Higher leverage results in an increase in expected return, which may not happen.

Debt investors in private and public markets for real estate expect promised cash flows and returns and do not partake in capital appreciation. The returns to equity real estate investors come in the form of both incomes from rental and capital appreciation from changes in the properties' underlying value. Potential diversification benefits can happen if returns to equity real estate investors are less than perfectly positively correlated with the returns to stocks or bonds, and investors can add real estate to their portfolio to diversify.

The categorization of real estate investment into the four quadrants allows finding the best investment aligned with their objectives, be it liquidity, professional management, or lower risks.

Example on Real Estate Diversification:
An ultra-high net worth investor wishes to add real estate to his portfolio for the first time. He has invested in a traditional portfolio that comprises 60% equity, and 40% fixed income and wishes to add a meaningful portion of his portfolio into real estate for diversification. He does not anticipate any liquidity need for the foreseeable future. Which is the most appropriate form of investment for the investor?

(a) Shares of REITs;
(b) Mortgage-backed securities (MBS);
(c) Direct ownership into residential and commercial real estate properties.

Solution:
Option **c** is correct.

REITs provide liquidity and require a lower investment amount than direct ownership of the real estate, but REITs are more correlated with stock. MBS does not provide much diversification as another debt is already in the portfolio. Direct ownership is much more illiquid, and many properties are required to provide a well-diversified real estate portfolio. Still, the investor does not have immediate liquidity concerns and has the resources to acquire a diversified property portfolio.

(1) Where does the return from real estate come from?

The value of real estate comes from rental charges, maintenance and repairs spending, and consideration for which purchase or lease provisions to be used to transfer certain rights, supply, and demand, etc.

Real estate increases in value during strong markets and decreases in value during weak periods. Macroeconomic issues that affect the real estate market include the interest rate levels, economic outlook, current demand and supply of space, and regional considerations.

Investing in real estate requires buying a selling correctly, but on top of that, choosing the right properties and managing them are essential as well.

(2) Important features and analysis

1. **Physical property:** A site survey can be taken to assess the property's quantity and quality. The survey involves accurate measures with drawings, inspection checks for defects, and review of contractual terms, including ownership of movable items.
2. **Rights to the property:** Legal rights like deeds, titles, easements, liens, and encumbrances need to be made clear and can be done by getting a standard inspection from a qualified lawyer.
3. **Time horizon:** A short-term investor might count on a quick drop in mortgage interest rates and future market expectations. A long-term investor would consider the potential population growth.
4. **Size and location:** The size and location of the investment are essential investment considerations.

(d) Determinants of Value

The major determinants of the value of real estate include:

- Demand;
- Supply;
- The property.

Demand: Demand for real estate is the need and ability to buy or rent a property. Some considerations include employment rate and job market outlook, enrollment rates in schools, expansion of companies and financial institutions, and retailers/wholesalers increasing sales. The upward trend of these may indicate an increase in demand.

Other factors include demographics and psychographics. Variables to consider within demographics are households' size, age, occupation, marital status, and other characteristics. Psychographics refers to aspects such as lifestyle and personality.

Interest rates broadly impact mortgage financing. High-interest rates may cause higher unsold properties, which causes the prices to decline, and low-interest rates will see a rise in prices. However, lower interest rates may not stimulate sales during poor economic conditions.

Lastly, government cooling measures like those implemented by the Singapore government can be promulgated to slow, heated markets. These measures can include a limit on income that can be used to service mortgage payments by individuals or families and increase development changes.

Supply: Examining competitors and sorting them by price and features are essential to analyze supply. The competition includes properties with similar characteristics. For long-term investments, competition can be analyzed with the substitution principle.

The principle is that properties are judged as a set of costs and benefits. Properties should fulfill the needs, which are driving the demand. Competition stems from properties that have similar features and locations. It is crucial to identify appeal factors and examine competitors' pros and cons.

The Property: Demand and supply conditions will be factors to determine real estate prices, which are governed by the needs and prices of available properties. To have a competitive edge for the property, the buyer should consider:

- Location;
- Improvements made;
- Site quality and size;
- Usage restrictions;
- Property management.

Location: "Location, location, and location" are the three most crucial real estate value criteria. Although location is not the single factor affecting value, a good location can increase the property's value and increase its investment potential.

Improvements Made: Improvements include subsequent additions, such as amenities, sidewalks, and buildings refer to the additions to a site such as buildings, sidewalks, and various on-site amenities. The quality of construction, amenities, and floor plans are some factors that affect the value of the property.

Site Quality and Size: Important features of the property include the site size and site quality. Some examples include parking space, land area, elevation, etc.

Usage Restrictions: Local laws and private contracts may limit property owners' rights. Such legal matters include zoning laws, building and occupancy codes, and health and hygiene requirements by the Government. Restrictions from private contracts include deeds, leases, and condominium by-laws, and operating rules. Before investing in a property, it is crucial to ensure that the purpose of purchase of property fits within relevant laws, contract provisions, and regulations.

Property Management: Skilled property management, such as day-to-day manning to ensure the smooth running of investment properties, can maximize cash flows.

37.4.2 *Valuation of Real Estate*

Rentals and lease payments make up the return for real estate investments. On top of that, price appreciation, or the selling price deducting the initial purchase price, takes up another part of the returns. Thus, it is important to ensure a fair price is paid during purchase, which should be the property's fair value. Some factors that affect fair value include:

- Demand;
- Supply;
- Property;
- Property transfer.

Market value for real estate is the actual worth, which is the indicative selling price under prevailing market conditions. Although properties may sell higher or lower than their true value, Here, are some points to note when estimating a property's fair value:

- Every property is different;
- Terms and conditions may vary for sale;
- Imperfect information of the market;
- Market exposure may take time, a luxury that some sellers may not have;
- Buyers may have to act sometimes quickly.

(a) Estimating Market Value

The cost approach, comparative sales approach, and income capitalization approach are three common approaches to estimate a real estate's fair value.

Cost Approach: The cost approach is based on the construction costs that would have been incurred to construct the property to the existing state. The cost of land is added, and the physical and functional depreciation costs are subtracted. Professional appraisers carry out valuation using the cost approach as it can be subjective.

Comparative Sales Approach: Similar properties in the recently sold locations are examined to determine the average selling price per square foot or the average capitalization rate. The existing property's value can be approximated using these metrics, with leeway for upward/downward adjustments due to external features like aesthetics, hence the subjectivity.

Income Capitalization Approach: This approach determines the value of an investment property based on income generated, based on an estimate of future net operating income that the property would expect to generate. These cash flows or net income is discounted to attain the present value, based on a discount rate. Professionals can make this approach with a good market understanding. Under the income capitalization approach, real estate value is

$$V_{RE} = \frac{NOI_1}{(1+r_{RE})} + \frac{NOI_2}{(1+r_{RE})^2} + \frac{NOI_3}{(1+r_{RE})^3} + \cdots$$

where r_{RE} is the discount rate appropriate for real estate and NOI is the net operating income of the property measured before interest expense, income taxes, and capital gains taxes, but after real estate taxes.

Net operating income is defined as the property's revenue, subtracting expenses excluding finance costs, depreciation expense, and capital expenditure.

Real estate or property taxes are operating expenses, but income and capital gains taxes are not. Thus, net income is a pre-tax cash flow concept.

If the net income is assumed to grow at a constant rate, the valuation formula can be simplified to

$$V_{RE} = \frac{NOI_1}{(r_{RE} - g_{NOI})} = \frac{NOI_1}{r_{CAP}}$$

where r_{CAP} is called the capitalization rate.

The market capitalization rate is usually approximated based on sale prices of similar properties sold recently:

$$r_{CAP} = \frac{NOI \text{ of properties surveyed}}{\text{Sales Price of Properties Surveyed}}$$

(b) Leverage in Real Estate

Since real estate properties' purchase bears high costs, buyers usually take on loans from banks and use leverage. Leverage can cause volatility in investor returns, which is larger than the volatility of the underlying real estate value.

Leverage is positive if the real estate asset's return is higher than the mortgage debt's pre-tax cost to finance the property. Return in the equity of the property exceeds the return on the asset.

Leverage is negative if the real asset's return is lower than the mortgage debt's pre-tax cost to finance the property. Return in the property's equity is lower than the asset's return.

(c) NPV of Real Estate Investments

Real estate incurs high investment costs, and before deciding to invest, the investor should conduct an NPV analysis.

Example:

Assume a property can be purchased for $4,000,000 of which 80% can be financed with a 9%, 155-year mortgage. The net cash flows produced by the property over the next 5 years, including $812,263 in cash expected from selling the property after paying off the mortgage in the fifth year are as follows:

Year	Net cash flow
1	$ 99,052
2	109,215
3	119,623
4	130,270
5	953,414

If the investment requires a 12% on equity, is the property a worthwhile investment?

If 80% of the $4,000,000 price is financed with the mortgage, the investor's equity would be $800,000. Therefore, NPV can be calculated as

$$\mathrm{NPV} = \frac{-800{,}000}{(1.12)^0} + \frac{99{,}052}{(1.12)^1} + \frac{109{,}215}{(1.12)^2} + \frac{119{,}623}{(1.12)^3} + \frac{130{,}270}{(1.12)^4} + \frac{953{,}414}{(1.12)^5} = \$84{,}432$$

Since NPV is positive, the investment is worthwhile.

37.4.3 *Real Estate Investment Trust*

Investment into physical real estate requires a high cash outflow. Another method to invest in the real estate sector is to buy shares in REITs.

(a) Overview of Real Estate Investment Trusts

REITs are collective investment schemes, which means that money is invested in a portfolio of real estate assets that generate income. Experienced professionals would manage the real estate assets. Public REITs trade like stocks on stock exchanges.

(b) Advantages of Owning REITs

REITs allow investors exposure to real estate asset investments. Listed REITs provide liquidity. Advantages of REITs ownership includes:

(1) Real estate assets exposure

- Real estate asset ownership, but with a smaller outlay of capital.
- REITs have access to capital and therefore acquire and build additional properties as part of their ongoing real estate business.
- Provides diversification into an existing portfolio, acts as a hedge against inflation, and thus adds stability to the investment portfolio.

(2) Liquidity and other features

- High dividend yields, with strong potential for increases in value with constant cash flows and the future addition of more properties into the portfolio.
- Owning REITs give a stake in the business, rather than just owning physical real estate assets.
- REITs are professionally managed by management teams who are knowledgeable.

(c) Types of REITs

There are two basic categories of REITs, equity REITs, and mortgage REITs.

Equity REIT: An equity REIT is a publicly-traded company with the principal business of purchasing, managing, renovating, maintaining, and sometimes selling properties. Acquisition and development of properties may be made during favorable economic conditions. It is not taxed at the corporate level, giving it a tax advantage.

Mortgage REIT: A mortgage REIT makes and holds obligations and loans secured by real estate collateral.

We will focus on equity REITs, as for individual investors, there are a few advantages:

- Less vulnerable to changes in interest rates;
- Better total returns historically;
- Relatively stable market-price performance;
- Lower risk;
- Higher liquidity;
- Allow for diversification geographically on top of the type of properties invested.

(d) General Investment Characteristics of REITs

Performance and Returns: REITs generally have a return equal to the return provided by the S&P 500 in the US. Though other stocks have had a higher return, the REITs are different because they have low betas, low market volatility, limited investment risk, and high current returns.

Low Betas: REIT betas average around 0.59. Although it has a low beta, REITs have historically produced low double-digits percentage returns. The low beta provides some cushion to market downturns. Also, REITs offer diversification benefits to the portfolio as it does not move in a perfect correlation with the rest of the equity market.

Low Volatility: Volatility is separate from beta, as a stock with high intraday volatility can have low volatility with the market over a more extended period. There is less concern over major negative surprises. REITs remain attractive with high dividend yields as investors can expect returns despite some short-term market fluctuations.

Low Risk: Ownership and management of Real Estate can bring many risks:

- Mall REITs are subject to the changing tastes and lifestyles of consumers.
- Apartment REITs are subject to overbuilding and declining job growth in the properties' geographical areas.
- Healthcare REITs are subject to politics, such as government cuts in healthcare reimbursement.
- Diversification in sector and geography can reduce these risks for property owners.
- Investment in high-quality REITs brings lower long-term risks than most common stocks.

High Current Returns: REITs' operating income is distributed as dividends to shareholders, on top of the benefit of diversification they provide. Although the dividend distribution will decrease the REITs' value appreciation due to lower reinvestment into the REITs, the high dividends offer a higher total return than many other companies.

Growth Potential: A REIT can grow through:

- Additional share or debt offerings;
- PE placements;
- Exchanging new shares or partnership units for properties;
- Loans from banks or insurance companies.

High-quality REITs usually have easier access to capital in most market environments. Selecting the strong REITs for investment is essential, as these REITs can attract additional capital, which provides high growth potential.

(e) REITs vs. Other Real Estate Investment Vehicles

Private Ownership: Private ownership can sometimes offer higher profits than investing in a REIT, but it requires time and experience to manage the real estate. Furthermore, private ownership usually brings about lower liquidity.

Private Partnership: A private partnership allows for delegating of management to experienced professionals. However, a private partnership is not extensive. Thus only a few properties are owned, which does not give a diversification advantage. The liquidity with the private partnership depends on the partners' financial solvency. Conflicts of interest and personal liability should also be considered if problems arise between partners.

Publicly Traded Limited Partnership: A real estate limited partnership is where a real estate promoter issues partnership shares to the public. The public partners are passive investors. However, due to the high fees and little to no profits for investors, they have failed. Sometimes, it can also be due to late buying into the real estate cycle or mediocre managers.

(f) Relationship of REITs and Fund from Operations

In choosing REIT for investment, the investors will have to look at the funds from operations generated by REIT. The current funds from operations and the prospects for growth in funds from operations will have to be studied.

Ordinary stock investors use net income as the measure of profitability. In REIT, the fund from operations (FFOs) is the most important profitability measure. Using FFO enables both REITs and their investors to correct the depreciation distortion by looking at net income before deducting depreciation expense or adding back depreciation expense to reported net income.

Important note: income from the sale of properties must be subtracted from the net income. Short-term maintenance expenses cannot be considered property-enhancing capital improvements and should be deducted from FFO to provide an accurate picture of a REIT's operating performance. Thus, the adjusted FFOs is used, which is calculated as follows:

Adjusted Fund from Operations (AFFO) are presented below:

- Revenues minus:
  - Operating expenses;
  - Depreciation and amortization;
  - Interest expense;
  - General and administrative expense.
- Net Income minus:
  - Profit from real estate sales Plus;
  - Real estate depreciation = FFO.
- FFO minus:
  - Recurring capital expenditures;
  - Amortization of tenant improvements;
  - Amortization of leasing commissions;
  - Adjustments for rent straight-lining = AFFO.

REITs do not report AFFO, but the investors should estimate AFFO from financial statements.

Dynamics of FFO Growth: A REIT must increase its FFO for the shares to offer a higher return than a less risky bond. Increasing FFO is required as returns on REITs depend on the fluctuation of long-term interest rates and investor perceptions of the REIT's ability to continue paying dividends.

Therefore, it is essential to analyze how a REIT generates growth in FFO per share.

FFO can grow in two ways: externally by acquisitions and developments or internally through a REIT's existing resources. External growth may not always be possible, while internal growth is in the management's hands.

Internal Growth: Internal growth is the growth of profits at the property level through increased rental revenues and reduced expenses at the REIT's properties. Management will break down how much of its increase in FFO derived from same-store rental revenue increases and how much from new stores, recent property developments, and acquisitions. Same-store rental revenues offset by related expenses determine NOI growth, which gives a good overview of how well the REIT is doing with its existing properties.

Avenues for Internal Growth:

- **Clauses in lease contracts**;
- **Percentage rent:** Used in retail-store leases allowing property owners to participate in store revenues if such revenues exceed certain present levels;
- **Rent bumps:** Lease clauses that provide for built-in rent increases every few years and used for long-term leases;
- **Expense sharing:** These clauses require the tenants to share some of the costs of operating the property, including property taxes, property insurance;
- **Tenant upgrades:** Used in retail store property management to replace mediocre tenants with attractive tenants;
- **Property refurbishments:** Upgraded and beautiful property will attract a more stable tenant base and higher rents;
- **Sale and reinvestment:** Sell properties with dim futures and reinvest in properties with better future.

External Growth: External growth can come from:

- Attractive property acquisition;
- Development;
- Expansion.

Acquisition prospects depend on:

- REIT's access to the capital market;
- Cost of capital;
- Strength of the balance sheet;

- Prevailing cap rates on the type of property it wants to acquire;
- The properties have significant NOI growth potential.

Internal Growth: REITs can achieve internal growth by increasing rental rates or decreasing operating expenses. Both of these will lead to an improvement in the profit margin and become more attractive to investors. Controlling operating expenses is the more reliable way of seeking the growth in "funds from operations" because it is independent of external acquisition or development of new properties.

The "same-store sales" metric is used to track a REIT's internal growth. Originally adapted from retail businesses, non-retail REIT sectors can also use the metric. Most REITs report their same-store rental revenues (and growth) quarterly. Same-store rental revenues consider occupancy rate changes after deduction of expenses. Also, this metric allows for comparisons of net operating income (NOI) and performance of REITs relative to previous periods.

REITs' tactics to generate same-store basis growth include rental revenue increments, improvement in tenant mix, and improvement in REITs' existing properties.

Increasing rental revenue is one of the critical drivers of internal growth. The ability of REITs to raise the rental rates and revenues will directly impact the financial performance of the REIT. The properties have to be attractive to tenants to improve the occupancy rate and raise rental income. However, raising rent may not always be feasible due to cyclical constraints in the real estate sector, such as high vacancy rates, which increase tenants' bargaining power in lease negotiations.

Rentals are also dependent on other factors such as supply and demand for that particular property, the economic environment, and the property's existing condition. The vacancy rate tends to rise in periods of recessions that coincide with lower rentals.

One solution to achieving higher rental revenue is focusing on the tenants' needs and financial capacity. Methods include using payment arrangements by percentage rent, rent bumps, and expense sharing and recovery. "Percentage-rent" clauses in retail-store leases allow the property owners to claim a certain proportion of store revenues exceeding a predetermined level. The property owner's bargaining power for such an arrangement arises from the property's location, the market supply, demand forces, the base rent, and the owner's ability to maintain and upgrade the malls to attract shoppers.

"Rent bumps" are contractual lease clauses that allow the property owner to raise their rents periodically. Escalation of rentals can be fixed dollar amounts or index-based, such as the Consumer Price Index. "Expense sharing" or "cost recovery" is an arrangement between the owner and the lessees whereby the cost of common area maintenance and other property maintenance expenses are shared. Cost-sharing clauses improve the NOI and thereby fund operations while reducing operating expenses fluctuations.

In the retail industry, we can also improve rental revenue by enhancing the tenant mix by replacing tenants seeing low sales with more attractive ones. Tenants that can offer innovative products at competitive prices can generate higher customer traffic and are therefore financially able to pay higher rents. Property owners can rebrand their malls through refurbishments to attract new tenants, obtain a better tenant mix, and increase customer traffic.

Occasionally, REITs re-evaluate their portfolio of properties to sell their non-performing assets. The proceeds would be put to better use by acquiring new properties to generate better returns. REITs can also use the proceeds from disposals to take on new developments or reduce debt obligations.

Other Sources of Growth: REITs can also generate growth by acquiring existing properties, expanding existing properties, property development, and joint venture participation. REITs can value-add to an acquired property by using their operating and management expertise to tighten expenses and obtain benefits from economies of scale.

Some REITs prefer to develop new properties to increase their FFOs growth. If the REIT undertakes a development project from scratch with little pre-leasing, the potential returns and risks will be higher. If successful, the REIT's operating income growth and NAV will increase. However, in developing new projects, construction risks such as development costs overrun can significantly reduce expected returns. The REIT can also over-estimate rental income and occupancy rates. Also, since real estate development is capital intensive, REITs face credit risk resulting from a sudden hike in interest rates.

REITs can buy and refurbish completed properties instead of developing new properties. The risks involved are significantly lower as the cost of adding new space to existing properties is less than creating a property from scratch and the percentage return on invested capital from the expansion is often less than building from the "ground-up".

REITs can also form joint ventures (JVs) with institutional partners to acquire, own, and develop properties. Participating in joint venture programs allow a REIT to:

- generate fee income from asset management, acquisition, and financing fees;
- improve their general and administrative cost structure;
- boost return on equity;
- diversify risk; and
- remain active even when market conditions may not be attractive.

Participation in joint ventures can generate additional fee income streams and improve funds from operations growth, thus enhancing shareholders' value. Each JV strategy needs to be evaluated on its own merits with risks and rewards consideration.

(g) Risk in REIT Investing

REITs investments have risks despite the attractive growth factors. REITs' returns are relatively more interest rate sensitive than equities but less sensitive than bonds. A higher yield is expected across all asset classes in a high-interest rate environment, which affects real estate values and REITS.

On top of that, an oversupply of properties in the market will adversely affect REITs' performance, as the underlying assets are ultimately properties. Occupancy rates and rental increment depend on the prevailing demand and supply. Furthermore, tightened liquidity and massive property sell-off in the market during financial crises to raise funds would impact REITs' performance.

References/Further Readings

Anson, M.J.P., Black, K.H., Kazemi, H., & Chambers, D.R. (2015). *Alternative Investments*, 3rd edn. John Wiley & Sons Inc., pp. 341–345, 351–363.

Anson, M.J.P., Fabozzi, F.J. & Jones, F.J. (2011). *The Handbook of Traditional and Alternative Investment Vehicles*. John Wiley & Sons, Inc., pp. 277, 299–312.

Geltner, D., Miller, N., Clayton, J., & Eichholtz, P. (2007). *Commercial Real Estate Analysis and Investments*, 2nd edn. South-Western Educational Publishing, pp. 620–621, 585–592.

37.5 Cryptocurrencies as an Investment Opportunity

We have observed extreme volatility in the cryptocurrency market, with bitcoin surging above the US$40,000 level. However, many continue to argue that cryptocurrencies have no intrinsic value and maybe the perfect vehicle for forming a bubble. They put forth this argument despite cryptocurrencies' payment utility.

Cryptocurrencies have very different characteristics than other digital currencies like the Central Bank Digital Currency (CDBC). We have discussed the CDBC in Module 1A1 Section 7.8. The CDBC is centrally issued, circulated within a community or geographical location, or tied to fiat currency or the organizations issuing them.

The cryptocurrency that uses blockchain technology solves the double-spending problem and does not require a trusted third party. As such, decentralization allows increased capacity, better security, and speedier settlement that overcome shortcomings of traditional financial processes.

To examine the potential of cryptocurrency as an investment opportunity, we can follow traditional finance by evaluating its diversification benefits if added to a portfolio of traditional assets. However, as cryptocurrencies are new and challenging to value, other attraction and risk measures need to be evaluated.

Learning Objectives

- Understand cryptocurrency as an investment opportunity.

Main Takeaways

Main Points

- While cryptocurrencies provide diversification benefits and good risk-adjusted returns, it is preliminary to consider them as an asset class of interest to institutional investors.

Main Terms

- **CRIX index:** The cryptocurrency index (CRIX) is a benchmark for the crypto market follows the Lespeyres construction.
- **Investor sentiments:** Investors' general mood regarding a particular market or asset. It can be generally gauged by reviewing price movement or trading volume.

37.5.1 *Findings and Opinions on Cryptocurrencies*

Adding cryptocurrencies to a portfolio of traditional assets has potential diversification benefits. Lee *et al.* (2018) found low correlations between traditional asset returns and a CRIX using historical data.

However, as cryptocurrencies are digital rather than real assets, investors have difficulties comprehending their fundamental values. As such, cryptocurrency prices are subjected to an investment sentiment factor, much like small stocks that are difficult to value. Assets susceptible to this factor are also difficult to arbitrage, giving rise to short-term fluctuations.

Overall, while good risk-adjusted returns are available, along with diversification benefits when combined with traditional assets, it is probably too early to conclude if indeed cryptocurrencies will be an asset class of interest to institutional clients.

Recently, many have warned that the sharp appreciation of cryptocurrencies is a bubble. Some have even said that cryptocurrencies are not an asset class and not an investment opportunity. Reasons given are: not generating cash, not having earnings, unrelated to global growth, unstable correlations, high volatility, and a poor inflation hedge.

In conclusion, we are still at an early stage. Cryptocurrencies do not look attractive when viewed through traditional lenses. However, given global concerns, like quantitative easing (see Module 1A1 Part B Section 7.6 Monetary Policy Tools), alternative opportunities to invest, transact or store value should be carefully examined, possibly using a different set of eyeglasses.

References/Further Readings

Fox, M. (2020). Goldman Sachs lists 5 Reasons Why Bitcoin is not an "Asset Class" nor a "Suitable Investment" Market BusinessInsider. Retrieved from https://markets.businessinsider.com/currencies/news/bitcoin-goldman-lists-reasons-why-not-asset-class-suitable-investment-2020-5-1029248469?utm_source=markets&utm_medium=ingest.

Lee, D.K.C., Guo, L. & Wang, Y. (2018). Cryptocurrency: A New Investment Opportunity? *Journal of Alternative Investments*, Winter, 20(3), 16–40.

37.6 Sample Questions

Question 1
Alternative investment funds are typically managed:

(a) actively
(b) to generate a positive beta return
(c) assuming that markets are efficient

Question 2
Which of the following hedge fund types is most likely to have a return closest to being risk-free?

(a) A market-neutral hedge fund
(b) A short-selling hedge fund
(c) A long/short hedge fund

Question 3
A merger arbitrage manager meets with a potential client. The manager states the fund has a Sharpe ratio of 2.30. The client remembers that there may be issues with using the Sharpe ratio. Which of the following explains why the Sharpe ratio may be inappropriate for hedge funds and which alternative measure is considered better?

	Reason	Alternative Measure
(a)	Returns are non-symmetric	Downside deviation
(b)	Returns are skewed	Standard deviation
(c)	Returns are normal	Downside deviation

Question 4
A hedge fund has the following fee structure:
Annual management fee based on year-end AUM 2%
Incentive fee 20%
Hurdle rate before incentive fee collection starts 4%
Current high-water mark $610 million

The fund has a value of $583.1 million at the beginning of the year. After 1 year, it has a value of $642 million before fees. The net return to an investor for this year is closest to:

(a) 6.72%
(b) 6.80%
(c) 7.64%

Question 5
An analyst wanting to assess the downside risk of an alternative investment is least likely to use the investment's:

(a) Sortino ratio
(b) Value at risk (VaR)
(c) Standard deviation of returns

Question 6
As part of his standard due diligence process for PE, Tony Tay constructs a scorecard to choose between several PE fund managers (A, B, and C). In going through his due diligence checkpoints, Tony should assess the highest weighting of the following facts?

(a) Many investment advisors have recommended manager A's strategies.
(b) Manager B's firm has had a minimal turnover in its administrative and upper-level staff.
(c) The return of Manager C's fund exceeded its target benchmark by 150 basis points over 2 years.

Question 7
PE funds are most likely to use:

(a) Merger arbitrage strategies
(b) Leveraged buyouts
(c) Market-neutral strategies

Question 8
The first stage of financing at which a VC fund most likely invests is the:

(a) Seed stage
(b) Mezzanine stage
(c) Angel investing stage

Question 9

As the loan-to-value ratio increases for a real estate investment, risk most likely increases for:

(a) Debt investors only
(b) Equity investors only
(c) Both debt and equity investors

The information below is used for Questions 10 and 11

Hui Lin is an investment manager looking to diversify his portfolio by adding equity real estate investments. Lin and his investment analyst, Maria Noor, discuss whether they should invest in publicly traded REITs or public real estate operating companies (REOCs). Noor expresses a strong preference for investing in public REITs in taxable accounts.

Lin schedules a meeting to discuss this matter, and for the conference, Lin asks Noor to gather data on three specific REITs and come prepared to explain her preference for public REITs over public REOCs. At the meeting, Lin asks Noor: "Why do you prefer to invest in public REITs over public REOCs for taxable accounts?"

Noor provides Lin with an explanation of her preference for public REITs and provides Lin with data on the three REITs shown in Exhibits 1 and 2.

The meeting concludes with Lin directing Noor to identify the critical investment characteristics and the principal risks of each REIT and investigate the three REITs' valuation. Specifically, Lin asks Noor to value each REIT using four different methodologies:

Method 1 Net asset value.
Method 2 Discounted cash flow valuation using a two-step dividend model.
Method 3 Relative valuation using property subsector average P/FFO multiple.
Method 4 Relative valuation using property subsector average P/AFFO Multiple.

Exhibit 1 Select REIT Financial Information

	REIT A	REIT B	REIT C
Property subsector	Office	Storage	Health Care
Estimated 12-months cash net operating income (NOI)	$350,000	$267,000	$425,000
Funds from operations (FFO)	$316,965	$290,612	$368,007
Cash and equivalents	$308,700	$230,850	$341,000
Accounts receivable	$205,800	$282,150	$279,000
Debt and other liabilities	$2,014,000	$2,013,500	$2,010,000
Non-cash rents	$25,991	$24,702	$29,808
Recurring maintenance-type capital expenditures	$63,769	$60,852	$80,961
Shares outstanding	56,100	67,900	72,300
Expected annual dividend next year	$3.80	$2.25	$4.00
Dividend growth rate in years 2 and 3	4.0%	5.0%	4.5%
Dividend growth rate (after year 3 into perpetuity)	3.5%	4.5%	4.0%
Assumed cap rate	7.0%	6.25%	6.5%
Property subsector average P/FFO multiple	14.4x	13.5x	15.1x
Property subsector average P/AFFO multiple	18.3x	17.1x	18.9x

Question 10
Based upon Exhibits 1 and 2, the value per share of REIT B using valuation Method 3 is closest to:

(a) $40.77
(b) $57.78
(c) $73.19

Question 11
Based upon Exhibits 1 and 2, the value per share of REIT A using valuation Method 4 is closest to:

(a) $58.32
(b) $74.12
(c) $103.40

Question 12

An investor is seeking an investment that can take long and short positions, use multi-strategies, and historically exhibit low correlation with a traditional investment portfolio. The investor's goals will be best satisfied with an investment in:

(a) real estate
(b) a hedge fund
(c) a PE fund

Solutions

Question 1

Solution: Option **a** is correct.

There are many approaches to managing alternative investment funds, but typically these funds are actively managed.

Question 2

Solution: Option **a** is correct.

Of the EH funds, market-neutral strategies should have a return that is closest to risk-free. However, they are not entirely risk-free and typically have exposure to systematic and unsystematic risks.

Question 3

Solution: Option **a** is correct

The returns of many hedge fund strategies are non-symmetric. Many suffer from negative skewness and positive excess kurtosis (fat tails). One alternative risk measure is the downside deviation. Skewness does make the Sharpe ratio a flawed measure. Standard deviation is an input to the Sharpe ratio, so it is not an alternative solution. The alternative measure is valid, but hedge funds may not have normally distributed returns.

Question 4

Solution: Option **c** is correct.

The management fee for the year is \$642 × 0.02 = \$12.84 million.

Because the ending value exceeds the high-water mark, the hedge fund can collect an incentive fee.

The incentive fee is {\$642 – [\$610 × (1 + 0.04)]} Å~ 0.20 = \$1.52 million.

The net return to the investor for the year is [(\$642 – \$12.84 – \$1.52)/\$583.1] – 1 ≈ 0.07638 ≈ 7.64%.

Question 5

Solution: Option **c** is correct.

Downside risk measures focus on the left side of the return distribution curve where losses occur. The standard deviation of returns assumes that returns are normally distributed. Many alternative investments do not exhibit a close-to-normal distribution of returns, which is a crucial assumption for the validity of a standard deviation as a comprehensive risk measure.

Question 6

Solution: Option **b** is correct.

Of the three facts given about PE fund managers, the only one specifically considered part of the due diligence checkpoints list is the evaluation of staff turnover. This checkpoint reflects the organization itself, and a lower turnover number will reflect positively on the firm's overall score. While it is positive, Option **a** is not a requirement for evaluation, and Option **c** is not covered explicitly as a due diligence checkpoint. However, the fund's return exceeds the benchmark.

Question 7

Solution: Option **b** is correct.

The majority of PE activity involves leveraged buyouts.

Merger arbitrage and market neutral are strategies used by hedge funds.

Question 8

Solution: Option **a** is correct.

The seed-stage supports market research and product development and is generally the first stage at which VC funds invest. The seed-stage follows the angel investing stage. In the angel investing stage, funds are typically provided by individuals (often friends or family) rather than a VC fund to assess an idea's potential and transform it into a plan. Mezzanine-stage financing is provided by VC funds to prepare the portfolio company for its IPO.

Question 9

Solution: Option **c** is correct.

The higher the loan-to-value ratio, the higher leverage is for a real estate investment, which increases the risk to both debt and equity investors.

Assuming normal probability distributions when calculating these measures will underestimate the downside risk for negatively skewed distribution. Both the Sortino ratio and the value-at-risk are downside risk measures.

Question 10

Solution: Option **b** is correct.

The value per share is \$57.78, calculated as:

Funds from operations (FFO) = \$290,612
Shares outstanding = 67,900 shares
FFO/share = \$290,612/67,900 shares = \$4.28

Applying the property subsector average P/FFO multiple of 13.5 × yields a value per share of: \$4.28 × 13.5 = \$57.78.

Question 11

Solution: Option **b** is correct.

The value per share is \$74.11, calculated as:

Funds from operations (FFOs)	\$316,965
Less: Non-cash rents:	\$25,991
Less: Recurring maintenance-type capital expenditures:	\$63,769
Equals: AFFO:	\$227,205
Shares outstanding	56,100 shares

AFFO/share = \$227,205/56,100 shares = \$4.05.

We are applying the property subsector average P/AFFO multiple of 18.3 × yields a value per share of \$4.05 × 18.3 = \$74.12.

Question 12

Solution: Option **b** is correct.

Hedge funds may use various strategies (event-driven, Relative value, macro, and EH), generally have a low correlation with traditional investments, and may take long and short positions.

Chapter 38

Portfolio Management

This section shall explain how investment managers actualize the real-world theory. This reading provides an overview of the concepts, techniques, and tools of managing a portfolio of assets. We will discuss the process of portfolio management, how assets are allocated, and performance measured.

38.1 Portfolio Management Process

Portfolio management is how portfolio managers can craft and keep track of the client's portfolio.

Learning Objectives

- Explain the process of portfolio management, the types of investors, and the investment policy statement (IPS).

Main Takeaways

Main Points

- The portfolio management process consists of a circular process of iteration which can be consolidated into three steps: Planning, Execution, and Feedback.
- There are two primary groups of investors: **Individuals** and **Institutions**.
- Individual investors have the most varied investment needs and characteristics, while institutions are organized to meet the different objectives, serve diverse clientele operating under various regulations.

Albeit being different, investment requirements and constraints are categorically similar.

- The risk and the return objectives are used to describe the investor's requirement.
- As circumstances differ across investors, their investment portfolios might vary. The cases that include requirements for liquidity, flow(s) of income from their portfolios, tax status, legal and regulatory restrictions, and unique circumstances impose constraints on investors' choices.
- The IPS is a mandate that guides the behavior and actions and specifies the portfolio manager's responsibilities.

38.1.1 *Overview of the Portfolio Management Process*

The portfolio management process is an integrated set of steps undertaken to create and maintain an appropriate portfolio (a combination of assets) to meet clients' stated goals. This process has been designed to be sufficiently flexible in applying to all types of portfolio investments, to various organizational types, to a full range of investors. It should be independent of manager, location, and investment strategy. The main iterative steps are:

- Understanding the client's objectives, constraints, and preferences;
- Understanding the macro-economic environment and capital market conditions;
- Constructing a policy portfolio through strategic allocation of assets;
- Selecting stocks through security analysis;
- Monitoring the environment and making tactical allocations;
- Portfolio performance evaluation.

These steps can be divided into three main phases: planning, execution, and feedback.

- **Planning**
  - 1(a) Identify and specify the investor's objectives and constraints. Create the IPS.
  - 1(b) Create the strategic asset allocation.
  - 2(b) Form market expectations.
- **Execution**
  - 3(a) Select specific assets and implement decisions. Carry out tactical asset allocation.

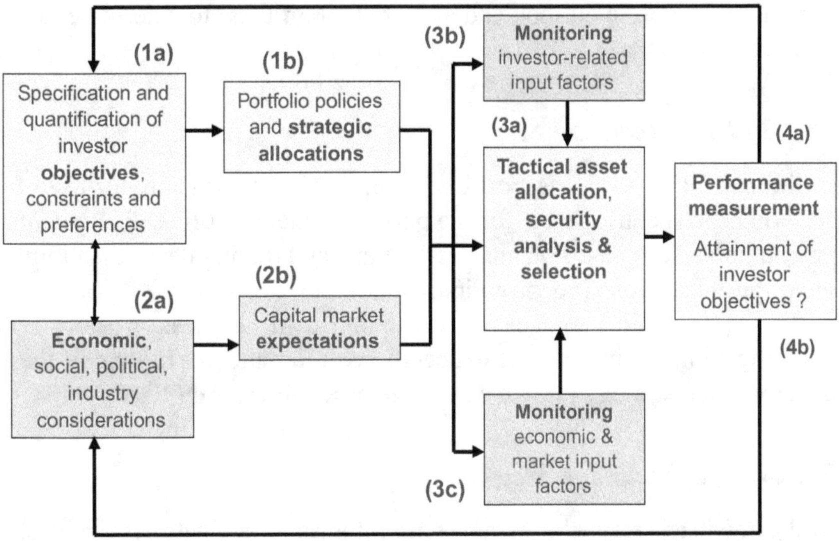

Figure 38.1: Portfolio management process.

Source: Maginn *et al.* (2007). *Managing Investments Portfolio: A Dynamic Process.* Wiley.

- **Feedback**
  4 Performance evaluation

Figure 38.1 illustrates this set of activities.

38.1.2 *The Planning Step*

The investment manager uses economic, market, and investor-related inputs to do three planning tasks. The first task is to identify and specify the investor's objectives, those that chiefly pertain to return and risk, and constraints, limitations on the investor's ability to take full advantage of particular investments. These objectives and constraints will formulate an IPS, which serves as the governing document for all investment decision-making.

The second task in the planning process is to form capital market expectations, long-run forecasts of risk, and return characteristics for various asset classes.

The final task in the planning process is determining the strategic asset allocation. Here the manager combines the objectives and constraints reflected in the IPS with the long-run capital market expectations (based on economic outlook and asset risk premiums) to determine target asset class weights.

38.1.3 *The Execution Step*

In the execution step, the portfolio manager constructs the portfolio by selecting the specific assets for the portfolio (the portfolio selection/composition decision) based on analysts' inputs, and trading desks then implement these decisions (portfolio implementation decision).

Also, portfolio managers may respond to differences in short-term and long-term capital market expectations in an attempt to exploit these differences, a strategy known as tactical asset allocation (TAA).

38.1.4 *The Feedback Step*

In the feedback step, the manager monitors and evaluates the portfolio compared with the plan, leading to revisions in the portfolio; thus, the feedback step interacts continuously with the execution step.

Performance evaluation assesses progress towards achieving investment objectives and assesses portfolio management skills. The assessment of portfolio management skills has three components.

1. Performance measurement: examine how the portfolio performed and calculate its return rate.
2. Performance attribution: understand why the portfolio performed as it did and involved determining the sources of a portfolio's performance.
3. Performance appraisal: shows the quality and consistency of performance and involves a statistical analysis relative to a benchmark (a comparison portfolio).

Example:
Which of the following is the *least* looked at during the planning stage? The client:

(a) Current securities;
(b) Investment constraints;
(c) Investment objectives.

Solution:
Option **a** is correct.

Current Securities are considered during the asset allocation step, which is part of the execution phase.

38.1.5 *Types of Investors*

We can broadly categorize investors into two groups: institutions and individuals. Each has its return requirements and risk tolerances unique to them, as shown in Table 38.1.

Institutional Investors: Institutional investors are entities that ultimately serve as financial intermediaries between individuals and financial markets. Investment committees or trustees typically make the investment policy decisions of institutional investors. Highlighted below are some of the institution groups that provide portfolio management services:

1. **Pension funds** contain assets set aside to support a retirement income promise, generally made by some enterprise or organization that sets

Table 38.1: Types of clients and their investment needs.

Summary of investment needs by client type				
Client	Time horizon	Risk tolerance	Income needs	Liquidity needs
Individuals				
Individuals	Varies by individual			
Institutions				
Pension Plans	Typically long term	High	High for mature funds, Low for growing funds	Varies by maturity
Endowments and Foundations	Very long term	High	Low: to meet spending commitments	Typically low
Banks	Short term	Low	Medium: to pay deposit interests and operational expenses	High
Insurance Companies	Short term for property and casualty, Long term for life insurance	Low	Low	High
Investment Companies	Varies by fund			High
Sovereign Wealth Funds	Varies by fund			

up the pension plan, referred to as the plan sponsor. Pension plans divide principally into one of two broad types. A defined-benefit plan is a pension plan that specifies the plan sponsor's obligations in terms of the benefit to plan participants. In contrast, a defined-contribution plan defines the sponsor's obligations regarding contributions to the pension fund rather than benefits to plan participants.

2. **Foundations and Endowments** are institutions with a very long-term view of the market. Foundations are typically grant-making institutions funded by gifts and investment assets. On the other hand, endowments are long-term funds generally owned by operating non-profit institutions such as universities and colleges, museums, hospitals, and other organizations involved in charitable activities.
3. **Insurance companies** can be classified as life or non-life (casualty) to consider investment policy. Many life insurance company liabilities such as annuity contracts are interest-rate sensitive.
4. **Commercial banks** are financial intermediaries involved in taking deposits and lending money. Still, universal banks combine commercial banking with investment banking (securities underwriting) and insurance under one roof. Nevertheless, the securities portfolio plays a vital role in managing a bank's risk and liquidity positions relative to its liabilities.

Individual Investors: Individual investors have diverse investment objectives, time horizons, and perceptions of risk, all subject to varying tax schedules. A distinguishing characteristic of private asset management is the wide range of personal concerns and preferences that influence the decision-making process. The terms individual investor, private client, and high-net-worth investor are used interchangeably to imply personal or family assets management.

Mutual funds serve the individual investor and, to a lesser extent, the smaller institutional market. Family offices are entities, typically organized and owned by a wealthy family, that assume responsibility for services such as financial planning, estate planning, and asset management, as well as a range of practical matters from tax return preparation to bill paying.

Examples:

Example 1:

On average, which of the following institutions have the highest need for liquidity?

(a) Banks
(b) Pension Funds
(c) Investment Companies

Solution:

Option **a** is correct.

Pension Funds generally have less need for liquidity than other institutions. Investment funds require a high demand for liquidity, but on average, banks have the greatest for it as they face the highest liquidity risk during times such as financial crises.

Example 2:

Which investor is most likely the one with the most extended time horizon?

(a) Endowment
(b) Individual
(c) Life Insurance

Solution:

Option **a** is correct.

Endowments are typically structured to have a perpetual lifespan and thus have the longest time horizon. Life insurance institutions also have a long time horizon but not as endless as Endowments and Foundations. Individual investors have vastly differing time horizons.

38.1.6 *Investment Policy Statement*

The planning process based on investor-related inputs culminates in developing the IPS. The IPS is a written document that sets out a client's return objectives and risk tolerance over that client's relevant time horizon, along with applicable constraints such as liquidity needs, tax considerations, regulatory requirements, and unique circumstances. Constructing an IPS is a dynamic process in which objectives and constraints are reconciled to produce realistic investment goals.

A typical IPS includes the following elements:

- A brief client description,
- The duties and investment responsibilities of parties involved,
- The statement of investment objectives and constraints,
- The schedule for review of investment performance and the IPS itself,
- Performance measures and benchmarks to be used in performance evaluation,
- Issues to consider in developing the strategic asset allocation,
- Investment strategies and style(s), and
- Appendices that include:
    - Strategic asset allocation,
    - Rebalancing policy.

An investor delegating portfolio management to an investment manager will communicate a mandate — a set of instructions detailing the investment manager's task and how his performance will be evaluated — that includes a specification of the manager's benchmark. For example, you have decided to invest 60% of a client's money in equities. The client wants to have equity exposure in the Asia Pacific region outside Japan. Hence, you recommend using a benchmark such as the MSCI AC Asia Pacific ex-Japan Index.

The IPS are the foundation of the portfolio management process. A properly developed IPS disciplines the portfolio management process and helps ensure against ad hoc revisions in strategy. A well-constructed IPS should be portable and executed by any portfolio manager the client might subsequently hire.

38.1.7 *Investment Objectives*

Two objectives are established during the planning phase: the risk objective and the return objective. This section will discuss each objective and examples of how it should be stated.

Risk Objectives: It is vital to ensure that the portfolio's risk is suitable for the client when conducting portfolio management. The IPS should clearly state the risk tolerance of the client. Risk objectives refer to the specifications for portfolio risk that represent the risk tolerance and can be split into three types of risk objectives: absolute, relative, or a combination of the two.

Absolute Objectives: These are objectives that are not tied to a benchmark. An example of this is a desire not to lose more than 6% of capital in 12 months.

Relative Objectives: Relate risk relative to one or more benchmarks presumed to represent an appropriate risk standard. For example, an investment in large-cap US equities can be benchmarked against the S&P 500 Index.

Overall, a client's risk tolerance is a combination of the client's ability to take the risk and his willingness to take the risk:

The ability to bear risk is measured primarily through objective factors such as expected income, time horizon, and capital relative to debt.

Willingness to take risks is based on more subjective factors based on their constraints or psychology. Examples of such factors include investment constraints, self-esteem, and personality type.

When combining above and below-average ability and willingness to take the risk, we arrive at the below matrix in Table 38.2.

When the ability and willingness to take risks are consistent, it is easy for a risk tolerance to be established. When the ability to take risk is below average, but the willingness to take risk is above average, the client's risk tolerance should be set as below average. When the opposite happens, the advisor may advise the client over how his ability to take risks is above average and explain the general consequences of not taking the risk, i.e., a decrease in expected returns.

Return Objectives: A return objective also needs to be set in the planning stage before any asset allocation can occur. Just like risk objectives, return objectives can be absolute or relative.

Table 38.2: Risk tolerance matrix.

Risk tolerance		
	Ability to take risk	
Willingness to take risk	Below average	Above average
Below average	Below average risk tolerance	Advise clients
Above average	Below average risk tolerance	Above-average risk tolerance

An example of an **absolute return objective** would be for the portfolio to achieve a rate of return of 5%. This return rate can be expressed in a nominal way or real way.

An example of a **relative return objective** could be that the portfolio would have returned 2% over the benchmark index.

The nominal rate of returns is not adjusted for tax or inflation. **Real returns** are adjusted for inflation. **Post-tax returns** are returns after taxes. Each has their purposes and are used for different investors. For example, some institutions are tax-exempt and thus have no need to use post-tax returns in their returns objective. When comparing against asset-class returns, the pre-tax nominal return objective can be calculated as follows:

$$\text{Pre-tax nominal return} = \frac{\text{After-tax real return} + \text{Expected inflation rate}}{1 - \text{Tax rate}}$$
$$= \frac{\text{After-tax nominal return}}{1 - \text{Tax rate}}$$

Internal rate of returns can also be used and are generally referred to as the level necessary return to achieve an investor's primary or critical long-term financial objectives. The desired return would be a return that can satisfy the client's additional considerations, including their secondary goals.

Ultimately, the return objective should incorporate both the required return and the desired return into a measurable annual total return specification. An investor's return objective should be consistent with that investor's risk objective and be sufficient to meet wealth objectives or liabilities that the portfolio must fund and spending needs. When an investor's return and risk objectives are inconsistent, a resolution is necessary.

Examples:

Example 1:

Consider the following objective: To have a return that exceeds the S&P 500 index by 150 bp.

What type of objective is this?

(a) Absolute return objective
(b) Relative risk objective
(c) Relative return objective

Solution:
Option **c** is correct.

As the return objective is benchmarked to an index, it is a relative objective.

Example 2:
We use personality quizzes to assess a client's:

(a) Ability to take risk
(b) Willingness to take risk
(c) Risk tolerance

Solution:
Option **b** is correct.

We judge the ability to take risks on more objective factors such as financial strength. Risk tolerance is the combination of ability and willingness to take the risk.

Example 3:
The portfolio manager should advise the client when they have this combination of willingness and ability to take the risk.

(a) Above average ability, Below average willingness
(b) Above average ability, Above average willingness
(c) Below average ability, Above average willingness

Solution:
Option **a** is correct.

Please refer to the risk tolerance table in Table 38.2.

38.1.8 *Investment Constraints*

Even with identical attitudes toward risk, different institutions and individuals choose different investment portfolios because of differing circumstances. These circumstances include differing liquidity requirements, flow(s) of income from the investment (time horizon(s)), tax status, various legal and regulatory requirements, and unique circumstances. The circumstances place constraints on investors' choices, which together with return and risk objectives determine investment policy and strategy.

Liquidity Constraints: A liquidity requirement is a need for cash above new contributions (e.g., for pension plans and endowments) or savings (for individuals) at a specified point in time. A portfolio manager should set aside part of the portfolio in liquid assets to anticipate such withdrawals. Liquidity requirements, which may be expected or unanticipated and recurring or non-recurring, include:

- Ongoing expenses, which should be met using a high degree of liquidity in some portion of the portfolio due to their high predictability and short time horizon.
- Emergency reserves serve as a precaution against unanticipated events such as sudden unemployment (individuals working in a cyclical environment may require a larger reserve) or uninsured losses.
- Adverse liquidity events, which are discrete future cash outflows and for which the need for portfolio liquidity rises as the time horizon to the event shortens.

If the investor's wealth and income base are large relative to his liquidity requirements, relatively less liquid assets can be held in his portfolio. In cases where an investor may face short-term liquidity needs, the amount of funds should be set aside and in short maturity instruments such as Treasury Bills and Money Market Funds.

Time Horizon Constraints: Time horizon refers to the period associated with the investment objective and may be short-term (<3 years) or long-term (>10 years). The longer horizon allows the investor to replenish investment resources by increasing savings. So, the investor can take more risk, with a larger proportion of funds allocated to risky assets.

The investment time horizon often shortens as investors move through various life stages.

A second issue relating to the investment time horizon is whether the investor faces a single- or multistage horizon. A multistage horizon is a combination of shorter-term and longer-term horizons. An example of a multistage horizon is funding children's education shorter term and the investor's retirement longer term.

Tax Constraints: Tax concerns arise for taxable investors because tax payments reduce the total return. Differences between the tax rates that apply to investment income and capital gains will influence taxable investors' choice of investments and the timing of their sales.

Although tax codes are necessarily country-specific, the following categories are widely recognized:

1. **Income tax:** It is calculated as a percentage of total income, often with different rates applied to various income levels. Wages, rent, dividends, and interest earned are commonly treated as taxable income.

2. **Capital gains tax:** Profits based on price appreciation resulting from the sale of an investment are often distinguished from income and taxed separately. The investment's cost basis is typically used to assess capital gains taxes.
3. **Wealth transfer tax:** It is assessed as assets are transferred without sale from one owner to another. Examples of wealth transfer taxes include "estate" or "inheritance" taxes paid at the investor's death and "gift" taxes paid on transfers made during the investor's lifetime.
4. **Property tax:** It refers to the taxation of real estate and generally assessed annually as a percentage of assessed value.

An investment adviser can recommend adopting the following tax strategies:

- **Deferral:** For the long-term investor, periodic tax payments severely diminish the benefit of compounding portfolio returns. When taxes are paid at the end of a given period, portfolio size is reduced by the tax paid, and funds that would otherwise compound at the portfolio growth rate are no longer available for investment. Therefore, many tax strategies seek to defer taxes and maximize the time when investment returns can be reinvested.
- **Avoidance:** Some countries have introduced special purpose savings accounts that may be exempt or deferred from taxation. Tax-exempt bonds are available as an alternative investment vehicle.
- **Reduction:** When the income tax rate exceeds the capital gains tax rate, a portfolio manager may emphasize securities and investment strategies whose investment returns are recognized as gains rather than income. If only net gains are taxed, loss harvesting, a policy to actively realize capital losses to offset otherwise taxable gains without impairing investment performance will reduce taxable net profits.

Legal and Regulatory Constraints: Regulations may limit the concentration of holdings in debt and equity securities for mutual funds, the holding of employer securities by pension plans, and the use of certain asset classes in retirement accounts.

For individual investors, legal and regulatory constraints most frequently involve transferring personal property ownership.

Unique Circumstances: Unique circumstances are internal factors (other than a liquidity requirement, time horizon, legal and regulatory requirement, or tax concern) that may constrain portfolio choices. Examples are ethical objections or social responsibility considerations for a university endowment; health needs and support of dependents for individuals; avoidance of non-domestic shares or derivatives; assets legally restricted from sale; directed brokerage arrangements; privacy concerns; and investor capability in terms of time, interest and technical expertise. It is also appropriate to note any assets excluded from the investment portfolio.

Reference/Further Reading

Maginn, J.L., Tuttle, D.L., Pinto, J.E., & McLeavey, D.W. (2007). *Managing Investment Portfolios — A Dynamic Process*, 3rd edn. John Wiley & Sons, pp. 1–19.

Examples:

Example 1:

Lady M is a 35-year old married lady with a healthy young son aged 5. She is currently employed at an educational institution and has been working there for 13 years. Her two financial goals are to provide for her child's college education and her retirement in the future. Her time horizon is best described as:

(a) Short term
(b) Long term
(c) Multistage horizon

Solution:

Option **c** is correct.

She has 2-time horizons.

Example 2:

A client is a director of a publicly listed firm. He is thus unable to trade that company's stock by law. When preparing the IPS, this trade restriction.

(a) Is not relevant
(b) Makes it illegal for the client to work with this portfolio manager
(c) Should be included in the IPS

Solution:

Option **c** is correct.

The restriction is a unique circumstance restriction and should be included in the IPS.

38.2 Asset Allocation

Asset allocation is the process of distributing an investor's wealth across various assets to achieve various investment goals. This section aims to explain the portfolio management process's asset allocation approach.

Learning Objectives

- Explain the asset allocation process, asset classes, and optimization approaches.

Main Takeaways

Main Points

- Asset Liability management includes liability management, while Asset-only approaches focus purely on maximizing returns.
- There are a few ways to quantify risk tolerance, such as the empirical or shortfall risk approaches.
- There are four classes of assets: equity, fixed income, alternative investments, and cash.
- The asset allocation steps are an iterative process that factors in market and investor factors to reach an optimized allocation.
- One approach to asset allocation optimization is the mean-variance optimization (MVO), which uses the available asset sets' efficient frontier.
- Implementation choices include the portfolio's activity and how to rebalance the SAA.
- Individuals are different from institutions as they have taxation requirements, have human capital, and two unique risks.

Main Terms

- **Strategic asset allocation:** It is a long-term strategy to meet the investment objectives. Long-term can means the next 3 to 5 years unless there is a significant change in market conditions or the client's situation. The portfolio should be managed broadly in line with the strategic asset allocation.
- **Tactical asset allocation:** It refers to the portfolio's active management, with deviations from the portfolio's strategic asset allocation (SAA) to take advantage of opportunities in the financial market. For example, after a natural disaster, the stock market is likely to trend downwards.

- **Asset and liability management (ALM):** It is the practice of managing financial risk that arises due to mismatches between the asset and liabilities as part of an investment strategy.

38.2.1 *Strategic Asset Allocation*

After an investor's objectives and constraints are found out (as mentioned in the previous section), the **SAA** is created by merging the above factors with long-term capital market expectations. Asset classes are then allocated target weights based on the client's desired exposure to undiversifiable risk.

TAA focuses on short-term adjustments to asset class allocations compared to SAA's long-term outlook. It creates active risk as it deviates from the SAA and is intended to capture (after-fee) alpha returns.

38.2.2 *Investor's Risk and Return Objectives*

When it comes to asset allocation, the first step is for the portfolio manager to understand the client's risk and returns objectives. Various institutions all have different characteristics and have different abilities to take on risk.

One important determinant of their risk-taking capabilities is the relative importance of funding one's liabilities. To that end, two asset allocation approaches are asset-liability management and the asset-only approach.

38.2.3 *Asset Only Approach*

Definition: The asset-only (AO) approach only considers assets in the asset allocation decisions. The impact of liabilities on portfolio selection is indirect at best. The objective is to earn the highest possible return rate without controlling liabilities. The AO approach has less precision in controlling risk related to liabilities' funding.

Example: The Black–Litterman Model (explained further below) starts with the global market value-weighted portfolio as the default SAA for investors before adjusting asset class weighting based on the investor's risk tolerances.

Advantages: Returns are maximized.

Who uses this approach? The AO approach is considered the "default" approach for individuals. Institutions with very long time-horizons can also use the AO approach.

38.2.4 *Asset Liability Management Approach*

Definition: On the other hand, the ALM approach explicitly includes liabilities into the model when making asset allocation decisions, along with assets.

Example: Traditional banks aim to maximize their risk-adjusted returns while ensuring sufficient liquidity to pay their depositor's interest.

Advantages: There are quite a few factors that would cause an investor to choose ALM over AO, such as:

1. Below average risk tolerance
2. High penalties when unable to meet liabilities
3. Legal and regulatory requirement/incentive to hold fixed-income
4. Tax incentives to hold fixed-income

Who uses this approach? Most institutions use the ALM approach due to the reasons stated above.

There are two dimensions to the ALM approach:

(a) Risk Dimension

The earliest ALM approaches aimed to be risk minimizing. These strategies aimed to be cash-flow matching and immunizing. A cash-flow matching strategy would be to invest in bonds with cash-flows that offset the planned outflows in the future, effectively matching the liability requirements.

The immunization approach aims to match the weighted average duration of the liabilities. Using immunization is a riskier approach relative to matching as duration is only a first-order approximation of interest rate risk and not a perfect match.

(b) Static versus Dynamic Dimension

The second dimension is regarding how dynamic the investor wants to be in their approach.

- A **dynamic approach** recognizes that an investor's asset allocation and actual returns and liabilities in a given period will affect the return and risk profile in subsequent periods.

- A **static approach** ignores any link between current and future performances. Asset allocation is set and infrequently revised.

With more substantial computing power, institutional investors prefer the dynamic approach. However, this approach is significantly more challenging, costly, and time-consuming. Despite this, investors with significant future liabilities often find that the dynamic method is worth the cost.

38.2.5 *Quantitative Measure of Risk Tolerance*

Generally, risk tolerances can be allocated into two camps: below and above average. However, to apply a qualitative approach to asset allocation, a more precise measure of risk tolerance needs to be established. Outlined below are four methods to quantify risk tolerance.

Numerical Scale: A numerical risk aversion score can be given to an investor after completing a questionnaire or interview. The investor expresses preferences among sets of choices involving risky and certain returns. Generally, a lower risk aversion score represents a higher risk tolerance level.

Empirical Approach: A mean-variance investor will evaluate an asset allocation mix using the utility curve (please refer to portfolio analysis for further explanation).

$$U = E(r) - \frac{1}{2} A\sigma^2$$

where U is the utility value, and A is an index of the investors' risk aversion.

Risk Acceptability Level: Another way to express risk tolerance is for the investor to quantify it in terms of the acceptable level of volatility he is willing to accept, usually measured by the return's standard deviation.

Shortfall Risk: Shortfall risk is the risk that a portfolio's value will fall below some minimally acceptable level during a stated time horizon.

The earliest shortfall risk criterion is Roy's safety-first criterion which states that the optimal portfolio minimizes the possibility over a stated time horizon that portfolio return, R_P, will fall below some threshold level R_L that the investor insists on meeting or exceeding. The safety-first optimal portfolio maximizes the safety-first ratio (SFRatio):

$$\text{SFRatio} = \frac{E(R_p) - R_L}{\sigma_p}$$

Steps in choosing amongst risky portfolios using Roy's criterion (assuming normality):

- Calculate each portfolio's SFRatio.
- Choose the portfolio with the highest SFRatio.

If an asset offers a risk-free return for the time horizon considered, and if R_L is less than or equal to the risk-free rate, then the optimal portfolio would be 100% risk-free asset. Holding the risk-free asset eliminates the chance that the threshold return is not met.

Examples:
Example 1:
Which type of investor would most commonly use the Asset Only approach?

(a) Individuals
(b) Investment Banks
(c) Pension Plans

Solution:
Option **a** is correct.

Institutions generally use the ALM approach.

Example 2:
Which statement is true?

(a) The ALM approach maximizes risk-adjusted returns without considering liabilities.
(b) The ALM approach is better for investors with a lower risk tolerance.
(c) The AO approach is generally harder to conduct.

Solution:
Option **b** is correct.

The ALM approach reduces the risk of the fund not meeting future obligations.

38.2.6 *Selection of Asset Classes*

An asset class is a group of assets with similar attributes, and asset classes should be specified to support SAA in diversifying and controlling risk. The following criteria help to specify an asset class effectively:

- Assets within an asset class should be *relatively homogeneous*.
- Asset classes should be *mutually exclusive*.
- Asset classes should *not have too high expected correlations with other asset classes* or a linear combination of the different asset classes to minimize risk exposures' duplication.
- The asset classes as a group should make up a significant portion of the world's investable wealth or help to complete the market.
- An asset class should have the capacity to absorb a significant fraction of the investment portfolio without seriously affecting the portfolio's liquidity.

While there may be many asset classes, investors may split large asset classes into distinct groups within their portfolio, such as separating domestic equity from international equity or dividing the fixed income classes into investment grade and high yield. The critical asset classes are:

(1) Equity,
(2) Fixed-Income,
(3) Alternative Investments,
(4) Cash/money market investments.

38.2.7 *Asset Allocation Steps*

As mentioned in Section 18.1, the portfolio management process is an iterative one. Similarly, the asset allocation process, which is the central part of the execute phase, is iterative. The asset allocation steps are outlined in Figure 38.2 and described in Table 38.3.

As time passes, the capital market conditions are sure to change. Changing conditions would affect asset prices and liabilities (banks, for example, may have interest liabilities subject to interest rate risks). Returns in one period also influence the investor's assets, liabilities, and net worth too. The feedback is represented by the loop from **A3 to I1**. Other factors, perhaps a sharp down-turn, may affect investors' risk appetite. The market return will also affect future capital market conditions (for example, current prices will become historical prices in the future), as shown by the loop from **A3 to M1**.

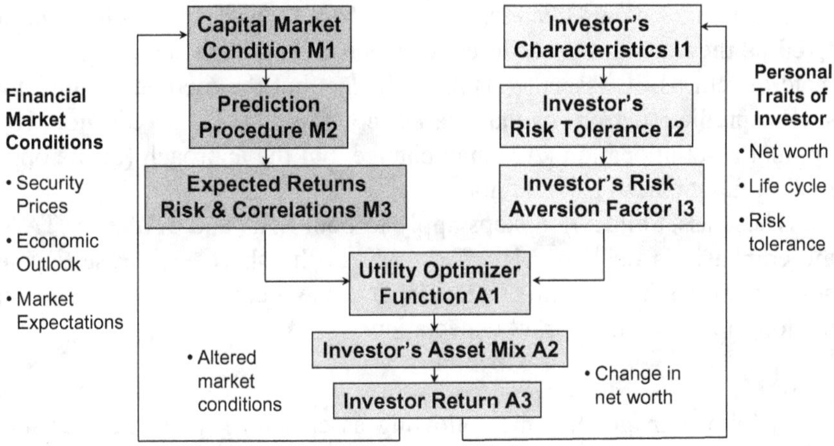

Figure 38.2: Asset allocation steps.

Source: Adapted from Maginn *et al.* (2007). *Managing Investments Portfolio: A Dynamic Process.* Wiley.

Table 38.3: Explanation of asset allocation steps.

Box identity	Remarks
M1	**Capital Market Conditions:** Available information that the portfolio manager has regarding the capital market at the time of asset allocation. Information includes current and historical prices, economic conditions, and market expectations
M2 (Procedure)	**Prediction Procedure:** Convert capital market conditions (M1) to estimates of returns on assets (M3)
M3	**Expected, Risks, and Correlations:** Obtain the estimates of returns on assets with correlations among the expected returns from the various asset classes
I1	**Investor's Characteristics:** Assess the factors that determine risk tolerance, including investor's assets, liabilities (if using ALM approach), net worth, and attitudes toward risk
I2 (Procedure)	**Investor's Risk Tolerance Function:** Assess the investor's risk tolerance function
I3	**Investor's Risk Tolerance:** Assign investor's tolerance for risk
A1 (Procedure)	**Optimizer:** By combining M3 and I3, use A1 to determine the optimizing function to determine asset allocation
A2	**Investor's Asset Mix:** Obtain the results from M1, the appropriate asset allocation or asset mix
A3	**Returns:** Shows actual returns. Given the investor's asset mix at the beginning of each period (M2), the returns plus additional contributions less withdrawals become the value of the investor's assets at the beginning of the next period. The cycle then reiterates

Most boxes would change, but boxes **M2, I2, and A1 should remain fixed** as they contain procedures (decision rules). For example, the estimate of returns on assets (M3) may change, but the method for making such a prediction from capital market conditions (M2) should not. The optimal asset allocation (A2) may change, but the approach (or the optimizing function, A1) should not.

These asset allocation steps apply to both SAA and TAA. For TAA, the emphasis is on how M1 affects M3 in the short term, resulting in adjustments to the asset mix M2. For SAA, the focus would always be on the long-term capital market expectations.

Example:
A portfolio manager has the following asset classes with the available correlations.

Correlations	US Equity	European Equity	Asian Equity	US Treasury
US Equity	1	0.9	0.6	–0.1
European Equity	0.9	1	0.5	–0.4
Asian Equity	0.6	0.5	1	–0.2
US Treasury	–0.1	–0.4	–0.2	1

When combined with the US equity asset class, which asset class will result in the largest diversification effect?

(a) European equity
(b) Asian equity
(c) US treasury

Solution:
Option **c** is correct.

US Treasury has a lower correlation with US Equity and will have the most significant diversification effect.

38.2.8 *Optimization*

There are multiple approaches to asset allocation optimization, for example, the Resample Efficient Frontier and Black-Litterman method. We shall elaborate on the default approach for this section: The MVO method. Most, if not all, of the other optimization approaches attempt to improve upon the MVO.

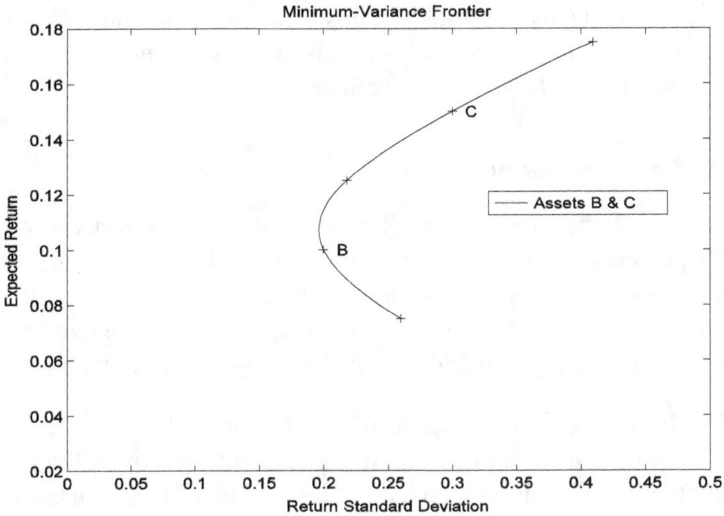

Figure 38.3: Minimum variance frontier.

Mean-Variance Optimization: MVO provides a quantitative way to the SAA approach. Recall the **efficient frontier** taught in an earlier module. According to the MVO theory, an investor should choose a portfolio on the efficient frontier as it offers the highest return for any specific risk, as illustrated in Figure 38.3.

We start from the left-most point of the graph representing the global minimum-variance portfolio (GMVP), or the portfolio combination with the smallest variance. Any combination below the GMVP is not worth considering, as, given the same risk, there are other portfolio combinations with a higher expected return. Portfolios on the curve that lies above the GMVP are called the efficient frontier. Those portfolios represent the highest expected return an investor expects to receive, given the risk he intends to take. Once the investor's risk tolerance is known, an efficient portfolio can be selected for him. The process is known as the MVO approach.

Advantages: It is a well-understood approach. It is also relatively inexpensive and allows the portfolio manager to quickly identify portfolios with the best risk to reward profile (for example, having the highest Sharpe ratio).

Disadvantages: It is a static approach that can only be used for that one period it is analyzing. Thus portfolios using the MVO methods need to be rebalanced frequently. It is also highly susceptible to estimation errors. Furthermore, it can yield asset allocations highly concentrated in one asset class, lessening portfolio diversification.

38.2.9 *Implementation Choices*

Passive and Active Investing: As part of the planning process, after the SAA approach gives the asset classes and weights to invest, the investor needs to decide on an **investment approach** for each asset class chosen. We can use four different strategies within each asset class: Passive Investing, Active Investing, Semi-active/Enhanced Indexing, or a combination of them.

Passive Investing: A tracking portfolio, derivative-based portfolio, or a combination of two with the intention not to interfere with the portfolio too much, if at all. This approach costs less to manage (as transaction fees are kept at a minimum) and demands less market forecasting from the portfolio manager. However, it loses out on opportunities to earn an excess return from short-term swings in the market.

Active Investing: The goal behind active investing is to take advantage of short-term price swings to generate 'alpha' on investments. By extension, this means the portfolio manager takes a much more proactive approach to manage the assets, pivoting in and out of the asset classes and individual assets based on what he considers an opportunistic situation.

Semi-active/Enhanced Indexing: A tracking portfolio that allows some under or over-weighting of securities but controlled tracking risk (deviation from benchmark weights).

Rebalancing to the SAA: There are two definitions of rebalancing:

1. Changes to the policy portfolio due to changes in the investor's objective, constraints, or long-term market expectations.
2. Adjusting the actual portfolio back to the SAA weightage when price changes have caused the weightage to deviate too far from the ideal weights. Adjusting back to SAA is the usual definition in industry practice and will be used when discussing rebalancing further.

Rebalancing can be done on a calendar basis (for example, yearly) or a percentage-of-portfolio basis when an asset class's weightage crosses a rebalancing threshold. The asset class is rebalanced to the target weight or a point between the target weight and threshold when the threshold is triggered.

38.2.10 *Strategic Asset Allocation for Individuals*

Individual investors differ from institutional investors in a few significant ways. This section will go through some of the differences.

Taxation: Individuals are taxable and should focus on their after-tax returns instead of the purely nominal returns their assets generate. Some tax-exempt institutions (e.g., some endowments) or institutions with different taxation schedules (like financial institutions) face other tax implications.

Human Capital: An investor's ability to take risk is based on the following:

- Personality,
- Current and future needs,
- Current and anticipated future financial situation, including all sources of income.

The last one involves human capital, defined as the present value of all expected future labor income. Unlike its economic counterpart, this capital is not as liquid and tradable. It is generally most significant in youth and decreases with age. The effects of human capital on asset allocation can be summarized as follows:

- Investors with safer human capital (from having a steady source of income which is unlikely to be cut soon) has a higher ability to take risk.
- Investors with a human capital highly dependent on the stock market (such as those in financial institutions) should aim to diversify this correlation with fixed income instruments.
- High labor flexibility tends to increase the ability to take risk.

Human capital can be quantified using the following formula:

$$\text{Human capital}\ (t) = \sum_{j=t}^{T} \frac{I_j}{(1+r)^{(j-t)}}$$

where t is the current age, I_j is the expected earnings at age j, T is the life expectancy, and r is the discount rate

Unique Risks: Finally, there are two unique risks that individual investors face that institutional investors generally do not, which are surprisingly at odds with each other.

1. **The mortality risk** is the risk of loss of human capital due to the investor dying prematurely. The investor's dependence will bear the effect of such a risk as their liabilities (which the investor was supposed to fulfill) are no longer accounted for with the sudden removal of human capital. Life insurance has been the default way to hedge such a risk. The impact of such a risk on SAA is minimal.
2. **Longevity risk** is the risk of outliving one's assets when in retirement. Unlike mortality, the investor will bear the effect of such a threat. Along with the fact that longevity risk is also related to income needs, this risk should be considered when preparing the SAA.

Reference/Further Reading

Maginn, J.L., Tuttle, D.L., Pinto, J.E., & McLeavey, D.W. (2007). *Managing Investment Portfolios — A Dynamic Process*, 3rd edn. John Wiley & Sons, pp. 230–327.

38.3 Portfolio Performance

In an extensive portfolio with multiple managers, there are typically decisions made by the fund sponsor and those made by the individual managers within the fund that affect portfolio performance. Performance evaluation can deconstruct return to show which decisions are made to create or destroy fund value. The fund sponsor perspective will capture all value created or destroyed. In contrast, the manager's perspective will focus only on what a particular manager did to add or lose value for the fund. While there are three components to the evaluation process, the focus will be on performance appraisal.

Learning Objectives

- Understand and calculate the various risk-adjusted performance appraisal measures.

Main Takeaways

Main Points

- There are three performance evaluation components: performance measurement, performance attribution, and performance appraisal.
- If we assume normally distributed returns, the risk is adjusted traditionally in one of two ways: by the market risk or by total risk.
- We discuss two measures utilizing market risk (Jensen's alpha and Treynor ratio) and one using total risk (Sharpe ratio).
- We examine the Sortino ratio that mitigates non-normal asset return.

Main Terms

- **Risk-adjusted performance measures:** These are sometimes also called reward-to-risk ratios to reflect that investors prefer to achieve a high return rather than a low return on their investment portfolio. All things being equal, they also like lower risk to higher risk.
- **Standard deviation:** It is a convenient measure of variability (or volatility) of returns around the mean.
- **Downside deviation:** It is calculated in almost the same way as standard deviation, but instead of using all the deviations from the mean, downside deviation is calculated only using negative deviations. It may also be calculated by focusing on outcomes that are less than a specified return target; this target does not need to be the mean.

38.3.1 *Performance Evaluation*

Performance evaluation comprises three main components: performance measurement, performance attribution, and performance appraisal.

- **Performance measurement** calculates return rates based on investment-related changes in an account's value over specified periods. The purpose of this component is to quantify the return.
- **Performance attribution** investigates both the sources of the account's performance relative to a specific investment benchmark and the importance of those sources. This component aims to identify the contributing factors that resulted in the return.
- **Performance appraisal** attempts to conclude the quality (that is, the magnitude and consistency) of the account's relative performance. The purpose of this component is to assess whether the return was due to skill (portfolio manager's decisions) or luck (overall market movements).

This section will only focus on performance appraisal and discuss basic risk-adjusted performance measures.

38.3.2 *Performance Appraisal*

Performance appraisal assesses whether the investment results are more likely due to skill or luck. Even the most talented managers can underperform their benchmarks due to poor luck. Conversely, ineffective managers may make correct decisions and outperform their benchmarks by good fortune.

Investment skill is the ability to outperform an appropriate benchmark consistently over time. The magnitude of the value-added returns relative to the variability of value-added returns determines a manager's skill.

38.3.3 *Risk-Adjusted Performance Appraisal Methods*

As we learned in previous sections, a higher expected rate of return is expected by accepting a higher level of risk. Thus, it is not enough to compare the nominal rate of returns without accounting for the investor's risk to achieve such returns. Two types of risk are generally applied to adjust ex-post returns:

- The account's market (undiversifiable) risk, measured as beta, β.
- The account's total risk, measured by the standard deviation.

There are many ways to assess risk using risk-adjusted performance measures or the reward-to-risk ratio. For this section, we shall describe four of them: Jensen's ex-post alpha, Treynor measure, Sharpe ratio. On the other hand, the Sortino ratio measure of risk is the downside deviation.

Jensen's Ex-post Alpha: The ex-post alpha (sometimes referred to as Jensen's alpha) is derived from the CAPM equation. The difference between the fund's actual returns and the expected return the investor should have gotten to compensate for the market risk he took on. First, we begin with the CAPM equation:

$$E(R_A) = r_f + \beta_A[E(R_M) - r_f]$$

where $E(R_A)$ is the expected return of the account, R_f is the risk-free rate of return, β is the account's beta, and R_M is the expected return of the market portfolio.

We then sub this expected return formula into Jensen's alpha's mathematical expression. The alpha can be positive or negative, given the portfolio manager's skill. A consistently positive alpha indicates the portfolio manager's good skills.

$$\text{Jensen's alpha} = R_A - E(R_A)$$
$$\text{Jensen's alpha} = R_A - \{r_f + \beta_A [E(R_M) - r_f]\}$$
$$\text{Jensen's alpha} = (R_A - r_f) - \beta_A [E(R_M) - r_f]$$

where R_A is the actual return of the account.

Risk-adjusted: **Market risk**

Treynor Measure: The Treynor measure (or the Treynor ratio) is like the ex-post alpha and will give you the same answer as Jensen's alpha as it measures excess returns to market risk as well. As a result, it also uses the ex-post SML to form a benchmark. Unlike Jensen's alpha, the Treynor measure measures excess returns per unit of market risk.

$$\text{Treynor ratio} = \frac{R_A - r_f}{\beta_A}$$

Therein lies the difference between the Treynor Ratio and Jensen's alpha. While Jensen's alpha can be taken on an absolute basis (for example, a negative Jensen's alpha implies a lack of skill of the portfolio manager), the Treynor ratio needs to be compared with other Treynor ratios to have any meaning. Thus, the Treynor ratio is most useful as a ranking tool where a larger Treynor ratio means more skill on the portfolio manager.

Risk-adjusted: **Market risk**

Sharpe Ratio: The Treynor ratio was originated in 1965. In 1966 Sharpe expanded upon Treynor's work to create the Sharpe ratio. The Sharpe ratio is almost the same as the Treynor ratio aside from one fundamental area: instead of measuring the excess return to market risk, it measures excess return to total risk, represented by the standard deviation of returns. The ratio goes as follows:

$$\text{Sharpe ratio} = \frac{R_A - r_f}{\sigma_A}$$

where σ_A is the standard deviation of the account's returns.

The benchmark, in this case, is the ex-post CML and is appropriate to use if the returns are normally distributed. Much like the Treynor ratio, it is best used relatively and ranked with other Sharpe ratios. The larger Sharpe ratio implies a better risk-adjusted return.

Risk-adjusted: **Total risk**

Sortino Ratio: The Sharpe ratio problem is accentuated by investments that do not have normally-distributed returns. An example of this is hedge funds that use dynamic trading strategies and options that exhibit skewness and kurtosis in their returns distribution.

We can use the Sortino ratio to overcome the Sharpe ratio's weakness in the presence of skewness and kurtosis.

The Sortino ratio is a variation of the Sharpe ratio that differentiates harmful volatility from total overall volatility by using the asset's standard deviation of negative portfolio returns, called downside deviation, instead of the total standard deviation of portfolio returns.

$$\text{Sortino ratio} = \frac{R_A - r_f}{\sigma_{\text{Downside}}}$$

where σ_{Downside} is the downside standard deviation.

As the Sortino ratio focuses only on negative deviation, it is thought to give a better view of an account's risk-adjusted performance as any positive volatility is beneficial.

Risk-adjusted: **Downside risk**

Example:

The return of a hedge fund A over the last 5 years is as follows:

		Sortino ratio	Sharpe ratio
Year, t	Return, R_A	Squared deviation $(R_A - \text{Average return})^2$	Squared deviation $(R_A - \text{Average return})^2$
1	20%	**Not Included**	0.02822
2	–7%	0.01040	0.01040
3	10%	**Not Included**	0.00462
4	–5%	0.00672	0.00672
5	–2%	0.00270	0.00270

Total	0.01983	0.05268
Total/(T–1)	0.00496	0.01317
Square root	7.04%	11.48%

The risk-free rate is estimated at 3%, and the fund has a minimum return requirement of 0%. Calculate the Sortino and Sharpe ratio of this account.

Solution:
The data point in years 1 and 3 are not included for the Sortino ratio as any returns above the minimum return requirements are not included.

The average return = (20%–7%+10%–5%–2%)/5 = 3.2%

T–1 = 5 − 1 = 4

Downside deviation $= \hat{\sigma}_d = 7.04\%$

Sortino ratio = (3.2% − 3%)/ 7.04% = 0.0284

Standard deviation = 11.48%

Sharpe ratio = (3.2% − 3%)/11.84% = 0.0174

Reference/Further Reading

Maginn, J.L., Tuttle, D.L., Pinto, J.E., & McLeavey, D.W. (2007). *Managing Investment Portfolios — A Dynamic Process*, 3rd edn. John Wiley & Sons, pp. 717–771.

38.4 Key Developments in Portfolio Management

In portfolio management, there has been a critical development that is likely to impact asset price performance significantly. That development is quantitative easing that was and still being carried out by Central Banks (see our Module 1A1 Section 7.6 Monetary Policy Tools). The critical question here is how quantitative easing affects asset returns and how investors need to adapt.

A second development is in the practice of multi-asset investing that is being suggested to improve the conventional structure. Asset management under the traditional design (based on improving the risk-return trade-off through diversification) includes a 60/40 portfolio in equities and bonds and the endowment model as discussed in Section 37.1. Over recent times, cross-correlations have increased with reduced risk premiums and increased volatility. Hence, asset managers seek to improve different aspects of their investment processes to accommodate more complex financial markets and new products and derivatives.

Learning Objectives

- Understand the impact of quantitative easing on investing.
- Understand developments in the practice of multi-asset investing like core-satellite investing.
- Understand the concept behind risk parity investing, in particular, the "All Weather" story and conditions where it fails to provide downside protection.

Main Takeaways

Main Points

- The continued use of quantitative easing has given rise to the disconnect between asset price and intrinsic value.
- Practical approaches to multi-asset investing have developed beyond the conventional method of the 60/40 portfolio and the endowment model. Among many, one approach is core-satellite investing adopted by large pension and sovereign wealth funds.
- Risk parity is another approach that Bridgewater Associates implemented as "All Weather" Investing. However, with near-zero interest rates, investors are faced with zero or negative premiums from taking interest rate risks.

Main Terms

- **Core-satellite investing:** A portfolio managed from this approach allocates some money to core asset classes with other funds allocated to the satellite ring to give the portfolio a chance to grow faster than the broad market averages.
- **Factor investing:** Investment styles that deliver high returns in the long-run. Risk premiums are available, given that losses may arise over shorter horizons. The most specific factors are equity and bond indices used as investors' benchmarks.
- **Risk parity** refers to portfolio construction based on the risk contribution of various component asset classes.
- **Risk Budgeting:** It is a type of portfolio construction in which the risk of the overall portfolio is distributed among the various asset classes to

maximize portfolio return while keeping total portfolio risk at a minimum.

- **Risk Contribution:** It is the contribution of each component of a portfolio to the risk of the entire portfolio.

38.4.1 *Quantitative Easing*

More than 10 years after averting a significant economic crisis in the wake of the Lehman collapse in 2008 through near-zero interest rates and large asset purchases, several advanced economies continue to operate below their natural rate. Currently, more quantitative easing is being implemented with the global pandemic. While QE has stabilized financial markets, global debt rise lays the groundwork for the next crisis as asset prices are disconnected from intrinsic value. Inflated asset prices have also increased income inequality (benefitting asset owners) and inflated pension liabilities due to the low-interest-rate environment.

More importantly, the last 10 years have demonstrated the difficulties of reversing QE and rebuilding the central bank's balance sheets. Such difficulty was shown in 2018 with the stock market collapse when the Federal Reserve of the US tightened interest rates and suspended asset purchases. Further, we expect a limit to QE's effectiveness, as demonstrated in Japan's case, where growth fizzled out quickly after several rounds of QE.

As we look to the future, many financial institutions are weak financially and may not withstand the next crisis. Further, these institutions need to manage their liquidity prudently, given the weak financial standing, hampering recovery. Lastly, with the disconnect between asset prices and their intrinsic value, asset prices are likely to revert to their mean. The interesting question is that, given the persistence in QE's use, attraction to other means to store value and facilitate transaction continues to increase?

38.4.2 *Core-Satellite Investing*

There is a great diversity in the asset management industry, sometimes inconsistent with the view that asset allocation provides the significant bulk of risk and return in a portfolio. To better explain this observation, Gupta *et al.* (2016) has shown an overall architecture covering the broad field of multi-asset investing, viz., any investment activity involving more than one asset class. This architecture includes details of the investment process that include: asset forecasting, allocation, portfolio construction, implementation, and risk diagnostics, focusing on the choice of asset buckets used for allocation purposes.

Within this broad framework, recent approaches to asset management, such as core-satellite investing, factor investing, and risk parity (see Module 4, Fixed Income), among others, can be examined.

One approach involves the core-satellite investing concept and considers all assets as consisting of two factors: the bond factor and equity factor. Based on clients' risk preferences, the "reference" portfolio is constructed, for example, with 65% equities and 35% bonds in the case of the Government of Singapore Investment Corporation (GIC). This reference portfolio is then risk allocated to a policy portfolio comprising of different buckets of assets managed by the investment managers. For the GIC, the buckets are Developed Market Equities, Emerging Market Equities, Nominal Bonds and Cash, Inflation-Linked Bonds, Real Estate, and Private Equity. Other variants can include segregating the policy portfolio into a passive core and investing into other asset classes, as adopted by Canadian Pension Plan Investment Board (CPPIB). Also, for CPPIB, the allocation of $1 in private equity is equivalent to $1.30 in public equity and a short position of –$0.30 in bonds.

38.4.3 *Risk Parity Investing and Risk*

Related to the previous discussion of multi-asset investing in Portfolio Management Another approach to allocating among different asset classes with a portfolio. One of the methods is Risk Parity Investing.

Definition of Risk Parity Investing: Risk parity can be defined as a portfolio construction process. On a broader scale, it can be viewed as a unifying principle to guide investment processes ranging from asset allocation, individual asset class investing, and factor-based investing.

The underlying concepts of risk parity are risk budgeting and risk contribution, whereby allocation amount assets are based on the risk that investment brings a portfolio of assets. Risk-based allocation is a concept well understood by investment risk managers. Risk parity investing is how one would use risk budgeting and risk contribution measures to influence the holding of different assets within a portfolio.

Examples:

Example 1: Allocation by asset weight and risk contribution

Two allocation approaches that have been used for SAA are the balanced 60/40 portfolio and an allocation using risk parity. In both approaches, they have approximately fixed weights between equities and bonds. A 60/40 portfolio rebalances to a 60/40 percentage irrespective of market conditions. A risk parity portfolio always rebalances equal risk between stock and bonds (resulting in a much larger weight in bonds).

We can calculate the percentage of risk contribution of equities p_e to a portfolio of equities and bond as follows:

$$p_e = \frac{w_e^2\sigma_e^2 + \rho w_e w_b \sigma_e \sigma_b}{w_e^2\sigma_e^2 + w_b^2\sigma_b^2 + 2\rho w_e w_b \sigma_e \sigma_b}$$

where w_e is the weight in equities or 60% in a 60/40 portfolio; w_b is the weight in bonds or 40% in a 60/40 portfolio; σ_e is the standard deviation of the equity asset class; σ_b is the standard deviation of the bond asset class; and ρ is the correlation coefficient between bonds and equities.

A simple numerical example assuming σ_e = 15% and σ_b = 5% with $\rho = 0.2$, gives = 91.8% demonstrating that equities contribution 91.8% of the risk to a 60/40 portfolio.

Example 2: Bridgewater "All Weather" portfolio

One specific use of the risk parity approach is the All-Weather investment strategy created by Bridgewater Associates. In this strategy, portfolios are constructed by balancing fundamental risk factors like growth and inflation (see Figure 38.4). This portfolio aims to be "all-weather". But we will see later do not avoid losses under extreme conditions.

The Important Question: The most frequently asked question about risk parity are questions about interest rates. That is, what happens when interest rates go up? In support of risk parity, several risk factors provide the risk premiums to compensate risk-taking in the risk parity constructed portfolio. Hence, the diversification benefits can offset the risk posed by interest rate exposure. Thus, we note that risk parity will fail when interest rates increase persistently, resulting in no or even negative premium for bearing interest rate risk.

There were at least two episodes where risk parity constructed portfolio performed poorly. One was in May 2013 when both the equity and

Market Expectation	Growth	Inflation
Rising	25% of RISK Equities Commodities Corporate Credit EM Credit	25% of RISK IL Bonds Commodities EM Credit
Falling	25% of RISK Nominal Bonds IL Bonds	25% of RISK Equities Nominal Bonds

Figure 38.4: Portfolio constructed by balancing fundamental risk factors.

Source: Bridgewater (2012). *The All-Weather Story*.

bond markets collapse. As a result of the pandemic's economic impact, the US Federal Reserve moved interest rates to near-zero levels. In the recent episode, Bridgewater suffered significant losses and was reported to shift away from corporate bonds to alternatives.

References/Further Readings

Ang, A. (2012). Factor Investing: The Reference Portfolio and Canada Pension Plan Investment Board, Columbia CaseWorks.

Ang, A. (2014). *Asset Management, A Systematic Approach to Factor Investing*. Oxford University Press, Chap 14.

Bridgewater (2012). *The All-Weather Story*. Retrieved from https://www.bridgewater.com/research-and-insights/the-all-weather-story

GIC's New Investment Framework, Report on the Management of the Government's Portfolio for the Year 2012-2013. Retrieved from https://www.gic.com.sg/wp-content/uploads/2014/07/0801-GIC-Report1213-Feature-2.pdf.

Gupta, P., Skallsjo, S., & Li, B. (2016). *Multi-Asset Investing: A Practioner's Framework*. John Wiley & Sons, pp. 1–7.

Lee, J. (2020). Bridgewater's Risk Parity Shift Jolts a 400 Billion Quant Trade. *Bloomberg*. Retrieved from https://www.bloomberg.com/news/articles/2020-09-02/bridgewater-s-risk-parity-shift-jolts-a-400-billion-quant-trade.

Qian, E.E. (2016). *Risk Parity Fundamentals*. CRC Press, Taylor & Francis Group, pp. 1–16.

Rajan, A. (2019). *Quantitative Easing: The End of the Road for Pension Investors*? Amundi Asset Management, UK.

Singleton, J.C. (2005). *Core-Satellite Portfolio Management: A Modern Approach for Professionally Managed Funds*. McGraw Hill, Chap 1.

38.5 Sample Questions

Question 1

1. Which of the following directly affects an investor's ability to take risks?
   i. Liquidity
   ii. Time horizon
   iii. Tax concerns
   iv. Legal and regulatory concerns
   v. Unique circumstances
      (a) i and ii only
      (b) ii and iii only
      (c) i, ii, and iv only

Question 2

Which of the following is not a role that the IPS plays in the portfolio management process?

(a) It protects both the advisor and the investor from misunderstandings.
(b) It disciplines the portfolio management process against ad hoc revisions in strategy.
(c) It guides the choice of clients for an investment manager.

Question 3

The stage an individual is in his/her life cycle will affect his/her

(a) Return requirements and risk tolerance.
(b) Asset allocation.
(c) All of the options are correct.

Question 4

Dr. Lee stated that "with the unrealized gains in my portfolio, I have almost saved enough money for my sons to go to university in 5 and 7 years, but university costs keeping going up." Based on this statement alone, which one of the following appears to be least important to Dr. Lee's investment policy?

(a) Time horizon
(b) Purchasing power risk
(c) Liquidity

Question 5

The Huey endowment fund has $20 million in assets with a targeted spending rate of 4.50%. The fund has been incurring 0.75% as management costs. The trustees would like to preserve the fund's purchasing power and curtail the risk in terms of the standard deviation to no more than 10%. The inflation expectation is 2% per year over the foreseeable future. The fund's required rate of return is closest to:

(a) 6.00%
(b) 7.40%
(c) 8.00%

Question 6

Suppose the standard deviation of equities is 15% and the standard deviation of bonds is 5%, and the correlation coefficient is 0.2. What is the risk contribution of bonds in a portfolio comprising 60% in equities and 40% in bonds? (Give your answers to the nearest 0.1%)

(a) 6.1%
(b) 7.2%
(c) 8.2%

Solutions

Question 1

Solution: Option **a** is correct.

The longer time allows an investor to take on more risk as the longer time horizon allows the portfolio to recover from short-term downturns. Further, suppose the investor has a significant need for liquidity. In that case, she will need to ensure that the portfolio includes sufficient liquid assets to meet such demands, affecting the investor's ability to take risks. The other constraints may or may not or indirectly affect the investor's ability to take risks. For example, suppose the investor has to hold a significant holding in her family's shares as a unique circumstance. In that case, this may affect the diversification of her entire investment portfolio. Solution **a** is the best choice among **a, b** and **c**.

Question 2

Solution: Option **c** is correct.

Options a and b have been explained as the reason for the need for a well-structured IPS. An investment manager is likely to be guided by corporate policy and regulation to clients' choice and suitability.

Question 3

Solution: Option **c** is correct.

The life cycle stage affects risk tolerance and affects return requirements and asset allocation.

Question 4

Solution: Option **c** is correct.

Liquidity is the least important. The question as to when significant withdrawals are required and having an adequate amount to meet the rising cost is the critical concern expressed.

Question 5

Solution: Option **b** is correct.

The required rate of return is: 4.50 + 0.75 + 2.00 = 7.25%. The closest is 7.40%

Question 6

Solution: Option **c** is correct.

The risk contribution of bonds in the portfolio is given by

$$p_b = \frac{w_b^2\sigma_b^2 + \rho w_e w_b \sigma_e \sigma_b}{w_e^2\sigma_e^2 + w_b^2\sigma_b^2 + 2\rho w_e w_b \sigma_e \sigma_b}$$

where w_e is the weight in equities or 60% in a 60/40 portfolio; w_b is the weight in bonds or 40% in a 60/40 portfolio; σ_e is the standard deviation of the equity asset class; σ_b is the standard deviation of the bond asset class; and ρ is the correlation coefficient between bonds and equities.

Substituting into the equation gives $p_b = 8.2\%$.

Global Fintech Institute - World Scientific Series on Fintech

(Continued from page ii)

Applications and Trends in Fintech II: Cloud Computing, Compliance, and Global Fintech Trends
David Lee Kuo Chuen (Global Fintech Institute, Singapore & Singapore University of Social Sciences, Singapore), Joseph Lim, Phoon Kok Fai and Wang Yu (Singapore University of Social Sciences, Singapore)

www.ingramcontent.com/pod-product-compliance
Lightning Source LLC
LaVergne TN
LVHW010539300926
849162LV00002B/182